THOMAS FRIEDRICH
HITLER'S BERLIN
ABUSED CITY

TRANSLATED BY STEWART SPENCER

YALE UNIVERSITY PRESS
NEW HAVEN AND LONDON

First published in

First published in

English translation copyright © 2012 Stewart Spencer

Originally published under the title *Die Missbrauchte Hauptstadt* by Thomas Friedrich ©
Ullstein Buchverlage GmbH, Berlin. Published in 2007 by Propyläen Verlag

For information about this and other Yale University Press publications, please contact:
U.S. Office: sales.press@yale.edu   yalebooks.com
Europe Office: sales@yaleup.co.uk   yalebooks.co.uk

Set in Minion Pro by IDSUK (DataConnection) Ltd
Printed in Great Britain by Hobbs the Printers Ltd, Totton, Hampshire

The translation of this work was funded by Geisteswissenschaften International –
Translation Funding for the Humanities and Social Sciences from Germany, a joint
initiative of the Fritz Thyssen Foundation, the German Federal Foreign Office, the
copyright collecting society VG WORT and the Börsenverein des Deutschen
Buchhandels (German Publishers & Booksellers Association).

A catalogue record for this book is available from the British Library.

Friedrich, Thomas, 1948–2011
  [Missbrauchte Hauptstadt. English]
  Hitler's Berlin : abused city / Thomas Friedrich.
    p. cm.
  Translated from the German.
  Includes bibliographical references and index.
  ISBN 978-0-300-16670-5 (cl : alk. paper)
  1. Berlin (Germany)—Politics and government—20th century. 2. Hitler, Adolf,
1889–1945. 3. National socialism—Germany—Berlin.   I. Title. II. Title: Abused city.
  DD880.F7713 2012
  943'.155086—dc23

                                                                        2011041772

ISBN 978-0-300-21973-9 (pbk)

10 9 8 7 6 5 4 3 2 1

Contents

Illustrations

Abbreviations

BVP	Bayerische Volkspartei (Bavarian People's Party)
DAP	Deutsche Arbeiterpartei (German Workers' Party)
DDP	Deutsche Demokratische Partei (German Democratic Party)
DHV	Deutschnationaler Handlungsgehilfen-Verband (German National League of Commercial Employees)
DNVP	Deutschnationale Volkspartei (German National People's Party)
DSP	Deutschsozialistische Partei (German Socialist Party)
DVFP	Deutschvölkische Freiheitspartei (German Nationalist Freedom Party)
DVP	Deutsche Volkspartei (German People's Party)
GDA	Gewerkschaftsbund der Angestellten (League of White-Collar Workers)
KPD	Kommunistische Partei Deutschlands (Communist Party of Germany)
KVP	Konservative Volkspartei (Conservative People's Party)
NSDAP	Nationalsozialistische Deutsche Arbeiterpartei (National Socialist German Workers' Party)
NSDStB	Nationalsozialistischer Deutscher Studentenbund (National Socialist German Students' Association)
NSFB	Nationalsozialistische Freiheitsbewegung
SA	Sturmabteilung (Storm Troopers)
SPD	Sozialdemokratische Partei Deutschlands (Social Democratic Party of Germany)
SS	Schutzstaffel (Protection Squad)

Preface

Bernhard Sauer begins his recent study of the history of the Storm Troopers (SA) in the Brandenburg district of Berlin by observing that historians have until now paid little attention to National Socialism in Berlin and, above all, to the history of the SA in the city.[1] This is true. Indeed, it defies belief that more than six decades after the end of the Third Reich there is still no comprehensive account of the National Socialists (NSDAP) in Berlin – the very city that had to be subjugated by the party before it could extend its murderous dictatorship to the remainder of Germany and, later, to much of the rest of Europe. This state of affairs is all the more grotesque in that the NSDAP itself needed little more than four years to publish an official account of the history of the SA in the Brandenburg district of Berlin, an account that appeared in 1937 on the occasion of the celebrations marking the seven hundredth anniversary of the founding of the city.[2] However meretricious as a piece of propaganda, it none the less contains interesting material on the organizational history of the SA's origins in Berlin and on the way in which it saw itself.

The present study makes no attempt to fill this gap, but by examining Hitler's relations with Berlin it seeks to examine the local variant of National Socialism and blaze a trail through the dense undergrowth of misunderstandings and prejudices that have long obscured that relationship. This undergrowth has for decades prevented historians from attempting an evaluation of the question based on a critical analysis of suppressed or unknown facts – in spite of, or at least in the face of, the growing flood of publications concerned with Hitler and National Socialism.

Also at stake is a mindless local patriotism that encouraged even Hitler's contemporaries to remark that, following the National Socialists' assumption of power, Berlin had been 'occupied by brown-shirted provincials',[3] implying that the local variant of National Socialism, far from emerging from within the city itself, had somehow been imposed on it from the outside. Fifteen years after the Nazi regime had been toppled, apologists were still claiming that the National Socialists' dictatorship was a superficial phenomenon in Berlin and that only elsewhere was its 'true' character to be found. In a brief overview of the city's history that was published in 1960, we read, for example, that 'the twelve years of National Socialism represent not just an episode in its history but also a break in its more authentic past, from whose deeper driving forces it was forcibly alienated during this time'.[4]

In what was for a long time arguably the most important biography of Hitler, Joachim Fest sought an alternative interpretation: rather than exculpating Berlin by seeing it as the innocent victim of external forces, he regarded Hitler, conversely, as a psychological misfit who, hostile to big cities, was confused by the modernism of Berlin:

> The hectic madness of Berlin, which was then entering its famous, or notorious, twenties, only heightened Hitler's dislike for the city. He despised its greed and its frivolity. [...] As if he were once again seventeen years old and arriving in Vienna, he stood baffled and alienated by the phenomenon of the big city, lost in so much noise, turbulence, and miscegenation. He really felt at home only in provincial circumstances and was, despite all his sense of being an outsider, permanently fixated upon provincial moral rectitude.[5]

As we shall see, this characterization of Hitler overlooks certain essential aspects of his personality. How could a man ostensibly terrified of the urban jungle at the same time have enjoyed visiting Berlin's Luna-Park? How could he have praised the Tiller Girls[6] and been an avid cinema-goer, a boxing fanatic and a man who was mad about cars? Hitler's undeniable aversion to certain aspects of the cultural life of the Weimar Republic, especially those found in Berlin, has often been seized on as evidence of his general aversion to the capital. Writers have argued that he was forced against his will to leave Munich, with its view of the Alps, and that he 'never liked Berlin'[7] and 'never concealed his dislike'.[8] Such claims are generally based on little more than a handful of quotations from *Mein Kampf*. A more recent study has described Hitler's dealings with Berlin as a 'love–hate relationship': his attitude to the city, we are told, was 'deeply divided' and 'invariably troubled'. Like most politicians of the extreme right, he felt 'an aversion to cities and to metropolises as such'. 'On the one hand, his rejection of modern – urban – forms of existence was fundamental to his whole outlook, while on the other hand he was fascinated by the organism of metropolises in general and of Berlin in particular."[9]

While earlier studies have sought to ascribe Hitler's attitude to Berlin to his alleged feelings of resentment, to his likes and dislikes and to psychological causes bound up with such emotions, the present study attempts a concrete analysis of the changing political situation in order to show how his attitude kept shifting. This does not mean that Hitler's emotional life will be excluded from our discussion, only that it is not the determining factor. Just as Hitler related his political, strategic and tactical decisions to the historical situation of the day, modifying or altering them where necessary, so his attitude to Berlin was dependent on the importance that he attached to the city in the light of changing political circumstances. Ultimately this was not an emotional relationship that could be measured on a scale extending from love at one extreme to hatred at the other. Rather, it was what one might call an instrumental relationship, albeit one that was susceptible to change. This explains why, in the days before he became a politician, Hitler regarded the city as 'wonderful' because it was an expression of visible power and grandeur. At the time when the party was being built up, it was a resource centre and a place to forge contacts and to plot conspiracies. In keeping with its function within the country's national, economic and social infrastructure, it was a place for party-political experiments, a place where variants of the National Socialists' claims to power could be enforced, a place where the SA could limber up and advance its claims to be the 'battering ram' of the workers' movement, a place, finally, where anti-Semitic attacks could be staged, Nazi rituals could be rehearsed and the conquest of the public arena could be planned in detail.

In order to describe this process of instrumentalization in all its various manifestations, I felt it advisable to concentrate on the years before the National Socialists' seizure of power, not least because the vast amount of available literature is in inverse proportion to the rise of the NSDAP from a tiny sect to a splinter group, and finally to a movement that embraced the masses. It is also this instrumentalization of the city for party-political ends that allowed Berlin to be 'violated' long before the transfer of power to the party made it possible for Hitler to treat the city as a kind of lab rat on which he could try out his architectural experiments and ideas on urban planning. From the outset, Hitler's view of Berlin as a living organism on which to conduct experiments intended to reconfigure it meant that he not only lost sight of the overall structure of a conurbation that numbered four million souls but that that infrastructure was in fact a matter of profound indifference to him.

The massive and mysterious concrete building that was erected on the border between Tempelhof and Schöneberg in the summer of 1941 in order to test whether the ground would support the weight of the triumphal arch that was planned for this spot continues to weigh figuratively on Berlin,[10] functioning as a symbol of the way in which the city remains oppressed by Hitler's legacy, a legacy that still affects Berlin and that will continue to do so for the foreseeable future.

Thomas Friedrich
Berlin, April 2007

1

'It's a wonderful city'

1916–18: HITLER'S EARLY VISITS TO BERLIN

Berlin (13º 23′ 54″ E 52º 30′ 17″ N), the capital of the kingdom of Prussia and of the German Reich, the principal residence of the king and Kaiser, the centre of government and, after London and Paris, the largest city in Europe. It lies on a sandy plain surrounded by low hills that rise to a height of between 105 and 160 feet above sea level on both banks of the River Spree, which is still navigable at this point. [. . .] On 1 January 1914 the city's population was 2,079,156 inhabitants. Clustered around it are also numerous suburbs and outlying villages, most of which are closely connected to it, so that a Greater Berlin exists with a population of more than four million.
Grieben's Travel Guide to Berlin, 1917[1]

The House in the Schonensche Straße

The building still exists. It is one of those countless blocks of rented flats that were built in Berlin and the surrounding area from around 1830 – the start of the Industrial Revolution in Germany. Even by that date the city was already growing exponentially. Each year another ten thousand immigrants would arrive, so that by 1877 the city's population was over a million. By 1905 that figure had doubled. After that, the growth rate declined, but only because better transport links meant that the suburbs and neighbouring communities were able to absorb the influx of new arrivals: the municipality of Pankow to the north of Berlin, for example, expanded from 38,000 inhabitants in 1908 to 58,000 in 1913. Like most of the city's other suburbs, Pankow was already so comprehensively merged with Berlin by this date that no one apart from the inhabitants of the districts on the edge of the city even so much as noticed the existence of a boundary.

Pankow lay on the northern side of the Schonensche Straße. Visitors arriving from the Schönhauser Allee will still find that no. 15 Schonensche Straße is the last house on the right. In 1917 it was still a part of Berlin. Named after a region in southern Sweden, the Schonensche Straße lay at the very northern edge of the city in postal district N 58. In the plan of Berlin published by Baedeker in 1908, it is in the square marked '28' at the top, squeezed between the Wisbyer Straße, named – appropriately enough – after a city on the Swedish island of Gotland, and the Kaiser-Friedrich-Straße. Whereas the Wisbyer Straße was in Berlin, the Kaiser-Friedrich-Straße was in Pankow. No. 15 was the last house to be built in the Schonensche Straße. Dating from 1909, it does not appear in the 1908 Baedeker guide, where the area in question is uncoloured, indicating that the plot of land was still undeveloped.

Each of the building's five floors was divided into four apartments comprising two rooms and a kitchen – not exactly palatial luxury. Hundreds of thousands of workers lived in such cramped quarters in Berlin, many of them families. The typesetter Fritz Arendt and his wife, Helene, lived on the third floor at 15 Schonensche Straße. They would have counted themselves lucky that the building was new rather than one of the older, dilapidated properties thrown up over the course of the previous decades. The flat was just big enough for them to find room for their twenty-two-year-old son, Richard, when he returned home on leave between 2 and 19 September 1917. Like his father, Richard Arendt was a trained compositor. Before the war he had lived in Augsburg, but now he was a non-commissioned officer in the Reserve Battalion of the Sixteenth Bavarian Infantry Regiment.[2] Soon after enlisting, he had got to know a volunteer who had been a member of the regiment since 1 September 1914.[3] The regiment was stationed in Alsace until the middle of October 1917. When Arendt returned from his two weeks' home leave, he presumably told his comrade about his experiences in Berlin. After all, the latter had for years taken a lively interest in the capital.[4] The conversation must have prompted Arendt to invite his comrade to spend his forthcoming two-week leave of absence with his parents in Berlin – his friend had repeatedly claimed that he had no wish to spend the time with members of his own family or to return to Munich, where he had lived prior to the outbreak of the war. In the German army no superior officer had the right to tell a volunteer where he should spend his home leave. Provided the latter observed the necessary formalities, remained within his country's frontiers and returned to the front on time, he could go wherever he wanted.

And so it was that, on Sunday, 30 September 1917, twenty-eight-year-old Corporal Adolf Hitler, holder of the Iron Cross (Second Class) and, since

17 September, of the Military Service Medal (Third Class), set off on an eighteen-day leave of absence – the first such leave in his entire life.[5] Travelling via Frankfurt and Leipzig, he arrived in Berlin on 2 October. Four days later he sent a postcard to his friend and fellow dispatch runner Corporal Ernst Schmidt:

> Dear Schmidt,
>
> Didn't get here till Tuesday. The Arendts are very kind, I couldn't have wished for anything better. It's a wonderful city. A real metropolis. Even now there's a tremendous amount of traffic. I'm out and about practically all day long. Finally have a chance to get to know the museums a little better. In short, I want for nothing. Every good wish, A. Hitler.[6]

For all its brevity, Hitler's postcard is none the less precise and to the point, comprising, as it does, an address, a characterization of the sender's hosts, his assessment of the city, an account of his activities, a summing-up and a colloquial salutation. But what did Hitler mean when he wrote that he had 'finally' had a chance to get to know the museums 'a little better'? Had he already had an opportunity to visit the city's museums and galleries before October 1917? Although this was his first leave of absence in Berlin, it was in fact his second visit to the city. But what drew a 'German Austrian', as Hitler liked to describe himself, to Berlin? And why does none of the published accounts of his life, including his own autobiographical writings such as *Mein Kampf*, contain even a passing reference to his home leave? Is it not strange that a man normally so keen to tell others about himself should have maintained a lifelong silence about his visit to this 'wonderful' city in October 1917, whereas his brief stay in the autumn of 1916 at least receives a six-line mention in *Mein Kampf*?[7] What reasons did Hitler have to be so unforthcoming about his relations with Berlin during the dying days of the Kaiserreich?

The Regiment as Home

Hitler was born in Braunau on the River Inn in 1889. In 1907 he applied for a place at the Academy of Fine Arts in Vienna but failed the entrance examination. In spite of this rejection, he moved to Vienna from Urfahr, a suburb of Linz, in 1908.[8] In October of that year he was not even allowed to re-sit the entrance examination. During the years that followed he led a life of indolence, incapable of coming to terms with his failure, while at the same time remaining convinced that he not only had the aptitude to become an architect but that he was positively predestined for the life of an artist.[9] In May 1913 – not 'the spring of 1912', as he erroneously claims in *Mein Kampf*[10] – he moved to Munich,[11] ostensibly to continue his studies.[12] Here he was forced to earn his living as a freelance architectural draughtsman, with a view to 'training to become an architect'.[13] In the event he did nothing that could be described as a serious attempt to further his education. Still less did his activities amount to regular employment or systematic, planned work.[14] He simply lived from hand to mouth.

Branded a failure and lacking any professional qualifications, the twenty-five-year-old Hitler was bound to welcome the outbreak of the First World War as a form of release. Although he was an Austrian citizen, he signed up for military service in Munich following mobilization and Germany's declaration of war on Russia. By the middle of August 1914 he had been summoned to report for duty at Recruiting Depot VI. During the days that followed he received his initial basic training, and by 1 September 1914 he had been assigned to the First Company of the Sixteenth Bavarian Reserve Infantry Regiment, often known as the 'List Regiment' after its first commanding officer, Colonel Julius List.[15] By 21 October the regiment was being transported to the Belgian front at Ypres and Becelaere, where the first military engagements took place before the end of the month, resulting in heavy losses. By 3 November Hitler had been promoted to the rank of corporal.[16] Six days later he was assigned to the regimental staff as an orderly, his duties from now until the end of the war being those of a dispatch runner – for whatever reason, he makes no mention of this in *Mein Kampf*.[17] By all accounts he was a courageous and reliable runner.[18] On 2 December 1914 he received the Iron Cross (Second Class).[19] In the middle of March 1915 the List Regiment was transferred to the front at Fromelles near Lille, where they fought in the trenches, defending a two-mile stretch of the front over a period of some eighteen months. According to Anton Joachimsthaler, 'the fighting at Fromelles resulted in many deaths and injuries among English and German troops alike, but the situation at the end was ultimately what it had been at the outset – in spite of two major skirmishes in May 1915 and July 1916 the front moved only a few metres throughout this entire period'.[20]

With hindsight Hitler came to regard his regiment as a kind of 'home'. After his aimless years in Vienna and Munich, he now found a sense and purpose in his life. He was part of a larger community that relieved him of the need to struggle to earn a living. A quarter of a century later he fondly recalled this period:

One thing is certain – your worries are never-ending. I had worries as a young man when I was dealing with denominations of 10, 20 or 30 marks. There was only one time when I didn't have any worries: my six years in the

army; people didn't take it all so seriously – you had your suit delivered, and
even if it wasn't a good one, at least it was respectable, and the same was true
of your meals, your accommodation and you had permission to lie down
wherever you wanted.[21]

Hitler's father had died in 1903, his mother in 1907. He had no contact with his
surviving relatives in Austria such as his sister, Paula, and his half-sister, Angela.
And from the middle of 1915 onwards he received no more parcels or post from
his few remaining acquaintances in Munich. He told his war comrades at this
time that his present home was his regiment and, inasmuch as he had no
relatives in Germany and had absolutely no desire to return to Austria, he 'felt
no great urge to go on leave'.[22] At the end of September 1916 the regiment left
Fromelles and moved to Cambrai. By 2 October they were already engaged in
the Battle of the Somme, which had been going on since the end of June. Only
a few days earlier the soldiers, who until then had worn spiked leather helmets
(in 1914 they had had only oilcloth caps), had been given steel helmets. The
regiment was positioned at Allaines, between Bapaume and Le Barque. The
regimental staff were accommodated in a dugout at Le Barque-Nord.[23]

In early October the dispatch runners moved into a tunnel so narrow and
low that they could barely sit upright or pass one another. The air was thick
and stifling. Pressed tightly against one another, mostly with their legs drawn
up against their bodies, they tried to sleep in spite of their discomfort. One of
the entrances was in the direct line of fire of the English artillery position. The
likelihood of a shell striking the narrow entrance at exactly the right angle was
negligible, and yet this is precisely what happened. A light grenade exploded,
causing shrapnel to fly down the passageway in which the dispatch runners
were sleeping. Six of them were injured, including Hitler, who sustained a
wound to his left thigh. It was not particularly serious, and when the regimental adjutant, Friedrich Wiedemann, startled by the explosion, arrived,
Hitler is said to have told him: 'It's not so bad, Lieutenant, I'll stay with you, I'll
stay with the regiment!'[24] Decades later Wiedemann described his impressions
of this incident: 'He lay there, wounded, and had no desire other than to be
allowed to remain with his regiment. He had no family and, if you like, no
homeland either. For Corporal Hitler, the List Regiment was his home.'[25]

From Field Hospital to the Reich's Capital

For the first time since moving to the front, Hitler now found himself – much
against his will – returning to Germany, where his injuries could be better

treated. As he himself put it in *Mein Kampf*, he now saw his 'home' again after two years – in the circumstances this was 'an almost endless time. I could scarcely imagine how Germans looked who were not in uniform.'[26] He arrived at the Red Cross hospital at Beelitz near Berlin on 9 October 1916. His bed was in Ward 34 in Section I.[27]

After months of fighting in the mud of the Somme, Hitler – by his own admission – scarcely dared climb into 'the white beds of this miraculous building'. He was disturbed by the strange atmosphere in the hospital. The whole scene was dominated by 'cowards'; 'a few wretched scoundrels' set the tone, 'the most unscrupulous agitators', who mocked the ideas of 'decent soldiers' and who even boasted that they were capable of mutilating themselves to escape from the front. One such inmate 'went so far in his insolent effrontery as to represent his own cowardice as an emanation of higher bravery than the hero's death of an honest soldier', an attitude that Hitler found so repellent that 'disgust mounted' to his throat. The managers of the hospital tolerated such 'agitators' on their premises and, even though the identity of these discontents was known, 'nothing was done' about them.[28] Eight years later, in his statement to the People's Court in Munich, Hitler tried to give an anti-Semitic gloss to his alleged horror at the way in which the hospital had secretly condoned the agitators' actions. But his mendacious account of his clash with a Jewish senior doctor presumably failed to achieve the desired result, for he made no attempt to relate the episode in *Mein Kampf*, which he wrote in 1924.[29]

A group photograph taken in the hospital grounds on 26 October 1916 shows Hitler with his usual staring eyes but, after two and a half weeks of medical treatment, he is by no means as hollow-cheeked as in earlier photographs taken on the front. And his moustache is no longer twirled up at the ends in the Wilhelminian manner.[30] Once he had recovered from his injury and was able to walk again, he was allowed to travel from Beelitz to Berlin. The Red Cross hospital lay right next to the extensive grounds of the Beelitz Clinics, which had their own station on the line from Wetzlar, making it easy for Hitler to take the train to the Friedrichstraße Station in Berlin in little over an hour. A postcard that he sent on 4 November 1916 to Franz Mayer – a fellow corporal in the List Regiment – congratulating him on the award of the Iron Cross, shows a view of the National Gallery in Berlin.[31] It seems likely, then, that Hitler visited Berlin for the first time in early November 1916, perhaps on Friday, 3 November.

Nor will it have been mere chance that the postcard showed the National Gallery. Hitler admired nineteenth-century German art and he could be certain that he would find works by at least some of his favourite artists at the National Gallery. We can imagine him arriving at the station early one morning during the first week of November 1916 and walking south along the Friedrichstraße, past the Central Hotel with its legendary Winter Gardens, and then turning either right along Unter den Linden in the direction of the Brandenburg Gate, or left in the direction of the Royal Palace and then aiming towards the city's cluster of museums on an island in the River Spree. If he took the second alternative, he would have passed, in turn, the Royal Library, the equestrian statue of Frederick the Great, the main building of the Friedrich Wilhelm University and, on the other side of the road, the Kaiser-Franz-Josef-Platz with the Old Palace of Wilhelm I and the Royal Opera, Schinkel's New Guard House fronted by marble statues of two Prussian generals, Gerhard von Scharnhorst and Friedrich Wilhelm von Bülow, the Princesses' Palace, the Crown Prince's Palace, the Commandant's Residence and the Arsenal, ending at the Schloß-Brücke. Arriving at the Lustgarten, at that date still a park, he may have headed northwards through the gardens themselves and, passing Schinkel's Old Museum with its columned front hall, reached the National Gallery on the Friedrichsgracht, a branch of the River Spree. Like the other museums and galleries on the island, the National Gallery was open from ten to three. Admission was free.

When Hitler came to describe this visit to Berlin in *Mein Kampf*, he saw it – remarkably enough – in a completely different light. Here he makes no mention whatsoever of his visit to the gallery but presents his stay in the city as a kind of political reconnaissance trip. 'Clearly there was dire misery everywhere,' he wrote of his impressions of Berlin in November 1916. 'The big city was suffering from hunger. Discontent was great. In various soldiers' homes the tone was like that in the hospital. It gave you the impression that these scoundrels were intentionally frequenting such places in order to spread their views.'[32]

Disquiet on the Home Front

Misery, hunger, great discontent – Hitler's summing-up of the situation in Berlin at this time cannot be faulted. Within six months of the outbreak of the First World War, the reports that had to be regularly submitted to the commander-in-chief of Berlin-Brandenburg by the Berlin police, together with other reports by the police and police informers, for all that they tended for the most part to gloss over the city's problems, none the less noted the growing shortages of foodstuffs and cases of profiteering, while the anti-war protests organized by the radically left-wing Social Democrats under Karl Liebknecht and Rosa Luxemburg were increasingly widely discussed. In his report of 16 January 1915 the local chief of police, Traugott von Jagow, had insisted that the constant increase in the cost of many basic consumer goods and other foodstuffs, especially peas, beans and fats, was in general being accepted with equanimity. People were starting to adapt to the inevitable; only the continuing high price of meat was causing ill feeling. But by 20 February 1915 Jagow was reporting that further increases in the cost of food had produced a mood of real depression. This, he went on, made it difficult for the Social Democrats to the right of the party to maintain their existing position, making it easier for the radicals to gain the upper hand. In a postscript dated 27 February 1915, Jagow noted with the dryness typical of the bureaucrat that the situation was 'not without its problems'.

From now on each report catalogued the growing discontent 'at rising food prices among the broad masses', the language used varying only in its propensity to increase or conceal alarm. Dated 6 March 1915, the thirty-second report noted that discontent had spread to the middle classes and that this, coupled with a sense of uncertainty regarding the duration of the war, had created a 'certain desire for peace' that had found repeated expression at Social Democrat meetings. The thirty-fourth report of two weeks later referred to a 'war-weariness' which, if not widespread, was undoubtedly present.[33]

Charged with surveillance operations, the police were particularly unsettled by the fact that from the spring of 1915 onwards radical women's groups had begun to emerge from the Social Democrats and that these women were 'attempting to agitate for peace among all sections of society'.[34] This was a trend that found public expression in demonstrations which, drawing only a few hundred women on 18 March 1915, had grown so much by 18 May that they could summon the support of over a thousand women, who demonstrated outside the Reichstag, expressing their disapproval of Philipp Scheidemann, a member of the Social Democratic Party (SPD) and, as such, a member of the right-wing majority government. By contrast, members of the house who were opposed to the war – and who included Karl Liebknecht – were roundly applauded. On 28 October 1915 a few hundred women gathered in the courtyard of the SPD's central offices, then broke into a meeting of the party executive with shouts of 'traitors' and demanded an immediate end to the war.[35] The first food riots took place in working-class areas of Berlin at the end of 1915, and there were anti-war demonstrations in the centre of the city, chiefly in Unter den Linden. According to the police report of 11 December 1915, these demonstrations were 'by no means widespread, and yet they prove that the influence of these agitators [in other words, the radical left] is not at all insignificant.[36]

In the course of the months that followed, basic foodstuffs grew increasingly scarce and prices continued to rise, leaving the city's chief of police with little choice but to report to the military commander a further worsening of the situation. The question of nutrition was more pressing than ever, he explained in his submission of 2 March 1916, and the mood of the masses was now such that unrest could break out at any time if prices continued to rise and nothing was done to address the problem of food shortages.[37] It goes without saying that the working-class women who for eighteen months had been struggling with constant shortages and even famine on the home front reported regularly and uninhibitedly on these daily experiences in their letters to their husbands, brothers and sons who were away on active service. Hitler, too, naturally learnt about the contents of these letters. But for a man who as a serving soldier himself had for the first time in his life been relieved of all material cares, these outpourings were merely 'complaining letters direct from home', flooding the front with 'poison dished up by thoughtless women at home who, of course, did not suspect that this was the way to raise the enemy's confidence in victory to the highest pitch, thus consequently to prolong and sharpen the suffering of their men at the fighting front'. Hitler's staggering conclusion was that, 'in the time that followed, the senseless letters of German women cost hundreds of thousands of men their lives'.[38]

If Hitler could blame a handful of 'thoughtless women' for the deaths of hundreds of thousands of soldiers, how would he judge the targeted political demonstrations that were organized in 1916? On 1 May the Spartacus Group – a radical anti-war organization that had emerged from the left wing of the SPD – held a demonstration on the Potsdamer Platz that was promoted by means of handbills and leaflets. Thousands of Berliners turned up for the occasion. The police were nervous, the mood tense. Karl Liebknecht – the principal leader of the Spartacus Group after Rosa Luxemburg and then the most recognizable figure in the radical anti-war movement – had barely left the Potsdam Station to deliver a speech on the terrace in front of the Café Josty when he was detained by plain-clothes policemen, before being arrested and taken away after repeatedly shouting: 'Down with the war! Down with the government!'[39] Within days he had been haled before the Berlin District Court and accused of high treason, prompting a show of force on the eve of the main proceedings when some 25,000 demonstrators demanded his release. On 28 June 1916 – the day on which the trial began – there was the first general strike of the First World War. Around 55,000 workers from the main ordinance factories in Berlin – AEG, Schwarzkopf, Borsig, Loewe and others – took part in the strike.[40]

Ever-closer links were forged between the increasingly well-organized anti-war protesters and large sections of the embittered population. It was a development that the military authorities viewed with apprehension and as a warning signal. In an attempt to emasculate the movement, they either took the leaders of the Spartacus Group, including Rosa Luxemburg, into 'protective custody' or enlisted them in the war. On the instructions of the commander-in-chief, the right-wing SPD party chairman replaced the largely left-wing editorial board and editor-in-chief of the local party newspaper, *Vorwärts*, with his own political stooges.[41] The authorities were also increasingly keen to curtail the activities of middle-class pacifist organizations such as the German Peace Society, the New Fatherland Alliance, whose most prominent member was Albert Einstein, the Association of Like-Minded Persons and the Central Office for People's Rights. Arrests were made, organizations were banned and individuals were deported.[42] For a time these measures did indeed succeed in limiting anti-war protests.

By the early autumn of 1916, however, the chief of police was alarmed to note that the supply problems were as bad as ever and that there was a 'widespread longing for peace'. The shortage of food was making life particularly difficult for families who were less well off, and the third winter of the war was already casting long shadows.[43] At the end of August 1916 Erich von Falkenhayn was replaced as chief of the general staff by Paul von Hindenburg, who wrote to both the chancellor and the Kaiser, proposing strict measures for mobilization, for securing the production of armaments and for improving the food supply. He knew, after all, that 'this question' would 'have a bearing on the outcome of the war'.[44] Month after month, the reports of the Berlin police returned with monotonous frequency to the catastrophic material situation of a growing cross section of the population. 'The mood in general is very depressed,' we read on one occasion.[45] And, on another: 'Many of the basic necessities continue to be obtainable only at exorbitantly high prices, if at all. [...] As a result, the number of people requiring mass feeding is considerably increased. Given the high prices even for woollen garments and for coal, there are grounds for serious anxiety if the coming winter proves to be severe.'[46]

Hitler's Denial of his Visits to Berlin in 1917 and 1918

By the date of this report – 14 October 1916 – Hitler had already been in hospital for several days at Beelitz. His own account of the suffering and discontent in Berlin, which we quoted earlier, was therefore largely the same as the picture presented by the chief of police. Of course, the authorities' assessment of the situation was based on information provided by police informers and on observations made by the police in the course of their daily contacts with the population. But what was the basis of Hitler's account? It is not inconceivable that he paid frequent visits to Berlin from the hospital – after all, he remained there for almost two months, until 1 December 1916, even though his injury was not especially serious. And yet the train connections between Beelitz and Berlin were such that he could have spent only a few hours in the city at any one time. And, even as a patient, Hitler was subject to military orders and was required to report to his superior officer each time he left the hospital and returned.

In Berlin, as in Vienna and Munich, Hitler was interested above all in architecture and art, including the holdings of the city's museums and galleries. The limited time available to him, together with his recent thigh injury, obliged him to concentrate on a relatively small part of the inner city, and we may assume that he had little time to indulge in any intensive exploration of the area between the Friedrichstraße Station and the museums on their island in the Spree. This area – known as Dorotheenstadt – contained hotels, restaurants and places of entertainment, together with offices and various tourist sights, but few people lived here. Certainly it was not a working-class district or a place where Hitler could have studied at first hand the growing unrest among the lower echelons of society in the face of the catastrophic shortages of food and other basic necessities. How, then, could Hitler have observed the severe shortages and the great discontent that affected the population on his journeys between the station and the museums? 'The big city was suffering from hunger.' No doubt this was true, but in the shops and restaurants along the Friedrichstraße he was more likely to meet people who had gained from the war.

How was it, then, that Hitler was able to offer such an apposite and by no means exaggerated account of social deprivation in Berlin in 1916 in *Mein Kampf* when it is extremely unlikely that he could have witnessed these conditions for himself on his flying visit or visits to the city towards the end of his period of hospitalization in the autumn of that year? Did he simply take over the description from a friend or army comrade and pass it off as something he had witnessed for himself? This is by no means out of the question. It is far more likely, however, that Hitler telescoped together the experiences of two different visits separated by about a year and wove them together to create a coherent narrative: the first visit or visits took place during his time in hospital in Beelitz between 9 October and 1 December 1916, while the second visit was his home leave, which he spent at the Arendts' between 2 and 17 October 1917.

In October 1917 Hitler did indeed stay in a part of the city that was predominantly populated by 'ordinary people'. The Berlin directory of 1917 divides up the households in the Schonensche Straße according to the professions of their heads. There were two compositors, two policemen, two draymen, two site foremen and two invalids, as well as a plumber, a moulder, a painter and decorator, a brewery representative, a revenue officer, a dispatch clerk, a plasterer, a chauffeur, an employee of the local overground railway, a saddler, a worker at the local gasworks, a senior postal worker, a cooper, a railway guard, a clockmaker, a master baker, a magistrates' clerk, a brewery worker, a greengrocer, a master mason, a master painter and decorator, a tram driver, a policeman specializing in criminal cases, a pub landlord, an office secretary, a widow and three seamstresses.[47] Among these artisans and black-collar workers, Hitler may well have had an opportunity during his two-week stay to see for himself 'the continuing difficult economic conditions under which the inhabitants of Greater Berlin are forced to live', to quote from an official report of 22 October 1917.[48] The same was true of his journey from the Schonensche Straße into the city centre. To reach the museums, he had to walk a couple of hundred yards to the nearest tram stop at the corner of the Schönhauser Allee and the Kaiser-Friedrich-Straße, where he would catch a no. 47 or 48 tram, which would then take him through the working-class districts of northern and north-eastern Berlin to the Hacke Market. In October 1917 he could not only observe at close quarters the conditions among the poorer members of society but also see for himself the reactions of the workers – 'a sense of turmoil and fermentation that revealed the shift from opposition to revolution', to quote one contemporary writer.[49]

In *Mein Kampf*, Hitler devotes more than a page to a description of his period of hospitalization in Beelitz and his attendant visit or visits to Berlin in the autumn of 1916, whereas his home leave of October 1917 is not mentioned at all. Nor does he refer to the fact that a year later, only a few weeks before the abdication of the Kaiser and the victory of the revolutionary workers' and soldiers' councils, he spent a second 'home leave' in the city, from 10 to 27 September 1918. But that is not all. He also fails to mention the growing discontent on the home front. Clearly he did not feel that it was worth referring to the fact that in April 1917 more than 200,000 employees working in the armaments industry at more than three hundred different factories downed tools,[50] while the two revolutions that broke out in Russia in 1917 feature only briefly as evidence of the 'Russian collapse'.[51] Nor does he have a single word to say about the United States' declaration of war on Germany on 6 April 1917, the 'peace resolution' of the Reichstag majority on 19 July 1917 or the unrest among the German fleet during the late summer of 1917. Instead, he waxes lyrical about the ostensible revival of the fighting spirit in the whole of the German army towards the end of 1917 and the newly awoken conviction that Germany would ultimately emerge from the conflict victorious: 'A glorious faith flowed again into the hearts of the millions, enabling them to await spring, 1918, with relief and confidence.' This mood of optimism is contrasted all the more graphically with the 'inner aim of the Marxist swindle of nations': 'While those at the front were undertaking the last preparations for the final conclusion of the eternal struggle [. . .], the biggest piece of chicanery in the whole war broke out in Germany. [. . .] The munitions strike was organised.'[52]

Hitler is referring here to the third and largest mass strike, which began on 28 January 1918 and spread from Danzig to Munich and from Leipzig to Hamburg. A total of 1.5 million workers, mainly in the munitions industry, went on strike.[53] In Berlin, where the number of striking workers reached half a million, the committee in charge of running the strike called it off on 3 February when the worsening siege of the city exacerbated the situation, specially convened courts handed down numerous terms of imprisonment and the military authorities started to enlist thousands of striking workers in the armed forces.[54] Writing in *Mein Kampf*, Hitler tried to give the impression that the strike convinced the enemy that they could still win the war and 'relieved the paralysing despair of the Allied front', 'an army believing all was lost', and which led to the deaths of thousands of German soldiers. Recognizing 'the possibilities for the future', the governments of the Entente 'approved unprecedented expenditures for continuing the propaganda to disrupt Germany'.[55] By the summer of 1918, Hitler concluded, petty squabbles and defeatist attitudes had reached the front, while supplies deteriorated, further reducing the armed forces' fighting strength. In August and September 1918 the 'symptoms of disorganisation' increased, and by the autumn the 'poison of the hinterland' began to take effect: 'And the younger recruit fell down completely – for he came from home.'[56]

At this point Hitler interrupts his account of the final weeks of the war on the western front in order to steer his narrative, in a dramatically more intense form, towards his own personal destiny. Early on the morning of 14 October 1918 he was the victim of a mustard gas attack on the heights south of Wervick, which was a part of the southern front near Ypres. For a time he was almost blind. On 21 October he was taken to the military hospital at Pasewalk in Pomerania. Here, on 10 November, he learnt that Kaiser Wilhelm II had abdicated and that the revolutionaries were victorious throughout the whole of Germany. In this way Hitler's own personal sufferings were a reflection of the 'monstrous' events that were taking place in the country as a whole, an act of 'madness' whose repercussions 'settled on all hearts' as a sense of 'the deepest dejection'. At the same time, however, those personal sufferings paled into insignificance beside 'the misfortune of the fatherland'.[57] Hitler's emotional and emotive account of the final chapter in the history of the First World War famously ends with the sentence: 'I, for my part, decided to go into politics.'[58]

Hitler's Retouching of his Autobiography

Many writers have pointed out the extent to which the autobiographical passages in Mein Kampf are marked by retouchings, distortions and downright falsifications. One of the most flagrant examples is Hitler's redating of his move from Vienna to Munich from May 1913[59] to the spring of 1912.[60] In the passage in Chapter 7 in which he describes the last two years of the war, Hitler essentially limits himself to a colourful account of the impact of enemy propaganda on the German soldiers serving on the western front. (The failure of German counterpropaganda, conversely, is ascribed to the mass strikes, which in turn are passed off, as noted above, as 'the biggest piece of chicanery in the whole war'.) The military actions themselves are described in vague and atmospheric terms. We learn nothing at all of Hitler's own role in these events. That he was a dispatch runner with the regimental staff from the outbreak of the war to the end of hostilities is nowhere mentioned.[61] Instead, Hitler uses extravagantly bombastic language to imply that for months on end he held out in trenches on the front line. Writing about his regiment in Flanders in July 1917, before the first major assault by the new English tanks, Hitler states that it 'clawed its way into the filthy mud, bit into the various holes and craters, and neither gave ground nor wavered'.[62] With his hankering after superficial effects, his portrait of the battles of the First World War effortlessly incorporates an account of his own two injuries of October 1916 and October 1918 and his subsequent weeks in the two military hospitals at Beelitz and Pasewalk. Thanks to his skilful interlinking of the universal and the particular, Hitler succeeds in forging a rigorous link between, on the one hand, the emotions that allegedly overwhelmed him while he was in hospital back home ('disgust' at the alleged shirking and 'hatred' of the ringleaders of the revolution) and his own political assessments and conclusions, which he claims to have drawn at this time, and, on the other hand, the overall course of the First World War.

This belated attempt to align political events with his own career – with a marked insistence on Hitler's own capacity for historiographical and political analysis and his ability to explain the world – reflects one of the basic drama-turgical concerns of *Mein Kampf*. It is also entirely typical of Hitler's general attitude towards his own person. If we are to believe *Mein Kampf*, then Hitler was only twelve and still at school when he first 'learned to understand and grasp the meaning of history'.[63] He was not yet twenty when, by his own account, there took shape within him 'a world picture and a philosophy which became the granite foundation' of all his actions. 'In addition to what I then created, I have had to learn little; and have had to alter nothing.'[64] Well aware of the falsehoods put about by the German propaganda services, Hitler claims to have been tormented by 'the thought that if Providence had put me in the place of the incapable or criminal incompetents or scoundrels in our propa-ganda service, our battle with Destiny would have taken a different turn'.[65]

Anton Joachimsthaler has summed up Hitler's autobiographical method by noting that, along with the various contradictions and demonstrably false assertions, what is striking above all is Hitler's 'constant attempt to bring forward his political ambitions to the earliest possible date'.[66] One could add that Hitler was no less concerned to draw a veil over certain sections of his life or at least to touch up the pictures of episodes that might have shown his political development in an unfavourable light. This would also help to explain why he could not admit that in the autumn of 1917 and again in 1918 he had been on home leave in Berlin in order to 'get to know the museums a little better'. More than a quarter of a century later he freely admitted as much to a small group of listeners in his headquarters in the Wolfsschanze one October night in 1941:

> I have always liked Berlin, and if it worries me that there is a lot there that is not very nice, this is only because the city means so much to me. During the war I spent ten days' leave there on two separate occasions. To spend such leave in Munich? The activities of the Blacks [Hitler is referring here to Christian politicians] would have robbed me of all pleasure in the place. On both occasions I went to Berlin, and it was at that time that I got to know Berlin's museums and collections.[67]

In the postcard that he sent to his friend Ernst Schmidt on 6 October 1917 Hitler had indeed mentioned that he was 'out and about practically all day long', getting to know the museums and galleries. On 8 October 1917 he wrote a second card to another friend, Sergeant Max Amann, who was later in charge of the National Socialist press empire, regretting that his days in the city were 'passing so quickly',[68] suggesting that he spent day after day visiting the museums and collections in the inner city.[69] He sent two further postcards to Amann on 11 and 12 October. The last one is a view of the monument to Kaiser Wilhelm I outside the Eosander Gate of the Royal Palace, only a stone's throw from the Lustgarten.[70] The various museums were situated at the northern edge of the Lustgarten, diagonally opposite the Arsenal with its Hall of Fame, which was used at this period as a museum for weapons and other memorabilia. This, too, would seem to indicate that during his first – and presumably also his second – visit to Berlin Hitler frequented the area around the city's museums, including the Royal Palace and the streets to the west of the Schloß-Brücke. It was here that the architectural jewels dating back to the age of Frederick the Great – buildings that Hitler particularly admired – were all to be found.

Writing in 1973, Joachim Fest examined the way in which Hitler portrayed his real or alleged impressions during the time that he spent in hospital in Beelitz and his first visit to Berlin in the autumn of 1916, and argued that it was at this period that he was 'prompted to enter politics'. According to Fest, Hitler observed the discontent and resignation that gripped the city and to his despair was forced to realize that with the passage of time the initial enthusiasm for the war had been stifled and 'the exalted sense of sharing a common destiny' had been replaced by factional divisions and social conflict. In short: 'It may be that his future resentment toward the city of Berlin had its origins in this experience.'[71] With the publication in 1980 of all of Hitler's surviving notes from the years between 1905 and 1924 and his 'Monologues in the Führer's Headquarters' of 1941–4, however, Fest's argument was effectively undermined. We now know that as late as 1917 Hitler was still insisting that Berlin was a 'wonderful', 'cosmopolitan' city and that in 1941 he even claimed that he had 'always liked Berlin' and had worried about it only because 'the city means so much to me'. As a result, it is no longer possible to sustain the argument that he felt a 'lifelong resentment' towards the capital.[72]

Conversely, it is hard to uphold John Lukacs' claim, advanced in 1997, that Hitler's thinking was effectively shaped by his 'experiences during the winter and the spring of 1918–19'. Only in the course of the 'German collapse' and the 'ridiculous and sordid episode of the Munich Soviet Republic' was his basic position and world view 'crystallized'.[73] In support of his argument Lukacs points out that until 1918 all of Hitler's notes, letters and postcards were – with a single exception, to which we shall return – 'apolitical'. A typical example is Hitler's postcard to Ernst Schmidt of 6 October 1917.[74] Lukacs argues that

Hitler's description of Berlin as 'wonderful' is an apolitical statement typical of the young Hitler. If we ignore Hitler's own self-portrait, this certainly seems plausible, at least at first sight.

A Fascination with the Monumental

Hitler's fondness for wartime Berlin was not, of course, directed at the city as such but at its function as the capital of the German Reich, a status that it had enjoyed since the foundation of the Reich in 1871. His claim in *Mein Kampf* that he left Austria primarily 'for political reasons'[75] is in many ways an implausible or at least one-sided explanation of his motivation in moving from Vienna to Munich.[76] And yet his choice of words is striking, implying, as it does, a choice in favour of Munich at the expense of Vienna: 'In addition to this, there was the heartfelt love which seized me for this city more than for any other place that I knew, almost from the first hour of my sojourn there. A *German* city! What a difference from Vienna! I grew sick to my stomach when I even thought back on this Babylon of races.'[77] In other words, Hitler's 'love' of Munich was politically motivated, whereas he repeatedly spoke of Vienna and its inhabitants in terms of the most abject loathing: 'I was repelled by the conglomeration of races which the capital showed me, repelled by this whole mixture of Czechs, Poles, Hungarians, Ruthenians, Serbs, and Croats.'[78] In consequence he never tired of stressing his 'inner revulsion' at the Habsburg state, even speaking of the 'Habsburg régime which I so hated' and of his view – acquired, of course, in his earliest youth – that 'Germanism could be safe-guarded only by the destruction of Austria, and, furthermore, that national sentiment is in no sense identical with dynastic patriotism; that above all the House of Habsburg was destined to be the misfortune of the German nation.'[79]

Unlike his aggressive anti-Semitism, Hitler's contempt for the Habsburg Empire – and his concomitant admiration for the Hohenzollern Empire – was not something that he picked up later from books. Nor was it the result of any subsequent political debate. This is clear from Hitler's only surviving letter from the war years in which he explicitly holds forth on political matters.[80] In this unusually long letter, written to a Munich acquaintance, the lawyer Ernst Hepp, on 5 February 1915, Hitler ends by admitting:

I think so often of Munich, and each of us has only one wish, that it may soon come to the final reckoning with the gang [i.e. of those opposed to the war], to the showdown, cost what it will, and that those of us who have the fortune to see their homeland again will find it purer and cleansed of alien influence, that through the sacrifices and suffering that so many hundred thousand of us make daily, that through the stream of blood that flows here day for day against an international world of enemies, not only will Germany's external enemies be smashed, but that our inner internationalism will also be broken. That would be worth more to me than all territorial gains. As far as Austria is concerned, things will happen as I always said.[81]

Anyone who longed for the downfall of the Habsburg Empire as ardently as did Hitler and who hoped that 'inner internationalism' would be smashed because only the destruction of the Austro-Hungarian Empire would make it possible for all German-speaking nations to be united in a single Reich 'cleansed of alien influence' – and at least until 1918 this inevitably meant an expanded Hohenzollern monarchy in Hitler's eyes – was bound to see Berlin, the capital of the German Reich, in a positive light. After all, Berlin, unlike Munich, was the home of the Hohenzollerns and, as such, the most important German city for Hitler, embodying, as it did, the power and grandeur of the Hohenzollern rulers and incorporating a greatness that was both geographical and numerical. How could Hitler not have found the capital of the German Reich 'wonderful'? After all, he often insisted at a later date that he could not marry because his love was directed at Germany alone.[82]

In Vienna, where Hitler still saw himself working in the future as an architect, he had been 'fascinated first and foremost by the buildings'. In the Wilhelminian architecture of Berlin he rediscovered something that had already caught his attention in the inner city in Vienna. In 1935 his early biographer Rudolf Olden observed that only the 'magnificence and power' of Vienna's architecture provoked a response in him and that he considered the buildings predating the neo-Baroque and neo-Classical structures of the second half of the nineteenth century not even worth mentioning: 'Strength and loveliness, everything original remains a closed book to him. Only the sleekly second-hand fills him with any enthusiasm.'[83] Hitler found examples of such second-hand architecture in abundance in the immediate vicinity of Berlin's museums and galleries: in the new buildings along the Kaiser-Wilhelm-Straße on the other side of the Spree.

In 1884, under Wilhelm I, a start had been made on redeveloping the medieval heart of Berlin in the northern part of the old city, a scheme whose magnitude can be compared only to the Haussmannization of Paris.[84] Under the overall control of private investors, the Kaiser-Wilhelm-Straße (now the Karl-Liebknecht-Straße) was laid out in an easterly direction, starting at the Spree. Dozens of houses were torn down and entire streets and apartment blocks disappeared. And, in keeping with contemporary taste, a space was opened up around the city's third-oldest church, St Mary's, by tearing down the houses to the north and west. The new boulevard was lined with houses and shops in the neo-Baroque style typical of Wilhelminian Germany. The street was also linked by the Schloß-Brücke to Unter den Linden, with its opera house and Arsenal, and beyond. For centuries Unter den Linden had ended at the Lustgarten in front of the Royal Palace, but now it formed part of an imposing new thoroughfare. The city's old 'triumphal way' had been designed to lead with magnificent inevitability to the Old Palace, but instead it was cut off at an angle and extended to run through the now-fragmented Lustgarten as far as the Spree. Here the old footbridge – the Sechserbrücke – was pulled down and replaced between 1886 and 1889 by the ostentatious Kaiser-Wilhelm-Brücke (now replaced in turn by the Liebknechtbrücke), which gave access to the new boulevard on the other side of the Spree.

The building of a new road bridge at this point was possible only because Wilhelm I gave his consent to the demolition of a third of the old Schloßapotheke, one of the oldest parts of the Royal Palace which dated back to the Renaissance. The old royal stables on the Schloßplatz were likewise demolished and replaced by a new building in the Wilhelminian style. In the mid-1890s all the houses on the Schloßfreiheit[85] in front of the Eosander Gate were torn down, thereby ensuring that, when seen from the west – from the direction of Unter den Linden – the palace acquired a far more monumental aspect. Schinkel's old cathedral gave way to a new building designed by Julius Raschdorff and constructed between 1894 and 1905, its massive forms in the style of the Italian High Renaissance completely dwarfing the architectural framework of the Lustgarten. The art critic Karl Scheffler called it the 'Reich's showpiece church' and in 1931 complained retrospectively that 'an age that dared to flaunt the specious magnificence of the Cathedral between Schlüter's Palace and Schinkel's Museum was ripe for major disaster'.[86]

As a result of more than two decades of systematic alterations to the area around the Palace, the well-planned Baroque axial design comprising Unter den Linden, the Lustgarten and the Palace that had survived until the end of the nineteenth century was sacrificed to a monumental redevelopment in the spirit of Wilhelminian Germany.[87] It was a process designed to impose a sense of uniformity appropriate to gala events, and it culminated in the inauguration of Reinhold Begas' national memorial to Wilhelm I on 22 March 1897 on the spot formerly occupied by the houses that made up the Schloßfreiheit.[88] The bombastic pretensions of the neo-Baroque monument are clear not least from the sheer size of the equestrian figure on a plinth in the middle of the square:

30 feet tall, it was three times higher than the equestrian statue of the Great Elector that had been designed for the Lange Brücke between 1696 and 1700 and which is now in the outer courtyard at Charlottenburg Palace. In all, the monument was 70 feet tall and covered an area of 260 by 130 feet, 'its tremendous triumphal architecture representing an apotheosis of national might, a monument in the theatrical style beloved of Wilhelm II'.[89]

One could add that, at least at this date,[90] Hitler, too, loved this same theatrical style, a claim based on a third postcard that he sent from Berlin on 12 October 1917, again to his regimental comrade Max Amann: 'I am sending you this picture postcard of the National Monument, Sergeant, and remain, with best wishes, yours sincerely, A. Hitler.'[91] In addition to what he already knew from Vienna, these early visits to Berlin provided Hitler with further examples of monumental urban architecture, and it was to these findings from the time of the First World War that he later returned when – at a meeting with representatives of the Reich's railways and Berlin city council in September 1933, for example – he announced that the 'only monumental buildings' in Berlin were 'Unter den Linden, the Palace and their immediate vicinity'. These, he went on, marked 'the high point of the city both culturally and in terms of its urban design'.[92]

For the present the barely thirty-year-old Hitler had little opportunity to devote himself to questions of urban development. And now, after the Kaiser had abdicated on 9 November 1918 and the Kaiserreich had been consigned to history, Hitler – suddenly a soldier without a war – had to contemplate the idea of being thrust back into an existence from which mobilization had freed him four years earlier. The period that followed was a time of 'terrible days and even worse nights – I knew that all was lost. [. . .] In those nights hatred grew in me, hatred for those responsible for this deed.'[93]

And Hitler was convinced that 'those responsible for this deed' were based in Berlin.

2

'Not away from Berlin but towards Berlin'

1919–25: A SOCIAL CLIMBER FROM MUNICH ON HIS WAY NORTH

'In the face of world history we shall have played our part when we have put an end to the November criminals. I was in northern Germany. Everyone is waiting for me.'
Hitler at an SA gathering in Munich, 4 March 1923[1]

'When I come to Berlin, it will be like Christ entering the Temple and driving out the money-changers!'
Hitler to Dietrich Eckart, early June 1923[2]

Hitler's First Aeroplane Flight to Berlin

Early in the afternoon of 17 March 1920 an open sports plane – even at this date a relatively antiquated model – landed on the airfield of the army's training ground at Jüterbog, some 45 miles south of Berlin. At the controls was twenty-eight-year-old Lieutenant Robert von Greim, one of Germany's heroes from the aerial battles of the First World War. A quarter of a century later he was briefly to become commander-in-chief of the German Air Force.[3] Until the second half of the nineteenth century Jüterbog had been a sleepy provincial town in the shadow of the industrial centre of Luckenwalde further to the north, but it had acquired a wider significance when the Prussian army laid out a training ground and shooting range there in 1864, after which date the facilities continued to grow incrementally.[4] The sports plane had taken off from Augsburg and needed to refuel, but as a result of landing in Jüterbog its passengers found themselves in a dangerous situation. For some days the airstrip, training ground and barracks had been in the hands of striking workers.

Early on the morning of 13 March 1920 a putsch had been set in train in Berlin in an attempt to overthrow the government. Its leaders were Wolfgang Kapp,[5] an East Prussian senior civil servant with a past involvement in nationalist politics, and General Walther von Lüttwitz, who was in charge of the First Group Commando. Their main support came from the Ehrhardt Brigade, which ought to have been disbanded under the terms of the Versailles Treaty of 10 March 1920. The deposed government fled to Dresden, later to Stuttgart, and within days millions of people had responded to the appeals of the Social Democratic members of the government, together with the leaders of the SPD and the trades unions, and organized a general strike designed to topple the new self-proclaimed chancellor, Kapp, and those sections of the armed forces that supported him.[6] This was also the situation in the small town of Jüterbog. The putsch was hastily prepared and badly carried out, and it failed after only a few days. On 17 March Kapp declared that he regarded his 'mission as complete' and that he was stepping down and 'handing back' the executive powers to the military commander-in-chief.[7]

This was the day on which the two passengers took off from Augsburg in order to offer their assistance to the putschists in Berlin. They were the fifty-two-year-old anti-Semitic journalist and editor of the weekly *Auf gut Deutsch* (Plain Speaking), Dietrich Eckart, and his companion, the thirty-one-year-old Adolf Hitler, whose first flight this was and who, not yet released from military service, had spent the last few months working closely with Captain Karl Mayr, running the armed forces' regional Information Department in Munich. The army had placed the pilot at their passengers' disposal.[8] Eckart had turned for help to his friend and sponsor, the Augsburg chemist and factory owner Gottfried Grandel, and it was Grandel who provided the aircraft, which came from the Rumpler Works at Augsburg.[9] Mayr and Eckart had already visited Berlin in early March in order to plan the putsch with Kapp and Lüttwitz, and on the night of 16–17 March Mayr held a lengthy telephone conversation with one of the representatives of the putsch at the Reich Chancellery.[10] According to Grandel, Eckart 'was in charge of the Bavarian preparations for the Kapp Putsch'. Eckart and Hitler's flight to Berlin and to the very heart of the attempted putsch was therefore no precipitate last-minute venture undertaken on the spur of the moment, as it is sometimes said to have been. Contact between the self-styled 'saviours of the fatherland' in Berlin and Munich had existed for quite some time.

In short, it was two delegates from the Munich supporters of the planned putsch who, landing at the military airstrip at Jüterbog, encountered workers who had occupied the airport as part of the general strike directed against the putsch. In the event Eckart and Hitler were well prepared for the situation in which they found themselves. Hitler was dressed half in civilian clothes, half in military dress, including puttees, and was also wearing a false beard – an unnecessary piece of disguise, for who would have recognized this political agitator outside Munich in March 1920? Be that as it may, he passed himself off as the 'book-keeper' of Dietrich Eckart, who in turn described himself as a 'paper dealer'. According to Hitler's early biographer Konrad Heiden, Eckart asked the strikers the quickest way to a large printing firm with which he was wanting to conclude a trade deal. 'With his goatee beard, Hitler stood modestly to one side as Eckart's book-keeper. They got through and arrived safely in Berlin.'[11] None the less, Eckart's paper business and Hitler's glued-on beard do not entirely explain why the striking workers allowed the two men to continue their flight after refuelling. It is likely that they were able to resume their journey because they had pre-emptively forearmed themselves with passes from both the German National People's Party and the Independent Social Democratic Party; it was the latter that helped the impostors out of their present difficulties. 'The Independent Social Democratic Party papers helped them on their way, and Dietrich Eckart spun them a tale about secret paper purchases for the party.'[12]

On their arrival in the capital, Eckart and Hitler found themselves facing a fait accompli, the members of the putsch already being in retreat. And yet their hazardous flight to Berlin was not entirely futile, and they did not return to Munich empty-handed.[13] Eckart had already introduced Hitler to high society in the Bavarian capital,[14] and he now proceeded to open a few doors to his protégé in Berlin – he had lived in the city between 1899 and 1915.[15] In this way Hitler came into contact with leading members of the right-wing nationalists, including Count Ernst von Reventlow, who was later to represent the NSDAP in the Reichstag, Walter Stennes, who was a former leader of the Volunteer Corps and now in charge of the Berlin constabulary (for a time he later became the SA commander in Berlin), and Captain Waldemar Pabst, who had been responsible for the murder of Rosa Luxemburg and Karl Liebknecht in January 1919 and whom Hitler was able to meet thanks to a letter of recommendation from Ernst Röhm in Munich. Röhm praised Hitler as a successful orator who was particularly effective when addressing soldiers and workers. Pabst is said to have been remarkably impressed by Hitler's appearance but to have sent him away again on the grounds that his Austrian accent rendered him unusable as a speaker in Berlin.[16] Eckart also introduced Hitler to the salon of the piano manufacturer Edwin Bechstein and to the latter's wife, Helene. Edwin remained a lifelong political ally, while Helene

smothered him with a mother's love.[17] According to Walter Görlitz and
Herbert A. Quint:

> It was through Reventlow and the widow of privy councillor Carl Albrecht
> Heckmann, a member of a large family of Berlin industrialists, that Hitler
> came into contact with Pan-German circles and at Frau Heckmann's home in
> the Maaßenstraße was introduced to General Ludendorff, an acquaintance
> that was to prove altogether momentous. [...] It was not without profit that
> Hitler returned to Munich. His prestige was in the ascendant and he had
> become what might be called 'well known'.[18]

And how quickly Hitler had risen to his position of newfound eminence!
According to his own version of events, it was in the wake of the news that
Wilhelm II had abdicated and that the revolution had triumphed in November
1918 that he had decided to become a politician, and yet he had initially done
nothing to implement that decision, preferring, instead, to devote his energies to
remaining in the army.[19] In early June 1919 he is known to have been ordered to
attend 'speakers' courses' and lectures organized by the Information Department
of the Fourth Bavarian Group Command under Karl Mayr. In August 1919
he addressed 'German prisoners of war returning home following their indoc-
trination with Bolshevik and Spartacist ideas' in the transit camp at Lechfeld,[20]
attracting attention through his spirited delivery and anti-Semitic outbursts.[21]

A few days after his return from Lechfeld, Hitler was asked by Mayr to
represent the armed forces at a meeting of the German Workers' Party (DAP),
which Anton Drexler had founded at the beginning of the year and which had
renamed itself the National Socialist German Workers' Party (NSDAP) on
1 February 1920. He was also asked to provide a report on the meeting, which
took place at the Sterneckerbräu on 12 September 1919.[22] Hitler joined the
DAP soon afterwards, and it was here, presumably towards the end of 1919,
that he was introduced to Ernst Röhm, who was to provide Hitler and the
party with sustained support during the coming years. Hitler first appeared as
a speaker for the DAP on 16 October 1919.[23] In the course of February 1920
Drexler and Hitler drew up the party's notorious twenty-five-point programme.
Within only a few months of his initial contact with the party and with the
politically active circles of the Bavarian Army, Hitler had succeeded, therefore,
in achieving a position in which he was found worthy of accompanying
Dietrich Eckart – already recognized as a leading figure in right-wing politics
in Bavaria – on a flight to Berlin to meet the leaders of the Kapp Putsch in
March 1920.

Confessions concerning Berlin

It is worth pausing at this point to ask whether Hitler's experiences of Berlin following the collapse of the Kapp Putsch influenced or even altered his view of the capital. A document that has survived from the period immediately before the putsch may be viewed as a programmatic response to this question on the part of the NSDAP. The document in question is a letter written jointly by Drexler and Hitler – here described as the 'recruiting officer of the party's local branch' – and addressed to Walter Riehl, who was the chairman of the Austrian National Socialists. Dated 1 March 1920, it states that the NSDAP's aim was to 'give the German nation the place on this earth to which it is entitled on the strength of its numbers and culture'. In order to achieve this goal, it was necessary to end the fragmentation of the German tribes and reunite the German nation. A permanent reunification was possible, however, only if steps were taken to ensure that the Reich was organized and administered around a central hub. And this led Drexler and Hitler to refer to Berlin:

> The shortcomings and disadvantages of Berlin do not strike us as inseparable from this city but only as a necessary consequence of a so-called culture whose basic nature is determined not so much by influences of a Germanic racial type as by their Jewish equivalent. It is only too natural that in the largest city in the Reich the curse of this cultural aberration should find its most pernicious expression, regardless of whether this city is Berlin or any other.
>
> That is why our struggle can be directed not at this city as such but at the general causes of this state of affairs. We regard the so-called 'Struggle for Berlin' as a mask for the goal of hurling Germany back into its former impotence and fragmentation by doing away with the Reich's capital and by creating equally large individual states that will fight with each other as equally powerful rivals, allowing the country to bleed to death in a perpetual civil war.[24]

In this way Drexler and Hitler made it clear that they had no desire to align themselves with the separatists who, relatively numerous in Bavaria, sought to break away from the Reich's central command structures. Rather, their hostility was directed simply at what they termed 'Judaized Berlin'. This attitude is easy to reconcile with Hitler's demagogic outbursts against the capital. On 6 April 1920, for example, he claimed: 'Of the many foodstuffs that are transported to Berlin, the worker sees and senses nothing, likewise the minor civil servant'.

His reproach was directed at the 'dirty East European Jew who has descended on the city' and whom Hitler had mentioned disapprovingly in his previous sentence.[25] This also explains why, in a different context, Hitler asked his listeners to 'stop insulting the north German tribes', for it was not his language that made the German what he was, but his heart. Elsewhere Hitler insisted that 'the Berlin of Frederick the Great has been turned into a pigsty by the Jews. You should first evict the Jews from Berlin and Munich and Vienna before you insult our German tribal brethren.'[26]

A speech that Hitler delivered on 24 November 1920 in which he attacked the 'dishonour dealt to the German nation' gives us an idea of where exactly in Berlin Hitler located this 'pigsty': all the misery 'comes from our fanatical left-wing parties in Berlin W'.[27] He was referring here to the postal district around the Kaiser Wilhelm Memorial Church and the Kurfürstendamm, with its relatively high percentage of Jews. Even before the First World War the phrase 'Berlin W' was a favourite cliché of anti-Semitic discourse, although the area can hardly have been a hotbed of fanatical left-wing thinking.

Other speeches by the tyro politician make it clear that it was not the city as a whole that Hitler had in his sights whenever he referred to 'Berlin'. A perceptive reporter from the *Rosenheimer Tagblatt* summed up Hitler's contribution to a debate at a meeting of the Bayernbund in the Hofbräuhaus in Rosenheim: 'Particularly moving was the fact that Hittler [*sic*] and, hence, the German Workers' Party repeatedly fulminated against the Jews in Berlin but had nothing to say about the centralism of the city.'[28] In referring to Berlin, therefore, Hitler aimed to awaken anti-Jewish, rather than anti-Prussian, feelings of resentment, notably when, in a historical retrospective, he argued that 'for the Jews' Jerusalem had simply been a headquarters 'just as – for all I care – Berlin and New York and Warsaw are today'.[29] On another occasion he attacked 'Jewish capitalism' by claiming – in a similar vein – that 'the Jew is ensconced in Russia just as surely as in Berlin and Vienna'.[30]

Fundraising Visits to Berlin

In 1920 Hitler paid at least one more visit to Berlin. Among his surviving correspondence is a postcard with an aerial view of the Reichstag building. It was written to his former landlord in Munich, Joseph Popp, and his wife Anna, and is dated 3 November 1920. But apart from its 'cordial greetings',[31] it contains no word as to the reason for Hitler's visit. Since he is known to have attended NSDAP meetings in Munich on 29 October and 5 November 1920,[32] he can have spent no more than a few days in Berlin. But we shall probably not be mistaken in assuming that Hitler renewed contact with members of the 'patriotic' groups he had met in March of that year.

But his visit to Berlin may also have been connected with attempts by the NSDAP to acquire the publishing house of Franz Eher and one of its titles, the weekly newspaper *Völkischer Beobachter*. The NSDAP concluded the deal on 17 December 1920 with the help of two loans, one from General Franz Xaver von Epp, who joined the NSDAP in 1928 and became governor of Bavaria in 1933, and the other from Gottfried Grandel, the Augsburg industrialist who had already financed Eckart and Hitler's flight to Berlin in March 1920.[33]

It is conceivable that, in Anton Joachimsthaler's words, Hitler returned to Berlin in December 1920 'to ask for financial support for the newspaper in the city's legal circles', but the claim is impossible to authenticate.[34] Beyond doubt, conversely, is the visit that Hitler and Eckart paid in June 1921, when the party's notorious financial difficulties prompted them to undertake a fund-raising trip to Berlin 'to find backing for the ailing *Völkischer Beobachter*'.[35] This was at least the sixth time that Hitler had been in Berlin, and the stay lasted several weeks, making it his longest to date.[36]

On this occasion, the visitors' travel expenses and accommodation were paid for by Edwin Bechstein, whom Hitler had known since the March of the previous year.[37] Hermann Esser, a member of the party since October 1919 and a speaker at numerous NSDAP rallies, accompanied Hitler on these fund-raising trips to Berlin. Decades later he confirmed that the aim of the visit in June 1921 had been 'to enter into financial negotiations with a whole series of prominent figures suggested by Heinrich Class'. Class ran the influential Pan-German League, which generally operated behind the scenes, and has been described as the 'political brains behind German chauvinism'.[38] His book *Wenn ich der Kaiser wär* (If I Were the Kaiser) was published in 1912 under the pseudonym Daniel Frymann and was reprinted several times. With its aggressively anti-Jewish programme, it represented one of the most important contributions to the debate among the extreme right in Germany and had a lasting impact on all *völkisch* nationalistic organizations of the early Weimar Republic.[39] Class evidently had access to unlimited funds and was willing to lend Hitler a helping hand.

The acting chairman of the United Patriotic Associations of Germany at this time was Fritz Geisler, who later reported that it had been the aim of the 'progressive nationalist circles in the north' to help the NSDAP, which had initially been limited to Munich, and to assist it in 'gaining access to northern Germany'. To this end a secret meeting took place in Berlin between Hitler,

Class, Geisler himself and Leopold von Vietinghoff-Scheel, who was the secretary of the Pan-German League. 'Following this discussion, Adolf Hitler was helped to gain entry to wealthy, nationally minded circles in Berlin in order to raise the funds that were needed to support the party's work in northern Germany.'[40]

Hermann Esser also recalled a number of other details about Hitler's visit to Berlin:

> Hitler and his companions stayed at the Hotel Sanssouci, a small and modest bed and breakfast hotel where leading members of the Ehrhardt Brigade, together with Major Pabst and other figures from the patriotic movement, including the Duke of Cobūrg, were permanent residents. During this visit Adolf Hitler also held discussions with others who held *deutschvölkisch* views, with [Reinhold] Wulle and [Albrecht von] Graefe.[41]

The seventy-room Hotel Sanssouci was situated at 37 Linkstraße, a small street near the Potsdamer Platz, and was far from being one of the leading hotels in the city. It is not even mentioned in the 1921 Baedeker guide to Berlin, while Grieben's guide lists it only under 'Other recommendable hotels (less luxurious)'[42] – an indication that Hitler still had limited resources.

Among the affluent backers in Berlin who shared an interest in politics and who promised to help Hitler at this time was the coffee manufacturer Richard Franck.[43] Even so, the financial proceeds of this extended visit to the city, which Hitler again used to visit its museums and galleries,[44] were clearly so meagre that by early August 1921 Dietrich Eckart, who had been appointed editor-in-chief of the *Völkischer Beobachter*, was afraid that it was already on the point of foundering. In a letter to his friend and contact in Berlin, Emil Gansser – a member of the NSDAP from 7 March 1920[45] – he complained that 'obtaining money is proving difficult. [...] Several days ago I wrote at length to Herr Frank [*sic*] in Berlin but have still not had a reply. [...] I have to obtain a relatively large contribution from somewhere or other within the next few days, otherwise I can't go on, not even with the best will in the world. If necessary I could return to Berlin at short notice.'[46] On 28 November 1921 he even sent a telegram to Gansser: 'Without immediate contribution of the most substantial kind, paper finished by day after tomorrow.'[47] In a further letter to Gansser of 13 August 1922, Eckart refers to more money worries: 'But ultimately Berlin must finally make a showing.'[48]

When questioned by the police at the time of the Hitler–Ludendorff trial in 1924, Helene Bechstein claimed that her husband had 'repeatedly – in other words, two or three times – given a helping hand to Hitler in order to assist him in his Munich newspaper enterprise, the *Völkischer Beobachter*'.[49] We can be relatively certain, therefore, that in the early years after its acquisition at the end of 1920, the party organ survived only thanks to constant contributions from sympathetic backers in Berlin. Some twenty years later Hitler himself confirmed this in one of his monologues in the Wolfsschanze, when he referred to Gansser:[50] 'Dr Gansser deserves to be remembered for ever by the party. I owe him for a whole series of extremely important introductions; without my acquaintance with Richard Franck [. . .] I would not have been able to ensure that the [*Völkischer*] *Beobachter* pulled through in 1923.'[51]

When Gansser died in Berlin in January 1941, the head of the Reich Chancellery, Heinrich Lammers, devoted a lengthy obituary to him. Gansser, he wrote, was one of the first people 'during the early days of the movement' to support Hitler and was also one of the few people to do so 'from the educated classes'. He never tired of introducing his protégé to others and of winning the latter over to the cause. These people then 'made available their extensive influence for the advance of National Socialism. Gansser deserves particular credit for introducing National Socialist ideas to northern Germany.'[52]

Hitler's Appearances at the National Club

Gansser was also the recipient of a letter that Hitler wrote on 29 November 1921 in which he gave 'a brief outline' of his career to date. It contains many of the phrases and idées reçues that were later to typify Hitler's – and other writers' – accounts of his life, from his alleged activity as an unskilled worker in the building and construction trade in Vienna to his membership of the DAP, which had once had only seven members.[53] On the one hand, the letter is extremely detailed when it comes to the military decorations and awards that Hitler received, whereas, on the other hand, it also includes a number of false statements such as the claim that Hitler moved to Munich from Vienna a whole year earlier than was in fact the case. As in *Mein Kampf*, Hitler knowingly drew a veil over his two visits to Berlin in the autumn of 1917 and the autumn of 1918. The letter begins with the sentence: 'Herr Eckart tells me that you have again taken an interest in my rise to party leader.'

Hitler presumably used the word 'again' because he had already made contact with Gansser before November 1921, whereas only now was he being asked to provide his correspondent with more detailed biographical information. In early December, shortly after receiving Hitler's letter, Gansser organized a meeting at the National Club near the Brandenburg Gate.[54] In the words of one of the National Socialists' later publications, the meeting was intended to provide Hitler with an opportunity to make 'initial contact with nationalist circles in northern Germany'. In the course of the session, he

> answered the various questions that were put to him as to the sort of solution he envisaged to the problem of the Marxists and Jews in the event of a takeover. Even at that early date he already indicated in broad outline what he was to implement in 1933, including the 'concentration camps' (this was the expression that he used), the necessity for which he particularly stressed if the takeover was to be carried out in as bloodless a manner as possible.[55]

Hitler's presence in Berlin between 8 and 14 December 1921 had to be kept a strict secret because he was afraid of the sanctions of Prussia's Social Democrat minister of the interior, Carl Severing.[56]

Hitler returned to Berlin between 8 and 29 March 1922, presumably to collect more money for the *Völkischer Beobachter* and to build up his political contacts with the city.[57] This would seem to be confirmed by a confidential letter that Gansser wrote to the director of Siemens, Karl Burhenne, on 8 March 1922 and that was evidently intended to prepare the ground for a private meeting between Burhenne and Hitler. Gansser enclosed with his letter a 'brief note on Hitler's movement based on my own observations of the last two years'. And he went on to suggest that it would be especially worthwhile if Hitler could address a relatively large gathering in the city. On the other hand, he did not think that at present any useful purpose would be served by 'just a single appearance'. Even if it was not possible to observe the crowd's reactions directly, the personal impression made by Hitler was 'such that anyone can easily explain his impact on the workers'.[58] Gansser clearly approved of Hitler, for in a subsequent letter to him he explained that Hitler was visible proof 'that the workforce is really glad to break free from the Red terror of the Jewish trades unions as soon as it is offered a sufficiently powerful hand'.[59]

Hitler's three-week visit to Berlin in March 1922 was followed by a month-long visit between 17 May and 15 June 1922. As before, he stayed at the Hotel Sanssouci.[60] And once again Gansser opened many doors for him. A confidential communiqué that he signed on 26 May reads:

> Monday 29 May 1922 at 8.30 in the evening
> Adolf Hitler from Munich

will address a select gathering at the National Club, 6 Sommerstraße, after dinner (7.30), on the National Socialist German Workers' Movement.

In view of the importance of this event for Germany's future, I take the liberty of asking Your Right Honourable self to grace this lecture with your presence. It would also be desirable if you would be kind enough to invite other German men of sociopolitical and economic importance to this lecture.[61]

In his lecture to the members of the National Club, Hitler left his listeners in no doubt as to his aims. They could gain power, he insisted, only on a completely new social and political basis, rather than by parliamentary or democratic means. The only way forward was through violence. Young people would have to be brought together and prepared for the task ahead. A national dictatorship must refashion Germany politically, economically and socially, while sidelining 'the pernicious influence of the Jews and Freemasons' as well as political Catholicism. The parties of the right did not fully appreciate the 'corrosive effect of these three international forces'. Only the NSDAP under his own command, Hitler went on, was free from the influence of these groups and, as a result, was destined to lead Germany to a better future.[62] One of those present on 29 May 1922 later recalled that the lecture 'left a very powerful impression on its listeners, who were mostly generals and older, high-ranking civil servants'. At the express desire of the 'extraordinarily enthusiastic members of the National Club', Hitler agreed to repeat his lecture at the same venue, which he probably did on 5 or 12 June 1922.[63]

Among those who turned up for the repeat of the lecture was Ernst von Borsig, the head of the Berlin locomotive and machine-building firm that bore his name. In 1937 Borsig's secretary of many years' standing, Fritz Detert, wrote to his employer's son to describe the effect that Hitler had had on his father:

Your father was so gripped by this experience that I was instructed to make contact with Adolf Hitler directly, without going through any third party, and to discuss with him how and with what resources the movement, which was at that time limited almost exclusively to southern Germany, especially Bavaria, could be expanded to take in northern Germany, especially Berlin. Adolf Hitler was happy to agree to your father's request for a private meeting.

As in March 1920, when Hitler's commanding officer, Karl Mayr, had met Wolfgang Kapp only days before the latter became the political head of the military putsch against the country's government, the meeting took place at the Rheingold wine cellar in the Bellevuestraße, close to the Potsdamer Platz. According to Detert, Hitler was pleased to receive Borsig's offer of support for his movement and suggested a plan for establishing and financing an office in Berlin. 'The active implementation of this plan,' Detert explained in his letter to Borsig's son, 'foundered on the composition of industry and commerce in Berlin, which was largely dominated by non-Aryan elements.' As a result, Borsig was reduced to 'talking to a number of tireless nationalists among his most intimate industrialist friends and persuading them to support the movement'. The not inconsiderable sums of money that were raised in this way were then taken to Munich by the factory manager at the Borsig plant in Tegel and handed over personally to Hitler's representatives in the Bavarian capital.[64]

'Our Movement Remains in Munich'

Detert's claim that the plan to set up an NSDAP office in Berlin came to nothing because commerce in the capital was dominated by 'non-Aryan elements' is called into question not least by the fact that such an office was indeed opened only a few years later, even though 'the composition of industry and commerce' had not substantially changed in the intervening period. Far more likely is the suggestion that in 1922 Hitler was not interested in shifting his party's focus of interest away from Munich. We know that he had bitterly resisted such moves in early 1921, when a number of leading members of the NSDAP had advocated a merger with Alfred Brunner's German Socialist Party (DSP).

Ideologically speaking, the DSP was almost indistinguishable from the NSDAP. It was largely focused on northern Germany, having its largest local branch in Hanover. In August 1920, at a joint meeting in Salzburg of National Socialists from Germany, Austria and the Sudetenland, the area north of the Main was allotted to the DSP as its field of political endeavour, while the area south of the Main was entrusted to the NSDAP. (The only exception was the DSP group led by Julius Streicher in Nuremberg.) But by the spring of 1921 a plan was afoot to merge the NSDAP and DSP as a single party under federalist management with its headquarters in Berlin. At the DSP's party rally in Zeitz in March 1921 it was also decided, with the approval of the NSDAP's representative, Anton Drexler, that the combined organization would henceforth be called the German National Socialist Party. An office was even opened in Berlin.[65] Only a short time afterwards, however, a circular letter from the DSP admitted that 'Munich rejects Berlin as its headquarters and is willing to agree to a merger only if the running of the unified party is transferred to Munich.

Our comrades in Munich have adopted this attitude not because of any hostility towards their colleagues in northern Germany but because of the system of government in Berlin.[66]

'Munich' was the shorthand form not of the leaders of the NSDAP, whose official chairman at this time was still Drexler, but of Hitler, who was bound to fear that his position within the party would be weakened if the two parties merged and their new head office was transferred to Berlin. He appealed to the party's constitution, according to which its headquarters were in Munich and must remain there 'once and for all'. In this way he was able to ensure that the agreement that had been signed in Zeitz 'in the face of all reason' was rescinded.[67] One result of this was that during his stay in Berlin during the early summer of 1921 a number of local party leaders openly criticized his political methods and his behaviour within the party. Also during this visit a serious rival appeared in the guise of the *völkisch* writer Otto Dickel, who was a popular and dynamic public speaker and who left a deep impression on the majority of the local leaders. Hitler was so furious at this development that on his return to Munich he resigned from the party on 11 July 1921, plunging the young NSDAP into its most damaging crisis to date.[68] Hitler then proceeded to insist on far-reaching conditions before he would consider rejoining the party: he was to be given 'the post of chairman with dictatorial powers', and it was to be 'laid down as a point of principle that the headquarters of the movement is Munich and will for ever remain so'. Moreover, he went on, the party's programme must remain inviolate; and all attempts at a merger were to be abandoned. Instead Hitler insisted on a form of annexation: all organizations that wanted to work with the NSDAP had to be subservient to it.[69] In little more than two weeks Hitler got his way with his demand for 'dictatorial powers'. And from now on he saw himself – as others did – as the 'Führer'.[70]

Following his victory over his adversaries within his own party and over his rivals outside the party,[71] Hitler was able to claim, triumphantly, at an NSDAP meeting on 29 July 1921: 'Our movement started out from Munich and it remains in Munich, not, as many troublemakers wish, in Berlin (never).'[72] As so often, he fulminated against 'the Jewish government in Berlin' and dismissed left-wing and liberal newspapers as 'dirty Jewish rags'. He also took part in demonstrations under the slogan 'For Germany – against Berlin'. On 18 September 1922 his tirades against the country's government culminated in the appearance of the term 'November criminals',* which he regularly used

---

* The expression used by the extreme right to vilify the members of the November Revolution of 1918 who had signed the peace treaty ending the First World War on 11 November 1918.

from now on.[73] And yet, in spite of all his attacks on 'Berlin's pernicious policies of fulfilment' and the 'Bolshevism that has been bred in Berlin', he
continued to protest against attempts to undermine Bavaria's loyalty and turn
the region into a separatist state. The party's watchword, he insisted, must
be 'Not away from Berlin, but towards Berlin in order to free the German
people from those who would lead them astray'.[74] One implication of this was
his continuing to maintain close contacts with representatives of extreme
right-wing and nationalist groups in Berlin.

And so we find Hitler again addressing members of the National Club in
Berlin on 12 October 1922 in the course of what was at least his seventh
visit to the city since the Kapp Putsch of March 1920. Among the 'nationalist
circles from northern Germany' were representatives of the United Patriotic
Associations, the Stahlhelm defence league, which was affiliated to the German
National People's Party, the German National League of Commercial Employees
and the German League, an anti-Semitic and *völkisch* 'order'. Hitler's address,
which was said to be 'very lengthy', was directed in particular at the imminent
battle for the Ruhr.[75] Following the French and Belgian invasion of the Ruhr on
11 January 1923, nationalist circles tried to create a united front against the
occupying powers, a front that would not fight shy of military attacks and acts
of sabotage. At a conference in Berlin in late February 1923,[76] Ludendorff
attempted to bring together conservative and extreme right-wing defence
leagues. He also arranged a meeting between the leaders of the various paramilitary organizations in northern Germany, including Generals Theodor von
Watter and Ernst von Oven, the leader of the Volunteer Corps, Gerhard
Rossbach, and Adolf Heiß, who was the head of the Reichsflagge and spokesman
for Röhm's Bavarian Working Group of Patriotic Fighting Associations.

Hitler, too, attended the meeting, at which Ludendorff expressed the view
that the government of Chancellor Wilhelm Cuno and General Hans von
Seeckt needed support since their main priority was now to join forces in
combating an external enemy. Hitler raised no objections to this assertion,
even though he had expressed the opposite view when speaking in public.[77] At
his trial in Munich, following his failed putsch of 9 November 1923, he
claimed to have asked the 'patriotic associations' whether they were prepared
to offer military training to the National Socialists' young Storm Troopers.[78]

Adolf Hitler – a Phantom

Even during his earlier visits to Berlin, Hitler already represented a threat to
the city's authorities, but the situation became worse after 15 November 1922,

when the NSDAP was banned in Prussia and a number of northern German cities passed a law designed to protect the Weimar Republic. Hitler now had a price on his head. The area in which he could legally operate was largely reduced to Upper Bavaria. (There were few local branches outside Upper Bavaria and Prussia.) The fact that at an NSDAP rally in Munich Hitler was able to threaten a 'general reckoning of the most unheard-of kind' and at an SA meeting was even able to ask what would happen 'if the German people were ever to pick themselves up and string up twenty-two of their November criminals'[79] without suffering any consequences throws significant light on conditions in Bavaria. If he had been recognized in Berlin, by contrast, he would certainly not have been left to roam the streets freely.

And yet who – apart from his political friends – could have identified Hitler in the capital? There was no official portrait of him until well into 1923. Not until the second half of 1922 did he become known outside Bavaria thanks to the growing strength of the NSDAP, and even then his fame was that of a local hero. National newspapers such as Ullstein's immensely popular weekly, the *Berliner Illustrirte Zeitung*, did not have a single photograph that they could have published under the heading of 'Portraits of the Day' or within the framework of their distinctly meagre political coverage. Many writers have attributed this to Hitler's well-considered attempts at obfuscation and to his desire to introduce an element of charismatic magic to his life.[80]

More compelling is an entirely pragmatic explanation: portrait photographs of Hitler could have been used to identify a wanted criminal, especially after the end of 1922, when the Weimar Republic's political and economic problems took a turn for the worse.[81] A decade later, when looking back on the risks involved in attending meetings in Berlin in 1923, Hitler's chief press officer, Otto Dietrich, explained why there had been no likenesses of his employer before that date:

Adolf Hitler had to get from Munich to Berlin at any price. Between the two cities, however, Red Saxony was in open rebellion. These were daring, hazardous journeys through an area controlled by Marxist tyrants who were on the trail of their hated mortal enemy. But Adolf Hitler still got through. The car number plate was smeared with oil and obscured by dirt to make it unreadable. [. . .] The car was stopped en route. Discovery would have been fatal. But Hitler wasn't recognized. At the moment of extreme danger his principle at this date of preventing any photographic likeness of himself from circulating proved its usefulness in the best possible way.[82]

In early April 1923, when Hitler was again in Berlin, his companion Ernst Hanfstaengl, who had known Hitler since the end of 1922 and who later became the NSDAP's foreign press officer, noted his superior's 'well-known secretiveness and refusal, as far as possible, to let anyone know where he was staying'. Hanfstaengl was reduced to despair by the bizarre conspiratorial conditions under which he and Hitler were in Berlin, looking for potential backers. Wherever they went Hitler 'said his little piece about helping the party'.[83] The steps that they took to conceal their true identities also emerge from a report of a later visit to Berlin in the middle of September 1923. On this occasion our informant is Hitler's personal bodyguard, Otto Graf. (By this date Hitler had paid at least ten visits to Berlin since the Kapp Putsch.) Graf describes the car journey to Berlin as 'nerve-wracking', for Prussia and 'bright Red' Saxony would both have 'loved to have seen Hitler behind bars, with the result that we all had good reason to be as careful as possible, for the Führer was in no doubt that if he had been caught there, he would not be seeing Munich again soon or, indeed, at all'.[84] The party spent a night in Hof on 16–17 September 1923, after which the car – according to Graf – had to be 'disguised' before they could continue their journey. Once they had crossed the border into Saxony, 'extreme vigilance was called for. For the Red police to have stopped and searched us and to have recognized us would have been our undoing'. Graf and another of Hitler's travelling companions, Christian Weber, carried around pistols with their safety catches off and were always ready 'to defend themselves'. On their arrival in Berlin, they booked into different hotels in order to avoid attracting attention. On their third day in the city, 'the Führer had a meeting during which I kept watch outside the house in question'. At the end of the meeting Hitler was recognized by two passers-by in the street, with the result that he and his companions immediately fled the city.[85]

At the end of May 1923 Germany's best-known, if not its best, satirical newspaper, *Simplicissimus*, devoted almost an entire page to the question 'What Does Hitler Look Like?'[86] The caricaturist Thomas Theodor Heine, who had been a member of the editorial board since the paper was founded in 1896,[87] offered his readers twelve individual drawings in the form of an illustrated broadsheet and invited them to guess which of them was the true likeness. 'Adolf Hitler refuses to allow pictures of himself to be reproduced,' Heine began. 'During my stay in Berlin, I was for ever being assailed by questions about his appearance.' He then proceeded to provide a series of satirical miniatures in response to the questions that may or may not have been put to him: 'What is so characteristic of his face is surely his fascinating eyes?' 'Or is his mouth his main feature?' 'Or the nose?'[88] Heine ended by stating that 'all these questions must ultimately remain unanswered. Hitler is not an individual at all. He is a condition.'[89]

Hitler's reluctance to be photographed produced some grotesque situations. At this early date, he apparently demanded that his companions seize an exposed plate from Heinrich Hoffmann after the latter had lain in wait for him outside the party's offices in Schwabing and taken a picture of him.[90] In the event, Hoffmann famously went on to become Hitler's official photographer. Konrad Heiden reports that Hitler was able to ensure that he was not photographed by 'making himself only half-visible' at meetings 'by means of elaborate lighting tricks'.[91] That he was prepared even as late as the spring of 1923 to stoop to more ruthless actions is clear from an episode that took place during another of his visits to Berlin. Hanfstaengl reports that the incident occurred while Hitler and his companions were visiting the Luna-Park, a popular place of entertainment on the Halensee between Charlottenburg and Grunewald:

> On the steps of the open-air restaurant where we were planning to have a beer and admire the view of Berlin's western approaches after our walk, we encountered a photographer who took aim at us with his camera. Even before I had realized what was happening, Hitler had already rushed over to the photographer, looking for all the world as if he was going to arrest him. What followed was deeply embarrassing: evidently in the belief that he was dealing with a photojournalist keen to have a snapshot of the spokesman of the nationalist cause taken against the backdrop of a mere place of entertainment in Berlin's Judaized and Communist hotbed of vice, Hitler threatened the man physically and demanded that he hand over the film.[92]

Remarkably enough, a second version of this incident has survived: it is the account of the photographer himself. Rudolf Herz takes up the story: 'Hanfstaengl did not know the press photographer, nor did he know that Hitler was already known to him. The man in question was Georg Pahl, who owned "ABC", the Berlin-based press illustration company, and who had once tried – in vain – to persuade Hitler to allow him to take his photograph in Munich.'[93] Pahl later recalled:

> I had just taken a number of photographs when I saw Adolf Hitler among the group of bystanders. I thought I was dreaming. My camera was at the ready and I was in position. About five yards away. Perplexed, Hitler looked at the camera and tried to turn away but the shutter had already been released, and Hitler was captured on the plate. He leapt at me and tried to smash the

camera with a stick that he invariably carried round with him. I held the camera behind my back, trying to shield it from his furious blows. The onlookers became aware of what was happening and Hitler backed away. My friend stood there, astonished. No one knew it was Hitler.[94]

According to Hanfstaengl, there followed a lengthy altercation in the course of which Pahl was persuaded to remove the negative 'without receiving a penny by way of compensation'.[95]

Within a few months of this incident, Hitler had not only lost his camera-shyness but had become positively addicted to the medium, a change that was almost certainly due to the gradual shift in his own perception of himself from a 'drummer' for the cause of 'National Socialism' to the dictatorial autocrat with control over a movement built up on the 'leadership principle'.[96] This was a development that began with the crisis that beset the party in July 1921 but more especially in the course of 1923–4. Although Georg Pahl had been attacked by Hitler in the Luna-Park in Berlin in the spring of 1923, it was none the less Pahl who finally succeeded in photographing Hitler at the German Day rally in Nuremberg on 2 September 1923. Shortly afterwards Hitler invited Heinrich Hoffmann to prepare a series of portrait photographs of him. Hoffmann had a good head for business and had already joined the DAP/NSDAP in April 1920.[97] He marketed the photographs in various formats so that they could be used as wall portraits, postcards and press pictures, thereby signalling the start of the cult of the Hitler portrait that was to last for the next two decades.[98]

The first published portrait of Hitler appeared in the *Berliner Illustrirte Zeitung* on 16 September 1923 and was captioned: 'Adolf Hitler, the leader of the Bavarian National Socialists, who has previously refused to be photo-graphed but who is now untrue to his principles.'[99] Three weeks later the same magazine published a second portrait by Hoffmann;[100] and on 11 November 1923 it reproduced a photograph showing Hitler 'addressing his people following a military-style exercise in the vicinity of Munich'.[101] On 25 November 1923 the portrait that had first appeared in September was reprinted, this time with the caption 'November storms'.[102] Presumably no new photographs were available.

Grosz Draws Hitler – and Misses the Mark

In the wake of these early reproductions of photographs of Hitler in the weekly *Berliner Illustrirte Zeitung* (the inferior paper used by the German dailies meant that it was still largely impossible for them to print images of him), picture postcards circulated widely, with the result that in turn graphic artists and caricaturists had a field day. In November 1923 the front page of the Berlin satirical journal *Die Pleite*, which had been appearing illegally since the summer of that year,[103] was given over to a full-page drawing by George Grosz entitled 'Siegfried Hitler'. The caption quotes comments that Hitler made at the Bürgerbräukeller on the evening of 8 November,[104] so that this particular issue can have been published only after his putsch. 'Siegfried' Hitler is seen staring grimly, his hands clasped behind his back, and wearing a bearskin and other attributes drawn from the world of Teutonic mythology. His arms and shoulders are bare, and on his upper left arm he has a swastika tattoo. By combining a caricature with a quotation from the speech that Hitler made on 8 November 1923, Grosz sought to expose a racist windbag to public ridicule.

With his sociocritical cartoons and implacable attacks on typical middle-class values and chauvinism, Grosz had been making a name for himself in Germany and beyond since the early 1920s.[105] Here he offers a striking likeness of Hitler's features or, to be more precise, the features that Hitler presented to the world at his first portrait session in Hoffmann's studio. His stance appears to be based on one of Hoffmann's postcards, depicting a three-quarter-length Hitler wearing a trench coat and hat and holding a walking stick.[106] This particular photograph already conveys a sense of the body language of the later images of the Führer and is manifestly very different from earlier private photographs of the young Hitler. According to Rudolf Herz, 'The new challenge facing Adolf Hitler clearly required a different type of picture. From now on, Hitler's rigid features and stereotypically grim expression became the characteristics found most commonly in portraits of him. The eyebrows drawn together over thick folds of skin were intended to signal fanatical strength of will, determination and rigour.'[107]

In his 1921 collection *The Face of the Ruling Class*, Grosz had needed only a few strokes of his pen to re-create the whole range of contemporary physiognomic possibilities from reactionary haughtiness to bourgeois superiority. For so perceptive an artist, Hitler's ostentatious grimness, coupled with what Herz termed his 'attitude of brutal resolve', must have been particularly striking. But Grosz does not exaggerate this feature in the manner common among most other satirists. Rather, he went a step further and became a political analyst, replacing the trench coat of his source with a bearskin and adding a polemical element by giving Hitler a new first name, Siegfried.[108] This is very much how Hitler would have been seen at the end of 1923, not only by the Socialist and Communist left but also by broad sections of society who would not have thought of themselves as *völkisch* or nationalistic. Here was a reactionary, hyper-German politician, a sectarian of the extreme right who glorified all that was German and whose political programme could be summed up as a nebulous 'return to our ancestors'. Grosz was well versed in depicting such ridiculous-seeming 'disciples of Germania', a skill developed in 1921 when he had illustrated the first volume of Hans Reimann's *Saxon Miniatures* with figures of this kind.[109]

But this satirical drawing of Hitler was fatally flawed in one important respect, for it failed to appreciate what was now his political role. The wild determination to which Hitler gave consciously histrionic expression may well have appeared absurd, not least because it was imposed on Hitler from outside. But it made no sense to draw attention to the bearskin that Hitler was meta-phorically wearing beneath his trench coat, as Grosz does in his caricature. In *Mein Kampf*, Hitler himself clearly ridiculed the sectarian members of the *völkisch* right, generally older men 'who try to estimate the value of a move-ment according to the most bombastic-sounding titles, most of which, sad to say, the vocabulary of our forefathers must provide. [. . .] If anything is unfolkish, it is this tossing around of old Germanic expressions which neither fit into the present period nor represent anything definite.' Striking a polemical note, he warns against 'those *deutschvölkisch* wandering scholars whose positive accomplishment is always practically nil'. The National Socialist movement should on no account be abandoned to some 'folkish Methuselah'.

As if looking directly at Grosz's caricature, Hitler continued in this same mocking vein, claiming that what was characteristic of these people was the fact that

> they rave about old Germanic heroism, about dim prehistory, stone axes, spear and shield, but in reality are the greatest cowards that can be imagined. For the same people who brandish scholarly imitations of old German tin swords, and wear a dressed bearskin with bull's horns over their bearded heads, preach for the present nothing but struggle with spiritual weapons, and run away as fast as they can from every Communist blackjack. [. . .] I came to know these people too well not to feel the profoundest disgust at their miserable play-acting.

Hitler's attempt to distance himself from people who are 'a real plague for all straightforward and honest fighters' culminates in his total rejection of the term *völkisch*, which he argues is too vague and semantically ambiguous.

In short, Grosz's satire sought to unmask Hitler as the sort of politician that he himself had no wish to be – one, indeed, that he vehemently opposed. Typical of Hitler's contempt for these 'folkish sleepwalkers' and 'antiquity enthusiasts' is a comment that he throws in more or less as an aside: 'I shall not even speak of the unworldliness of these folkish Saint Johns of the twentieth century or their ignorance of the popular soul. It is sufficiently illustrated by the ridicule with which they are treated by the Left, which lets them talk and laughs at them.'[110] They are left to talk and then they are laughed at. But this, of course, was the aim of Grosz's caricature, which was intended to present a figure at whom the world could laugh. This attitude also involved a certain sense of superiority at the pitiful figure that Hitler cut, at least in Berlin, following his failed putsch in the Munich Bürgerbräukeller. Above all, Grosz's caricature reveals the way in which the danger posed by Hitler was underestimated at this time. If people saw in him simply a latter-day variant of the long-familiar type of right-wing enthusiast for early Germanic virtues, then they were seriously mistaken about both Hitler and the NSDAP and failed to appreciate what was fundamentally new and even modern about his movement. Its very modernity placed it beyond the *deutschvölkisch* methods and programmes of the pre-war period and their imitators since 1919.[111]

While Grosz and many other liberal and left-wing intellectuals and artists in Berlin were underestimating the threat posed by Hitler and in that way were making him seem harmless, the leaders of the country's Communist Party, meeting on 3 November 1923, barely a week before the Munich putsch, demonstrated their complete inability to engage in any kind of serious political analysis. In view of the hardening of attitudes towards the Socialist and Communist coalition in Saxony and Thuringia on the part of the German government, aided and abetted by the chief of the army command, General Hans von Seeckt, the Communist Party's leaders felt that it was 'Fascists' who were in power in the shape of the armed forces. In the principles agreed to at the November conference, the party argued:

The November Republic has been abandoned to Fascism in every part of Germany that remains unoccupied. Power has been placed in the hands of the military authorities [. . .] in order to saddle the defenceless proletariat with the unlimited power of the bourgeoisie. [. . .] The victory of Fascism over bourgeois democracy has assumed forms other than those expected by the working class, with the result that that victory was not immediately clear to them. While the working class saw the heart of Fascism in Bavaria, the Fascist centre established itself in Berlin as the dictatorship of General von

Seeckt, behind which we find not only the Reichswehr [the German army]
but also decisive sections of the German bourgeoisie.[112]

This was the first time that the leaders of the German Communist Party had
applied the term 'Fascism' not only to the dictatorial use of force against the
left but also to other forms of state and military force used against them. It was
an example of terminological confusion that was to have disastrous consequences during the years that followed, especially towards the end of the
Weimar Republic.

Among the intellectuals who lived in Berlin and who held Socialist or
Communist convictions, there were a few less dogmatic souls and even a
number who could be described as far-sighted. Among the most distinguished
of these was Ernst Bloch, who at the end of the trial of Ludendorff and
Hitler published an essay, 'Hitler's Force', in *Das Tage-Buch*, a journal edited by
Stefan Großmann and Leopold Schwarzschild.[113] Bloch began by conceding
that the threat posed by Hitler and the NSDAP had initially been underestimated: 'At first we ignored it, dismissing it and shrugging our shoulders at the
malicious pack that crawled forth and at the Red posters with their drivelling
sentences, but with knuckledusters behind them.' There was no doubt that
these people were rabble, riffraff and police informers. However: 'He who
knows only this knows nothing as yet of the whole. [. . .] For separate from the
hideous gawpers and accomplices, new youth glows at the core, a very vigorous
generation.'

Hitler, Bloch went, did not deserve to be spared by his judges and by 'this
farcical trial', and yet there was 'no getting at him even with the wit of Berlin
lawyers'. 'Hitler the tribune is undoubtedly a highly suggestive type' with 'the
strength of a collective will, a vital pressure and a talent for inflaming others,
a fanatic with a vision that makes his disciples see him as akin to Bernard de
Clairvaux or even the Maid of Orleans':

> The extent to which Hitler has young people on his side should not be
> underrated. We should not underestimate our opponent but realize what is a
> psychological and inspirational force for so many. [. . .] Hitler himself here
> ignited or at least fanned a thoroughly unbourgeois movement in bourgeois
> youth, and shaped a certain ascetic energy. [. . .] Fascism in Germany and the
> whole non-Russian world is, as it were, the crooked governor of the revolu-
> tion, an expression of the fact that the social situation is by no means static;
> the younger members of the bourgeoisie sense this for themselves and keep
> the process alive.[114]

Bloch's insight into the 'ecstasy of bourgeois youth' was extremely rare at this time. It was an ecstasy, he went on, which 'characterologically and formally' was 'profoundly revolutionary', but in its aims it was an expression of counter-revolutionary aspirations on the part of social strata that were sinking out of sight. In his analysis of the contradictory nature of the National Socialists, whom he saw as 'disgusted by the lack of ideals in this dull Republic' but at the same time as filled 'with the most lifeless nationalism' and haunted by 'the feudal ghosts that they have brought with them', Bloch used consciously crass images in an attempt to make clear the dangers posed by Hitler and his move-ment, drawing attention to the fatal fascination exerted by the latter, taking it seriously instead of merely holding it up to ridicule, and issuing an urgent warning not to underestimate it.

Mocked by the Capital's Press

The danger posed by Hitler was also underestimated in bourgeois and demo-cratic circles. In early October 1923 the journalist Leo Lania claimed to have been sent by the Italian Fascists to gain access to the NSDAP's headquarters in Munich, where he interviewed Hitler and got to know the party's inner sanctum. He was then forced to stand by and watch as his alarming reports in the German press attracted only limited interest. Published by Ullstein-Verlag in Berlin, the *Vossische Zeitung* printed a much-abbreviated account of Lania's visit to the NSDAP's high command, adding that his political conclusions and above all his view that Hitler represented a threat to the Republic were 'absurd'. The editor-in-chief of the *Berliner Tageblatt*, Theodor Wolff, whose editorials were obligatory reading for all politically minded Berliners, was 'literally appalled', according to Lania himself, 'that I had equated the National Socialists with Fascism and that I could compare an illiterate adventurer like Hitler with a man like Mussolini, who, after all, was a statesman and a highly cultivated and cultured individual'.[115] If the paper reported Hitler's prophecy – made in the course of a speech at an assembly meeting in July 1923 – that the swastika flag would flutter over the dome of the Royal Palace in Berlin within a matter of only four years, it was, to quote the paper's editorial, 'merely for curiosity's sake'.[116]

The *Berliner Tageblatt* was the flagship title of Rudolf Mosse's publishing empire, whose portfolio included another widely read paper, the venerable *Berliner Volks-Zeitung*, which, under its editor-in-chief, the co-founder of the German Democratic Party, lent the Weimar Republic its powerful journal-istic support.[117] Above all, Carl von Ossietzky, who ran the paper's editorial

department from 1920 to 1924, ensured that the note that it struck was belligerent, radically democratic and anti-militaristic. Ossietzky was one of the
earliest writers to offer an accurate analysis of the dangerous political situation
in Bavaria. In September 1921, for example, he was forcibly struck by 'appeals
from the strange "National Socialist Workers' Party" crudely disparaging the
German government' that he found pasted to billboards in Munich.[118]

Ossietzky had been sent to Munich as the *Berliner Volks-Zeitung*'s special
correspondent and at the end of September 1921 he devoted an entire article
to the NSDAP, reporting that 'this obscure factional entity' had formed groups
of regular Storm Troopers who had been used to break up public gatherings in
the most brutal manner imaginable.[119] After describing the political situation
in Bavaria, he went on to examine the various extreme right-wing groups,
noting that

> the National Socialist Party of a certain Hitler – generally regarded as the
> protégé of the chief of police – deserves a chapter unto itself in any account
> of these mysterious organizations. Outside Bavaria observers have seen in
> this 'party' little more than a gang of hooligans that is the human equivalent
> of a chair-leg guard. This is a mistake: we are dealing here with a secret
> society that works in extremely sophisticated and highly unscrupulous ways,
> *shock troops of the counterrevolution*, albeit a ragbag of inexperienced youths
> and elderly Catiline conspirators, all of whom are none the less desperate and
> capable of anything.[120]

This does not sound like a failure to appreciate the true significance of the
NSDAP. But when, in the course of 1923, Hitler's reputation spread far beyond
the confines of Bavaria, it became clear that in his assessment of Hitler's
political significance Ossietzky was essentially of the same view as Theodor
Wolff. In Ossietzky's opinion, the right-wing radicals lacked leaders – 'Herr
Hitler is ultimately only a miniature Mussolini', he wrote in early March
1923.[121] Only a few months later he was still calling Hitler 'a pitiful street
demagogue',[122] a characterization that he repeated immediately after the
attempted putsch of 8/9 November 1923. Hitler, he wrote, had been 'unmasked
a thousand times over as a scarecrow': the Germans were 'not interested in
raising to the level of a German dictator a confused street demagogue like
Hitler, who has been using primitive anti-capitalist phraseology to undeniably
good effect'. With the defeat of the putschists a 'wretched bogey' had been
destroyed. 'The ghost of National Socialist demonstrations is no longer a
threat, and unbridled laughter everywhere greets their comic turn in the

Bürgerbräusaal.'[123] *Vorwärts*, the central organ of the German Socialist Party, came to the same conclusion, and in its evening edition of 9 November 'Berlin's popular paper', as it styled itself on its masthead, described the failed putsch as 'November Shrovetide shenanigans in Munich's Bürgerbräu.'[124]

It may have been a turbulent year but, by the end of 1923, the view from Berlin was more or less the same from whichever quarter one looked, whether it be the radical left and the Social Democrats or the bourgeois and republican camp. Only the conservative right preferred to bide its time, while the extreme right was disorientated or disappointed by Hitler. In general, then, Hitler was seen as a figure of fun whose movement was politically finished. But developments during the first few months after the putsch, from the Hitler–Ludendorff trial to the events of the summer of 1924, should have provided food for thought for those who had initially felt relieved. Admittedly, the *völkisch* movement seemed by the end of 1923 to have been splintered and destroyed, but Hitler himself emerged from the trial much strengthened, and in certain sections of the population he was – in Ian Kershaw's words – 'almost deified'.[125]

The Electoral Potential of the Extreme Right

At least for a time there was an electoral alliance between the Deutschvölkische Freiheitspartei (the German Nationalist Freedom Party; DVFP) and the National Socialists. In Bavaria the Großdeutsche Volksgemeinschaft (Greater German National Community) was set up by leading National Socialists, including Alfred Rosenberg, Hermann Esser and Julius Streicher, as a refuge for members of the banned NSDAP, while in northern Germany, National Socialists and supporters of the DVFP joined forces under Ludendorff in the Reichstag elections on 4 May 1924, after which date they formed a single faction in the Reichstag. The National Socialist Freedom Movement, as the combined parties called themselves, won 6.5 per cent of the vote in the country as a whole, but in Greater Berlin, which had come into existence in 1920 as a parliamentary constituency comprising twenty wards, it won only 4.8 per cent. Within the individual wards, the results were extremely varied, in keeping with the city's social make-up. In working-class areas of Berlin, they were well below the urban average, the only exception being Spandau, where the alliance claimed 8.7 per cent of the vote. But in middle-class districts, the Freedom Movement generally did much better. The solid middle-class district of Zehlendorf provided its best showing, with 9.8 per cent, followed closely by Steglitz, which was an area dominated by civil servants and members of the upper-middle class. Here the Freedom Movement won 9.5 per cent of the vote.[126]

Above all, however, one is struck by the fact that the electoral potential of the far right was even higher in Berlin, for if we add to the 106,559 votes cast for the National Socialist Freedom Movement the 83,970 votes won by Richard Kunze's German Socialist Party, the total of a little over 190,000 votes works out at 8.6 per cent of the 2.2 million voters in the Reich's capital city. In the light of these figures we can only agree with Bernd Kruppa when he writes that 'even by the early 1920s there was already a statistically significant group of voters in Berlin who could be mobilized in times of economic crisis and who were ready to entrust a political mandate to the right-wing radicals'.[127] And there were further deviations from the link between social make-up and electoral result. In the largely working-class districts of Kreuzberg, Friedrichshain and Lichtenberg, for example, Kunze's German Socialist Party obtained highly respectable results, with the Freedom Movement and the German Socialists together winning almost 7 per cent of the votes in Kreuzberg.[128]

A little over six months later the voters were called to the polls again, and now it was possible to see the effects of the country's attempts to control inflation. A tentative economic recovery was in progress, and the relative stabilization of Germany's economy[129] was reflected in a partial stabilization of the political picture. In the elections to the Reichstag on 7 December 1924 the liberal German Democratic Party increased its share of the vote in Greater Berlin from 8.9 to 10.9 per cent, while the Social Democrats shot up from 20.4 to 30.3 per cent. Only the Communist share of the vote dropped slightly, from 17.9 to 16.3 per cent. At the same time, the German National People's Party (DNVP), whose members were right-wing conservatives, achieved its most impressive showing to date, moving up from 22.6 to 23.9 per cent of the vote.

Of course, the DNVP was so successful only because the two extreme right-wing groups that took part in the poll lost out to it: the National Socialist Freedom Movement won only 2.0 per cent of the vote, and the German Socialist Party only 1.6 per cent – less than half of their share of the vote in the elections in the May of that year. The National Socialist alliance achieved its best result – 4.2 per cent of the vote – in the middle-class district of Zehlendorf. If we add together the votes of both groups, the percentage won by these extreme right-wing parties ranged from 7.5 per cent in the middle-class district of Steglitz to 1.7 per cent in the working-class district of Wedding; in the most densely populated district, Kreuzberg, they won just under 3 per cent of the vote.[130]

The 'Movement' in Crisis

If the *völkisch* movement was already in crisis by the end of 1924, the months that followed marked a veritable meltdown. In the middle of February, Albrecht von Graefe, who had originally been a conservative member of the Reichstag but who became the spokesman of the *deutschvölkisch* faction after 1918, formed the Deutschvölkische Freiheitspartei (the German Nationalist Freedom Party; DVFP) as a focus for right-wing aspirations in the north of the country. In his inaugural address he criticized Hitler for believing that he 'had to strike out on his own'.[131] Meanwhile, the latter had organized a regrouping of the NSDAP following his release from prison in December 1924,[132] prompting the two substitute organizations, the Völkischer Block and the Großdeutsche Volksgemeinschaft, to disband. Four members of the Reichstag – Hans Dietrich, Gottfried Feder, Wilhelm Frick and Gregor Straßer – immediately declared their support for Hitler and at the end of April resigned from the DVFP.[133]

This rift was triggered by a visit that Hitler paid to Berlin on 13 and 14 March 1925. According to a police report on his stay in the capital, a meeting took place in the Reichstag on 13 March that was attended by Hitler, Straßer, Frick and Feder, on the one hand, and, on the other, by four *völkisch* members of parliament, Reinhold Wulle, Ernst zu Reventlow, Franz Stöhr and Karl Fahrenhorst. After Hitler had tried in vain to persuade the DVFP to support Ludendorff's candidacy for the country's presidency, he addressed his supporters in the city, almost certainly on that same day. In the course of his speech Hitler admitted that Ludendorff's candidacy was to a certain extent a gamble, but what was at stake was not just 'the existence of the NSDAP' but also the party's 'loyalty to our leader, His Excellency General Ludendorff'.[134] Hitler went on to say that he reckoned that Ludendorff would receive two million votes.[135] In the event the first round of voting on 29 March 1925 ended in ignominy for Ludendorff, who was supported by Hitler and the NSDAP but not by the *deutschvölkisch* members of his own NSFB party. He received only 286,000 votes, or 1.1 per cent of the total. His total tally of votes in Berlin – 9,222[136] – represented 0.42 per cent of the votes cast in the capital, a disastrous result that reflected badly on Hitler's electoral strategy. Only in the NSDAP stronghold of Spandau, where he received 760 votes, did Ludendorff's share of the vote rise above 1 per cent.

Once the ban on the NSDAP had been lifted in Prussia, a certain Erich Thimm – one of the founder members of the Greater German Workers' Party in November 1922 – helped to re-establish a local branch on 17 February 1925, its reconstitution being confirmed by Hitler on his visit to the capital on 14 March of that year.[137] Under its Gauleiter, Ernst Schlange, the group is believed to have boasted 350 members at this date. Its headquarters were at 172 Kaiserallee (now the Bundesallee) in Wilmersdorf.[138] The party seems to have led a pitiful existence and to have developed only fitfully as an organization. All the evidence suggests that, in Bernd Kruppa's words, Berlin's population 'took little notice of the tiny handful of National Socialists' in its midst,[139] a statement that receives some support from the remarkable fact that in the whole of 1925 the *Berliner Tageblatt* did not carry a single report on the activities of the NSDAP in the city.[140] On 26 September 1925 Hitler was officially banned from speaking in Prussia, making it impossible for him to make any further public appearances in Berlin, appearances that had undoubtedly been effective in terms of the publicity they had generated. The ban was not lifted until the end of September 1928.[141]

The municipal elections of 25 October 1925 finally revealed the pitiful state of the extreme right-wing parties, all of which appeared to have sunk to the level of splinter groups: the DVFP won only 1.5 per cent of the vote, Kunze's German Socialists only 1.4 per cent. Their combined support amounted to no more than 53,000 votes out of a total of more than 1.85 million. The Berlin branch of the NSDAP was now so weak that it could not even afford to take part in the elections to the city council. It fielded only one candidate in the elections for the individual district councils, garnering a total of 137 votes in Spandau.[142]

Writing in *Die Weltbühne* before the elections for the country's presidency, Heinz Pol had proclaimed 'the end of the *völkisch* movement', arguing that its decline had begun with Hitler's term of imprisonment: 'What went on in the brain of this talented political circus clown during his time in prison remains a secret known to him alone.' Hitler had fallen out with every leading *völkisch* politician and tried 'one last time' to stage-manage a movement: 'But no one showed up.' At the first speech that he gave after his release, there had been only expressions of disappointment 'for Hitler no longer had a programme, and even his voice was no longer as fine-sounding as before. He stepped down from the podium, and people shouted the odd bravo. [. . .] Since then there has been the silence of the grave.'[143]

Other facts confirm this assessment. In early November 1923, for example, the NSDAP had still had more than 55,000 members,[144] but by the end of 1925 this figure had fallen to around 27,000.[145] By the end of 1924 Carl von Ossietzky had noted with regard to the *deutschvölkisch* parties that the crisis was now a full-blown catastrophe: 'Time itself has declared its opposition to these people. Just as the period of stabilization is dealing financially with the ghosts of inflation, so it is also doing intellectually and politically. The romantic gang leaders and Adolf Hitler, their fine-sounding brass instrument, were the children of a desperate age. [...] The Rentenmark [the currency issued on 15 November 1923 to counter hyperinflation] has defeated the inflamed demagogues and power-crazed officers.' The sudden collapse of these swastika-touting louts, Ossietzky concluded, was 'by no means uninteresting from a sociological point of view, but it barely impinges on the world of politics'. As so often, Ludendorff had missed the opportunity to retire from the political stage in an even remotely impressive way. 'The rest belongs in the satirical newspapers.'[146]

Ossietzky may have been thinking of *Simplicissimus*, which had picked up the subject in the wake of the failure of the putsch on 9 November 1923. Some time after Hitler had been transferred to the prison at Landsberg, he had received a visit from Ernst Hanfstaengl,[147] who took with him as presents a number of volumes containing reproductions of Old Masters from the art galleries in Munich and Dresden. Hitler found them relatively uninteresting, at least when compared with another of the gifts that Hanfstaengl had brought with him: the issue of *Simplicissimus* for 1 April 1924, the title-page of which depicted Hitler himself entering Berlin on horseback. The Brandenburg Gate can be seen in the background.[148] Hanfstaengl is said to have given Hitler the caricature in an attempt to cheer him up, allegedly adding: 'Just look at this, Herr Hitler, I think this is the model we need right now. It wouldn't be the first time that a caricature had predicted a historical development.' Hitler apparently stared at the image for some time, lost in thought, before replying: 'That might still happen as long as we remain sufficiently dogged.'[149]

Perhaps Hitler was reminded at this moment of the time when he had spoken at the German Day rally in Coburg on 14 October 1922: 'Our symbol is no club membership badge but a victory banner. It must and shall one day flutter over the Berlin Palace just as surely as it flutters over the peasant's lowly hut.'[150] At the end of October 1923 he had even proclaimed that 'for me, the German question will not be solved until the black, white and red swastika flag flutters over the Berlin Palace'.[151] A few weeks before his attempted putsch, he returned to a city that he described as a 'hotbed of sin'[152] and, together with his bodyguard Ulrich Graf, climbed to the top of the Victory Column, which at this date still stood on the Königsplatz[153] between the Reichstag and the Kroll Opera. Graf later recalled Hitler pointing down to the sea of houses below them and, indicating the Palace and Reichstag, saying: 'When our swastika flag flies over these wonderful buildings, I shall be the leader of our whole nation.'[154]

3

'It is the Gau's tragedy that it never had a real leader'

1922–6: SETBACKS IN BUILDING UP THE NSDAP IN BERLIN

'We often come to Berlin nowadays because it is clear to us in Munich that the great movement must start out from Berlin.'
Hermann Esser, *Völkischer Beobachter*, 9 November 1925

'This whole vast city had to be captured for our movement. [. . .] Until then we had been ignored in Berlin, they didn't know us, they took no notice of us, they snubbed us.'
Joseph Goebbels, speech at an NSDAP rally in Munich, 19 December 1927[1]

The Politicization of the Freikorps

The history of right-wing extremism in Berlin during the early post-war period is not just a tale of political organizations and parties that necessarily evolved in public and in the broad light of day. For long stretches it is also a tale of secret allegiances, conspiratorial circles and putschists who did all they could to remain hidden from public view until the moment of planned or actual attack. There were times when their activities resembled nothing so much as a scene from a Ruritanian operetta, notably in the case of the Freikorps leader Gerhard Roßbach, who shortly before the Kapp Putsch in March 1920 rented a villa at 22 Hohenzollernstraße, close to the Armed Forces Ministry in the Tiergarten district of Berlin, and opened the elegant Tiergarten Club, employing a staff of around thirty. Both the staff and the members consisted largely of men who had once belonged to Roßbach's Freikorps division.[2] On the morning after the putschists took up their positions, the *Berliner Tageblatt* reported that the club suddenly ceased to be a club but became the fortified headquarters of the Roßbach Regiment. In addition to a black, white and red flag there also fluttered from the roof a long white flag with the large black 'R' of the regiment. Lieutenant Roßbach had put on his uniform and assumed command, while his secretaries and waiters likewise wore uniforms and Storm Troopers' helmets and carried swords and hand grenades. The windows were fortified with machine guns. There seemed to be munitions aplenty, and cars were available for patrols.[3]

The military clubs in and around Berlin that placed themselves at Kapp's disposal in March 1920 were disbanded soon after his amateur coup had failed, but many of the officers and soldiers from these units continued to remain in contact with one another and even formed new paramilitary groupings, concealing their true identity beneath descriptive names such as 'work teams' and 'working groups'. These were stationed on estates as far afield as Mecklenburg and Pomerania that had been placed at their disposal by well-to-do supporters. The 'Roßbach Working Group' with its headquarters in Berlin provided them with their central point of reference.[4] It was not long, of course, before the state's surveillance services noticed that these 'working groups' were constituted along military lines with a particular chain of command. Above all, 'it is in the nature of these organizations that when they are deployed, it is envisaged that it will be with weapons in their hands'.[5]

By this date these clandestine Freikorps associations were already being steered inexorably in the direction of right-wing politics while at the same time welcoming virulent anti-Semites into their midst.[6] Even so, the Ehrhardt Brigade, for all that it was central to the Kapp Putsch and predominantly extreme right-wing in terms of its membership (its marching song referred to 'the swastika on the Storm Trooper's helmet'), had as yet no direct party-political affiliations, even though there is evidence that there had been initial contacts between right-wing extremists in Berlin and the NSDAP leadership in Munich as early as 1920.[7] The more notorious Hitler later became and the more significance he acquired within the network of right-wing organizations and defence associations in Bavaria, the more he attracted the sympathies of the 'eternal warriors' from the Freikorps movement. But as long as Hitler's scope for public action was confined to Munich and Upper Bavaria, it was only in Bavaria that the NSDAP benefited from this development.[8]

The Pan-German Workers' Party as a Cover

Some fifteen years later, an official account of the 'NSDAP's struggle to win over Berlin' could claim with total honesty that National Socialism had gained a foothold in northern Germany only relatively late in the day, at least when compared with Munich and Bavaria.[9] It took years for the SA to come to the capital, and even the NSDAP had to wait until the end of 1922 before it could think of opening a local branch, a move that in the event was thwarted by the decision of the Prussian Ministry of the Interior to ban the organization within the Free State of Prussia. As a result, supporters of National Socialism in Berlin were forced to set up a cover organization. In this way the Pan-German Workers' Party was founded on 19 November 1922 at the Reichskanzler Restaurant at 90 Yorckstraße in Kreuzberg. According to the *Berliner Tageblatt*, this new party defined itself in its constitution as *völkisch* and declared war on 'the corrupt parliamentary system' and the 'Jewish-materialistic mentality'. Membership was open to 'every ethnic German who is morally beyond reproach'.[10]

The ban on the NSDAP meant that a National Socialist group in Göttingen was forced to seek refuge beneath the skirts of this newly constituted cover organization in Berlin. The party programme that it published on 9 December 1922 reflected that of the NSDAP on every essential point. In order to 'save the nation', the Pan-German Workers' Party demanded the 'creation of a Greater Germany' and 'an end to our enslavement to interest rates'. Only 'ethnic Germans' could be citizens of the new state; 'everyone else must be treated as an alien'. All East European Jews who had come to Germany since 1914 were to be deported forthwith 'in order to end the housing shortage'.[11]

The party's official version of events appeared in 1937 and mentions the presence of a 'representative of Adolf Hitler' at the meeting in Kreuzberg on 19 November 1922 when the Pan-German Workers' Party had first been summoned into life.[12] Somewhat surprisingly, the name of this representative is nowhere mentioned, even though the names of even the most insignificant 'old warriors' from the 'fighting days of the movement' were as a rule itemized in meticulous detail, including a note of dates and addresses. This unusual degree of discretion can be explained in terms of the fact that the representative in question later had a falling-out with Hitler in the mid-1920s and was officially ignored by the NSDAP thereafter. His name was Gerhard Roßbach, the Freikorps leader who had come to prominence at the time of the Kapp Putsch in March 1920. Although his Roßbach Working Group was officially disbanded in November 1921, it was reconstituted only two weeks later as an 'association for hiking trips, a national savings society and an organization for professional agricultural training'.[13]

Lieutenant Roßbach was a consummate chameleon, with an ability, honed over many years, to keep changing his organizational identity. According to Bernd Kruppa, the authorities had 'barely banned one of Roßbach's organizations before a new one was formed under a different name'.[14] Members of his 'Working Group' were based for the most part on estates in Mecklenburg and Pomerania and had independent access to weapons. He supervised them from Berlin, where he ran a 'German Information Office' that gathered information and provided surveillance and armed escorts.[15] Members of his own association and other Freikorps units first came into contact with the Bavarian National Socialists during the fighting in Upper Silesia in the spring of 1921.[16]

The *Berliner Tageblatt* hit the nail on the head when, citing the Official Prussian Press Service, it reported only days before the formation of the Pan-German Workers' Party that Roßbach represented Hitler in northern Germany and that his organization was affiliated to the NSDAP in Munich, sharing a publication in the form of the *Völkischer Beobachter*.[17] In an undated report submitted to the Ministry of the Interior, Roßbach was described as the 'representative of the leader of the National Socialists in Berlin'.[18] Meanwhile, another Freikorps leader, Heinz Oskar Hauenstein of the 'Heinz Organization', had lost no time following his release from police custody (it had been impossible to prove his involvement in the murder of the foreign minister Walther Rathenau in June 1922) in issuing an appeal to the members of his former regiment in which he stated: 'I have decided that together with the leader of the former Roßbach Volunteer Storm Troops, Lieutenant Roßbach, I shall bring the National Socialist movement to northern Germany.'[19]

A 'group of leaders' of north German members of the NSDAP, made up entirely of officers from the Freikorps, met Hitler in Munich in August 1922 and agreed with him about their mission in northern Germany.[20] The group included not only Roßbach and Hauenstein but also Albert Leo Schlageter, who later became the idol of German nationalism.[21] Schlageter played a leading role in the attempts of Roßbach and Hauenstein to build up a local branch of the NSDAP in Berlin. The surviving list of founder members of the Pan-German Workers' Party runs to 194 names and includes, at No. 61, 'Albert Schlageter, 107 Seestraße, Friedrichsh[ain], businessman, 12 Aug. 1894'.[22]

This list also allows us to draw a number of conclusions about the make-up of the Pan-German Workers' Party. First, Roßbach's name is conspicuous by its absence. In view of the fact that he was currently under investigation for founding and propagating secret organizations, it is easy to see why he would have preferred to avoid public exposure.[23] Of the 132 members whose date of birth is given, fifty-six were twenty-five or younger, seventy were between twenty-six and fifty, and only six were over fifty. Of the total 194 members, a mere five were women. Only 122 gave their profession; of these, forty, or 32.8 per cent, were office workers, and twenty-five, or 20.5 per cent, were businessmen and self-employed people. Only twenty-two (18 per cent) described themselves as skilled or unskilled workers. The rest of the list comprises eleven civil servants, eleven students, eight freelancers, three military men, a farmer and an office manager.

In short, the Pan-German Workers' Party was a male-dominated, middle-class organization set up by ex-members of the Freikorps and made up for the most part of younger people. These findings are reflected in the distribution of its members around Berlin: the majority – 104, or almost 58 per cent – lived in middle-class or lower-middle-class districts, only thirty-eight members (21.1 per cent) came from Steglitz, while the working-class district of Wedding fielded only six (3.3 per cent), and Neukölln only one.[24]

It did not take the authorities long to realize that the Pan-German Workers' Party was a cover for the NSDAP, and on 10 January 1923 the Prussian minister of the interior, Carl Severing, banned it. Shortly afterwards steps were also taken to prevent Roßbach's people from attending the NSDAP party rally in Munich. On 26 January 1923 a few hundred of them – mostly, no doubt, from Mecklenburg and Pomerania – were stopped at Gera en route from Berlin and taken back under armed guard. By the time they got back to the Anhalt Station, they had been stripped of their swastikas. Surprisingly, perhaps, Roßbach's men were found to have 'considerable amounts of money on them'.[25]

Two Different Kinds of Conditions in Munich and Berlin

Roßbach made a number of further attempts to circumvent the ban on the NSDAP by setting up other cover organizations before he and his followers joined the German Nationalist Freedom Party (DVFP) on 10 February 1923. The latter had been formed as recently as 16 December 1922 as a splinter party from the radically nationalist wing of the German National People's Party (DNVP).[26] Although this development represented a further fragmentation of the extreme right-wing parties, the mere existence of the DVFP allowed the NSDAP's supporters in Berlin to find a legal cover for their activities at least for a time. Roßbach quickly rose to a leading position within the new party and was able to continue to run two of the organizations that he had set up in

1921 and that together had more than 1,200 members in Berlin: the military-style Völkische Turnerschaften (Nationalist Gymnasts' Association) and the Jugendbund Graf Yorck von Wartenburg (Count Yorck von Wartenburg Youth Association). In both cases, moreover, he was able to rely on the support of the Reichswehr leadership to help with their military training.[27]

By the middle of March 1923, however, it was becoming increasingly clear to the Prussian police that Roßbach and the DVFP were planning a putsch. A search of various apartments and of the party's offices at 6 Dessauer Straße in Kreuzberg yielded so much incriminating evidence, including weapons, that on 23 March the Prussian minister of the interior decided to ban the DVFP, along with all its ancillary organizations and youth group, arguing that it was no more than a secret successor of the NSDAP in Prussia and that its aim, like that of the NSDAP, was the abolition of parliamentary government. In pursuit of this goal, the party was said to have 'secretly made extensive preparations for a National Socialist putsch'. The only purpose of the party's youth movement had been to prepare young people theoretically and practically for civil war and to this end exercises had been held on Berlin's parade grounds. A whole series of leading officials and staff, not only of the DVFP but also of the Olympia Sports Association, were arrested and accused of high treason and of forming military gangs.[28]

Roßbach was taken in for questioning in Leipzig but was released on bail on 15 October 1923 as it was not believed that he would try to flee. In the event he did precisely that and decamped to Munich.[29] Although the proceedings against him continued,

> it was impossible to arrest him in Bavaria. On 18 [*recte* 19] October Roßbach rightly made fun of the German authorities in a speech that he gave in the Löwenbräukeller. The putsch of 9 November found an enthusiastic supporter in him. Following its failure he fled to Vienna on a false passport and was arrested there in February 1924 but was allowed to remain in Austria.[30]

In Austria, Roßbach was appointed the SA's deputy chief of staff by Hermann Göring, another 'émigré' member of the NSDAP. But he soon formed an independent 'free youth movement' and formally parted company with Hitler and the NSDAP in 1926.[31]

The case of Gerhard Roßbach is a good example of the parallels and, even more so, the differences in the conditions that obtained in Munich and Berlin during the early years of the NSDAP. In both cities the NSDAP was set up by the Reichswehr or at least by circles closely associated with it, being protected and materially assisted in the process. Both groups, moreover, were made up for the most part of members of the Reichswehr or former Freikorps units and as a result were permeated by militaristic thinking. And yet the two parties evolved in completely different ways. Whereas conditions in Bavaria allowed the party to develop almost unhindered, the situation in Berlin, where the party entered the arena some three years later, meant that it was forced into becoming an illegal organization or else into operating in the guise of a cover organization, so repressive were the measures taken against it on the basis of the laws designed to protect the Republic. In Munich, Hitler could address thousands of listeners, often in several halls in a single evening, whereas Roßbach and Hauenstein had only a few months in which to speak to small gatherings of supporters in Berlin, and even then their meetings were often raided, ending in the arrest of the participants and their appearance before the chief of police at his headquarters on the Alexanderplatz.[32] Nor could the two Freikorps leaders hold a candle to Hitler in terms of their gift for oratory. They may have been competent soldiers and organizers, but they were no popular tribunes.

By the end of 1922 the NSDAP in Bavaria could already boast more than twenty thousand members, and during the crisis year of 1923 this number rose to more than 55,000.[33] By contrast, the membership in Berlin stagnated at only a few hundred.[34] The dominance of former Freikorps fighters and the need to remain under cover affected the whole character of the Berlin NSDAP, not just in its initial phase but for a long time afterwards. Even as late as the early 1930s the militaristic defence association atmosphere was still causing conflict between its 'politicians' and its 'soldiers'.

As Germany's political and social crisis grew worse during the final months of 1923, so the NSDAP increasingly became what Anton Joachimsthaler has termed 'an activist military party' in Bavaria too. Formed in March 1923, its SA's supreme command under Göring operated with ever greater autonomy and at the same time consumed vast sums of money. In order to be able to finance the party, the SA and the *Völkischer Beobachter*, Hitler was repeatedly obliged to undertake round trips to Berlin and elsewhere,[35] most recently in the middle of September.[36] But the ban on the NSDAP in Prussia and lack of time prevented him from building up the party outside Bavaria and meant that these trips were limited to political discussions among only a handful of supporters and begging-bowl visits to possible backers.

At an NSDAP rally at the Zirkus Krone in Munich on 5 September 1923, Hitler had declared: 'It is now a question of taking the national idea to circles that have not yet grasped it. Beyond the confines of Bavaria, to central Germany, Saxony, Berlin and beyond. To the whole of Germany! And this is something that only we National Socialists can do, something that only our propaganda, only our fighting press can achieve.'[37] But this was merely verbal posturing, for there was simply no opportunity for the sort of show of organizational strength that such words presupposed. Only if the phrase 'taking the national idea' to new parts of the country was understood to mean military action could the speech acquire any meaningful significance, and it was precisely this idea to which Hitler returned at the end of his speech when he announced: 'We mean to be the bearers of the dictatorship of national reason, the bearers of national resolve, of national brutality and determination. [. . .] There are only two possibilities: either Berlin marches on Munich, or Munich marches on Berlin!'[38]

Hitler's conviction that Germany's future lay down one or other of these roads appeared to be confirmed on 26 September 1923 when the country's president, Friedrich Ebert, and the government of Gustav Stresemann declared an end to the policy of passive resistance against the French and Belgian troops occupying the Ruhr and transferred executive powers to the minister for the armed forces.[39] The end of passive resistance caused outrage among members of the extreme right and arguably triggered an attempted putsch by the 'Black Reichswehr' – paramilitary organizations intended to circumvent the provisions of the Versailles Treaty – under Bruno Ernst Buchrucker, who tried to occupy the fortress at Küstrin on 1 October. According to the official account of the putsch, 'Major Buchrucker seems to have intended to take the fortress by surprise and in that way to persuade like-minded individuals in the rest of the Reich to launch an indiscriminate attack. [. . .] It is difficult to say with any certainty on which circles he was counting.' The leaders of the Reichswehr feigned innocence, and it was said that the political aims of the putschists emerged only in the course of their interrogation.[40]

The putsch failed, as did Buchrucker's attempt two days earlier to occupy the government district of Berlin with two hundred of his men. And yet the latter failed not because Buchrucker was a military dilettante but because he was politically naïve enough to believe that by pressing ahead with his putsch he could signal the start of the 'national uprising' that had been long in the planning.[41] One of his commanders, ex-captain Walter Stennes, was more successful in carrying out Buchrucker's orders to take the fortress at Spandau. Surrounded by Reichswehr troops, Stennes capitulated only when he received an assurance that he and his men would not be prosecuted.[42]

No Hitler Putsch in the Capital

It was Stennes who is said to have been instructed by Buchrucker to 'make contact' with Hitler and the Bavarian branch of the 'United Patriotic Associations',[43] and although the public was largely excluded from Buchrucker's trial, comments made by the state prosecutor none the less trickled out: the defendant was accused not only of having repeatedly met the leaders of the DVFP in Berlin but also of having held discussions with Hitler and Ludendorff in Munich about the exact timing of the putsch.[44] There is indeed evidence that a meeting took place at Ludendorff's home in Munich at the end of August 1923 and that it was attended by Hitler, the latter's adviser Max Erwin von Scheubner-Richter, Buchrucker, Stennes and, as a representative of the 'Black Reichswehr', Kurt Jahnke, who had co-ordinated the passive resistance in the Ruhr. On the agenda were the kinds of measures that might be taken to establish a national dictatorship in the event of the resistance in the Ruhr collapsing. In the face of Hitler's initial veto, it was agreed that the 'Black Reichswehr' should be the first to intervene. Until then, all the other associations should hold back and do nothing to provoke the situation so as not to disrupt the preparations that were taking place in the north of the country.[45]

In short, the events at Küstrin were by no means an isolated phenomenon but were 'the start of a well-organized radical right-wing attempt to overthrow the government and the Republic'.[46] According to a later report, the leaders of the 'Black Reichswehr' were motivated by the idea

> of establishing a right-wing dictatorship by means of a putsch once the government had abandoned its resistance in the Ruhr. The whole of the 'Black Reichswehr' – officers as well as men – were aware of this goal, which was regarded as altogether self-evident. This idea was no doubt also closely linked with the actions of right-wing circles in Bavaria. [. . .] There were also links with Roßbach's organizations and the other nationalist defence organizations, some of which had sent their men to join the 'Black Reichswehr'.[47]

The teams that made up the 'Black Reichswehr' were in charge of the Reichswehr's secret stock of weapons and provided it with secret reinforcements. They were entitled to wear the uniforms of the Reichswehr and occasionally saw active service. There is a certain irony in the fact that they even did turns of sentry duty outside government ministries and offices, including President Ebert's palace in the Wilhelmstraße.[48] Some of these soldiers on guard duty are said to have declared that 'if it gets to that point, we can take him prisoner at once'.[49] A sentence handed down in the case of a lynch-law killing in 1926 described the recruiting practices of the 'Black Reichswehr' as follows: 'Only men who were hostile to the existing form of government, in any case not in favour of it, were considered "nationally reliable". [...] If individual leaders, because of lack of candidates or out of kindness, accepted other people [...] it was considered a grave mistake'.[50]

It is no wonder, then, that in spite of the premature actions of Buchrucker's battalions these right-wing extremists cheerfully continued to prepare for their putsch. On 22 October 1923 the leader of the Pan-German League, Heinrich Class, met Gustav von Kahr, Bavaria's general state commissar, to discuss 'individual measures for the great coup': in other words, which troops should be sent north by way of an advance force. It was agreed that General Otto von Below, who had a number of regional commanders and north German Freikorps leaders on his side, should lead the putsch in Berlin. They planned to launch their attack on the night of 8–9 November without letting Hitler know in advance. A great speech by Kahr about Germany's reawakening was to usher in the overthrow.[51]

On 3 November the chief of the Bavarian state police, Hans von Seißer, met leaders of the ultra-reactionary Reichslandbund in Berlin, when he was assured by Lieutenant Fedor von Bock, the chief of staff of the Third Wehrkreiskommando, that the Küstrin Putsch was more or less in the past and that the various organizations that had been involved in its planning had returned to the fold of the Reichswehr. At the same meeting, a Colonel Friedrichs, who described himself as the 'leader of the Kampfbünde in Berlin', announced that there were five battalions in Berlin, only one of which was made up of National Socialists.[52] Seißer also spoke with General Hans von Seeckt, now the chief of the army command and arguably the most influential man in Berlin, who insisted that they must remain within the law.[53]

In Munich, meanwhile, confusion had degenerated into chaos. It was said that 'things' could change at any moment. In other words, the putsch could be launched. But by whom? With whom? And against whom? The triumvirate of general state commissar Gustav von Kahr, Reichswehr commander Otto von Lossow and chief of police Hans von Seißer evidently shared the same goals, but they omitted to spell these out to Hitler, the 'political leader' of the 'German Fighting League' that had emerged in early September 1923 from the NSDAP and the two defence associations, the 'Oberland League' and the 'Reichsflagge' (or 'Reichskriegsflagge'). Hitler's ally, General Ludendorff, was likewise left in the dark. The pressure from the SA to attack continued to grow, causing Hitler to panic, so afraid was he that he and Ludendorff would be excluded from a 'national dictatorship' that was supported by the Reichswehr. The 'triumvirate' had the police and army at its beck and call and was willing to play for time, whereas Hitler was no longer prepared to delay and risk losing the initiative.[54]

At an event arranged to welcome Roßbach to Munich on 19 October 1923, Hitler had told the local SA that the rule of parliamentary law must go: the nation longed not for a new coalition but for heroes: 'Our cross will triumph and our banner will fly from the Royal Palace in Berlin.'[55] And on 23 October he addressed a gathering of SA leaders, not only giving free rein to his anger at the politics of the 'triumvirate', which he claimed had led to hopeless confusion, but also outlining the aims of the planned putsch:

> Reopening the *German* question at the last minute, starting out from Bavaria; the call for a *German* freedom army under a *German* government in Munich. The planting of the black, white and red swastika flag as the symbol of our struggle against all that is un-German. [...] Taking the battle to the *whole of Germany* and hoisting the black, white and red swastika flag on the Reichstag in Berlin to symbolize the liberation of a Greater Germany.[56]

Hitler was able to implement the first part of this 'programme' in Munich's Bürgerbräukeller on the evening of 8 November 1923, but he came to grief over the next point on his agenda: the formation of a new government. And what were people to make of the idea of a 'freedom army'? Was it to be a merger between the Reichswehr and the defence associations? And by 9 November there could no longer be any question of 'taking the battle to the whole of Germany'. Quite the opposite. The National Socialists in Berlin seem to have been reduced to a state of utter confusion by these events. The local branch of the NSDAP, which is believed to have had around seven hundred members in the autumn of 1923, was kept informed of Hitler's instructions by four couriers, Kurt Daluege, Waldemar Geyer and two others known only by their surnames, Schlockermann and Wolfermann.[57] But it was apparently only after it had failed that NSDAP members in Berlin learnt from the newspapers about the putsch in Bavaria. Decades later, one of those involved recalled that, on receiving the news, 'seventy or eighty men gathered in the colonnades outside the Supreme Court in the Potsdamer Straße and, together with their weapons, got into the Munich train under the leadership of Wolfermann and Schlockermann. But they were taken off the train again in Gera, where they were disarmed and taken into custody.'[58]

If none of the potential fellow combatants in northern Germany had been told about the exact timing of the putsch by those who initiated it in Munich,[59] this would certainly help to explain such senseless actions. But there are indications that Munich's National Socialists had been in close contact with Berlin. The *Vossische Zeitung*, for example, reported on a conversation between the Berlin correspondent of the Italian *Corriere della Sera* and a 'leader of the National Socialist movement who is maintaining links with southern Germany from a Berlin suburb'. The text of the interview was published in Rome on 8 November and claimed, ominously, that a march on Berlin was by no means necessary.[60]

And the aforementioned Völkische Turnerschaften had almost certainly been tipped off on the evening of 8 November, for, according to J.K. von Engelbrechten's official 1937 history of National Socialism, two 'small groups of National Socialist activists' gathered in Fort Hahneberg near Spandau and in the fortress at Spandau and waited 'for the signal to attack'. (The Völkische Turnerschaften was one of Roßbach's organizations, while Roßbach himself – briefly Hitler's 'representative' in Berlin – became one of Hitler's closest associates following his flight to the Bavarian capital and, as such, knew every last detail about the planned putsch.) According to the leader of the exercise, Kurt Daluege, writing in the NSDAP's official newspaper, the *Völkischer Beobachter*, twelve years later, the 'optimistic resolve' that the would-be putschists initially felt in Berlin turned to sombre despair when they received instructions to retreat on 9 November.[61] Daluege had succeeded Roßbach as Hitler's confidant in Berlin but, unlike Roßbach, he remained loyal to the party leader and had a great career ahead of him.

As a result, there was no real putsch outside Bavaria on the night of 8–9 November 1923.[62] The most obvious reason for this is that in Munich the coup crumbled very quickly. And yet there were former members of the Ehrhardt Brigade and the Consul Organization ready to act in Berlin. Under surveillance by the police and by the public prosecutor's office, the Consul Organization's leader, Hermann Ehrhardt, a former lieutenant commander, had been forced to take evasive action six months before the planned putsch and had set up the speciously legitimate Wiking League in Munich on 2 May 1923, the official aim of which was 'the revival and rebirth of Germany on a national and ethnic basic through the spiritual education of its members'. In July 1923 Ehrhardt himself managed to escape from police custody in Leipzig thanks to the help of a group of his supporters. He then turned up in Bavaria and formed a tense liaison with the putschists, including Hitler. In the autumn of 1923 he established a number of military units in the Coburg area. Mainly made up of his own men from the Wiking League, they were kept in constant readiness to march on Thuringia, while maintaining close contact with the Berlin branch of the Wiking League, which had several hundred members at this time. But these preparations for the 'March on Berlin' were likewise frustrated by the failure of the putsch in Munich.[63]

Conflicts over Party Strategy

On 9 November 1923 the chief of the army command, General Hans von Seeckt, was entrusted with the exercise of executive powers by the country's president. Two weeks later he announced a nationwide ban on the NSDAP and DVFP (as well as the German Communist Party). As a result Hitler found himself on the horns of a dilemma that was entirely of his own making. In 1921, in his desire to maintain complete political control over the NSDAP, he had vehemently insisted on making Munich the party's headquarters and had clung tenaciously to that resolve since then. Since the autumn of 1922, however, more and more National Socialist associations had sprung up outside Bavaria, albeit not as part of any purposeful and systematic process. But if even the Munich NSDAP, with its five-figure membership, could not prevail over the will of the state police and the Reichswehr, what chance of playing a politically dominant role did the party have elsewhere, at least within an extreme right-wing setting? In Berlin, for example, the authorities noted that the Wiking League was closely associated with the National Socialists, even to the extent of having been implicated in the attempted putsches in Küstrin and Munich, but that by the end of 1923 a rift had opened up between the political positions of the two groups, making it difficult for them to operate as one.[64] In the whole vast teeming mass of sect-like secret societies and putsch-planning pacts, of conspirators and mercenaries in the 'Black Reichswehr', of organizations set up in the wake of the disbanded Freikorps and of the sort of *völkisch* and anti-Semitic groups and defence associations and nationalist circles that existed in Berlin, it was difficult to see how a National Socialist German Workers' Party stood out, even if its specifically Munich manifestation may have seemed distinctive.

Hitler's dilemma intensified when, in the course of the proceedings against him at the People's Court in Munich, he proved surprisingly successful at enhancing his own reputation in right-wing circles outside Bavaria. In court he had ample opportunity to make propaganda speeches, and the right-wing press reported them at length. The more popular Hitler became in nationalist circles, the more glaring was the contrast between the image of a radiant, self-assured and patriotic hero and the impression of fragmentation and inner division presented by the various groups that were attempting to continue the traditions of National Socialism either openly or covertly. Hitler later described the year – actually it was closer to ten months – in which he 'failed' the party by dint of his imprisonment as 'naturally harmful to the movement'.[65] Following his release at Christmas 1924 he had even been forced to concede that the party had 'dissolved into warring factions'.[66]

In a tactically skilful move in early July 1924, while he was still in prison, Hitler had issued a 'Public Declaration' in which he announced that he had stepped down as leader of the National Socialist movement and that as long as he remained in prison he would abjure all political activity. The reason for his decision, he explained, lay 'in the present impossibility of assuming any practical responsibility'.[67] In this way Hitler avoided tying himself down on two contentious points that had emerged during the winter of 1923–4, when the National Socialists had attempted to resume their activities by circumventing the ban on the party. The first point concerned the attempts of the DVFP to take over National Socialist groups in northern Germany, a move bitterly resisted by the illegal NSDAP branch in Hanover in particular, which preferred to adopt a strictly anti-parliamentarian course of action.[68]

The second bone of contention related to the question of the form that might be assumed in the future by the SA, which had likewise been declared illegal. Immediately before he had begun his term of imprisonment, Hitler had issued instructions to the SA appointing Röhm as its 'military leader' and no more.[69] But Röhm had other plans. Under Ludendorff's patronage he founded the Frontbann in May 1924, a nationwide paramilitary organization whose ranks were made up for the most part of former members of the SA but which was specifically intended to 'remain outside the party conflict and provide support for the whole of the fragmented nationalist movement'. In other words, it was not to be affiliated to the NSDAP.[70]

Hitler lost no time in unceremoniously rejecting the plans of both Röhm and Ludendorff when they were presented to him during a prison visit in Landsberg at the end of May 1924. He was afraid above all that he would lose control of the SA and become involved in paramilitary activities that would jeopardize his chances of an early release on parole.[71] At the same time his dealings with Ludendorff, who more than ever saw himself as the real leader of the *völkisch* camp, were proving increasingly strained, and there is little doubt that he was painfully mindful of a phrase in the guidelines for reconstituting the SA drawn up on 24 May 1924: 'Supreme Command (Munich or Berlin), Commander Röhm.'[72] Röhm had been released from prison on 1 April

1924. Hitler could not bear the thought of his rival lording it over the SA in Munich or even in Berlin while he himself continued to languish in Landsberg.

On the other hand, Hitler had no concrete plans for a scheme of his own to replace that of Röhm. He was still dealing with his own emotions in the wake of his failed putsch and hardly in a mood to consider the respective merits of a putsch or more lawful processes. Rather, he was seeking a political strategy designed to free him from his dependence on unreliable allies, on the one hand, and, on the other, politically naïve but strong-willed members of the military. His as yet vague plans for the future[73] needed to be fleshed out in the light of far greater experiences than those that he had acquired in Munich in 1923. In this way his bid for power would become a question of realpolitik. In 1942 he recalled that 'the SA has become something that I had previously not envisaged. I had many ideas about the party but not about its defence organizations.'[74] Hitler's well-developed awareness of questions of political tactics soon allowed him to realize that paramilitary organizations with their overemphasis on military forms were not suitable for the sort of political battles that had to be fought every day, as he imagined would be the case in the future. His conception of the SA as functionally related to the party organization and dependent on it for carrying out the party's work was diametrically opposed to Röhm's, whereby the SA was an independent organization of a traditional kind and in no way subservient to the party's leadership.[75] The argument ended, for the present, with Röhm resigning from all his posts in early May 1925. (Not until September 1930 did Hitler reappoint him as head of the SA.)

Eighteen months later, on 1 November 1926, Hitler made his views on the SA unequivocally clear when setting up the 'Supreme SA Leadership' and explaining his model to the SA's newly appointed commander-in-chief, Franz von Pfeffer:

> The training of the SA must reflect the aims of the party rather than a military standpoint. [...] The organizational structure of the SA, together with its clothing and equipment, must be modelled, therefore, not on those of the old army but in a way that is appropriate to the task in hand. [...] What we need are not one or two hundred daring conspirators but a hundred thousand or, indeed, hundreds of thousands of fanatical men and women prepared to fight for our view of the world. We must operate not in secret conventicles but in huge mass demonstrations, and neither by dagger nor poison nor pistol can a path be cleared for the movement but only if we take to the streets. We must teach the Marxists that National Socialism is the future master of the streets just as it will one day be master of the state.[76]

The Frontbann as a Substitute Party

At the end of 1926 Hitler's aims for the SA were no more than a pipe dream. Once he had re-established the party in February 1925, there was a period when the Frontbann in some places assumed the function of a substitute party or at least an organizational precursor of an SA built up from scratch in the spirit intended by Hitler. This was the case above all in Berlin,[77] where Röhm had founded the Northern Frontbann in August 1924 in the Reichstag building itself – the rooms normally used by the National Socialist members of the Reichstag were placed at his disposal. By the beginning of March 1925 the Frontbann had some six hundred members in Berlin, while Berlin-Brandenburg could boast around two thousand. It clearly served as a kind of catchment for the *völkisch* organizations' extreme right-wing splinter groups that were under threat and also for members of the disbanded 'Black Reichswehr'.[78]

The nature of the Frontbann in Berlin and the surrounding area emerges to startling effect from an advertisement that the organization produced in 1924. It shows a man carrying a large flag with the Frontbann symbol consisting of a black steel helmet overlaid on an obliquely angled black swastika on a white circle. In the background are the rays of the sun rising over the outlines of Berlin – among the buildings that can be identified are the Brandenburg Gate and the Victory Column. In the upper right-hand corner is a portrait of Hitler probably based on a contemporary photograph. At the bottom are the words 'Follow the German workers' leader Adolf Hitler! Join the Northern Frontbann!' As a symbol of the strictly militarily structured defence associations, the steel helmet has been overlaid on the political symbol of the swastika, and any substantive message has been replaced by Hitler as a workers' leader seen as a nebulous figure of light.

Tributes to Hitler by Kurt Daluege and Waldemar Geyer reveal the extent to which even at this early date the members of the Frontbann were held together by their positively cultic veneration of the Führer in spite of the diffuseness of their political views. Writing in 1936, Daluege struck a remarkably enthusiastic note when describing the

handful of National Socialists who had organized themselves into the banned Frontbann in the capital and who at that date [the spring of 1925] were the earliest champions of Adolf Hitler's ideas in Red Berlin. [. . .] We can nowadays only imagine how this handful of permanently hounded men had the temerity and unshakeable idealism to create a new party from scratch up here in northern Germany on the basis of a large number of associations, alliances and tiny groups. Hardly any of them had actually seen Adolf Hitler but perhaps knew him only from photographs, and yet they were committed to him body and soul. [. . .] They did not even have a fixed goal but were simply resolved to oppose the bigwiggery of Weimar and the Bolshevist terror with a bellicose mentality inspired by their experiences on the front.[79]

Geyer, who in 1936 was promoted to the rank of SA brigade leader, added that the Northern Frontbann was the only fighting force to stand up to other organizations with uncompromising resolve. Its flags had been emblazoned with the symbols of the Third Reich, and with its battle songs it had taken Hitler to its heart. 'Fewer than two dozen men from the Frontbann were members of the NSDAP at this period and these were scattered across the whole of Berlin-Brandenburg. Our opponents never spoke of the Frontbann, however. They always referred to us as "Hitler's servants" or "Hitlerians".'[80]

When Geyer stressed the Frontbann's refusal to compromise with other organizations and even mocked those whom he called 'also-nationals', by which he meant people who 'secretly eked out their anxious existences', he was alluding to the extreme right in Berlin, which had been fragmented for years. It was not only the German Nationalist Freedom Party, or DVFP, and Kunze's German Socialist Party that attempted to keep their party machinery running, there were also secret societies that operated behind closed doors and paramilitary organizations that dreamt, undeterred, about putsches – these included the Wiking League. And yet the refusal to compromise noted by Geyer was to a certain extent the result of a belated wish to gloss over the truth, for there was initially a tendency in the Frontbann to cling to Ludendorff's patronage, while another group was tempted to join one of the defence associations that operated under the umbrella organization of the United Patriotic Associations which included the Stahlhelm, the Wiking League and the Olympia Sports Association.[81] As long as none of the extreme right-wing groupings achieved political dominance over the others, membership of these different organizations was bound to be unstable.

The Wiking League's leaders in Berlin were two retired army majors, Major Günther and Major Hans von Sodenstern. The latter was a member of the National Association of German Officers and edited its journal, *Deutsche Treue* (German Loyalty).[82] He was also for a time editor-in-chief of the *Deutsche Zeitung*, a newspaper acquired from Heinrich Class's Pan-German League in 1917 which openly promoted an extreme form of nationalism and was markedly anti-Semitic and anti-democratic in its views.[83] By May 1925 the Berlin branch of the Wiking League had around five hundred members, most of whom were grammar-school pupils and students who performed military and gymnastic exercises and practised using small-bore rifles. It was no wonder, then, that the Berlin branch of the Wiking League maintained excellent relations with the Reichswehr, which even allowed the Wiking League and Olympia Sports Association to hold regular military exercises around Berlin in the summer of 1925.[84] Not until May 1926 were these two defence associations banned by the Prussian Ministry of the Interior when detailed military deployment plans were discovered revealing that, 'if things became serious', both were prepared to take control of the capital and revoke parliamentary democracy.[85]

The Formation of the Berlin SA

The National Socialists in Berlin must have thought that their time had finally come. A large number of members of the banned defence organizations had sought refuge in their ranks. In July 1926 the monthly report by Reinhold Muchow, an NSDAP activist in Berlin, noted that 'many' new members had joined from the disbanded Olympia Sports Association.[86] Moreover, the NSDAP's two main rivals, the German Socialist Party and the German Nationalist Freedom Party, were already in decline. Between March 1926 and March 1927, for example, the German Socialist Party in Berlin lost three thousand of its four thousand members, while the DVFP fell from three thousand to two thousand members between April 1925 and April 1926.[87] To the extent that they remained politically active, the majority of those who left these two parties switched their allegiance to the National Socialists.

The NSDAP had one inestimable advantage over its rivals in that the Reichswehr lost interest in supporting organizations that harboured any ambitions to mount a putsch, a development that went hand in hand with the stabilization of the country's economy once the crisis of 1923 had been overcome.[88] But financial and logistical support from the Reichswehr was the lifeblood of organizations associated with the 'eternal putschists', with the result that smaller groups such as Olympia disappeared immediately while a larger one like the Wiking League survived only until 1928. The age of a 'politicized military' gave way to one of 'militarized politics'. Extreme right-wing activists now had to base their decisions on political programmes and align themselves either with the Stahlhelm, whose members had close links with the DNVP,[89] or, if they preferred not to side with any of the smaller 'national revolutionary' parties, with the National Socialists, who were bitterly opposed to the DNVP, branding it 'reactionary'.[90]

As if anticipating the way that things would develop, the leaders of the Frontbann in Berlin who felt an affinity with the NSDAP convened a meeting on 22 March 1926 under the heading 'Frontbann or SA?'. As Karl Daluege explained in 1936, this was not a question of deciding for or against Hitler, but of deciding how to restructure the Frontbann in the spirit of Hitler, which meant joining the SA. Having been appointed the first head of the SA in Berlin, Daluege was determined

> to put an end to the aimless confusion and bring all fighters into line with the party of Adolf Hitler. I explained to the men that if things went on as they were, we could not achieve our great goal together and that only by combining all our resources in a single clearly structured entity under the leadership of Munich could we continue our work in the future.[91]

This first SA in Berlin – the term *Sturmabteilung* (Storm Division) was not used, the organization preferring to style itself the 'NSDAP's Sports Association for Greater Berlin' – is said to have boasted 350 members from across sixteen of the city's administrative districts. The Spandau group had eighty members and for a long time was the largest. For the present no groups could be set up in Köpenick, Weißensee, Pankow and Reinickendorf.[92]

It is interesting to see the extent to which National Socialist historians later rewrote the story of the Berlin SA along party lines. According to this version of events, the sixty-strong Stettin Station group, which was made up for the most part of 'workers and fighters', could trace its antecedents back to the Frontbann and thence to the 'Sportvereinigung Maikäfer', which itself was a successor to the 'Gruppe Frundsberg' of the 'Black Reichswehr' and of the Stettin Station branch of the 'Association of Nationally Minded Soldiers', which had been banned in the wake of the murder of Walther Rathenau.[93] In short, it was not only during the early years of its existence that the Freikorps and its successors in the guise of the 'Black Reichswehr', the defence associations and their youth groups provided most of the members and leaders of the Berlin SA.

The SA's first leader in Berlin, Kurt Daluege, was born in 1897 and volunteered for active service in 1916, later becoming a divisional commander in Roßbach's Freikorps. Between 1920 and 1923 he played a leading role in each of Roßbach's organizations. He joined the Munich NSDAP and the Greater German Workers' Party in 1922. From 1924 he was also one of the organizers and leaders of the Frontbann in Berlin. At the end of 1926 he was appointed deputy Gauleiter of the Berlin NSDAP, switching to the SS in 1930 and taking over as its leader in the city. From 1931 to 1933 he was the leader of the Eastern

Group of the SS. He made his career under Göring from 1933 and later under Himmler, becoming SS senior group leader in 1934. In 1936 he even reached the rank of police general and was in charge of running the 'Order Police', the regular German police force that dealt with all aspects of law enforcement under the Third Reich. In 1942 he became deputy Reich protector of Bohemia and Moravia. It was Daluege who gave the orders for the massacre at Lidice. He was tried and executed in Prague in 1946.[94]

Sooner or later other Freikorps members turned up in the SA or NSDAP in Berlin. These included Bruno Ernst Buchrucker, who had organized the Küstrin Putsch in 1923 and who joined the party in 1926, leaving it again in 1930; his battalion commander Walter Stennes, who until the revolt against Hitler was head of the SA in Berlin; and Röhm's successor as leader of the Frontbann, Count Wolf-Heinrich Helldorf, who became head of the SA in Berlin in 1931 and chief of police in 1935. Among other members of the Roßbach Freikorps were Rudolf Höss, who later ran the Auschwitz concentration camp, and Martin Bormann, who went on to become head of Hitler's secretariat and minister in charge of party headquarters.[95] Especially significant were the younger members: Hans Maikowski, who led the infamous Charlottenburg SA-Sturm 33 and who was a former member of Olympia; and Horst Wessel, who was a member of the Wiking League from the end of 1923 and who joined the SA and NSDAP at the end of 1926.[96]

The way in which the Berlin SA was described in official accounts of the party throws light on its prevailing mentality:

In Berlin-Brandenburg we soon see a particular manifestation of the typical 'political soldier', or SA man: the so-called 'thug'. He is fired by the greatest revolutionary fervour, his life is one of radical socialism and the harsh regime of a soldier. He is to be found among the proletariat that has always existed in the organizations in Berlin and the larger towns of the Brandenburg Marches, where he makes up 80 per cent of the membership, and he is to be found among the agricultural workers who come over to the SA in equally high percentages, in the smiths and cartwrights, the labourers and gardeners, and in the soldiers from Berlin and Brandenburg – the cradle of the Prussian German army – whose thinking is conditioned by their blood and by their history. Of course, the 'tone' of these 'thugs' and their 'socialism' is not to the liking of the petty bourgeoisie. But this is intentional, and it is good that it is so. For the battle over Red Berlin [. . .] can never be fought by a group of weaklings whose feelings are dictated by aesthetics and whose actions are over-refined, but only by men who know life and who can write with their fists.[97]

In order to avoid any possible misunderstanding, Daluege added that 'the initial aim was to gain the respect for Adolf Hitler's followers that every honest man must always offer an honest opponent. This was possible only by resisting brute force with a clenched fist.'[98]

To the extent that the majority of members of the newly formed SA had previously belonged to the Frontbann, they knew what was expected of them in their new organization when they heard the phrase 'clenched fist'. They were now 'party soldiers', but for the present their challenges and the types of action that they might undertake remained the same. Writing in 1936, one 'old warrior' recalled that the Frontbann had taken part in the two elections for the Reichstag in 1924, sharing a platform with the National Socialist Freedom Movement – the electoral pact between the NSDAP and the DVFP – and 'in response to direct instructions from the Führer it also took charge of the propaganda for General Ludendorff, the National Socialist candidate in the 1925 election for the country's president'.[99] Far more important than its involvement in the elections, however, were the violent demonstrations that it organized against 'the Marxist enemy' and 'the insolent Jews'. On 9 August 1925, for example, the Frontbann 'again held one of the demonstrations that were so popular with the radical right wing in Berlin from 1919 onwards and that regularly ended in fist fights and attacks on innocent passers-by'.[100] This particular demonstration took place in the area around the Memorial Church. On 15 February 1926 the Frontbann and the Communists fought a running battle on the corner of the Badstraße and Pankstraße in the working-class district of Wedding.[101]

The SA took over where the Frontbann left off. According to the NSDAP's monthly report for June 1926:

> At the end of the month the whole of the SA organized a demonstration that was intended as Berlin's contribution to the Weimar party rally [of the NSDAP]. It passed through the western part of the city, the 'elegant Jewish ghetto' where those Galicians [i.e. Galicia in Eastern Europe] now own princely villas, Galicians who had once lived in the greasy, dirty Grenadierstraße, a collecting point for East European Jews. The blood-red swastika flags betokened a terrible awakening for the international vultures who, anxious and fearful for their lives, looked down through their curtains on the animated street below them.[102]

Members and sympathizers of the NSDAP could read no less malicious anti-Semitic tirades in the *Berliner Arbeiterzeitung*, which appeared for the first time on 1 March 1926 and was published every Sunday by Gregor and Otto Straßer's Kampf-Verlag. Regarded as the official organ of the NSDAP in Berlin, it initially had a print run of three thousand copies. In May 1926, for example, it attacked the satirist Kurt Tucholsky as 'that Galician Jewish swine Ignaz Wrobel'.[103]

From August 1926 the paper's masthead also described it as 'the only workers' newspaper in Berlin that is not in thrall to financial capital'. But side by side with its aggressive hostility to the Jews it also revealed, in often amusing ways, the cultic veneration that Hitler enjoyed among his supporters in Berlin even at this early date. Typical of this tone is the bombastic appeal addressed to the paper's readers on 11 April 1926 by the Berlin Gauleiter, Ernst Schlange:

> National Socialists! German men, German youth, German frontline fighters! [...] At a time when the country's needs were greatest [in 1923], you who spent more than four years protecting your homeland, fatherland and nation with your lives, you looked up with ardent hearts and an expression of longing in your eyes to the *one* man who had given you and the entire German nation a new political doctrine and a whole new view of the world. From the man who reawoke in you your faith in Germany and in the German nation, you expected the salvation and deliverance of Germany. That man is our own Adolf Hitler! [...] A year ago Adolf Hitler breathed new life into the NSDAP. [...] It is now a question of creating the well-wrought power that Adolf Hitler needs. All who see their leader in Adolf Hitler belong in the NSDAP and its sports divisions! [...] We National Socialists are fully resolved to fight for a National Socialist Greater Germany under the leadership of our own Adolf Hitler. Heil![104]

The same edition of the paper invited members of the party to turn up in force at 105 Berliner Straße in the Charlottenburg district of the city on 21 April 1926. 'This is the birthday of our leader Adolf Hitler [in fact, Hitler was born on 20 April; the 21st that year was a Saturday, presumably chosen as being preferable to a workday] and it will be festively celebrated in the Hohenzollern Rooms. Come, then, to Charlottenburg. Contribution towards expenses: 1 reichsmark.'[105] Under the heading 'Adolf Hitler's Thirty-Seventh Birthday', the paper also regaled its readers with a poem signed simply 'K. H.':

> Der Du so stark und rein vor uns erscheinst
> Und 'furchtlos' deutsche Volksgenossen einst,

Der Du Gestalter jener Lehre bist,
Die deutsche Mannen führt und nie vergißt,
Daß sie alleine nur berufen ist
Den Kampf zu fechten gegen Trug und List,
Heil Dir! . . .[106]

[You who appear so strong and pure and 'fearless' to us national comrades, you who shaped that doctrine that guides all German men and never once forgets that it alone is called upon to fight against deception and base trickery, all hail to you!]

The Collapse of the NSDAP in Berlin

And yet the admiration that all its members felt for Hitler could not prevent violent arguments from breaking out within the party – at this date 'an almost completely insignificant, tiny club'.[107] Or perhaps it would be more accurate to say that these arguments were between the party and the SA. Writing retrospectively in 1942, the journalist Julius Lippert, whose sympathies in the 1920s lay entirely with the NSDAP, claimed:

> The only thing that was still in any kind of order was the SA, which under its leader, Kurt Daluege, occasionally allowed itself to be seen in public and held meetings. [. . .] Otherwise the party had very few members, and even these could never agree among themselves. In the circumstances it was no wonder that the leading members of the party failed to make any headway. There were almost permanent arguments of every kind between individual groups, and petty squabbles of a disagreeable, personal nature were the order of the day.[108]

The arguments escalated at a meeting of the leaders of the NSDAP and SA in Berlin on 25 August 1926. Attempts were made to vote the incumbents out of office and install a new set of leaders. In the end the disputants came to blows.[109] In October 1926 the party's internal report even had to concede that 'the situation inside the party has not been good this last month. A situation has arisen in our Gau that is now so bad that we must reckon on a complete collapse of the Berlin branch. It is the Gau's tragedy that it never had a real leader, something indispensably necessary in a city numbering several million inhabitants.' Gauleiter Schlange, the report went on, had worked himself into the ground but had failed to give the Gau a clear and unified line, not least because he was said to be a poor speaker.

Schlange had handed over the running of the organization to a deputy, but it had then turned out that the latter was 'even less able to deal with the confused situation with any real resolve'. Although the opposition within the party had severely criticized this unfortunate state of affairs, they had failed to put forward any positive counterproposals and had not nominated a new Gauleiter from within their own midst. The party's self-destruction had encouraged the opposition to announce that the former leaders were no longer in control and that their function had been taken over by Heinz Oskar Hauenstein. Since it was impossible to impose any sense of order on the confusion and the two groups were blocking each other's actions, 'negotiations were begun with the party leaders in Munich with a view to appointing a new Gauleiter'.[110]

Within eighteen months of his party's re-emergence, then, Hitler saw himself faced with the complete meltdown of the Berlin branch of the NSDAP. The Frontbann that Röhm had landed him with while he was in prison could have been replaced by a branch of the SA which would have been under party control, but the NSDAP in Berlin was now under the leadership of Heinz Oskar Hauenstein, a man who, as a former Freikorps commander, had already led the party in the capital in tandem with Gerhard Roßbach in 1922–3, when the NSDAP had been banned.[111] A rival to Hauenstein now emerged in the person of Otto Straßer, the chief ideologue of a specifically north German variant of the NSDAP, whose leading representatives, writing in their journal *Nationalsozialistische Briefe*, argued for greater emphasis on the 'socialist' and 'proletarian' character of the party and advocated a pro-Soviet foreign policy, drawing up plans for a new party programme and in general promoting the idea of a left-wing version of National Socialism that was hostile to Munich and above all to Hitler.[112]

For Hitler, this was tantamount to choosing between two equally unattractive alternatives. For a number of years the ghost of the old Kampfbünde and defence organizations had continued to bedevil the SA and even took the form of internal party revolts until Hitler finally acted to put a stop to them, which he did with extreme brutality. To have appointed Hauenstein as the new Gauleiter in Berlin would have meant restoring the local NSDAP to the state in which it had found itself in 1922, while the SA would have reverted to being a defence organization, a situation that, as Hitler knew very well, would have proved a disaster in the light of the changed political conditions within the country at large. Conversely, Straßer's ideas for combining anti-Semitism, nationalism and social revolution may have worked in the Ruhr Valley, where they would have helped to lure a few proletarian voters away from the Social

Democrats and above all from the Communists,[113] but to have taken over these ideas as the basis of the party's entire programme would sooner or later have frightened away the NSDAP's middle-class voters and sympathizers, all of whom were deeply anti-Marxist and who would have been driven into the arms of the DVFP and DNVP. And it was very much here that Hitler hoped to enlist many more new members, a hope that in the event was to prove well founded.

Although Hitler may have had a reputation for procrastinating where staffing decisions were concerned, he wasted little time in making up his mind in the present case: after all, the post of Gauleiter in Berlin was immensely important in terms of the future growth of the NSDAP. And his decision on such a fundamental point of political strategy turned out to be both surprising and at the same time highly intelligent. He began by offering Gregor Straßer, the organizational head of the 'North Germans', the task of running the party's propaganda bureau and, later, the post of its organizational leader – a move designed to render Straßer harmless. Straßer accepted the post 'in the hope of being able to win Hitler back to socialist thinking, but in doing so he committed the error of believing that Hitler was being deceived and misled by the people around him'.[114] This was a view that was initially shared by the Gauleiter of the Ruhr Valley, Joseph Goebbels, who had joined the NSDAP in August 1924, and who, following Hitler's appearance at a meeting of National Socialist leaders in Bamberg on 14 February 1926, had noted in his diary: 'What kind of Hitler? A reactionary? Amazingly clumsy and uncertain. [. . .] Arguably one of the greatest disappointments of my life. I can no longer wholly believe in Hitler.' At the same time, however, he suggested that he and Straßer could go and see Hitler 'to impress on him that he must not allow those rogues down there [in Munich] to tie him hand and foot'.[115]

Hitler had been kept fully informed about the state of the north German opposition and gradually succeeded in winning over Goebbels, initially by means of his extreme attentiveness and friendliness, with the result that by 13 April 1926 we find Goebbels writing in his diary: 'I like him a lot. He is embarrassingly kind to us.' Hitler also flattered Goebbels' vanity: 'At the end [of his speech], Hitler embraced me.' And, finally, he sought by dint of rational argument to undermine Goebbels' own convictions. 'His line of reasoning is compelling,' we read on 16 April. 'But I don't think he has fully recognized the problem of Russia. I too must revise my thoughts on a number of points.' Within weeks Goebbels was enthusing over Hitler's speeches and their conversations together. 'It's impossible not to like him as a person. And then there is this towering intellectual figure,' he noted on 16 June. 'As a speaker a wonderful harmony between gesture, facial expressions and words.' 'Hitler speaks', we read on 6 July, 'about politics, ideas and organization. Deep and mystical. Almost like a Gospel. With a shudder one walks with him past the bottomless pit of existence. The last word is said. I thank fate for giving us this man!' By the end Goebbels' language had acquired a positively hymn-like tone expressing a commitment and devotion that bordered on the religious. 'He is a genius,' Goebbels wrote on 24 July. 'The self-evidently creating instrument of a divine destiny. I stand before him, shaken to the very core of my being. [. . .] Above us in the sky a white cloud assumes the shape of a swastika. [. . .] A sign of destiny?' And on the 25th: 'A star shines forth in our hour of deep distress. I feel bound to him for ever. Now my last remaining doubts have vanished. Germany will live. Heil Hitler!'[116]

By now Hitler had Goebbels almost where he wanted him. On 27 August 1926 the latter noted in his diary: 'Offer from the party leadership: I am to take over the Gau in Berlin on a temporary four-month basis. I am thinking hard about it.' But by the next day he had written to Munich, 'half turning down the offer – I've no wish to kneel in the dirt'.[117] Since the Political Police in Berlin were keeping a close eye on the activities of the local NSDAP, a surveillance report of 28 August allows us to reconstruct in some detail the events that led to the approach to Goebbels. The leaders of the NSDAP's Gau for Greater Berlin gathered on 25 August. It was a meeting that reflected the internal divisions within the local party. In the course of it, a party member by the name of Knodn reported on discussions with Hitler concerning the crisis within the party in Berlin. The negotiations, which had taken place in Munich, had lasted several hours and had included an account of the situation in the capital, ending in a request for Hitler's urgent assistance. Hitler had replied to the effect that it was impossible for him to take a view of the situation from Munich and told the leaders in Berlin to sort out the matter themselves. Once they had done so, he would either come to Berlin in person or ask someone to report on the steps that had been taken. He would then make contact with the proposed leader and, if he agreed with the choice, would confirm him in his new post.[118]

But Hitler was reluctant to leave the matter to the Berliners themselves and so it occurred to him to send Goebbels in as temporary Gauleiter. The latter travelled to Berlin in the middle of September 1926, at a time when the party's situation was critical. Goebbels noted only 'discontents' and 'grumblers'. The mood also affected his perception of the city itself: 'We then stroll through the streets. Berlin at night. A den of iniquity! And I'm supposed to plunge headlong into this?'[119] But he now found himself overtaken by events. In a letter dated 16 October, the city's acting Gauleiter, Erich Schmiedicke, wrote to Goebbels, imploring him to accept the post: throughout the violent upheavals that had shaken the party in recent months, he had been assailed 'from all quarters by cries for you to be appointed the new Gauleiter'. And as if these entreaties were not enough, Schmiedicke ended with a dire warning:

> On a purely personal note, I should like to say on the basis of my knowledge of the psychology of our party comrades in Berlin that if you do not take over the running of the Gau on 1 November, their disappointment will be so great and their faith in the NSDAP so badly undermined that there will be no question of Berlin playing a part in the movement as a whole for the foreseeable future.[120]

Beneath the date the letter bears a note: 'Dealt with, 19.10.26.' The matter had been dealt with by Goebbels agreeing to the request, presumably in response to pressure from Hitler. His diary contains an entry for 16 October: 'I'm now minded to take over in Berlin and govern there. That's the end of the matter!'[121] Two days later we read: 'Finally off to Berlin on 1 November. I'm looking forward to it. After all, Berlin is the control centre. For us too. An international city.'[122] One wonders if he was merely repeating a phrase that he had heard on Hitler's lips. In the course of a propaganda trip, Goebbels found himself in Plauen on 30 October, and it was here that he received a letter from Hitler, giving him every reason to celebrate: 'Berlin is perfect. Hurray! I'm off to the capital in a week's time. Goodbye, Elberfeld!'[123]

On 7 November 1926 the *Berliner Abendzeitung* published the following announcement:

> 1. With effect from 1 November 1926 the Gaus of Greater Berlin and Potsdam will be disbanded and a new Gau of Berlin-Brandenburg formed from them. The local branches of Cottbus, Landsberg an der Warthe and Müncheberg in the Brandenburg Marches that were formerly independent will become part of the Berlin-Brandenburg Gau.
>
> 2. I hereby entrust Party Comrade Dr Goebbels of Elberfeld with the running of the Berlin-Brandenburg Gau. He will be responsible to me alone for running the Gau in terms of its organization, propaganda and politics.
>
> 3. All details relating to the disbandment of the Gaus of Greater Berlin and Potsdam and the transfer of their offices will be dealt with by Party Comrade Dr Goebbels in direct consultation with the previous Gauleiters.

4. The SS and SA of the new Gau are placed under the explicit political control of the Gauleiter. Their leaders will ultimately be appointed by the SA leadership in Munich only in response to his suggestion.

Munich, 26 October 1926

Adolf Hitler[124]

4

'A second headquarters'

1926: GOEBBELS TAKES OVER THE RUNNING OF THE PARTY IN BERLIN

'Party comrades were devoted to him. The SA would have done anything for him. Goebbels was like Hitler to them.'
Horst Wessel, *Politik: Aufzeichnungen aus dem Jahre 1929*[1]

'We owe this successful launch of a new and decisive battle plan first and foremost to Adolf Hitler's judicious perception as leader, for he recognized that, after consolidating the great flank defences in the Ruhr and in Saxony, he needed to set up a second headquarters in Berlin and fill it with his best men.'
Berliner Arbeiterzeitung, 21 November 1926[2]

In Search of a Leader

In an autobiographical note that he was invited to contribute to *Kürschner's German Reichstag* in 1928, Joseph Goebbels, who had been elected to the Reichstag as a member of the NSDAP on 20 May of that year, described himself as a 'writer from Friedenau' and explained that he had been politically active 'since 1922'.[3] This was not in fact true, but why should Goebbels – born in the Rhineland town of Rheydt on 29 October 1897 and head of Berlin's National Socialists since November 1926 – not bring forward the date of his 'decision to become a politician', just as his lord and master, Adolf Hitler, had brought forward the date of his move from Vienna to Munich in *Mein Kampf*? Why should he not emulate Hitler and tailor the facts of his life to fit the picture of himself that he needed to project for propaganda purposes? Having taken his doctorate in November 1921,[4] he had, after all, published a series of articles in the *Westdeutsche Landeszeitung* between January and March 1922 in which, echoing ideas that he had picked up from Oswald Spengler's *The Decline of the West*, he had spoken out against materialism, which, he claimed, was to blame for the 'political, intellectual and moral confusion of our own day'.[5] And even as early as the spring of 1922 he had argued that 'salvation cannot come from Berlin'. Rather, there were times when he felt that 'a new sun is about to rise in the south'.[6]

It is doubtful, however, whether Goebbels was thinking of the situation in Bavaria, still less of the emergence of Hitler and the NSDAP in Munich. Although the 'reminiscences' that Goebbels jotted down in the summer of 1924 mention his state of mind in 1922 and 1923, it is impossible to find a single concrete reference to any political activity during this period.[7] True, there are signs of his incipient anti-Semitism at the end of 1922, when his lover, the teacher Else Janke, told him that her mother was Jewish. Goebbels' reaction in his reminiscences was: 'She admits her origins to me. Since then the initial magic has been destroyed. I am sceptical about her.'[8]

In January 1923, more than a year after completing his dissertation, Goebbels found work at the Dresdner Bank in Cologne but was soon complaining about the 'pitiful wages' and suffering another crisis in his private life, which he linked to the apocalyptic conditions in Germany at this time:

> Banking and stock market. Industrial and stock market capital. My gaze grows clearer through suffering. Revulsion at the bank and at my work. Desperate poems. Jews. I think about the money problem. [. . .] The Jewish question in art. Gundolf. Intellectual clarification. Bavaria. Hitler. Come home early from work. Diary entries to Else. [. . .] Revolution inside me. Pessimism towards everything. At the opera *Palestrina*. German music. Wagner. Turning away from internationalism. [. . .] Despair. Thoughts of suicide. The political situation. Chaos in Germany. [. . .] Cologne an abomination, the bank completely meaningless. Wages practically nil. Sick in body and mind. Can't hold out any longer.[9]

Hitler's name is mentioned as casually as a visit to a concert or a recital ('Hugo Wolf. St Matthew Passion'), hardly suggesting any great political affinity. Goebbels lost his job at the bank in September 1923 and moved back in with his parents in Rheydt, where he continued his litany of complaints: 'Wild days of drinking brought on by despair. [. . .] The decline of the German idea. I can't bear this torment any longer. I have to expunge this bitterness from my heart.'[10]

Goebbels' bitterness – which, politically speaking, drove him increasingly to the right at this time – was additionally due, almost certainly, to the fact that his attempts to find work as a dramaturge or editor were unsuccessful. He was even shameless enough to apply to Jewish newspaper publishers in Berlin, including Ullstein-Verlag's *Vossische Zeitung* and Rudolf Mosse's *Berliner Tageblatt*, which among extreme right-wing readers was the most hated German newspaper after the *Frankfurter Zeitung*.[11] He was now twenty-six years old and unemployed. But at least he was at home and could live off his father's income. He did not have to whine endlessly but could now commit his thoughts to his diary, which he started in the early summer of 1924 and continued until the very end of his life. In the morning he read Wagner's essay *On Conducting*, then continued his reading of 'Prozesse', the third volume of *Köpfe* by the journalist Maximilian Harden ('alias Isidor Witkowski', Goebbels dutifully noted in his diary). Harden's prose infuriated him: 'What a hypo-critical bastard this blasted Jew is! Knaves, blackguards, traitors! They're sucking the blood from our veins. Vampires!' In his entry of 27 June he continues without drawing breath: 'I am sitting in the newly installed arbour and enjoying the beautiful summer day. Sunshine! Beautiful mild weather! The smell of flowers! How beautiful this world of ours is!!!'[12]

Two days later an old school friend, Fritz Prang, who had been a member of the NSDAP since 1922, took Goebbels to Elberfeld for an event organized by the German Nationalist Freedom Party. Goebbels was deeply disappointed by all the 'blather', but by now he was sufficiently well informed to note the begin-nings of the rift between the DVFP and the NSDAP, which in May 1924 had stood on a single ticket in the Reichstag elections, representing the 'Völkisch-Sozialer Block' in the Rhineland. Indeed, he even predicted the outcome of the rift: 'Munich and Berlin are at war. One can say the same about Hitler and Ludendorff. As to which side I may join, there can really be no question. To the young people who actually want the new man. [. . .] I'm bound to prefer Munich to Berlin. If only Hitler were free!'[13]

The political uncertainty that Goebbels bewails at this period ('One hope after another is crumbling away inside me') goes hand in hand with a contin-uing lack of any real prospects for the future ('I'm waiting for ever for a posi-tion and for money. Despair! Scepticism! Collapse! I don't know which way to turn').[14] This mixture of private and political depression produced a desire for authoritarian leadership: 'In Germany we lack a strong hand. [. . .] Germany is yearning for the one man who is like the earth in the summer after it has rained. [. . .] Lord, reveal a miracle to the German people! A miracle!! A man!!!'[15]

A few weeks later, Prang made it possible for Goebbels to travel to Weimar, where the party rally of the National Socialist Freedom Movement – the

völkisch-National Socialist alliance – took place under Ludendorff's chairmanship on 16–17 August 1924. On this occasion Goebbels was much taken by the
prevailing atmosphere. The opportunity to sit alongside 'a certain elite from
Germany' was a source of 'great assurance and contentment'. When he heard
Julius Streicher – the 'fanatic with the pinched lips', as Goebbels called him –
delivering himself of one of his anti-Semitic tirades, he felt not a little alienated
and described the speaker as 'a bit pathological', but consoled himself with the
thought that 'We need these people as well. To grip the masses. Hitler is said
to have something of this about him.'[16] He was impressed by his first sight of
Ludendorff ('I felt something amounting to a shock'), and yet his meeting with
the 'great man' elicited little more than a vague sense of admiration at the fact
that 'at his age and in his position he has thrown in his lot with young people
and with the nation'. 'Yes, we are looking for the born leader. But,' he admitted,
'we mustn't lapse into Byzantinism.'[17] At the end of his visit to Weimar,
Goebbels summed up his reaction by noting that 'the *völkisch* question' was
now becoming associated in his mind with 'all manner of intellectual and
religious questions'. He was beginning, he went on, to think along *völkisch*
lines. This, he argued, had nothing to do with politics but was a 'world view:
I am starting to find firm ground. Ground that I can stand on.'[18]

   Only a few days later in München-Gladbach (now Mönchengladbach)
Goebbels founded a local branch of the National Socialist Freedom Movement
of Greater Germany, and for a few months from the end of September 1924 he
worked as the editor of the party's weekly newspaper, *Völkische Freiheit*. It was
at this period that he discovered his gift for public speaking. And so he threw
himself into politics: as a talented journalist and an eloquent official, he could
certainly hope to rise quickly through the ranks of an extreme right-wing
party in which such doubly gifted individuals were distinctly thin on the
ground. Admittedly, he was sometimes aware that he 'must look round for a
paid position' because he was still a drain on his father's finances and playing
a 'pitiful role'.[19] And there were times when he doubted whether he was 'on the
right path'. At such times he would long to find 'a rock-like and unerring
faith'.[20] But when the NSDAP broke free from the DVFP and formed its own
independent party in the Rhineland, he lost no time in joining and by March
1925 was already the secretary of the North Rhineland Gau.[21]

   For Goebbels, Hitler was 'the fixed pole around which all National Socialist
thinking turns', a 'real man'.[22] Following the latter's release from Landsberg
Prison, Goebbels hailed him as a 'leader and hero', a 'voice calling out in the
conflict, a drummer for the rebirth of German faith and German fervour' and
'the incarnation of our faith and our idea'.[23] His first encounter with Hitler

probably took place on 12 July 1925 at a meeting of NSDAP leaders in Weimar. The text of Hitler's speech at this meeting has not survived, but it appears from the report in the *Völkischer Beobachter* that he spent two hours expatiating on 'questions of fundamental importance'. According to the paper, the 'irresistible logic' of Hitler's remarks 'confirmed each and every listener in the belief that in its general outlines the leadership of the movement could not be in better hands'. The 'tremendous cheering' at the end of the speech had been tantamount to an 'oath of allegiance'.[24]

But Goebbels' faith in Hitler was then called into question. Under the influence of Gregor Straßer, who was building up the NSDAP in northern and western Germany, he dismissed the NSDAP's headquarters in Munich as 'a complete and utter shambles'. Hitler, Goebbels concluded, was surrounded by 'all the wrong people'.[25] On reading *Mein Kampf*, which he found 'utterly gripping', he asked himself: 'Who is this man? Half-plebeian, half-God! Actually Christ or just John the Baptist?'[26] But when he met Hitler for the second time in Braunschweig in early November 1925 and the latter shook his hand 'like an old friend', Goebbels was overwhelmed by 'these big blue eyes', which struck him as being 'like stars'. Hitler had everything it took to be king: 'The born tribune of the people. The coming dictator.' And Goebbels' delight was no less great when they met again in Plauen on 20 November 1925: 'How I love him! Such a fellow! [. . .] How small I am! He gives me his picture. [. . .] I'd like to have Hitler as a friend. His picture stands on my desk. I couldn't bear to have to doubt in this man.'[27]

'A Terrible Stone Wasteland'

If Goebbels met Hitler in Braunschweig and Plauen, it was because with effect from the autumn of 1924 he was one of those peripatetic speakers whom the NSDAP sent all over the country to ensure that people heard of the party through its propaganda machine and that new members might be persuaded to join.[28] Between 1 October 1924 and 1 October 1925 Goebbels gave no fewer than 189 speeches both within the Rhineland and further afield.[29] He travelled to Berlin for the first time at the end of October 1924 and spoke to the party faithful about the '*völkisch* idea'. He passed through the city again in early March 1925, spending only a few hours there, but it was enough to convince him that Berlin was 'a terrible stone wasteland with perfume and female flesh displayed in a shameless manner. The Siegesallee. All these large, fatuous stone masses. And the terrible people!'[30] What a contrast between this reaction from the twenty-seven-year-old Goebbels in 1925 and the enthusiastic response of the twenty-eight-year-old Corporal Adolf Hitler, who had described the city as 'wonderful' when he visited it in the autumn of 1917.

Goebbels returned to Berlin at the end of November 1925 and delivered another speech, ostensibly 'before thousands' and 'hugely successful', as the self-infatuated diarist recorded. His only comment on the city was that it was 'a den of iniquity'.[31] It was a view that remained intact in the course of his subsequent visits to the capital. Indeed, his account of his visit in early February 1926 culminates in the comment: 'O terrible anguish! Is this life? I hate Berlin!'[32] Between February and October 1926 his work as a party official and public speaker took him back to the capital on no fewer than seven occasions for shorter or longer periods. On 8 June 1926, for example, he addressed an audience of two thousand in Spandau (again with 'tremendous success'), noting that the local Gauleiter was in despair at his inability to deal with 'defiant and refractory people', especially the SA. 'Everyone', he wrote smugly in his diary, 'wants me in Berlin as their saviour. I am grateful for the stone wasteland.' A few sentences later he refers again to Berlin as 'a great wasteland'.[33] Some years later he freely admitted that in the mid-1920s Berlin had been a book with seven seals and that on his 'occasional visits' it had always seemed 'a dark, mysterious puzzle, an urban monster made of stone and asphalt' that he preferred to avoid.[34]

In the speech that he gave in Munich's Bürgerbräukeller on 27 February 1925 to mark the 'reconstitution' of the NSDAP in the city, Hitler, too, had referred to Berlin when he entreated his listeners to heed 'the vital question that concerns the German nation'. The greatest danger, he went on, was the 'poison of foreign peoples that is in our bodies'. All other questions were bound up with the age in which they lived, which was why he wanted to take his audience

> to Berlin for no more than a moment and look around the Friedrichstraße. You will then see Jew boy after Jew boy arm in arm with German girls. And then you must realize that each night thousands upon thousands of children of our blood are destroyed for ever in a single moment, and our children and our children's children are lost to us for good.[35]

Whereas Goebbels dismissed the city in general as a 'den of iniquity' and a 'stone wasteland', Hitler limited his remarks to the propaganda commonplace of Berlin's 'Judaized' culture and society whenever he spoke about the Friedrichstraße and other places in the capital.[36] This is particularly striking whenever his anti-Semitic outbursts give him an opportunity to draw a contrast between examples of 'Aryan' cultural achievements and 'the corrosive work of the Jews':

> Go to the city, to Berlin. There you will see on the one hand the Royal Palace, the museums and galleries, all the buildings created by the Aryan spirit, by the man who works with his hand in union with the man who works with his brow. And then look between all these great objects and see the filth and sewage of the big city, and allow your eyes to wander to the little man down there, selling journals on his cart: on the one hand, there is imperishable beauty and, on the other, the most wretched filth, the most common dirt. Here there is the Aryan, there the factory owner of the other persuasion, here the names of great Germans carved in stone, there the names of a Veilchenblühen, Nebeltau and Morgenstern written on paper.[37]

Goebbels still had to acquire Hitler's gift for drawing distinctions of this kind. Hitler could think along historical lines, his point of view always geared to a strategic goal, but this was an ability that Goebbels initially did not share. Whereas Hitler could appreciate the capital's importance and influence and see it as a political centre entirely worthy of prestigious official events, Goebbels was evidently indifferent to such considerations. And while Hitler was able to see that 'one day a clenched fist will come and clean out this whole mess',[38] the morally censorious Goebbels ('Every woman makes my blood boil')[39] could see only a 'den of iniquity', from which he turned away in horror. Every day he was capable of producing memorable phrases by the dozen, but Hitler could articulate complex sentences, equally brilliant as a journalist and as a speaker. Goebbels simply did not have it in him to be a theorist or strategist for the NSDAP.

Presumably Goebbels knew or at least suspected this, for we occasionally find him expressing his contempt for politics as a 'day job' that was 'repugnant' to him or that made him feel 'unproductive'.[40] It was for this reason that he submitted to Hitler as 'the greater man, the political genius'.[41] He wanted to be a prophet, a preacher, and from an early date he found himself hailed as a 'born speaker'. As fearless as he was audacious, he gradually emerged as one of the NSDAP's most capable propagandists, with the result that Hitler hit on the idea of appointing him Gauleiter of Berlin, even though he was not from the city. Almost sixteen years later in the Wolfsschanze, Hitler recalled that Goebbels had the two qualities needed to master the situation in Berlin: eloquence and intellect. At the same time Hitler told his listeners that Goebbels had asked for – and been given – the power 'to cleanse the party of all unedifying elements',[42] which he was able to do without recourse to the mechanisms that existed within the party for dealing with such eventualities. Goebbels duly travelled to Munich on 2 November 1926 'to speak to Hitler about taking over in Berlin'. Before setting off on his journey, he noted in his diary that there were 'enormous problems' in the capital and that his role was 'to play the saviour'. His first meeting in Munich was with Bruno Heinemann, at that time the chairman of the NSDAP's Investigation and Arbitration Committee, and the two men discussed the party organization in Berlin, where the situation was described as appalling. 'And I'm supposed to act the part of Hercules in these Augean Stables,' Goebbels noted in his diary with his usual mixture of self-pity and self-gratification. He finally met Hitler on the 5th, when the latter 'signs everything over to me regarding Berlin'. He would now be decamping to the capital, 'to the great asphalt wasteland of Berlin'.[43]

Throughout the years that followed, Goebbels returned again and again to the image of an 'asphalt wasteland' both in speeches and in leading articles. On the day before he set off for Berlin, he noted in his diary: 'Off to battle! Berlin! Asphalt or fulfilment?' And shortly after his arrival he characterized the capital as 'the city of the intelligentsia and of asphalt'.[44] His later comments, too, repeatedly echo the sense of unease that had initially assailed him in Berlin, and even after years of increasing successes in the city, his attitude towards it never lost the hint of violence that is an expression of deep-seated insecurity. Time and again he described the capital as an 'urban monster', most notably in the foreword to his 1934 book *Das erwachende Berlin* (Berlin Awakening). Here he introduces his description of the capital with the words: 'The city lies before you like a stone monster immeasurable in its dimensions and full of riddles and secrets'.[45] As a result he felt himself to be an intruder, a conqueror who, sword in hand, penetrated a city 'completely ruled by Marxism and Jewry'.[46] He was a dragonslayer who would kill the monster that was Berlin. Much the same spirit informed his later choice of words:

It is with profound inner emotion that I still recall that evening when, completely unknown, I travelled to a meeting in Berlin on the open top deck of a bus with a number of comrades from the early days of our struggle. On the streets and in the squares the ant-like swarm of the city. Thousands upon thousands of people on the move, seemingly aimlessly. Everywhere the flickering glow of this urban monster. Someone asked with genuine concern if it would ever be possible to force the name of the party on this city and – with or without the city's consent – to hammer home our own names too.[47]

Whether the city wanted it or not – this was one of the ideas that Goebbels brought with him to Berlin. It is hardly surprising to find him moved to comment, when an event was not 'a tremendous success' because the audience sang the Internationale at the end: 'Lumpenproletariat that refuses to be converted. Force will have to be used to make them happy.'[48]

Transfigured Arrival in Berlin

Goebbels arrived in Berlin to take up his new post on 9 November, a date that invested his appointment as Gauleiter with a very special solemnity: 'A momentous day for Germany itself as well as for our own movement! It is three years to the day since the machine guns rattled in the Feldherrnhalle in Munich and the marching columns of a young Germany were rounded up and shot by the forces of reaction.'[49]

'Straightforwardness has not been granted to him,' Konrad Heiden observed when quoting from Goebbels' final article for party comrades in the Ruhr. Far from announcing simply that he had been transferred to Berlin as the city's new Gauleiter, Goebbels wrote that he was 'striking camp with silent sadness, and by the time that these lines are in your hands, the rushing steam train will already be carrying me to the great asphalt wasteland of Berlin.'[50] He struck a similar note in his account of his arrival in the city: 'It was a typical November evening, heavy and grey and oppressive, when the express train puffed into Potsdam Station. Within two hours I was already standing on the stage that was so often to be the starting point of our subsequent political development. I found myself speaking to the party in Berlin.'[51] Another contemporary source – the monthly report written by Reinhold Muchow of the Neukölln branch of the NSDAP – claims that Goebbels arrived in the city two days earlier than was in fact the case: 'Party Comrade Dr Goebbels arrived at Anhalt Station on the seventh inst., and on that day a new chapter in the history of the Gau began. By the ninth inst. he had already given his first official speech at the Gau's Memorial Service for the Dead in the Kriegervereinshaus.'[52] It is unclear why a native Berliner like Muchow should have claimed that Goebbels arrived at Anhalt Station, as if he were coming from Munich rather than Elberfeld. Goebbels himself states that he 'puffed into' Potsdam Station. Anhalt Station was the terminus for trains from the south, not for those arriving from the west.

In *Vom Kaiserhof zur Reichskanzlei* (From the Kaiser's Court to the Reich Chancellery), Goebbels wove a further strand into the official party legend. The book consists of a series of diary-like entries. The one for 15 November

1932 reads: 'Six years ago to the hour I founded the party in Berlin as a young Gauleiter with three hundred people.'[53] Goebbels was referring here to his first test in the capital, a general meeting of the party in the Seitz Conference Rooms in Spandau, which in fact took place on 11 November 1926. The following day – the 12th – he noted in his diary:

> The battle is over, and I have won all along the line. That stool pigeon Hauenstein, who is my very antithesis, tried yesterday evening to terrorize everyone and break up the party. His people had to leave the hall, all fifty of them. I'm finally rid of these perpetual grumblers and criticasters. [. . .] I then spoke for three hours, as it were with the tongues of angels, and it ended with a great show of trust.[54]

In another account of these events, Goebbels claimed that it was in Spandau that Berlin's National Socialists 'had their most solid support at this time'. And yet the hall, according to Goebbels, was by no means full, for the party's local members were hostile to him. When he again demanded strict discipline, about a fifth of the party's members resigned.[55]

In this way Goebbels passes off the meeting – which for him went very well – as the occasion on which he formed a new party in Berlin. During the years that followed, he likewise rewrote history along the lines of his Munich model and portrayed the period as a series of 'historic' events from the party's 'time of battle'. No less remarkable is the little-known fact that, after signing the papers setting out the conditions under which his new Gauleiter would take over in Berlin, Hitler accompanied Goebbels to Berlin on 9 November, rather than simply sending him off into battle on his own. They met for lunch the next day at Edwin Bechstein's, as Goebbels himself reports. And Hitler called on him again on 14 November. Goebbels initially stayed with Hans Steiger, one of the editors of Alfred Hugenberg's *Berliner Lokal-Anzeiger* and a friend of Otto Straßer. Steiger had a large apartment at 5 Am Karlsbad, not far from the NSDAP offices in the Potsdamer Straße.[56]

Hitler no longer needed to interfere in the party's internal politics, Goebbels having already solved the problem to his satisfaction. This point is confirmed not least by the fact that Goebbels' diary entries for November 1926 in which he discusses his conversations with Hitler contain no mention of developments within the local NSDAP. Presumably Hitler felt that it was far more important at this time for him to speak to the NSDAP's remaining representatives in the Reichstag in order to discuss the future course of the party and, more especially, its relations with the DVFP.[57]

The Reorganization of the Berlin NSDAP

On taking up his new post in Berlin in November 1926, Goebbels first had to worry about the party's internal affairs. He already knew that it had 'collapsed under the weight of internecine struggles' and scarcely deserved to be called a party at all, being 'a bunch of people thrown together in wild confusion'.[58] This party, he later wrote, 'wasn't manoeuvrable – they couldn't be used in the decisive political battle simply on account of their goodness, quite apart from their numbers [according to Goebbels, they numbered 'a few hundred']. They first had to be uniformly shaped, they had to be given a common will and fired by a new and ardent impulse.'[59]

Goebbels was by no means unfamiliar with the situation that he found in Berlin. When he began to take an interest in politics in the summer of 1924, he became caught up in a movement in which the members of the *deutsch-völkisch* parties had long been at loggerheads with the National Socialists. Their electoral pact began to fall apart when Hitler reconstituted the NSDAP in February 1925 and made it unmistakably clear that his aim was leadership, not a merger. In the NSDAP's North Rhineland Gau and beyond, Goebbels knew only groupings in which individual members and divisive factions were in a state of constant conflict, fomenting intrigue, sowing mistrust and struggling to achieve a position of power by all manner of tricks and other machinations.[60] The problems in Berlin differed only in that here the disputants did not shy away from physically attacking their comrades and even challenging them to a duel.[61]

Predated 9 November 1926, the decisively worded 'Circular No. 1' made clear Goebbels' readiness to use harsh methods in restructuring the party. He was even prepared to discipline its members. He refused to see party members 'about gossip and so on' and would agree to speak to them only on factual matters. The party offices, he went on, were a place of work and as a result 'should not be confused with a waiting room or a place to keep warm'. Remarkably, he not only kept on Kurt Daluege as the leader of the Berlin SA but even appointed him deputy Gauleiter, while stipulating that every public appearance by the SA and SS had to be agreed with him in advance.[62]

For obvious reasons, Goebbels painted a bleak picture of the situation at the time of his appointment, but within a short time of taking up his new post he seems to have managed to inspire party members to work with him, a development that he brought about with a skilful mixture of censure and praise. The *Berliner Arbeiterzeitung* – the NSDAP's official weekly newspaper in Berlin-Brandenburg – was jubilant:

The Berlin Gau is standing. The ghosts have vanished. Swept away. The Berlin-Brandenburg Gau is standing. The terrible 'Kaiser-less' age is over! The new and definitive Gauleiter, Party Comrade Dr Josef [sic] Goebbels, has finally come and is here. 'Hitler's confidant', the capitalist *Berliner Tageblatt* whispers anxiously in its characteristically Yiddish way. [...] With all the events that it held, the party made such a powerful start, demonstrating such a unified passion for battle and revealing such a trusting subordination to the will of our God-given Führer, Adolf Hitler, that the Jewish-*völkisch* press could do nothing but remain silent. [...] The Berlin Gau is standing! Our headquarters in the north are now occupied. Now the winter may come! Like winter, we shall collect our forces underground. Until the solstice. But then the wheel of the sacred sun will thunder through the streets of this citadel of an inferior race, and he who resists its fiery spokes will be crushed.[63]

The Berlin NSDAP was also in a bad way financially, and so Goebbels hit upon the idea of setting up a National Socialist Freedom Alliance to demand excessive material sacrifices from its members – a similar method had been used with some success in the Ruhr in May 1925.[64] In Berlin the whip-round ensured that the party – or, rather, its new Gauleiter – was able to move into new offices. Goebbels also sought to form a new orchestra for the Gau. But the real selling point was

the acquisition of cars that will be permanently on call with the aim of intervening quickly, securely and inexpensively in propaganda marches, riots, etc., with a special commando of party comrades. Challenge will follow challenge until the Freedom Alliance – according to Party Comrade Dr Goebbels – is given its final task and the order comes to occupy and raid the Reichstag![65]

But with a single exception, to which we shall return shortly, Goebbels was initially unwilling to put even the most modest public acts on the agenda. For weeks and months he was completely preoccupied with reorganizing the party. By his own admission, his aim was to consolidate it, with the result that his work was directed towards its internal reorganization rather than any external concerns. Week after week he signed up more and more party members as well as other sympathizers and fellow travellers, which he did not so much in an attempt to deal with pressing political questions as to

examine the programmatic principles of our view of the world and drum them into our party comrades so effectively that they could repeat them in their sleep. In this way the initial nucleus of the party came together to create a very tight structure. The organization had a support, the idea was pursued with tireless educational work. Everyone knew what was involved, the goal was set, and all our resources could now be concentrated on it.[66]

Propaganda March through the Working-Class Quarter of Berlin

The goal was 'set'. But what exactly was that goal? Given the state of the Berlin NSDAP during the winter of 1926–7, the idea of occupying the Reichstag and taking over the reins of power was a non-starter. But were there other demands that could be realized in the shorter term and that Goebbels could have turned into the object of a political campaign? One possible aim would have been to overturn the ban on Hitler speaking in public, which was still in force in Prussia. Goebbels spoke out against it at almost all of his public appearances. And during the early months of 1926 the Greater Berlin Gau printed thousands of posters protesting at it. At the end of April the *Berliner Arbeiterzeitung* even published an appeal inviting readers to sign a petition demanding 'freedom of speech for Adolf Hitler'.[67]

But the campaign had then become bogged down in internal party wranglings and been unceremoniously ignored. And Goebbels had absolutely no intention of reviving it. Neither he nor Hitler wanted the NSDAP to appear indistinguishable from any other extreme right-wing party or organization. No one who examines the documents relating to Goebbels' early period in office in Berlin will find any trace of substantive arguments: there was no clear-cut programme, no attempt to engage with and propose a solution to the concrete questions of the day, and no draft proposals for the future direction of Berlin, Brandenburg, Prussia and the Reich. Dated 9 November 1926, Goebbels' first circular as Gauleiter contained eight points, all of which were concerned with purely organizational matters.

Admittedly, the columns of the *Berliner Arbeiterzeitung* were filled week after week with the most virulent anti-Semitic attacks on politicians, writers, journalists, artists and individuals working in the theatre and the film industry. There were cries of indignation at 'Germany's enslavement by the system of Versailles'. And there were polemical outbursts directed against the burden of reparation and litanies of complaints at Germany's decline since the 'November criminals' had come to power. Such matters were also discussed at meeting groups and various other events. But anti-Semitism was by no means unique to the NSDAP, being common to many extreme right-wing, *völkisch* and ultraconservative groups. And this was even more true of the party's

anti-democratic, anti-parliamentary, militaristic stance and its refusal to countenance any form of reparation. The only difference lay in the degree of rejection, hatred and aggression. What, then, might make the Berlin NSDAP a
distinctive force and guarantee its political influence?

The only event that Goebbels organized between early November 1926 and
the end of January 1927 that might be regarded as an initial attempt to answer
this question was a march that took place on Sunday 14 November 1926, when
some three hundred members of the Berlin SA – presumably all the men that
it could muster – marched through the working-class district of Neukölln.
Alongside Wedding, this was regarded as the 'Reddest' in Berlin – in the
elections for the municipal assembly on 25 October 1925 the SPD and the
Kommunistische Partei Deutschland (KPD) had together polled more than
two-thirds of the vote.[68] The paramilitary marchers set off from the railway
station on the Kaiser-Friedrich-Straße (now the Sonnenallee) and made their
way to the Hermannplatz, then over the Hasenheide and finally to the
Hallesches Tor. Since there was no real reason for the march, it must have been
regarded as an act of provocation in a working-class district like Neukölln.
And it was as such that it was intended. The SA called it a 'propaganda march',
and wore uniforms and carried flags and standards, although there was no
chanting and no banners. Scuffles broke out at the edges of the march, and the
marchers were evidently heavily outnumbered, but a police riot squad was
standing by at the Hermannplatz and, according to the SA's official account of
the episode, 'swept the Reds away'. The report ended: 'There were thirteen
more or less serious injuries among the Berlin SA, but this first march through
Neukölln has been a success.'[69]

In fact, this first 'march through Red Neukölln' was almost certainly not a
'success' – either the event was badly prepared or the new Gauleiter had
misjudged the conditions at the time. Whatever the case, the march became no
part of the legend surrounding the 'battle for Berlin' that was to form the
subject of the book that Goebbels published under this same title five years
later.[70] Muchow's monthly report on the NSDAP in Berlin did not mention it,[71]
nor did any of the leading local newspapers. The only reference to it occurred
in a small, right-wing suburban paper which claimed that the march caused a
'tremendous stir'.[72] The fact that a march took place at all is remarkable in that
Goebbels had no illusions about the state of the Gau when he assumed control
of it earlier in the month. 'We were a risibly small association,' he later
admitted. 'People did not even know our name.' Nothing, he went on, was
more difficult to accept than the fact that 'people treated us at worst with
provocative indifference and at best with a pitying smile'.[73]

Goebbels found himself on the horns of a dilemma, at least in the short term. The party organization was urging action at a time when in his own view it was not yet sufficiently powerful. He later claimed to have done everything possible to resist such a course of action 'even if it meant a certain temporary unpopularity', because he could not 'appear in public with an organization that in the eyes of that public could simply not hold its head above water. The organization first had to be internally sound before we could take the battle for Berlin out into the streets.'[74]

Indoctrination through 'Mass Meetings'

In order to give at least the impression that his activities were outward-looking, Goebbels held weekly 'mass meetings' which generally took place in the Great Hall of the Kriegervereinshaus in the Chausseestraße, a venue that had an air of familiarity about it. 'And yet', as he himself conceded,

> they deserved to be described as 'mass meetings' to only a limited extent. Only in exceptional cases were masses of people activated. Audiences of between one thousand and fifteen hundred men and women were recruited mainly from fellow travellers and sympathizers from all over Berlin. For the present this was an acceptable solution for us. In this way we had an opportunity to express our views candidly among ourselves without running the risk of being put off our stride at the very beginning by confusing and dangerous discussions with party-political opponents. Here we introduced the broad masses of party comrades to the basic ideas of National Socialism, ideas that were sometimes understood in very vague and confused ways. [...] If the party itself, and especially its old guard, was subsequently safe from all outside attacks and was effortlessly able to overcome every crisis that beset the movement, this was due to the fact that party comrades were brought up to believe in a unified and fixed dogma and were thereby able to resist any temptation into which our enemies sought to manoeuvre us.[75]

Goebbels was in fact deluding himself when he claimed in this later report – it was written in 1931 – that the party was capable of 'effortlessly' dealing with every crisis that befell it, for the Berlin branch of the NSDAP overcame several crises after 1929 only with great difficulty. But Goebbels' rhetorical gifts must already have been sufficiently well developed by the winter of 1926–7 for him to hold the attention of the NSDAP's supporters, week in, week out, over a relatively long period of time and bind them to the party through his 'intensive schooling'. Evidently he sought to appeal not just to the immediate circle of members and sympathizers but to all right-wing extremists, especially those who were disappointed in the other parties. At the end of 1926, for example, an otherwise unidentified Max Tölle appealed through the columns of the *Berliner Arbeiterzeitung* 'to all former Freikorps fighters', while launching a particularly vicious attack on the policies of the DNVP. 'Many of us did not know where to turn because we were leaderless', Tölle went on:

> But then a man appeared who wanted to lead us to the freedom to which we aspired, a man who fought for that freedom and who is ready to lay down his life for it: Adolf Hitler! *Heil*! Our leader lives! All who have not yet buried their ideals and who are still willing to fight for the freedom of our German fatherland should follow this leader. Join the ranks of the NSDAP. Let us fight for Adolf Hitler, shoulder to shoulder as we once did, and let us achieve victory through battle. Let us set Germany free! Heil![76]

In the first issue of 1927, the paper's editor-in-chief, Gregor Straßer, who was also the NSDAP's head of propaganda, paid further tribute to the cult of Hitler by ushering in the new year 'with a greeting of Heil to our revered leader'. It was the great secret of the movement, Straßer went on, that 'inner devotion to the idea of National Socialism and an ardent belief in the victorious power of this doctrine of liberation and redemption' were combined with 'a profound love of the person of our leader'. The tremendous superiority of the NSDAP as a fighting force over all other groups that were 'instinctively' pursuing the same goal of liberating Germany and ensuring the rebirth of the German nation lay in the fact that 'we have the towering figure of the Führer, who is not only in supreme command but who enjoys the love of his followers as a far more powerful binding force'.[77]

To a certain extent this was true. In the longer term neither the DVFP nor the DSP could compete with the NSDAP and the fascination exerted by Hitler over the whole of the nationalist camp. But in Berlin, where Hitler was still banned from appearing in public, Goebbels had for the time being to stand in for his leader as a speaker. Initially this policy evidently worked very well, but ultimately the city's Gauleiter could not be satisfied with preaching to the converted at 'mass meetings'. 'The real public battle' began on 25 January 1927, when, to quote Goebbels, the 'first mass meeting that really deserved this title' was held in Spandau, the party's chief support base in Berlin.[78]

Violence in Halls and in the Streets

The NSDAP's monthly internal report describes the events that unfolded at the meeting in the Seitz Conference Rooms:

> Party Comrade Dr Goebbels gave a talk that was also attended by 200 to 250 Communists who wanted to break up the meeting. During the talk, word came that forty Communists in the street outside had attacked a single party comrade, which was the signal to throw out the Communist Party members in the hall, all of whom landed up outside in the street, bruised and bloodied. The Berlin SA then marched off in closed formation, after which the small commando groups of the Spandau SA remained on lookout until five in the morning, cleaning up the streets and beating up all members of the RFB [Red Front Fighters' League] whom they recognized by their uniforms.[79]

It is clear that the Communists who were present had been lured into a trap. Published five years later, Goebbels' own account of the incident doubles the number of Communist Party members to 'more than five hundred', then candidly describes the method (the 'virtuoso tactics adopted in the course of the meeting') that enabled the SA to turn every subsequent meeting of the NSDAP into an indoor battle:

> We declared in advance that we were willing to hold an open discussion with every honest comrade and that every party would receive adequate time to speak but that the way in which the meeting was conducted would be dictated by us, since we held the householder's rights to the building, so that anyone who refused to comply would be ruthlessly sent packing by the SA.

Goebbels then goes on to say how impressed the audience was by his speech, so that 'at the end a solemn calm of collective excitement descended upon the whole gathering':

> The discussion then began. A Red rabble-rouser mounted the speaker's podium and was just about to start inciting his listeners to resort to violence with his blood-chilling phrases, when from outside came the alarming news that Red riot squads had attacked two of our party comrades who were returning home early, beating them bloody and stabbing them; one of them had to be taken to hospital, where for a time he fought for his life. I immediately rose to my feet and informed the gathering of the enormity of this

incident, declaring that the NSDAP considered it beneath its dignity to continue to lend an ear to representatives of a party whose followers loitered outside under the cowardly cover of darkness and sought to use clubs and daggers as a substitute for their evident inability to make their case by means of rational arguments. This account of such a base and despicable attack had already roused the whole assembly to the point at which their indignation was ready to boil over, while the last remaining Communists, no doubt oppressed by their guilty consciences, began to fall silent. The categorical announcement that the NSDAP was not willing to allow itself to be misused in this way elicited deafening cheers and enthusiastic agreement on the part of every decent listener. Without our intending it, the Red rabble-rouser, still stammering a few protests, climbed down from the podium, whereupon he was passed from hand to hand and finally evicted into the fresh air. [...] The meeting ended in a victory all along the line.[80]

Goebbels' account of his own achievements needs to be seen in the light of the fact that, as with the march through Neukölln, none of the local newspapers reported on the incident. Only the *Spandauer Zeitung* carried an official police report to the effect that there had been agitated exchanges 'during the debate' (a debate that, according to Goebbels, never took place) and also, following the meeting, outside in the street, 'but the police were initially not required to intervene. [...] Then, at a quarter to one, a scuffle broke out on the Stresowplatz that ended only with the arrival of police officers.'[81] The police had nothing to say about seriously injured members of the public 'fighting for their lives'.

But Goebbels, who was later to coin the slogan 'Forward over graves!', seemed almost desperate for the death that would allow the movement in Berlin to honour its first martyr. In an appeal written in February 1927 and headed 'To our Friends in the Reich', he declared that 'the last two weeks have cost us more than twenty seriously injured members. Two of them are dying. It is now a question of offering them our final comfort and the final greeting of their comrades.'[82] Goebbels was referring, on the one hand, to an event that the NSDAP held in Spandau on 25 January and, on the other, to the SA's involvement in the Lausitz Day of Freedom organized by the NSDAP in Cottbus on 30 January. According to the SA's official account of the later incident, 'serious rioting broke out with the police [...] and there was a bitter confrontation with the Reds. Seventeen SA men were injured, one of them so seriously that he had to be taken by stretcher to Berlin.'[83]

However carefully worded, the NSDAP's own internal report again reveals that these later accounts are a travesty of the truth and that the members of the

SA, far from being the victims of terror, were in fact responsible for those acts of violence:

> The crowd became agitated, a number of SA comrades wanted to apprehend the alleged provocateurs, the police became nervous, and the result was a fist fight – the police laid into our men! The SA became very worked up. We were unwilling to be struck down for no good reason by the Social Democratic Party of this 'Free State', and so a few police officers were attacked with their own rubber truncheons, leaving them unfit for combat. The police now attacked the SA columns with extraordinary savagery. Needs must when the devil drives, and our party comrades defended themselves with their iron flagpoles, having first ensured that the flags themselves were safe from being impounded.[84]

The written account of a nineteen-year-old member of the SA confirms that this 'bloody massacre' unfolded along lines very different from those described by Goebbels: 'Above all, the police had had enough of us. After we'd beaten six police officers black and blue in Cottbus and shot another one to pieces and wounded several in Pasewalk, they were finally mobilized against us.'[85]

The Berlin branch of the NSDAP was furious to discover that once again only a single local newspaper had reported on the events in Cottbus. In the words of the party's indignant internal report: 'the whole of the Jewish press in Berlin drew a veil over our march through Cottbus, remaining completely and utterly silent on the subject.'[86] After three months in his new post, Goebbels was extremely sensitive about this lack of response in the local press. 'Berlin needs a sensation just as a fish needs water,' he later wrote. 'The city draws its lifeblood from this need, and every form of political propaganda will fail to achieve its aim if it does not recognize this fact.' The NSDAP, he concluded, had discovered this far too late and only in the wake of many bitter experiences.[87] There initially seems to be some truth in the claim advanced by one of Goebbels' more recent biographers to the effect that what followed was Goebbels' reaction to the silence of the 'Jewish press in Berlin':

> Impatient and dissatisfied with what his propaganda had achieved until then, Goebbels decided to hold his first great demonstration in the lion's den of the 'Red' district of Wedding. The event was intended from the outset as an act of provocation designed to bring on the great battle with the Communists and ultimately achieve the publicity that he hoped for. The place that Goebbels chose was the Pharus Hall in a courtyard off the Müllerstraße,

where the Communists traditionally met for their meetings and where the Twelfth Party Congress of the Communist Party was to meet two years later under its chairman, Ernst Thälmann.[88]

The Battle in the Pharus Hall

The truth of the matter is that if Goebbels decided to hold the event on 11 February 1927, it was not out of anger at the fact that none of the SA marches and indoor battles that he had stage-managed since taking office had met with much of a response in the local press. Rather, his provocative act of holding a 'mass event' in Wedding – the part of Berlin in which the Communists were about to overtake the SPD in the polls and become the biggest party[89] – was the outcome of a plan on which he had been working for several weeks, details of which can be inferred from NSDAP documents published in the *Berliner Arbeiterzeitung*. A schedule of the Gau's activities that appeared in the issue of 9 January 1927 already announces the event in the Pharus Hall and gives the exact time and place ('eight o'clock in the evening').[90] Allowing for the newspaper's deadline and taking account of the fact that the hall first had to be hired, we may assume that the venue had already been agreed upon during the second half of December or by early January at the latest. And it did not require the gifts of a prophet to see that such a provocative gesture ('It was an open declaration of war,' wrote Goebbels; 'that is how it was intended by us, and that is how it was interpreted by our enemies')[91] was bound to end in the way that all previous NSDAP events had ended. Although the rise of the party since 1919–20 had been based in no small measure on Hitler's mass appeal as a speaker, it had also been linked from the outset with a second form of propaganda: terror and physical violence.[92]

This was as much as admitted in 1933 by Eugen Hadamovsky, a colleague of Goebbels who, echoing the relevant phrases from *Mein Kampf*, wrote:

> Propaganda and violence are never total opposites. The use of force can be a part of the propaganda machine. [...] Propaganda and the graded use of force must work together in a particularly skilful way and use the unifying forms of the masses. [...] The National Socialist movement very quickly drew a distinction between discussion evenings, when debates could be held, and mass demonstrations, when all discussion and every hostile interjection was frowned upon. These demonstrations were grandiose and uplifting in character. [...] The most effective force at any mass demonstration is the visible form that it assumes as an expression of power, in the first place the

number of participants, the extent of the demonstration and, beyond that, those elements that figure as power: armed and uniformed men, weapons of every kind. [. . .] All force – indeed, arguably even more force than is actually present – must be shown and demonstrated.[93]

Goebbels was familiar with these principles from *Mein Kampf*, which he had studied assiduously. He also knew them from Hitler's own spoken comments to himself and to others. We may assume that the two men discussed how this link between propaganda and violence could be applied to the conditions in Berlin. In the aforementioned appeal 'To our Friends in the Reich', Goebbels had already hinted at the fact that he had a particular short-term goal in view when he announced, in terms as vague as they are bombastic: 'The struggle in Berlin has begun all along the line. Now there is *no going back*. In only a few months' time we shall have pulled through.'[94] As for the methods that he planned to use in this struggle, he left his readers in no doubt in a second appeal that appeared in the same issue of the *Berliner Arbeiterzeitung*:

> Our party comrades are hereby instructed to defend their lives in the most brutal possible manner if they are attacked by murderous Red bandits, no matter whether or not our enemies slander and besmirch us the next day in their press. As of today we are in a permanent state of self-defence! The police cannot and will not help us! You must help yourselves! *Needs must when the devil drives!* [. . .] We mean to fight for our ideas. If the Jew, in his disguise as a Red, forces us to resort to the most brutal terror, then he and his cronies must learn that where others have arms and fists we ourselves do not have liver sausages![95]

Set up in this way, the Pharus Hall meeting went entirely to plan. According to the NSDAP's internal report for February 1927, the audience was 'made up politically of four-fifths SA and one-fifth KPD'. The meeting was chaired by Kurt Daluege, who opened the proceedings by stating that it was the NSDAP that would dictate the order of business. When this triggered noisy protests, Daluege announced that if they interrupted him again, the troublemakers would be ejected from the hall. At this point the supporters of the Communist Party who were present 'became artificially excited'. 'In the meantime,' the report goes on,

> the SA had slowly isolated the source of the trouble, and the Communists, noticing the danger, suddenly resorted to violence. What followed was all

over in three or four minutes. In a flash, chairs, beer glasses and even tables had been picked up, and a wild battle broke out. The Communists were increasingly driven under the gallery, which had wisely been occupied by us, and it was not long before chairs and glasses were likewise raining down from there. The battle was soon over: the Communist Party retreated with eighty-three of its men more or less seriously injured; in other words, they were unable to descend the stairs quite as cheerfully and as 'harmlessly' as they had ascended them. On our own side we had three comrades who were seriously injured and around ten to twelve who were not seriously hurt. By the time the police arrived, the fighting was already over. The Marxist terror had been bloodily put down. [. . .] At the end Party Comrade Dr Goebbels gave the word to march off in closed formation. [. . .] And at around half past eleven the procession of some five hundred SA men set off through streets that had been cordoned off by the police. The men disbanded at a central location. The battle had been fought. The victory of National Socialism in Wedding was ours.[96]

Outnumbering their opponents by four to one, the Berlin SA had won a victory that consisted of provoking its enemies into an act of violence, after which those members of the SA who, forewarned and forearmed, were cunningly distributed around the hall, encircled their opponents and drove them from the building by force. When Goebbels later gave his own account of this incident, he claimed that the hall had been 'two-thirds full of Red Front Fighters' who had made the mistake of 'positioning only scattered groups inside the hall'. Forced together 'in a tight knot', they had occupied a place 'on the right-hand side at the back of the assembly'. According to Goebbels, the SA and SS troops distributed around the hall and massed in front of the platform had then 'shown great daring and bravery in launching a counterattack', whereupon the 'Red mob' had been forced to flee, 'howling, bawling and cursing'. Never before or since had he spoken 'in such rousing circumstances'. 'Behind me, groaning in blood and pain, lay our badly injured SA comrades. Around me were shards of glass, shattered chair legs, broken beer glasses and blood. The entire assembly petrified in icy stillness.'

In his memoirs Goebbels devotes several pages to a detailed portrait of this bloody inferno, when 'for the first time' he spoke 'the word about the unknown SA man'.[97] Elsewhere he defined the type of person he meant by this: 'the aristocrat of the Third Reich who day after day goes about his business, obeying a law that he does not know and barely understands.'[98] He was pleased to note that from now on he was acknowledged 'as a leading and dependable authority' in the Berlin party organization.[99] He could also be pleased that at least a section of the Berlin press finally reported on the 'Pharus Hall Fight', as the event was to become known in the party annals. On the other hand, the prestigious *Vossische Zeitung* did not go into details, nor did the no less prestigious *Berliner Tageblatt*, which dismissed the incident in a mere twenty lines.[100] The most detailed account appeared in the Communist *Welt am Abend*, although it is clear from its report that it was unfamiliar with the term 'SA', referring instead to the 'swastika-touting assembly guard' and 'Hitler's hall guard'. The *Berliner Morgenpost* even described the organizers as the 'German Socialist Workers' Party'.[101]

The 'Lichterfelde Bloodbath'

On 20 March 1927 another 'clash' took place which 'overshadowed everything that had occurred before it', to quote from a police report written shortly after the event in question.[102] On the evening of 19 March hundreds of members of the SA set off from Anhalt Station for Trebbin, a small town less than 20 miles south of Berlin, where Goebbels delivered a speech by firelight marking the first anniversary of the formation of the Berlin branch of the SA. A 'special report' written as a supplement to the NSDAP's usual monthly bulletin describes the atmosphere on this occasion:

> The speech became a form of worship. The sons of the Brandenburg Marches listen to the words of our leader [Goebbels], who is bound to us in life and death. [...] Barely 20 miles away lies the Moloch that is Berlin, a Judaized centre, a place of terror, a place of blood and ignominy. Harsh and keen-edged is the ring of Party Comrade Dr Goebbels' words: 'Forward over graves!' In whatever way is necessary, within a year Berlin *must* be in our grip!

The next day the SA held a rally and a mass meeting in Trebbin, after which its members set off for the station to return to Berlin. As it turned out, the train in which they were to travel contained members of a brass band belonging to the Red Front Fighters' League, who clenched their fists in their customary Red Front greeting. According to the 'special report', the Communists smiled as they did so. 'We regarded this as a provocation.' The report then claims that the members of the Red Front Fighters' League were carrying revolvers, which they aimed at the SA:

At each of the stations on the journey, we launched a volley of stones at the Communist carriage. Each stone hit home, as the fourth-class carriage had no side divisions to it, and its occupants were standing huddled together. Within a trice each pane of glass was shattered. Standing on the steps of the carriage we tried to force our way inside during the journey. From the roof we thrust a flagpole through the windows and caused a lot of injuries.

The 'special report' claims that when the SA members left the train at Lichterfelde-Ost in the south of Berlin, shots were fired from the carriage containing the members of the Red Front Fighters' League, whereupon the SA responded with a further salvo of stones. The riot squad then arrived, and

the carriage doors were opened by us and by the police, presenting us with a picture of the worst possible kind. All the Communists had been injured by the stones, almost all of them seriously, their musical instruments were smashed to pieces. Throughout the carriage lay shards of glass, pools of blood, splinters of wood and more than two hundred stones. The first person to be brought out was a civilian, the Communist member of the Landtag, Paul Hoffmann. His face was a shapeless bloody mass. One of the real ringleaders who was impossible to catch. He has received his just reward. The other revolver-toting heroes will never attack another National Socialist. Their musical instruments are stamped on. Our two [injured] SA members are taken at once to the Vincent Hospital in Lichterfelde. The SA leaves the station.[103]

Had it not been Goebbels himself who had given the orders the previous evening with his slogan 'Forward over graves'? According to the later indictment drawn up by the public prosecutor's office on the basis of police reports, all that was left at the scene of the incident was a completely wrecked railway carriage,[104] the broken instruments that had belonged to the brass band and sixteen wounded individuals, six of them seriously so, ten of them less so.[105] When he had spoken of 'graves', Goebbels had not only meant the graves of his party's political opponents, of course, but also those of his own party comrades. However, his SA members had attacked the Red Front Fighters with unprecedented brutality, not even giving them a chance to defend themselves properly. As a result, Goebbels still had no martyrs to his cause. On the other hand, the Berlin press gave wider and more detailed coverage to the incident than it had accorded to any other act committed by the local National Socialists. Under the headline 'Serious Clashes at Lichterfelde-Ost Station', the *Berliner Tageblatt* referred to the National Socialists' vast superiority in numbers.[106] The *Vossische Zeitung* stressed that, according to the police, the NSDAP 'bore most of the blame for the clashes'.[107] *Vorwärts* quoted an eyewitness according to whom the National Socialists had behaved 'like vandals'.[108] Unlike the liberal and Social Democratic press, the German-nationalist papers that were part of the Scherl empire and that included *Der Montag*, the *Berliner Lokal-Anzeiger* and the *Berliner illustrierte Nachtausgabe* all blamed the Communists for the violence, but the *Welt am Abend*, which had Communist sympathies, insisted that the 'Lichterfelde bloodbath' was the result of an attack by the National Socialists that had been long in the planning.[109]

The breadth of the political spectrum represented by Berlin's newspapers at this period emerges from the position adopted by the reactionary, Pan-German *Deutsche Zeitung*, which not only took over the version of events peddled by the National Socialists but also observed that things had now reached the point where

> not just uniformed National Socialists but every decent citizen can now venture out of Berlin on a Sunday only by taking the greatest precautionary measures because, thanks to their reign of terror, Communist gangs are making it unsafe for Berliners to go to any of the places habitually favoured by them for their Sunday outings. [. . .] The defenceless Berliner who holds right-wing views can therefore prepare to be attacked sooner or later by the Red rabble and to be taken to hospital, seriously injured.[110]

While the extreme right was declaring the members of the SA the lamentable victims of 'Red terror', it was emerging from the reports of impartial eyewitnesses that it was in fact the National Socialists who had provoked the clashes. The *Vossische Zeitung* also drew attention to the clear disparity in numbers: 'It already seemed highly unlikely that a Communist orchestra consisting of twenty-three men and their valuable instruments would have attacked 650 National Socialists.'[111] But the most remarkable aspect of all is the political interpretation placed on the affair by the *Berliner Tageblatt* three days after the bloody 'battle': 'The new need for activity on the part of the National Socialists is clearly attributable to the involvement of a certain Göbels [*sic*] who, coming from the Ruhr, has the task of breathing new life into the dying National Socialist movement by means of crude excesses. The police will presumably be taking an interest in him.'[112] This was the first time that the *Berliner Tageblatt* had mentioned the name of a man who years earlier had applied to the paper as an editor. He had now been NSDAP Gauleiter in Berlin for four and a half months, and he was presumably profoundly insulted that the liberal paper, read all over the world, could not even spell his name correctly. On the other hand, the brutal excesses of the National Socialists had at least made it onto the paper's front page. If the report did not appear until three days after the event, this was evidently because it took so long for the paper to recognize the full import of the events at Lichterfelde-Ost. The *Welt am Abend* had already published a second article on the 'Pogrom at the Memorial Church' on the day after the 'Lichterfelde bloodbath', but the *Berliner Tageblatt* had clearly needed time to register the fact that there was now a new element of violence to the National Socialists' agenda. 'These swastika-bearing hooligans have outdone themselves in terms of their brazenness and baseness, far surpassing the worst of their earlier heroic activities and giving the impression that they now feel to be in total control of the streets.'[113]

Anti-Semitic Attacks on the Kurfürstendamm

Following the attack on the Red Front Fighters, the SA had not simply left the station and returned home, for in the course of the afternoon about a thousand other members of the NSDAP, generally not in uniform, had gathered on the station forecourt, waiting for the arrival of the train and then helping to attack the Communists. Goebbels had in fact already invited members of his party to take part in a march through Berlin, setting off from the station at Lichterfelde-Ost. The Gauleiter and other National Socialist officials had driven back from Trebbin by car and were waiting at the station for the SA members to arrive. At around eight o'clock in the evening Reinhold Muchow reports that a procession was formed, made up of more than eight hundred uniformed members of the SA, and that there were more than one thousand party comrades 'who accompanied the procession'. The columns then marched through Steglitz and Friedenau, with the demonstration finally ending on the Wittenbergplatz, where between eight and ten thousand people gathered to hear Goebbels' 'rousing speech'.[114]

Although these numbers may be much exaggerated, Goebbels was right when he later wrote that 'this was the first time that the cobbles of the capital had rung with the tread of SA battalions; the SA was fully conscious of the magnitude of this moment'.[115] Nor was it mere chance that the marchers took the route that they did. According to Konrad Heiden in his early account of the history of the NSDAP, 'the actual headquarters of the National Socialists in Berlin were the middle-class suburbs of Friedenau and Steglitz, old German-national domains'.[116] They had attacked a Communist orchestra, outnumbering it by more than twenty to one, and had then marched in uniform through parts of the city where they knew that they could count on a good deal of sympathy for their actions. All that they needed for their contentment to be complete was a display of anti-Semitism.

Since the police made no attempt to interfere, it was easy for the marchers to stage-manage an anti-Jewish outrage as a sort of sideshow. Muchow's report of the party's activities notes simply that 'insolent Jews were beaten up on the spot'.[117] The Gau's weekly newspaper, the *Berliner Arbeiterzeitung*, made a sincere attempt to outdo even the mendacity of the extreme right-wing *Deutsche Zeitung* in its account of what had taken place, heading its report 'Bloody Sunday in Berlin' and describing the SA's attack at the station in Lichterfelde-Ost: 'The compartments in which the Marxist assassins were hiding were stormed by our SA, who were provoked by them into acting. And, one by one, the murderers were pulled out. The Communist member of the Landtag, Paul Hoffmann, had to pay with his blood for the spilt blood of German workers.' Jewish passers-by who had allegedly made disparaging remarks while the SA were marching past 'were beaten bloody by the embittered crowd', and it was only with difficulty that the SA had succeeded 'in maintaining any degree of order'.[118]

Many years later, Wilfrid Bade, who was to become a close colleague of Goebbels, drafted an interesting report that says much about the ways in which the SA 'maintained order' in Berlin. The 'Doctor' – Goebbels was always referred to as 'the Doctor' by the SA in Berlin and elsewhere – had had only one thing to say when the marchers left the station: 'SA men! We are marching to Berlin! Anyone who opposes us must be shown what SA fists are!' The writer then goes on to say that the SA knew exactly what this meant and had answered with a single impassioned cry. It will be recalled that we are talking here about Berlin on 20 March 1927.

> And then they march. To the left and right of the column is the 'wadding' –
> these are the civilian marshals who are intended to keep order and who are
> known as the 'wadding'. They provide protection for the brown-shirted
> procession on the pavement. [...] They are a chosen group of powerfully
> built SA men in civilian clothing. They are not wearing any insignia. [...]
> They are men of steel and iron and to a certain extent are ruthless. They
> march along the pavement beside their uniformed comrades. The crowd that
> is cheering the brown battalions is not even aware of them. At most, the
> occasional police report mentions that during an SA march fighting broke
> out among onlookers accompanying the procession. In this way the 'wadding'

does its duty. [. . .] The SA is not made up of aesthetes. The SA is made up of soldiers. And on this particular evening the SA intervenes for the first time. From the Kaiserplatz in Wilmersdorf to the Wittenbergplatz the 'wadding' reacts in an extremely unfriendly way to every Jew that it encounters. The uniformed SA in the middle of the road do not even turn to watch. It is of no concern to them. They are bearing the flag and carrying the idea of Adolf Hitler through the west of Berlin, an area known as the 'Jewish west'. At this moment in time their only task is to represent the great threat that is posed to these people by the Führer.[119]

And here we have it in so many words: the great threat that is posed by the Führer. The report ends by describing the final demonstration on the Wittenbergplatz and notes how 'the profoundly shocked west of the city' had witnessed its first National Socialist demonstration and heard the Gauleiter of Berlin speak for the very first time.[120]

The *Berliner Arbeiterzeitung* struck a particularly enthusiastic note in its report on the demonstration in the Wittenbergplatz, describing how Goebbels addressed a crowd of ten thousand people 'with thrilling words', and how

thousands raised their hands as one, swearing not to rest until the bloody attack had been avenged and the rabble-rousing Jew, grinning behind the assassins, had been called to account and the third Reich of the German working classes had become a reality. The crowd listened to the leader's words and understood what he meant: they were not to repair to the Kurfürstendamm and kill the Jews there but should wait until we have won control of the state. With a thunderous cry of 'Heil' to Adolf Hitler, the leader of the German workers, this shattering demonstration ended.

In spite of Goebbels' admonition, the report ended, there had indeed been clashes on the Kurfürstendamm, allegedly 'caused by the provocative behaviour of the Jews there when they were rude to our party comrades as the latter were returning home'.

Following the demonstration in the Wittenbergplatz, Goebbels later recalled that 'late in the evening a few brazen Hebrews who were evidently incapable of controlling their unwashed mouths were thanked for their pains with a few stout punches'.[121] The report in the *Berliner Arbeiterzeitung* culminates in the observation that, following these 'Jewish insults', 'our people' had ensured that such scenes would never be repeated, with the result that 'the Kurfürstendamm was very soon free from Jews'.[122] Wilfrid Bade, the aforementioned SA 'expert', also reports that the 'wadding' had done its duty here too:

> Many people disappear on the Kurfürstendamm. He who belongs to this land in respect of his race does not think of disappearing. The SA watches angrily as the broad thoroughfare empties. The civilian guard makes a slight detour to visit the Romanisches Café. [...] They go in and out very quickly and with that there is no one left in the café whom they do not wish to see there. A pane of glass is shattered in the process, but more remain to be broken, they think.[123]

There is no doubt that not only was this the first time that Goebbels had held out the promise of a 'Third Reich' for his fanatical followers, it was also the first time that the shadow of that Third Reich had fallen across the capital.

5

'The alternative Berlin is lying in wait, ready to pounce'[1]

1927–8: THE SUCCESSES OF A DANGEROUSLY MISJUDGED SPLINTER GROUP

'We demand that Berlin should again be a German city!'
From an NSDAP campaign leaflet at the time of the Reichstag election, May 1928

'We must fight for our first surprise victory in the Jewish Babel that is Berlin.'
From Goebbels' appeal to the Berlin NSDAP, 14 May 1928[2]

Hitler's Début at the Clou

The photograph shows a man no longer in the first flush of youth. He is wearing a trench coat, his hair is carefully parted and he is staring ahead of him with a particularly serious, even a surly expression. Nothing about the photograph reveals the fact that he has just completed a rhetorical tour de force. Followed by his chauffeur, Julius Schreck, he is seen leaving a side entrance at the Clou restaurant in Berlin's Zimmerstraße and forcing his way to his car past a crowd of policemen, journalists, curious onlookers and a handful of party members. The man in question is the thirty-eight-year-old Adolf Hitler. The date is Sunday, 1 May 1927. Since he was still officially banned from speaking in Prussia, the only way he could address his supporters in the capital was to hold a private event open only to party members.

The morning edition of the *Berliner Tageblatt* had announced:

The National Socialist Workers' Party is also holding a series of demonstrations. Dr Goebbels, the National Socialists' new head of propaganda, has invited his friend Adolf Hitler to be the day's main speaker. As readers will know, Hitler has not been allowed to address public gatherings in Prussia since 1925. Only in Bavaria and Baden, where he had until recently also been banned from speaking, has the ban been lifted in certain circumstances, notably on the condition that he undertakes nothing that is directed against the state. Hitler has agreed to these terms. In view of the Prussian ban on his speaking in public, he will attend the National Socialists' public demonstration at the Clou at eleven o'clock in the morning only as a guest and will not speak. In the evening a closed meeting of members of the National Socialist Workers' Party will be held at a venue in Spandau, when guests will also be present. Hitler will speak at this meeting. The police will take adequate steps to ensure that the law is not infringed and that Goebbels' National Socialist SA – their Sports Divisions[3] or, to be more accurate, their Raiding Parties – are prevented from making any active contribution to the proceedings.[4]

Evidently the paper had been misinformed, for the meeting that took place at the Clou was open only to members of the NSDAP.

Hitler had spoken at the Zirkus Krone in Munich on 13 April 1927, when the audience, according to the local police report, numbered some seven thousand.[5] With the exception of two smaller events in Rosenheim and Hattingen, Hitler's next major appearance was at a party rally in Essen on 24 April, when the police reported a 'brisk attendance', with between 3,000 and 3,500 party members arriving from out of town. According to the *Völkischer Beobachter*, Hitler addressed an audience of fourteen thousand.[6] Goebbels was aware of these figures as he himself had been in Essen to speak at the party rally. As a result, he was under considerable pressure to prove that the party in Berlin had grown much stronger under his leadership than it had been on the occasion of Hitler's last documented visit to Berlin on 13–14 March 1925,[7] when the branch was still tiny.

The Clou was a concert hall as well as a restaurant. As the venue for Hitler's first speech in Berlin, it can hardly have been chosen at random. It was built in 1886 as a market hall between the Zimmerstraße and Mauerstraße but in 1910 it was converted into an 'enormous restaurant', to quote from a 1912 travel guide.[8] An extensive programme of modernization was carried out in around 1925. Covering an area of over 40,000 square feet, it had seating for three thousand people, making it the city's largest restaurant.[9] It was thus ideally suited to the sort of gesture designed to impress not only Berlin but also Hitler. We may assume that invitations were extended to party members not only in the city itself but also from further afield and also, perhaps, to close sympathizers from the extreme right generally in and around Berlin.

Goebbels certainly succeeded in mobilizing his supporters, the *Berliner Arbeiterzeitung* reporting that 'more than four thousand National Socialists celebrated the First of May as a German festival' and did so, moreover, 'solemnly and cheerily'. The *Völkischer Beobachter* even thought that there were as many as five thousand party members present, while the official account of the party's history in Berlin was later to settle on 'more than five thousand'. The 'solemnity of the occasion' was reflected in the tone adopted by the party's newspaper in its description of the atmosphere that reigned in the Clou:

> Speeches, singing, a flag-waving entry, drum rolls, a poem – and yet all this must fade into insignificance when compared with the excitement and expectation in the minds of all who were present: '*He* will speak today.' For the first time since the movement was founded, Adolf Hitler will speak to his loyal followers in Berlin. – All heads are suddenly jerked upwards. To the gallery. And then the first words of this warm, powerfully controlled voice resonate through the hushed hall.[10]

Announcement of a War of Conquest

Hitler behaved in an entirely statesman-like manner. He began his speech, for example, by declaring that he had no wish to address 'the so-called questions of the day because in examining these questions it is all too easy for the nation to lose sight of the truly great problems that constitute its struggle for existence'. Rather, there was a question that, raised by destiny itself, was the starting point of the National Socialist view of the world. In examining the 'genuine, solitary and solid principles of the life of a nation', one came across only one question:

> What is the relationship between the number of people who make up the nation and the land on which those people find themselves? Is the land on which they find themselves in a position not only to support the total population at the time in question but also to enable the nation to continue to increase, or is the relationship between the land and the number of people an impossible one, allowing one to predict with mathematical certainty that either today or at least in the future this nation will no longer be able to maintain an existence on this land? This problem is of immense importance.

As always, Hitler went on, the 'great question posed by destiny is: can you support yourselves?' In contradistinction to Germany's current foreign policy, whose 'successes' consisted in 'driving our finest human material' out of the country, he argued that the land should be made to fit the number of people in the country – 'if need be by fighting'.

> This is the natural way that providence, too, has laid down for us, providence which has given people the world not so that it can be ruined by pacifism but so that our energies may be protected through the eternal struggle with each other and so that the most active and most powerful nation may one day be granted the greatest freedom.

The speech's essential political message was to be found in its conclusion: 'We shall not be able to intervene in our own destiny until the German nation once again represents a factor in the power equation.' Unfortunately, he explained, the nation was now divided in thought and deed, torn, as it was, into two conflicting halves: 'On the one hand, there is the bourgeoisie, on the other hand, the workers.'

It is remarkable that Hitler did not take this opportunity to attack the Socialists or the Communists as well as the bourgeoisie, who, he claimed, 'no longer had any thought of conquest' and had abandoned any serious belief in victory in the future. Unsurprisingly Hitler praised the NSDAP as the one force that would overcome this division:

> We shall give our nation a new philosophy that everyone can embrace. Once we follow this road together, the politics that deals only in the questions of the day will cease to exist, and a cry for freedom will go up all over Germany. We do not want to be bourgeois or proletarian. We want to be Germans in our motherland, Germania, and in that way we shall hasten to victory.

This was the cue for a ritualistic, pseudo-religious peroration that allows us to imagine Hitler the demagogue, his facial expression, tone and body language all coming vividly to life: 'As a soldier on the front I first prayed to God: Lord, do not let me be a coward! However things may turn out for us, whether victory or defeat, we should also pray to God for the battle that we are fighting tenaciously and implacably: Lord, let us not be cowards!'[11]

Reactions in the Berlin Press

Although Hitler spoke of 'land expansion' and 'conquest' in his speech at the Clou, he wisely omitted to mention the direction that any such expansion might take. If a journalist writing in the National Socialist press described Hitler's goal as 'new space in Central Europe', there were limits even within the party's own ranks to the extent to which this was 'unequivocally clear' in May 1927. The liberal *Vossische Zeitung* noted only that Hitler had 'avoided the threatening cliffs of internal politics' and had expressed disapproval of the country's current foreign policy, while predicting that in only a few years' time Germany would be united under the NSDAP. The *Berliner Tageblatt*, by contrast, seemed distinctly slow on the uptake when it reported merely that at a closed meeting of the party Hitler had spoken of 'the goals of National Socialism in an exceptionally moderate tone'.[12]

In short, a National Socialist journalist was still in the dark about the basic and, indeed, the most important thrust of Hitler's strategic thinking, while the liberal *Berliner Tageblatt* was able to refer to Hitler's 'moderate tone' as he proclaimed a future war of conquest. Against this background it is interesting to see how the Social Democrat and Communist press reacted in Berlin. The Social Democrats' official organ was *Vorwärts*, which devoted a total of nine lines to Hitler's speech, heading its article 'Hitler's End. No Longer Successful and No Longer Attractive'. Hitler, readers were informed, had spoken to members of his 'party' (the paper used quotation marks around the word) about the increase in the number of people living in Germany and an increase in the area of German land. 'The meeting listened to him in silence, applauded a few anti-Semitic outbursts and then went home. The atmosphere of the beer hall was missing.' But Hitler had eschewed all 'anti-Semitic outbursts' for tactical reasons, otherwise the *Berliner Tageblatt* – owned by the Jewish publishing magnate Rudolf Mosse – would scarcely have spoken of his 'moderate tone'. *Vorwärts* took a further step in the same direction when it concluded: 'Hitler is finished. His first appearance in Berlin was one big yawn for his audience: there is no more certain sign of his political end.'[13]

Somewhat surprisingly, *Die Welt am Abend* – the extremely successful paper from the publishing house of the Communist deputy Willi Münzenberg – came to a similar conclusion. 'Hitler the Clown at the Clou' was the headline of a piece which, not much longer than the one in *Vorwärts*, declared that in the course of a speech lasting two hours Hitler had repeatedly offended against sound common sense and reason. 'According to Hitler, Germany is too small and can be saved only by the National Socialists. And, of course, people need him, Adolf Hitler, the beer-hall speaker from Munich, who has now brought joy to Berlin, too – not that Berlin has taken much notice of him. Little is being said about the clown at the Clou.'[14]

One wonders what might have happened if these journalists of the bourgeois and left-wing press had been told on 1 May 1927 that in less than six
years' time this 'clown', far from being 'finished', would be living as chancellor
in the nearby Wilhelmstraße. And the same prophet would surely have been
met with little more than a pitying smile or a shake of the head if he had gone
on to predict that, as a consequence of Hitler's policies as chancellor, less than
a generation later a wall would be erected along the Zimmerstraße only a few
yards from the side entrance to the Clou, a wall that would divide Berlin in
two. To say nothing of other developments, such as the fact that on 27 February
1943 the Clou, long since closed and empty, would be turned into a makeshift
collection point for hundreds of local Jews destined to be transported 'to the
east'. No, in the spring of 1927 journalists who did not hold extreme right-wing
views were simply unable to see in Hitler anything other than one of those
countless men and women who founded the sort of sects that thrived at the
time of the Weimar Republic.[15]

Conversely, supporters and members of extreme right-wing groups in
Berlin saw in Hitler 'the man of the future'. The *völkisch* and anti-Semitic
Pan-German *Deutsche Zeitung* spoke rapturously of the 'admirable impression'
created by Hitler's Brownshirts, adding that 'There is a mass of coiled strength
in Nationalism. The spirit of the meeting was purely manly. Hitler's ability to
inspire the masses is limitless.'[16] As early as April 1927, in the run-up to
celebrations for Hitler's birthday, the *Berliner Arbeiterzeitung* had already
made it clear to what extent the 'myth of Hitler'[17] was alive and kicking in the
local NSDAP. Gregor Straßer had again proclaimed in hymn-like terms that
God had given the Germans a man who embodied National Socialism's 'idea
of redemption' and who was its 'herald and leader: Adolf Hitler'. Party
members were entreated to do their duty in the Kriegervereinshaus on the
Chausseestraße and ensure that the hall was filled for the birthday celebrations. A poem, 'Germany's Leader', by Dietrich Eckart, who had died in 1923,
was specially reprinted for the occasion. It ended with the words: 'The force is
here before which night must flee!'[18]

The rest of the paper's report on Hitler's appearance at the Clou suggests
nothing so much as a political apotheosis:

> It happened countless times – each time the words struck home, the darkness
> was lit up and there was endless applause. Finally he would raise his hands
> in entreaty and ask to be allowed to continue. And then there was the end
> of the speech, when everything that had previously cast its shadow over
> the thought processes of reason burst forth in all its glory: feeling, the

heart, concern for his starving people. The warrior's anger. And so the very last image of Hitler as a soldier on the front was an image of battle: Germania, which may yet look on as its children fight this final battle. And survive. The man who stepped forth between walls of raised hands, beneath the lowered flags of battle, will restore freedom to Germany! We are certain of that![19]

Carl von Ossietzky, the editor-in-chief of *Die Weltbühne*, which was the favourite reading matter of Berlin's left-wing intellectuals, did not devote a single word to Hitler's début in the capital. He was far more exercised by the Stahlhelm march planned to take place on 8 May 1927, the 'Reich's Day of Frontline Soldiers', when at least eighty thousand demonstrators were expected. The aim of the exercise, he wrote, was 'to show the capital of the Republic that the balance of power has shifted'. 'Red Berlin' had felt little of the political upheavals in the provinces and was to be made to see what had changed: 'It will register with astonishment the May celebrations of reactionary politics.' But when the Stahlhelm march – by its own estimate, it attracted 120,000 participants – passed off peacefully and without any of the clashes with left-wing organizations that the authorities had feared, Ossietzky summed up his feelings as follows:

> Throughout the whole of the march it was impossible to avoid the feeling that this massive show of strength was going nowhere. Things that we have for years experienced with a shudder are once again presented to us as an eerily empty form. [. . .] But the nation clearly expresses its disapproval. Perhaps these armies will one day return in a different guise, not wrapped in cotton wool by a solicitous police force. Perhaps they will then take their revenge and hang us from the lampposts for this evident lack of respect. But they will never conquer this city.[20]

Ossietzky was not far wide of the mark in his assessment of the political appeal of the Stahlhelm in particular and the German National People's Party in general. The traditional right wing in Germany did indeed suffer from a lack of initiative and a shortage of rousing slogans, but above all it lacked ideas that would allow it to extend its reach beyond its habitual membership and make an impression on other social strata. But neither Ossietzky nor the journalists of 'republican' and 'Communist' Berlin could imagine that the political force that would achieve this aim in the years to come already existed on the extreme right wing in the form of Hitler, his party and, above all, the SA – the 'brown army', which, largely unnoticed by the public at large, was already being built up in certain parts of Berlin.

None the less, there is an exception to every rule. Journalists and editors of the influential Central Society of German Citizens of the Jewish Faith regularly reported on right-wing activities in their weekly paper, the *C. V.-Zeitung*. There they noted with increasing concern the doggedness with which the NSDAP and SA were now pursuing their goal in Berlin, too, and attempting to provide a solid basis for their organizational structures. 'Hitler's latest stronghold. Berlin is not to be allowed to rest. – Hooligans on the Kurfürstendamm – who is putting up the money? Goebbels in his limousine – Berlin the great hope.' Thus the paper began its report on 18 May 1927. The writer then went on:

> One really needs to have seen for oneself a Hitler meeting in Berlin to recognize the danger for the capital that comes from this particular make-up of listeners. Far more than half of the lads are under twenty-one, the sort who are to be found wherever trouble is to be expected. [...] Five hundred of these people form the core of every National Socialist demonstration. Around them are many elderly men and women from the petty bourgeoisie who hope or are even convinced that Hitler will one day pay them back the war loan that they signed away and do so, moreover, in coin of the realm. The storm troops that Goebbels has mustered in only a few weeks – some two thousand men carefully trained in what are known as National Socialist sports divisions – constitute the danger on the streets of Greater Berlin. They gather in side streets and venture out when they have established that the coast is clear. [...] Several times a week huge National Socialist posters can be seen from afar on all the advertising pillars, catching the attention of passers-by. Large sums of money – indeed, vast sums – must be flooding into Berlin to cover these immense costs. Who are these donors? [...] Berlin is Hitler's great hope. If he is pouring so much money into his business in Berlin, then he, as an enemy of capital, must already know why he is doing this. Even so, we must admit, if we are honest, that he has already achieved a number of successes in Berlin.[21]

Goebbels could make nothing of such 'praise'. Indeed, there was not a single sentence in this liberal Jewish newspaper that he would have quoted in public. Not only were the Jews, in Hitler's words, 'the most terrible danger in the life of all nations', but the whole of the journalistic response to Hitler's appearance at the Clou was bound in the final analysis to leave him feeling dissatisfied. Even the German-national *Lokal-Anzeiger*, which generally avoided publicly upbraiding the National Socialists, struck a note of carping criticism, noting that 'fighting is, of course, physically easier than working' and deriding the 'primitive doctrine of the leader of the National Socialists'.[22]

The Ban on the NSDAP in Berlin

On 4 May 1927, three days after Hitler had addressed the NSDAP in Berlin, Goebbels attacked the Berlin press in general and individual journalists in particular at another 'mass meeting' convened at the Kriegervereinshaus. The writer of the 'basest and most hateful' article – it appeared in *Germania*, the official organ of the Centre Party – was dismissed as a 'common Jewish pig'. Goebbels explained that he was deliberately expressing himself in such terms in the hope of teasing out the true name and address of the writer, who he claimed had penned the piece pseudonymously. His party comrades would then have a chance to pay the journalist a visit and 'thank him in kind'.[23] Earlier, a member of the audience had shouted out, 'Where does the black-guard live?', prompting Goebbels to hand out the address of a second journalist and to add: 'I have no wish for this man to receive a National Socialist scalp massage, but we shall certainly be taking a closer look at him.'

Goebbels' speech and his audience's effusive reaction caused one listener – as it turned out, a former clergyman – to call out, 'Yes, yes, you're quite the Germanic youth', whereupon Goebbels 'took some time to collect himself', as the public prosecutor later put it in his indictment of the Gauleiter, who then went on to say, 'I guess you want to be thrown out.'[24] During the ensuing silence, the man repeated his remark, at which SA members threw themselves at him 'with their tankards'. Battered and bruised, their victim staggered out of the hall 'streaming with blood and to the sounds of roaring and howling', to quote from a right-wing newspaper report.[25] He then made a statement at his local police station, where a number of shards of glass were removed from his blood-soaked head.[26]

The heckler had evidently been referring to Goebbels' physical deformity – his club foot – and, indeed, to his appearance in general: he was small in size and had dark hair. No amount of political polemics could provoke Goebbels as much as an allusion to his appearance, a point to which we shall return in due course. For the present, it is enough to add that in his own account of this incident, which he published only a few years later, Goebbels made no mention of his earlier anti-Semitic abuse but insisted that he 'had given no cause for such uncouth behaviour'. He also drew a veil over the actual content of the remark, merely describing it as 'insulting in the extreme'. He had, he went on, interrupted his speech 'for two or three seconds' and 'asked the troublemaker in a dismissive tone' whether he wanted to be thrown out. When 'the person in question' had then attempted to continue his provocative remarks, 'a few hearty SA men went over to him, boxed his ears a couple of times, then, seizing him by the scruff of the neck and his backside, carried him out of the hall'.[27] By his own account, Goebbels had 'attached no importance to the whole affair'. Even when the police arrived at the end of the meeting to look for weapons, he had not felt that there was any cause for disquiet: the matter struck him as 'settled'.[28]

The behaviour of the members of the SA whose task was to maintain order in the hall hardly suggests that the methods used by the National Socialist thugs had grown appreciably more violent when compared with their earlier attacks, which could just as easily have ended in fatalities. But until then the local police had handled the SA and NSDAP with kid gloves and had been conspicuous by their absence during the party's more brutal attacks, with the result that Goebbels was presumably not prepared for the fact that what in his eyes had been a trivial incident in the Kriegervereinshaus now persuaded the police to come down on him with the full force of the law. In its evening edition of 5 May the *Berliner Tageblatt* was already reporting that a search of the party members at the meeting had uncovered knuckledusters, sticks, cudgels, daggers, knives and guns and that a total of thirty party members had been arrested. Moreover, the Prussian Ministry of the Interior and the local chief of police were already considering 'further measures against the National Socialists'. The paper added that in view of the way in which people who held different opinions were beaten to within an inch of their lives, there was only one course of action that would help to deter these 'gangs of hooligans' in the future – 'such ruthless intervention by the police and the other authorities that these gentlemen lose all desire to ruin the good reputation of the Reich's capital by habits more appropriate to a low dive'.[29]

By the following day the *Berliner Tageblatt* was able to announce the chief of police's decree with the headline 'The National Socialist Workers' Party for Berlin Banned'. Underneath we read:

On the basis of Article 124 of the Reich's Constitution, § 2 of the Reich's Law, governing Clubs and Societies and § 10, II, 17 of the German Land Law I have disbanded the Berlin-Brandenburg Gau of the National Socialist Workers' Party together with its subsidiary organs, the Sports Division [SA], the Defence Unit [SS], the National Socialist Freedom League, the National Socialist German Students' Association (Berlin branch) and the German

Workers' Youth Movement in Berlin (Hitler Youth) because the aims of these organizations run counter to criminal law. This order comes into force with immediate effect. In consequence the members of these disbanded organizations are banned from any form of society activity, in particular the holding of meetings and gatherings of every description, both in closed rooms and in the open air. They are also banned from organizing public processions and demonstrations.[30]

The ban was not only unexpected, it was also – to quote Goebbels' later formulation – 'a blow that we could barely get over'. Then, showing his usual boundless overestimation of his own importance, he added that the ban had come into effect at the very moment when the movement was starting 'to take its rightful place in the ranks of the great mass organizations'.[31] (A later close colleague of Goebbels, the journalist Hans Schwarz van Berk, calculated that at the time of the ban the NSDAP had 1,400 registered members in Berlin.)[32] Goebbels had left no stone unturned in his attempts to mobilize all his resources for Hitler's appearance at the Clou and to show off his newly acquired 'mass support'. But was Hitler not likely to have been annoyed at the ease with which Goebbels had compromised the legal existence of the party in Berlin? And, following the refounding of the party, had not Hitler himself done everything in his power to get rid of its old image as a party of putschists and to ensure that it was run on strictly legal lines even in the face of 'disobedient' SA leaders?[33] For the journalist Konrad Heiden, who wrote an early history of the NSDAP, there was no doubt that 'Hitler wanted nothing more than to be able to speak in public again in Prussia' and that he was 'very angry at his doctor's accident'.[34]

Gauleiter Goebbels Toes the Führer's Line

On 30 July 1927 Hitler addressed a general meeting of the NSDAP and offered an overview of the party's development since it had been refounded, even claiming that the ban on his speaking in public that had been imposed in March 1925 had lost its force by the winter of 1925–6 and that the party had been able to use it for propaganda purposes, 'especially in Prussia today'. He also pointed out that a number of the party's branches had made great progress in 1927. Here he explicitly referred to the 'great successes' in Berlin.[35] At no point does he imply even a hint of 'annoyance'. Quite the opposite. In his *Kampf um Berlin*, from which we have already had occasion to quote on several occasions, Goebbels claims explicitly that Hitler was in complete agreement with the way he was running the party in Berlin: 'That same night [5–6 May 1927] I held a brief discussion with Adolf Hitler, who was currently staying in Berlin. He immediately grasped the entire situation and saw exactly how it had led to the ban. We agreed that the movement must now prove that it could also deal with this serious test.'[36]

It was no accident, of course, that Hitler was in Berlin. Following his appearance at the Clou on 1 May, he had gone the next day to the Feurich Hall at 76 Lützowstraße in the Tiergarten district of Berlin[37] in order to address the members of the National Socialist Freedom Alliance, a group of well-heeled party supporters whom Goebbels had brought together in the hope that they would be willing to make substantial financial sacrifices for the NSDAP. Some five hundred supporters were present. Hitler naturally reminded them of their 'obligations towards the future, obligations that demand sacrifice upon sacrifice from us'. According to the *Berliner Arbeiterzeitung*, he also described 'the brown army of Third Reich fighters whose weapons are sacrifice and boundless devotion to the idea', for 'we know only one thing – the German nation for whom we fight in a spirit of sacrifice'. The paper ended by noting the 'thunderous' applause of the audience: 'With cheers and promises, men reach out their arms to our leader, our Hitler. [. . .] We shall be free through sacrifice.'[38]

As in previous years, Hitler must have focused all his attention during the days that followed on persuading others to demonstrate their boundless devotion to the 'idea' and, hence, to the party. It is no wonder, then, that Goebbels met Hitler for a brief discussion that same night. In fact, Goebbels' account of the conversation is somewhat lacking in substance, encouraging Heiden and later writers to assume that Hitler had initially been annoyed at the ban on the NSDAP in Berlin.

It is beyond doubt that there was a group in the Berlin NSDAP that was far from agreeing with Goebbels' methods for building up the party, and this was the group around Otto Straßer. Their dissenting views must have been discussed at a meeting of the NSDAP in Munich on 20 June 1927, for Goebbels travelled from Berlin especially to attend the meeting. The standard edition of Hitler's speeches and writings insists that the text of his speech on this occasion could not be found,[39] but another account states that Hitler did not in fact take part in this event,[40] a claim that is entirely plausible when we recall that he was always keen to avoid conflict and hated taking decisions. According to his biographer Ralf Georg Reuth, Goebbels began his speech by striking 'a moderate and even an apologetic note'. He then went on to explain that, when he had arrived in Berlin nine months previously, it had been clear to him that the capital could not be won over in a matter of months. His aim had been to spend his first six months ensuring that the movement became better known in Berlin, a goal that he had achieved. The reproach of the Straßer brothers that his own agitational policies were to blame for the ban on the NSDAP in Berlin was easily countered, he went on: the ban was unreasonable, and it was clear from the increase in membership that he was on the right track.[41]

A detailed report by the Reich commissar for the supervision of public order for the autumn of 1927 presents us with a rather different picture and indicates that Goebbels adopted a far less conciliatory tone at this meeting, 'occasionally expressing criticism of the Stahlhelm Day in Berlin: if he – Goebbels – could march through Berlin with 120,000 men as the Stahlhelm had done, he would not have given the assurance, as the Stahlhelm's leaders had done, that the march would pass off peacefully. He was certain that 120,000 National Socialists would not leave Berlin as they had found it.'[42] In adopting this position, Goebbels left no one in any doubt that he had any intention of curtailing his activities in Berlin or of toning down the aggressive policies that had led to a ban on the party in the city after only a few months. In short, Goebbels' position was in no way at odds with the aims of his party leader.

Such a difference of opinion is in any case highly unlikely because, in referring to his willingness to use violence, Goebbels was merely repeating what Hitler had already said at an NSDAP meeting in Munich four weeks earlier, when his remarks had been intended as a vague threat for the future. On the occasion of a South Bavarian Republican Day that the Social Democratic Reichsbanner organization had planned for 28–29 May 1927,[43] he had pointed out that the NSDAP, unlike the Reichsbanner, was growing all the time. By 1928, Hitler went on, he would demand the same right for the NSDAP as the Bavarian government currently accorded the Reichsbanner and would hold a German Day or a party rally in Munich. By 1929 there might also be a march through Berlin 'and instead of 100,000 members of the Stahlhelm there will be 100,000 Brownshirts, but they would not simply promenade through the streets like the Stahlhelm, these 100,000 men would one day be fighters'.[44]

In *Mein Kampf*, too, Hitler had already indicated the tactics that had been 'infinitely important' for expanding the SA during the early years of its existence. In his view, it was because of the brutality of the SA in Munich in the late summer of 1922 ('Red republican defence corps [. . .] were within a few minutes scattered with bloody skulls by SA detachments') and in Coburg in October 1922 ('for ten whole minutes a devastating hail fell from left and right, and a quarter of an hour later, there was nothing Red to be seen in the streets') that the SA doubled its membership in Munich, while in Coburg the 'Red

terror' was broken.[45] Ultimately, then, all the signs are that Goebbels had
not struck out on his own in Berlin but that in the autumn of 1926 he and
Hitler had discussed the strategy and tactics that they felt were necessary to
build up the NSDAP in Berlin. Or, rather, Hitler had given his new Gauleiter
instructions to take back with him to the capital.

In short, the last thing on Goebbels' mind was the idea of inviting members
of the SA and of his party in general to show restraint. (He later justified this
by claiming that the ban had made it impossible for the movement's leaders to
'exercise a calming influence on the masses', making 'excesses inevitable'.)[46]
Exactly a week after the ban the National Socialists tried to hold an event in
the Hohenzollern Rooms in Charlottenburg, arguing that it was an 'electoral
meeting' for two of their deputies in the Landtag. The police refused to allow
the event to go ahead, however, leading to scuffles inside and outside the
building. According to the *Berliner Tageblatt*, 'evidently disappointed that
the meeting had been prevented from taking place, some 150 National
Socialists marched to the Kurfürstendamm and taunted passers-by between
Joachimsthaler and Schlüterstraße. In some cases they also resorted to violence.'
As a result the police had to intervene and a total of thirty-four supporters of
the NSDAP were arrested.[47] Seven days later National Socialist troops tried to
break up an event organized by the Reichsbanner in the Tiergarten district,
resulting in further arrests.

It soon became clear, however, that the decisive steps undertaken by the
police might be set at naught by the judiciary, whose representatives were
largely reactionary and hostile to the Republic. Of the twenty-three NSDAP
supporters to be haled before the courts, all but two were acquitted, even the
public prosecutor declaring that the actions of the accused could not be
described as dishonourable: they could not be reproached for 'not abandoning
practices that are now to be found all over our fatherland' and for allowing
themselves to be provoked into rioting. A young woman who had repeatedly
egged on others by shouting out phrases like 'Jewish pig' was likewise
acquitted. The two rioters who were found guilty were fined 70 marks, a
punishment considerably less than the one demanded by the public prosecutor, who had asked that the four ringleaders be sentenced to at least five
days' imprisonment.

According to one witness statement, the members of the SA who broke up
the rival demonstration had received money 'from the party which, although
officially disbanded, had by no means ceased to exist', while the NSDAP had
promised 'unconditionally' to pay their fines.[48] One of the two SA leaders who
was fined was later to make a name for himself in the party. Werner

Studentkowski was twenty-three at the time that he was charged. He had got to know Goebbels in October 1926. By the winter of 1927–8 he was already one of the Gau's public speakers in Berlin-Brandenburg. In 1933 he was elected to the Reichstag, and in 1938 he became director of the Saxon Ministry of Education, finally being appointed to a senior post in the Reich Ministry of Information and Propaganda in 1941.[49]

The Growing Appeal of the NSDAP

Described in a Berlin Political Police report of 28 March 1927 as a 'propaganda leader for the province of Brandenburg', Werner Studentkowski was only one of the young supporters whom Goebbels had gathered around him since taking over as Gauleiter in November 1926. Since then membership of both the party and the SA had risen continuously, and in March 1927 alone there had been four hundred new applications to join the party, which now had some three thousand members.[50] Most of them were right-wing students and schoolchildren. While Goebbels' talk of an imminent transformation into a 'large-scale mass organization' was a wild exaggeration, there was some truth to his assertion that 'membership numbers were increasing', as he told the NSDAP rally in Munich on 20 June 1927 when defending his aggressive course of action in Berlin.

One thing led to another, as the case of the young Horst Wessel illustrates. Wessel was fifteen when he joined the Bismarck Youth in 1922. This was the youth organization of the DNVP, the most influential right-wing party at this time. But by the end of 1923 he had joined the Wiking League, the extreme right-wing defence association whose 'ultimate aim', in Wessel's own words, was 'the establishment of a national dictatorship'. When its leaders started to show signs of at least tolerating the parliamentary system, the now nineteen-year-old student of jurisprudence resigned from the Wiking League and became a member of the SA and NSDAP, where he could finally satisfy his urge for violent action.[51]

Wessel explained his political development in his diaries:

Bismarck League, that was pleasure and enjoyment, the Wiking League was adventure, the atmosphere of the putsch, playing at soldiers, albeit against a background that was not without its dangers. But the NSDAP was a political awakening. [. . .] The movement's centrifugal force was tremendous. [. . .] One meeting followed hard on the heels of the last one, each more tempestuous than the last. [. . .] Street demonstrations, recruiting drives in the press, propaganda trips into the provinces creating an atmosphere of activism and high political tension that could only help the movement.[52]

Shortly before joining the party, Wessel had explained in a letter that more than two-thirds of the people who had served under him in the Wiking League had already joined the SA and NSDAP.[53] In doing so, he indicated one of the main reasons why the NSDAP's membership numbers were rising in Berlin: Goebbels had succeeded in creating the 'atmosphere of activism' that attracted more and more of the younger members of right-wing organizations, young men and women who felt increasingly disenchanted by the lack of prospects, the passivity and the sheer opportunism of their own parties and associations.

Under Goebbels' leadership the NSDAP drew under its sway a number of older activists and even entire organizations. Wilhelm Kube was a professional politician who left the DNVP in 1922 to join the DVFP. When he resigned from the latter, it was to found his own Nationalist Social Working Group in Berlin, which by early 1927 had around 1,500 members. In the late autumn of 1927, Kube switched his allegiance to the NSDAP, 'bringing to the party his seat in the Reichstag and the members of his association'.[54] Even more sensational, at least as far as the general public was concerned, was the decision by the then fifty-seven-year-old Reichstag deputy and editor of *Der Reichswart*, Count Ernst von Reventlow, to leave the DVFP and join the NSDAP in February 1927. According to Reventlow himself, he had attempted to lend a 'keener voice to the German National People's Party and also tried to create a radical social German spirit, in other words a socio-revolutionary spirit', but with the passage of time he had been forced to admit that his 'socio-revolutionary aspirations would never have any prospect of success' within the DVFP.

Reventlow also explained what he found so attractive about the NSDAP, namely, the fact that it had now achieved the status of a party capable of leadership:

I have gone over to the National Socialist German Workers' Party without any so-called leadership claims and without any reservations. I subordinate myself unquestioningly to Herr Adolf Hitler. Why? He has demonstrated that he can lead; he has created a party out of his views, his will and the unifying idea of National Socialism, and he leads it. He and the party are one, and they offer the unity that is the unconditional premiss of success. The last two years have shown that the National Socialist German Workers' Party is on the right road, that it is on the march, that it possesses unbroken and unbreakable socio-revolutionary resolve.[55]

The *Berliner Arbeiterzeitung* was a little premature in its announcement that this move spelt the 'end of the German Nationalist Freedom Party', although it was certainly the beginning of the end. Its leading politicians created the impression of complacent dignitaries and in the longer term could offer nothing to match the leadership cult around Hitler or compete with his party's aggressive propaganda and the young and dynamic SA. Fifteen months later the results of the Reichstag elections on 20 May 1928 revealed just how meaningless the German-*völkisch* parties had become, when, forming an electoral pact as the *Völkisch*-National Bloc, they won barely 0.9 per cent of the votes in the city. By the beginning of the 1930s they had vanished almost completely from the electoral scene.[56]

The increasing tendency of the NSDAP to acquire a position of dominance among right-wing extremists was evidently not impaired by the ban on its activities, and by the end of July 1927 Hitler was able to announce that the party had been particularly successful in 'bringing about an end to so-called *völkisch* separation', referring specifically to Berlin in this matter.[57] Had the ban on the NSDAP in Berlin failed to have any impact at all? How, then, was it that Goebbels was later able to claim that the ban on his speaking in public had affected him 'extraordinarily deeply'? By his own account, he had had no other opportunities to maintain the necessary contact with his party members and had been robbed of any chance of influencing his followers. Indeed, he had 'lost all contact with the masses'.[58] Not that this prevented the disingenuous demagogue from admitting in the same breath that the city's chief of police had 'now and again' done him the 'favour' of allowing him 'to speak in public', thereby giving him an opportunity 'to vent the feelings pent up in his heart'. And yet this favour had been granted so infrequently, Goebbels concluded, that the political value of such generosity was for the most part 'nonexistent'.[59]

Of course, Goebbels used his ostensible total isolation to develop a perfidious line of reasoning that he hoped would enable him to refute the press's charges relating to the riots organized by his supporters in the west of the city. Under the headline 'End the Kurfürstendamm Riots', the popular *B. Z. am Mittag* had demanded that, in view of the 'SA's well-known fondness for the Kurfürstendamm', the police should not wait for rioting to break out but should take the 'necessary precautions' to prevent such brawls from taking place each time the National Socialists gathered for one of their demonstrations.[60] Goebbels hypocritically complained at the 'noise and screams of the threatened Jews', who were trying to give the impression 'that pogroms were being organized on a daily basis in the heart of a peace-loving city, as if the

NSDAP had set up some secret headquarters where these excesses were routinely planned'. 'To the extent that these events have taken place at all', the blame must be laid firmly at the door of the chief of police for preventing him, Goebbels, from making contact with his massed supporters. Ultimately, he insisted, the National Socialist movement rested on the 'idea of a leader'. It was up to the leader whether he maintained party discipline or allowed his party to sink into a state of anarchy. 'If a party is deprived of its leaders, then the masses are made headless, and thoughtless acts are always the consequence. [. . .] The masses became rebellious, so one could hardly complain when they resorted to violence.'

The way in which the ban had been implemented, Goebbels went on, had produced such 'a mood of hatred and anger' in the ranks of the NSDAP that it had been easy for

> paid police informers and agents provocateurs to stir up the headless and leaderless masses and incite them to commit acts of violence against the police and against people who held different political views. Generally small demolition squads would break away from the indignant masses and seek their political pleasures by going to the Kurfürstendamm and venting their anger on innocent passers-by who happened to look like Jews and whom they hit in the face and sometimes even beat up.

Goebbels became so carried away on the tide of his own rhetoric that he even claimed that National Socialist demonstrations were a 'safety valve for the ruling class. Thanks to this safety value the indignation of the masses found a way of expressing itself. Whenever this valve is prevented from operating, anger and hatred are forced back into the masses, where they simmer and seethe uncontrollably.'[61]

To describe the political agitation organized by the NSDAP as a safety valve and a way of channelling popular anger into legitimate courses of action is simply an affront to reason, a topsy-turvy attitude to responsibility, surpassed only by Goebbels' explanation that even the worst excesses of violence were to be blamed on one's political opponents because the 'headless masses' would be susceptible to 'cunning demagogic insinuations, especially those of Communist spies'[62] if the 'people' were robbed of leaders who were 'the representatives and interpreters of their sufferings'.[63] We shall encounter many more examples of the NSDAP's 'guilt transference', a method that it frequently used to shift the burden of responsibility to its enemies of the day whenever it found itself in a disagreeable situation.

Goebbels' Power Struggle with the Straßer Brothers

Meanwhile the National Socialist leaders demonstrated that they would not shy away from malice and slander even in their personal dealings with party comrades. At the end of April 1927 an article appeared in the *Berliner Arbeiterzeitung* and other papers from the Straßer stable that was headed 'Consequences of Miscegenation'. Goebbels immediately saw it as a reference to himself. Miscegenation, the author wrote, caused spiritual disharmony, which in turn led to physical disharmony in the guise of illness and deformity, including misshapen limbs. The article culminated in the claim: 'Talleyrand had a club foot. His character is well known. Indeed, it is difficult to apply the word "character" to him at all.'[64]

Goebbels spoke to Hitler on the subject of the article when they met at the NSDAP rally in Essen. According to a letter that he subsequently wrote to Hitler, the latter had initially been angered by the 'malicious' piece and had promised to speak to the Straßers. Goebbels went on to note that, in view of the critical state in which the party currently found itself, he could fully under-stand why Hitler had done nothing to resolve the matter, but he himself could no longer remain silent. They were dealing with a 'dastardly act committed in a cowardly and calculated way, with the single aim of destroying me within the movement' because the Straßers did not like him as Gauleiter in Berlin. As if in response to a secret command, the 'whole of the Jewish press' was now speaking of a rift between Hitler and Goebbels – the internal workings of the party could have been revealed to the press only by his enemies within the party. If Hitler was to demand that for reasons of party discipline he should say nothing about this 'new villainy', then he must ask Hitler to relieve him of his post as Gauleiter of Berlin-Brandenburg.[65]

In a second letter to Rudolf Heß, who was then Hitler's private secretary, Goebbels claimed that 'the Jewish press' was reporting 'serious differences' between himself and his 'boss', who was said to have 'spoken out on various occasions' against Goebbels' 'working methods'. Hitler was also said to have seized the opportunity presented by their recent meeting to 'dress him down'. Heß was asked to persuade Hitler to issue an unequivocal denial of these rumours and publish it in the *Völkischer Beobachter*.[66]

Worse was to come. At a meeting of NSDAP officials and Goebbels' supporters in Berlin, Goebbels demanded that all present should 'unanimously declare their trust in him, just as he himself expected a declaration of Adolf Hitler's trust in him, for he would otherwise not remain in Berlin a moment longer'. According to the minutes of the meeting, one of Goebbels' supporters

claimed that Otto Straßer had 'Jewish blood' in his veins, a claim he substanti-
ated by reference to Straßer's curly red hair, hooked nose and fleshy face.[67] In
turn Gregor Straßer wrote to Heß on at least two occasions, complaining at
Goebbels' 'outrageous claims' and objecting to his 'incitement' and 'inaccurate
statements'. He ended by demanding that Hitler 'put an end to the matter'.[68]
The deputy Gauleiter, Emil Holtz, even wrote to Hitler to point out 'the danger
of destroying the movement in Berlin' and asked him not only to reach a quick
decision but 'as a matter of urgency to examine the whole situation in Berlin
and try to sort it out'.[69]

A declaration signed by Hitler duly appeared in the *Völkischer Beobachter*,
insisting that all the claims about a 'fraternal duel in the house of Hitler' were
an invention on the part of the 'Jewish gutter press', as was any alleged critique
of Goebbels' methods in Berlin. The reasons for such libels were 'transparent'.
Nothing whatever had changed in Hitler's relations with Goebbels, who
continued to enjoyed his leader's 'complete trust'.[70] Hitler left it at that and
evidently did not feel it necessary to travel to Berlin to resolve the matter. But
he demonstrated his support at least indirectly by allowing Goebbels to
continue with his preparations for a new National Socialist weekly newspaper
in Berlin, even though the city's deputy Gauleiter had drawn the party's attention to the fact that many members of the NSDAP had said that if they bought
the new newspaper, they would stop reading the *Berliner Arbeiterzeitung*,
which Gregor Straßer had been publishing since March 1926, with the result
that the latter title would fold.[71] In short, Hitler's non-intervention meant a
weakening of the Straßer brothers' position.

Of course, the present controversy was not at root about club feet or curly
red hair but about a power struggle within the Berlin NSDAP. It was no accident that, in his letter to Hitler, Goebbels had specifically drawn attention to
the fact that this was no private matter. It was about the position of the
Gauleiter of Berlin, 'who since the Bamberg rally [of the NSDAP on 14
February 1926] had clearly moved the party away from the Straßer circle and
towards the head of the party himself'.[72] In turn, Gregor Straßer mentioned in
his first letter to Heß that he had held a meeting with Hitler in Munich in the
course of which Hitler had referred to 'the neutral character of the new paper',
meaning the plan to publish a National Socialist weekly in Berlin under
Goebbels' editorship. But Goebbels was regarded by Berliners as 'Adolf Hitler's
representative' and could hardly be the editor of a 'neutral' paper, Straßer
noted complacently.[73] Straßer had good reason to be angry for he had invested
a considerable amount of his own private capital in his publishing house, a
sum that had also helped to finance the *Berliner Arbeiterzeitung*, which had

been appearing every week under his brother's editorship since 1 March 1926. Being privately financed, it was exempt from the ban on the party. Even so, the paper never tired of stressing its character as the NSDAP's official organ in Berlin.[74] If Goebbels was preparing to launch a second weekly newspaper only a short time after the party had been banned in Prussia, then Straßer was bound to regard this as a declaration of war and, indeed, as a threat to the very existence of his own publishing empire. And that is exactly what Goebbels intended.

Der Angriff

Until now Goebbels' party appeals and his announcements as Gauleiter, together with the party's calendar of events, had routinely appeared in the pages of the *Berliner Arbeiterzeitung*. But this was by no means enough for Goebbels. He wanted a paper of his own, a paper whose political orientation would be determined by him alone. He alone would write the editorials, not Otto Straßer. In order to conceal his self-interested motives he later – and with some success – put about the story that the ban on the NSDAP had effectively forced him to 'defend himself against gutter journalism. We lacked a newspaper. We were not allowed to speak, and so we had to be able to write. [...] The predicament in which we found ourselves led for the first time to the idea of founding our own newspaper.'[75] *Der Angriff* (The Attack), which began to appear every week from 4 July 1927 onwards, was initially 'nothing more than an act of revenge by Berlin's Gauleiter directed against the Straßer press,'[76] an attempt to 'destroy the competition' represented by the *Berliner Arbeiterzeitung*.[77] Even after the ban on his party's activities, Goebbels had still had access to the columns of this last-named paper, notably when he announced that he was setting up a new cover organization, his 'School for Politics'.[78]

It is extraordinary how successful Goebbels was in persuading contemporaries and even posterity that his own misleading account of the genesis of *Der Angriff* was true. The lies begin with his touching tale of the way in which he decided to make a 'desperate attempt to create a paper of our own without any money and without any fixed membership'. Since the NSDAP – Goebbels suddenly describes it in this context as 'this risible pygmy party' – had no money of its own, he resolved 'to borrow the sum of 2,000 marks for which I myself was willing to stand surety. This sum was to help safeguard our young enterprise as it took its first steps in life. [...] For days at a time I had to run round raising this sum among friends of the party by means of well-chosen words and entreaties.'[79]

The legend that Goebbels set up his own weekly paper on 2,000 marks' credit has been handed down through the decades from biography to biography, as well as taking on a life of its own in other accounts of the period.[80] The first editor-in-chief of *Der Angriff* was the journalist Julius Lippert, who had previously edited the *völkisch Deutsches Tageblatt*. In the volume of reminiscences that he published in 1942, Lippert offered a rather different version of events, insisting that he managed to persuade the first printer of the *Deutsches Tageblatt* – like Lippert himself, a recent convert to the NSDAP – to risk 'taking over the printing and distribution of *Der Angriff* at his own expense for an initial period of three months'.[81]

Even more fanciful is the tale of the three 'blood-red' posters that Goebbels claimed to have put up 'on the advertisement pillars of Berlin' in order to trail the publication of his new weekly paper.[82] The first poster featured only the name of the paper and a large question mark, the second bore the words 'The Attack follows on 4 July' and the third finally revealed that *Der Angriff* was a newspaper: 'The German Monday paper in Berlin'.[83] Beneath this phrase were the words 'For the Oppressed – against the Exploiters'. With typical immodesty, Goebbels noted that his poster campaign was 'effective and calculated to have an impact'. Even the first of the posters had caused 'great astonishment' in Berlin, while the series as a whole had familiarized readers with the name of the paper even before it had begun publication.[84]

Only much more recently has Goebbels been accused of peddling a version of events that is 'a masterpiece of propaganda', a 'highly aggressive, very modern form of marketing'.[85] But it remains unclear why he should have lavished such expense on a publicity campaign for a new weekly paper with an initial print run of only two thousand,[86] especially when a glance at the records kept by the advertising agencies of the time reveals that a three-day campaign using Berlin's 3,190 advertising pillars cost 2,587.50 marks. A series stretching over nine days would have cost almost 7,800 reichsmarks.[87] If we are to believe Goebbels' own version of events, *Der Angriff* could be launched only because he himself had struggled to raise a loan of 2,000 reichsmarks. Is it plausible that the impoverished and 'risible pygmy party' should then have spent almost four times that amount on a poster campaign? There is much to be said for the claim that Goebbels' alleged loan is another of the tear-jerking legends that litter his own accounts of his life. After all, we know that even in 1927 the National Socialists spent often considerable sums of money on advertising public meetings.[88]

Shortly before the ban on the NSDAP was lifted, an article appeared in the *C. V.-Zeitung* in which Artur Schweriner once again expressed his surprise at the financial resources available to the party in the capital:

The National Socialists in Berlin have a lot of money. Their leader, Göbbels [*sic*], must know of sources that never run dry. His baby is *Der Angriff* and undoubtedly demands huge sums of money, the gigantic advertising campaign on the city's advertisement pillars must be devouring untold thousands over the course of several months, and anyone familiar with the societies and organizations in Berlin is bound to wonder where Herr Göbbels gets the money to hire the city's largest halls and mainly to fill them with people who do not pay for that pleasure.[89]

During its early phase in the summer of 1927, Goebbels' new weekly paper was by no means as innovative as later writers have occasionally claimed. The *Berliner Arbeiterzeitung* provided not only the odd editor and editorial idea but also various design elements. As a result, the visual appearance of *Der Angriff* owed a great deal to the caricatures of Hans Schweitzer, who published his work under the name of Mjölnir and whose depictions of bull-necked SA men with muscular torsos, huge fists and faces distorted by rage were a source of unalloyed pleasure to Goebbels, who saw in them the beginnings of 'a new artistic style for the young movement, a style that we had longed for with a vague presentiment and which here found its first animated and stirring expression, simple, grand and monumental and requiring no instructions from ourselves'.[90] Goebbels was very friendly with Schweitzer but he certainly did not 'discover him among party comrades in Berlin'.[91] The illustrator had often provided the *Berliner Arbeiterzeitung* with his crude cartoons, and it seems likely that Goebbels used him now because of his ability to produce easily grasped stereotypical images, especially anti-Semitic caricatures, that were useful in rounding out the polemical leading articles that Goebbels published in every issue of *Der Angriff*.

Mjölnir's hallmarks include not only his representations of the typical SA man from Berlin,[92] but also his idiosyncratic treatment of the ideas underpinning the National Socialists' propaganda, which were reduced to the language of cartoons and geared to the particular conditions in Berlin. Members of the Communist Red Front Fighters' League were invested not only with the attributes of the city's underworld, but the 'criminal Red' was generally also depicted standing in front of a fat and insidious individual with all the features habitually associated with Jews. Mjölnir's caricatures were intended to show that these 'Bolshevik sub-humans' were acting in the pay of the 'Jewish world of finance'. Representatives of what Goebbels called 'this horde of Asiatic freebooters' could be depicted, where needed, as the slimy seducers of frivolous German virgins ('Kurfürstendamm Jews') or as rapacious 'warehouse Jews'.

In entirely characteristic language, Goebbels described one such scene:

Three German members of the proletariat, all of them frontline soldiers, return home tired after work. Their journey takes them from the lovelessly empty stone wildernesses of the East End to the Kurfürstendamm, which twinkles with a thousand lights. Overhead, the evening sky is heavy and grey as they walk with regular tread over the shiny asphalt. Embittered, they stare at all the splendour. Jews are strolling to and fro, with flaxen-haired German girls on their arms. [. . .] When one of our working-class heroes happens to brush against a round and fat son of the people of the wilderness mincing along with painted nails and scent, the latter breathes on him as if he is the lord and master of this city. [. . .] Our local hero then takes out his calling card emblazoned with his trademark and plants it on the Hebrew's face in a way that is not open to the least misunderstanding.[93]

Der Angriff offered a local variant of this anti-Semitism, which by now was no longer merely verbal. 'Cheeky Orje' was a figure from the city's art world invented by one of the editors of *Der Angriff*. In one of his commentaries Orje explains in the local dialect how 'a Jewish boy, a particularly cunning rascal', addressed a 'nice little girl, pretty, blonde and blue-eyed', and 'put his arm playfully round her waist'. Orje ran over to help, whereupon the 'Jew boy' spoke to him in the most 'shameless' manner. Orje boasts of his subsequent heroic act: 'I hit him a couple of times so that he got a nosebleed.'[94] The columns of *Der Angriff* likewise made it absolutely clear that the National Socialists were willing to use violence in dealing with their political enemies. The term 'Fascists', which had been used by the Communists' official newspaper, *Rote Fahne*, was taken up by *Der Angriff*: 'Yes, we are "Fascists", if by that you mean the enemies of your corrupt system. And with your spitting and hissing you shall revile our name for the final time on the day when a German fist forces your teeth down your gullet.'[95]

Goebbels was very proud of this particular brand of journalism. *Der Angriff*, he wrote, should be 'belligerent and aggressive'. The paper was written for the people and must therefore use the language of the people. 'And the masses read only what they understand,' he argued, here too revealing himself to be Hitler's best pupil. Above all, however, he was convinced that with *Der Angriff* he had created not only a new kind of leading article, which he wrote himself, but also a new kind of weekly political review and political cartoon. When taken together with all the 'journalistic details' contained in the paper, this had produced 'an inflammatory standard that was irresistible in its impact'.[96] Goebbels' self-regarding evaluation of *Der Angriff* has far too often been taken over and repeated unquestioningly by historians, biographers and other writers with an interest in media studies. He is said, for example, to have succeeded in founding 'an effective fighting journal for the party in Berlin',[97] while his leading articles allegedly had been characterized by their 'lively, aggressive and yet simple, popular style'.[98] Another writer, finally, has praised Goebbels for inventing 'new techniques of mass communication' and creating 'an efficient instrument' of a kind 'never previously seen in a city famous for its newspapers'. *Der Angriff* is said to have 'achieved respectable sales'.[99]

But these – involuntary – admirers of Goebbels' newspaper project have overlooked the Gauleiter's later admission that, 'after briefly lighting up the scene, the paper failed thanks to the general lack of public interest in our work' and because 'it was impossible to extend its influence beyond the circles of our own party comrades'. Moreover, the number of subscribers was 'pitiful and completely inadequate', while 'the street sales of our paper, which appeared every Saturday evening, were negligible'. Propagandist that he was, Goebbels then immediately swept aside this unwonted element of self-criticism by insisting that what had initially been a 'wretched local rag' soon became a 'respectable and excitingly polemical paper'.[100]

These remarks were likewise intended as propaganda and should not be taken unduly seriously. The 'irresistible impact' that Goebbels ascribed to *Der Angriff* was limited to the fact that initially, at least, the paper succeeded in calming the nerves of party members unsettled by the ban on the NSDAP and that it offered a substitute for the absence of demonstrations, while 'restoring contact between the leadership and its followers', as Goebbels himself expressed it. The shop had to be kept open, and a weekly paper was enough to achieve that end. The SA provided the vendors and at the same time amused itself by forming more and more new cover organizations intended to pull the wool over the eyes of the local police.[101] For a time it was also able to satisfy its need for action by means of propaganda marches through the province of Brandenburg, where the ban did not apply.

Paradoxically, the Gauleiter of the banned NSDAP was able to express himself as brutally and as offensively as ever in his new weekly paper – not once in its history was *Der Angriff* banned by the authorities. The opening sentence of Goebbels' very first editorial set the tone for what was to follow: 'Germany has become a colony of international Jewish financial capital for its own exploitative ends.' Goebbels then went on to speak of 'the cockroaches in parliament' and to complain that 'today the Jew and his German henchmen are cutting their belts from our flesh'.[102] Years later an NSDAP journalist freely admitted that the paper was given 'an almost unbelievable degree of freedom'.[103]

At the end of October 1927 the ban on Goebbels speaking in public was lifted, and 'mass meetings' could be held once again, the first of them on 8 November. Within weeks the situation had reverted to the one that had existed before the ban was imposed on the party as a whole – a ban, it should be added, that continued to exist in theory.

On 13 January 1928 the Reichstag deputy Wilhelm Kube gave a lecture in the Kriegervereinshaus under the title 'The Jewish Plague in Germany'.[104] Shortly afterwards, the *C. V.-Zeitung* reported:

> The activities of the clubs and meetings in Greater Berlin are currently domi-
> nated by a thousand National Socialists attending meetings. Anyone who has
> a chance to attend these events, which are organized with a great deal of
> ballyhoo by Herr Goebbels, who is known in Berlin as 'a little Hitler', will see
> the same brown jackets, the same four hundred professional attendees, no
> matter whether the meeting is in the north or the south of the city. They are
> variously joined by a few hundred embittered pensioners on low incomes, a
> handful of unemployed people, fanatical students, immature schoolboys and,
> above all, vacillating figures from the working class, men who today hail the
> Communists and tomorrow swear by Hitler. We are far from overestimating
> the danger posed by the National Socialists. [. . .] If we none the less raise our
> voices by way of a warning, this is because of the impression of the whole way
> in which Herr Goebbels and his supporters dare to appear in public in Berlin.

The Jewish-run newspaper went on to describe the anti-Semitic insults habitually levelled at the Jews at NSDAP meetings: 'Anyone who is allowed to speak
and write in this way at meetings and in the press must create the impression
in innocent readers and listeners that Herr Goebbels is already Hitler in Berlin
and that he holds unlimited power and thumbs his nose at the law and at
public order.'[105]

The Reichstag Elections of 1928

It came as no surprise when the chief of police in Berlin revoked the ban on
the NSDAP on 31 March 1928, giving as his reason for doing so the party's
need to take part in the electoral campaign for the Reichstag elections on
20 May. The party's supporters celebrated Hitler's thirty-ninth birthday on
20 April in a packed Kriegervereinshaus with march music played by the
Fuhsel Brass Band and a ceremonial tattoo reminiscent of the days of the old
Kaiser.[106] In early May the *C. V.-Zeitung* noted that the National Socialists were

by then 'the most active party in Berlin', Goebbels being a gifted organizer and as a result a very real danger. The paper had in front of it a copy of the NSDAP's election leaflet, hundreds of thousands of copies of which had been distributed throughout the city. 'Germans!' it screamed in large letters. 'Are you again going to vote for the Jewish-Masonic henchmen of Germany? Do you want the Jew and his capital to own everything and for the non-Jew to be dispossessed? Do you want German men in the guise of Masons to do the Jewish will?'

Beneath was a fifteen-point programme:

We demand:

    1. The restoration of German honour!

    2. A German state instead of today's slave colony!

    [. . .]

    5. Land for our people! Work for hands and brows!

    6. Peace among honest workers! War on the rapacious!

    7. Jews out of German administration and commerce!

    8. Berlin must again become a German city! The workers must return to the Kurfürstendamm, and the Jewish parasites must go back to today's proletarian districts!

    9. An end to parliament's lies! German representation for workers of hand and brow!

    [. . .]

    11. The rights of the frontline soldier over those of the Galician [i.e. Galicia in Eastern Europe] intruder!

    12. Peace among Christian denominations, but war on the Jewish money race!

    [. . .]

    15. A kingdom of honour and social justice![107]

The NSDAP electoral campaign culminated on 17 May 1928 – Ascension Day – in a 'great propaganda march' when all four hundred of the party's Storm Troopers paraded from the Stößenseebrücke to the Stettin Station, passing through Spandau, Henningdorf, Heiligensee, Tegel, Reinickendorf and Wedding. In a message to the local party before the final week of campaigning, Goebbels urged his supporters to use their last remaining resources of money and propaganda 'to win our first great surprise victory in the Jewish Babel of Berlin'. In his leading article he expressed confidence that the elections would be a day of 'decisive triumph' for the National Socialists.[108]

In the event, the last thing that the National Socialists achieved was a decisive triumph. In the country as a whole they won only 2.6 per cent of the vote, and in Berlin only 1.6 per cent – 39,052 out of a total of 2,481,138 votes cast. When divided according to sex, the figures were 1.8 per cent for men, 1.3 per cent for women. The party's greatest success came in the district of Steglitz, where it won 2.9 per cent of the vote, while Spandau, Schöneberg, Wilmersdorf and Charlottenburg were also slightly above the average. If we may speak of National Socialist 'successes' in Berlin, they were in the west and south-west of the city, areas notable for their middle-class and lower-middle-class populations. The more working-class areas fielded far less impressive results, the most pitiful of all being in Wedding, where the party won only 0.8 per cent of the vote. Here the Communist Party won 40.4 per cent, ahead of even the SPD on 34 per cent.[109]

It is hard to draw any comparison with the Reichstag elections of 1924. On that occasion the NSDAP had entered into an electoral pact with the DVFP, but now it stood on its own as an independent party. When one of Hitler's early biographers claims that 'Goebbels first really opened up the working classes and the urban masses to Hitler's movement',[110] this assessment can hardly apply to the elections of 20 May 1928. Even the assumption that Goebbels' principal aim was to 'drive away the supporters of Communism and, by winning them over, turn them into his own followers and create a fighting force based on the Communist model'[111] ignores the balance of political power in Berlin in the spring of 1928, for it was precisely here that, as Konrad Heiden put it in 1934, the results of the election revealed 'the extent to which successes at meetings and at SA parades had given a misleading impression of the NSDAP's political significance'.[112]

Gregor Straßer, who had been head of operations at the NSDAP since 1927, clearly recognized this weakness in his analysis of the election result. National Socialist voters, he noted, were recruited for the most part from the lower-middle classes[113] and the rural, peasant classes, the former for reasons of anti-Semitism, the latter for reasons of nationalism. The proletarian percentage 'that our particular brand of Socialism has brought over to us' made up a far smaller part:

This is demonstrated not only by the results in Bavaria, Hanover, Thuringia and Schleswig-Holstein, on the one hand, but even more clearly by the figures for the industrial parts of Berlin, Central Germany and the Ruhr, on the other hand. But if one shares Adolf Hitler's view that the victory over Marxism is the most important and, all in all, the *only* task of National

Socialism, then we must acknowledge that the elections on 20 May cannot be a cause for satisfaction for us.[114]

Straßer concluded by asserting that the party must change its whole approach. Goebbels did what he could to put on a brave face and in his initial reaction – at least the one designed for public consumption – he stated that he believed he could 'reasonably hope that many of those who think as we do may have listened on election night, delighted and happy, to the official despatch on receivers and loudspeakers, while the Jews and their lackeys will have listened to the same reports trembling and with fear in their hearts'.[115] A week later he added: 'Why should the Reichstag concern us? We have nothing in common with parliament.' He was not in fact a member of the Reichstag, he went on, but only a 'bearer of immunity, the bearer of a free travel pass'.[116] As one of the NSDAP's twelve elected members of the Reichstag, Goebbels enjoyed protection from prosecution, making it easier for him to fight an ongoing electoral battle.

Expansion in the Extreme Right-Wing Camp

Goebbels may have put a brave face on the situation, but the election results had shown that his propaganda methods, centred, as they were, on anti-Semitic vituperation and, increasingly, on physical attacks on Jews, had emphatically not helped the NSDAP to challenge the Communists' position in the capital. However well conceived and modern the means that he applied, *Der Angriff* continued to behave in a demagogic and underhand way: eighteen months of demonstrations, marches, leading articles, leaflets and posters had done nothing to alter the fact that the NSDAP was a splinter group in Berlin. None of its attempts at propaganda and none of the vast expense lavished on promoting the image of an omnipresent, hyperactive organization had produced any appreciable response in a city of several million inhabitants.

And yet we should be wary of generalizations. For the meagre electoral result does not reveal one important fact that becomes clear on much closer inspection. Once again it is the journalist Artur Schweringer who, writing in the *C. V.-Zeitung* in June 1928, provides the best assessment of the situation at this time. There was no doubt, he wrote, 'that the NSDAP in Berlin is gradually absorbing the right-wing radical groups and in the process making considerable progress in terms of building up its numbers'.[117] In his appeal to the party on 31 December 1927, Hitler had announced that, organizationally, spiritually and 'ideologically', the NSDAP's 'battle for hegemony' had long since been decided 'within the so-called *völkisch* movement'.[118] In the autumn of 1927 *Der Angriff* had already called on its members to launch the decisive battle against the remainder of the city's extreme right-wing organizations and parties, and only a short time later it was able to report on its success in 'absorbing' rival groups. In the course of 1927, for example, the thousand or so remaining members of Richard Kunze's German Socialist Party joined the NSDAP.[119]

The NSDAP pulled off another coup in the spring of 1928, when the Wiking League, officially disbanded since 1926, abandoned its attempts to continue to operate as an illegal organization and joined the SA.[120] The National Socialists could also report on a series of successes in systematically winning over Berlin's student population, most notably by means of frequent speaking engagements by leading members of the movement, including Reventlow and Goebbels himself. Established in May 1928, the National Socialist Student Association won 791 of the 5,146 votes cast in the elections for the Student Council at the University of Berlin in the June of that year, winning fifteen of the one hundred seats contested.[121]

These were results that could be held up in an attempt to persuade party members to forget the disappointing outcome of the Reichstag elections, even though the Berlin branch was once again riven by internal conflicts. The arguments between Goebbels and Otto Straßer remained unresolved, while the SA continued its familiar attempts to break free from the party apparatus. 'The military organizations are doing their best to destroy the party,' Goebbels noted in his diary on 21 June. By 1 July he was even writing: 'I am on the point of handing in my resignation. I've had enough of this whole business in Berlin.'[122] When Hitler returned to the city on 13 July 1928, more than fourteen months had passed since his last appearance at the Clou. He spoke at a closed session of members and in the course of a lengthy conversation is said to have sided with Goebbels '100 per cent'. Goebbels expressed his satisfaction, even though Hitler, as usual, failed to reach a decision.

On this occasion the rally took place not in the centre of the city but in the Friedrichshain Rooms in the East End. *Der Angriff* reported that by half past seven the hall, 'which holds 3,500, including the galleries, was full to overflowing'.[123] Two days later a report in the *Völkischer Beobachter* claimed that there were 'around five thousand' people present for the meeting, the same number as the previous year, when Hitler had first addressed the party faithful in Berlin. It is striking that, although *Der Angriff* mentions Hitler, it gives no indication of the cult of the Führer of the sort that was to become customary only a short time later. The reporter merely states that following the showing of a film about the party rally in Nuremberg in August 1927 and a few marches, the cry of 'Hitler! Hitler!' had suddenly rung out in the hall. At the end of the evening the same reporter describes the party members pouring out of the hall 'into the warm and balmy summer night': 'As we made our weary way home, we none the less felt that around our brows there wafted the enchanted breath of cool consideration, clear knowledge and a cheerful hope for the future, a hope that nothing could dampen. A great day in the history of the movement in Berlin had come to an end.'[124]

This hardly suggests euphoria, but Hitler's all too statesman-like manner may have been to blame for this. The subject of his speech was German foreign policy. Just as he had the previous year, he lectured his audience on the relationship between the country's population and its surface area, raised the question of possible pacts with Great Britain and Italy, and from there moved on to the problem of South Tyrol. Here he had to defend himself against recriminations from the 'nationalist camp' that he was abandoning it to Mussolini and that this represented an act of betrayal. After three hours in this vein, Hitler finally came to the point:

> You say that German culture is being suppressed in South Tyrol. Yes, but who is poisoning our culture most of all, and where is it being poisoned the most? Do you have the right to set yourselves up as the guardians of German culture? Just look at the culture here at home. Negro dancing, the shimmy, jazz bands, pitiful Cubism and Dadaism, literature hounded to the point of extinction, wretched theatre, miserable cinema: wherever you look, culture has been destroyed. You do not see this. In a single city like Berlin, more Germans are corrupted every year, more are alienated from their people and more have their blood poisoned than there are Germans living in South Tyrol.[125]

Much of Hitler's speech was taken up with the question of 'degenerate art', so much so that one wonders if he had spent the previous day visiting the Great Berlin Art Exhibition at the regional exhibition hall at Lehrt railway station, where the paintings on display were the work of the 'International Association of Expressionists, Futurists, Cubists and Constructivists', together with pieces by the November Group. The Deutscher Werkbund was also presenting its travelling exhibition 'International Architecture', showcasing designs by Le Corbusier, Walter Gropius and Mies van der Rohe.[126] Hitler would have taken little pleasure in such an exhibition. But art is a question of taste, and as for Hitler's comments on the problem of South Tyrol, there was nothing that would have justified the Berlin police in continuing the ban on his speaking in public, a ban that had now lasted for three years, and it was duly lifted on 28 September 1928. From then on, Hitler could speak wherever and whenever he wanted. Goebbels chose 16 November as the date for Hitler's first unrestricted appearance in the capital. The venue was the Sportspalast at Schöneberg.

At this date, Berlin's mayor, Gustav Böß, was working on his book *Berlin von heute: Stadtverwaltung und Wirtschaft* (Berlin Today: Administration and Commerce), which was to appear in the spring of 1929. One of his colleagues, Willy Müller-Wieland, collated the statistical material, providing him with dry dates and columns of figures. In Chapter Four, 'The Major Challenges Facing Berlin's Administration', Böß began by examining the city's social policies and its welfare provisions for the unemployed. Müller-Wieland proved extremely competent, and just before the book went to press he was able to obtain the very latest figures for the period between 1922 and 1928.

When Böß saw the figures, his face darkened. He had intended to conclude his remarks on the two-page table of statistics with the sentence: 'The number of unemployed persons for 1928 is only slightly smaller than that for 1927.' But when confronted by the current data, he decided to add a further sentence: 'At the end of 1928 the unemployment curve is moving sharply upwards. On 15 December 1928 there were 113,594 persons receiving their principal support from National Insurance, 12,629 from emergency welfare payments. By 29 December 1928, these figures had risen to 132,672 and 13,930 respectively.'[127]

Böß cast another look at the findings. During the last two weeks of the year the number of unemployed had risen by more than twenty thousand, an increase of 16 per cent. It was, he feared, the unmistakable sign of the start of a new economic crisis. He could not know, however, that the figures that he had added to his manuscript at the very last moment were the harbingers of an avalanche that was to overwhelm and bury the capital of the Weimar Republic within a matter of only a few years.

6

'The movement is now gaining ground in worrying ways'[1]

1928–30: THE BREAKTHROUGH AS THE DOMINANT PARTY OF THE RIGHT

'Everyone who is still striving honestly for a German future increasingly wants to see and hear the leader of the National Socialist movement, a figure more and more lit by the brilliant light of success.'
Der Angriff on Hitler's first public appearance at the Sportpalast in Berlin, 19 November 1928

'There is no doubt that National Socialism is currently in the ascendant.'
Fritz Sternberg, August 1930[2]

The Sportpalast as a Venue for Demonstrations

It is now several decades since the Sportpalast ceased to be one of Berlin's most recognizable landmarks. All that remains is a legend. Built in the Potsdamer Straße in Schöneberg at the end of 1910 as the biggest indoor ice-skating rink in the world, it could equally be converted for use as a boxing arena, ballroom, roller-skating rink, velodrome, theatre, hippodrome or meeting place.[3] It gained its legendary aura by 1925 at the latest, when the architect Oskar Kaufmann redesigned the building, adding curved lines and a new rear wall, repainting the interior in yellows and reds and investing the structure with an intimacy that gave the Sportpalast an elegance hitherto unknown in the city's other venues. On completion of the rebuilding work, the *Berliner Tageblatt* wrote enthusiastically about the city's new sight: its current guise was not only novel but artistically exceptionally attractive.[4]

But we may well doubt whether 'the particular atmosphere of the Sportpalast, which contemporaries described as unique,'[5] was the result of Kaufmann's work on the structure, for even before this date the Sportpalast, or at least its interior, had attracted the interest not only of artists and cartoonists but also of poets and journalists, a sure sign that the place already had a special aura. In 1922, for example, Kurt Tucholsky had penned one of his typically caustic quatrains about one of the many boxing matches involving the heavyweight champion Hans Breitensträter, who was immensely popular in his day:

> Es dampft Berlin. Bei schönstem Sommerwetter
> ist knackend voll der ganze Sportpalast.
> Das macht: Es boxt doch heute Breitensträter!
> Na Mensch, wenn du das nicht gesehen hast![6]

> [Berlin is steaming. For the finest summer weather, the Sportpalast is full to overflowing. And that's because Breitensträter is boxing today! Man! You really should see it!]

As early as 1912 the dramatist Georg Kaiser had set one of the scenes in his Expressionist play *From Morning till Midnight* in the Sportpalast, and in March 1923 Egon Erwin Kisch wrote one of his famous journalistic pieces on the Tenth Six-Day Race* that was held in the building, publishing it under the title 'Elliptical Treadmill'.[7] The Six-Day Race – the 'circus of madness' – was also a popular subject with satirists such as Walter Mehring and Erich Weinert, for whom it was synonymous with the most advanced form of modern mass entertainment.[8] For today's audiences, the most potent symbol of the venue's fascination is the Sportpalast Waltz by Siegfried Translateur, who moved to Berlin from Upper Silesia in 1900–1. Originally titled *Life in the Vienna Prater*, the piece was chosen in 1923 as the unofficial anthem of the Six-Day Race.[9] It is worth adding at this point that Oskar Kaufmann was Jewish. Sixty years old when he had to emigrate to Palestine in 1933, he died in Budapest in 1956.[10] Translateur, too, was Jewish. He was deported by the National Socialists to Theresienstadt, where he died in 1944.[11]

Goebbels' choice of the Sportpalast as the next stage in the NSDAP's 'campaign of conquest' was entirely deliberate. For Hitler's earlier visits to Berlin in May 1927 and July 1928, when the latter had spoken at closed sessions of the party, he had been able to fill the Clou restaurant and the Friedrichshain Rooms respectively, on each occasion attracting an audience of several thousand. Now, in his own words, he wanted to find out 'if the

---

* This was an indoor bicycle race, originally an American idea but which was very popular in Germany from before the First World War.

movement is as firmly anchored in the broad masses here in Berlin as it is elsewhere'.[12] Initially he planned to hold the event without Hitler as a draw – the ban on Hitler's public appearances in Prussia had only just been rescinded. It was a reflection of the low level of Goebbels' understanding of politics that he measured success by whether or not he could fill the Sportpalast. 'We plan to pack the Sportpalast and fill it to the rafters, but it will involve a lot of hard work,' he noted in his diary on 6 September 1928.[13] Kaufmann's restructuring of the interior meant that the second balcony could also be used. Moreover, new seating had been fitted, resulting in a capacity for meetings and boxing matches (but not for cycling races) of almost ten thousand, which was to remain the case until the building was destroyed during the winter of 1943–4.[14] If Goebbels was to fill the hall 'to the rafters', he would have to more than double the attendance figures for the NSDAP's two earlier internal events addressed by Hitler.

Goebbels' Conflict with the SA in Berlin

Goebbels once again proved himself to be a capable organizer and had the inspired idea of declaring the meeting in the Sportpalast the culmination of the NSDAP's 'Third Day of the Brandenburg Marches', giving him a pretext to mobilize the membership not only of the Berlin branch but also of the whole of the province of Brandenburg and possibly even beyond. At the same time it served his propagandist aims to have those members who lived outside the capital take part in a 'March on Berlin', as the exercise was dubbed in the press. In this way he was able to conceal some of the discontent that had been simmering in the ranks of the SA since the early summer of 1928 and at least for the present to nip in the bud a threatened SA revolt. On the very day that Hitler returned to Berlin after an absence of over a year – 12 July 1928 – Goebbels had had a 'serious row with the SA leadership', as he noted in his diary. On the 17th, while Hitler was still in Berlin (and the two men presumably discussed the 'question of the SA'), he was forced to admit that 'the defence associations have turned the whole thing into a fiasco. They've now come to us and are trying to repeat the same fiasco with our SA.'[15]

The tensions between the party leadership and the SA were to bedevil the day-to-day activities of the NSDAP in Berlin for years to come. For a time Goebbels managed to get his way, as he did during his preparations for the 'Day of the Brandenburg Marches'. On 8 August 1928 we find him writing in his diary:

Bad day yesterday. Had to spend most of it making clear to the soldiers [!] of the SA that marching on Berlin in August is sheer madness. In the end they saw this for themselves. We're now marching on 30 September. In the meantime we can prepare every last detail. And so this embarrassing business has now been sorted out. The SA continues to be a source of great concern to me. [. . .] They're gradually becoming too independent, and when fighting men start to make their own policies, the result is always nonsense. You have to rap them on the knuckles and do so, moreover, in good time.[16]

The decision to postpone the march 'on' Berlin – as Goebbels significantly described it in internal party documents – did little to ease the crisis. Rather the opposite, in fact. With the resignation of Walter Stennes and several other standard-bearers a few days later, the problems escalated into a 'crisis with the whole defence association such as I predicted long ago', as Goebbels confided in his diary on 13 August.[17] The SA's chief of staff, Franz von Pfeffer, had to travel to Berlin from Munich. It turned out that 3,000 marks was missing, obliging Goebbels to discuss the matter with Stennes at a meeting whose outcome he noted in his diary: 'Solution. Hitler will appear twice in Berlin. I'm accepting 3,000 marks on credit. Great relief. Discussion with Munich. Good. Speak to SA leaders. Everyone satisfied. Crisis over.'[18]

If Hitler was to speak twice in Berlin in an attempt to calm the SA and contribute decisively to a resolution of the problems that beset the NSDAP in the city, one must assume that he was to address the leaders of the SA in Berlin in addition to his planned public appearance in the city.[19] In other words, it was felt that a second appearance would help to calm frayed nerves and keep the SA on a tight rein, an indication of the divisions that had already opened up between the party leadership and the SA by the summer of 1928. Later, too, it was to prove necessary to deal with a similar situation in the Berlin SA by combining financial compensation with Hitler's personal intervention. In view of the self-imposed need to fill the Sportpalast 'to the rafters' on 30 September, Goebbels had no choice but to 'work together' with Stennes and the SA. As he noted in his diary following a meeting with Stennes on 14 September, he would do his best 'to maintain a truce'.[20]

In spite of the ban on its activities, the SA had lost very few members. By 31 March 1928, when the ban was lifted, it had – by its own official estimate – some eight hundred members.[21] From the middle of the year onwards, it took on a new lease of life, not least as a result of defections from the defence associations, which, as we have already noted, were increasingly being disbanded. In the middle of April, the Political Police calculated that the total number of men in the SA in Berlin was two thousand, but this was clearly an overestimate. None the less, this figure does indeed seem to have been reached in the capital by the spring of 1929.[22] In short, Goebbels could rely on a good 1,500–2,000 Brownshirts when mobilizing the whole of the Berlin and Brandenburg SA for his Sportpalast demonstration.

Der Angriff weighed in as best it could:

> On Sunday our SA will be marching on the capital. At four in the afternoon the biggest National Socialist mass demonstration ever seen in Berlin will be held at the city's Sportpalast. It goes without saying that you will be there. How many acquaintances and friends will you be bringing with you? The Sportpalast is the biggest meeting hall in Berlin. Our watchword is: 'Closed by the police on account of overcrowding.'[23]

The ostensibly impoverished NSDAP again invested vast sums of money in a poster campaign with which Goebbels had every reason to be pleased: 'Our posters are everywhere.'[24]

Goebbels' diary contains an account of the day in question, the events being recorded in his usual disjointed style:

> Sunday morning. Out to the airport. A magnificent military spectacle unfolds there. Pfeffer inspects the troops. To the sound of music. Crush of people. We drive back quickly to Berlin. Then to meet the train. In Lichterfelde. No end to it. These wonderful boys! No end to the cheering. To the town hall in Steglitz. The crowd – tens of thousands – sings the national anthem with bared heads. Through the West End. To frenetic cheering. Congratulations from Hitler. In the Sportpalast. Closed by the police on the grounds of overcrowding. Fifteen thousand people. Music and speeches. Kube, Reventlow, [Friedrich Wilhelm] Heinz, [Josef] Wagner and I speak. Endless enthusiasm.

Goebbels also commented on the following day's reactions in the newspapers: 'We have a brilliant press. Everyone on our side except those that are completely Jewish. Back to work without delay. We're on the march. Hurray!'[25]

The report in *Der Angriff* reads as if it had been dictated by Goebbels himself:

> Like a brown worm, the army winds its way into the vast hall, greeted by endless cheering. Drums are beaten loudly. Deafening music.

'Prussia's Glory' accompanies the flags to their places to the right and
left of the main box. The crowds continue to stream in. The passageways
fill up. The steps are turned into seats. Finally the hall is so full that the
police are obliged to prevent anyone else from entering. This has happened
only once before in the history of the Sportpalast – at the election for the
Reich's president. Fifteen thousand people fill every last seat in the vast
oval arena.[26]

Given the hall's capacity, the figure of fifteen thousand may well be an
exaggeration, and yet the demonstration on 30 September can be regarded as
a success if we see it as a dress rehearsal for Hitler's first public appearance
in Berlin. 'Letter from Hitler', a self-satisfied Goebbels could note in his
diary on 4 October. 'He is with me all the way. Full of praise for me. "Berlin,
that's your job." How pleased I was to read this!' The next day he was able to
keep the SA happy ('In the evening I shall speak in the Red quarter at the
Alexanderplatz. There'll be riots'). 'Everyone is again looking to Berlin,' he
summed up the situation. 'We are at the heart of things.'[27] A few days later he
felt that this assessment had been confirmed when Richard Kunze announced
that he was joining the NSDAP. Also known as 'Cudgel Kunze', Kunze had until
recently been the leader of the German Socialist Party and as such the National
Socialists' keenest rival in Berlin. 'What's taken you so long, my friend?'
Goebbels wrote in his diary. 'Everything is in good shape. Things are rolling
along.'[28] That same day Hitler – the 'Chief', as Goebbels called him – paid a
surprise visit to his Gauleiter in Berlin and announced that he was 'full of
enthusiasm' for all that was going on in the city. Goebbels was given the
authority to do whatever he wanted. Hitler was also said to be 'delighted' with
Der Angriff.[29]

Staging the Cult of the Leader

From now on Hitler's visits to Berlin became more frequent. Indeed, he was so
anxious to make the best impression that he spent weeks practising how to use
a loudspeaker in the Sportpalast.[30] And Goebbels felt that the responsibility
that he had to bear for organizing his leader's first public appearance in Berlin
was his 'sternest test' to date.[31] His feeling was well founded. After all, electoral
success seemed as far away as ever, at least in the capital: the party was
anything but 'anchored in the broad masses'. By this date, of course, Goebbels
had revealed a virtuoso ability to appear in force with members of his party
and the SA. To quote Martin Broszat:

This not only made the National Socialists extremely visible to the outside world, it also had a lasting impact on the emotional experience of party members and confirmed them in their future willingness to act, as Hitler knew that it would. Both of these factors were important preconditions for the way in which the hopes, longings and resentments of anxious and disorientated people from all walks of life could crystallize around this extreme right-wing party during the coming crisis.[32]

Described by the *C. V.-Zeitung* as 'the Hitler of the north',[33] Goebbels invented the term *Großkampftag* (literally, 'great day of battle') for the forthcoming event in the Sportpalast.[34] One of his diary entries for this period sheds light on his frame of mind while he was preparing for Hitler's highly important visit:

National Socialism is a religion. All that we still lack is the religious genius who's needed to throw out the old superannuated formulas and create new ones in their place. We lack any form of ritual. National Socialism must one day become the state religion of the Germans. My party is my church, and I believe that I may best serve the Lord by doing His will and freeing my downtrodden people from their chains. That is my Gospel.[35]

It was entirely in this spirit that *Der Angriff* announced in its issue of 12 November 1928 the subject of Hitler's first speech in Berlin following the lifting of the ban on his speaking in public: 'The Struggle That Will Sometime Break the Chains'. From this point of view, the Sportpalast – Berlin's largest meeting place – was an obvious choice as the church of this new religion. But admission to this church was not free. Tickets cost 1 mark in advance, 1.20 marks on the night.[36]

From now on *Der Angriff* adopted a positively hushed and reverential tone in discussing all the to-do bound up with Hitler's public appearances in the city. The report on his first such appearance was headed 'Military Review in Berlin':

Mild and humid air fills the streets of the whole vast city. It had rained all morning. Now a bright blue sky peers through the ragged, scudding clouds. Night has not yet sunk over the sea of houses, but already thousands upon thousands of Berliners are hurrying from every quarter of the country's capital to the Sportpalast, Berlin's enormous festival hall. On every street corner huge red posters on the advertisement pillars have been shouting out since last Monday: 'Adolf Hitler is speaking at the Sportpalast on Friday. For

the first time in public in Berlin!' Now the great day has come. [...] At
the entrance to the venue SA divisions are out in force, investing even the
building's exterior with a unique and thrilling character.

The paper was pleased to note that the press had not previously taken such a
'tremendous interest' in an NSDAP event: the reporter for *Der Angriff* counted
more than one hundred other journalists. One after the other, almost all
the party's representatives in the Reichstag and the Landtag filed in. The paper
was particularly delighted to see that numerous prominent figures from other
parties had also turned up: 'Above all one notices the many German Nationalist
deputies who responded to our invitation to attend. Alongside them are
respected leaders of the Stahlhelm and also Richard Kunze, one of the oldest
socially minded early *völkisch* champions in Berlin.'

The *Völkischer Beobachter* put the number of participants at eighteen
thousand, evidently in an attempt to imply that the event had drawn a larger
crowd than the 'dress rehearsal' on 30 September.[37] The reporter of the Jewish
C. V.-Zeitung, Artur Schweriner, thought that there were around twelve
thousand present – undoubtedly a more realistic assessment – and at the same
time provided a number of additional details that help to explain the huge
crowds:

> One sees only an infinitesimally small number of Brownshirts but a largely
> middle-class audience of both sexes that is looking forward to celebrating
> Hitler's first appearance in Berlin. A Werwolf unit [...] appears in closed
> formation. They have come out of sympathy for Hitler, as have several
> hundred members of the Stahlhelm, who have donned their insignia to mark
> the occasion.[38]

It seems, then, that the large turnout was prompted, on the one hand, by the
audience's desire for sensation and, on the other, by a growing interest among
other right-wing organizations, an interest that initially extended only to
Hitler rather than his party.

There is little doubt that it was Goebbels himself who stage-managed the
events in the Sportpalast, but he will not have needed to invent any new ideas.
After all, the standard scenario was familiar to him from the frequent speeches
that he had heard Hitler deliver in Munich. He simply had to provide a copy
of what he had witnessed there, albeit tailored to the local conditions in Berlin.
In short, the evening ran along lines identical to those that it was to follow in
this same venue throughout the ensuing period:

1 The National Gallery on Berlin's Museumsinsel, postcard (*c*.1912)

2 The National Monument to Kaiser Wilhelm I, with the Royal Palace's Eosander Gate to the right, postcard (*c*.1910)

3 The Arsenal at the eastern end of Unter den Linden, postcard (*c*.1912)

4 View from the tower of Berlin Town Hall looking towards the Royal Palace and (r.) Unter den Linden,
postcard (*c*.1924)

Judenhetze in Berlin?

Arbeiter und Soldaten!

Man hetzt gegen die Juden, weil Marx, Lassalle, Haase, Bernstein, Rosa Luxemburg, Viktor Adler u. a. Juden sind!

Man belügt Euch jetzt, wie man Euch stets belogen hat.

Die Juden sollen den Krieg gemacht und verlängert haben!

Wer saß zu Beginn des Krieges an der Regierung? Wer im Auswärtigen Amt? Wer in den Gesandtschaften?

Kein Jude!

Wer saß im Kriegsministerium? Wer im Generalstab? Wer im Militärkabinett?

Kein Jude!

Wer hat den Krieg verlängert? Wer hat während des Krieges am lautesten den deutschen Schwert- und Machtfrieden gefordert? Wer hat jeden Verständigungsfrieden als Hungerfrieden und Judenfrieden geschmäht?

Etwa die Juden?

Die Juden sollen sich aus dem Schützengraben gedrückt haben. Glaubt Ihr, daß es Frontsoldaten sind, die so etwas schreiben? Weiß nicht jeder Frontsoldat, wie unzählige Juden als Eure treuen Kameraden draußen begraben sind?

Unter den Machthabern der **Reaktion** gab es **keine Juden!**

Unter denen, die für **Freiheit und Recht** eintreten, gibt es **viele Juden!**

Was ist der **Zweck der Hetze?**

Die Aufmerksamkeit von den **Schuldigen** abzulenken!

Was wollen die **Hetzer? – Unruhen anzetteln!**

Sie wissen, daß die Ordnung mit allen Mitteln geschützt werden wird, für wen und gegen wen es immer sei!

Man hetzt gegen die Juden, man meint die **Volksherrschaft,** die **Republik!**

Die Reaktion, die ihr Spiel noch nicht verloren glaubt, versucht es noch einmal, diesmal mit der Judenhetze!

Arbeiter und Soldaten Berlins!

Laßt Euch nicht betrügen!
Laßt Eure neue Freiheit nicht beschmutzen!

Druck: Deutscher Stadtverlag G. m b H., Berlin.

5 Flyer protesting about anti-Semitism in Berlin (early 1919)

6 George Grosz, 'Siegfried Hitler', line drawing on the title-page of the magazine *Die Pleite* (November 1923)

HUNGER IST HOCHVERRAT

Die Pleite

Preis: 20 Goldpfennige

Nr. 8, November 1923

SIEGFRIED HITLER:

„Ich schlage vor, daß die Leitung der Politik der deutschen Regierung ICH übernehme."

„Der morgige Tag findet entweder in Deutschland eine nationale Regierung oder uns tot. Es gibt nur eins von beidem."

7 Adolf Hitler, probably photographed in Berlin (autumn 1923)

8 The Sanssouci in the Linkstraße, close to the Potsdamer Platz (c.1910). It was here that Hitler stayed when he was in Berlin until 1931

9 SA propaganda march on the outskirts of Berlin (*c*.1928)

10 Hitler leaving the Clou following his speech (1 May 1927)

11 Publicity flyer for the 'Frontbann Nord', one of the SA's cover organizations in north-eastern Germany (1924)

12 Joseph Goebbels speaking in the Berlin Sportpalast (1930)

13 Karl Holtz's design for the cover of the periodical *Neue Revue* (15 October 1930)

14 Hitler at the Prinz Albrecht hotel during his address to NSDAP members of the Prussian Landtag (19 May 1932)

15 'He's destroying everything! Vote him down!' Election flyer (1930 or 1932)

16 and **17** Hitler's headquarters in Berlin: the first and third pages of a report in the *Neue I. Z.*
(January 1932)

Suddenly a tremendous cheer breaks out near the entrance and quickly spreads to the whole of the rest of the vast hall. Hitler is coming! The Führer is here! Accompanied by men from the SS[39] and followed by Berlin's Gauleiter, Dr Joseph Goebbels, he strides along the narrow passageway. Like a roof of honour, arms rise above him in greeting. The cheering is endless. And suddenly it starts up all over again when, to the strains of deafening music, the sacred insignia of the movement, the standards and flags, are borne in by immensely tall SA men. To the right and left of the raised podium they rise resplendent in their colours of flame. Again there is renewed cheering. Dr Goebbels has stepped onto the podium. In a clear voice he declares the meeting open. [. . .] Now Adolf Hitler sets foot on the stage. The shouting and cheering show no sign of ending. His dazzling blue eyes flash at the masses in front of him. Finally he is able to speak. It is a speech so powerful in form and content and so thrilling in its noble fanaticism that even we ourselves are not used to from him. Time and again thunderous applause rises up from the tens of thousands below. And when he finishes, a storm rages through the high-vaulted hall such as the Sportpalast can never have known. The Führer has spoken![40]

The same issue of *Der Angriff* included a piece by Goebbels himself: 'When Hitler Speaks'. For the first time in public, the city's Gauleiter celebrated the cult of the Führer with all the linguistic refinement of which he was capable. He began by drawing a distinction between 'genius' and mere 'talent'. It is in the nature of genius, he writes, to be able 'to see what is great and necessary', whereas talent achieves its results through hard work, perseverance and innate abilities. Genius, conversely, is 'self-creative only through grace. [. . .] Whatever hard work, knowledge and book-learning are incapable of solving, God proclaims through the mouths of those whom He has chosen'. Invested with God's grace, Hitler is one of the elect, and so 'all resistance crumbles before the magical effect of his words. One can be only his friend or foe. [. . .] There are people who when they heard him for the first time were his most ardent foes but who after ten minutes became his most impassioned supporters'. And in what does Hitler's genius consist? Goebbels describes him as 'the great simplifier, a man who in a few words strips away all inessentials from the strife-torn problems of Germany today and reveals them in all their bitter, naked and implacable hideousness. In his presence no empty phrase can survive'.

Goebbels' reference to the 'strife-torn problems of Germany today' may perhaps be excused as an example of the rhetorical device of hypallage, or transference of epithet, but it still seems strange that he should hold up Hitler as a man of few words and an enemy of empty phrases. After all, the speech that Hitler had given in Munich only the previous week in which he had declared that 'a front of procurers and deserters' had 'stabbed Germany in the back' in November 1918 runs to more than twenty pages in its printed version.[41] But for Goebbels, Hitler was not just a genius chosen by God:

> The statesman must be an orator and an organizer as well as being capable of insight and understanding. We find all three of these gifts in Hitler. That is why his propaganda today is more than mere eloquence. It is a political statement even though he is in opposition. He is the mediator between insight and political organization. Many are capable of insight, even more are capable of organization, but to be able to create political values for the future on the strength of a portentous understanding gained through the power of words is something that only he can do in Germany today. [. . .] That is why we believe in him. Above and beyond his infectiously thrilling human form we see destiny exerting its benevolent influence in this man, and we cling with all our hopes to the idea that he embodies and, hence, to that creative force that drives him and all of us on. To the future![42]

Hitler's First Appearance at the Sportpalast

In his speech in the Sportpalast on 16 November, Hitler repeated one of the ideas that had been central to his speech in Munich the previous week and, indeed, to many of his other speeches: he had ridiculed the November revolution as an 'armed theft of weapons' that had caused 'the deepest harm'. When the war had broken out in 1914, there had been only one question:

> Will Germany remain free, or are seventy million people condemned to endure the country's economic collapse? On that occasion it was possible to fight only with weapons or share certificates. The first cost blood, the other hunger, but in the case of both the end is the same in the event of defeat: the death of the people. The people felt this, otherwise they would not have held out for four and a half years.

Hitler then went on to embellish a point that he had made dozens of times already in *Mein Kampf* and in other speeches, raising the question of blame for the war, the 'stab in the back' and honour, cowardice and the betrayal of Germany, while seeking to forge a link between them and create a line of argumentation.

There followed a section that might be described as the 'party narrative', which Hitler repeatedly worked on in the course of the years that followed:

It was then that we came together, seven men,[43] workers and soldiers, all of us fired by the desire to combat the madness of class divisions and bring the nation together again as a community of decent men and women. All who are German by blood, all who live decent lives and engage in honest toil can and must stretch out their hands to their neighbour. On the basis of this front of decent men and women, a national community will grow once again.

Jews were, of course, excluded from this 'national community' as they could never be German 'by blood' in the *völkisch* – racist – understanding of that term.

Hitler went on to explain that, 'above and beyond all denominational divisions and concepts of class', all that mattered to him was 'to belong to the community of seventy million that has been singled out by destiny', whether in good times or 'in bad'. And he left his listeners in no doubt about what he meant by this alternative. 'The premiss of freedom is power; its premiss in turn is faith and the value of the nation, a value without which there can be no leaders and personalities. No nation can survive if it does not have a certain percentage of heroes, and no state can exist if its leaders are not heroic. If anyone shows the German people his fist' – and Hitler made no attempt to conceal his threat – 'we shall break it open and force him to be our brother.' Once Jews and others who were 'not desirable' for reasons of 'blood' had been excluded from the German 'national community', there could be no question of the way in which he and other 'heroic leaders' in his entourage planned to deal with their political opponents and force them to become part of the 'community intended by destiny'.

Particularly remarkable is the fact that Hitler devoted so little space to the 'Jewish question'. Instead, he left it at a brief reference to the need to belong to the 'national community' through blood. The rest, we must assume, went without saying. Two weeks earlier he had given a speech in Nuremberg on the subject of 'Race and the Future',[44] and expatiated at immoderate length on the 'Jewish parasites feeding on the body of the German people'. In Berlin he wisely refrained from making any such remarks.[45] Instead, he chose to speak at length on the 'racial shame' that in his view was gaining ground all around them. The 'bastardization' of the great states had already begun, while the 'Negroization' of culture, morals and blood was also all-pervasive. The 'poison' of pacifism was likewise everywhere, the world having forgotten that battle is the father of all things. And yet, Hitler went on:

The nation that resists pacifism by insisting on the idea of battle will with mathematical certainty become the master of its own destiny. A nation that resists the bastardization of its spirit and blood can be saved. The German nation has its specific value and cannot be equated with seventy million Negroes. [. . .] Negro music is dominant, but if we put a Beethoven symphony alongside a shimmy [Hitler invariably misspells this as 'jimmy'], then victory is clear. If we recall the German soul, then faith, creativity and tenacity will not desert us. Our nation has always found the men necessary to destroy need. [. . .] From our powerful faith will come the strength to help us to resist this bastardization.

This was his first appearance before a wider public in the capital, so Hitler also spelt out what he saw as the programmatical implications of his party's name:

This is the goal that the NSDAP has set itself. We have to strip the terms 'Nationalism' and 'Socialism' of their previous meaning. Only that man is a nationalist who stands by his people, and only that man is a socialist who stands up for the rights of his people both internally and externally. As a result, the NSDAP is no longer just nationalist and socialist, no longer just middle class or working class. No, it sees before it people who honestly want to create a national community and rid themselves of their class pride and arrogance in order to fight together. As a result the party is a movement that with pride can call itself a workers' party for it contains no one who does not toil and work at the life of the people. Even now the proletarian stands alongside the bourgeois, a single army of brow and fist, forged together to achieve a single goal.

No, Hitler could not tolerate empty phrases in the presence of a party made up of 'workers of brow and fist'. Who would have been prepared to object that non-manual workers use not their brows but their brains, whereas manual workers use their hands and arms and muscles, 'fists' being the preferred form of expression of members of the SA as they went about their political 'business'? Bloodless intellectuals and others remote from the people might object that Hitler's definition of 'National Socialism' lacked all substance, but they simply did not understand what the NSDAP was all about: 'Hundreds of thousands stand by us, what matters for them is not consensus but the authority of the Führer, and these hundreds of thousands know that democracy as such is a mistake.'

This was a view that Hitler was keen to share with others, no doubt in the knowledge that only weeks after the lifting of the ban on his speaking in public he was not threatened by any sanctions. In his Sportpalast speech he went on to claim that the movement had created for itself a model of what lay in store for the country as a whole. It was 'German, pure-blooded and consciously aristocratic in its structure' and had no wish to be objective but only 'subjectively German'. With reference to the SPD and KPD he predicted that the coming confrontations would lead to an increase in the force 'that destroys all classes and triumphs over Marxism – not for the middle classes to triumph but for the German people to live'. At this point Hitler avoided any mention of the 'conquest of *Lebensraum*', although this goal was clearly implied by his remarks that 'we mean to create room and bread, for now we are enslaved by the world economy, slaves on our own land and soil. We admit that our aim is to give the nation land once again.'

Hitler went on to stress that the movement could not be sidelined by repressive measures undertaken by the state ('A three-year ban has filled the biggest hall in the Reich' – by which he meant, of course, the Sportpalast). He then indulged in a rhetorical trick that he was to use on various subsequent occasions, allowing his speech to create the greatest possible impact: 'Let us now repeat our profession of faith,' he declared.

> We feel a great love for our people alone. It is our belief that this people has the right to live. And it is our hope that our merciful Lord is watching over our struggle and that He will say that we deserve to report for battle. We have the will that we need to resist each and every temptation, to endure all oppression and not to break down in the face of calamity, which is why with our will we shall cut through our chains and end our present plight.[46]

All that was missing was the word 'Amen', an omission that Hitler was to make good on many subsequent occasions.

'The Chief is very happy,' wrote Goebbels. 'He keeps smiling at me, and then we congratulate each other.' He felt that Hitler's appearance at the Sportpalast was his 'greatest success so far'.[47] Hitler too was evidently impressed by the crowd. Two weeks later, in a speech in Hersbruck in Franconia, he even described the packed Sportpalast as living proof of his own personal ascendancy and the rise of his party: 'When I started in Munich, there were only seven of us. At that date I had no prospect of ever speaking in Berlin. [...] A few days ago I appeared for the first time in Berlin after I had for years been banned from speaking there. And the result? Berlin's biggest hall was packed with more than eighteen thousand people.'[48] He described the occasion in his 'Weekly Politics' column:

> The National Socialist German Workers' Party held a meeting in the Sportpalast in Berlin which, all in all, may be regarded as the greatest political demonstration not only of the movement itself but also in the whole history of the Reich's capital. Around eighteen thousand people were present, but in spite of this there was overwhelming discipline and unanimity. Not a single heckler disturbed this huge demonstration.[49]

The Argument over the 'Stahlhelm Question'

But Hitler did not rest on his laurels. As long ago as the end of January 1929 he had already registered the exceptional increase in the number of unemployed. Flourishing the relevant statistics, he predicted that the full extent of the disaster allegedly caused when the Reichstag had accepted the Dawes Plan as a way of dealing with the country's war reparations was still to make itself felt. 'German industry is on the point of collapse, agriculture faces a crisis unlike anything it has seen before, unemployment is assuming the most insane forms. [. . .] The new year is starting bitterly and will end badly.'[50] From now on these predictions of impending disaster were a part of Hitler's regular repertory of rhetorical flourishes in all his speeches and writings. Nor, of course, had he failed to note the changes taking place within the DNVP since it had suffered a heavy defeat in the Reichstag elections in May 1928, when its share of the vote had fallen from 20.4 per cent in December 1924 to 14.3 per cent.[51]

On 20 October 1928 the DNVP had elected a new leader in Alfred Hugenberg, the chief representative of the wing of the party that hoped to move the German nationalists in the direction of right-wing extremism, whereas most of the DNVP's deputies in the Reichstag, led by Kuno von Westarp, were still willing to remain within the parliamentary framework and even to share in government. In the longer term two such contradictory positions within one and the same party were impossible to reconcile, and by the autumn of 1928 the internal divisions had grown markedly worse. By the summer of 1929 the party was falling apart and several of the DNVP's representatives in the Reichstag turned their backs on the party, while others founded new parties, including the People's Conservative Association. It soon became clear to Hitler that these developments would lead to a fundamental shift in the balance of power between the different extreme right-wing parties.

(Following the Reichstag elections in May 1928, the DNVP had had six times as many deputies as the NSDAP.) As a result he hoped to exploit the situation to the advantage of the NSDAP, and an opportunity to do so arose in the summer of 1929.

According to Goebbels, Hitler had given his work in Berlin a ringing endorsement when they saw one another at a meeting of NSDAP leaders in Weimar in the middle of January 1929, allegedly saying: 'I shall never take away your burden in Berlin. I cannot imagine another leader in the city!' But Goebbels' diary for this period contains no indication that he shared his leader's awareness of a deep-seated economic crisis in Germany or that he had drawn any conclusions from this concerning the future strategy and tactics of the NSDAP. On 1 February 1929 he noted that the crisis in the parliamentary system was growing unstoppably worse, and at a 'vast meeting' in Friedrichshain he registered a 'far larger audience' than the party had drawn hitherto.[52] But he was simply unable to analyse the crisis that was unfolding before his eyes. His reactions to his parliamentary 'work' include entries such as 'Reichstag uninteresting' and 'boring nonsense'.[53] In response to the ensuing 'confusion' in the Reichstag he could offer only banalities: 'Open crisis of government in the Reich. Little else remains but the dissolution of the Reichstag or a dictatorship. The drama may well suit us. Whatever happens we shall be the heirs.'

In his continuing attempts to build up the NSDAP in Berlin, Goebbels seems to have assumed as a matter of course that he could call on Hitler's services whenever he required them: 'He should speak in Berlin at least once every two months, not as a propagandist but as our leader on programmatic points. Not in the Sportpalast but in the Kriegervereinshaus.'[54] For the early autumn Goebbels had particularly ambitious plans that look very much like a continuation of his earlier practices in organizing demonstrations, the only difference being one of scale. 'At the end of September we're holding a great NS week in Berlin with a mass demonstration in the Stadium. Capacity fifty thousand. Hitler speech in the Sportpalast, theatre, cinema, chamber music and eight mass meetings.'[55] It never occurred to him that the party was now entering a third phase in its history, the first having been the period during which he had had to restructure and consolidate the tiny and inwardly divided party, and the second having witnessed the deliberate deployment of the SA as a way of turning the NSDAP into the dominant party of the extreme right.

Hitler, conversely, not only sensed that there was a crisis, he was also conscious of the fact that the NSDAP needed a new sense of direction and new methods if it was to become a genuine party of the masses. The terrain occupied by the *völkisch* parties was already taken, with the result that National

Socialist propaganda now had to find a new audience. It is conceivable that Hitler was unaware of the fact that the SA's 'march on Berlin' and the NSDAP's first event in the Sportpalast on 30 September 1928 had also witnessed the involvement of the Stahlhelm,[56] but it is hardly plausible that when he himself spoke at the Sportpalast on 16 November he could have failed to notice that 'several hundred members of the Stahlhelm' turned up to hear him, such was their interest in him.[57] Hitler knew, moreover, that the Stahlhelm already had more than 200,000 members and that their numbers were increasing.[58] As such, they might provide a bridge to the DNVP, with its millions of members and voters.

Goebbels had proved himself to be an excellent organizer, at least to the extent that he had made Hitler's ideas his own and applied them to the conditions in Berlin. But he was not a party strategist with original ideas of his own. In the spring of 1929 he discovered to his dismay that, however much Hitler might praise him, he was not a member of that inner circle of leaders with whom Hitler discussed strategic decisions. 'I see from indications in the [Völkischer] Beobachter that the Chief is initiating closer dealings with the Stahlhelm,' he noted on 17 March. 'I consider this to be very dangerous. [. . .] No one should be allowed to contest our right to be at the forefront of the political opposition.' Confused by these developments, he spoke to a close confidant about the party's relations with the Stahlhelm and the DNVP, admitting that he had grave concerns: 'The Chief seems to be seeing things in rather too optimistic a light. We mustn't allow ourselves to be robbed of our right to be at the forefront of the political opposition as a result of any compromise. The Chief isn't answering any questions. What's going on?'[59]

After complaining for a second time that he had not heard from Hitler in spite of his 'urgent entreaties in the matter of the Stahlhelm', Goebbels finally received an answer from Hitler's private secretary, Rudolf Heß, at the end of March. For the present, it set his mind at rest, Heß having assured him that they were merely striving to develop friendlier relations with the Stahlhelm but that there could be no question of 'the insane policies of an alliance'.[60] And yet the 'Stahlhelm question' continued to obsess Goebbels: 'The Chief seems to want to take in the forces of reaction. As long as he doesn't get taken in himself.'[61] At the end of April he decided to write an article on the subject, and it duly appeared in Der Angriff on 13 May 1929 under the title 'Against the Forces of Reaction'. At no point in the last five years, he wrote, had the political situation been as favourable to the NSDAP as it was now. In terms of its domestic and foreign policies, the 'system' – the Weimar Republic – was 'on the brink of a major catastrophe'. Predictions made by the National Socialists 'ten years ago' were now starting to come true, with the result that 'the awakening German people recognizes in us the movement which, unwavering and without regard for momentary success, foresaw this development, which is why it alone can be considered to be worthy of taking the great decisions that are now having to be made'.

The emphasis is on the word 'alone', for Goebbels now attacks the 'clever old hands in the bourgeois camp' and the 'venal newspapers of the black, white and red [i.e. the Republic's] moneybags' who, speculating on the economy, have presumed 'to cheat us out of our own well-earned harvest'. And once again he stresses the National Socialists' claim to be regarded as the only party of opposition:

> Anyone who wants the same as us should form an orderly queue behind us. There is still enough room. [. . .] The gentlemen in question will love this! We have sown the seed, and this has cost us effort, sacrifice and blood, and now we would like to harvest it. [. . .] A revolutionary idea – and the idea of National Socialism is revolutionary – tolerates no compromises. On its own, it is intrinsically right, but with outside additions it is wrong. Only one person can be right. And this means that all the others are wrong.[62]

Two weeks later Goebbels adopted an even more unequivocal tone in a piece headed 'United Front'. 'United fronts' were created when one party asserted itself and the others submitted to its sovereign will: 'When you have forced an opponent to his knees, he has no right to be treated as an equal but has to capitulate. This is the case with you. No doubt you will feel disconsolate when you think of the immediate future. The great migration has begun, not from us to you, but from you to us.'[63]

Goebbels' attitude was that of a sectarian politician, demanding that those of his enemies who were still to be won over should immediately submit to his will, even though the superiority of the NSDAP over the rest of the nationalist camp still had to be proven. Here he could apparently appeal to Hitler's memorandum of 24 April 1929 in which the Führer had rejected the Stahlhelm's invitation to join the latter in its referendum to change the country's constitution, a rejection he had justified not only on tactical grounds but also as a point of principle. Goebbels was delighted when he read this memorandum, finding Hitler's reasons for rejecting the approach 'utterly compelling and, thank God, expressed with a refreshing clarity towards the pack of bourgeois politicians'.[64] Evidently he had failed to notice that, although Hitler had dismissed the constitutional changes proposed by the Stahlhelm in its referendum as 'unimportant'[65] when set beside the 'inner regeneration of the nation' and the 'establishment of a powerful and outward-looking state' that his own movement was seeking, he had ended not only by praising the Stahlhelm's leadership for its 'honourable nationalist attitude' but also by expressing the 'sincere hope' that 'the possibility of our co-operation might present itself on some other occasion'.[66]

When Hitler returned to Berlin at the end of May 1929, Goebbels met him and Heß at the Hotel Sanssouci, where Hitler always stayed. In the course of the meeting he was asked to take over the running of the party's nationwide propaganda machine. According to Goebbels' diary, Hitler also expressed his 'caustic views on the Stahlhelm. [. . .] The Chief thinks that the political situation is extremely favourable. We must now learn to wait and avoid a ban at all costs. [. . .] It is late by the time the meeting breaks up. As always in complete agreement'.[67] Goebbels was pleased. And yet his diary for the following days contains two entries noting that Hitler was still in Berlin, even though he evidently did not know the reasons for such an extended visit.[68] The 'Stahlhelm question' continued to smoulder throughout the next two weeks, during which time Goebbels and, presumably, the majority of the NSDAP in Berlin took exception to the fact that the party's official newspaper in Munich was publishing 'stupid provocative articles on the Stahlhelm Day'. In Goebbels' view, the people in Munich 'are bourgeois and always will be'.[69]

Hitler returned to Berlin on 4 July and again asked Goebbels to run his propaganda machine. 'I'm still thinking it over,' Goebbels commented in his diary. At the same time Goebbels suggested the idea of a daily newspaper for the NSDAP in Berlin – Hitler's reaction has not survived. Later that evening, the two men met again for a convivial get-together at the Rheingold wine bar on the Potsdamer Platz, and 'the Chief' mentioned almost in passing that within the next few days he would be meeting the chairman of the DNVP, Alfred Hugenberg. On 19 June Goebbels had noted in his diary, almost by way of an afterthought: 'The DNVP is organizing a referendum against the Young Plan.'[70] Now, two weeks later, he discovered that Hitler had arranged all this some time previously and that the NSDAP was involved. In an evident attempt to boost his own morale, Goebbels noted: 'We shall force our way to the top and tear the mask from the face of the DNVP. We're strong enough to win in the event of a pact.'[71]

The following day he accompanied Hitler on a visit to the artist Ernst Heilemann, 'who had painted a good likeness of Hitler' (no other details are known), and thence to a student meeting. 'He talked for an hour. Good. [. . .] A devastating repudiation of the system.' After that the two men discussed questions relating to a new constitution for the country. 'The Chief takes his cordial leave. We'll be seeing each other again in Nuremberg [at the party rally in early August]. I've again learnt to love and respect him.' Goebbels then returned home to pack, for he was setting off the next morning on his summer holiday, which he was to spend at Prerow on the Baltic. Torrential rain greeted his arrival. And yet: 'I am happy and content. I shall now sleep, sleep, sleep!'[72]

The Temporary Pact with the DNVP

While Goebbels was relaxing on the Baltic, Hitler was in Berlin, preparing to implement his plan for his party's change of fortune. He addressed a meeting of the National Socialist German Students' Association in the Kriegervereinshaus on 5 July 1929, the first time that he had spoken there. The NSDStB had been founded in January 1926 and by May 1927 already had more than fifteen different branches in universities up and down the country. The Berlin branch took part in the elections to choose student representatives for the University of Berlin's governing body for the first time during the summer term, polling 118 votes, or 2.3 per cent of the total. By the following year its share had risen to 14.6 per cent. In July 1929 that figure was 19.2 per cent, 1,377 students having voted for the National Socialists. (Of the eleven thousand students entitled to vote, only a little over seven thousand exercised that right.) After only three and a half years in existence, the NSDStB had grown in size to become the second-largest student party at the University of Berlin, allowing the NSDAP to exercise influence of a kind that it was not to achieve among the wider electorate until the autumn of 1930.[73]

In the course of his speech Hitler compared the present day to the period between 1806 and 1813, when German professors, foremost among them Johann Gottlieb Fichte, had fanned a desire for freedom in the student population. Nowadays, Hitler went on, German students and teachers were banned from speaking out against 'the lie about blame for the war', while the police with their rubber truncheons attacked young people who made no secret of their love of their country. Here Hitler was alluding to riots at the University of Berlin and in particular to a demonstration organized by nationalist students on 28 June protesting at the Treaty of Versailles, a demonstration that had been broken up by the police.[74] He went on to predict that every blow was bringing the party closer to the day 'when we shall wield the rubber truncheon with exactly the same legitimacy as others do today'.[75] If he then felt able to issue his first threats for the period when the NSDAP had won control of the country, it was because he was not only aware of the growing influence of his party in the 'nationalist camp' during the early summer of 1929 but because he now reckoned on finally penetrating the circle of 'influential politicians'. Over the coming years he was increasingly to play the part of a forward-looking statesman.

His first opportunity to play this part came at the end of April 1929 at a demonstration held by the Reich Committee for the German Referendum which had been formed by the Stahlhelm, DNVP, Landbund and Landvolk Party. In his attempt to persuade the NSDAP to join his 'National Opposition Bloc', the DNVP's chairman, Alfred Hugenberg, made a carefully calculated tactical move in mid-June and added a further point to the referendum that the Stahlhelm was planning and that Hitler had already rejected in his afore-mentioned memorandum. In addition to the demand for changes to the country's constitution, it would now include a question about the 'lie' concerning Germany's responsibility for the war. Hugenberg then took steps to ensure that the resolution announced for the meeting that was to take place in Berlin on 9 July would include as its second point the decision to 'place at the forefront of its tasks the battle to combat the Paris tribute plan based on the extorted confession of responsibility for the war'. In particular, he would use the referendum to prevent the Young Plan from being 'imposed on the German nation as if it had the force of law'.[76]

Hitler now declared his willingness to join forces with Hugenberg and others in order to combat the 'tribute plan'. As he later freely admitted, his decision to work alongside them was based on tactical considerations:

> At the time it seemed to me that we needed to look beyond the framework of our party, which even today continues to be limited in scope, and to mobilize the entire German nation against this new and monstrous attempt to enslave us. [. . .] At that date we thought that these tactics would be of more use to the German people than if we fought the Young Plan in isolation.[77]

The Reich Committee met in the former Herrenhaus,[78] not far from the Potsdamer Platz, for a 'working session' on 9 July 1929. The meeting was introduced by speeches by the leaders of the Stahlhelm, Franz Seldte, and the DNVP, Alfred Hugenberg. In the course of his speech, Hugenberg declared that 'we have created a great national front from a group of people of the most disparate parties, professions, religious denominations and walks of life, including representatives of great organizations such as the Stahlhelm, the Landbund, the Patriotic Associations, the German National People's Party, the Christian National Farmers' Party and the National Socialists'. He described the meeting in the Herrenhaus as 'the start of a new national offensive'.[79]

The fifth speaker was Hitler, who announced that the National Socialist movement was joining the struggle to overturn the 'Parisian diktat', to which end it was appealing to the German people. The day was bound to come, he went on, when the Germans were no longer prepared to sacrifice the nation's honour and future to the right to live in the present. Ultimately, the German people would not 'shake off their chains by fulfilling the terms' of the Treaty of Versailles but only by casting aside 'the vice of cowardice and disunity'. 'If this nation is to rise up again, then it is up to us. [. . .] It is merely slumbering. It is up to us to waken it again.' The early sections of Hitler's speech were repeatedly interrupted by the parliamentary cry of 'Hear! Hear!', but by the end it had elicited 'tempestuous applause', to quote from the reports in the Pan-German press. The resolution was unanimously adopted by all three hundred of the delegates present, Seldte, Hugenberg and Hitler all being elected to serve on a 'working party' with a similar degree of unanimity.[80]

Hitler's seat on the Reich Committee raised his profile in the nationalist camp overnight. The Berlin journalist Adolf Stein, who contributed a weekly column to the *Tägliche Rundschau* under the pseudonym of 'Rumpelstiltskin' (the articles were also syndicated to other right-wing newspapers and published in book form every year), was delighted to note an end to the divisions among the millions of nationalists who wanted to break free from 'the chains of Versailles'. The great miracle had taken place: 'As for the petition for a German referendum against the Paris diktat, all the right-wing groups, however small, have formed a united front. They do not suspect one another. They do not denounce one another. [. . .] By the same token, Hitler is not listened to in embarrassed silence but greeted with thunderous applause.'[81] Goebbels, conversely, had the shock of his life when news reached him on the Baltic coast that a petition demanding a referendum had been drawn up:

The prime mover is Hugenberg. Adolf Hitler stands in the middle. This cuts me to the quick. Our task is to ensure that the wool isn't pulled over our eyes and to see that we get to run this whole business and leave the rest of them trailing in our wake. We'll achieve this, even though the danger of political reaction is now greater than ever with us. I find it hard to overcome my most serious misgivings. Names have been put to the appeal! Dear God! In Hitler's case one can only say: 'How it grieves me to see you in such company!'[82]

Increasing Party Propaganda with Outside Help

Far more important than any gain in prestige for Hitler was the sudden increase in the NSDAP's opportunities to disseminate its message. Alfred Hugenberg, who had initiated the idea of a referendum against the Young Plan, was not only the party chairman, he was also a major industrialist and a press baron. In 1916 he had taken over Scherl-Verlag, one of Berlin's three major newspaper empires – the other two were the publishing houses of Mosse and Ullstein, which together were branded the 'Jewish press' by the right. Hugenberg's empire included three daily newspapers in Berlin, the *Berliner Lokal-Anzeiger*, the *Berliner illustrierte Nachtausgabe* and *Der Tag*. He also published the weekly *Der Montag* and an illustrated magazine, *Die Woche*, in addition to *Scherl's Magazin*, and ran a news agency, a news service and an advertising firm.[83] By agreeing to support Hugenberg's project, Hitler suddenly found himself in a position to introduce party policy to sections of the population who had previously remained inaccessible to the National Socialist press and propaganda. In September 1929, for example, the *Berliner Lokal-Anzeiger* announced on its front page that there would be a demonstration against the Young Plan at the Sportpalast that would be addressed by Hugenberg, Seldte and the leader of the Stahlhelm in Berlin, Franz von Stephani. Immediately below was a note to the effect that the NSDAP, too, would be holding a demonstration under the title 'The New Front against Young', at which the speakers would be Franz Xaver von Epp and Goebbels. The programme would also include the first showing of a film about the Nuremberg party rally.[84]

In short, Goebbels' wish that the other parties would end up in the 'wake' of the NSDAP had come true, at least indirectly and as far as the range and resonance of the party's propaganda were concerned. Only six months earlier he had been happy to note that *Der Angriff* had signed up over three hundred new subscribers and that from now on each issue would have twelve pages, turning it into 'a real paper'.[85] With more and more people joining the party, it became possible after 1 October 1929 to publish the paper twice weekly.[86] And yet even during the second half of 1929 *Der Angriff* remained pitifully insignificant among the city's newspapers. By the end of the year it had a print run of 25,000 at best, more or less the same as the pro-NSDAP *Deutsche Zeitung*. The three Hugenberg dailies, by contrast, were selling around half a million copies in all. Of these, the *Berliner Lokal-Anzeiger* was the most successful, selling some 225,000 copies a day, which made it Berlin's second-biggest daily paper after Ullstein's *Morgenpost*.[87] By comparison, the National Socialist press was of negligible importance, and there is little doubt that both Hitler and Goebbels sensed that there was a problem with the movement's underdeveloped presence in the printed media.

At the end of 1928 Hitler had already appealed to party members and spoken of his 'burning ambition' to see the *Völkischer Beobachter* 'among the ranks of the great daily newspapers',[88] encouraging Goebbels to turn his mind to the idea of starting up a National Socialist daily in Berlin. For several months during the first half of 1929, the project preoccupied Goebbels' thoughts in a whole series of variant forms. Sometimes he would plan a new daily newspaper for the NSDAP in Berlin, at other times he thought of expanding *Der Angriff*, which was still appearing twice weekly. A Berlin edition of the *Völkischer Beobachter* was also mooted. Time and again he invited Hitler to acquire the new daily, with himself as editor-in-chief, but each time he was rebuffed. Presumably Hitler's aversion to the idea stemmed from his desire to launch a Berlin edition of the *Völkischer Beobachter*. As a result he kept Goebbels dangling until the end of January 1930, when the latter vented his frustration in his diary: 'Still no answer from Munich in the matter of the daily paper. I'll send him a telegram today. As usual Hitler won't reach a decision. It's enough to make you sick! He needs to get away from Munich, which is stifling him.' Within days, however, Hitler had announced his intention of starting up an eight-page daily that would appear under the title of the *Völkischer Beobachter für Groß-Berlin* with effect from 1 March 1930. It would initially be printed in Munich, but it was hoped that by 1 October production would have been transferred to Berlin, requiring a new publisher, editor and printer.[89]

In the circumstances it proved a blessing for the Berlin branch of the NSDAP that the party had access to publications far more influential than the still-insignificant *Der Angriff* when in the late summer of 1929 it launched its campaign in support of a referendum to combat the Young Plan. Opponents of the plan – in Goebbels' eyes, this ultimately meant the whole of the middle-class and nationalist camp to the right of the National Socialists – had at their disposal a platform that could fight a sustained and determined battle not only against the system of reparations but against the whole of the 'Weimar system' and that consisted above all of the various papers that made up the Hugenberg stable. In this context, the apparently large and powerful DNVP proved the inferior rival, not least because it was increasingly riven and weakened by internal divisions. The German Nationalist bigwigs would occasionally turn out for major events and seek to imitate the National Socialists with their flags and marches and their increasing tendency to refer to Hugenberg as their 'Führer', but it was the NSDAP that was the real 'party of demonstrations', not least as a result of its members, who were for ever willing to play an active role and who on average were much younger than the elderly German Nationalists.

In their detailed minutes of the extraordinary general meeting that they held at the Neue Welt in Neukölln at the end of November 1929, Berlin's National Socialists proudly reported that they had held 850 events since the start of the year: 199 public meetings, 325 public discussion groups, 21 gala events and 305 members' evenings. A total of 62 speakers had taken part. At their head was Goebbels, with 93 appearances, followed by the young SA leader Horst Wessel, with 56. According to the report, the average attendance at the discussion groups was 150, at the party's meetings 1,500.[90] On two occasions – 27 September and 20 October – Goebbels had again managed to fill the Sportpalast with demonstrations on two related subjects, 'The Popular Front against Young' (along with Goebbels himself, the other speaker was Hermann Göring, making his first such appearance in the city) and 'The Final Thrust against Young!' The later event took place without Hitler, even though he was in Berlin between 19 and 22 October.[91]

The party's ceaseless activities during the autumn of 1929 certainly helped to raise its public profile, but there was a further factor that drove increasing numbers of Berliners into the arms of the NSDAP and SA at this time, and that was the worsening economic crisis and resultant sense of social and political uncertainty, especially among the commercial middle classes, tradesmen and white-collar workers.[92] During the month between 16 September and 15 October 1928, 109,000 men and women had been registered as receiving income support either from National Insurance or from welfare payments. By the same period in 1929 – in other words, even before the worldwide economic crisis had begun to take effect – that figure had risen to almost 154,000. By the end of 1929 it had practically doubled to 293,000.[93]

But the politics of organized resentment, as pursued by the NSDAP, acquired a particular resonance thanks to the Sklarek Affair, a corruption scandal which for some considerable time dominated the news in Berlin. In 1926 the firm of Sklarek had taken over the existing stock of the former municipal clothing company. Bribes handed out to various councillors meant that the company had then received generous loans and the contractual right to supply uniforms to all of the city's departments. There were also irregularities in the company's bookkeeping. All told, the city's losses were reckoned at a total of 10 million marks.[94] When the fraud was uncovered in September 1929, the city's mayor, Gustav Böß, was on a visit to the United States. Once it was discovered that his wife had bought a fur jacket from Sklarek but that the firm had not invoiced her for it, it was not long before the popular press was painting a picture of wholesale corruption on the council, a situation not helped by Böß's inept handling of the media. In turn, the local affair came to be seen as symptomatic of a wider, national malaise 'in which it was above all the political opponents of the Weimar system who were pursuing their own agenda', to quote Böß's biographer.[95]

For the propagandists of the NSDAP, the Sklarek Affair was a godsend, for not only were the Sklarek brothers Jewish, but the scandal also stoked the fires of the party's anti-Marxist outlook and its hostility to the 'system' in general. (Böß was a member of the German Democratic Party, while the municipal council consisted for the most part of paid councillors from the SPD, its unpaid members being two representatives from the KPD and three from the DNVP.)[96] Hitler reacted swiftly to the scandal, commenting on it in the middle of October in his regular weekly column in the *Illustrierter Beobachter* and drawing a comparison between 'the Germany of the Sklareks etc.' and 'the Germany of honour, honesty and decency'.[97] When Böß returned from his visit to America, he found himself confronted by a crowd numbering several thousand Berliners, whose hostile reception included physical assaults on him. He and his wife were attacked as they made their way from their car to their front door.[98] The liberal *Berliner Börsen-Courier* complained about the 'scenes of rioting prepared with cold calculation'. The paper was evidently unaware of the fact that these 'dark heroes of the street' who could be seen 'at every ugly demonstration' were not 'the sort of rabble who are ready to riot in every city at any given moment',[99] but members of a party that had just begun to prepare for the elections to the municipal assembly. As Gauleiter Goebbels noted in his diary on 1 November 1929, 'Böß was welcomed back by us National Socialists yesterday. With insults and whistling. Which is fine by us.'[100]

The NSDAP's First Seats in the Municipal Assembly

In the elections for the Berlin municipal assembly on 17 November 1929, the NSDAP won a total of 132,097 votes (70,204 men and 61,893 women), or 5.8 per cent (6.4 per cent from men, 5.2 per cent from women).[101] In comparison to the pitiful results that the party had achieved in the Reichstag elections in May 1928, this represented an increase of 93,000, three and a half times more than its previous share of the vote. Not all the parties in the assembly lost out. Although the SPD slipped back from 73 to 64 seats, the Communists made considerable gains, increasing their number of seats from 43 to 56. The German Nationalists slumped from 47 to 40 and suddenly found themselves sitting alongside 13 representatives of the NSDAP.[102]

As before, the NSDAP's performance reflected Berlin's deep social divisions and the make-up of its individual wards. In working-class districts such as Neukölln and Friedrichshain the National Socialists achieved below-average results and once again came off worst in the Communist-dominated district of Wedding, where they won only 3.1 per cent of the vote. Conversely, they did considerably better than average in the more affluent parts of the city to the west and south-west – Zehlendorf, Charlottenburg, Schöneberg and Wilmersdorf. And yet it is worth noting that even in Charlottenburg and Schöneberg there were hotbeds of Communism. Only in the district of Steglitz, with its large population of civil servants, did the NSDAP reach double figures, with 10.3 per cent of the vote.

There is no doubt that overall the results represented a major success for the NSDAP. 'I telephone twice to the Chief', Goebbels noted in his diary. 'Like me, he's extremely happy and altogether beside himself with delight.' 'Yesterday was a day of congratulations. They pour in from Berlin and the rest of the Reich. [. . .] The whole of the Reich is looking at Berlin in amazement.'[103] In order to assess the true extent of the NSDAP's success we need to compare the result of November 1929 with the Reichstag elections in May 1924, when the National Socialist Freedom Party had stood on a single ticket with the German Socialist Party. The election in 1924 had likewise taken place against the background of an economic and political crisis, even if the worst of it was already over by this date. The comparison reveals that the figures for 1929 are only a little above those for 1924; in some districts they were even a little lower.[104]

In short, it still seemed that the extreme right had failed to make inroads in Berlin, and yet such an assessment overlooks a new quality that characterized the National Socialist organization in Berlin during the winter of 1929–30, an organization that in a certain regard was now without a rival. In his evaluation of the election results, the editor of Der Angriff, Dagobert Dürr, sought to draw a veil over the party's lack of success in the working-class districts of the city, while at the same time claiming quite openly:

We have no wish to hide the fact that for us the mass of electors represents no more than a sounding board that must of course be widened as far as possible. The ultimate decision is taken not by this mass of electors but by a strictly organized and properly deployed minority which in turn obviously needs this sounding board in order for it to be able to achieve anything.[105]

When the new assembly met for the first time on 12 December 1929, the NSDAP members entered the chamber in closed formation as a single brown-shirted body, creating a 'deliberately provocative' impression, as Goebbels noted gleefully in his diary.[106] The group was made up exclusively of men.[107] They described their professions variously as writer, lathe operator, civil servant, fitter, inspector, editor, white-collar worker, secondary-school teacher, building contractor, bank employee, engineer, student and auditor. At least as far as its officials were concerned, the workers' party was made up for the most part of desk-workers.[108] The splinter group of 1928 had become a minor political party that had for the first time managed to gain entry to the Red House, as the city's town hall was then known.[109] And yet the DNVP, in spite of its losses, remained a powerful rival, with three times as many representatives in the municipal assembly.

The elections may have been over, but this was of little consequence to the NSDAP – the 'party of demonstrations'. The string of public events continued unbroken. On 6 December 1929, for example, Goebbels once again spoke at the Kriegervereinshaus, which, as he noted in his diary, was 'insanely full'. On 18 December the SA held a demonstration in the Fehrbelliner Platz, where Goebbels spoke 'before a vast crowd of people'. Among the slogans that members of the SA used to chant and that became traditional at this period, especially when the SA travelled on open lorries, was 'Who'll set us free? The Hitler party!'[110] On the afternoon of 28 December five hundred members of the SA marched past the headquarters of the SPD with burning torches, and on 6 January 1930 a women's meeting was held 'with an extensive programme'.[111]

Horst Wessel – the Legend of a Martyr

Late on the evening of 14 January 1930 Goebbels received news that a group of Communists had attacked Horst Wessel. The twenty-two-year-old SA leader had been hit in the mouth by a bullet. He died on 23 February from septicaemia caused by the injury.[112] When the main culprit, Albrecht ('Ali') Höhler, was arrested in Berlin on 6 February, Goebbels noted in his diary: 'Wessel's murderer caught'[113] – two and a half weeks before the victim was dead. Mere wounds do not a martyr make. A list that the NSDAP later drew up, a 'Roll of Honour of Those Members of the Movement Who Have Been Murdered', contains three names for the period between Goebbels' appointment as Gauleiter and the end of 1929.[114] In one case Goebbels had tried in vain to fabricate the legend of a martyr. In the other two cases he had not even considered it worth his while to make the attempt, in spite of the fact that his party insisted that the men in question had been murdered. In the case of Horst Wessel, however, he suddenly saw his chance to elevate the dead man to the status of an SA saint whose cult could be venerated by the faithful.

A former member of Wessel's notorious SA unit, Sturm 5 (Friedrichshain), later wrote:

> Horst made Adolf Hitler's principle his own: terror can be destroyed only by counterterror. [. . .] The places where the KPD met were often visited by a mere handful of loyal supporters, and our standpoint was made unequivo-cally clear to the landlord and all who were present. In the East End [of Berlin] Horst Wessel opened up a route through which a brown storm tide poured in unceasingly and conquered the area inch by inch.[115]

Goebbels shied away from such openness. It was now the thwarted writer of religious tracts who penned Wessel's obituary for *Der Angriff*. When he had visited Wessel in hospital, he wrote, he had noted a contorted look on his face, but Wessel himself had still believed that he would recover. Appropriating the phrasing of a well-known chorale, Goebbels wrote of 'a young and radiant smile beneath the blood and wounds'. Later, when Wessel died, Goebbels noted: 'Horst Wessel has passed away. After the combat and conflict of life, his mortal remains lie here silent and motionless. But I feel an almost physical certainty that his spirit has risen and will continue to live in us all.'[116]

Following Wessel's burial on 1 March 1930, Goebbels wrote a further article for *Der Angriff*, this time insisting even more forcefully on the Christian typology:

> He was ready to make the ultimate sacrifice. [. . .] Leaving his mother and parental home, he went into the midst of those who mocked and spat on him. I am one of you! [. . .] A Christian Socialist! A man who calls out through his deeds: 'Come to me, I shall redeem you!' [. . .] A divine element works in him, making him the man he is and causing him to act in this way and no other. One man must set an example and offer himself up as a sacri-fice! Well, then, I am ready! [. . .] Wessel drained the cup of suffering to its dregs. He refused to let it pass from him but took it willingly and devotedly. I drink these sufferings for my fatherland! Raise him aloft, the dead man, and reveal him to all the people. And call out repeatedly: *Ecce homo!* [. . .] Another Germany rises up. A young, new country! We already bear it within us and above us. The dead man who is with us raises his weary hand and points to the dim distance: Forward over graves! Germany lies at our jour-ney's end![117]

At the end of February, Goebbels was still assuming that Hitler would attend the funeral, but when he explained the situation to him on the telephone – the police had imposed restrictive conditions and the KPD had announced a counterdemonstration – Hitler decided against travelling to Berlin for the service. Months later, when Wessel's mother complained to Goebbels that 'Hitler had neither visited her nor written even so much as a line to her', Goebbels replied to the effect that he too found this 'incredible' but blamed Hitler's private secretary, Rudolf Heß, for the lapse.[118] Ernst Hanfstaengl later recalled that Hitler had discussed the matter with Göring in Munich and that Göring had emphatically discouraged Hitler from travelling to Berlin and delivering a speech at Wessel's graveside, justifying his decision by claiming that any advantage gained by such a demonstrative gesture was outweighed by the danger of exposing Hitler to an attack 'in the Reddest corner of Berlin'.[119] Since Göring was becoming increasingly important at this time as a result of his manifold connections and was helping to prepare the political ground for Hitler in Berlin,[120] it is understandable that Hitler should have concurred with his assessment of the situation.

For the rest he contented himself in his weekly political column with declaring that 'the fighting men who are torn from our ranks today will be the victors of the future. The martyr's blood of Horst Wessel and his comrades' would create the desire to ensure that the revolution of November 1918 was 'worthily expiated by world history'.[121] Almost three years were to pass before Hitler spoke at the grave of the 'martyr to the movement', when a commemorative stone was unveiled on 22 January 1933. That same evening he addressed a Horst Wessel Memorial Service in the Sportpalast, which, according to Hitler, 'presented the picture of a large and mighty church', the front part of it having been turned into 'a sublime altar' with laurel trees, branches, candelabra and a larger-than-lifesize portrait of Wessel himself. Before the speech, the Kampfbund Orchestra under Gustav Havemann played the Funeral March from Wagner's *Götterdämmerung*.[122]

While the NSDAP may have been able to report a palpable success in the elections,[123] the Berlin SA struggled to increase its membership, in spite of its often violent activities. By the end of 1930 it still had fewer than 2,300 members.[124] Although Goebbels had claimed in February 1929 that it was making inroads in the city's working-class districts,[125] the results of the elections on 17 November 1929 belied the party's propaganda machine, which had asserted that appreciable numbers of members of the SPD and KPD were 'switching' to the NSDAP. At best the party had had some success in recruiting 'nationalist elements' in working-class areas as elsewhere. In Wedding, for example, it was not until May 1928 that the party had been able to set up a branch, and even then it could boast only eighteen members. By the summer of 1930 that figure is said to have risen to 'around 250'.[126]

A later account of the party's history freely admitted that it was initially difficult for the NSDAP 'to gain a foothold in the predominantly Red parts of Berlin', a claim that receives support from the fact that in the elections in November 1929 not a single National Socialist was elected in the 'Red' districts of Wedding, Prenzlauer Berg, Friedrichshain, Neukölln, Treptow, Köpenick, Lichtenberg, Weißensee and Pankow.[127] In these 'strongholds of Communism', the SA was largely limited to carrying out terrorist outrages, acts that were passed off as 'self-defence' and 'counterterror':

> In Schöneberg the Red terror has become so bad that Sturm 9 has decided on counterterror. One night, all our men donned their riot gear and converged on the Communist venue the Rote Insel in the Sedanstraße, and before the Communists knew what had hit them, the venue had been stormed and smashed to pieces. [. . .] In Weißensee, four SA men were taking their leader home after he had been repeatedly attacked, when twelve armed Marxists accosted them in the Naugarder Straße. In self-defence they drew their pistols: two Communists were shot.[128]

The SA's claims to control the area around Görlitz Station in the south-east corner of the old city centre were incongruously enshrined in doggerel verse:

> Arbeiterviertel – tiefste Not!
> Dennoch der Glaube an Deutschland nicht tot.
> Roter Südosten, Unterwelt!
> Jede Woche ein Opfer fällt!
> Trotzdem steht Hitlers Fahne fest
> Mitten in Moskaus Mördernest.[129]

[Working-class district – deepest misery! And yet the belief in Germany is not dead. Red south-east, underworld! Every week a victim falls! In spite of this Hitler's flag stands firm in the midst of Moscow's den of murderers.]

As long as the SA was attempting in this way to plant 'Hitler's flag' in the working-class districts of Berlin, relations between the leaders of the SA and their political masters remained strained, although these tensions seem not to have amounted to anything more than 'disagreements' during the first half of

1930. But the situation deteriorated with the question of the plans for a National Socialist daily in Berlin. On 13 January 1930 Hitler saw himself obliged to issue a declaration to the effect that there were no plans to transfer the *Völkischer Beobachter* to Berlin in an attempt to thwart Goebbels' wish to turn *Der Angriff* into a local daily. Rather, Hitler claimed to welcome any attempt to develop *Der Angriff*.[130] The truth of the matter is that, with effect from 1 March 1930, the *Völkischer Beobachter* also appeared in a special Berlin edition. The situation was especially difficult for Goebbels in that the Straßer brothers launched a second National Socialist daily on the very same day, *Der Nationale Sozialist*.[131]

Der Nationale Sozialist proved popular, and this, combined with the failure of his own plans and Hitler's prevarications, left Goebbels so annoyed that he expressed his anger in his diary: 'Munich, including the Chief, has lost all credit in my eyes. I no longer believe them. For whatever reason, Hitler has broken his word to me five times. This is a bitter realization, and I shall draw my own conclusions from it. Hitler hides away, taking no decisions and no longer providing leadership, but allowing things to drift.' Goebbels' litany of woe went on for weeks, culminating in the question: 'What's going to happen when he has to play the dictator in Germany?'[132] By 25 April 1930 he had made up his mind to resign as Gauleiter. Three days later the situation changed when Hitler suddenly agreed to be pinned down at a meeting of National Socialist leaders in Munich and he came down in favour of Goebbels. As a result, Goebbels got his way on the question of a new daily, and within a few months the Berlin edition of the *Völkischer Beobachter* had ceased to appear and *Der Angriff* was published daily, starting on 1 November.

The NSDAP Gains Control of the Political Right

Meanwhile the economic crisis was growing worse. By March 1930 the unemployment figures for the country as a whole still stood at over three million. By June they had fallen slightly but by September they had risen again to over three million – the comparable figure for September 1929 had been 1.3 million. By the end of December 1930 they had risen above four million for the first time.[133] In the course of the year, moreover, output fell, with the result that the urban middle classes, on the one hand, and farming communities, on the other, found themselves substantially poorer. Workers and the unemployed alike were affected: wages fell and income support was reduced.[134] Month after month these developments drew more and more anxious and desperate Germans into the arms of the National Socialists – in the first instance, it was not the unemployed who swelled the ranks of the NSDAP but those who feared the loss of their economic livelihood and a resultant loss of social standing. The social and economic crisis was exacerbated by political chaos, with the result that from November 1929 the world of right-wing politics increasingly changed to the advantage of the NSDAP, a situation from which the party was quick to profit.

Only 10.02 per cent of the electorate petitioned for a referendum on the Young Plan, barely above the minimum of 10 per cent that was needed to force the issue. But scarcely had the 'Law against the Enslavement of the German People'[135] (the 'Freedom Law') been introduced to the Reichstag when the DNVP fell out over the punishments set out in the draft bill for the chancellor and his ministers and possibly also for the president himself, all of whom were accused of high treason. The argument ended with twelve members of the house resigning in protest at the Hugenberg line adopted by the DNVP. Hitler immediately predicted that, even if the party did not lift a finger, the NSDAP would benefit from the stance taken by the German Nationalists in the Reichstag to the tune of 'half a million votes at the next election'.[136]

In the event, only 13.8 per cent of electors voted against the Young Plan in the referendum of 22 December 1929, a humiliating result that the NSDAP was able to use in its propaganda against the disunited and disorganized DNVP, while presenting itself as the only party that had fought with any consistency to resist 'the enslavement of the German nation'. On 27 March 1930 the government of Chancellor Hermann Müller of the SPD resigned and was followed for the first time by a cabinet – under Heinrich Brüning of the Centre Party – that did not enjoy a parliamentary majority. The rump of the DNVP continued to argue over the whole attitude of Brüning's government and over a number of its planned laws and emergency degrees enacted under article 48 of the constitution. By the middle of July there had been more resignations from the party, leaving only thirty-one of its original seventy-eight parliamentary representatives.

Meanwhile various attempts were made to bring together the different centre and right-of-centre parties but by the summer of 1930 these had failed,[137] leaving the whole of the middle-class, conservative and right-wing nationalist camp inwardly torn and lacking in direction, a situation that could not escape the notice of increasing numbers of outside observers. Only on the extreme right, they noticed, was there a force that exuded vitality, youth and reckless energy. Above all, that party was led by a man who in the midst of the worsening crisis had succeeded in attracting the attention of people from the most disparate social backgrounds, people who until then had held moderate views or in some cases been simply apolitical.

This meant that the NSDAP was occasionally able to fill the Sportpalast even when Hitler himself was not speaking. According to *Der Angriff*, 'fifteen thousand people packed the hall' on 7 February 1930, when a 'mass demonstration by an awakening Berlin' was addressed by Goebbels and Göring – both of them members of the Reichstag – and by the retired army general Karl Litzmann. Writing in his diary, Goebbels described it enthusiastically as 'the biggest and best demonstration we've ever had in Berlin'. When, in early April, Hitler announced that the NSDAP was withdrawing its support from the committee set up to debate the 'petition for a German referendum', Goebbels was able to report this tactical move at a demonstration in the Sportpalast at which his fellow speakers were Wilhelm Kube, now a member of the Prussian Landtag, and Wilhelm Frick, a member of the Reichstag, who, following the NSDAP's success in the elections in Thuringia, became the first National Socialist minister in a regional government. The demonstration was held under the slogan 'The German Freedom Movement Facing New Challenges!' Goebbels noted that he was 'on the best possible form'. 'Everyone bowled over. Huge ovations in the street.'

When Hitler himself spoke at the Sportpalast on 2 May 1930 – it was the first time he had done so for almost eighteen months, his only public appearance throughout the whole of 1929 having been at a National Socialist Student Association meeting on 5 July – the hall, according to Goebbels, was 'absolutely packed'. Hitler's speech was 'authoritative, great, thrilling [. . .] There is nothing but blissful happiness at this glorious success.'[138] Eloquently titled 'National Socialism Is Germany', Hitler's speech was preceded by a documentary film, *The Somme*, which was then showing in cinemas in Berlin and which included images of the fighting on the Somme in the summer and autumn of 1916. This provided Hitler with a welcome opportunity to regale his listeners with yet another account of his 'movement' from its modest beginnings. Now, he boasted, it had between two and a half and three million followers. Within a year, he predicted, this number would have doubled. The party's supporters were motivated by 'the misery of our German people and their fear of a hopeless future'. No nation had such a 'tragic destiny' as Germany. The Germans had been turned into a 'nation of slaves' with 'too little room', a 'shortage of land' that they must end: more land must be 'fought for and retained'. The National Socialists would train the nation for the 'life's struggle' that lay ahead and ensure that the Germans saw what was 'so essential about maintaining the strength of the people'. This meant representing the people's rights abroad in order to safeguard the individual's rights at home. There was no mistaking the threat in his next remark: 'We admit that we are resolved to destroy the madness to the right and left. He who refuses to conform will be broken.' The members of the Berlin SA whose presence in the hall was impossible to over-look will have been pleased to hear this. According to a liberal paper of the period, the party's militaristically organized troops had ensured that Hitler's arrival at the hall was impressive in the extreme. He was accompanied onto the stage by Prince August Wilhelm of Prussia (popularly known as 'Auwi'), who had recently joined the party.[139]

'The Socialists Are Leaving the NSDAP'

Hitler had barely returned to Munich from Berlin when he found himself obliged to issue a further denial in the pages of the *Völkischer Beobachter* after a Munich paper had reported that during his visit to the capital there had been internal party arguments. There were no divisions, Hitler insisted, not even a difference of opinion between himself and Deputy Straßer.[140] Hitler was fortu-nate in that the newspaper had confused Gregor Straßer, who was a member of the Reichstag, with his brother, Otto, whom Goebbels had been trying for some time to expel from the party. There had indeed been simmering argu-ments for some time between Hitler and Otto Straßer, and these were soon to become public knowledge. At a meeting of NSDAP leaders in Munich in late April, Hitler had left his listeners in no doubt about what he did *not* mean by 'National Socialism': the movement owed nothing to the idea of a 'universal morality of pity' but implied an awareness of the need for a German 'master race'. That was why the roots of National Socialism did not lie in socialism as a universal panacea, nor was it a nationalist variant of that idea. Rather, it was a completely new political concept with a totality that could not be divided into separate components.[141]

This programmatical explanation, demarcating National Socialism from all the socioromantic and sociorevolutionary ideas of 'National Socialists', was aimed above all at the group of people surrounding Otto Straßer in Berlin: Straßer, after all, was propagating the idea of a kind of 'National Socialism of the left' and therefore able to count on the sympathy or support of sections of the SA in particular.[142] Back in Berlin, however, Goebbels fell into a trap of his own making: on the very day that Hitler was conclusively redefining National Socialism at a meeting of NSDAP leaders in Munich, *Der Angriff* published a piece in which Goebbels defended himself against the reproach raised 'in the bourgeois gutter press' that the National Socialists were 'half Bolsheviks'.

Known for his radical phraseology and pseudo-revolutionary social dema-
goguery, Goebbels had to back-pedal. On the one hand, he pointed out that
the National Socialists had been fighting every form of Marxism for the last
ten years – 'and not just in cheap newspaper articles and on harmless bourgeois committees [this was a reference to the Reich Committee from which the
NSDAP had just withdrawn] but in those places where Marxism is really to be
found: among the people themselves'. And, on the other hand, he issued a
vague demand for 'a new relationship between the broad masses and Germany's
national possessions', a relationship that would allow 'German workers' to win
the place they deserved in the forthcoming national community. He demanded
'sacrifices and dedication', insisting that if necessary these must be extorted by
force, and he condemned 'the rule of the moneybags', which, he said, would be
replaced by 'the principle of labour'. 'We do not want a state based on profit,'
he proclaimed, 'but a state based on work!'[143]

This was a lot to swallow in the light of Hitler's warning at the NSDAP
leaders' conference that the National Socialist mission demanded the inner
unity of the movement, a movement 'in which every political or tactical difference of opinion would be senseless'. Hitler also wanted to ensure Goebbels'
allegiance by giving him a leading post, much as he had done four years
earlier: 'At the end of the speech Hitler gets to his feet again and to breathless
silence announces my appointment as head of Reich propaganda.'[144] Goebbels
now saw himself obliged to do a U-turn and assure Hitler of his loyalty. When
Hitler next appeared in Berlin at the aforementioned rally in the Sportpalast,
the two men parted on cordial terms. Hitler was 'very moved and happy',
Goebbels himself was relieved: 'We've sorted things out again!'[145]

A few days later *Der Angriff* published another piece by Goebbels, headed
'Radicalism among Men of Letters' and making it clear that he had realized
very quickly that Hitler was on the point of settling old scores with the socialists in the NSDAP. It was time, he wrote, to warn the National Socialist movement about a particular type of person: the 'man of letters', the 'political snob'
with his 'scribblings', his 'clatter of words', this 'rabble', these 'vain fops', who,
'skilled only in hackwork', tried 'to compromise the good revolutionary name
of our party by running amok in their hyper-radical way'. Moreover, 'those
who talk a lot about revolutions rarely undertake them. And as for our
socialism, we do not prepare for it in bombastic paper programmes and
boastful written manifestos but by creating a true community spirit within our
party.'[146] In short, the party's tactical retreat had already been printed by the
time Hitler and Otto Straßer met for a final verbal exchange of blows at the
Sanssouci Hotel – still Hitler's hotel of choice whenever he visited Berlin – on

21–22 May 1930. Goebbels himself was not present. But after reading his outburst, Straßer 'could no longer have been in any doubt about the fact that Goebbels' attack was directed and sanctioned by Munich'.[147]

The basic differences between Hitler and Otto Straßer became strikingly apparent when Straßer asked what Hitler would do with Krupp and similar companies in the event of his assuming power. Would everything remain unchanged in terms of ownership, profits and management? 'But of course,' Hitler is said to have replied. 'Do you think I'm mad enough to destroy the economy?' Only if 'people' failed to act in the national interest would the state intervene. But this would require no expropriation and no right to participate in the decision-making process. Straßer was dismayed. If Hitler was planning to retain the capitalist system, he could hardly speak of 'socialism'. After all, the supporters of the NSDAP were first and foremost socialists. Hitler retorted that the term 'socialism' was 'intrinsically bad' and repeated his view that companies could be nationalized only if they failed to act in the national interest. 'As long as this does not happen, it would simply be a crime to destroy the national economy.' By the end Hitler had realized that there were irreconcilable differences of opinion between him and Straßer and that the latter's ideas on 'co-ownership and the right to take decisions' were 'simply Marxist'. He himself believed that 'only the state that is run by a higher social stratum' had the right to exercise this kind of influence.[148]

Enough had been said by both men to make their respective positions clear, but in spite of this Hitler did not immediately throw Straßer out of the party. Nor did Straßer demonstrate great aplomb by announcing his resignation. He seems to have interpreted Hitler's slowness to act as a further sign of his irresolution, but it was in fact the result of calculation. New elections to the Saxon Regional Assembly were due to take place on 22 June 1930, and Hitler cannot have been keen to fall out with Straßer's many supporters in Saxony during the election campaign. The results marked a day of triumph for the NSDAP, which won 14.4 per cent of the vote, an improvement on the barely 5 per cent that it had won in the May of the previous year, making it the second-largest party after the SPD in the Saxon Landtag. A week later Gregor Straßer resigned as editor of Kampf-Verlag's various newspapers and aligned himself with Hitler. Three days after that, Der Angriff published an open letter from Hitler to Goebbels pointing out that for months there had been a sustained attempt to foment disunity and confusion in the ranks of the NSDAP, but as long as he was its leader, the party would not be 'a debating club for rootless men of letters or chaotic salon Bolshevists'. Rather, he now regarded it as necessary to 'throw these destructive elements out of the party ruthlessly and without exception'.

In the second section of his letter, Hitler addressed his Berlin Gauleiter directly:

> My dear Dr Goebbels, several years have passed since I raised you to the most difficult position in the Reich in the hope that with your energy and vigour you would succeed in turning the confused mass of National Socialist aspirations in Berlin into a unified and taut organization. You have met this challenge in a way that has ensured you the gratitude of the movement and, above all, my own supreme appreciation. Today I must ask you to continue this task and undertake a ruthless purge of the party in Berlin by removing all those elements whose views are essentially the same as those of our enemies and who are now trying to obtain a hearing for these views of theirs by breaking down party discipline. [...] Act mercilessly and swiftly. [...] You have behind you the whole organization of the movement, the whole of the leadership, the whole of the SA and SS and all of the party's representatives in public corporations. Against you, you have half a dozen professional grumblers and men of letters. And so you must act![149]

It was rather more than half a dozen party members who, responding to an appeal that appeared the following day in Straßer's *Der Nationale Sozialist* under the heading 'The Socialists Are Leaving the NSDAP!', formed the Fighting Community for Revolutionary National Socialists on 8 July 1930. As Goebbels conceded in a speech on 30 June, there were some four hundred 'professional grumblers and men of letters' in Berlin and the surrounding area. In the Reich as a whole that number was closer to four thousand. And yet the new organization failed to attract mass membership and by May 1931 had only 2,500 paid-up members, after which it disintegrated into a number of internally divisive groups. During the second half of 1931, the organization enjoyed something of a revival, but it was never able to provide a serious challenge to the NSDAP.[150]

Approaching the Government Quarter

At the meeting of NSDAP members that was held at the end of June 1930 Goebbels had announced that the NSDAP now had ten thousand members in Berlin, a spectacular increase on the figure of four hundred in 1926.[151] Developments during the early summer of 1930 seemed to justify his optimism that the departure of the Straßer group had produced no more than a passing outcry in the press.[152] On 1 July the Greater Berlin Gau held an 'end-of-summer demonstration' in the Sportpalast, an event that prompted one of Goebbels' usual self-congratulatory entries in his diary: 'Sportpalast. Again packed to the rafters. A wonderful atmosphere. The speakers are Studentkowski, Wagner, Göring and me. All were good, but I was in particularly fine form.' According to the report in the *Berliner Lokal-Anzeiger*, each of the speakers had called on the masses to be ready to take control of the reins of power once the present government system had broken down. It also noted that, although the Sportpalast was 'full', it was by no means 'as packed as previously'.[153]

But Goebbels could be pleased with himself as he set off for his summer break. The Berlin branch of the NSDAP had survived the Straßer crisis more or less unscathed, and the party was again in the ascendant. Since early May the Gau had had new offices at 10 Hedemannstraße, not far from the government district.[154] Six large swastika flags were attached to the gable, encouraging Goebbels to note gleefully that they were 'lighting up the whole of the Wilhelmstraße'.[155] It was here, in the Wilhelmstraße and its immediate vicinity, that the country's president and chancellor resided and most of the ministries had their offices. In the event Goebbels' summer vacation was by no means undisturbed, and the 'end-of-summer celebrations' in the Sportpalast were far from the end of the matter. On 18 July 1930 a proposal by the Social Democrats in the Reichstag that the latest emergency decrees announced by Chancellor Brüning be repealed was accepted with the help of the votes of the SPD, KPD, NSDAP and a part of the DNVP. Brüning then prorogued the Reichstag and set a date for new elections on 14 September.

The election campaign thus began all over again, and the NSDAP held three demonstrations in the Sportpalast on 29 August and on 3 and 10 September. (Hitler spoke on this third occasion.) On the 14th the party organized what it called 'election celebrations with brass-band music', in the course of which the election results were announced as they came in. According to the *Völkischer Beobachter*, the mood was one of unmitigated jubilation, Goebbels demanding that the NSDAP be entrusted with the Home Office and Defence Ministry as well as the Prussian Ministry of the Interior and, above all, the post of chief of police in Berlin. He also called for new elections for the Prussian Landtag. The editor of the *Völkischer Beobachter*, Alfred Rosenberg, ended his front-page article with the words: 'Victory is ours! Now fasten your helmets even tighter!'[156]

One of the former party members who shortly beforehand had left the NSDAP with Otto Straßer was the journalist Herbert Blank. He lost no time in publishing a pseudonymous attack on Hitler in which he described the mood of euphoria produced by the election results:

The night of 14–15 September 1930. On old and threadbare couches, at wooden desks, in salons, on country estates and in tenement buildings, the German middle classes crouched before their radio sets, which time and again blared out 'National Socialists! National Socialists!!'

Uncomprehendingly, pencils noted down the huge figures from the elections. By dawn, it was clear: 6,400,000 for Hitler.

And by the early hours of the 15th, fur-coated landowners, worthy civil servants with imperialist and republican views, manual workers, company secretaries, students, soldiers and courtesans on the Friedrichstraße were tearing copies of the *Völkischer Beobachter* from the hands of newspaper vendors: 'The paper of *our* party!'

The middle classes are jubilant. They stand there as if rooted to the spot. In the editorial offices in the Kochstraße [in the city's newspaper quarter] there is a sense of bags being packed. [. . .] Around the Memorial Church there is much chattering of teeth.[157]

7

'Hitler is standing at the gates of Berlin'[1]

1930: THE NSDAP BETWEEN LEGITIMATE TACTICS AND OPEN VIOLENCE

'The National Socialists' poster campaign in the streets has misled many people into hopelessly overrating this playground party.'
Theodor Wolff, editor-in-chief of the *Berliner Tageblatt* on the day of the Reichstag elections, 14 September 1930[2]

'Of course, Fascism will try to concentrate all its forces on Berlin.'
KPD chairman Ernst Thälmann following the elections in September 1930[3]

'The new year will see us in power.'
Joseph Goebbels, diary entry, 23 December 1930[4]

Course Set without Gauleiter Goebbels

'Well, delight on our part and dismay on that of our enemies,' Goebbels noted in his diary two days after the sensational result of the Reichstag elections on 14 September 1930. 'One hundred and seven seats at a stroke. No one had expected that of us. [. . .] Hitler is beside himself with glee.' The NSDAP had captured 18.3 per cent of the vote. 'We just need to stay calm! I have to break off for a couple of days, and then our work can continue. I have already started to reorganize the Gau.'[5] Even on election night the 'revolutionary' Gauleiter had reacted to the count like a typical party official by demanding a ministerial post. Between then and four o'clock in the morning he had visited all the SA venues in Berlin and noted the 'joy and fighting spirit' that obtained there. But in spite of the radical shift in the balance of power, he seems not to have been tempted by the thought of any more subversive revolutionary activities. The NSDAP's opponents and rivals were in a state of profound shock, but neither this nor the temporary total paralysis of the government and its state machinery encouraged him to think that it might now be possible to seize power. No, he felt only 'blissfully calm' on the day after the National Socialists' breakthrough and planned to 'recuperate' before proceeding 'cautiously' to restructure the party organization. 'During the coming months,' he knew, 'things will hot up. [. . .] We must go on as we are, never tiring, never flagging. Our watchword is battle. Whether in opposition or in government, we shall fight for a new Germany.'[6]

Was Otto Straßer right, therefore, when he left the NSDAP with his 'revolutionary National Socialists' in July 1930 and published his account of his confrontation with Hitler under the polemically provocative title of 'Ministerial Post or Revolution?', only then to attack the NSDAP leadership for acquiring a 'bourgeois' outlook under Hitler? Straßer's reproach seemed to be confirmed a week after the elections, when Hitler returned to Berlin to discuss the formation of a government and – if we can believe Goebbels' diary entries – laid down two conditions: he would not tolerate a 'cabinet of experts' – non-political specialists with no party affiliations – and he demanded an end to the coalition government in Prussia. The DNVP, he added, had also agreed to these conditions. The NSDAP was demanding the Foreign Ministry, the Home Office and the Defence Ministry. Goebbels apparently believed he would be offered 'temporary control over Prussia'. 'Then we'll have a proper clear-out.'[7]

Goebbels was clearly convinced that the Prussian government would soon be toppled, a conviction to which he gave public expression in one of his articles in *Der Angriff*:

> The key to control over Germany lies in Prussia. Whoever has Prussia has the country. And the way to gain power in Prussia involves the conquest of Berlin. A national cabinet that is not at one with the Prussian government is merely the prisoner of the chief of police in Berlin. That is why it is naïve nonsense to believe that national policies can be pursued in the country while international organizations guilty of high treason [Goebbels is referring here to the SPD, which had provided Prussia's prime minister in the person of Otto Braun] exert a decisive influence on the government of the greatest of all the German regions.[8]

Both in his public pronouncements and in the private context of his diary, Goebbels sought to pass himself off as a far-sighted political strategist invariably in direct contact with Hitler and in agreement with him on all the major questions.[9] In doing so, he conveniently overlooked the fact that on important strategic matters he was never consulted by Hitler. As Martin Broszat has noted: 'he was clearly unsettled by Hitler's tactical decision to pursue a course of strictly lawful action but he was no less disturbed by Hermann Göring's opportunistic activities – Göring was making himself increasingly useful in Berlin as Hitler's political governor and seeking to make contact with members of the conservative elite and leading industrialists.'[10] As had been the case with Hitler's tactical volte-face in the run-up to the referendum against the Young Plan, Goebbels was again slow to realize that 'the Chief' had moved the goal-posts in the face of the new situation. Goebbels' apparent slow-wittedness was simply due to the fact that he continued to be excluded from the party's inner circle, a circumstance that he invariably refused to admit.[11]

Shortly after the elections for the Reichstag, Hitler had in fact given a public and, indeed, ostentatious demonstration of his determination to remain within the law when he took the stand as a witness in the Supreme Court in Leipzig in a case against three army officers from Ulm accused of high treason. He had then declared under oath: 'After two or three more elections in Germany, the NSDAP will have a majority. There is bound to be a National Socialist uprising, and we shall create the state just as we want it to be.' Within three years, he insisted, the NSDAP would be the biggest party. As a result, the movement did 'not need to use force'. When the chairman of the court ventured to sound a sceptical note and asked how Hitler imagined he would establish a Third Reich, the latter replied that

> the National Socialist movement will seek to achieve its goal by constitutional means. The constitution merely prescribes our methods, not our goal. We shall attempt to reach the decisive majorities in the legislative bodies by constitutional means in order that as soon as we achieve our goal we may cast the state in the form that corresponds most closely to our ideas.[12]

Appeasement by the Capital's Press

Hitler's vocal rejection of any form of violence in his quest for power seemed plausible enough, even to some of his enemies on the political left and in the republican centre. On the actual day of the elections the editor-in-chief of the *Berliner Tageblatt*, Theodor Wolff, homed in on the widely expected increase in the NSDAP's share of the vote. As always, he chose his words carefully – his leading articles were highly regarded across a broad political spectrum – and yet there seemed to be something almost bad-tempered about his opening remark that the National Socialists' poster campaign had 'misled many people into hopelessly overrating this playground party'. People were cudgelling their brains in an attempt to work out just how many deputies Hitler's followers would have by the end of the day 'as if this were really all that mattered'. But sensible people would not be troubled by a National Socialist 'victory' – Wolff even used quotation marks round the word 'victory', arguing that the outcome was bound to be 'something like a so-called victory'. If a couple of dozen more deputies of this kind were to find their way into the Reichstag, they would merely provide another two dozen examples of the fact that 'this is a collection of incompetents. It is a form of theatrical magic that can briefly entertain an audience of big children, old women and numskulls but which is seen to be mean and shabby when transferred to a serious stage.' Today might be the high point in the lives of the National Socialists, but a decline would inevitably follow.

Writing in his own periodical, *Die Weltbühne*, at the beginning of 1930, Carl von Ossietzky had described the National Socialists as storm troopers who had been let loose on the world by the DNVP's chairman, Alfred Hugenberg, and who were creating a noisy but utterly harmless anti-capitalist spectacle. In Ossietzky's eyes, the liberal papers were overestimating the importance of the electoral losses suffered by Hugenberg's party as a result of the growth of the NSDAP. Indeed, Ossietzky even went so far as to portray Hitler as entirely dependent on the grace and favour of his powerful patron:

> Hugenberg will not want his golem Hitler to become too independent. As soon as he no longer needs him, he will simply shut off all contacts, and the National Socialist movement will disappear as mysteriously as it came into being over these last two years. They are no more than hired hands who are chased away when, their task accomplished, they demand not only coin of the realm but also a share in power.[13]

Remarkably, perhaps, this assessment by a radical democrat like Ossietzky, who saw Hitler as Hugenberg's 'golem' and the NSDAP as the 'hired hand' of the DNVP, was echoed by a writer of a very different political hue. Friedrich Hussong was the chief political commentator of the *Berliner Lokal-Anzeiger* – the flagship of Hugenberg's press empire – and held trenchantly right-wing views. He, too, saw the election results of 14 September 1930 as a confirmation of the NSDAP's alleged lack of independence: 'The German Nationalists have maintained and consolidated their position as the only powerbase among the nationalist middle classes that is still capable of action. And the National Socialist extreme right can exert a positive influence on the state only with them and through them.'[14]

Here, too, Ossietzky agreed with the views of the German Nationalist
Hussong, arguing even after the Reichstag elections that the NSDAP was in a
dependent relationship with Hugenberg and the DNVP. Hugenberg's influence
in the Reichstag, he insisted, must be 'greater than in the election campaign,
when he often seemed no better than a hostage designed to guarantee his
party's good behaviour. As soon as capitalism is at stake, he will ensure order,
and the new Nazi deputies, still wet behind the ears, will learn the full serious-
ness of life soon enough.' Ossietzky was convinced that the NSDAP posed no
immediate threat. Did their success in the elections mark 'the start of a Fascist
dictatorship'? By no means. If Hitler had wanted to mount a putsch,

> he would have had to attack on election night, when the streets of Berlin
> belonged to the Nazis and everywhere the mindless roar of the words
> 'Germany, Awake!' could be heard. Rumours that the government had been
> overthrown circulated in the editorial offices of all the major papers. The
> march on Berlin had started! Suddenly doubts were cast on the reliability of
> the Prussian police and the army. Had people not placed their hands in the
> fire for both of these organizations? Now, at the first false alarm, neither of
> them was effective any longer. People were trembling with fear and talking
> about an initial contact between Hitler and senior army commanders. It was
> now being said that the Ministry for the Armed Forces had promised its
> neutrality. While these hideous reports were circulating freely, the victors
> were celebrating in the Sportpalast. The extent of their success has taken
> them by surprise.

No, Ossietzky concluded, Hitler was not planning a new putsch. 'For a long
time Hitler has been striving for legality. The Third Reich will emerge not from
the rejuvenating bath of a nationalist revolution but from the usual ministerial
portfolios.'[15]

The same issue of *Die Weltbühne* contained a second article that put forward
a similar argument to Ossietzky's. Pseudonymously signed 'Quietus', it argued
that the NSDAP's policies no longer had anything in common with the party's
erstwhile revolutionary language:

> As a result any fear of a Fascist overthrow proves relatively groundless. If
> Hitler had considered anything like this during the elections, the night of
> 14–15 September would have been the right time to attack, the night on
> which National Socialist voices rained down like blows on listeners and spec-
> tators from the loudspeakers and projection screens outside the major

publishing houses. Adolf did not seize the moment. He knew why. He knew that the petty bourgeois does not like being shot in the stomach; he knew that the petty bourgeois likes calm and order; and he knew that the army would not come to his assistance. [. . .] Hitler as the dictator of Germany remains no more than a pipe dream.

Contemporaries might have objected to this that the petty bourgeois, especially when wearing an SA uniform, had no inhibitions about shooting Communists and members of the Reichsbanner in the stomach. But 'Quietus' went a step further and assured his readers:

Anyone who believes that these people will now make a serious attempt to implement their anti-Semitic ideas may be reassured. There is absolutely no reason to start applying for passports and packing your bags. In order to get back at the Jews, there would need to be a change to the constitution. Where is the necessary two-thirds majority? And even a dictatorship of which Hitler would be only one part would not tolerate anti-Semitic excesses for anti-Semitism is now no more than an advertising slogan, and Hitler's fellow dictators would merely smile at him. The stock market has understood this. It is not alarmed.[16]

The NSDAP Expands While the KDP Resorts to Empty Phrases

Among journalistic reactions to the election results of 14 September were caricatures in the various satirical journals and comic periodicals, from *Simplicissimus* to the Social Democratic *Der wahre Jacob*. In many ways the most remarkable attempt to satirize recent events was a caricature that appeared in the *Arbeiter-Illustrierte-Zeitung aller Länder* (*A-I-Z*), an illustrated weekly published by Willi Münzenberg, one of the Communist Party's elected representatives in the Reichstag. Unlike the party's official publications, especially the dry-as-dust *Rote Fahne*, the *A-I-Z* contained interesting and varied material, its print run increasing in direct proportion to the party's increasing share of the vote. By 1930 it was the most successful illustrated weekly in Germany, with a print run of 450,000 copies.[17] In the February of that year it gained a new contributor in the person of John Heartfield, an active member of Berlin's Dada scene and a friend of George Grosz, Walter Mehring and other left-wing artists and intellectuals. He had already come to prominence during the First World War, and by the mid-1920s was known for his photomontages which served as publicity on the dust jackets of books published by the legendary Malik-Verlag. It was his wish to use photography and the still-uncommon technique of photomontage as a 'political weapon' that persuaded Heartfield to widen his audience, and the *A-I-Z*, which was produced using a rotogravure process, was a welcome forum for his polemical views. His work almost always filled an entire side and often appeared on the front page of the periodical in question.

After his first six such montages, generally directed at the SPD, Heartfield turned his attention to Hitler in the first of a long series of works aimed at the NSDAP. It was headed: 'Six Million Nazi Voters: Fodder for a Big Mouth'. A second caption beneath the image read: 'And I voted for the shark!' The cartoon depicts a shark on the point of devouring a smaller shark against a dark background.[18] Consciously or otherwise, Heartfield was replicating a topos already used by Pieter Bruegel the Elder in his 1556 moralizing allegory *Big Fish Eat Little Fish* and repeated countless times since.[19] In Heartfield's case the larger fish had a dollar sign on its back and wore a top hat surmounted by a swastika, while the words 'With God for Hitler and capital' appeared along the side of the smaller shark. More than sixty years later the art historian Hanne Bergius, writing in an exhibition catalogue devoted to the artist's work, argued that Heartfield had 'wanted to illustrate capitalist Darwinism with the fish that eat each other'.[20] But what conclusions would have been drawn by the readers of the *A-I-Z*, the majority of whom tended to support the KPD, if this was how they interpreted it in the autumn of 1930? What 'Fascist great white shark' – especially one emblazoned with a dollar sign – was devouring which 'smaller Fascist'?

The leaders of the KPD had for some time been defining the term 'Fascism' in a remarkably open-ended way. In June 1930, for example, the party's 'Polbüro'[21] had adopted a resolution declaring that Fascism in Germany was by no means limited to the National Socialists, the Stahlhelm and so on, but rather covered

all the important bourgeois parties. The transformation of Germany into a Fascist state is due both to the Fascist fighting organizations and to the bour-geois state machinery and its socio-Fascist agents. [. . .] The war against Fascism is unthinkable, therefore, without the most determined war on the Social Democratic Party and its leaders, who represent a decisive weapon in the transformation of Germany into a Fascist state.[22]

In the light of such a definition, it was only logical that representatives of the left wing of the SPD should be described as 'left-wing social Fascists' and that an attempt by Leo Trotsky, now banished by Stalin from the Soviet Union, to form a united front with the Communists and Social Democrats should be denounced by Willi Münzenberg as 'Trotsky's Fascist proposal for the creation of a KPD–SPD bloc'.[23]

In view of all this, we should not be surprised to read the comments made by the KPD chairman, Ernst Thälmann, in his analysis of the election results, especially with regard to Berlin:

> Let us, for example, look at the fact that here in Berlin support for Fascism has not risen as much as it has in other parts of Germany. There is no doubt that this is no accident. Here in Berlin, the headquarters of the Central Committee, the decrees of the Politburo relating to the war on Fascism that have been approved and underlined by the plenum of the Central Committee filter down through the party with all the greater speed and effectiveness. That is why it is easier here in Berlin to strike a blow at Fascism and hasten its dissolution.[24]

Taken to its logical extreme, Thälmann's line of argument meant that the NSDAP's failure to increase its share of the vote in Berlin as dramatically as it had been able to do in other parts of Germany was due to the accelerated 'dissolution of Fascism'. Under Thälmann, the KPD had scored a great success in Berlin on 14 September by returning more party representatives to the Reichstag than the local Social Democrats, albeit by the narrowest of margins, and becoming the most powerful political force.[25] Equally undeniable was the fact that with barely 400,000 votes, or 14.6 per cent of the total cast in Berlin, the NSDAP had achieved a share of the vote that was markedly lower than in the rest of the country, where the figure was 18.3 per cent.[26] But the NSDAP could in no way be said to be falling apart: after all, it had succeeded in sixteen of the city's twenty electoral wards in polling more votes than the DNVP, with the result that it was now the dominant right-wing party in Berlin. Only in Wedding, where the KPD and SPD had together won 71 per cent of the vote, had its own share been as low as 9 per cent, but this statistic merely serves to underline the fact that the NSDAP was still relatively weak in the working-class areas of Berlin but that it had already left far behind its status as a splinter group, which is how it had appeared as recently as the Reichstag elections of May 1928.[27]

When Hitler came to Berlin on 5 October 1930 – it was his third visit since the elections – in order to discuss the formation of a new government, his meeting with Brüning sparked a rumour that if the NSDAP were to be allowed to serve in government, he had assured the chancellor that he would disband the SA.[28] The discussions took place at the home of one of the ministers in Brüning's government, Gottfried Treviranus, who lived on the Reichskanzlerplatz (now the Theodor-Heuß-Platz). The NSDAP was additionally represented by Wilhelm Frick and Gregor Straßer, but not Goebbels. The meeting was planned with all the secrecy of a conspiracy, with the result that press photographers and reporters waited in vain outside the Chancellery in the hope of gleaning sensational news. Prior to the meeting, Brüning had spoken in confidence to the leaders of the other parties and informed them that he would be discussing the government's programme with the NSDAP leadership too.

Hitler responded to Brüning's introductory remarks with an hour-long monologue, in the course of which the chancellor became aware of SA troops marching back and forth along the Heerstraße and Reichsstraße outside. The precondition for any successful foreign policy, Hitler insisted, was the annihilation of the KPD, the SPD and the 'forces of reaction'. When this battle began, he would be prepared to join the cabinet with three other ministers but without committing himself to any of the government's measures. Brüning was neither willing nor able to accept this, and the meeting broke up after three hours. Brüning later recalled that he then 'took a taxi and drove past the singing SA divisions, who acclaimed Hitler as he drove ahead of me'.[29] The next day Goebbels was reassured to note that, at the end of a long and substantive meeting ('Hitler seems to have left a powerful impression on Br. He was altogether delighted'), the NSDAP would remain in opposition: 'Praise be to God. But it means that this Reichstag will have a very short life.'[30] Goebbels was so confident of victory that he was already predicting that the recently re-elected Reichstag would fail even before it had convened for its first session on 13 October.

Anti-Semitic Riots Mark the Opening of the Reichstag

The streets were again calm this morning. There was plenty of traffic in the Leipziger Straße, on the Potsdamer Platz and in the neighbouring side roads. The city had changed. The police could be seen patrolling the inner town, and cars filled with police crews constantly drove through the streets. Many onlookers had gathered to see the shop windows that lay in ruins. By lunchtime today the Leipziger Straße in particular was crowded with people watching the columns of glaziers going about their business.[31]

The casual reader might assume this to be a description of the inner city on the morning after Crystal Night on 9–10 November 1938. Indeed, the two scenes were outwardly so similar that decades later a photograph showing the police outside the broken windows of a shop was still being described by a well-known picture library as dating from 10 November 1938.[32] In fact, the account is taken from a press report of the mood in the centre of Berlin on 14 October 1930, a day after the riots that had marked the opening session of the new Reichstag, which was meeting for the first time since the elections on 14 September. Another contemporary report describes the scene as follows:

The opening of the Reichstag took on an air of the sensational as a result of the entry into the chamber of the 107 National Socialist deputies marching in closed formation, all of them wearing brown uniforms. Outside the building the National Socialists organized demonstrations. The police were quick to intervene, and when some of the demonstrators were driven back, they retaliated by breaking the windows of many Jewish firms in the Leipziger Straße. The National Socialists claimed that these excesses were the work of Communist agents provocateurs.[33]

These same events were reported in detail by the *Berliner Lokal-Anzeiger*, Hugenberg's biggest-circulation paper:

By the time the Reichstag was opened, some four to five thousand people had gathered around the building. They arrived from every direction in very small groups and took up their positions around the Bismarck memorial.[34] Large numbers of police were positioned in the vicinity of the Reichstag and tried to drive back the crowd. Time and again the officers used their rubber truncheons and initially arrested twenty-seven of the demonstrators. Finally two hundred extra policemen and a detachment of mounted police assembled in the Platz der Republik and began systematically to clear the square. The crowd was forced back along the Friedensallee and the Siegesallee to the Charlottenburger Chaussee, where they regrouped and made a further attempt to march on the Reichstag, an attempt that again came to nothing. The police called for further reinforcements and by four o'clock in the afternoon had cleared the whole of the Tiergarten.

A three hundred-strong group of demonstrators gathered in the Stresemannstraße and initially made for Dobrin's pâtisserie and coffee shop on the corner of the Friedrich-Ebert-Straße and the Tiergartenstraße. The demonstrators raised their fists threateningly at the occupants of the shop, forcing the latter to withdraw into the rooms at the back, so much did they fear an attack. Suddenly a hail of rocks and stones flew through the air in the direction of the café. Within moments all its windows had been shattered. [...] Only by a stroke of good luck was no one injured. The crowd then moved on to the Potsdamer Platz. The traffic police tried to bar their way but were driven back. On the Leipziger Platz the demonstrators threw stones at the windows of the Wertheim department store. They had previously taken up their positions on the pavement outside the store and at an agreed sign threw their stones at the windows in a concerted action, so that all were smashed within seconds. Since the shop was full of customers, the result was a mood of panic. Shoppers ran out of the exits in their search for a means of escape. [...] Leaving behind them a scene of devastation, the crowd moved on, threatening Herpich's Furrier's, smashing three windowpanes at Grünfeld's linen store and destroying a window display at Bette, Bud und Lachmann's. At Cord's and Adam's, too, a number of very large windows bit the dust. Only now did the police appear and drove the demonstrators back with their rubber truncheons. [...]

More rioting broke out on the Potsdamer Platz towards seven o'clock in the evening. The crowd wanted to hold a meeting there but they were prevented from doing so by the police and driven back. A smaller group of demonstrators broke a number of windows in the Darmstadt & National Bank in the Kronenstraße and another group smashed the display window of Behrendt's clothing emporium in the Charlottenstraße. [...] Throughout the whole of yesterday evening the Potsdamer Platz remained exceptionally tense. Between seven and eight the situation seemed to have calmed down sufficiently for the police chief on duty to move his forces back, but the rioting broke out again by half past eight. [...] The scene in the Potsdamer Platz in front of the station was even more animated. Here several hundred demonstrators had gathered and, shouting loudly, gave every sign of preparing to march on the Vaterland pâtisserie.[35]

By now there was rioting along the whole length of the Leipziger Straße, the main shopping street in the old city centre: at a quarter past nine two youths smashed the windows of Tietz's department store on the Dönhoffplatz at the eastern end of the street.[36]

Almost all the stores and businesses attacked by the mob belonged to Jews. In particular, firms like Wertheim's at the western end of the Leipziger Straße and Tietz's at its eastern extremity were favourite targets among National

Socialist and anti-Semitic groups who had set their sights on what they called 'rapacious Jewish capital'. On 29 November 1929, for example, Hitler had declared the NSDAP's opposition to department stores on the grounds that they 'led to the demolition of tens of thousands of small businesses'.[37] It comes as no surprise, therefore, to read the report drawn up by the city's chief of police and discover that, of the 106 individuals who were detained during the riots, forty-five were members of the NSDAP and fifty-five were sympathizers. It appears that the demonstrators chanted 'Germany, Awake!' in front of the Reichstag and threw stones at the security forces.[38] But the police were unable to determine the exact circumstances in which the demonstration had been planned and executed. In April 1931 a thirty-six-year-old member of the SA was arrested as one of the 'ringleaders', but the police investigation established that the crowd was not directed by a single individual but had been made up of 'groups of young lads who pulled stones from their pockets while shouting and making an exceptional amount of noise'. They had then 'thrown these stones at the large plate-glass windows of many shops and offices while running at high speed'. The report emphatically denied that the rioting had been planned at the highest party level.[39]

As early as January 1929 Goebbels had recorded a conversation with the young SA activist Horst Wessel in which the latter complained about the 'lack of action on the part of the SA', a complaint that obliged Goebbels in turn to lament the fact that he was 'in a jam: if we become active in Berlin, our people will smash up everything, and Isidor [Goebbels' name for the city's deputy chief of police, Bernhard Weiß] will then be only too pleased to ban us. For the present we need to marshal our forces'.[40] Had the party not 'marshalled its forces' with its electoral victory in September 1930, when it had become the second most powerful party in the Reichstag? But in the days before the house met, Goebbels was far too busy saving his own skin to give this question much thought. After he had failed to appear to hear the charges against him at the Charlottenburg criminal court, the court issued a subpoena demanding his appearance on 13 October 1930. 'I'm leaving today,' Goebbels wrote in his diary in response to the request. 'Where? To escape from the public prosecutor. I'll be back on Monday. As a member of the Reichstag with immunity from prosecution [only when the house reconvened on 13 October could he no longer be prosecuted].'[41] On the day in question, he forced his way into the Reichstag, past the waiting detectives, noting only that 'outside the masses are seething'. Only later did he discover that the demonstrators had 'gone completely mad in the city centre. Thousands of windows smashed. Mayhem in the press. [...] Things look terrible in the Leipziger

Straße. Crowds of black-clad marchers singing and chanting. To the Görings. Lots of people there, including Hitler. He is very nice. Many beautiful women. [...] We remain there until late at night.'[42] It does seem, therefore, that neither Goebbels nor the other party leaders in Berlin had planned the riots.

Strangely enough, the Berlin police appear not to have been aware that there had long been a rift between the party leaders and the SA in the city and that the situation had suddenly become worse as a result of the Stennes Putsch only weeks before the riots.[43] The whole of the north-east German SA had been growing increasingly restless, and its disquiet had come to a head shortly before the Reichstag elections. After Walter Stennes, the supreme commander of the SA in north-eastern Germany, had tried in vain to have some of the SA leaders under him added to the NSDAP's list of candidates and after the SA's chronic lack of funds had assumed catastrophic proportions,[44] the tensions came to the surface at the end of August, when members of the SA loyal to Stennes occupied and demolished the party's offices in the Hedemannstraße. There was also fighting among the SA and with the SS. Hitler hurried to the capital and held a series of discussions with the leaders of the local NSDAP and SA, starting on 31 August. Within three days he had managed to resolve the conflict, at least for the present, by taking over the running of the SA and SS from Franz von Pfeffer, who had stepped down on 29 August, and by granting the SA certain financial concessions.[45]

On 1 September Hitler spoke at the Kriegervereinshaus in the presence of more than two thousand SA men, informing them that the NSDAP would gradually take over all the positions of power within the state and occupy one police headquarters after another. Even though they would do so by legal means, Hitler also insisted that the National Socialist movement reserved the right to defend itself, a right enshrined in the country's penal code. Towards the end of his speech, Hitler again worked himself up into a mood that teetered between sentimentality and religious kitsch, assuring his listeners that he would always make himself available for 'his' SA. According to a police report, Hitler concluded the meeting by

> appealing to the loyalty of his SA. His voice rising to an almost hysterical scream, he then struck a distinctly theatrical note: 'Let us swear in this hour that nothing can part us, as God can help us against all devils! May our Almighty God bless our fight!' The audience began to shout 'Heil', but Hitler gestured to them to stop and, clasping his hands, he listened to his own words, as if sunk in fervent prayer.[46]

At the time it seemed obvious that the 'groups of young lads' throwing stones were organized by the SA and that the latter was keen to mount a parallel action to that of the NSDAP's deputies in the Reichstag. Given the 'tradition' of anti-Semitic excesses in the city, such an explanation is by no means implausible. Writing in *Die Weltbühne* immediately after the riots, Carl von Ossietzky was in no doubt that, 'according to the opinion of those in the know', the fighting had been fomented not by the party leadership but 'by Captain Stennes and his Storm Troopers'. Stennes, Ossietzky explained, had been passed over in the selection of parliamentary candidates and had 'recently made his dissatisfaction known in no uncertain terms' when speaking to his commanding officer – since 2 September, Hitler himself.[47] None the less, as Dirk Walter has pointed out, it is striking that 'in public comments on the rioting little significance was paid to the role played by anti-Semitism in the street fighting'.[48] If Berlin's journalists were aware of the militant anti-Semitism of the NSDAP, they certainly downplayed its importance.

The very next day the leadership of the NSDAP in Berlin issued a statement in which it simply played dumb, claiming that the riots in the city centre were the result, above all, of nervousness on the part of the police who 'for no good reason' had erected stupid barricades around the Reichstag and attacked the crowds with their rubber truncheons. It was only natural, the writer went on, that there had been National Socialists present as they wanted to salute their leader, Gauleiter Goebbels. The resultant riots

> had as little to do with the National Socialist German Workers' Party as with any other party. As a result, they were as much of a surprise to the political leaders of the NSDAP and the leaders of the SA as they were to the public at large. In our own opinion, they must be seen as a spontaneous expression of anger on the part of thousands of people and should also be attributed in part to carefully prepared acts of provocation by Communist elements. Among the crowd, it was possible to identify several well-known anti-Fascists, who were seen to egg on the crowd artificially by shouting National Socialist slogans.

Other bystanders who were not party members had also seen 'Communist hooligans urging the crowd to attack the police'.[49]

Paying Lip-Service to Non-Violence

Immediately before the Reichstag met for the first time, Hitler himself had addressed the NSDAP deputies in one of the assembly rooms in the Rheingold wine bar just off the Potsdamer Platz.[50] For him, the riots were by no means welcome for they were bound to raise or even confirm doubts about his claim that he was determined to remain within the confines of the law. In consequence, the account of the rioting that he gave to a reporter from a foreign news agency in an interview conducted on 14 October differs substantially from that of the party leaders in Berlin. According to Hitler, the smashing of shop windows on 13 October was no 'spontaneous expression of anger', as they were claiming. Above all, he was bound to be keen to condemn the intentional disregard for private property as a criminal activity and to distance himself from it in the name of the NSDAP. In his words, the attacks were carried out 'for the most part by hooligans, shoplifters, looters[51] and Communist agents provocateurs. These people have nothing in common with our movement. We reject every use of force with the exception of the God-given right to defend ourselves. We do not need to use violence, as our movement will triumph without it.'

After Hitler had declared the NSDAP a more or less peace-loving party, he had to find some explanation for the undeniable fact that among the people arrested by the police were many of his own party members. He therefore divided the previous day's riots into two distinct parts:

> The first part was an innocent demonstration outside the Reichstag, when the police, exceptionally nervous, provoked the crowd, whereas in other countries people would have been allowed to go about their business in an open-air park. It was here that all the National Socialists who were arrested were taken into custody. But a clear distinction must be drawn between these events and the ones that took place in the Leipziger Straße. So far the police have not been able to give us a single name of a National Socialist involved in smashing the shop windows there. We know that none was present because no one who is a part of our movement and who has grasped its underlying idea would be capable of such an act. If a National Socialist were proved to have done such a thing, he would be thrown out of the party within ten minutes.[52]

Hitler's explanation was in flagrant denial of the party's history, above all the history of the SA, whose appeal lay not least in the deliberate and systematic use of violence. True, the party and the SA had admitted to the use of force in exceptional cases, when they had portrayed such actions as acts of self-defence in the face of 'terror' organized by their political opponents. In Hitler's eyes the mere existence of organized 'Marxism' and 'Bolshevism' in the guise of the Red

Front Fighters' League and both its successor and the Reichsbanner represented a permanent threat to the 'body of the German people', with the result that the NSDAP and SA were in a perpetual state of emergency. But the events that unfolded in Berlin on 13 October 1930 forced Hitler to twist his own line of argument with regard to that part of the 'nationalist camp' that still had to be won over: after all, the attacks had clearly not been directed against parts of the organized workers' movement. Hitler could not simply play down the significance of the riots or pass them off as an act of self-defence because to have done so would have left his middle-class audience profoundly unsettled.

But almost immediately Hitler had even greater difficulty explaining away a strike by Berlin's metalworkers, some 126,000 of whom downed tools in the second half of October over a wage dispute. Writing in the *Illustrierter Beobachter*, Hitler carried off the feat of simultaneously condemning lower wages as 'destroying the strength of the body of the people' and arguing that from an economic point of view any strike at the present time could 'only end badly'. The NSDAP, he went on, had to fight on two fronts:

> It has to stand up for the worker as far as possible by defending his justified and practicable demands, but it must also be honest and teach him what ultimately may destroy him rather than raise him up. Above all, it must stigmatize those criminals who are to blame for the worker's present misery – the Marxists who are cheating the people![53]

In the light of Hitler's vacillation, it is hardly surprising that the NSDAP had difficulty gaining support among Berlin's industrial workers.

In a second interview – this time given to the Berlin correspondent of *The Times*, Stanley Simpson, who spoke to the NSDAP leader at the Hotel Sanssouci[54] – Hitler assured his interviewer that the NSDAP was a 'strictly disciplined movement' and that it

> discountenanced violent anti-Semitism. Herr Hitler would have nothing to do with pogroms, and that was the first word that had always gone forth from him in turbulent times. Their doctrine was 'Germany for the Germans', and their attitude towards Jews was governed by the attitude of Jews towards this doctrine. They had nothing against decent Jews, but if Jews associated themselves with Bolshevism, as many unfortunately did, they must be regarded as enemies. The party was against all violence, but, if attacked, it was ready to defend itself.[55]

Hitler's determination to play down the party's anti-Semitism as part of his movement's commitment to remaining within the law was not without its risks, as it prevented him from protecting the SA and forced him to ascribe its anti-Semitic excesses to self-defence. In this way he confirmed the view of those members of the SA who had for some time been accusing him of undue subservience to the parliamentary system and even of abandoning the National Socialists' 'revolutionary' goals. But in order to distance himself from the reproach that he was attacking middle-class property values, he was obliged either to criminalize the riots or to lay the blame for them at his opponents' door.

In this he was supported in the most perfidious way by the German nationalist press. The *Berliner Lokal-Anzeiger*, for example, did everything in its power to encourage the belief that the rioting was caused by 'Communist agents provocateurs', even providing its readers with a particularly entertaining demonstration of the 'proof' of its remarks: when the local chief of police, Karl Friedrich Zörgiebel, emphasized in an interview that 'the only firms to be attacked were those that the rioters believed were Jewish', this was by no means remarkable but merely reflected the fact that people were 'trying to blame the National Socialists for the riots': 'If this was the aim of the exercise, it is understandable that the agents provocateurs went looking for businesses that they believed to be Jewish.'[56]

Another writer who embarked on a damage-limitation exercise was the aforementioned Friedrich Hussong – the chief commentator of the Hugenberg press and, as such, the German nationalist counterpart of Theodor Wolff, who was the liberal editor-in-chief of the *Berliner Tageblatt*. The police reports, he insisted, were contradictory and failed to support the suggestion that 'the rioting and stone-throwing that had broken out and died down again with singular speed were anything other than the messy exploitation of a tense situation by hooligans spoiling for a fight'. Hussong then tried to turn the tables by attacking the 'impudence and willingness to jump to overhasty conclusions of democratic journalists'. (For Hussong and his like, the word 'democratic' was a term of abuse.) The proceedings on the opening day of the Reichstag's new session were in any case yet further proof, in Hussong's eyes, of 'moribund parliamentarianism' with its 'unfruitful, negative and whimsical tendency to indulge in the sort of aimless self-mockery that is a sign of national decline'.

Hussong's leading article is a good example of the insidious change in tone that became apparent in nationalist writers in Germany, whose views mutated from secret sympathy for the 'Hitler movement' to barely concealed admiration for its seemingly unstoppable triumphal march at this time:

It was with a fixed smile that the democrats of all persuasions observed the Brownshirts with their swastika armbands who have added this decisive feature to the face of the new Reichstag. When these Brownshirts entered the chamber in closed formation, the Social Democrats were seen to make a few failed attempts at enforced joviality. But these attempts were quickly stifled by the ever-growing brown sea that overwhelmed the right-hand side of the chamber. Yes, the Reichstag now has a new face.[57]

Now the National Socialists needed only to choose an object for their attacks that would allow any remaining German nationalists to identify with the conceptual thrust of a National Socialist 'propaganda of action'. When that happened, the NSDAP would be able to extend its organizational superiority to the point at which it could sway opinion within the right-wing camp.

Thomas Mann in the Right Wing's Line of Fire

By 17 October 1930 – only days after the riots accompanying the reopening of the Reichstag – the extent to which the 'nationalist press' concurred with the slogans of National Socialism had become even clearer. This was the day on which Thomas Mann, who had received the Nobel Prize for Literature only ten months earlier, gave a speech in Berlin's Beethoven Hall[58] that was published shortly afterwards under the title 'German Address: An Appeal to Reason'.[59] The fact that Mann had chosen the occasion of the recent Reichstag elections to inveigh against the policies and ideology of the National Socialists was in itself sufficient to cause a stir, but even more sensational was the admission of his conviction that 'the political place of the German bourgeoisie' was now 'on the side of social democracy'.[60] In conservative and nationalist circles, this was bound to sound like a declaration of war.

As was only to be predicted, Mann's enemies fell back on crude polemics, the tone of which was all too typical of the brutalization of the whole of the right-leaning camp. None the less, it was still possible to discern occasional differences in responses to the speech, for whereas *Der Angriff* made no secret of its anti-Semitic views, heading its article 'Thomas Mann with the Jews',[61] Hugenberg's *Berliner Lokal-Anzeiger* spoke of an audience 'with the character-istic qualities familiar from Piscator's productions', a slyly and cryptically coded image that made sense only to the initiated. The paper described Mann's lecture as a 'public act of intellectual and political suicide' and claimed that, 'in terms of its expression and ideas', the text had been 'intolerably stilted, mannered and elitist'. Above all, it was an utterly failed attempt to characterize

National Socialism. Whereas *Der Angriff* sought to trivialize the attempts by right-wing members of the audience to disrupt the meeting ('But the good Germans who had wandered into the lecture by accident booed Thomas Mann to their heart's content'),[62] Hugenberg's paid hack had no hesitation in issuing an unconcealed threat to those members of the audience who had applauded the speaker and evicted hecklers such as the writer Arnolt Bronnen: since the 'brazenness of the Berlin rabble' was growing to a remarkable degree, it would henceforth be 'necessary to find a suitable occasion to remind people of the intolerance that was shown yesterday in so uninhibited a way'.[63]

It could almost have been Goebbels who wrote these lines. Indeed, there seems to have been an almost deliberate attempt to outdo him on the part of Curt Hotzel, who, writing in the *Deutsche Tageszeitung* – another newspaper with German nationalist views – summed up the day's events:

> It is with envy and hatred that this type of person [Thomas Mann and other leading Social Democrats] looks upon the impassioned storms that rage creatively in young Germany's soul, inspiring a sense of self-sacrifice in those souls and drawing the best and bloodiest from the ranks of the unspoilt labourers – in all likelihood the grandsons of peasants – before sweeping them away to a time of new and tremendous departures.[64]

Almost a quarter of a century later Arnolt Bronnen published his memoirs, in which he sought to play down the significance of the events in the Beethoven Hall and turn them into a basically harmless affair. Bronnen had once been a friend and colleague of Bertolt Brecht (hence his preference for the spelling 'Arnolt') and had come to be regarded as one of the leading nationalist writers on the strength of historical novels such as *O. S.* (1929) and *Roßbach* (1930) which glorified the Freikorps fighters of the early post-war period. He and a number of other right-wing writers, including Ernst Jünger, had apparently arranged to attend the lecture in order to 'start a debate'. But without his knowledge Goebbels had dispatched twenty members of the SA to the hall. Unfortunately, Bronnen went on, he had been unable to countermand Goebbels' orders as the party leadership had bought the tickets and 'hired twenty dinner jackets for the twenty members of the SA on payment of a deposit'. Disorder had broken out in the hall in response to 'a few brief interjections' and a mere 'Oho!' from Bronnen and his colleagues, at which point the police had escorted him from the hall but later allowed him to return. There the disturbances had continued ('everyone was shouting at the same time'), the only people to remain silent being Mann himself and the twenty members of the SA, who had been afraid to get their hired dinner jackets dirty 'as it had been borne in upon them by means of dire threats that their involvement was not to be physical'.[65] Goebbels' diary entry following the event was as brief as it was unequivocal: 'Our men spat on Thomas Mann's head'.[66]

Goebbels under Pressure to Succeed

Although the disturbances that had accompanied Thomas Mann's lecture in Berlin may have generated a few more headlines, they could hardly be regarded as a major factor in the mobilization of the NSDAP as they met with little interest outside intellectual circles and were scarcely calculated to generate strong feelings in a mass audience. In spite of this, Bronnen later claimed that, as a result of the Thomas Mann scandal, Goebbels had 'had a taste of blood and realized that this kind of cultural war could be used as propaganda'. And Bronnen believed that Goebbels 'thought his time had come' when, six weeks later, the film *All Quiet on the Western Front* – based on Erich Maria Remarque's successful anti-war novel of the same name – was shown at the Mozart Room on the Nollendorfplatz in Schöneberg: 'I was to work with him not only on disrupting the performance but also on preventing it and subsequent performances from going ahead.' With his usual tendency to trivialize events, Bronnen claims that he refused to do so because the whole affair was 'much ado about nothing – no one knew what was involved, having heard of neither Remarque nor the film'.[67]

Conversely, if we may believe Goebbels' diary, the opposite was the case, Bronnen being held up as the instigator of the planned action. By now Bronnen was in any case serving increasingly as the Gauleiter's close friend and adviser. It was for Goebbels, for example, that he came up with the idea of a 'political spectacle' in the form of a piece that he would co-author with Goebbels. The two men also went to the cinema together and on the eve of the proposed attack on Remarque's film they spent a convivial evening in the company of guests from outside Berlin and a number of NSDAP deputies whom Goebbels described as his 'raiding party', presumably because he was planning to exploit their parliamentary immunity.[68]

Goebbels needed his 'raiding party' as he was hoping to mount a coup. By early December 1930 he was in desperate need of a success on the most spectacular possible scale. The National Socialists' deputies had met in Berlin on 3 December, when they had again been addressed by Hitler at the Rheingold wine bar and had agreed to abide by the NSDAP's tactical and political guidelines as defined by Hitler himself.[69] The following day he spoke at a meeting of the National Socialist German Students' Association in the main room at the Neue Welt restaurant on the edge of the Hasenheide in Neukölln. According to *Der Angriff*, more than five thousand students from the University of Berlin and the Technical University were present to hear Hitler speak on the subject of 'The Way of the New Germany and the Challenges Faced by Young Students'. As usual, he scrupulously avoided all the burning political issues of the day but used empty phrases such as 'idealism must necessarily triumph over materialism', complained about the 'lack of a sense of community', demanded that the opposition between bourgeois and proletarian members of society be overcome and prophesied that his new 'heroic ideas' would be implemented, allowing everyone – peasants, students and workers – to say: 'We are a nation. The eternal bond of the blood that we have in common will enfold us.'

The more perspicacious members of Hitler's audience might have noticed the implications of his prophecy concerning the nation's future rise: 'Our nation must apply all its reserves to resisting other nations, but it is not with the best economic theory and good-quality products that a nation asserts itself but only if it is ready to lay down its life in the most tremendous way imaginable. Ultimately it is always the sword that decides.' Hitler ended by appealing to the young students to find their 'way to the German worker'. It was terrible to read newspapers reporting on the election results of the NSDAP and writing: 'Victory of the bourgeois right! No, no and no again: German victory!' According to the *Völkischer Beobachter*, loud cheering broke out at this point, and five thousand students showed the Führer that they wished to distance themselves from the bourgeoisie and to be 'only Germans, nothing but Germans and comrades of their fellow workers in the factories'.[70] In the audience this particular evening and cheering Hitler with the best of them was a twenty-five-year-old assistant lecturer at the Technical University, Albert Speer. According to his later reminiscences, it was his students who encouraged him to attend the meeting, which he claimed was his 'initiation' into National Socialism, although the truth of the matter is that he had been a sympathizer for some time.[71]

Goebbels, who for years had been familiar with the set-pieces that made up Hitler's speeches, thought that his superior had not given of his best but had seemed 'very tired'. During the morning Hitler had showered Goebbels with reproaches ('lengthy argument with the Chief').[72] Goebbels was also uneasy about the position of the SA in Berlin, a situation that now struck him as more serious than he had previously believed. The case was similar to the one that had developed some months earlier, leading to a clash of ideologies and weakening Goebbels' position vis-à-vis Hitler and the other party leaders. On that occasion, too, Goebbels had felt that 'the rulers of the SA are right to oppose the scandalous pigsty in Munich. Hitler is surrounded by all the wrong people. He needs to be freed from his petty bourgeois cronies.' On the other hand, he had misgivings about Stennes' plans to deal with the 'oligarchy of bigwigs' in Munich. At the same time he also saw this as a pretext, for in the background lurked a 'Stennes Freikorps'.[73]

Ever since the time of the 'Stennes Mutiny', Goebbels had been treated with a certain reserve. A new crisis with the SA was expected to flare up at any time. And he, Goebbels, was isolated in the Reichstag ('It seems that they are trying to exclude me from the parliamentary party').[74] Against this background, Goebbels had somehow to enhance his own reputation and regain Hitler's acceptance of him, while at the same time temporarily reducing the SA's need for aggression and weakening the position of the SPD-led government in Prussia and, with it, that of the chief of police in Berlin. It is difficult to know if he realized that this aim could be achieved by launching a sustained and vicious attack on the Remarque film. Whatever the answer, we find him writing in his diary on 3 December 1930: 'On Friday [the 5th] we're off to the cinema to see *All Quiet on the Western Front*. We'll teach the eunuchs a lesson. I'm looking forward to it.'[75]

All Quiet on the Western Front as the Object of Right-Wing Hostility

Goebbels had read Remarque's novel over a three-day period in July 1929, six months after it was published. 'A vulgar, corrosive book' was how he described it. 'The wartime reminiscences of a conscript. Nothing more. In two years from now no one will be talking about this book. But it has had an effect on millions of hearts. It's contrived as a book. That's why it's so dangerous.' Two days later he returned to the attack: 'A wretched and tendentious sham. You notice that in the second part above all. None of us can be taken in by this book any longer.'[76] Goebbels was spectacularly wrong in his belief that the book would be forgotten within two years. Indeed, it was the commercial success of the novel and its impact on readers which meant that both the book and its author became so reviled by the nationalistic and militaristic right. It was almost certainly because of this widespread hostility to the book in right-wing circles that Goebbels was persuaded to act. The rioting on 13 and 17 October had clearly helped to bring the NSDAP's name to the attention of a wider public but it had failed to bring together the various groups that were not already affiliated to the party. If the NSDAP were now to launch a

campaign whose aims might attract right-wing support, the party would have
a chance of winning the backing of the whole of the right, becoming one of its
mouthpieces and ultimately uniting the entirety of the 'nationalist camp'
beneath its banner. If this really was Goebbels' strategic aim, then he was
finally abreast of the times.

On 6 December 1930 one of the smaller liberal newspapers in Berlin headed
its report on the previous evening's events 'Riot at Remarque Film'. The film
had opened on the 4th with a showing for invited guests only which had
passed off without incident:

> The second performance, which began at seven o'clock, was attended by a
> number of National Socialists, including several Reichstag deputies led by
> Dr Goebbels. Initially the showing passed off without trouble. But during the
> second act there is a sequence of scenes that have met with frequent criticism,
> and it was during these that the most tremendous noise broke out. The
> National Socialists threw stink bombs and at the same time released hundreds
> of white mice, while shouting 'Jews out!' and 'Germany, Awake!' There was
> the most indescribable pandemonium in the cinema and the performance
> was stopped, the lights turned back on in the auditorium and the large audi-
> ence fled to the sound of continual shouting from the National Socialists,
> leading to violent confrontations, jostling and fist fights.[77]

Goebbels' version of events reads as follows:

> Within ten minutes the cinema resembles a madhouse. The police are power-
> less. The embittered crowd takes out its anger on the Jews. The first break-
> through in the west. 'Jews out!' 'Hitler is standing at the gates!' The police
> sympathize with us. The Jews are small and ugly. The box office outside is
> under siege. Windowpanes are broken. Thousands of people enjoy the spec-
> tacle. The screening is abandoned, as is the next one. We have won. [. . .] The
> newspapers are full of our protest. But not even the B[erliner] T[ageblatt]
> dares to call us names. The nation is on our side. In short: victory![78]

It is worth noting that even in his own diary entries Goebbels stresses the anti-
Semitic aspect of the 'cinema war'[79] that he had started. The National Socialist
propaganda machine in Berlin, where Goebbels' position had dramatically
improved since 1 November 1930, when *Der Angriff* had started to appear
daily, was essentially anti-Jewish in outlook. Between 6 and 10 December *Der
Angriff* reported interminably on the 'mass protests' against the film, regaling

its readers with headlines such as 'German Frontline Soldiers against Perverse Jews', 'Unanimous Storm of Indignation at Sloppy Jewish Film', 'Impudence of Film Jews', 'Police Protect Profiteering American Film Jews', 'Protests against Shameful Jewish Film' and 'Jewish Press Demands Ban on Demonstrations'.[80]

It is striking that throughout the whole of the period under discussion Hitler did not make a single anti-Semitic remark in any of his speeches. As we have already observed, he stressed 'ideational values' and positive thinking in the speech that he gave to the National Socialist German Students' Association on 4 December, while referring only in the vaguest terms to 'inferior forces' and to 'bad elements that continue to eliminate peoples and destroy nations'. His only concession to the anti-Semites in his party occurs in a speech that he made the following day at an SS gathering in Munich, when he demanded that the NSDAP's political actions be dictated by the sort of principles 'for which Christ was born and for which he was persecuted and crucified by the Jews'.[81] Otherwise, the position that Hitler adopted was singularly free from the rabid anti-Semitism that was so symptomatic of Goebbels' propaganda in Berlin at this time.

Given the NSDAP's new position and its possible involvement in government, Hitler was evidently keen to cultivate the image of a statesman, so Goebbels, dividing up the party's workload, took over the role of the revolutionary agitator giving the street protesters their sense of political direction. A whole series of demonstrations took place in and around the Nollendorfplatz, the Wittenbergplatz, the Kurfürstendamm and what is now the Ernst-Reuter-Platz. Hailed by *Der Angriff* on 10 December as a 'vast parade on the part of a city conscious of its Germanic traditions', as a 'march-past by the battle-grey front' and as 'columns of men marching with iron tread', the marchers were initially made up essentially of the few thousand members of the SA and National Socialist students whom Goebbels had been able to deploy since the late 1920s whenever he needed to put on a show of military might. As a result, the demonstrations against *All Quiet on the Western Front* were what Goebbels termed a 'breakthrough in the west'. By this he meant not so much the extent of the western half of the city's political sympathy for the National Socialist movement, which had in any case been greater in the middle-class districts of Berlin than it had been in the working-class areas, as an increase in the threat level to 'Berlin W', the 'new west', with its disproportionately high number of Jews. Until now this 'Judaized' part of Berlin had been pilloried by Goebbels and Hitler only in their propaganda, whether in the form of speeches or newspaper articles. Now it was time to confront the 'Kurfürstendamm Jews' on their home turf, not only giving them the shock of their lives but demonstrating the extent to which the power of the National Socialists had already grown in Berlin.

In singling out Remarque's film as the object of their contumely, the National Socialists found a perfect target, and the *Neue Preußische Kreuz-Zeitung*, for example, expressed its support for their demonstrations against a film 'that poisons the nation' (7 December). In a similar vein to two of the German Nationalist deputies, Alfred Hugenberg and Ernst Oberfohren, who sent a telegram to President Hindenburg on 9 December complaining about it, the *Berliner Lokal-Anzeiger* spoke of a 'rabble-rousing film' that should be banned, a sentiment echoed by the *Deutsche Tageszeitung*, which dismissed *All Quiet on the Western Front* as a 'pseudo-war film', claiming in all seriousness that 'certain left-wing radicals' were using the 'isolated excesses to discredit the national demonstrations in the eyes of the general public' (9 December). But it was the journalist Adolf Stein who best summed up the mood of the 'nationalist united front' with his use of expressions such as 'grubby vulgarity', 'film propaganda for Ullstein's publishing house', 'it is enough to make one sick', 'journalistic scribblings' and 'a scandal'. Widely circulated in the form of syndicated reports made available to local newspapers, Stein's opinionated views reached the remotest corners of the German provinces.

Commenting on one of the demonstrations organized against the film, Stein noted:

Last Monday National Socialists, members of the Stahlhelm and German Nationalists assembled at Goebbels' bidding. He is a revolutionary by nature but, fortunately for us, he does not have Red credentials. [...] The columns of marchers are quickly formed and set off, marching in step. The battle hymn rings out, and a well-disciplined army of mostly young people, students and workers is on the move [...] 'Germany, Awake!' and 'Death to all Jews!' Windows are darkened far along the Kurfürstendamm and their roller blinds pulled down, the inhabitants overwhelmed by one wave of quaking anxiety after another. The battle song. A military march. Finally *Deutschland, Deutschland über alles*, ruling over everyone in the world! It can be heard several streets away. The strains merge together over the roofs of the great department stores. In the course of the orderly march the whole of Berlin W hears the singing. [...] Is this a shift in the fortunes of the world? The masses can feel dully that such a change is in the offing. The nation is starting to march.[82]

'Rumpelstiltskin' thought that there were 8,000–10,000 demonstrators, while Goebbels put the figure at 20,000–30,000. By the following demonstration on

9 December, he calculated that some 40,000 people had been on the move. 'This marks the start of the revolution,' he wrote on 9 December. By the next day he was convinced that 'tomorrow's showing will be cancelled. If it is, then we'll have won a victory that couldn't be greater. The N[ational] S[ocialist] tail is wagging the government dog.'[83] By 11 December 1930 the chairman of the German Board of Film Censors had announced that *All Quiet on the Western Front* risked 'jeopardizing Germany's standing and offending German sensibilities', with the result that the film could no longer be shown in Germany.[84] That same day Hitler gave a speech in which he made his first passing reference to the 'disgraceful film that pours scorn on German soldiers'.[85]

Goebbels was triumphant, and as usual he was unstinting in his self-praise: 'Congratulations are pouring in from all sides.' – 'The film has become an international sensation overnight. It's the talk of the continent. Great excitement in the international press. We are again at the centre of public interest.' – 'The Republic is furious at our victory over this film. [. . .] In the eyes of the general public it is we who are the stronger party.' And, above all: 'Spent a long time with Hitler. We are in total agreement. [. . .] My standing in Munich has grown immeasurably as a result of the Remarque affair.'[86] Now he again felt at his ease among the leaders of the SA: 'They are great lads. They just need to be properly handled. There are times when Munich has evidently failed to do this.'[87] Within months Goebbels was to be proved spectacularly wrong on this point. Moreover, although he had succeeded in increasing the NSDAP's appeal through his 'film war' and ensured that the party was now taken seriously by the rest of the nationalist camp, Hitler was far more preoccupied with the defeats in the Reichstag, where all the motions put forward by the various parties opposed to Brüning's government, including one proposed by the NSDAP on 6 December, were thrown out.[88] He was also attempting to ensure the involvement of the National Socialists in the formation of any new government.

In a leading article headed 'Remarque Film' and published in *Die Weltbühne*, Carl von Ossietzky drew up a balance sheet that was bound to be a bitter pill for the NSDAP's enemies to swallow. With the ban on the film, Fascism, he wrote, had won its first major victory since 14 September. 'Today Fascism has killed off a film, tomorrow it will be something different.' Berlin was still Communist and republican, but 'where is the Reichsbanner? Where are the young Socialists? Where are the Communists? The gentlemen in question are normally quickly on the scene, whenever it is a question of a confrontation using their applied faculties. But here it was a question of defending a breach in the wall of Fascism, which will spare none of them, none of them.'[89]

8

'He hates Berlin and loves Munich'

1931: THE CAPITAL AS THE BUTT OF RIDICULE AND VITUPERATION

'[T]he cities and the mentality associated with them determine and guide our political actions, and this big-city mentality is a disaster, poisoned and bestialized, as it is, by a thousand superficial impressions – cheap neon advertising, sham politics everywhere you look. Our nation has completely forgotten how to think along sober and matter-of-fact lines. The result is a hysterical mass of men and women.'
Hitler, speech at an NSDAP meeting in Weimar, 8 February 1931[1]

A New Offensive by the SA

It seemed as if the new year in Berlin was going to begin as 1930 had ended: with attacks by the SA. In December 1930 the SA had formed the active nucleus of the 'indignant nationalist masses' that Goebbels had succeeded in mobilizing over a period of several days, leading to the street riots that had resulted in the ban on all further screenings of *All Quiet on the Western Front*. Although the new year also brought with it 'a certain amount of annoyance' after two members of the Reichsbanner had been 'shot by some of our own men', Goebbels was able to put a positive gloss even on this, claiming that it made people respect them. It was others who started the terror; they were merely defending themselves.[2] Hitler struck a similar note only a short time afterwards in the course of a private conversation with an influential landowner and NSDAP sympathizer: 'I am waging a ruthless war on Marxism using all the means – even the most extreme ones – that the law allows us, including the right of self-defence, until this plague that is afflicting the German people has been fully and finally rooted out and exterminated.'[3]

Two days earlier, on 22 January, Goebbels had held an event in the Friedrichshain Rooms in the course of which the Berlin SA once again demonstrated what it understood in practice by the term 'self-defence to the point of annihilation'. According to the SA's official report of the occasion, the audience of five thousand had included more than a thousand Communists. The way in which the report is worded gives the game away:

> The Communists go on the offensive. And within seconds the SA are breathing down their necks. One of the longest and bloodiest indoor battles rages. All the furnishings – tables and chairs, mirrors and curtains – are destroyed, all the windows smashed. The fighting even extends to the toilets. The SA does a good job, and not even the three hundred policemen who storm the hall can prevent them from doing so. This attempt to terrorize us costs the Reds some sixty injuries of greater or lesser severity.[4]

Goebbels was both proud and delighted that the press reported at length on 'the sensation of our indoor battle. [. . .] Everyone is talking about us.'[5] This 'battle' in the Friedrichshain Rooms – a venue that Goebbels had already tried using in 1928 as part of his assault on the city's 'Red' East End[6] – was not an isolated incident but was part of 'an avalanche of National Socialist meetings designed to overwhelm every part of the country's capital', to quote from the official history of the SA in Berlin-Brandenburg.[7] This 'avalanche of meetings' was accompanied by additional attempts on the part of the SA to make inroads into the working-class areas of Berlin, an aim achieved not least through the systematic expansion of the organization's network of 'storm centres', the exact function of which is described at length in the aforementioned history:

> A 'storm centre' [*Sturmlokal*] is, as it were, a fortified position within the battle zone. It is the place on the frontline that allows our fighters to rest and which offers them protection against our enemies and provides us with a place of relaxation and refreshment after the toils of active service.
>
> Thanks to the storm troopers' evenings that are held here, these centres are at the very heart of the SA's duties. In consequence, they are also, in a figurative sense, a place where the spirit of the SA may be sustained, preserved and renewed. In these storm centres our menfolk can experience something that they almost invariably lack at home: a warm heart, a helping hand, an interest in them, and the harmony of feeling and thinking that exists within their community. They experience comradeship and, with it, a sense of home and a true zest for life.

The storm centre thus becomes the solid moral and material bulwark against the Communists and the forces of reaction. But this also places it on the front line. Thus the battle around the storm centres, the attacks on them, the attempts to storm and close them down are all worthy of being placed alongside the indoor battles and street fighting.[8]

Quite how this worked out in practice emerges from the following passage in the SA's official history:

> The new storm centre of Charlottenburg Company 33, Robert Reisig's Zur Altstadt at 20 Hebbelstraße, lies at the very heart of the working-class district of Alt-Charlottenburg, in the midst of those grey blocks of houses demarcated by the Sophie-Charlotten-Straße in the west, the Spandauer Straße in the north, the Berliner Straße in the east and the Bismarckstraße and Kaiserdamm in the south. Wretchedness and despair dwell here. And here the Red terror prevails. Furiously it beats against the new National Socialist bulwark. Not a day passes without attacks, without scuffles and stabbings, without bullets fired insidiously from dark ambuscades. But the company holds its ground. It sets up guard posts and goes on patrol, keeping the closest of eyes on its enemies and in that way being in a position to defeat each and every attack with bloody resolve. [...]
>
> Wednesday 28 January [1931]: In the evening six heavily armed Communists attack the storm centre of Charlottenburg Company 33. They are thrown out, one Red is stabbed in self-defence. [...]
>
> Saturday 31 January: [...] Around three in the morning the company commander sets off home with two comrades. Then, on the corner of the Hebbelstraße and Schloßstraße, they are attacked by some thirty Communists. [...] They are already encircled, blows are raining down on them, knives and pistols are flashing. In their dire situation, two comrades come to their assistance. Two Communists are injured, one of them shot.

While describing these instances of 'self-defence', the SA's official chronicle also made a point of mentioning the help that was afforded by their women-folk, including the landlady of the storm centre who had a 'magnificent' gift for 'hiding away under her counter certain forbidden objects belonging to the SA, swiftly concealing them beneath the bread bin or in the oven'. When haled before the courts, she had simply repeated the phrase: 'I can't divulge that.' Nor could the chronicler overlook the girls who in times of greatest danger – as they walked home after closing time, often with comrades but also on their own through these apparently quiet streets – were there for them. They strode along on the other side of the street in order to provide the necessary weapons when the time was ripe and to spirit those weapons away again immediately afterwards.[9]

The SA was clearly well prepared, and weapons were to hand. In this it was helped by the fact that the number of NSDAP sympathizers and supporters had grown considerably in the ranks of the local police. As early as the summer of 1925, during one of Hitler's visits to the capital, Rudolf Heß had referred to 'information received from our secret followers in the police force'.[10] Two years later the liberal press felt moved to complain about the commander-in-chief of the police inspectorate in Charlottenburg, Alfred von Majewski, who appeared to be indifferent to the National Socialist riots on the Kurfürstendamm: 'His political views are of no interest to us; but when he refuses to do his duty and intervene whenever radical right-wing elements are involved, then he should at least be transferred to a less responsible post'.[11]

On 12 March 1930 Goebbels recorded a conversation that he had had with a senior police officer who had told him 'some very interesting things about the police'. 'How many followers we already have in the force!' he noted contentedly in his diary.[12] Twelve months later, at a meeting of the Association of Republican Police Officers on 30 March 1931, fifty to sixty National Socialists, including police officers, announced their membership of the NSDAP by unleashing a brawl, in the course of which chairs and beer bottles were thrown.[13] The extent to which the NSDAP had gained support in the city's police force emerges from figures relating to the votes cast by members of the force living in police accommodation in the elections for the Reichstag on 14 September 1930. Although the SPD continued to be the dominant party in four divisions and in the police hospital, where they won 50 per cent of the votes, the NSDAP managed to win between 15 and 30 per cent of police votes.[14]

SA Violence in Hitler's Calculations

On 1 April 1931 the NSDAP's elected representatives declared their unwillingness 'to work any longer in a house that has sanctioned an organized breach of the constitution' and walked out of an institution widely reviled as 'the Young Parliament'.[15] Only a few days earlier, Goebbels had explained his interpretation of the term 'legality' at a full session of the house:

In the person of its leader, the National Socialist movement has expressed the view that it is legal. But what this means is that according to the constitution we are committed only to the legality of the means, not to the legality of the goal. We plan to seize power by legal means. But what we shall do with this power once we possess it is our own affair.[16]

This was not only a thinly veiled threat, it was also part of a propagandist high-wire act on the part of the NSDAP, the origins of which can be traced back to the early days of the SA.

By the time he came to write *Mein Kampf*, Hitler had settled on a systematic explanation of this political concept and its implementation in terms of party propaganda. One of the ways in which he achieved this aim was to head his final chapter 'The Right of Emergency Defence'. Looking back on the tense situation that had existed in 1923, he argued that the most important prerequisite for any successful political action on the part of the NSDAP and, indeed, of the whole of the nationalist camp was 'the elimination of the Marxist poison from our national body'. A 'truly national government' should have sought out and found the forces 'that were resolved to declare a war of annihilation on Marxism, and then given these forces free rein'. Time and again he had tried 'to make it clear, at least to the so-called national circles, what was now at stake' and had 'begged them to give free rein to Fate, and to give our movement an opportunity for a reckoning with Marxism; but I preached to deaf ears'.[17]

For Hitler, however, this opportunity to dispose of Marxism was by no means confined to the past but remained a part of his ongoing agenda: 'A Germany saved from these mortal enemies of her existence and her future would possess forces which the whole world could no longer have stifled. *On the day when Marxism is smashed in Germany, her fetters will in truth be broken forever*.'[18] Essentially, it was the SA that was to be used to 'smash' Marxism. But the SA could not be allowed to become involved in a war on two fronts, fighting both Marxism and the power of the state as embodied in the Reichswehr. As a result, it must have a strictly political, not a military, character. This, and this alone, was the essential lesson that Hitler had learnt from his failed putsch of November 1923.

Organizationally speaking, the function of the SA found expression in the SABE 1,[19] the first order that Hitler gave to the newly appointed head of the SA, Franz von Pfeffer, on 1 November 1926. His aim was not only to stress the SA's non-military, party-political character but also to define its task as being to serve as the main instrument in his 'war of annihilation against Marxism, together with all its organizations and the men who were pulling its strings'.[20] But as the NSDAP grew in political strength, the SA developed a far more aggressive profile, with the result that Hitler frequently found it difficult to explain away its function to the police and other state bodies, including the government and Reichswehr, to say nothing of his German nationalist allies and influential representatives from the world of industry and commerce. Throughout his attempts to win over the latter to his political aims, he repeatedly had to contend with open scepticism towards the SA and its apparently 'socialist elements'. Whenever the SA became embroiled in arguments with organizations representing the workers' movements, especially the KPD, it often seemed to outsiders as if it was merely fighting over the right to be seen as the true and legitimate voice of 'anti-capitalism'. Industrialists in particular feared that an organization perceived as 'revolutionary' might be used for aims other than the 'annihilation of Marxism'.

It was against this background, then, that Hitler tried by means of internal directives and public assurances to balance the conflicting interests of strict legality and the exceptional use of violence for reasons of self-defence. In a letter written to all the Gauleiters in April 1930, for example, we find him stressing the claim that ever since the reconstitution of the NSDAP he had been making every effort to 'clarify and demonstrate the non-military character of the party and especially of the SA'. Both he himself and the SA leadership had repeatedly drawn attention to 'the need to avoid all illegal actions, all illegal behaviour and every unlawful deed'.[21] He never tired of stating that every act of violence on the part of the SA was the result of simple self-defence or, at worst, an involuntary transgression of the bounds of self-defence. On the other hand, he had no choice but to concede that if the principal aim of the SA was to 'annihilate Marxism', then the organization needed to find a foothold in those places where Marxism was particularly deeply embedded – chiefly in the country's industrial centres. And to the extent that the Berlin of the Weimar Republic was the largest industrial centre between Paris and Moscow and inasmuch as it had for decades been the headquarters of the labour movement in Germany, the SA was condemned, as it were, to strike at the very heart of all the strongholds of the workers' movement using every means in its power.[22] And these means had to include more than electoral representation, for, as we have seen, the National Socialists had fared comparatively badly in the elections in the Communist quarters of the city.

In short, the political significance of the SA was particularly great in Berlin, where it served as a kind of 'pile-driver' against the 'Red districts'. It was here, accordingly, that the clashes in lecture halls and in the streets proved especially violent, with battles being fought over areas of control, above all in the vicinity of the 'storm centres'. According to one contemporary account, 'the SA troops are the "clenched fist of the movement". In other words, they carry the often violent political struggle into working-class areas, where the socialist workers' movement that is our enemy must be attacked, intimidated and driven back on its own ground'.[23] In turn this meant that the SA tended to take on a life of its own within the party, a tendency that was diametrically opposed to Hitler's ideas of its role. Time and again he was required to trivialize the acts of violence committed by the SA, which he did in speeches and newspaper articles, where there was never any risk of a rejoinder, but sooner or later he would be required to appear as a witness in court, where he would have to account for himself.

This is precisely what happened on 8 May 1931. Four members of SA Company 33 appeared at the Moabit District Court in Berlin, where they were accused of involvement in an armed attack on a KPD event in the Eden Dance Palace on 22 November 1930 and of shooting three Communists. Hitler was subpoenaed to appear as a witness, and the presiding judge initially gave him an opportunity to expatiate at length on the legitimacy of the NSDAP in the context of his explanation of the term 'raiding party'. Hitler stressed that he and his party 'emphatically' rejected the use of violence. The SA, he went on, had been formed with the aim of protecting the party from 'left-wing terror' and of representing it at propaganda rallies. Any attempt to gain power by circumventing the Weimar constitution was misguided, Hitler insisted, for it would mean that blood would be spilt. Although he had not created the constitution, which he did not regard as a good one, he would none the less pursue a legal course 'on the basis of the innermost conviction of the need for legality'.[24]

When Hitler declared that he had never even heard of SA Company 33, Hans Litten, representing the joint plaintiffs, interrupted him. Still only twenty-eight, Litten had been the legal representative of the Rote Hilfe Deutschlands (German Red Aid) since 1929. Hitler typically used Litten's questions to 'launch into elaborate political explanations', as the press later put it.[25] When Litten noticed this, he started to ask more concrete questions, making it impossible for Hitler to evade the issue and embark on flights of rhetorical fancy. Litten then confronted him with a series of quotations from one of Goebbels' pamphlets, leaving Hitler visibly shaken and reduced to giving evasive or formal answers, including making the claim that the pamphlet in question did not bear the party insignia and had 'not been officially sanctioned by the party'. When asked if Goebbels had been Gauleiter in Berlin since 1926, Hitler replied that he could not be certain of the date.[26]

When Litten insisted that the pamphlet must have been sanctioned by the party since it was on sale at all of Goebbels' meetings and available at all the party's bookshops, Hitler became so angry that he finally 'turned a bright red' and shouted at Litten: 'How is it, Herr Litten, that you can say this is an invitation to illegality? There is no proof of this explanation!' At this juncture, the judge helped Hitler out of his impasse by interrupting Litten and preventing any further questioning.[27]

By his own admission, Goebbels spent the entire day 'awaiting the outcome of Hitler's testimony with beating heart' and knowing only too well that Hitler's answer to Litten's questions contained a 'flaw' inasmuch as the pamphlet did indeed contain a 'compromising sentence'. Only when the two men met that evening did it suddenly occur to him that the sentence in question had been 'cut from the second expurgated edition'. 'This is a cause for celebration. Hitler literally dances for joy. With this we are proved right. Hitler and I will write a stiff letter to the court.'[28] Hitler never forgot this incident in the Eden Dance Palace case. Hans Litten was arrested in 1933 and spent the next five years being moved between prisons and labour camps before taking his own life in the Dachau concentration camp in 1938.[29]

The Failed Stennes Mutiny

Hitler was not used to having his torrent of words interrupted, still less to being asked awkward questions. As a result, the scenes in the court in Moabit became associated in his mind with a sense of deep humiliation. It was a feeling made worse by the fact that the court had also referred to the turmoil within the ranks of the Berlin SA in the weeks leading up to the trial. Only a little more than six months after the Stennes Revolt of the late summer of 1930, arguments within the SA had reached the point where a far more serious crisis was inevitable. The sense of euphoria that had gripped the SA following the party's triumphs in the Reichstag elections on 14 September had increasingly evaporated as it became ever clearer that Hitler was pursuing his policies chiefly through diplomatic manoeuvres, behind-the-scenes discussions and wheeling and dealing with the German Nationalists and the Stahlhelm. The NSDAP's demonstrative walkout from the Reichstag did little to alter this state of affairs.

A further source of annoyance was the fact that the party leaders were spending vast sums of money enlarging their central offices in Munich. In one of his diary entries Goebbels expresses his dismay that Hitler seemed to be so focused on redesigning the Palais Barlow, which the party had acquired in

1930, and turning it into his party headquarters or 'Brown House'. Indeed, he was afraid that as a result a 'new row' would break out in the Berlin SA.[30] A week later he recorded his local SA's profound antipathy 'to Munich' on the subject of 'tactics and legality'. Moreover, 'the party house alone is too small for the most powerful party in Germany'. In the wake of a lengthy discussion with Hitler on the political situation in general, Goebbels even noted that 'he is too soft for my taste, too keen to make compromises. Wants power in any circumstances, and wants it now'.[31] A diary entry of 28 March 1931 hints at the coming confrontation: 'Trouble brewing again in the SA. Stennes won't let up. But Munich, too, is making some serious mistakes. The party house will yet be our undoing'.[32]

Events followed hard on each other's heels. In Munich the SA's new chief of staff, Ernst Röhm, whom Hitler had summoned back from Bolivia and appointed to the post in early 1931, ordered Stennes and his people to be thrown out of the organization, but Stennes' men refused to recognize the order and occupied the Berlin offices of the NSDAP as well as the editorial offices of *Der Angriff*, which they briefly published themselves. On 2 April Stennes pilloried Hitler for his 'breach of faith', claiming that he had the trust of the SA officers under his command and that he had ordered the SA to assume control of the movement in the provinces of Mecklenburg, Pomerania, Brandenburg-Ostmark, Silesia and Berlin itself. The political leaders of the NSDAP in Munich, he went on, had turned their backs on the 'ideals' of the party, ideals for which thousands of the finest SA men would willingly have laid down their lives. The 'revolutionary momentum' of the SA had been compromised by 'bourgeois and liberal tendencies' on the part of the NSDAP's leaders, who were trying to turn the National Socialist 'fighting force' into a party indistinguishable from any other. 'Even the erection of the Brown House by the exit to a storm centre is typical of the irresponsibility that is already gaining ground.' Stennes ended his piece by attacking the party's acceptance of parliamentary customs and habits, its willingness to compromise and its desire for ministerial appointments.[33]

That same day Hitler authorized Goebbels to purge the Berlin party of all 'corrosive elements'.[34] Two days later he published a piece in the *Völkischer Beobachter* headed 'Adolf Hitler's Revenge on the Rebels', in which he justified his decision to expel Stennes and his followers from the party and indignantly rejected all criticism of the Brown House, which externally and internally would constitute a single act of homage to the movement's great fighting spirit. Hitler repeatedly referred to Stennes disparagingly as 'former police chief Stennes', who was said to be pursuing his vendetta against Hitler's authority by trying to stir up the most baleful opposing forces that had ever existed in the whole of German history: 'Using a subtle methodology, he plays off Berlin against Munich and Munich against Berlin, Prussian-ness against Bavaria and vice versa. But Herr Stennes must know better than anyone that Prussian-ness is not a geographical but a moral concept. [...] The Prussians of today's Germany are the National Socialists, no matter where they may be.' And Hitler ended by repeating his insistence on pursuing a legitimate course and by demanding: 'Away with the traitors!'[35]

As a result of the rigorous countermeasures undertaken by Hitler, the Stennes Mutiny collapsed within a matter of days. By 3 April Stennes' supporters had been forcibly removed from the rooms that they had occupied after the party headquarters in Munich had placed an official request with the Berlin police to intervene. Within weeks Stennes' group was reduced to around two thousand members, and although they joined the Straßer group in early June 1931 to form the Fighting Community of Revolutionary National Socialists, the resultant organization was quickly condemned to little more than a sectarian existence.[36] The vast majority of SA members, especially in Berlin, were not to be swayed by any battle for hearts and minds: most of them simply had no interest in programmatical statements and complicated arguments. 'The crucial point about the SA's view of the world', Peter H. Merkl has aptly summed up the situation, 'was usually its disjunctive pursuit of the idolatrous cult of Hitler and its violent loathing of the "Marxist enemy".'[37]

There are few texts that provide us with a more striking expression of this idolatrous cult of Hitler, as found in the SA and NSDAP in Berlin, than the one that introduces the collection of articles originally published in *Der Angriff* and reprinted in book form under the title *Der kesse Orje* (Cheeky Orje) in 1931, with a preface by none other than Goebbels himself. Like all of the satirical Orje texts, 'Our Führer: A Sermon of Mine' is written in a rather stilted Berlin dialect intended to point up the links between the National Socialists and 'ordinary folk'. Orje is evidently a somewhat older SA man who learnt his love of march music and uniforms under the Kaiser but whose narrowly nationalistic views find their truest expression only when the Führer speaks. For the Führer brings out something very special in Orje, a hitherto hidden longing for a quasi-religious sense of fulfilment achieved through politics:

When you know that our Führer is coming, the mood is solemn and expectant, just as it is before Holy Communion. Although you know that you can expect something great and powerful and beautiful, you still don't know exactly what it will be like. You hear people saying lots of things about it, but it is all so mysteriously vague that you know only that it is bound to grab you by the heartstrings.

Yes, it's just like Holy Communion: when you hear the Word, it puts you in the mood. In our case you need only to say 'Hitler' and you already feel that you have to salute him. It gives you a jolt. Something great stands before us.

'Hitler' – you think of granite, of something hard, something unshakeable. With a name like that we know that here is a man, a hero, a leader.

'A man?' someone asks. 'Why emphasize that?' 'Yes,' I say, 'a man who follows such a straight course is rare indeed. And he's so strong and bold that his word of honour is enough, without any other epithet: a man!'

And a hero? Yes, indeed. Someone who on his own puts forward a new idea, imposing it on millions, fighting for it, suffering and bleeding bloody wounds for it, without ever recoiling – that man is a hero. For only a hero fights on his own against the great mass of humanity until he wins through.

And a leader? If 100,000 men are ready to die for a single person, then he is a leader. There's no more to be said on the subject. But that's already enough.

And so: when we hear that our leader Adolf Hitler is coming, then we know that something great is about to happen, and the mood is like the one before Holy Communion. And when he speaks to us, it means more to us than when the Kaiser used to speak to us.

What used to happen back then? Music, cheering, hats thrown in the air, 'To my people', and then you went home, you'd seen something nice, military orders and uniforms, it was all very nice, but you then went to bed without giving it any further thought. It was undoubtedly the Kaiser, but it wasn't your Kaiser, it wasn't our Kaiser, it was something alien, something you listened to and looked at. You felt nothing. But when our Hitler speaks, it's very different.

You know you come from the people, and so does your leader. What he says is felt by everyone. You don't shout 'Heil' because everyone else is shouting 'Heil' but because you have to, because it feels so good, so truly great to have a man standing there who wants to save you and your people. Because you realize that he can because he wants to and because he is honest. You're overcome with enthusiasm and at the same time moved.

If your leader is here now, it is not by chance or because Daddy's loaded or because of anything else. No, he has come from the same place that you have, from the people, and he now speaks to you and is so great that he simply has to be your leader.

This is our Hitler. And since there is no one who can compare with him, we are proud of him. We are no Byzantines, as they say of idolaters, for we don't need to be – we serve him willingly and because a man like Adolf Hitler cannot be idolized, he is revered.

If a stranger is unwilling to recognize our leader, we grow impatient, for there's nothing we wouldn't do for our leader. There's no alternative.

There, I've got myself all worked up again, but when our leader comes and speaks to us, then that is the best sermon for me.[38]

For this kind of SA man, the mere idea of rebelling against Hitler and joining Stennes for political reasons would have been tantamount to apostasy: as a course of action, it was simply inconceivable to the majority of members of the Berlin SA. This also explains why the repeated attempts on the part of the KPD to appeal to what it regarded as the misdirected 'proletarian class instincts' of the SA were doomed to fail.

The Kaiserhof – Hitler's New Headquarters in Berlin

But it was not only the appeal to the 'class consciousness' of the simple members of the SA that found them unresponsive. Equally unsuccessful were the attempts of republican journalists and various politicians to uncover concrete evidence of the rift that separated the image that Hitler presented to the public gaze from his actual lifestyle and to prove by rational means that he was violating the proclaimed principles of a modest way of life and in that way to discredit him in the eyes of his own supporters. Perhaps the most eloquent example of this is the campaign waged by the republican Berlin weekly *Die Welt am Montag* in its effort to discover the true cost of Hitler's visits to the capital.

With effect from February 1931 Hitler no longer stayed at the Hotel Sanssouci on the Potsdamer Platz but at the Kaiserhof, an elegant establishment situated at 1–5 Mohrenstraße on the Zietenplatz in the immediate vicinity of the Wilhelmplatz and much frequented by diplomats.[39] Hitler was now the leader of the second most powerful party in Germany and no doubt felt that it was beneath his dignity to put up at the second-rate Sanssouci, with its limited facilities, when he met the country's other leaders or gave interviews to foreign journalists. His decision may also have been influenced by the fact that the Kaiserhof had been one of those hotels that flaunted their anti-republican views in August 1927 on the Day of the Constitution, when the hotel management had refused to fly the black, red and gold flag of the Weimar

Republic.[40] Above all, however, the Kaiserhof was situated diagonally opposite the Chancellery and the residence of the country's president, a location symbolic of the fact that, in taking up a position so close to the heart of the government district on the Wilhelmstraße, Hitler was preparing an onslaught on the very centre of power. His chief press officer, Otto Dietrich, later described this move as follows:

> The name of his hotel on the Wilhelmsplatz in Berlin remains closely associated with the history of the NSDAP and with its decisive battle for power. Every child knows that it was here that the Führer set up his headquarters in recent years each time that he was invited to the capital to discuss important questions with the country's leading figures. [. . .] Why did the Führer choose this hotel as his workplace? In itself, the atmosphere of such a place meant little to us and still less to the Führer himself. It was entirely for reasons of expediency that he made this choice.
>
> At this point in the struggle, the Führer owed it to the movement to take account of the mentality of his negotiating partners and adapt his approach to their own psychological attitude. In this sense the Kaiserhof was a 'prestigious' venue.
>
> Another important reason, however, was the Kaiserhof's symbolic position in illustrating the ideological battle being fought between two opposing views: the ultimate struggle between the new Germany and a system that was on its last legs. From his office, Adolf Hitler could look out across the Wilhelmsplatz at the old Chancellery building in which the countermines were laid and where, insidiously and maliciously, the occupants brooded on ways of preventing the onrushing movement from gaining power.
>
> The terrified cry of 'Hannibal ante portas' that once brought fear and terror to Rome was repeated here in a figurative sense the moment that Adolf Hitler entered the Kaiserhof. Even the outward picture of the way in which the negotiations unfolded revealed an obvious parallel. Adolf Hitler stood at the gates – not of Berlin, for he had long since conquered the city's heart. Rather, he laid siege to the gate of the house from which Bismarck had ruled the German Reich in order to take possession of it in turn.[41]

Dietrich was belatedly attempting to counter the 'infamous witch-hunt' by the 'establishment press' following Hitler's choice of this hotel as his headquarters. Accordingly, he stressed the fact that Hitler's visits to the capital were all related to his work and that the hotel rooms were correspondingly functional:

During his time in this building the Führer rarely left his office on the upper floor in the rearmost corner of the long corridor, and when he did emerge, it was to go downstairs to the round table in the corner on the right that was reserved for him and for his companions and his visitors. Normally he remained in his first-floor rooms, where he generally took his meals. In his reception room, he would hold one meeting after another until late at night. In the antechamber the telephone never stopped ringing. Calls came in incessantly from all over the world. Such was the rate at which we worked that we often forgot about mealtimes and on many occasions ate nothing all day. Although we were in Berlin, we saw nothing at all of the city. There were times when we did not leave this stone colossus all week.[42]

The same picture emerges from a report in a popular illustrated magazine in January 1932: here, too, Hitler is portrayed as a hard-working party leader, dictating letters and receiving innumerable visitors. No doubt journalists were admitted to the hotel only on condition that they peddled this version of events.[43]

Dietrich himself mentions that those journalists who were hostile to the NSDAP in Berlin regularly used the phrase 'the workers' leader in a luxury hotel' when complaining about Hitler's lifestyle in the city. And there was some truth in the accusation. In the spring of 1932 *Die Welt am Montag* reproduced a hotel bill 'for the NSDAP for the attention of Adjutant Heß', accompanied by the headline 'This Is How Hitler Lives! An Invoice from the Kaiserhof!' The bill for a total of twelve rooms over a ten-day period, including breakfast, meals and beverages, came to 4,048 marks. (Telephone calls, linen and baths were charged separately.) The paper commented as follows on the story:

This document is no ordinary sensation. It throws a significant light on the contrast between the lifestyle of the leader of a 'workers' party' and the general poverty of our age. For weeks on end Herr Hitler and his closest staff live in the same luxury accommodation as that which, for reasons of prestige and at state expense, the government has offered to the country's most important visitors in recent years. The cost of one of these twelve rooms for a single night is the maximum that two unemployed persons can claim for an entire week's support. Little would be gained by comparing the price of daily breakfast – 2.30 marks – or a meal without wine – 5 marks – with the income of an unemployed man on income support. In the language of the *Völkischer Beobachter*, Herr Hitler's life at the Hotel Kaiserhof could be described as one of 'oriental extravagance'. Even within the ranks of his own supporters Herr Hitler has now forfeited the right to call himself the leader of a workers' party.[44]

Other workers' organizations, not to mention the whole of the republican and democratic press, used arguments such as these to appeal to the reason and moral sensibilities of supporters of the NSDAP and SA. But in doing so, they overlooked the fact that the idolatrous veneration felt for Hitler rendered those supporters immune to rational and moral objections. A demigod can do whatever he likes, including taking rooms at a luxury hotel with all the attendant comforts. With this kind of critique, *Die Welt am Montag* could reach out only to those readers who had not already succumbed to Hitler's appeal or who, like the small group of supporters of Stennes and Otto Straßer, were still relatively open to a critical and rational approach to social and political issues. If the critique were couched in the language of satire, the message would reach only a tiny handful of like-minded individuals. With hindsight we can only look on in helpless dismay at the many attempts by liberal and left-wing satirical journals in the early 1930s to ridicule Hitler through cartoons and caricatures.

Even so, Hitler was unable to dismiss incidents such as the Stennes Mutiny as simply harmless. The constant squabbles in the Berlin party organization and in the local SA found him at his most vulnerable for they effectively questioned his power and authority. As the national and government crisis worsened in 1931, it became increasingly necessary to rely on the SA as an instrument of menace and as a tool in any potential civil war. An SA that refused to obey its political leaders and that risked countermanding their instructions for tactical or more idiosyncratic reasons would discredit Hitler in the eyes of possible and actual supporters and allies – allies whose goodwill, or at least neutrality, was crucial if he was ever to come to power. The ongoing unrest and unreliability of the SA and its umbrella organization in Berlin was bound to be a source of considerable annoyance to him.

'Americanized and Lacking in Culture'

It is hard to assess the effect that these local crises had on Hitler's attitude to Berlin. When Goebbels – apparently – explained to him in a conversation that the party must be 'more Prussian, more active and more socialist', Hitler is said to have understood what he, Goebbels, meant but at the same time to have expressed 'tactical reservations'. In spite of these misgivings, he had promised that he would 'come to Berlin more often and give greater attention to the question of socialism', whatever that may have meant.[45] Only three weeks later, however, Goebbels again had occasion to note that Hitler was 'giving too little time to Berlin'. Worse, Goebbels then tried to explain that Hitler 'must throw his personal weight' behind Berlin 'more than he has done until now', only for him to realize that Hitler 'does not really want to do so: he hates Berlin and loves Munich. That's the crux of the matter. He refers to Potsdam, Washington and Angora [i.e. Ankara]. But why Munich? I don't get it.'[46]

Yet Goebbels must have noticed the extent to which Hitler's thoughts revolved around his plans to turn the Palais Barlow into the heart of the NSDAP's new party headquarters. When the Brown House was officially opened in February 1931, Hitler announced quite openly: 'What the movement needs is a home that must become as much a part of our tradition as the headquarters of the movement have become a part of our tradition.'[47] His references to 'small capitals' such as Washington and Ankara alongside major cities like New York and Istanbul that were not their country's capital evidently left Goebbels unimpressed, as did his remark that Frederick the Great preferred Potsdam to Berlin. But how was Goebbels to explain Hitler's 'hatred' of Berlin, when only six years earlier Rudolf Heß – a man undeniably close to the Führer – had been able to write: 'The bustle associated with the centre of the country is certainly impressive. And in its way I'm very fond of this magnificent city. The Tribune [Heß's term for Hitler] loves it to distraction!'[48]

How can we explain this emotional volte-face? Should we attribute it to Hitler's anger at the NSDAP's still relatively modest successes in Berlin and at the perpetual arguments with the local SA leaders, whose units remained difficult to control? Was it ultimately no more than a passing mood caused by his defeat in his courtroom duel with 'that shameless Red lawyer Litten' in the Eden Dance Palace trial? This would seem to be the conclusion to be drawn from a remark recorded by one of Hitler's close confidants at this time, Otto Wagener, when the NSDAP's Department for Economic Policy, which Wagener had built up from scratch, was moved to Berlin in the autumn of 1931. Not only was Hitler in full agreement with this move, Wagener later recalled, the Chief had even declared:

> We have to start putting in a more powerful appearance in Berlin. The more offices we have there attesting to the party's activities, the more people will talk about us and the more our political enemies will feel that the NSDAP is getting closer to the place of government. The choice of the Hotel Kaiserhof as my headquarters in Berlin, diagonally opposite the Chancellery building, has already left the men there profoundly shaken. And these impressions will also have an impact on the members of our own party.[49]

But the remark that Hitler made to Goebbels that convinced him that the Führer 'hated' Berlin is unlikely to have been a single thoughtless slip or the result of some passing annoyance. In short, it was not an irrational emotional response. The Italian consul in Munich, Capasso Torre, records Hitler making a further dismissive comment about Berlin during this same period. On 18 June 1931 Hitler told Torre that in Berlin he could never find the peace and quiet that he needed to work: it was a city without traditions, half Americanized and half lacking in culture.[50]

Why should Hitler have commented on what he saw as the unfavourable working conditions in Berlin? In what exactly did his work in the city consist? In order to answer this question, we need to examine the ninety-nine documents that have survived from the first six months of 1931 and that are reproduced in the complete critical edition of Hitler's speeches and writings.[51] With the exception of two witness statements in court and four interviews (excluding those with foreign newspapers and news agencies), these documents all show Hitler to have been a 'party worker' pure and simple: from his base in Munich, he guided the actions of the NSDAP and SA by means of ten letters, fifteen appeals and declarations and twenty-five orders. The nine articles that he wrote during these six months were all published by the party in its newspapers and other publications. He also appeared at twenty-four meetings of the NSDAP and SA – on average almost one such meeting a week. Half of these meetings took place in Munich. Throughout this period he appeared in public only twice in Berlin, once as a witness in court, on 8 May, and once as a speaker, on 19 May – hence Goebbels' request begging him to come to Berlin more often. But Hitler had no intention of acquiring a second home in the capital (instead, he stayed at a hotel), still less of having his own rooms in the Gau's offices,[52] where he would effectively have been Goebbels' tenant – an idea that Hitler could never seriously have entertained. Even after the NSDAP had become Germany's second most powerful party, he insisted on keeping its headquarters in Munich in spite of the fact that with the single exception of the Bavarian People's Party all the other important parties relocated to Berlin.[53]

In short, the inadequate working conditions that Hitler found in Berlin were entirely of his own imagining. In much the same way, his claim that the city had no traditions of its own is hard to explain, at least at first sight. At his public appearances in Berlin he had frequently spoken positively about Prussia and Prussian traditions. On one occasion he explicitly aligned himself with this tradition when, striking an emotionally bombastic note, he had declared: 'Perhaps fate has decreed that we should assume the role of a Friedrich Wilhelm I, which is to say that we must prepare the ground for someone who will come after us [Frederick the Great].'[54] And the only speech that Hitler gave in Berlin during the first half of 1931 was reprinted in *Der Angriff* under the title 'Prussian-ness and National Socialism'.[55] To a packed Sportpalast Hitler had declared:

> If the spirit of revolution had really asserted itself in 1918, the idea of Prussia as a moral state would have been lost without trace. Prussia is the cornerstone of Germany's development, the nub and nucleus of its racial being. National Socialism has once again taken up all that is best about the traditional idea of Prussia. It has drawn it up from the mud and morass into which it had been thrust down.[56]

If, by his own admission, the NSDAP had breathed new life into all that was great about Prussia, how was it possible for Hitler to describe its chief city, Berlin, as lacking in tradition? At least an indirect explanation may be found in his identification with the views of Frederick the Great as expressed in his comments to Goebbels. Here Hitler was thinking of Frederick's avowed dislike of Berlin, a 'vast official residence', in comparison to Potsdam.[57] Inasmuch as Hitler associated the Berlin of the Weimar Republic solely with its rejection of all that was great about Prussia and with its espousal of the degenerate culture of the modern day, it was only logical that he should describe the city as lacking a sense of tradition. Years later, he claimed that although Berlin still boasted all the monuments from the days of Frederick the Great, it was the city's misfortune that it was 'now colonized by people from Lower Saxony and Frisia who encompassed all manner of different elements but who had failed to produce the sort of soil on which a culture could flourish'. The last person to represent that culture as a living force was Friedrich Wilhelm IV (1795– 1861). Kaiser Wilhelm I had lacked taste, Bismarck had had no interest in the arts, and although Wilhelm II had had taste, it had been 'altogether bad'.[58] This view found its most extreme expression in early 1942, when he voiced his conviction that a quintessentially Prussian government architect could not be commissioned to redesign Berlin: 'If I want a genuine culture to be extended northwards and eastwards, I must begin by employing people from the south.'[59]

Hitler's characterization of Berlin as 'half Americanized' reflects a cliché among cultural conservatives of the 1920s, the term being used first and foremost to describe the rise of such varied forms of industrialized mass culture as an enthusiasm for sport, the cult of the film star and a fondness for light music and fashionable dances, all of which were regarded as symptoms of the way in which German culture was being swamped by foreign influences and falling into moral decline.[60] Hitler's endlessly dismissive references to jazz and jazz-inspired dance forms are only the most obvious expression of this attitude. On 8 November 1930, for example, we find him making a speech in which he voiced his high regard for German music, including German dance forms, but spoke disparagingly of 'Negro music', which he claimed was alien to the German character.[61] It was no accident, he declared on another occasion, that

> the achievements of today are insignificant when set alongside those of the past, when our nation was inspired to create things on the basis of its own essential nature. If we think that as American halfcastes we have to write American jazz music, our achievements will necessarily remain pitiful. We shall then be beaten by those who create this art from their innermost being. Ultimately, however, a German symphony is worth more than all the jazz music in the world.[62]

A Tactical Critique of the Big City

Throughout this period, remarks such as the foregoing are regularly associated in Hitler's speeches with dismissive references to big cities. He calls such cities 'excesses [!] on the body of the nation'. Their inhabitants are 'rootless' and 'unnerved' by the 'psychoses and neuroses' unleashed by the big city. People who move to the cities see 'only factories, chimneys, shops, neon signs, export and import, trade and commerce, international finance and international trade'.[63] Here Hitler picked up on ideas that he had already expressed in *Mein Kampf*, ideas that were part of a conservative cultural discourse that was critical of the 'impoverishment' of all contemporary art, especially architecture.

The first volume of *Mein Kampf* had appeared in July 1925 under the heading 'A Reckoning'. In its tenth chapter Hitler examines what he sees as the causes of the collapse of the Reich in November 1918,[64] beginning with a whole series of 'symptoms of decline' and 'signs of morbidity' that had already been visited upon the German nation in the years before the outbreak of the First World War.[65] Here Hitler typically uses medical metaphors in referring to 'toxins', 'pathogens' and 'diseases of the body of the nation',[66] before moving on to the world of business. In spite of the rapid population increase, the country had ignored the only correct solution to the problem – 'the acquisition of new soil' – and succumbed instead to the 'lunacy of world economic conquest', resulting in 'an industrialization as boundless as it was harmful' and in 'the weakening of the peasant class'. At the same time, the urban proletariat had continued to increase in size until 'finally the balance was completely upset'.

This 'economisation of the nation' led not only to discontent and bitterness but, worse, to 'the domination of money', which, sanctioned by the Kaiser,[67] meant that the entire economy had passed into the hands of public limited companies, resulting in the triumph of the stock market and 'greedy finance capital' in an unholy alliance with the 'Marxist movement' – and, hence, with social democracy.[68]

After expatiating on 'the gravediggers of the monarchy' at the court of Wilhelm II, on the 'mass-poisoning of the nation' by a press which, 'mainly of Jewish origin', was 'slowly ruining' the country',[69] on syphilis and tuberculosis and the 'infection and mammonisation of our love lives' – a point on which Hitler lingers at prurient length – and on the need for the sterilization of the incurably ill, Hitler finally comes to the question of culture. And here he has particularly harsh words for what he terms 'Art Bolshevism', for the 'decline of the theatre' and the tendency to 'besmirch and befoul the past'. His tirades culminate in the demand that German culture be purged of all its impurities: theatre, art, literature, the cinema, press, posters and window displays must be cleansed of the symptoms of a putrid world and placed in the service of a moral idea of the state and of culture.[70] It is entirely typical of Hitler's attempt to deal with Germany's cultural development that he ends his outburst with a devastating critique of present-day architecture and urban planning:

> In the nineteenth century our cities began more and more to lose the character of cultural sites and to descend to the level of mere human settlements. [...] This is partly connected with the frequent change of residence caused by social conditions, which do not give a man time to form a closer bond with the city, and another cause is to be found in the general cultural insignificance and poverty of our present-day cities *per se*. [...] No one will be particularly attached to a city which has nothing more to offer than every other, which lacks every individual note and in which everything has been carefully avoided which might even look like art or anything of the sort. [...] All our cities are living on the fame and treasures of the past. For instance, take from present-day Munich everything that was created under Ludwig I, and you will note with horror how poor the addition of significant artistic creations has been since that time. The same is true of Berlin and most other big cities.[71]

It is not surprising that Hitler names Munich and Berlin here. He knew Berlin's inner city from his two periods of army leave in autumn 1917 and autumn 1918, but above all from his frequent visits between 1920 and 1923; thanks to a remark that he made in 1933, we know that he regarded 'Unter den Linden, the Castle and its immediate vicinity' as the only points of significant architectural interest.[72] His fondness for the age of Ludwig I is clear from his praise of the Bavarian ruler in the second volume of *Mein Kampf*, which appeared at the end of 1926:

> By pushing Munich from the level of an insignificant provincial capital into the format of a great German art metropolis, he created a spiritual centre. [. . .] It is not the 'Down with Prussia' shouters that made Munich great; this city was given its importance by the King who in it wished to bestow upon the German nation an art treasure which would have to be seen and respected, and which was seen and respected.[73]

In Vienna, where Hitler spent his youth and early adulthood, he particularly admired the buildings on the Ringstraße: 'For hours I could stand in front of the Opera, for hours I could gaze at the Parliament; the whole Ring Boulevard seemed to me like an enchantment out of *The Thousand-and-One-Nights*.'[74] In much the same way, the part of Ludwig I's Munich that impressed him the most was Leo von Klenze's Königsplatz with its three monumental structures of the Glyptothek, the Propyläen (both designed by Klenze himself) and the Exhibition Hall (now the Museum of Antiquities, a building designed by Georg Friedrich Ziebland). When, in 1930, the opportunity arose for Hitler to acquire the neo-Classical Palais Barlow, situated in the Briennerstraße between the Königsplatz and the Karolinenplatz, he seized it with both hands, turning it into the party's Brown House in 1931 and creating a nucleus for all of the NSDAP's subsequent building activity in this particular part of the city.[75]

At the end of his speech in Weimar, Hitler had rounded off his indictment of city life by advocating a rejection of exports in favour of 'home-grown produce'. He then returned to the image of the 'big-city mentality': 'baleful, poisoned and bestialized, as it is, by a thousand superficial impressions – cheap neon advertising, sham politics everywhere you look.'[76] Between 13 and 18 October 1928 dozens of buildings in the centre of Berlin – not just public buildings but also privately owned department stores such as KaDeWe – had been floodlit as part of a series of events advertised as 'Berlin in the Light'.[77] Since then the use of light in architecture and the subject of neon advertising had proved an emotive topic in the city. Goebbels, too, had contributed to the discussion in the pages of his diary: 'Berlin in the light?! What kitsch!'[78] Hitler himself had always been interested in architecture and urban planning. He arrived in Berlin on 13 October[79] and must have witnessed the city's 'week of light' for himself. It is possible that he was already following the debate: after all, the possibility of using the front of business premises for night-time advertising had given rise to lively discussions not only in professional circles but among the wider public following Erich Mendelsohn's proposal to redesign Herpich's Furrier's in the Leipziger Straße between 1924 and 1928.

Of particular interest in this context is the city authorities' reason for initially rejecting Mendelsohn's design: it was said that the planned building, rising to a height of 100 feet, would impact on the street as a whole and impair 'the monumental impression of the public buildings in the vicinity'.[80] One novel aspect of the new design was the close link between architecture and advertising:

> At night, it was not only the name of the firm that was illuminated, the balustrades on the upper floors were also lit indirectly by lamps on the string courses. The city's mayor, Gustav Böß, initially refused to give planning permission for Mendelsohn's design, which was felt to be too progressive, but he finally agreed to it following protests from colleagues who supported the project.[81]

Illuminated advertisements in the form of superstructures on the roofs of shops and business premises had been known in Berlin since before the First World War, generally in the Potsdamer Platz, but this was the first time that they had been an integral part of a building's façade.[82] And now it was advertising that played a decisive role:

> Advertising signs dominate the city, both new and old buildings are fitted with large advertising hoardings, advertising signs light up the darkness, and everywhere there are advertising towers. Businesses attract their customers with lights in exactly the same way as cinemas, which are equally indebted to the world of dreams and backstage reality and which create their own worlds on façades and interior walls by using lighting effects.[83]

This systematic use of light to create an urban nightscape was inspired above all by American models, especially New York's 'Great White Way' along Broadway and around Times Square, where the theatres were lit up at night. It was Mendelsohn's 1926 monograph, *Amerika: Bilderbuch eines Architekten*, that helped to introduce German audiences to this new 'architecture of the night'.[84] His introduction to the volume includes a photograph of Times Square taken at night and captioned, significantly, 'Typically American'.[85]

Hitler's Attitude to Contemporary Architecture in Berlin

These experiments in the use of light were only one aspect of developments in architecture and urban planning that became known as the 'Neues Bauen' (new architecture) and that created something of a stir in Berlin from the middle of the 1920s. The term was initially applied to a trend found throughout Europe and referred to an avant-garde style that was not introduced to a wider, American audience until 1932, when the Museum of Modern Art in New York organized an exhibition under the title *The International Style: Architecture since 1922.*[86] In the light of all that we know about Hitler's interest in questions of design and his personal preference for the architecture of his youth,[87] it is easy to see why he would condemn current developments in architecture in Germany, especially in Berlin,[88] and why he would regard them as symptomatic of a process of 'Americanization' that was 'fundamentally alien to German culture'. In the debate over high-rise buildings, there was, after all, a widespread belief that specifically 'German solutions' must be found to the problem of contemporary architecture and that American trends must be resisted, a view held not only by conservative architects.[89] This attitude received quasi-official backing at the 1931 German Building Exhibition held in Berlin. In the accompanying catalogue, the senior building adviser on the city council, Walter Koeppen, declared that 'on no account do we want streets darkened by skyscrapers, as in America, we want no courtyards deprived of light and air and unprecedented traffic jams'.[90]

But Hitler's response to the architecture of his age was dictated by very different criteria. At the end of his philippic in *Mein Kampf*, in which he inveighs against the alleged cultural impoverishment, not to say the total lack of culture, of early twentieth-century German cities, he asks a number of basic questions about the role of architecture in our lives. It was his avowed conviction that public buildings were far more important than those erected by private individuals and private businesses, for they reflected the power of the state and the culture that it promoted. It was a sign of weakness and cultural decline, he believed, when a state like the Weimar Republic put up few new buildings in its capital – buildings, moreover, that were stylistically unadventurous. Monumental designs were an expression of strength in Hitler's eyes, while private buildings must remain understated in comparison. Architectural proportions should reflect the primacy of politics over commerce: the authority of the state must find expression in weighty architecture. The powerful gesture and architectural imperiousness had Hitler's unqualified support. And so we find him writing as follows in *Mein Kampf*:

Our big cities of today possess no monuments dominating the city picture which might somehow be regarded as the symbols of the whole epoch. That was true in the cities of antiquity. [. . .] The characteristic aspect of the ancient city did not lie in private buildings, but in the community monuments which seemed made, not for the moment, but for eternity. [. . .]

Only if we compare the dimensions of the ancient state structures with contemporary dwelling houses can we understand the overpowering sweep and force of this emphasis on the principle of giving first place to public works. [. . .]

Even the Germanic Middle Ages upheld the same guiding principle, though amid totally different conceptions of art. What in antiquity found its expression in the Acropolis or the Pantheon now cloaked itself in the forms of the Gothic Cathedral. [. . .]

Yet how truly deplorable the relation between state buildings and private buildings has become today! If the fate of Rome should strike Berlin, future generations would some day admire the department stores of a few Jews as the mightiest works of our era and the hotels of a few corporations as the characteristic expression of the culture of our times. Just compare the miserable discrepancy prevailing in a city like even Berlin between the structures of the Reich and those of finance and commerce. [. . .]

Thus, our cities of the present lack the outstanding symbol of national community which, we must therefore not be surprised to find, sees no symbol of itself in the cities. The inevitable result is a desolation whose practical effect is the total indifference of the big-city dweller to the destiny of his city.

This, too, is a sign of our declining culture and our general collapse. The epoch is stifling in the pettiest utilitarianism or better expressed in the service of money.[91]

This belief in the need 'to set political power in stone and bronze' and 'to create dominant centres for the community intended to express a political will to power and a political idea' was to be repeated in many of Hitler's public pronouncements during the years that followed. In a speech given at an NSDAP meeting in Munich on 3 April 1929, for example, he examined a whole series of instances from the Acropolis and the Ringstraße in Vienna to the 'truly magnificent example in Italy, where Fascism immortalizes forces in monumental works'. He also mentioned Berlin in this context:

And we can see the same in Berlin. The little principality of Brandenburg has tried to acquire the necessary prestige by means of outstanding public buildings. Frederick the Great tried to win the status he needed by building on a grand scale. He proclaimed this explicitly. He had buildings erected with the sole aim of signalling the political power of the state to the outside world. And when the Wars of Liberation were over, this same Berlin set out once again on the same course as before. Finally, the Germany of the Kaisers tried to complete this process, even if it was not always successful in this regard.[92]

In short, Hitler had no difficulty accepting the public buildings of Berlin from the time of the Great Elector and Frederick the Great to the age of Schinkel in the early nineteenth century. Only in the case of the public buildings of the later nineteenth century did he harbour any reservations. His contempt for the city's more recent architecture, which he condemned in *Mein Kampf* for the wretched disproportion of public and private buildings, was directed at the products of the early twentieth century and was based on the impressions that he had gleaned during his visits to Berlin between 1917 and 1923, a time when the capital was singularly lacking in architectural lustre. By 1917 practically all building work in the city had come to a standstill, and the only public building to be completed during the first half of the Weimar Republic was the offices designed by German Bestelmeyer on the Oranienstraße in Kreuzberg and dating from 1919–24, the Reichsschuldenverwaltung, whose function, ironically enough, was to regulate the reparations to be paid to the victorious powers in the wake of the First World War.[93]

The new buildings that dated from the first two decades of the twentieth century that Hitler must have noticed on his perambulations of the inner city on account of their monumental design[94] were either the large banking houses in the city's financial district to the south of Unter den Linden, which were inspired in the main by the palazzos of the Italian Renaissance,[95] or the vast 'cathedrals of commerce' on the major shopping thoroughfares. Here pride of place must go to Alfred Messel's Wertheim department store with its 800-foot frontage overlooking the Leipziger Straße. Dating from 1904–6, its main section on the Leipziger Platz was an icon of early modern architecture and widely regarded as one of the city's most famous landmarks until it was destroyed by Allied bombs at the end of the Second World War.[96]

By Hitler's lights, buildings such as these were a declaration of state bankruptcy when compared with private commerce. By the second half of the 1920s the trend was not only being continued, but the sense of disproportion observed by Hitler had increased immeasurably. Only a single public building was erected during this time, the Chancellery being extended along the Wilhelmstraße between the Palais Borsig on the corner of the Voßstraße and the Baroque Chancellor's Residence. Dating from 1928–30, the extension was the work of the architect Eduard Jobst Siedler. Although the design was relatively understated, the Cubist, asymmetrical form, the flat roof and the natural stone that was used to clad the exterior were bound to disturb many lovers of traditional forms amid so many Baroque and neo-Classical buildings in this part of the city. Certainly Hitler saw in it a confirmation of his view that the Weimar Republic was weak and not in a position to produce powerful, monumental buildings. Privately he later joked about Siedler's extension, likening it to the 'headquarters of a soap company'.[97]

With the end of the period of inflation and the resumption of economic growth, private architecture flourished, resulting in a whole series of new buildings, from private houses and business premises to the administrative offices of large companies, dance halls and cinemas, department stores and company headquarters, all of which were popularly described as 'high-rise buildings' and regarded as examples of architectural Americanization. All were built in the style of the New Objectivity and were up to twelve storeys high. In particular, pictures of New York were hard to avoid at this time, thanks to countless articles in newspapers and magazines reporting on that city's skyline and describing such legendary projects as the Chrysler Building (begun in 1928), the Rockefeller Center (1929) and the Empire State Building (1931). Of course, the industrial high-rise buildings that began to appear in Berlin between 1924 and 1928 could not begin to compare with their counterparts in New York, but by local standards their size and appearance gave them an 'American feel'.[98] This was particularly true of the Borsig administrative offices, the Klingenberg Power Plant, Ullstein's new printing works at Tempelhof and the Siemens & Schuckert factory, which, ten storeys high, was the first high-rise factory in Europe.

This impression was increased when several offices and other businesses moved into high-rise buildings in or near the inner city between 1929 and 1932. Designed by the architect Philipp Schaefer and completed in 1929, the new Karstadt department store on the Hermannplatz in Neukölln inspired one contemporary guide to modern architecture in Berlin to speak of 'a department store on the grandest scale, imposing through its sheer size and also by the technical perfection of its fittings. [. . .] The American model seems to have been achieved. But the neo-Gothic style of American high-rise buildings has also found an echo in the exaggerated verticalism of these designs'.[99] The fascinating impact of this vast structure was further increased at night by the use of skilful lighting, which the company also sought to exploit for the purposes of advertising.[100] The Europahaus complex that from 1926 began to appear directly opposite the Anhalt Station in the Stresemannstraße (until 1929 the Königgrätzer Straße) can hardly have escaped Hitler's attention since he invariably stayed in the nearby Hotel Sanssouci, at least until the beginning of 1931. Designed by Otto Firle, the ten-storey central section was erected during the second phase of the building programme and was described as follows by the guide from which we have already quoted: 'The building itself is a tall, smooth cube. Little could be said against it, were it not for the fact that it recalls the beginnings of the problematical development of the American skyscraper.'[101]

Those commentators who were critical of the changing face of Berlin's architecture must have been particularly disturbed by the Columbus Building, which was built to designs by Erich Mendelsohn on the Potsdamer Platz in 1931–2. For Mendelsohn, the main problem had been to find a suitable form for the steel-framed building, a problem that he solved by adopting the model of the American high-rise building:

> Taking the American model as his starting point, he has given his steel-framed building a simple, functional and smooth shell, which fits snugly over the structure. Erich Mendelsohn evidently learnt a lot about American architecture during his visit to the United States in 1924: he under-stands that the steel frame of the high-rise building needs to finds adequate formal expression and has designed a clear, functional shell for the Columbus Building whose language is plainly intelligible.[102]

Years later the building became the object of anti-Semitic tirades:

> It is not only that these vast buildings with their flat roofs and walls consisting of little more than windows and glass are intrinsically ugly, they are not even suited to the local climate. The sooner they disappear from the landscape of a city where they do not belong, the better. [. . .] They are a reflection of all that is bad about the Jewish world of business under the present parliamen-tary system: namely, the foreign and the racially alien.[103]

As early as 1930 the *Völkischer Beobachter* was already using the language of anti-Semitism to attack the 'new architecture', albeit not yet in any personal-ized way, inveighing against the 'architectural squalor' of the present day and reviling the 'box-ticking studios under foreign ownership' whose designs had only one merit: 'that of showing the next generation that it was not their own fathers but foreigners who have created this amalgam of steel, glass and flat roofs.'[104]

But arguably the greatest sensation was caused by the Shell Building, whose design remains unique to this day. The work of the architect Emil Fahrenkamp, it was built on the Landwehrkanal to the south of the Tiergarten in 1930–1 and was soon being mentioned in guidebooks as one of the sights of the city,[105] a status that it still retains. According to more recent accounts, it 'occupies an important place in architectural history',[106] creating 'a magnificent impression'[107] and even constituting 'a stroke of genius'.[108] In an article published in a French architectural journal in 1932–3, the twenty-eight-year-old architect and writer on architecture Julius Posener, who eighteen months earlier had worked on the Columbus Building with Erich Mendelsohn, summed up the importance of the Shell Building in terms that go beyond any aesthetic component and stress its significance for the city's urban development:

> The Shell Building is in the Tiergarten district of Berlin, a part of the city whose character is not defined by offices but by elegant private houses and luxury villas.[109] But following the end of the war the street[110] along the Landwehrkanal on which the building is situated has become an important thoroughfare connecting the old inner city with the business quarter around the Zoo. A number of the old villas and houses in this street have now vanished, and others have been turned into offices. The Shell Building is merely the first part of a radical plan to transform the entire street. Rising to a height of over 100 feet, it towers above the row of low houses between the Potsdam Bridge and the Bendler Bridge.[111] In short, the question of urban development was extremely delicate. Fahrenkamp has solved it in a wholly personal way by treating the entire façade along the canal as a single complex running in a zigzag line, rising from a relatively low level – the 'Tiergarten level' – by degrees of approximately 45 feet each to the highest corner of the building on the corner of Bendlerstaße.[112]

In other words, Posener stressed the function of the building within the contemporary context of the city's urban planning, laying emphasis on the 'delicate' position of the building within the city as a whole rather than singling out its aesthetic qualities as a solitary tribute to modern design within older architectural forms.[113]

A Letter on Contemporary Urban Planning

By the early 1930s Hitler was in regular contact with the country's chancellor, the leaders of the Reichswehr and even the president of Germany himself.[114] But did his interest in the problems of Berlin's urban development extend beyond mere name-calling and dismissive references to 'Americanization' and the policy of using light in advertising? One searches in vain for any critical comments on the 'new architecture' before 1933. As one recent writer has noted, Hitler 'never attacked modern architecture directly'.[115] When the NSDAP began to take an interest in the debate about modern architecture in 1930, it was not Hitler, but the editor of the *Völkischer Beobachter*, Alfred Rosenberg, who took the initiative. Nor did Hitler make any public pronouncements on individual buildings in 'new Berlin'[116] or on the whole of the debate over the city's development during this period, a time when Berlin was becoming a modern cosmopolitan capital,[117] and a new business centre – the 'new West End' – was emerging around the Tauentzienstraße, the Memorial Church and the Kurfürstendamm. Only Goebbels and *Der Angriff* regularly inveighed against the area commonly known as 'Berlin W', at least to the extent that they were able to score anti-Semitic points by attacking this part of Berlin for the disproportionately high percentage of Jews who lived there.[118]

There is only one surviving example of Hitler making an entirely negative comment about an outstanding example of modern architecture in Berlin, and it comes in the form of a personal insult hurled at the architect Emil Fahrenkamp: 'You're the man who committed the crime of the Shell Building.'[119] It is hardly a surprising remark, coming, as it does, from a would-be architect like Hitler, whose own architectural fantasies belonged entirely in the nineteenth century. But we may well be right in assuming that he held similar views on the other iconic examples of the 'new architecture' in Berlin. That he was familiar with the central themes that were currently being debated in urban development, especially in the context of Berlin and of designs such as the Shell Building, and that he was even able to use those arguments for his own ideological ends emerges from a document that was not published in its entirety until 1996. While undertaking research for a survey of the NSDAP buildings on the Königsplatz in Munich,[120] Iris Lautenbach discovered a long letter written by Hitler to the Bavarian minister of the interior, Karl Stützel, on 7 August 1931. The local planning department had threatened to turn down permission for an extension to the Brown House in the pre-existing grounds of the building, prompting Hitler to write a letter of complaint. His intervention was ultimately successful.[121]

In his letter Hitler points out that the changes that had taken place in the part of Munich where the new building was planned and where all new buildings required special planning permission had reached the point where they could no longer be held back. In the Briennerstraße especially, numerous former town mansions had been turned into offices after the war because of unavoidable financial constraints. As a result, Hitler went on, the transformation of former residential avenues into streets of shops and offices was the practical precondition for maintaining at least the outward semblance of the city; in the longer term, it was impossible to continue to use these properties for residential purposes. To grant an applicant special permission could make sense only if an attempt was being made to preserve the outward appearance of this once-elegant quarter and avoid damaging its artistic value. In acquiring the Palais Barlow, he himself had been fully conscious of the need 'to maintain the Classical picture of the city to the extent that this picture still exists in this street'.[122]

In order to ensure that his appeal was favourably heard and the NSDAP's plans were allowed to go ahead, Hitler then went on to examine the artistic aims of the Bavarian royal family, at least as he himself interpreted them, and to express his fundamental belief in the absolute primacy of public architecture, a point he had already laboured in *Mein Kampf*:

> Like every other leading authority in public or religious life, the royal family has always seen its artistic mission only in part in maintaining artistic values as such. To a far greater extent, it has seen in art a means of glorifying and ultimately of consolidating the royal institution. [. . .] But the glorification of kingship through art also helped to invest the institution of the monarchy with a power that found expression outwardly in pomp and ceremony, inwardly in subservient admiration. The art of the monarchy was only one aspect of the *impressive pomp* of this institution vis-à-vis the people and, in a wider sense, the outside world. For this outer show also involved the visible form of courtly ceremonial, the *demonstration of power* – in short, the whole style of courtly life.

When the monarchy ceased to exist, royalty forfeited not only its ceremonial function but also its role in urban development. All that now remained was to preserve the artistic property created in the interests of the monarchy.[123]

Hitler then goes on to examine contemporary trends that have led to changes in people's perception of the city, and here it is no accident that he cites the example of Berlin:

From a purely artistic point of view, the Schloßplatz in Berlin and the Schloßfreiheit[124] have retained more of their outward appearance than any other aspect of the city. The street Unter den Linden was once conceived as the most elegant approach road to the Royal Palace but has become a shopping street filled with noisy traffic. Ultimately the ceremonial ambitions of the [Prussian] royal family could not resist the life-governing laws of a city whose population now exceeds two million. The changes brought about simply by modern traffic are so far-reaching that the stylistic appearance of this street must necessarily be changed in consequence and will indeed be changed.[125]

Hitler's disquisition on the architectural upheavals that were taking place in Berlin in the years around 1930 culminates in a passage that suggests that what Karl Arndt has called Hitler's 'obsession with architecture' included his familiarity with contemporary writings on the subject, especially architectural journals:

On top of this necessary change in the character of any town- or cityscape that is caused by general traffic and so on, we must also add the shift in the city's financial focus. The residential streets of yesterday are the thoroughfares of today, while the thoroughfares of a bygone age often fall into decay and become depopulated in the space of only a few decades. A kind of urban architecture can be observed in all the cities of the world, with all its technological consequences for traffic. [. . .] Indeed, it is an irony of fate that what appears to be the starkest contrast with today's world of business and commerce ultimately leads to the same result. In practical terms, the accumulation of museums, galleries and other public buildings produces the same outcome as the agglomeration of offices and business premises.[126]

Hitler's ability to argue his point in his letter to Karl Stützel indicates that he was fully abreast of contemporary writings on town planning. The term 'urban architecture', for example, is one that could be used only by someone who had examined the relevant material and was able to demonstrate its context and its consequences in the plausible way seen here. In the light of the actual appearance of the Brown House and in view of what we know about Hitler's fundamental conviction that state power must find expression in architecture as an exhibitionist gesture, we can also imagine what German cities and especially the capital might look like once Hitler had assumed control.

In 1926 Goebbels had met Hitler on the Obersalzberg and expressed his wonderment in a diary entry: 'In the evening he talks about what the country's architecture will look like in the future – he is the architect through and through.'[127] In the autumn of 1930, too, shortly before the Reichstag reconvened with the NSDAP as the second-largest parliamentary party, Goebbels was expressing his amazement at the 'fantastic plans' that Hitler had devised for 'new buildings: he's one hell of a guy!'[128] Two years earlier, on 18 December 1928, Rudolf Heß had claimed that 'as an architect Hitler already has ideas for developing Berlin and turning it into the great metropolis of the new German Reich – in some cases this takes the form of some wonderful individual designs that he has already set down on paper'.[129]

But the rise of the NSDAP to the point where it could harbour very real claims to power meant that in the eyes of Hitler's immediate circle his architectural ambitions were reduced to the level of a kind of casual conversation reserved for off-duty evenings. It is unlikely that Göring, Heß or Goebbels suspected even for a moment that it was in anything but daydreams that Hitler saw himself as an architect or thought his 'wonderful individual designs' to be a great deal more than the eccentric expression of a private passion. In fact he was preparing for the completely new machinery of power that would be established in the 'coming Reich' where it would play a demonstrative role in signalling the country's new architectural pretensions.

Although Goebbels shared Hitler's enthusiasm for the cinema, he had absolutely no interest in questions of architecture and urban planning. In consequence, his dreams were directed not at the redevelopment of Berlin but at the office of Prussian prime minister. Following the disappointments that he had suffered during the early part of 1931, he was again feeling optimistic and on 12 June 1931 he noted in his diary: 'We'll be in power sooner than we think.' On the 13th he observed that 'the political situation is again extremely complicated. [Chancellor] Brüning is fighting for his survival. If he falls, it'll be our turn. Disaster is impending.'[130] Following the summer break, however, Hitler seems to have taken Goebbels' advice to heart, for in early September Heß was able to announce that Hitler was now 'spending more time in Berlin than in Munich. He has set himself the task of undermining those props that are still supporting the present government in the worlds of industry and banking. He is pursuing his goal with great success. Even leading bankers have expressed their belief that H[itler] is the only person who can still save the situation.'[131] Had Hitler learnt his lesson and realized that such influence could not be exerted from Munich alone? If Hitler was on the point of taking control of 'the citadel of Berlin', then he already had plans for redeveloping it.

The 'Kurfürstendamm Pogrom'

Meanwhile, the events of the summer of 1931 had shown that Goebbels had misjudged the balance of political power. Although he was pleased to note on 16 June that the number of NSDAP members in Berlin was already more than twenty thousand and that two months later the print run of *Der Angriff* was ninety thousand,[132] the failure of the referendum of 9 August calling for the dissolution of the Prussian Landtag as demanded by the Stahlhelm and NSDAP revealed that the power to mobilize the 'nationalist opposition' was still extremely limited: only 9.8 million voters – 36.8 per cent of the total – had voted yes, whereas the parties who supported the referendum polled 12.3 million votes in the Reichstag elections on 14 September.[133] The NSDAP leadership drew what seemed to be the obvious conclusion from this setback and renewed contact with Hugenberg's DNVP and the Stahlhelm,[134] leading in October 1931 to the creation of the 'Harzburg Front'.

In a letter to the NSDAP's Gauleiter in Brandenburg, Ernst Schlange, Gregor Straßer described this move as one that 'falls under the heading of tactics not principles'. The road to a National Socialist government, he went on, must necessarily

> involve the stage of a right-wing cabinet at least to the extent that such a route
> is legally possible. It is of no consequence whether we like this or not, the main
> thing is that we achieve our goal and that once we are in power we can set about
> implementing the fundamental idea of National Socialism on a far stronger and
> more powerful basis. This is the politics of the so-called nationalist opposition.

This was a point determined by the Führer himself. 'The fact that this nationalist opposition must manifest itself through a far greater degree of co-operation with the Stahlhelm and the German Nationalists goes without saying, but this does not mean that we shall thereby alter our basic attitude or our attitude to these associations.'[135]

Goebbels was unenthusiastic about this tactical reorientation of the NSDAP, so keen was he to leave his own particular mark on the party in Berlin. With effect from 1 September 1931 the new watchword was 'Into the factories!', the aim being to sign up ten thousand new members from among the workers before the end of the year. To achieve this, the party needed 'to distance itself more clearly from the forces of reaction. This is now being vigorously implemented. The whole party will follow. Within two weeks the plans for action will have been worked out. Then we'll set to work again.'[136]

Exactly a month later it became clear what Goebbels meant by this kind of 'action'. The event in question has gone down in history as the 'Kurfürstendamm pogrom' and took place on the evening of 12 September 1931, when members of the Jewish community were celebrating their new year in their synagogues, including the synagogue in the Fasanenstraße, only a few yards to the north of the Kurfürstendamm, where a large crowd of National Socialists – estimates range from five hundred to 1,500 – had gathered from all over Berlin and where they mingled with the pedestrians. The traffic police soon noticed that something was amiss:

> Young men, simply dressed, were circling the Memorial Church in small groups of between three and four. Some were wearing brown jackets, so-called climbing jackets, others wore brown trousers, some so-called bear boots, while many wore blue caps and insignia such as swastikas, spears and steel helmets. The authorities later reckoned that in the end there were around five hundred SA men present from at least eighteen SA units. Soon after the nearby police stations had been informed at around 20:20, there was a sudden eruption of demonstrations and acts of violence. Groups of National Socialists chanted slogans such as 'Heil Hitler', 'Germany, Awake' and 'Death to All Jews!' and attacked the passers-by.

A non-Jewish eyewitness later described how he was on his way from the Fasanenstraße to the Memorial Church when he was suddenly confronted by a group of forty to seventy individuals. He managed to get out of their way and cross to the other side of the street, where he immediately came face to face with another group, one of whose members broke away and struck him in the face. When he tried to defend himself, several other members of the group laid into him with such force that 'not a part of him remained unhurt. His face was smashed in, his teeth loosened, his feet bloodied and his suit covered in blood'.[137]

Within days thirty-four arrests had been made. All the accused were tried by a summary court. The *Berliner Tageblatt* reported on the first day's proceedings:

> It was clear from the evidence of the second of the accused, a Herr Bonin, that the rioting had been planned in advance. He is a member of SA Company 49 and had heard from comrades that Jews were celebrating their New Year on the Kurfürstendamm and wanted to show them that there are still some Germans around. He had told the police that his commander had instructed him to go to the Kurfürstendamm. They had also been instructed

to walk up and down in small groups but not to commit any acts of violence. In court today the accused claimed that no such orders had been given and that he had merely discussed the matter with some of his comrades.[138]

It is also clear from the report in the Jewish *C. V.-Zeitung* that the National Socialist demonstration was well planned:

> During the evening a thousand or so National Socialists suddenly arrived. Although they were not wearing uniforms or carrying any insignia, they were immediately identifiable as members of the SA to everyone in the know. They proceeded to accost Jewish passers-by and others who simply looked Jewish, including those Jews who were emerging from their places of worship. They struck down innocent pedestrians without rhyme or reason and, hurling anti-Jewish insults and battle cries, they forced their way into a confectioner's shop [the Café Reimann] whose owner is a Christian but which is frequented by many Jews. Here they smashed windows and destroyed marble tables and crockery. The police arrived in force shortly after the attack began. They prevented any further attacks on other restaurants and dispersed the SA, but they were unable to prevent the latter from reforming in smaller groups of three or four individuals and continuing with their tried-and-tested tactics by mingling with the pedestrians on the stretch between the Memorial Church and the Knesebeckstraße, including the Nollendorfplatz and the Wittenbergplatz. These squads sought out businesses according to a prearranged plan. Their vocabulary on launching an attack ran the whole gamut of abuse from a witty 'Happy New Year!' and 'Sarah, pack your bags' to 'Your synagogue's on fire', 'You never dreamt that we'd call on you today!' and the usual 'Death to all Jews!'[139]

The *Völkischer Beobachter* achieved the remarkable feat of turning these events into an 'act of spontaneous self-defence' when 'young Germans, strolling along the Kurfürstendamm in righteous indignation on the Jewish New Year's Day, smashed the windows of these whores' temples and in a spirit of truly Christian anger called to account the Jews and other creatures in their dens of iniquity'.[140] The *C. V.-Zeitung*, conversely, wondered who had organized the pogrom:

> Some uncertainty still surrounds the role of Count Helldorf and his companions. Count Helldorf is the leader of the Berlin SA. Throughout the unrest he drove up and down the Kurfürstendamm in his car with his chief of staff, [Karl] Ernst. Passers-by saw him giving instructions from his car and insisted

that he be apprehended. For everyone with any understanding of what was going on, it was he who organized the whole business.

But the paper also asked who else was responsible, noting that their identity was 'all too apparent': 'invisible, but known to everyone', it was the 'anti-Semitic, rabble-rousing press whose editorials had created the mood that found such violent expression on the Kurfürstendamm'. Among the accused, the paper identified

> the 'great' leaders of the NSDAP, Goebbels, Streicher and Ley, all of whom have spent years systematically fuelling anti-Jewish passions. Also among their number was Adolf Hitler himself, a man who once said that 'nothing ever happened in the party without his knowledge or against his wishes' and who therefore bears the responsibility not only for the witch-hunt that has been directed against the Jews in the basest form by certain National Socialist newspapers but also for the bloody excesses that have now resulted from it.[141]

Helldorf and his adjutant, Karl Ernst, went into hiding on the day after the riots, turning up in Munich to attend a meeting of SA leaders on 15 and 16 September but handing themselves over to the state prosecutor in Berlin on the 21st, when they were taken into custody. What happened next can be understood only against the background of the growing political influence of the NSDAP, an influence that now extended to the highest echelons of government. Although the public prosecutor received intelligence indicating that a leading role had been played not only by Helldorf but possibly by Goebbels as well, and although his indictment stressed that 'the action was prepared and executed according to a predetermined plan', the case quickly became bogged down in lengthy legal arguments, with the result that it was not until 26 October 1931 that proceedings against Helldorf and others finally began.[142] In his reminiscences the then chancellor, Heinrich Brüning, admits quite openly that Goebbels visited him on 25 September and expressed his concern at the possible severity of Helldorf's sentence. Goebbels went on to assure him that there would be no SA demonstrations during the forthcoming visit to Berlin by the French foreign minister, and in the light of that assurance Brüning asked to see the secretary of state in the Ministry of Justice, Günther Joel, and the secretary of state in the Prussian Ministry of State, Robert Weismann. Together with them, Brüning found what he later described as 'a way of postponing the Helldorf trial without violating the legal constitution so that the case had to be handled by other judges'.[143]

On 7 November Helldorf, Ernst and Wilhelm Brandt – one of the leaders of
the Stahlhelm who had also taken part in the riots – were sentenced to six
months' imprisonment and a fine of 100 marks for breach of the peace and
insulting behaviour. Both the public prosecutor's office and the defence
lawyers immediately appealed against the sentence; at the appeal hearing on
9 February 1932 the district court acquitted all three men of the charge of
organizing the riot. Brandt was sentenced to four months' imprisonment for
breach of the peace, while the other two were fined 100 marks for insulting
behaviour after they had been heard calling a passer-by a 'Jewish banker'.[144]

In justifying its ruling, the court wilfully 'obscured the responsibilities of the
parties involved, rendering them unrecognizable'.[145] It also placed a grotesque
gloss on the arguments for and against the accused. According to a contemporary newspaper report on the court's oral judgement,

> a whole series of facts might support the argument that Count Helldorf was
> guilty of leading the riot, but there was also a whole series of factors that
> seemed to the court to be so weighty that the accused was acquitted. It was
> said that Helldorf had arrived extremely late at the Kurfürstendamm and
> then driven round in his car. It was clear to the police from his clothing that
> he was the SA's commander-in-chief. This in particular gave the lie to the
> claim that he had been planning to lead a demonstration that had been well
> prepared in advance. [. . .] Count Helldorf had himself been surprised by the
> events that unfolded on the Kurfürstendamm and had intended to single out
> the SA demonstrators and restore order. From an objective standpoint his
> actions did indeed constitute a breach of the peace, but from a subjective
> point of view it could not be proved that he was conscious of the fact that his
> presence might increase the danger.[146]

It is worth stressing that this passage is taken from a court document setting
out the case for granting Helldorf's appeal. In spite of appearances, it is not a
satirical text.

As for Hitler, an internal police report quotes a comment that he made at
the SA leaders' meeting in Munich to which we have already referred. On this
occasion he expressed his views at least indirectly on the events in Berlin and
did so, moreover, in the presence of Helldorf and Ernst. He admitted that

> in the light of the necessarily slow advances being made by the party, the SA
> leadership in the big cities was often placed in the position of undertaking
> actions designed to placate people's revolutionary mood. But these actions

must assume forms that did not jeopardize the outwardly legitimate policies of the NSDAP. The party must not be burdened with such actions. For the SA leaders it went without saying that they must protect the party and as a matter of principle deny that the party was connected with such events. Only if there were no alternative should they themselves accept responsibility for these incidents. The SA leaders in question must also understand that in the wake of such incidents the party must of course turn its back on the leaders concerned and demonstratively drop them. But they could be certain that the party would not forget them and would reinstate them as soon as the moment was right.[147]

In Helldorf's case such an offer was unnecessary for he remained the SA's leader in Berlin and continued to run an organization that had recently completed a remarkable transformation from a mere splinter group to a body that now enjoyed the support of the masses. In the spring of 1931 the Stennes Mutiny had resulted in the loss of several hundred members, but since the autumn of that year its ranks had been swelling day by day, with the result that between November 1931 and April 1932 membership of the Berlin-Brandenburg SA rose from 9,000 to 27,000. And it was Berlin itself that could claim the biggest increase in membership, the number leaping from 3,557 to 9,923 between October and late November 1931. In his account of the growth of the SA in Berlin and Brandenburg between 1926 and 1934, Martin Schuster has noted that 'this increase of six thousand men in a matter of only a few weeks' was 'unique within the country as a whole'.[148] The Central Association of German Citizens of the Jewish Faith (C. V.) had been watching these developments with mounting concern and reported on the planned relocation of SA units to Berlin, a move about which the Berlin police 'knew nothing', encouraging the Association to dismiss the report as 'no doubt inaccurate'.[149]

But the figures could not be disputed. The Berlin SA entered 1932 – a year described as 'decisive' by a later writer on the subject[150] – as a numerically far more powerful organization which had emerged against the background of a steadily worsening economic and political crisis. Throughout the second half of 1931 there had been repeated rumours that the SA was preparing to launch a civil war or a coup d'état. But the majority of Hitler's supporters and opponents were agreed on one point at least: the question *Deutschland – so oder so?* (Germany – like this or like that?), which featured on the jacket of a widely read book by an American journalist that was published at the end of 1931,[151] would be answered in Berlin in 1932.

9

'The power struggle is just beginning'

1932: THE START OF A DECISIVE YEAR

'After the Truce – a New Wave of Attacks. But Hitler Will Never Triumph.'
Headline in the liberal *Welt am Montag*, 4 January 1932[1]

'Last Monday tens upon tens of thousands of Berliners who are not members of Hitler's party none the less took part for the first time in one of his demonstrations in the Lustgarten and as night fell filled the Sportpalast and the Friedrichshain Brewery. A quarter of a million people from Berlin and the surrounding area have risen up, fired by the great popular anger that throughout the country is directed at our present rulers.'
Adolf Stein ('Rumpelstiltskin'), 7 April 1932[2]

A Confused Picture

By the start of 1932 Berlin's population had stagnated at 4.29 million. As had been the case during other economic crises, most recently in 1923–4, the city had lost its attraction for potential immigrants, while the increasingly difficult jobs market had persuaded many others to leave, so that the population had sunk by about sixty thousand over a two-year period and was now lower than it had been in 1929. The unemployment figures, conversely, continued to rise, from around 466,000 in January 1931 to 595,000 in January 1932 and 615,000 by the middle of February 1932. By the end of 1932 the figure was 636,000. After Breslau, Berlin had a higher proportion of its workforce unemployed than any other German town or city.[3]

On 8 December 1931 President Hindenburg signed a fourth emergency degree banning the wearing of uniforms, a ban that continued to remain in force. But the 'Christmas truce' that was announced in this same context, and which declared unlawful all public political gatherings and marches and prohibited the dissemination of political posters and leaflets, ended on 3 January 1932.[4] Within twenty-four hours the National Socialists had launched what they termed a new 'wave of attacks', and SA units proved true to their watchword of 'hunkering down in every street, wherever possible opposite a KPD meeting place'.[5]

On 5 January *Der Angriff* published a report on two NSDAP meetings headed 'Battle for Berlin: Yesterday the Decisive Wave Began in Berlin'. Goebbels had made it clear that all would be lost if the movement did not now play its trump card. The year 1932, he went on, was decisive, involving, as it did, 'the death or resurrection of Germany'.[6] Three days later the party held another demonstration in the Sportpalast. The SPD's official newspaper, *Vorwärts*, which was published in Berlin, noted

the usual picture – alongside the token general from the old army, the gentlemen in their monocles, the student bearing the scars of a duel like some badge of honour and, not least, the representatives of a well-fattened bourgeoisie, we also saw young unemployed people seduced into joining the party by poverty and lack of insight. When we also saw the ladies in their place of honour holding up their lorgnettes and ogling and appraising the SA men who, because of the ban on uniforms, were dressed in civvies, we were bound to ask ourselves how a class-conscious member of the proletariat could ever wander in here by mistake.[7]

It was at this demonstration that 150 members of Unit 7 of the Wilmersdorf SA lined up, two abreast, and, accompanied by the Fuhsel Band, first sang Arno Pardun's new SA battle hymn, *Volk ans Gewehr* (Folk, to your Rifles):

Siehst du im Osten das Morgenrot,
Ein Zeichen zur Freiheit und Sonne,
Wir halten zusammen auf Leben und Tod,
Mag kommen, was immer da wolle.
Warum denn noch zweifeln, hört auf mit dem Hadern,
Noch fließt uns deutsches Blut in den Adern.
Volk ans Gewehr, Volk ans Gewehr![8]

[When you see the dawn in the east, a sign of freedom and sun, we'll stick together in life and in death, no matter what may befall us. Why, then, should we doubt? We should stop our complaining, for German blood still flows through our veins. Folk, to your rifles! Folk, to your rifles!]

In his New Year radio broadcast, President Hindenburg spoke of the 'serious-ness of the age' and appealed to all Germans to 'face the future undaunted, hand in hand, for difficult decisions lie ahead'. No one should succumb to faint-heartedness; all should be sustained by an unshakeable faith in the fatherland. 'God has often saved Germany in its time of need,' Hindenburg assured his listeners. 'He will not abandon us now!'[9] In his own appeal to party members on 1 January 1932, Hitler claimed that God was on the side of the NSDAP: 'Through His merciful will, the Almighty Himself creates the condi-tions to save our people – by annihilating the half-hearted middle ground, He will grant us victory.'[10] A rather different view was taken by Otto Wels, who had been the chairman of the SPD since 1931 and who struck a confident note in *Vorwärts*, claiming that National Socialism was 'simply an army of troopers blown together by the gale of the economic crisis' but destined to be scattered by the next 'gust of wind' unless it was first allowed to gain a firm foothold 'by a victory rich in plunder'. The present year would pass 'without Fascism succeeding in seizing power. Its disappointed masses will abandon the prophets of today as quickly as they joined them.'[11]

A less optimistic note was struck by Theodor Wolff, the editor-in-chief of the *Berliner Tageblatt*, in a leading article in which he addressed the question of the ease or otherwise with which the NSDAP could be defeated: 'The main battle between the present state and National Socialism' – which Wolff described as 'a movement that is no more than a mental aberration' – would 'be fought in the month of May at the Prussian elections and the country's presidential election.' If Hitler failed to achieve his goal by then, he would never succeed. It was here that the goal of all National Socialist aspirations lay, but many ships had sunk when passing the Cape of Good Hope. 'The psychotic fear and fatalistic belief on the part of cowardly citizens that Hitler is a fate that cannot be avoided' had not grown appreciably less in the final weeks of 1931. Now 'the ruling figures and all who want to preserve the state' had four months in which to 'shake citizens from their psychosis' and make it clear to them in word and deed that it was a 'foolish superstition' that 'the Third Reich is inevitable'.[12]

But Wolff did not know what had been going on behind the scenes in terms of the discussions taking place over a period of several weeks between the Chancellery, the Defence Ministry, the President's Office and various party leaders. For some time the country's rulers had been trying to harness Hitler and the NSDAP to their own particular agenda, while studiously avoiding saying anything to the country about the imminent threat of a Third Reich.[13] In early January 1932 the press had reported at length on a proposal to change the constitution in order to allow Hindenburg to remain in office after May 1932 – for this to happen, a two-thirds majority was needed in the Reichstag, which would require the agreement of the extreme right-wing parties: namely, the DNVP and NSDAP. Under the headline 'Hindenburg Must Stay', the *Vossische Zeitung* reported that the government had drafted the relevant bill. In the hope of reaching an agreement with the 'most important right-wing parties', Chancellor Brüning had made contact 'in the first instance with the National Socialists'. According to the paper, the negotiations with Hitler had already begun: he had been invited to Berlin by the defence minister, Wilhelm Groener, and the two of them had already held 'a lengthy discussion'. A second meeting, between Brüning and Hitler, would shortly take place.[14]

'This meeting had tremendous consequences for German politics', Konrad Heiden, one of the leading authorities on National Socialist strategy, was to write two years later, while living in exile in Switzerland.[15] It took place at Groener's home at 16 Sedanstraße in Steglitz. Brüning began by informing Hitler that he had not yet held talks with any other party, which meant that this was Hitler's big chance to 'take a leading role in politics' by being the first to champion the president's re-election. According to his memoirs, Brüning felt that Hitler was 'still hesitating over whether to succumb to the temptation to capture a leading political position by peaceful means or whether to risk an open conflict in his pursuit of total control'.[16]

Brüning's initiative and his offer to Hitler ushered in the final phase in the struggle for power in Germany. As far as the public at large were concerned, these meetings – a web of intrigue, secret discussions, open and veiled calumnies, opportunistic allegiances and flagrant breaches of trust – remained largely impenetrable. 'The power struggle is just beginning', Goebbels noted in his diary. He was also remarkably accurate in his assessment that it would 'perhaps last all year'.[17] At least it was clear that the battle would be fought in Berlin and that Hitler could no longer afford to avoid the city for months at a time. The Kaiserhof now became his headquarters in the capital, and between early January 1932 and the end of January 1933 he stayed there at least once a month, frequently more often and sometimes for more than a week at a time, the only exception being the summer months. According to a later official account of this period, Hitler spent almost one hundred nights at the Kaiserhof in the course of twenty separate visits.[18]

It was from a position of strength that Hitler was able to haggle over the reins of power. After all, the elections of recent months had shown that the NSDAP was far from having exhausted its potential for winning votes. In the elections for the Hamburg City Council on 27 September 1931, for example, it had polled 25.9 per cent of the total votes cast and become the second largest party, only a little behind the Social Democrats. And in the elections for the Hesse Landtag on 15 November 1931 it had scored its greatest success of all, winning 37.1 per cent of the vote and leaving all the other parties far behind. But the chancellor's offer to Hitler to join forces with the German Nationalists in order to prolong the president's period in office placed the NSDAP leader in a difficult position, for Brüning's government would first need to fall before he himself could hope to seize power. If he agreed to the proposal, he would unwillingly be helping Brüning to increase his own prestige and bolstering a chancellorship that lacked a parliamentary majority and remained unstable in consequence.[19] But if he turned it down, he would equally involuntarily take some of the lustre away from the myth surrounding Hindenburg and undermine the president's position of authority. If he adopted this course, he risked setting in motion a train of events that would force him to put himself forward as a candidate, possibly against Hindenburg himself, a man 'for whom we fellow fighters in the Great War feel only reverence and gratitude as the field marshal of our armies' – thus Hitler expressed his feelings for Hindenburg in the letter that he wrote to Brüning turning down the latter's proposal.

In justifying his decision, Hitler began, bizarrely, by listing his detailed misgivings about the country's constitution, and it was only at the end of his letter that he explained what had really persuaded him to say no: Brüning's proposal was merely an attempt to patch up a system 'that must be destroyed if the German nation is to have any chance of surviving'.[20] Instead, Hitler wanted the Reichstag to be dissolved as the NSDAP's recent successes in the polls had convinced him that if there were new elections the National Socialists would emerge as by far the strongest party. But his attempts to persuade Hindenburg to dismiss Brüning and call for new elections proved futile. 'We've lost the first round. Brüning will triumph all over again,' he noted afterwards.[21] The *Berliner Tageblatt* struck a sarcastic note in commenting that 'Hitler evidently considers his Berlin mission over as he has now returned to Munich'.[22]

The Cult of Hitler in Berlin

But Hitler was back in Berlin by 16 January to appear in the Berlin-Mitte County Court on a charge of insulting behaviour brought by Walter Stennes following his expulsion from the party. Hitler's co-defendant was the editor-in-chief of *Der Angriff,* Julius Lippert. Following the suppression of the second Stennes Mutiny and his exclusion from the NSDAP in April 1931, Stennes had been accused by the NSDAP press of being a police informer, an accusation repeated by Hitler in a lengthy article in the *Völkischer Beobachter.*[23] In court Hitler expressed his disbelief at having to answer for a piece that he had neither written nor commissioned and of which he had not even been aware. As the paper's publisher, he could not accept responsibility 'for every last article'. He was responsible only for the pieces that he himself signed, otherwise it was the editor. Thanks to this line of argument Hitler did indeed succeed in having the charges against him dropped, whereas Lippert was fined for libel. Both Stennes' lawyer and the court had evidently failed to notice that Hitler had himself used the term *Lockspitzel* – a spy who acts as an agent provocateur – in his article. They had consulted the wrong edition of the *Völkischer Beobachter,* not the one dated 4 April 1931 in which Hitler used the expression in question, but the one from the following day.[24]

In view of the heightened tensions in Germany's internal politics, the case against Hitler was no more than an insignificant sideshow, although the conditions under which it took place reveal the extent of the fascination that Hitler was able to exert on the mass of the population. Hugenberg's *Berliner Lokal-Anzeiger,* for example, reported that queues had started to form outside the courtroom in Moabit at two in the morning. In spite of the time of year, they had not moved from the spot but 'waited patiently until eleven in the morning, when they were finally admitted to the courtroom'.[25] It was under the headline 'Hitler a Star in Moabit' that the *Berliner Tageblatt* described the atmosphere inside and outside the building:

> The criminal court in Moabit resembles a beehive today. The unusual occurrence of the appearance of the prima donna Adolf Hitler has mobilized the court officials in all the different rooms. The leader's supporters are meanwhile standing outside in the street in an orderly line as demanded by the police. [. . .] At the door Hitler is of course greeted by cheering on the part of his followers. [. . .] When he later leaves the courtroom, the onlookers stand and raise their hands in a Fascist salute. In the street he is received with shouts of 'Heil!' With a friendly smile the leader of a workers' party then climbs into an elegant Mercedes cabriolet.[26]

Hitler's next two appearances in Berlin, in January and February 1932, reveal the extent to which support for what people viewed as the NSDAP's political programme[27] was increasingly taken to include the cult of Hitler as a person

– and not just within the party's immediate membership. Both events were merely the start of a vast wave of propaganda that assumed very different dimensions as the year progressed. In the run-up to the elections for the Berlin Student Council between 18 and 23 January, the National Socialist German Students' Association had called a meeting in the Wilmersdorf Tennis Halls close to the Fehrbelliner Platz, and it was here, on 17 January, that Hitler addressed an audience of several thousand – six thousand according to *Der Angriff*, ten thousand according to the *Völkischer Beobachter*.[28] He began by commenting on the course of German history since 1871 and on the way in which Germany was now 'internally divided', words that, according to *Der Angriff*, were greeted 'with tremendous cheers' in the form of 'an unconditional vow to remain loyal in the battle for the fatherland, which was threatened from without and within'.[29] Hitler then turned directly to the students who were present. For them, it was not a question of 'growing old in the service of political science' but of 'becoming a part of the people'. As students, they belonged in the forefront of the 'popular movement, *our* popular movement'. Alluding to their future chances of professional employment, Hitler then went on to say: 'He who does not take part in the struggle will not have a share of the victory!' The students should not stand to one side or think themselves too good to don the SA's brown shirt but must be ready to stake their lives on the 'great cause': 'There is a desire among the people, a desire for unity!'[30]

The reporter for the *Vossische Zeitung* did not think that Hitler's speech had been a political sensation. Instead of saying anything about the events of the last few weeks or even the forthcoming presidential election, Hitler had merely 'spouted a flood of rhetoric' of a kind that he had 'been churning out for years for the benefit of his right-leaning "national" opposition' – the report was headed, significantly, 'A Sandwich-Board World View'. Even so, the writer went on, no one will have been bored among the 'thousands of party members for whom even the prospect of hearing the "German leader" is a Godsend or even among the few professional critics who can still worry about the mystery of this form of mass worship'. The big question was simply 'how Hitler himself managed to get through a speech that he has already given several hundred times with only minor modifications'.

At this point, the reporter, who signed himself only 'O. H.',[31] added a few thoughts of his own, thoughts highly unusual in the context of a report on a party-political meeting:

It is almost impossible to reproduce the contents of language like this, for it amounted to nothing more than the vaguest of concepts, nothing more than images and comparisons that were purely emotional in character and that were hurled forth with ever-increasing effusiveness, culminating time and again in a catchword or emotionally charged term of entreaty that the crowd found infectiously uplifting. There was absolutely no attempt to tackle any concrete political, economic or social questions. All that emerged from the whole one-and-a-half-hour speech was the familiar political picture of the world, the primitively simplistic and unsubtle nature of which may help to explain the mass suggestion of National Socialist propaganda: there are only two parties – those who betray their fatherland and those who defend it; and there is only one choice – a vote for Marxism means Germany's downfall, a vote for Hitler means Germany's rise.

For the students who had convened the meeting, Hitler had not had a single word: nothing he had said had taken into account 'their special position and their obligations in the Germany of today'. There was not 'the slightest hint of the sort of intellectual engagement that the young people of today are conducting with the state and the forces that shape our society'. The whole speech could be reduced to a simple appeal to join the National Socialist front: 'Worker and student walking hand in hand – a heroic picture-postcard ideal – represent the new idea of the state. With this recruitment programme for the SA, the speech passed effortlessly into a military march, a flag-waving parade and a storm of cries of "Heil".[32]

The reporter for the *Vossische Zeitung* was by no means alone in feeling a certain sense of bewilderment at the 'mystery of this form of mass worship'. His colleague on the *Berliner Tageblatt*, Rudolf Olden,[33] expressed a very similar view. In his introduction to a collection of his essays published in 1932 under the title *Das Wunderbare oder Die Verzauberten* (The Wondrous, or The Enchanted Ones),[34] Olden freely admitted to being perplexed, and yet he had stolen a march on his contemporaries by at least acknowledging his bewilderment. 'Where no one else sees that there is a problem, I can show them one that is unsolved and present. I have called it "wondrous" on account of its apparent insolubility.'[35] Olden's satire was directed only in part at all the miracle-workers, the founders of new sects, the quacks and the charlatans who appear in his collection of essays as what he calls 'prophets in the German crisis.' At the same time he was by no means indifferent to 'the fate of our own times and the policy of forcing on all who want to think for themselves the rule of the wondrous. In the brief history of the German Republic such a tremendous shift has taken place from the rational to the irrational that even a blind

man must see it.' Of course, no political party could get by without some form
of irrationality.

> But there is arguably something unique about the decisive and unmistakable
> way in which a nation has turned its back on reason and in the here-and-now
> embraced something that is openly declared to be wondrous. [. . .] The irra-
> tionality of the means has been combined with the impact of the personal to
> produce the egregious success of the National Socialist party.

Ultimately, Olden went on, the NSDAP's programme was unimportant.
Rather, it was the means employed by the party that proved most effective,
confirming the sense of a community by dint of 'flags, symbols, uniforms,
columns of marchers in step with each other and music, all of which spread a
feeling of unity and create a mass out of individuals'. Of decisive impact was
the influence of the leader on the masses. 'The wise would at this point cry out
with a liberating laugh: the suggestive power of a great orator.' And, indeed,
they would be right, Olden conceded. But in what did this suggestive power
consist? Why did one man succeed in this and not another? What was Hitler?
A great speaker? 'Here we are again, back with the terms "transfer" and "identification". All the common and not-so-common terms that are used to
describe the various stages between cause and effect merely detain us unnecessarily. What remains every time is the wondrous.' Politics could be defined
as a 'permanent struggle between reason and the wondrous'. In any crisis,
reason is 'squeezed and its weapons, which had until recently cut very
keenly, suddenly become blunt. Doubt eats away at it, and it emigrates or is
locked up.'[36]

The sense of bewilderment to which independent writers such as Olden
admitted was in no way reduced by the result of the elections to the Student
Council. Under the headline 'Hitler Elections at the University', the *Vossische
Zeitung* reported that, of the 5,801 votes counted, 850 had gone to student
societies, 1,155 to the German Nationalists and the Stahlhelm, and no fewer
than 3,794 to the National Socialists. With sixty-five out of a hundred seats, the
NSDStB had missed gaining a two-thirds majority by only the narrowest of
margins. In an attempt to reassure its readers, the paper explained that the
Student Council was 'in reality a private organization of radical right-wing
students'. Moreover, the total number of students enrolled at the university
during the current term was twelve thousand, suggesting that since only a
small proportion had chosen to vote, 'the majority of students' had 'absolutely
no time for any such radical goings-on'.[37]

But to infer from the number of students who voted that the majority rejected Hitler and his policies was risky in the extreme, and there was no contesting the fact that the 'Hitler students', as they were called by the liberal and left-wing press, had captured the University of Berlin before their leader had succeeded in doing the same with the machinery of state. Academic circles were disproportionately affected by the mood of crisis that was gripping the country, allowing the NSDStB to become by far the most powerful political student body. Encouraged by their electoral victory, National Socialist students now adopted a much more provocative approach to other students whom they took to be Jewish, republican, socialist or Communist,[38] leading in extreme cases, such as the riots of June 1931, to bloody street battles that required the intervention of the police and forced the university to close for a time. On 8 February 1932 Berlin's newly established summary court handed down sentences of several months' imprisonment to seven National Socialist students for breaches of the peace.[39]

Concern over the Loyalty of the Capital's SA

Hand in hand with the growing aggressiveness of National Socialists at the university went an increase in the number and severity of the attacks launched by the SA on 'the Commune', as members of the Communist Party and its various organizations were generally known in right-wing circles. But another frequent target for violence was the 'Iron Front', an umbrella organization formed at the end of 1931 by the Reichsbanner from republican parties and trades unions with the avowed aim of 'defeating the Fascist danger'. In early 1932, according to the official history of the aims of the Brownshirts in Berlin,

> the SA is carrying the battle forwards and becoming increasingly effective in combating the Red terror. [. . .] In addition to helping with propaganda and protecting halls, it is moving in two great directions: first, it is recruiting men and strengthening our units and, second, it is evicting the Commune and the Iron Front from their venues, which it then makes its own or at least sets up its own bases there.[40]

The KPD inevitably fought back, leading to increasing numbers of serious injuries on both sides and even to deadly attacks. From early 1932 onwards the newspapers were full of reports like the following:

There were repeated confrontations among radical elements in Berlin on Saturday night. Communists and National Socialists attacked each other throughout the city, and in many cases the police had difficulty restoring order. In total the police arrested 150 individuals in the course of the night, 109 of whom turned out to be National Socialists. [. . .] One Communist was shot and killed, and one National Socialist was so seriously injured during a fight in the Danziger Straße that he died from his wounds that same evening.[41]

There was a highly charged atmosphere, therefore, when Hitler returned to Berlin on 9 February, his third visit of 1932. On this occasion, however, his aim was not to hold discussions with representatives of the government or with other parties and organizations but to issue his first 'general appeal'. That same evening he addressed a meeting of SA members at the Sportpalast – according to the *Völkischer Beobachter*, the audience numbered fifteen thousand. The title of his harangue, 'We Are the Iron of the Nation', was a direct attack on the Iron Front, which, dominated by Social Democrats, had held a similar rally in the Sportpalast on 31 January under the banner 'For People's Rights – against Dictatorship'.[42] This meeting, too, is said to have drawn an audience of fifteen thousand. Hitler began by declaring that he had come to 'greet his SA comrades' and at the same time to thank them. He then launched straight into an account of the history of the local SA. 'About a year ago,' he explained, alluding to the Stennes Mutiny of late March and early April 1931, 'certain groups, including the press, hoped that the National Socialist movement was about to fall apart and in particular that the SA was on the point of disintegrating.' The present rally was the party's answer to the flood of mendacious reports at that time, all of them intended to 'undermine trust in the leadership' of the party – by which Hitler was referring, of course, to himself – and also in the leadership of the SA: 'The Berlin SA is still standing and will not be shaken or broken by anything.'

After an uncharacteristically brief account of the party's history that was in marked contrast to his usual rambling disquisitions, Hitler turned his attention to the specific situation in Berlin, 'where the movement has had to survive four stages. The first was the period when our enemies cut us dead. They then began to ridicule an organization that they hated, but they soon had to find other weapons in the form of lies and calumny. [. . .] What lies they made up about us here!' The party's enemies had even stooped to inventing a struggle between the Führer and the SA's chief of staff – between the party's political leadership and the head of the SA.[43] To which the only possible answer was that 'within a year I and my chief of staff have restored the organization to the state you now see before you'. The SA was inviolable now that it had survived 'a perpetual purgatory of attacks and lies'. The 'fourth stage in the battle' had been the most difficult for the SA. This was the 'age of terror'. In Berlin especially, the SA knew how the terror had spread – Hitler was referring, of course, to the 'terror' of the SA's enemies, not the terror that it inflicted on others. But this, too, would be overcome. Finally, Hitler painted a picture of the future in which a 'new German Reich' would replace the 'regime of the parties of November 1918' and the 'whole German people' must and, indeed, would 'march' behind the flags and symbols of the SA.

Of course, this prophecy was hardly new, and Hitler had not come specially to Berlin to assure fifteen thousand members of the SA that the organization was, as he put it, 'more powerful and more self-confident than ever'. The real message he had come to impart was mentioned almost in passing after his account of the 'four periods' in the SA's history and his prophecy of the new Reich:

We can look forward to the coming events with the greatest confidence. [. . .] All who are familiar with this organization know that it contains none of what constitutes the life of other political parties that rack their brains over the decisions that we ourselves now have to take. These gentlemen struggle in vain. Our own decision will be taken at the right time and announced at the opportune moment. [. . .] My friends, if you are standing here today, it is because I know what brought you here. It is no blind order but your own will. It is your own belief that has brought you here, your own inner life, just as it is my belief in you that has brought me here. This is something that our enemies do not understand. [. . .] That also explains their failure to understand the conformity in our thinking. My dear SA man, I know exactly what you will be thinking at the moment of the forthcoming election, just as you know what I myself shall be thinking.[44]

It was no accident that there was a sense of mass suggestion and crowd hypnosis about Hitler's language. After all, how could the 'dear SA man' know the tactics that his leader had chosen to adopt in the forthcoming presidential election? Indeed, Hitler himself had still to decide on a particular course of action: if people wanted Hindenburg to be re-elected, that could only happen under very particular conditions, but there was also the possibility that Hitler himself might be a candidate or that the various parties belonging to the 'nationalist camp' might enter into any number of different pacts. Since 18

January Goebbels had repeatedly pleaded with Hitler to put himself forward as a candidate, but on 9 February he was told by the latter: 'everything is still in the balance.'[45]

One way or another Hitler saw himself obliged to ensure that the SA – in the first instance the members of the SA in the capital and at the seat of government – were unconditionally loyal to him personally. In view of the forthcoming electoral campaign he could not afford another SA rebellion, and the exclusion of Stennes' supporters from the party in April 1931 following the Stennes Mutiny had by no means removed the potential for conflict between the SA and party officials, including its leaders. The *Vossische Zeitung* was in no doubt about Hitler's reasons for courting what it called his 'Praetorian Guard'. Among the tensions that existed between the party and its troops, the paper, citing a 'well-informed source', drew attention to the way in which

> the opposition felt by the SA (the party's defence association) and by the SS (the party police) to the party's 'Septemberlings' is being exploited in private battles among the leaders of the NSDAP. The mistrust of the SA and SS is directed at the influence of more recent party members who, abandoning the party's principles, are 'busily haggling over a role in government'. As soon as these people win party office, they are described as 'Konjunkturpolitiker'*.[46]

According to the *Vossische Zeitung*, this explained why Hitler was so keen to make such close contact with the SA and SS and assure himself of their support in the coming weeks.

The ritualized form that this close relationship had assumed becomes clear from the events that followed on from Hitler's speech, which lasted only an hour and ended with his call of 'SA Berlin! Sieg Heil!' According to *Der Angriff*, the band now struck up and played a march to accompany the Führer's review of his troops assembled inside the Sportpalast:

> Its strains thunder through the vast hall as the Führer begins to review his troops. Directly alongside him in their place of honour are the wounded of the SA. Adolf Hitler extends his hand to each of them, and beneath the shattering force of his powerful gaze the eyes of these brave young men fill with tears. They will never forget this day. Although the troops are ranged four deep, it still takes exactly two hours for the Führer to pass them all in review. Time and again he stops and speaks to individual comrades. When he finally

---

* A term for politicians specializing in economic policy.

reaches the Horst Wessel Unit at the top of the third tier, the glorious song of the dead commander rings out loudly and movingly throughout the whole of the arena, a symbol of all the party's dead.[47]

As if this were not enough, a second 'Berlin Appeal before Adolf Hitler'[48] was held the very next day, the number of members of the SA in Berlin having increased so dramatically since the previous autumn that the SA alone was enough to fill the Sportpalast. On the 10th, then, some seven thousand members of other National Socialist organizations in Berlin – mainly the SS and the Hitler Youth movement – gathered in the Wilmersdorf Tennis Halls to hear Hitler deliver a second speech, preceded by a review of his supporters, which again took about an hour. An official from the Moabit branch of the Hitler Youth movement later recalled an event that he described as 'the greatest and most wonderful experience for our comrades in the Hitler Youth movement':

Hitler inspects us. We five from the Beussel district of Moabit step forward from our group. The Führer inspects the line of soldiers. When he reaches us, the Reich Youth Leader [Baldur von Schirach] introduces us to him. The Führer gives me his hand, and for a few seconds our eyes meet. He then hands me an award for 'Bravery and Loyalty'. He greets the others, too, by shaking their hand and gives them his picture. Before he goes on, he comes back to me and pats me on the shoulder. This was the best day of my life. [. . .] I gazed into the Führer's eyes, read a great deal in them, and will always keep faith with him![49]

Hitler could take stock: at his two appeals, more than twenty thousand predominantly young members of National Socialist organizations in Berlin had sworn 'undying loyalty' to him, no matter what he might choose to do in the future. On 10 February Hitler himself described the situation in which he found himself: 'We have known for *twelve years* what we are fighting for, and you can be certain that in the *thirteenth year* – the year of *decision* – we shall not forget what our goal was!'[50]

But was more at stake than the forthcoming electoral campaign, however important that might be? And when Goebbels noted after the first of the two appeals that 'the Berlin SA is on standby' and that his men were 'waiting unwaveringly for the signal to march',[51] did he not mean those propaganda marches that for years had been a regular part of the SA's public displays of its military might? By the 10th, he was expressing himself in less equivocal terms: 'The

Kaiserhof is again our great headquarters. Here, during the afternoon, influential figures from the NSDAP come from the whole country to gather around their leader.' At the two appeals, Hitler 'inspects his troops in Berlin before sending them into battle. In the evening all the SA and SS leaders are with him at the Kaiserhof.' A small group of close associates then remained, 'gathered around the Führer until the grey light of dawn. Plans are hatched as if we are already in power.'[52]

Staging the Presidential Candidacy

By this date, Hitler – like his regional leaders – was convinced 'that somehow or other we shall soon reach our goal'.[53] In the wake of his failed attempt to topple Brüning's government and force new elections, he tried to find common ground with Alfred Hugenberg and other representatives of the extreme right. While he remained in Munich to attend a meeting of leaders of the local Gau, Göring, acting on his behalf, entered into discussions with Hugenberg and the head of the Stahlhelm, Franz Seldte, over the possibility of helping with Hindenburg's re-election in the event of Hindenburg's agreeing to a radical cabinet reshuffle. But the discussions came to nothing as Göring continued to demand that the NSDAP be given the posts of chancellor, minister of the interior and minister of defence.[54] Within a short space of time a definitive list of candidates for the post of president had emerged. As it had done in 1925, the Central Committee of the KPD put forward the name of its party chairman, Ernst Thälmann, when it met on 12 January.[55] On 15 February, Hindenburg declared his willingness to stand for re-election,[56] and on 22 February the DNVP and Stahlhelm proposed the Stahlhelm's deputy leader, retired colonel Theodor Duesterberg, as the joint candidate for the 'Black, White and Red Fighting Bloc'.[57]

As for Hitler, his initial reaction to Hindenburg's candidature was an appeal to members of the NSDAP on 16 February 1932 stating that, 'true to the aims of its war on the Weimar system', the National Socialist movement 'must reject this candidacy. The hour has struck when we must confront the representatives of our present system of government.'[58] This was a remarkable statement. After all, had not the NSDAP been confronting the 'representatives of the system' since its foundation? Two days later Hitler returned to Berlin for his fifth visit of the year. By now he knew that the German Nationalists and Stahlhelm were proposing a single joint candidate. Goebbels hurried to the Kaiserhof and after a long private conversation with Hitler was able to note that 'the decision has now been taken'.[59]

The following day – 20 February – Hitler gave an interview to the Berlin correspondent of the *Giornale d'Italia*. Asked if the NSDAP would be contesting the election for the post of president as a matter of life and death, Hitler replied:

> Yes, indeed. National Socialism is the expression of a national consciousness that rebels against a system that has enslaved and humiliated us. It can no longer tolerate such a situation. As a person, Hindenburg has come to embody this system. We shall fight him, although it is a matter of great personal regret that we see the field marshal, whom we respect as the commander of our armies, driven into such a disagreeable position.

In response to 'a more precise and more personal question' at the end of the interview, the correspondent explained that he had received an answer that he was not allowed to publish.[60]

Presumably Hitler had been asked about his own candidacy and had answered in the affirmative. Although the propaganda department of the NSDAP had moved from Munich to Berlin on the previous day 'as a precautionary measure', as Goebbels put it,[61] Hitler was still unwilling to announce his decision to the world. Possibly Hugenberg was still trying to find a joint candidate in the 'nationalist camp' who would be palatable to Hitler,[62] but it is more likely that Hitler had yet to acquire the basic prerequisite for his own candidacy: German citizenship. Leading NSDAP politicians in coalition governments throughout the country had been trying to obtain German nationality for him by having him appointed to public office, the best-known example being the attempt by Wilhelm Frick, the leader of the NSDAP representatives in the Reichstag, to have Hitler appointed gendarmerie commissar at Hildburghausen. Frick was minister of the interior and national education in Thuringia at the time, but he failed to consult the cabinet.[63] Following the failure of various other attempts to engineer this step, the State Ministry of Braunschweig, which was then ruled by a coalition of German Nationalists and National Socialists, finally managed to have Hitler appointed a government councillor on 25 February 1932. As a civil servant, he acquired German citizenship automatically and was entrusted 'with carrying out the duties of a specialist at the Braunschweig embassy in Berlin', with particular emphasis on 'obtaining commissions for the Braunschweig economy'.

The very next day Hitler attended an official ceremony at the embassy on the Lützowplatz in the Tiergarten district of Berlin, where he swore an oath to perform his duties conscientiously and received his credentials. It goes without saying that there is no evidence that Hitler ever carried out a single duty as a Braunschweig government councillor.[64] Indeed, his first official request in his new post was to ask for extended leave of absence until the end of the presidential elections, a request that was granted without further ado. Later the Braunschweig envoy was 'pleased' to extend this period.[65] The French ambassador in Berlin, André-François Poncet, commented wryly that 'the general public is laughing; but in Germany ridicule is not fatal'.[66] It would in fact have been more accurate to refer in this context to those members of the German public who were not National Socialists. Welcoming him as their 'redeemer', Hitler's supporters did not take it amiss if he stayed at a luxury hotel and drove a Mercedes cabriolet. Why should they begrudge him the title of Braunschweig government councillor?

It is more than likely that Hitler already knew that the 'Braunschweig solution' would confer German citizenship on him several days before the actual appointment, otherwise he would hardly have informed Goebbels during a conversation at the Kaiserhof on 22 February that he could announce his candidacy at a general meeting of members of the Greater Berlin Gau in the Sportpalast that same evening. For tactical reasons Goebbels preferred not to state simply that Hitler was a candidate in the way that Thälmann, Hindenburg and Duesterberg had already proclaimed their candidacies. Instead, his speech built to a dramatic and rhetorical high point consisting of the words:

> Today, party comrades, I can tell you that Hitler will be our country's new president! [. . .] I know that you are aware of the greatness of this moment. I also know that you will understand me when I say that Hitler will be our country's president, rather than saying that he will be our candidate. For if I say that he will be our candidate, I also know that he will be our president.[67]

According to Goebbels' diary, this announcement was followed by a storm of enthusiasm lasting almost ten minutes and accompanied by 'wild demonstrations of support for our leader' and by an 'incredible frenzy of rapturous delight'. At the end, Count Helldorf, the head of the SA in Berlin, stepped up to the microphone and in the name of the SA swore an oath of loyalty to the Führer.[68]

From now on Hitler moved the focus of his activities from Munich to Berlin, at least at certain periods. It was symptomatic of this development not only that he instructed Goebbels to announce his decision in Berlin, at the Sportpalast, but also that in the course of February 1932 he spent a total of sixteen days in the capital. He also chose Berlin as the place to launch his presidential campaign. On 27 February he spoke at the Sportpalast, a speech relayed to the Tennis Halls in Wilmersdorf, where he travelled for a further rally at midnight. In a special edition published to mark the event, the *Völkischer Beobachter* claimed that the audience at the two venues had numbered 25,000 in all. It was Goebbels who opened the rally in the Sportpalast. The extravagant dimensions that the cult of Hitler had assumed by this date is clear from the Gauleiter's speech:

> In the whole history of the world's nations, there has probably never been another man who, called upon to assume the highest national and state office, has been so sustained by the yearning and love of his people and raised aloft by such sheer and profound enthusiasm on the part of the people themselves as is the case with Adolf Hitler, a man from the people who will lead the Germans to freedom. Millions upon millions of hearts among the tormented and downtrodden people and, indeed, in the whole world beat for him in hope and utter confidence, prepared, as they are, to give him their last remaining strength and to sacrifice everything for the nation that has taken on living form in his person.

Nor was the reporter of the *Völkischer Beobachter* at a loss for superlatives when describing the atmosphere in the hall:

> Who can find the words to describe the flood of enthusiasm that poured over the leader of the young Germany and the country's future president for several minutes after Dr Goebbels had dispatched the old system with razor-like precision to the sound of thunderous applause and our new leader entered the Sportpalast and made his way to the platform through the vast crowd? This was not the road taken by a man who until yesterday had been stateless but the journey of a victor. Through the symphony of enthusiasm and battle-resolve, the elemental cry of an entire nation rang out, demanding that they be led to freedom and rescued from nameless misery.

Goebbels had greeted Hitler 'in the name of German Berlin'.

'Showered with flowers thrown from the gallery', Hitler began his speech by stressing that in the 'tremendous battle' in the coming weeks far more was at stake than the presidency. The battle involved 'the concept of 9 November 1918', and it could end 'only with the annihilation of this 9 November 1918 and its aftermath'. The representatives of the 'Weimar system' were insisting on remaining in place 'at any price', but Hitler's watchword was: 'We shall topple you, no matter what it costs!' He believed that the decision was now at hand: the first day of the elections, 13 May, would be 'a day of battle for us, and I am convinced that this battle, my comrades, will end in the way we deserve'. Hitler went on to claim that he believed in a higher justice and that 'the arm of the Almighty will be removed from those who seek only to hide among others'. After this new appeal to the Almighty, Hitler touched on the sore point regarding his confrontation with Hindenburg. He was, he claimed, obliged to say to the 'old field marshal': 'Old man, we revere you too much to see others line up behind you whom we mean to destroy. However much it grieves us, you must step aside, for they want to fight, and so do we.'

But even now Hitler had not finished. Instead, he ended with a fundamental 'historico-philosophical' appeal to his followers, summing up the essence of his political thinking and, with it, the National Socialists' programme:

> And so I would ask you to go forward into the coming weeks and do your duty! Look on this month of March as more than a month in German history. Rather, you should see in it the day that first makes it possible to open the book of world history once again and to tear out the pages for the period between 1918 and 1932. It must no longer be said that the German people took part in a revolution but that, following our army's great feat, the German nation has won back its honour. So that the following pages can remain as they are, glorious and honourable for our people and a story of which our German youth can be proud. Not a story to make them blush with shame. The hour is coming. Do your duty, and the victory is bound to be ours.[69]

In short, the whole of German history from Kaiser Wilhelm II's abdication and the victory of the revolutionary workers and soldiers in Berlin on 9 November 1918 was to be wiped out and replaced by 'our army's great feat'. This could mean only one thing: taking up the First World War where it had been left off or at least rewriting its historical outcome. In short, a Second World War was implied by Hitler's speech. This time, of course, he would take steps to ensure that the country avoided the mistakes which in his view had been committed by its political and military leaders during the First World War and which he had described in elaborate detail in *Mein Kampf*.

In the course of his speech, Hitler also suggested a reason why until now he had not had the backing of the entire nation in spite of his 'complaints about this system'. Those sections of the population who had not yet been won over were being 'held in a state of hypnosis by the press', which in turn was being manipulated by 'people with an interest in maintaining the status quo of

9 November 1918'.[70] He was referring here to the bourgeois, liberal and left-wing press which, at least in Berlin, was still in a majority in 1932 and, as such, more influential than the extreme right-wing papers that were essentially German Nationalist and National Socialist. Time and again Hitler would pepper his speeches with insults directed at his enemies in the press. As we have already observed, he was even more appalled by the papers owned by Jewish publishers – especially Mosse's *Berliner Tageblatt* and Ullstein's *Vossische Zeitung* – than by the ones owned by the organized workers' movement, notably the SPD's *Vorwärts* and the KPD's *Die Rote Fahne*, and related newspapers such as *Die Welt am Abend*, which was owned by the KPD politician Willi Münzenberg. In fact, any predominance that these papers enjoyed consisted solely in their high circulation figures. It must have infuriated Hitler that even after years in the capital, the NSDAP had failed to establish a paper challenging the hegemony of what Goebbels called the 'asphalt press', the 'Jewish hacks' and the 'rotary synagogue'.[71] The party had simply been unable to make its publications sufficiently attractive to be able to compete with the great Berlin newspapers.

In 1932 the *Berliner Tageblatt* still had a daily circulation of 140,000, a figure that on Sundays rose to 230,000, whereas Goebbels' *Der Angriff* had probably only just passed the 100,000 mark. Two of Hugenberg's titles, the *Berliner Lokal-Anzeiger* and the *Berliner illustrierte Nachtausgabe*, each sold a little over 200,000 copies, making them more successful than Ullstein's *BZ am Mittag* (165,000 copies) and the newspaper *Tempo* (125,000 copies). But by far the most popular of the dailies, even with falling sales in the wake of the country's economic crisis, was Ullstein's flagship, the *Berliner Morgenpost*, which in 1932 was still printing around 560,000 copies a day. In 1932 the four major newspaper empires in the city were publishing thirteen of the capital's twenty most popular papers. If one adds together the circulation figures of all these papers, a fairly clear picture of the relative sizes of the various publishing houses emerges: the five liberal Ullstein papers enjoyed a total circulation of 970,000, the three equally liberal papers from Mosse's publishing house around 280,000. The three newspapers published by the German Nationalist Scherl–Hugenberg group reached a total circulation of 475,000, while the equivalent figure for the two Communist papers published by Münzenberg was 260,000.[72] In 1932, therefore, the circulation figures for the newspapers from the two democratic publishing houses, on the one hand, and the figures for the National Socialist *Der Angriff*, on the other, were bizarrely disproportionate given the relative strength of the parties with which they were most clearly associated. In view of the National Socialists' poor showing from a journalistic point of view, it is easy to understand why Goebbels was planning to wage the coming 'electoral war', as he called it, 'mainly through posters and speeches' but also through the rather more unusual media of gramophone records and films.[73] The NSDAP was simply unable to compete with the support shown by the Ullstein and Mosse papers for Hindenburg, with that of the German Nationalist papers for Duesterberg and that of the Communist Party papers for Thälmann. In the longer term, a passionate newspaper-reader like Hitler was bound to regard this as a personal humiliation.

Political Agitation in Working-Class Areas

But there was another factor that proved a headache for Hitler. On 26 January 1932 he had delivered a two-and-a-half-hour speech at the five-star Düsseldorf Park Hotel, where he had addressed up to eight hundred members of the Industry Club and tried to assure them that they had nothing to fear from his party's economic policies. He offered a crudely simplistic picture of the balance of power in Germany: how could a nation influence foreign policy when half of it comprised Bolsheviks, the other half Nationalists or anti-Bolsheviks? If the present trend were to continue, Germany would one day end up in Bolshevik chaos. In order to prevent this, the nation must be 'subjected to a school of iron discipline and slowly be cured of the prejudices of both camps'. It was, Hitler went on, a 'difficult process', but one that 'we cannot avoid!' He had already described the NSDAP's strategic contribution to this task when he spoke of 'young Germany' continuing to march and one day 'reclaiming the German road for the German people'. In order to avoid any misunderstanding on the subject, Hitler also repeated the maxim that he had been proclaiming for years: 'And if people accuse us of impatience, we shall proudly admit to this charge – for we have taken the implacable decision to eradicate Marxism from Germany, root and branch.'[74]

However often the party may have claimed success in this regard, the fact of the matter is that even at the beginning of 1932 the NSDAP had been largely ineffectual in its battle to root out Marxism in Berlin. Goebbels, too, had admitted this, albeit in a grotesquely contradictory manner, in a diary entry of 5 February 1932. Following a meeting with the 'old guard' of the local NSDAP, he had noted that 'these fine old comrades' had helped National Socialism to 'overcome every obstacle in the city', only to add that 'once this Red bulwark falls and the country's capital is won back for the Germans, then it will be them alone that we have to thank'.[75] In short, the 'Red bulwark' was far from having fallen. Although new members were joining the NSDAP and SA every day during the early months of 1932, their greater attractiveness was by no means synonymous with a perceptible weakening of the position of Marxism in its strongholds in the city – in the course of the months that followed, the KPD gained in influence, albeit often at the expense of the Social Democrats. In keeping with Hitler's aims, then, the SA had to intensify its 'battle with Marxism', a demand that led in turn to an increasing number of acts of violence directed against it, mainly by the Communists. A week before the elections, the SA's Company V/6 duly organized a propaganda march through Moabit. Before 1914 this area had been in the hands of the Social Democrats, but by the early 1920s it had become a Communist stronghold.[76] Tensions in the area suddenly escalated when Herbert Norkus, a fifteen-year-old member of the Hitler Youth movement, was stabbed by Communists on 24 January 1932 while distributing propaganda leaflets.[77] During the march there were two separate clashes. According to the party's official history, the shooting went on for ninety minutes and left one SA member seriously wounded, with several lesser injuries on both sides.[78]

The SA's 'propaganda marches' were not political demonstrations with banners, slogans and chanting but military shows of strength organized along the most formal lines. A high-ranking SA leader described their impact as follows:

> Anyone who has ever taken an interest in propaganda knows that with the German nation in particular nothing creates a more powerful impression than marching columns, men who, well ordered and stiff-backed, are uniformly dressed, marching together, disciplined, not looking to their right or left, not talking, but staring straight ahead with thoroughbred, resolute faces. The sight of such columns causes the heart of every German man, every German woman and every boy and girl to beat a little faster.[79]

By holding these marches, the SA was particularly well placed to fulfil its function as an anti-Marxist terror machine, not only drumming up business for the future world order but also, to quote the historian Gerhard Paul, 'mounting a show of strength designed to unsettle, frighten and provoke their political enemies, who would finally be driven from public view. [. . .] In particular the psychology of the authoritarian character confirmed how the show of physical might appealed to this character type above all.'[80]

There is no doubt that a similar psychological predisposition and similar psychological needs existed among the inhabitants of Berlin's working-class districts, even if only among a minority of their younger members. And these young people could be activated by the organized exploitation of their emotions and by persuading individuals to join National Socialist groups, not least at a time when the crisis of the early 1930s was affecting family relationships. The idea of young people looking for a sense of direction was central to the novel *Der Hitlerjunge Quex* by Karl Aloys Schenzinger, which describes how the carpenter's apprentice Heini Völker joins the Hitler Youth movement in Berlin. At the start of the novel, Heini looks out of one of the windows in his parents' house in the Beusselstraße and sees a policeman standing there. The boy likes policemen, for

> they always looked so neat and tidy and so strapping in their shiny leather uniforms. They reminded him of the order and discipline that he could read about in all the old stories. But he liked the army even more, especially during the changing of the guard or when the guard of honour presented arms at the Reichstag. [...] The policeman wore leather gaiters. Leather gaiters were also worn by the young lads who had marched past him one day, all of them spick and span, bursting with vitality, a flag at their head. He had run alongside them for a whole hour; his only desire was to be able to march with them in the same ranks, with these same boys, who were as young as he was and who sang songs that almost made him cry.

Later, he is taken on a trip outside Berlin by a group of young Communists, a 'clique' with whom he feels uncomfortable, and here he meets 'these lads' again. That night he slips into their camp and hears them talking about their 'movement' and their 'leader', and when they sing the German national anthem round the campfire,

> he feels a hot wave overwhelm him with a thousand voices, and he thinks: I'm a German. [...] He wanted to join in, but his voice failed him. This was German land, a German forest, and these were German lads, and he saw that he was standing to one side, alone, helpless and not knowing what to make of this sudden great feeling.

He then wonders why he does not simply go over and ask if he can join them.

> Was it because he did not know what they wanted? Because he did not know what they meant by their 'leader' and by their 'movement'? Heini broke off a branch and struck the air with it. He knew very well that this was not the

reason. There was nothing else that he needed to know. He felt that he would like to join these lads and that here was the exact opposite of what was going on in the clique: here there was order – he could not get the word out of his head.[81]

Heini finally becomes a member of the Hitler Youth movement and a 'blood sacrifice of the movement' – a martyr: on his way home, he is attacked – although the author does not say so in as many words, he implies that the attackers are Communists. He is struck by a knuckleduster and dies from meningitis. Schenzinger offers an upbeat ending, claiming that on Reich Youth Day – which, historically, took place in Potsdam on 1–2 October 1932 and which Quex had helped to prepare – '75,000 lads marched past their Führer with their brightly shining faces'.[82]

It was above all in the working-class areas of Berlin that the SA and Hitler Youth movement recruited boys like Heini Völker, boys who were prepared to march without demanding to know 'anything more'. Conversely, they were relatively unsuccessful in persuading members of the organized workers' movement to change sides. Instead, they proved attractive to a type of person who had already existed in the Kaiserreich but who as a general rule had been ignored by the traditional right-wing parties and organizations. The National Socialists were the first to appeal explicitly to 'the nationally minded employed' and to press them into service in their aggressive demonstrations. In this context it is significant that anti-Semitism plays no part in *Der Hitlerjunge Quex*. Instead, the author stresses how in his daily life Heini feels only revulsion at most of the people living around him in his working-class district of the city. While walking along the Beusselstraße, he finds the children at play to be 'rude and badly brought up' and feels 'a great desire to punch one or other of these little brats'. On seeing the adolescents standing around in groups and often discussing politics, he observes that

> they carried on in their pretentious way as if they were the source of all wisdom. [...] They went on and on about dictatorship and capitalists, they were always fighting, and every third sentence started with 'Down with ...'. For him, this was all no more than a way of showing off. They were incompetents and idlers. The less they could do, the bigger their mouths. [...] One of them was standing on the corner of the Huttenstraße and holding forth. [...] The things he was spewing out they had heard before until they were sick of it. They had read it on leaflets and on advertising pillars. He had had all that he could take of these brothers.[83]

During the early years of the SA in Berlin, most of its members were still part of the tradition of the Freikorps and defence associations that had been markedly anti-Semitic in character. During the period of 'conquest of the Red districts', by contrast, there had been an appreciable increase in the number of young men who came from the proletariat or from a background of skilled manual work. By the beginning of 1932, therefore, there were thousands of young, often unemployed and bitterly resentful skilled and unskilled workers and public employees concentrated in the working-class areas of Berlin with a potential for violence that Hitler could deploy in his 'war on Marxism'. Both the SA and the Hitler Youth movement knew that they could provoke their enemies into attacking their own columns – and they did so. As one later writer has noted, the SA differed from other paramilitary organizations in that 'its marches were not simply propaganda or symbolic acts of violence. Rather, the SA had the effortless ability to use its marches as a form of provocation and to break out of its march formations in order to commit acts of thuggish brutality.'[84]

So tense was the political atmosphere in the run-up to the first round of the presidential elections and so swift the descent into economic chaos that the activities of the SA were bound to give the impression of a deliberate attempt to exacerbate the situation in the 'Red' districts of the capital. There were even reports that the SA was planning a putsch, with the result that the Prussian minister of the interior, Carl Severing, was obliged to issue a directive to the police authorities on 11 March:

> For several days, information, news and rumours have been circulating freely among the population, claiming that radical groups, especially the National Socialists, are planning a violent overthrow of the government on 13 March immediately after the elections for president and without regard to the outcome of the same. It is the task of the police to counter these nervous reports. But I would ask you as your particular duty to ensure that as a preventative measure each and every attempt to disturb the public order is nipped in the bud with all possible dispatch.[85]

The city's chief of police, Albert Grzesinski, announced that with effect from the morning of 12 March the police were on high alert and that all demonstrations planned for 12 and 13 March were banned. Members of political organizations were also prohibited from riding in lorries. The police would use all the means in their power to ensure that the voting remained free and that public order was not violated:

Passers-by are urged to avoid standing still unnecessarily and not to go near larger gatherings of people. The peace-loving inhabitants of Berlin are asked to keep out of the way of the danger that exists for innocent bystanders in the event of clashes and of riots requiring police intervention. They should overcome their natural curiosity and after exercising their right to vote await the outcome of the poll calmly and in their own homes. The results will be broadcast on the radio quickly and reliably.[86]

Peculiarities in the Voting Patterns in Berlin

On the actual day of the elections – a Sunday – the city in fact remained calm. Rumours of a putsch appeared to have evaporated, and a local midday paper was pleased to note:

> In the capital police carrying carbines had patrolled the streets only hours before the polling stations opened, making one fear the worst, but in the event the picture that presented itself to us on a carefree spring morning was one of the population enjoying the fine weather and performing their electoral duties generally within the context of a pre-Easter walk. Only in the strongholds of left-wing radicalism – in this sense there are no out-and-out Nazi centres in Berlin – was the mood tense. But this was due in the main to memories of May 1929. [. . .] In the west and south of the city there was little trace of an election mood, and only the posters outside the polling stations suggested that this was polling day.[87]

Hindenburg emerged as the clear victor with 49.6 per cent of the votes cast, missing an absolute majority by the narrowest of margins but none the less necessitating a second round of voting. The Communist Party's candidate, Ernst Thälmann, received 13.2 per cent of the vote, the Stahlhelm leader, Theodor Duersterberg, 6.8 per cent. In both cases these were disappointing results. Adolf Gustav Winter, the candidate of the sectarian party styling itself the 'Victims of Inflation', won only 0.3 per cent. Hitler's share of the ballot – 30.1 per cent, or 11.3 million votes – was clearly better than the NSDAP's result in the Reichstag elections on 14 September 1930 (6.4 million votes, or 18.3 per cent),[88] but the party's propaganda machine, screaming 'Hitler will be president!', had raised expectations to such a pitch that the actual result was bound to come as a shock to his supporters.[89]

As had long been the case, the results in Berlin departed in often substantial ways from those in the country as a whole. Here, too, Hindenburg was clearly the winner, albeit with only 45.1 per cent of the vote. Conversely, Ernst Thälmann did far better than the national average, with 23.6 per cent of the vote, although this was still less than the 27.3 per cent that his party had polled in September 1930. With 8.0 per cent of the total vote, Duersterberg, too, exceeded the national average. But the most remarkable result of all was Hitler's modest 23.0 per cent. Although this marked an improvement on the NSDAP's result in September 1930, when it had won 14.6 per cent of the vote, it still fell strikingly short of the party's average for the country as a whole. In the Communist stronghold of Wedding, the NSDAP's avowed aim of 'smashing Marxism' had once again proved to be a pipe dream: here Hitler won only 15.2 per cent of the vote. Duesterberg took 5.2 per cent, while Thälmann, on 38.6 per cent, was only marginally short of Hindenburg's total of 40.1 per cent. At the same time, the extreme political divisions in Berlin may also be seen in the fact that Hitler beat Thälmann in ten out of the city's twenty electoral wards.[90]

The Central Committee of the KPD reacted to the results in an entirely predictable way, spouting phrases about 'Social Fascism' and insisting that the party had not yet succeeded in 'making clear the character of the SPD as the moderate wing of Fascism and the twin brother of Hitler's Fascism'.[91] For his part, Hitler sought to counter any sense of resignation in his party and appealed to his members, including those of the SA, the Hitler Youth movement and a number of subsidiary organizations, demanding that they should 'immediately' begin to prepare for the second round of the elections.[92] But those sections of the press that had supported Hindenburg – the Social Democratic *Vorwärts*, a number of the smaller left-wing liberal newspapers and, above all, the papers that were part of the Mosse and Ullstein empires – declared the 'battle' already over. Writing in the *Vossische Zeitung* under the headline 'Counterattack!', the historian Veit Valentin began his editorial with the words: 'The election on 13 March marks a turning point in the history of our age. It is compensation for the disastrous elections in September 1930. Since 13 March the spell of National Socialism has been broken.'[93] And Theodor Wolff summed up the situation in his first leading article after the election: 'The strident prophecy that appeared on so many posters, claiming "You can do what you like, Hitler will still be president", has suffered the same fate as all the other vainglorious claims on the lips of the National Socialists and is now no more than a risible memory.'[94]

By 21 March Hitler was back in Berlin, where he addressed a meeting of the party's press and propaganda chiefs at the Kaiserhof. Not only was the text of his speech not published, but even the meeting itself was kept secret.[95] But at least part of the contents of Hitler's address has survived in the published reminiscences of the journalist Albert Krebs, who until May 1932 was one of the leaders of the Hamburg branch of the party. Krebs begins by recalling the ill feeling among all who were present at the meeting and who vented their annoyance at their electoral defeat in mocking and rebellious remarks. Even 'the overbearing gilded stucco decorations of the hotel' were a source of anger, until Hitler rose to speak and eventually managed to overcome at least some of the frustration that was felt by party activists. He described the course of the election campaign and set out what he saw as the reasons for the party's failure. According to Krebs, these consisted above all in the 'shortcomings of the middle- and lower-ranking party authorities' and serious difficulties with the party press machine. Hitler ended his speech by demanding that his press officers derive more political capital from the death of members of the SA.[96]

It seems from Krebs' account of the meeting that Hitler's harangue was designed to nip in the bud all criticism of his own contribution. In an interview with the correspondent of the *Daily Express* in Berlin, Sefton Delmer, he evinced a striking degree of demonstrative and pugnacious optimism in advance of the second round of voting. Delmer explained to his readers that Hitler had just returned to Berlin to resume his work as a government councillor in the employment of the Braunschweig embassy. When asked if he was 'downhearted', Hitler said that he was not. He had won five million more votes than in the Reichstag elections and was confident that in the second round he would increase his share still further. Indeed, he went on, he would show the world an electoral campaign such as it had never seen before. The government had ordered a suspension of campaigning over the Easter period,[97] which left only a week in which to work before the vote on 10 April. 'But in the six days left I shall make history. I shall address at least a million people. I shall have an airplane and fly in it from one town to another, speaking at four or five meetings a day.'[98]

An Electioneering Marathon

Beginning on 3 April 1932, the NSDAP propaganda machine organized a feat that was without precedent in the history of German politics, a feat that it then went on to repeat during the week of campaigning for the Landtag elections in Prussia, Bavaria, Württemberg and Anhalt between 16 and 23 April. Above and beyond the usual flood of brochures, leaflets and posters, Hitler's electoral campaign focused on a series of twenty-three rallies in twenty-one towns and cities the length and breadth of Germany attended by a total of almost a million people.[99] But what gave this particular campaign its symbolic edge was the fact that, as he had explained to Delmer, Hitler travelled almost everywhere by aeroplane, a development trailed by the party's propaganda machine as the 'Führer's flight over Germany'. Hitler's admirers could later buy a slender volume with fold-out plates 'documenting' Hitler's first two flights. The text was the work of a staff writer on the *Völkischer Beobachter*, its overwrought tone apparent from its very opening sentences:

> If the mountains and seas, the blue of the sky and the stars of the night could tell a story, they would have to tell how the German people is rising up in rebellion. [...] Just as the swallows and the starlings, the auricula and the anemone announce the arrival of spring, so millions of people from the mountains to the sea were able to attest to the German spring and the awakening of the German people when they paid tribute to Adolf Hitler, cheering him with indescribable enthusiasm and in thrall to the deepest emotion.[100]

It was Goebbels himself who was placed in charge of the National Socialists' propaganda machine.[101] The importance that the party attached to Hitler's appearances in Berlin is clear from the fact that, in the course of his first series of flights between 3 and 9 April, he spoke no fewer than three times in a single day in the city: late in the afternoon of 4 April at the Lustgarten between the Royal Palace and the Old Museum, and twice during the evening, first in the Sportpalast and then in the Friedrichshain Rooms. As with Hitler's appearance at the Sportpalast in 1928, Goebbels had held a sort of dry run at the Lustgarten on 9 March, an event that, according to his diary, attracted eighty thousand visitors,[102] encouraging him to book the historic venue again a month later. After all, Hitler's name and the sensational circumstances of his first *Deutschlandflug** were bound to ensure a heightened level of interest. Hitler, too, was aware of the political significance of the Lustgarten as a parade ground capable of attracting vast numbers of people, a point that he had elaborated in *Mein Kampf* in the context of the use of symbols in political propaganda:

> Then, after the War, I experienced a mass demonstration of Marxists in front of the Royal Palace and the Lustgarten. A sea of red flags, red scarves, and red flowers gave to this demonstration, in which an estimated hundred and twenty thousand persons took part, an aspect that was gigantic from the purely external point of view. I myself could feel and understand how easily the man of the people succumbs to the suggestive magic of a spectacle so grandiose in effect.[103]

---

* Hitler's aerial speaking tours of Germany during his election campaigns. For the first of these, 3–9 April 1932, he used a hired plane.

In Wilhelminian Germany the Lustgarten was the place where new recruits traditionally took their oath of allegiance, but under the Weimar Republic it became a venue for large-scale political demonstrations and rallies, often attracting as many as half a million people, notably at the SPD and KPD's May Day rallies.[104] An impressive mass demonstration was held here on the day after Walther Rathenau was murdered in June 1922, when Count Harry Kessler wrote in his diary of 'more than 200,000 people, a sea of people above whom countless red and black-red-and-gold flags wafted'.[105] Following his tryout on 9 March 1932, Goebbels was proud to note that 'we've conquered this historic meeting place for the first time'.[106]

The NSDAP propaganda machine was confident that Hitler's appearance at the Lustgarten would mark a further step on the road to 'capturing the Red bulwark'. The author of the aforementioned volume *Hitler über Deutschland* wrote:

Two hundred thousand people, a crowd stretching further than the eye could see, a single black mass, extended from the Palace across the vast square and as far as the Cathedral, the Museum, thence to the bridge and Arsenal and even into the broad approach roads. Not since the November Revolution had the Lustgarten seen such crowds. The evening was already drawing its veil across the heavens. Only down below, above the tops of the trees, where the Brandenburg Gate lies, was there still a broad strip of light. It was there that the Führer was expected. Above the heads of the crowd of 200,000 people an aeroplane flew. On its wings was emblazoned a single word that brought hope to millions: 'Hitler.' Two large red swastika pennants fluttered along its fuse-lage. There was then a roar in the distance, a roar that drew closer as arms were raised like ears of wheat in a cornfield, the flags stiffened in the wind, a storm of jubilation seized hold of the vast army of people in the Lustgarten and the Führer's automobile drove between the walls of people. It was this crowd that Adolf Hitler now addressed.

The Lustgarten had witnessed far larger rallies than this, but from its very title to the whole way in which it was stage-managed, the rally was a model for all later events of its kind.

Hitler's speech was remarkably indecisive. In the main he spoke about 'the Weimar Republic's lie that women are being stripped of their rights by National Socialism'. (The country's propaganda chiefs had insisted on demanding an 'explanation' from the NSDAP on its 'particular attitude to women', which had then been turned into one of the main emphases of the campaign.)[107] Hitler's observations on the subject culminated in the claim that throughout the ages 'men' had been obliged to ensure that 'women' could not only earn their daily bread but that 'both together can form the eternal bond of matrimony. The child should not be felt as a bitter burden as a result of social conditions but as a source of genuine happiness.' At the end of his speech he relapsed into quasi-liturgical language, appealing to his audience to 'lift up your hearts and draw new faith from the resurrection of our people. [. . .] Ultimately we shall live to see the kingdom of freedom, honour and social justice. Long live Germany!'[108]

From the Lustgarten Hitler drove straight to Potsdam, where he addressed another gathering at the Airport Stadium. After spending some time reviling the 'party system' and assuring his listeners that he would continue to fight against this system 'for one year or if necessary for another ten', he issued what amounted to an endorsement of the whole of the Prussian tradition. Hitler had frequently expressed his admiration of the Prussian electors and kings of the seventeenth and eighteenth centuries, but never had he drawn such a clear parallel between the rise and character of Prussia, on the one hand, and the growth and political programme of the NSDAP, on the other:

> I am speaking to you this evening on soil that is sacred to us National Socialists, for this clod of earth was once the starting point for a very small movement that was initially ignored and mocked and ridiculed, but this little state of Brandenburg has become Prussia, and Prussia has ultimately become Germany. And this is something that we, too, can acknowledge with pride: we were small when we began and were despised and mocked, but we slowly became the National Socialist movement and now have more than eleven million men and women behind us. [. . .] It was here on this soil that the attempt was first made to turn the state into the servant of the people. It was here that the attempt was first made to overcome classes and social divisions. [. . .] In the space of two centuries something grew up that we all recognized as the great German Reich's invincible army.[109]

Great was the memory of the Prussian Brandenburg army, but greater still was the memory of King Frederick, 'who never failed even in adversity but who always remained steadfast, never yielding and never capitulating'. Hitler ended his speech with the words: 'We wish and hope that this spirit of Prussia will one day be the spirit of our own age, too.' He was already on his way back to Berlin for further appearances at the Sportpalast and the Friedrichshain Rooms while the organizers in Potsdam were holding a particularly spectacular send-off: 'Five thousand torches shone in the faces of the Brandenburg peasants. The SA and SS pay homage and greet their great king.'[110]

Exactly 301 days later the SA of Berlin-Brandenburg was again to hold its torches aloft.

10

'German Berlin is on the march'

1932–3: THE ROAD TO POWER

'When the SA goes marching again in its brown shirts, the Depression will all be over, and our enemies will soon sink to the ground beneath our blows.'
Joseph Goebbels, diary entry, 8 May 1932[1]

'While we were driving through the beautiful countryside on Sunday, the unbridled and organized terror of the Nazis left another seventeen victims dead and almost two hundred injured. Day in, day out, Sunday after Sunday, it is a St Bartholomew's Day Massacre.'
Count Harry Kessler, diary entry, 12 July 1932[2]

'We shall conquer this city – not without Hitler and not in spite of him, but under his leadership.'
Joseph Goebbels at an NSDAP rally in the Sportpalast, 20 January 1933[3]

No Cause for Panic

The second round of voting in the presidential elections produced the expected result when Hindenburg won an absolute majority with 53 per cent of the vote and was duly re-elected. But the turnout was lower than in the first round, and the Communist candidate, Ernst Thälmann, now won just 10.2 per cent of the vote as compared with 13.2 per cent only a few weeks earlier. Meanwhile, Hitler's share had gone up from 30.1 to 36.8 per cent, adding more than two million votes to his overall total.[4]

The press that supported the 'state front', as the parties and other organizations that backed Hindenburg were often called, was clearly relieved, claiming that the majority of the German people had announced their determination to reject all experiments, no matter which side they came from.[5] Commentators more or less refused to acknowledge the fact that almost 37 per cent of the German people were willing to countenance a 'Hitler experiment'. In Berlin, too, relief at Hindenburg's victory outweighed all other considerations, although the results in the city were in some ways even more problematic than in the rest of the country, not least because, although Hindenburg topped the poll here, too, he won only 48.1 per cent of the votes cast in the capital. Thälmann came a poor third, with 20.7 per cent of the votes cast, while Hitler increased his proportion of the vote by more than eight percentage points to 31.2 per cent – a greater increase than the NSDAP's national average. Even in a Communist stronghold like Wedding he managed almost 22 per cent, while in the NSDAP hotbed of Steglitz he won 46.2 per cent of the vote, slightly more than Hindenburg.[6]

If there were no obvious signs of panic in non-National Socialist circles, this may have been due to the fact that at the time of the second round of elections it looked as if the police and the public prosecutor were ready to take decisive steps to combat the SA's preparations for civil war. On 17 March the police had already raided the offices of the NSDAP and SA on the orders of the Prussian minister of the interior, Carl Severing. According to one official communiqué, the police were obliged to act because it had been established that in the event of an electoral victory the SA was known to be planning a series of violent attacks on the rest of the population, including the political enemies of the National Socialists, and was also intending to take over certain official positions. SA units had been placed on high alert on election day. It was allegedly the National Socialists' 'high command in Munich' that had ordered these measures, presumably a reference to the SA leadership under its chief of staff, Ernst Röhm. It was immaterial, the communiqué went on, whether the leaders of the NSDAP – in other words, Hitler – approved or disapproved of these preparations for civil war. There could be no doubt that at least several of the SA's group leaders were intent on committing serious acts of violence.[7]

In Berlin alone sixty different premises were searched. Lorryloads of police officers arrived outside the NSDAP offices in the Hedemannstraße in Kreuzberg at around half past ten in the morning, and officers from both the ordinary constabulary and the criminal investigation department occupied the building. Searches were also undertaken of all the offices run by individual SA units and the private apartments of National Socialist leaders.[8] In its initial report on its actions, the Prussian government drew attention to the discovery not only of internal SA orders relating to polling day but also of numerous weapons. The report went on:

Particular light is shed on all these observations by notes found a few days ago during the searches in Berlin. According to these plans, units of the SA would move into position in the city, where, supported by other units brought into the capital from the surrounding area, they would blockade the city. The plans were being prepared and prosecuted with great care.

There were also 'emergency orders' including detailed instructions for mobilizing and positioning individual units of the SA at particular points, and plans to impound weapons, to have council leaders and local policemen arrested by special command units, to occupy telephone exchanges and to guard all roads into and out of the city. 'Emergency orders were also found in the Hedemannstraße, the NSDAP's main offices in Berlin, the wording of which made it abundantly clear that they were meant for the first round of voting in the presidential election and were designed to blockade Greater Berlin.'[9]

The word used in the report to describe this blockade was *Zernierung*, a military term derived from the French *cerner* and generally used to refer to the blockade of a fortress. How did Goebbels react to the rumours of a putsch? On 11 March 1932 he had written in his diary: 'I do not believe it. Once we are in power, we should think less of getting out of Berlin than of stopping others from leaving.'[10] The *Berliner Tageblatt*, conversely, did not mince its words, commenting on the police finds by noting that the National Socialists' warlike preparations had nothing to do with politics or the work of politicians but were the first stages in a civil war, which could not be concealed beneath the pretext that they were preventative measures designed to counter any unrest on the part of the Communists:

They are playing with fire in the most irresponsible manner imaginable, a game that the government cannot continue to observe from afar for much longer. [. . .] The Prussian government is certainly not minded to stand idly by while an army is equipped whose only aim is to establish the domination of a minority over the majority of the population and which, whether it is activated or not, remains a source of profound disquiet for the whole of the public at large.

The paper concluded by expressing the hope that, as a result of the evidence that had been brought to light in this way, the government might finally be persuaded to act.[11]

Banned as Expected

Many observers asked themselves why the police had taken so long to act – after all, the SA had for years made no secret of its willingness to commit acts of violence and brutality – but the police could only conduct searches and provide evidence, of course. The government alone could enforce a nationwide ban on the SA. Writing in the *Berliner Tageblatt*, the legendary theatre critic Alfred Kerr used a free-verse form to pillory the state's reluctance to intervene:

> Sie rüsten zum Putsch in Nebel und Dämmer,
> Gepackt der Tornister, die Feldküche dampft;
> Wir bleiben friedlich wie die Lämmer.
> Und blinzeln wie die Tauben sanft. [. . .]
> Es fragt sich: wie wir einschreiten sollen.
> Es fragt sich, ob –, es fragt sich, wann;
> Warten wir, bis die Köpfe rollen.
> Immer langsam voran.
> Immer langsam voran.[12]

[They're arming themselves for the putsch in mist and in darkness. The knapsack is packed, the field kitchen's steaming. We remain as quiet as lambs. And blink like gentle doves. [. . .] The question is: how should we intervene? The question is: whether and when? Let's wait till the heads start to roll. Slow and steady wins the race. Slow and steady wins the race.]

Unknown to Kerr, there was in fact behind-the-scenes activity: on the day before his poem appeared in print, a meeting had taken place in Berlin under the chairmanship of the minister of the interior, Wilhelm Groener, at which various regional representatives, including the Prussian minister of the interior, Carl Severing, and the Bavarian minister of state, Karl Stützel, demanded a ban on the SA and SS and a number of subsidiary organizations not only in individual regions but in the country as a whole.[13] But Groener himself continued to hesitate: whereas it made sense to get rid of the SA, 'the thousand men who were members and who had only the best of intentions' should not be 'repudiated by the state'. Rather, they should be given a chance to 'join the state'. After all, the 'outward impression' left by these people was an 'altogether good one – you have only to look into their eyes'. Behind Groener's remarks was the belief on the part of leading members of the Reichswehr, including Groener himself, that in the longer term the SA should not be allowed to continue to operate 'in a political form' but should be turned into 'a kind of militia under the aegis of sport' and that other 'organizations that cannot be tolerated in the long run' should be incorporated into it. In general, this seems to have meant the Iron Front, which was dominated by Social Democrats.[14]

In the end Groener gave in to pressure from the various regions and persuaded Heinrich Brüning and ultimately Hindenburg, too, to sign an emergency decree on 13 April 1932 ordering the immediate disbandment of all of the NSDAP's 'paramilitary organizations', in other words, 'the Storm Troopers (SA), the Protection Squads (SS) and all the staff and other organizations belonging to them, including the SA Observers, SA Reserves, Motorized Storm Divisions, Marine Storm Divisions, Cavalry Storm Divisions, Flying Corps, Motorized Corps, Ambulance Corps, Führer Schools, SA Barracks and Ordnance Units'. The justification for the ban ended by claiming that no German government could tolerate any party attempting to create a state within a state.[15] For the National Socialists, however, 'the ban came as no surprise for they were extremely well informed about every stage of the government's consultations and had made all the necessary preparations to disguise the true identity of the SA'.[16] This was confirmed by a letter sent to Groener by Wilhelm Abegg, the secretary of state, a week after the decree was issued. In it he was forced to admit that attempts to impound incriminating objects, as demanded under the emergency legislation, had been 'successful to only a limited extent because the leaders and premises in question had been tipped off the previous day about the planned measure and had therefore had ample time to remove all the relevant objects'. A whole series of other documents showed that 'the NSDAP had known about the planned decree by 12 April 1932 at the latest and was evidently even aware of its exact wording. In other words, it had clearly been informed by one of the country's civil servants.'[17] Abegg had hit the nail on the head, for Goebbels had noted in his diary on the 11th: 'I have to telephone the Führer late at night. The government is planning a nationwide ban on the SA. But it is playing with fire. After making further enquiries, I am able to give the Führer more information at five the next morning.'[18] Hitler was at the Kaiserhof from the 12th – two days after the completion of the electoral campaign for the country's presidency. He seems not to have been particularly perturbed by the impending ban. On the evening before it was officially announced, he gave an interview at the Kaiserhof to Sefton Delmer, the Berlin correspondent of the *Daily Express*. Asked his opinion of a possible ban on the SA, Hitler adopted an attitude that was half-threatening, half-relaxed: ' "If they dissolve the storm troops organisation," he said, "then they will relieve me of my responsibilities for them. I shall not, as up to the present, have these 400,000 men under my control. I cannot be held accountable for what they will do in such a case." ' And what would Hitler do in the event of such a ban? ' "Let them declare them dissolved if they like," was his answer. "They cannot cut off the heads of my men, and as long as they have heads and hearts my men will remain loyal to me." '[19]

On the day of the ban, Hitler addressed an appeal to his 'former comrades in the SA and SS', inviting them to give 'the present authorities' no occasion to call off the elections that were planned for 24 April for the regional assemblies in Prussia, Bavaria, Württemberg and Anhalt or for Hamburg City Council. 'Our response to this new act of desperation on the part of the system will not be a parade but a blow. The 24th of April is the day of reckoning.'[20]

According to a later official account of the rise of the 'brown army' in Berlin, 'men who can be trusted by the movement' occupied 'the highest posts in government'. Tipped off by these officials, the SA had plenty of time 'to remove or destroy all the important evidence', not only in Berlin but in the country as a whole, with the result that 'the officials in question generally found only empty cupboards, boxes and crates'. Striking a note of smug self-satisfaction, the author went on:

> The Storm Trooper units were quickly transformed, mostly into sports organizations. Schöneberg Reserve Storm Unit 3, for example, became the Brandenburg Sports Society, Storm Unit 8 of Prenzlauer Berg formed a foot-ball club and joined the German People's Sports Association. [. . .] Troop 105 from Wedding, on the other hand, set itself up as a bowling club, and Storm Unit 122 from Prenzlauer Berg became the Small-Bore Rifle Association.[21]

Hitler himself returned to the campaign trail. On 22 April he addressed an audience reckoned to number sixty thousand in Frankfurt an der Oder, followed by 75,000 in Neuruppin and then, later that evening, he was back in the Sportpalast in Berlin for a rally described with the usual hyperbole by the campaign's official chronicler: 'The 25,000 men and women in the Sportpalast receive their Führer with countless flowers and tumultuous cheering. Only after almost fifteen minutes of uninterrupted clapping and stamping and shouting was he finally able to begin his address.'[22] For the most part it was the same speech that he had been delivering several times a day since the start of the campaign, the only difference being the degree of clarity with which he was now prepared to spell out his party's aims: 'I come to the only reproach that they [Hitler's political opponents] can rightly level at me: I want to destroy all parties; I hereby acknowledge: Yes, this is what we want to do.'[23]

On 25 April one of the local newspapers was able to head its report: 'Election Day in Berlin Passes Off without Incident.' Even in the 'proletarian' north of the city, there had been little sign of unrest. 'As the ultimate novelty, the red flags displayed a black, red and gold insert, and in the Red northern part of the city the swastika banners handed out by the National Socialist Party disappeared behind the flags of the Communists.'[24] Throughout the city the NSDAP had confirmed expectations and improved on its poor showing in the last elections for the Prussian Landtag on 28 May 1928, when it had polled only 38,000 votes. That figure was now 766,000. The SPD won 798,000, the KPD 649,000, while the number of votes cast for the German Nationalists – previously exceptionally popular in Berlin – had fallen from 438,000 to 226,000. All the other parties were left far behind. A more informative guide to the political mood in Berlin is offered by a comparison with the results in the second round of elections for the presidency, which had taken place exactly two weeks earlier, when Hitler had received 864,000 votes. The turnout had been more or less the same, but the NSDAP had lost almost 100,000 votes, probably to the German Nationalists, whose candidate had not taken part in the elections on 10 April.[25] The NSDAP now had 162 representatives in the new Prussian Landtag, compared with only nine in 1928. The SPD had 94 (137 in 1928), the Centre Party 67 (71), the KPD 57 (48) and the DNVP 31 (71). The remaining parties were reduced to the status of splinter groups.[26] The resultant stalemate could have been resolved by a coalition between the NSDAP and the Centre Party, but for the time being the existing government continued in office under its SPD prime minister, Otto Braun. 'There is no doubt', wrote Theodor Wolff in the *Berliner Tageblatt*, 'that this time, too, National Socialism had had a brilliant run for its money, at least as far as the final furlong from home. But this is the hurdle that the Brownshirt is unable to take.' The 'nationalist opposition' had triumphed, but 'without taking the prize'. It had not received 'the key to the castle', and its gunpowder had been expended in vain.[27] Wolff's assessment of the situation is typical of that of large groups of liberal, republican observers: as with the presidential election, the successes of the NSDAP were written off on the grounds that the party had not achieved its goal of an absolute majority.

Even before the decree banning the SA had been announced, it had already been criticized and even rejected by influential sections of the Reichswehr, including Major General Kurt von Schleicher, who was chief of the ministerial office in the Defence Ministry.[28] Its implementation led to a serious loss of trust not only in the defence minister, Wilhelm Groener, but increasingly in the whole of Brüning's cabinet. Immediately after its promulgation, Goebbels had learnt that Schleicher did not approve of Groener's course of action,[29] with the result that barely a week later the first contacts had taken place between Schleicher and a representative of the NSDAP in the person of the commander of the SA in Berlin, Wolf-Heinrich Helldorf, who was increasingly popular with the party's leaders following his 'dashing appearance' as the organizer of the Kurfürstendamm progrom in September 1931.[30] Their initial meeting was followed very quickly by a second one.[31] Schleicher soon made it clear that he wanted nothing less than a change of government in Prussia. Goebbels immediately suspected that the 'aim of the other side' was to 'turn the Führer away from the party' and so he 'reported on the situation by telephone',[32] with the result that a direct exchange of views between Schleicher and Hitler now became imperative. By 28 April, Goebbels was able to note: 'the Führer has been to see Schleicher. The conversation went well.' In spite of this, he felt that as far as the situation in Prussia was concerned the NSDAP leadership could 'still see no way out of its difficulties'.[33]

Schleicher's Plot

Once the conspiracy[34] had been set in train, however, it quickly developed in a direction that both parties found entirely to their liking. According to a contemporary account by two journalists known for their investigative reporting, Schleicher's intrigue was 'in every respect so subtle that it has so far proved impossible to uncover every aspect of it'.[35] Not even they had been able to discover what had taken place behind the scenes in Berlin on 7 May 1932. The local press had been reporting vaguely on 'rumours of a crisis' in the capital since the beginning of the month.[36] On the 6th, Hitler left the Obersalzberg and took the night train from Munich to Berlin, where he met Schleicher for secret talks on the 7th. Deliberately avoiding taking rooms at the Kaiserhof and seeking to escape the attention of the rumour-mongers in the city, he continued his journey that same night to the estate of a party member in Mecklenburg. His brief stay in Berlin on his return on 10 May likewise passed unnoticed by the public at large.[37] Goebbels was excluded from the meeting with Schleicher, which involved 'a number of gentlemen from the president's immediate circle',[38] but he none the less heard enough about this 'important discussion' to be able to note that 'everything is going well. The Führer spoke compellingly. Brüning is expected to go within the next few days. The president will withdraw his trust in him. The plan is to install a presidential cabinet; the Reichstag will be dissolved. [. . .] It is gratifying to think that no one suspects a thing, least of all Brüning himself.'[39] The public at large learnt nothing about all these plans and secret agreements. According to one later writer on the NDSAP, Thilo Vogelsang, 'domestic politics became increasingly focused on an ever-smaller circle in the capital',[40] while his fellow historian Albert Krebs noted how 'Hitler was forced to seek his road to power through the back door'.[41] Meanwhile four NSDAP deputies beat up a journalist in the Reichstag restaurant.[42] In the main chamber of the house the NSDAP members shouted down Wilhelm Groener, while Brüning confined himself to matters of foreign policy.[43]

On 12 May, Groener offered to resign his ministerial post, leading to speculation in the press about Schleicher as his possible successor, 'either to allow a wider cabinet reshuffle – a number of people are hoping that the Prussian National Socialists may be included in order to produce a shift to the right – or without any such changes taking place'.[44] While the journalists of the republican press could only speculate on the motives of the 'general's camarilla', which they rightly suspected of being behind Groener's fall from power, Goebbels was able to write in his diary that same day: 'We received news from General Schleicher – the crisis is going as planned.'[45]

On 19 May, Hitler addressed the NSDAP members of the Prussian Landtag – although he himself was not a member, he could hardly resist the opportunity to speak to them as their party leader. The 162 newly elected representatives met at the Prinz Albrecht Hotel in Berlin, a building situated at 9 Prinz-Albrecht-Straße, diagonally opposite the Prussian Landtag at no. 5. This had the advantage from the NSDAP's point of view of occupying a symbolically threatening position similar to that of the Kaiserhof vis-à-vis the Reich Chancellery.[46] The National Socialist movement, Hitler told his audience, had not fought for thirteen years simply to perpetuate the current state of German politics by means of some coalition or other. Rather, it was conscious of its responsibility to its thirteen million voters who wanted change. The battle was not being fought in order to occupy certain ministerial posts or to enter government at any price. There could be no government in Prussia that did not want to include the NSDAP. At present the movement's group of representatives in Prussia was one of its most powerful instruments, the 'troops with which the final battle may be fought'. The party's enemies hoped that it would lose its nerve, but this hope was delusional. The NSDAP would allow its policies to be dictated 'only by the coldest of considerations'. Hitler ended his speech by appealing to the deputies to work tenaciously and fulfil their obligations 'to the movement and to the nation as a whole'. He had 'complete confidence' in them and in their leadership and showed his indebtedness to each and every one of them 'by shaking their hands'.[47] In his speech, Hitler astutely left open the question whether his rejection of any coalition and his refusal to 'enter government at any price' referred only to Prussia or to the country in general. He left straight afterwards and between then and 17 June appeared in a total of eighteen different venues, delivering election speeches as part of the campaigns for the regional assemblies in Oldenburg, Mecklenburg and Hesse.[48]

Brüning announced the resignation of his entire cabinet on 30 May 1932, a resignation accepted by Hindenburg on the 31st. By the following day the president had appointed Franz von Papen as his new chancellor.[49] In the wake of his meetings with Hitler, Schleicher was convinced that the two of them had agreed on a 'political deal': 'Reacceptance of the SA and SS and dissolution of the Reichstag or toleration of a government that is either shuffled or reformed.'[50] But even before Brüning's fall from power, Groener had realized that there were doubts concerning the extent to which the 'political deal' was mutually binding. As he wrote on 22 May, 'Schleicher has long been resolved to rule with the help of the Reichswehr and without the Reichstag. But his plans, which he is, of course, no longer confiding in me, are extremely vague, and it is entirely possible that the Nazis are his superiors in matters of cunning and mendaciousness.'[51]

The Illusion of Integration

With the Oldenburg regional elections behind him – the NSDAP had won 48.4 per cent of the votes and gained an absolute majority in a regional assembly for the first time in its history – Hitler could be sufficiently confident of victory to drive to Berlin, where he and Hermann Göring were received by Hindenburg in the early evening of 30 May to discuss the formation of a new government. According to notes kept by the president's office, Hitler was asked to comment on the political situation in general. 'It was necessary,' he explained,

> to form a powerful political basis within the country; this could be achieved only by new elections to the Reichstag, which must be held as soon as possible. On this basis a national government could work forcefully and effectively in the longer term; a government that had the trust of the people could also demand more sacrifices than the previous one. In principle he and his movement were prepared to work together on this basis, without his laying down any conditions for the makeup of the cabinet. The only precondition for a productive working relationship with a new government formed by the president was, first, that the Reichstag should be dissolved as quickly

as possible and new elections held for a Reichstag that reflected the mood of the people and, second, the immediate suspension of the various decrees that defamed the NSDAP, especially the ban on the SA.[52]

Both sides interpreted this declaration in the way that suited them best. Hindenburg, Papen and Schleicher regarded it as Hitler's assurance that he would tolerate the new government and that this would entail a shift towards the right, which was what they themselves were striving for. Hitler, conversely, saw the future government as no more than a 'transitional cabinet', and at a further meeting with Schleicher on 3 June he even refused to provide a written guarantee that he would tolerate Papen's cabinet.[53]

In the belief that the NSDAP was committed to working with them, the other parties to the agreement made haste to comply with the first of Hitler's demands. On 4 June 1932 Hindenburg dissolved the Reichstag with immediate effect and two days later set a date for new elections – 31 July. This was the latest possible date that he could have announced and as such was calculated to annoy the NSDAP, which was in any case unhappy with the ponderous pace of developments.[54] Also on 4 June the new minister of the interior, Wilhelm von Gayl, announced that all existing provisions for maintaining law and order would be redrafted 'within the shortest possible space of time' and that 'all the present injustices towards the nationalist move-ment' in all their various forms would be resolved.[55] Time and again during this period Hitler put in brief appearances in Berlin to demand that his conditions be met. On 13 June, for example, he discussed the matter with the chancellor and, according to Goebbels, was 'more insistent than ever' that the ban on the SA be lifted, a move resisted in particular by the regional govern-ments in the south of the country.[56] The following day the ban was still in place, prompting Goebbels to telephone a furious Hitler half a dozen times and to note in his diary that they had no alternative but to take the most drastic steps:

In the evening, in spite of the ban, I go with forty or fifty SA officers in full uniform to a large café on the Potsdamer Platz in order to provoke a response. Our one and only desire is to be arrested by the police. [. . .] Unfortunately the Alexanderplatz [the headquarters of the city's chief of police], which has done us so many other favours, refuses to oblige. Around midnight we walk very slowly across the Potsdamer Platz and Potsdamer Straße. But not a soul stirs. The police stare at us, nonplussed, and then look away again in embarrassment.[57]

Finally, on 16 June, a 'presidential decree against political excesses' was announced. In spite of its name, this lifted the ban on the SA and SS that had by then been in place for just two months.[58] On the 18th, Hitler gave orders for the SA to be 'set up again', a task with which he charged his chief of staff, Ernst Röhm. The SS would likewise be 're-established by Reichsführer H[einrich] Himmler'. At a meeting of NSDAP leaders in Weimar on the following day Hitler repeated his long-familiar remarks on his party's policy of 'self-defence', but now there was no denying the note of menace that lay behind them. Commentators feared the worst in the days and weeks ahead: 'We shall fight with every legal means to defend our right. But' – and here Hitler raised his voice – 'if anyone in Germany should believe that they can entrench injustice by a breach of the constitution, they will learn to see us from a different side.' Thunderous applause greeted this statement. 'We are fighting in the strictest possible legal way and in the course of this lawful battle we shall use every means to overthrow those who violate the law.'[59] Three weeks later, when the latent threat of civil war risked becoming a real one as a result of the SA's determination to exercise its 'right of self-defence', Hitler offered an even starker assessment of his understanding of the concept of strict legality:

> The brown battalions that are marching across the whole of Germany at a strength of half a million will greet every German and hold out their open hand to him, but beware if it ever reaches the point where our hand becomes a fist as a result of our need to defend ourselves. We shall never relinquish the road to which we have a constitutional right: people may regard this as a provocation a thousand times over. For us, there is only one provocation: when Moscow's hordes march along our German streets.[60]

By the same token, the SA's 'propaganda marches', which started up again with alarming alacrity, were bound to incite not only 'Moscow's hordes' – in other words, the followers of the KPD – but others, too, to acts of retaliation. Throughout the province of Brandenburg, towns and villages were filled with Brownshirts whose units 'marched in serried ranks, parading through the streets in their beloved brown uniforms for all the world to see', while for the rest of the population, too, the return of the Brownshirts was bound to create the impression that the fires of an already tense situation were being stoked to produce yet further incendiary heat. Commenting on the atmosphere in Berlin during the early summer of 1932, one journalist wrote:

It begins with insults directed at their uniforms, followed by scuffles and stone-throwing. Finally a knife or a dagger is pulled from one of the parties' pockets. The new brown jacket that is flaunted by the SA men has the effect of a deliberate provocation, especially in the working-class parts of Berlin. New 'gear' at a time when support for the unemployed is being cut! It is then only a short step from insults to acts of violence.[62]

But it was not just the daily displays of provocative violence on the part of the SA that led to a worsening of the political crisis. No less inflammatory was the aggressive response of the Communists, who reacted to the reappearance of the SA with a wave of generally armed attacks on National Socialists and SA venues as well as with other forms of action. And whereas there were a number of KPD leaders capable of analysing the NSDAP's lasting success with greater or lesser precision and of couching their concern in the language of moderation,[63] the party's practical response continued to be dictated by the 'assessment' of Ernst Thälmann, the chairman of its Central Committee, according to which the 'bourgeoisie is increasingly turning to the NSDAP as the party of toleration, whereas the SPD is still the bourgeoisie's main social prop'.[64] Against this background, nothing could be more welcome to the NSDAP than the undeniably offensive acts of violence on the part of the KPD directed at the National Socialists, especially in the former's strongholds in Berlin. After all, these attacks played an important role in the plans that the NSDAP was formulating for the days and weeks leading up to election day on 31 July.

As early as 20 June – immediately after the NSDAP had reported a further success in the elections to the regional assemblies[65] – Hitler returned to Berlin and in the course of a meeting with the minister of the interior, Wilhelm von Gayl, announced that, 'in the light of the increasing number of acts of terror perpetrated by the Communists and in view of the failure of the country's police authorities', the National Socialists 'would have to claim their right of self-defence if the country did not act quickly and rigorously to curb the excesses of the Communists'.[66] Even during the early weeks of Papen's government, therefore, there were increasingly clear signs of the position that Hitler was both keen and able to adopt on his road to power under the existing conditions which were far more favourable to his party. His would be a dual role, supported, on the one hand, by the growing National Socialist potential for violence in the form of his 'brown army' and, on the other, by the undeniable political weight of the NSDAP throughout the whole of the country, including Prussia, a weight demonstrated most recently by the regional elections in Mecklenburg-Schwerin and Hesse.[67] This dual role also found expression in practical ways, allowing Hitler to act on two different levels, as it were. During the daytime he was a statesman and the leader of the most powerful political party in Germany, wearing an elegant dark-blue double-breasted suit and holding meetings both in public and in secret with secretaries of state, ministers and the chancellor as well as with other prominent figures, urging and even forcing decisions upon them. During the evening, by contrast, he donned his SA uniform and became the supreme commander of his own private army, issuing instructions to a force that now numbered tens of thousands, giving them their marching orders and enjoining them to obey a leader singled out by 'Providence'. These two functions were by no means mutually exclusive but were different sides of the same coin and, indeed, were complementary. In particular, the SA's function as a 'battering ram' against the organized workers' movement – 'Marxism' – at its centre in Berlin was necessarily bound up with the party's goal of gaining state power. It was a function that Hitler himself had given voice to on frequent occasions, when he had insisted that the NSDAP was not simply one party among many vying to gain overall control or to exercise power in a coalition. Rather, it had a 'historic mission' to fulfil by re-establishing a robust and unified 'body of the people', a move that presupposed the 'destruction of Marxism'. None of the other paramilitary organizations in Germany had a political function remotely comparable to that of the SA. The Reichsbanner and the Iron Front, for example, had been formed with the intention of defending parliamentary democracy. And although the Stahlhelm may have included a number of officers, including among its higher echelons, who gazed fondly in the direction of a coup d'état, there were never any concrete plans for such a course of action. Indeed, the Stahlhelm's ability to mount a successful putsch is very much open to question, not least because it was not merely the 'military arm' of the German Nationalists. The Communist Battle League against Fascism was a replacement for the Red Front Fighters' Association, which had been banned in 1929, but its activities were limited to street fighting with the SA, and it never progressed beyond vague plans for 'armed insurrection'. The decisive strategic factor in political developments prior to the Reichstag elections on 31 July was the SA, which in certain circumstances was capable of far more than propaganda marches and calls to arms, especially in Berlin.

Only a few days after the ban on the SA was lifted, Schleicher – now the country's defence minister – was required to defend himself against the reproach, levelled against him by the Social Democratic *Vorwärts*, that he had implicated the Reichswehr in the world of day-to-day politics,[68] encouraging the *Vossische Zeitung* to comment as follows on the new situation:

It is said that General Schleicher came to some arrangement with Hitler in advance of the formation of a new government. Confirmation of this may be seen in the government's generous mood, a generosity that appears to be far from exhausted. But Hitler has failed to keep his side of the bargain and has not accepted a share of the responsibility for what is happening. The premature dissolution of the Reichstag has freed him from the constraint of having to pursue a policy of tolerance, and his SA is marching into the election campaign more uninhibited than ever, with plans for total control already packed in their knapsacks.[69]

It is clear from a random selection of the headlines that appeared in the *Vossische Zeitung* during the period between the lifting of the ban on the SA and the start of the election campaign that the political situation in Berlin in particular had reached boiling point: 'Return of Rioting: Clashes Everywhere on First Day of Resurrected SA', 'Bloodshed in Berlin', 'Planned National Socialist Attack. Shots Fired from "Fischerkietz"', 'Clashes in the City. Shots Fired from Crowd', 'More Bloodshed in Berlin', 'Armed Attacks in Berlin', 'Not a Day Passes without Bloodshed' and 'More Night-time Shootings'.[70]

The clashes reached a new low on 25 June 1932, when dozens of Storm Troopers forced their way into the offices of the Social Democratic *Vorwärts* in the Lindenstraße in Kreuzberg. In the subsequent shoot-out, two bodyguards and a member of the SA were seriously injured.[71] Shortly afterwards the NSDAP in Berlin published a flyer, demonstrating the depths to which the party's propaganda machine was now capable of sinking:

The Jew-boy fears of the synagogue brethren employed by *Vorwärts* have been transferred to the Reichsbanner to such an extent that they did not even wait until their own comrades were out of the line of fire. Perhaps it was even a Jew boy who fired the first shot. [...] But you German workers, comrades of the people, do you intend to allow these Jew boys to lie to you any longer and lead you by the nose? [...] The feelings that have been building up in 400,000 SA men will not tolerate any further increase. Our patience is at an end. We are no longer prepared to stand idly by while our comrades are butchered by this bestialized rabble.[72]

It is no wonder that at the end of June the *Vossische Zeitung* voiced its suspicions that this increase in the number of 'acts of brutality' represented more than 'the usual repertory' of excesses. Rather, the systematic use of cheap propaganda by the right-wing press cast these events in a far more sinister light: 'One has the impression that these acts of terror are being encouraged by the right so that when the moment is opportune they can speak of a "failure of the Prussian police".'[73]

The political editor of the *Vossische Zeitung* sounded almost resigned in his summing-up of the situation:

> Shots are to be heard in the street. Every day the injured are taken to hospital as the victims of the troublemakers, and deaths, too, have been reported, much to our dismay. It is as if people have been seized by a frenzy that demands blood even though only a few years have passed since the great period of bloodshed ended.

Here the writer was clearly referring to the end of the First World War.[74] At almost the same time, Goebbels took the night train to Munich to plan the election campaign with Hitler and other Gauleiters. In the course of his journey he and a number of other SA leaders discussed the 'serious situation in Berlin', where there was 'the latent risk of civil war' and where 'no opportunity should be missed' to ensure the party's safety and 'if necessary to seize the reins of power'. On his way back to Berlin, Goebbels reports a conversation with the SA's group leader in Brandenburg, Wolf-Heinrich Helldorf, regarding 'the measures to be taken in Berlin to combat the Red terror'. He and Helldorf agreed: 'If we have to, we shall present the government with a fait accompli.'[75]

Planning Step by Step

The next stage in the 'Prussian scenario' was ushered in by Berlin's National Socialist students on 30 June 1932, when they sang songs that included *Volk ans Gewehr* (People, to your weapons) in the vestibule of the university and chanted slogans such as 'Jews out!' The chairman of the National Socialist student group declared that it was 'dishonourable for a German to be in the same room as a Jew'. The day ended in serious fighting, and the university was temporarily closed, a process that was to be repeated on the days that followed.[76]

But the leaders of the NSDAP and SA in Berlin were keen to offer their members and their supporters more than merely riots and an increase in popular resentment. In an appeal published on 8 July 1932 in a special edition of *Der Angriff*, Goebbels announced that the 9th was to have been 'a day on which to honour the SA in Berlin and Brandenburg'. Its members were to have responded to a general rallying call, wearing the brown dress of honour of the German liberation army and appearing in the presence of their supreme leader, Adolf Hitler. Forty thousand SA and SS men wanted to gaze into the eyes of the leader of the new Germany and with arms raised swear undying loyalty. They wanted to march along the historic Unter den Linden in a mighty demonstration of their strength and then file past Adolf Hitler in the Siegesallee.

But the march had been banned by the minister of the interior, preventing National Socialist Germany from doing 'what the leaders of the November system had dozens of times allowed the Reichsbanner, the Iron Front and similar organizations representing pacifism, racial degeneration and the German collapse to do in recent years'. The minister was now depriving National Socialist Germany of the right to march along streets that 'because of their historical importance belong uniquely to our demonstrably great and weighty party organization and our proud and invincible SA and SS'. The party was now calling out to the government: 'Our SA and SS will march along Unter den Linden and through the Brandenburg Gate and file past their leader when our hour comes and Adolf Hitler holds the reins of power in his hands.' Following the ministerial ban, the planned rallying call was cancelled, and the SA would instead take part in a mass demonstration of the Berlin Gau in the Lustgarten.[77]

Hitler had returned to Berlin for a further meeting with Schleicher on 8 July 1932 and apparently gave Goebbels the green light to declare war on Papen's cabinet.[78] As the electioneering began, the NSDAP certainly lost no time in distancing itself from the cabinet – the very government that had 'staked everything on Hitler' in its struggle to hold on to power, especially in its conflict with the south German regions, which had opposed the lifting of the ban on the SA.[79]

The first speaker to address the crowd at the NSDAP's demonstration in the Lustgarten on 9 July was Wolf-Heinrich Helldorf, who began by attacking the minister of the interior, Wilhelm von Gayl, and blaming him 'for every injured and dead SA comrade from within our ranks. [...] If it were not for the SA, Herr von Gayl, the Red hordes would now be making trouble here in Berlin, at the Brandenburg Gate and along Unter den Linden.' Helldorf finally turned to what he called 'the final government act of Minister von Gayl', exclaiming:

You, my comrades in the SA, shall one day – after years of an unprecedentedly harsh and desperate struggle – march in uniform past your supreme leader, Adolf Hitler. The SA wanted to assemble here in the Lustgarten, wanted to lower their flags and standards in front of the monument to the first National Socialist, Frederick the Great, and wanted to gaze into the eyes of our supreme SA leader, Adolf Hitler, as we marched past him. Minister von Gayl has banned this planned march-past. After a fight that has lasted decades we have no reason to hide our dress of honour – the brown dress of honour of the new Germany – on side streets. We want everything or nothing! That is why the SA rallying call has been abandoned. But we hereby declare that we shall march through the Brandenburg Gate, that we shall file past our leader on the Siegesallee and render homage to him, and that we shall do so when Germany is ruled by National Socialists and not by bourgeois weaklings.[80]

Helldorf wisely avoided mentioning that the minister, no doubt attempting to uphold a last remaining vestige of legality, had been forced to ban the march because the route chosen by the SA would have taken it through the area to the south of the Reichstag where demonstrations were permanently prohibited.[81]

Helldorf's harangue was followed by an address by Goebbels beginning with the words 'German people of Berlin!' and larded with clichés and kitsch ('You have emerged from the dark and joyless tenement buildings'). He claimed to be standing before a crowd of 'twice one hundred thousand', although in his diary he reduced this number by half, and went on to insist that 'never before' had the capital 'witnessed a popular uprising of such demonstrative power'. The poet's words 'The nation rises up, the storm breaks loose!' had come true, Adolf Hitler was beating at the gates of power, and the time of shame and humiliation was drawing to a close.[82] In the minds of the SA in Berlin, however, the thought of assuming control was now irrevocably associated with the idea of marching through the Brandenburg Gate and rendering homage to Hitler.

The election campaign now became more intense, and the NSDAP leaders adopted an even more belligerent language in addition to their tried-and-tested propaganda methods. Above all, they issued a clear threat that from now on cast its shadow over the political horizon. At a party rally at the Sportpalast on 15 July 1932 Hitler's 'political representative', Hermann Göring, repeated the threat of violence that had already been uttered a day earlier in Weimar: the 'murderous rabble', he declared, still had to reckon with the discipline of the National Socialists. They knew, of course, that there were orders forbidding the SA from carrying weapons. 'But I say to you that this is now at an end!' Sustained applause greeted Göring's remarks:

When the Führer returns from Eastern Prussia during the coming days, I shall ask him and the other party leaders – and I know that this request will be met – to countermand this instruction. Within three days our right of self-defence will be re-established, our Brownshirts will be free, and the cowardly rabble will crawl back into their holes to die. In three days' time the streets will be free again.[83]

In the face of this ultimatum to the government, the *Vossische Zeitung* asked its readers in some bewilderment if there could be any further doubt as to 'where responsibility for the terrible events of the last few weeks' lay and 'how far we have travelled down the road to the total barbarization of public life'.[84] Was this merely empty rhetoric and a put-up job, or did Göring genuinely not know that Papen's government was preparing to solve the troublesome 'Prussian question' before the election took place? Since 11 July 1932 the cabinet had been discussing how to proceed against the government, which was still led by the SPD, and appoint a 'commissar for Prussia'.[85] Rudolf Diels, who worked for the Prussian police, targeting political radicals, had changed sides in the hope of advancing his career and provided the government with material about the alleged plans for a pact between the SPD and KPD (the 'Abegg Affair').[86] In his submission to Hindenburg on the latter's estate at Neudeck, Papen had addressed the internal political situation and especially conditions in Prussia, but his subject matter, dubious in the extreme, merely served to exacerbate the psychotic fear of Communism felt by the whole of the nationalist right and in that way helped to convince Hindenburg that it was high time to restore the authority of the state which had been seriously under-mined in Prussia. Here, Papen argued, Communism was being combated only 'inadequately', while National Socialism was being unjustly targeted in ways that were not desirable. Order must be restored to policing in Prussia.[87] Suitably impressed, Hindenburg 'gave the cabinet carte blanche and, omitting only the date, signed an "order re-establishing law and order throughout Prussia", together with a further order declaring a state of siege, a move unprecedented in the history of the Weimar Republic'.[88] But some excuse was needed before Hindenburg's legal powers could be used. It was found in the events of 'Bloody Sunday', which occurred in Altona on 17 July 1932, when armed Communists and National Socialists clashed during an SA propaganda march through Altona, at that date still an independent town belonging to Prussia. A running battle followed,[89] resulting in eighteen deaths among the civilian population, most of them caused by ricocheting bullets.[90] In general, writers have failed to note the significance of the identically worded telegrams that Hitler sent on the night of 17–18 July to Hindenburg, Papen, Schleicher and Gayl, complaining about the 'monstrous provocation' by the police during the election speech that he gave at an NSDAP rally in Königsberg on 17 July and drawing the following conclusion:

> Since these incidents are repeated every day and there is no guarantee that the population, needlessly attacked, will always display the same degree of discipline and restraint, I believe that if the Prussian police continues to adopt this attitude and act in a way that is conceivable only as a response to direct orders from the government, a bloody catastrophe may occur at any moment. It is high time that the government put an end to this irresponsible behaviour by the police, whose policies can lead only to tumult and turmoil.[91]

Hitler's complaint was backed up by a letter that Hanns Kerrl, the NSDAP president of the Prussian Landtag, wrote to Papen on 18 July 1932 in which Kerrl declared that there was now a state of emergency in Prussia which, given the balance of political power, could not be resolved by the Landtag but had to be sorted out if genuinely constitutional conditions were to be re-established. This sounded like an order, and in his reply of 22 July Papen, signing himself his correspondent's 'most humble servant', permitted himself to draw Kerrl's attention to the president's emergency degree, which Papen had now dated.[92]

The Prussian Coup

The 'decree concerning the restoration of public law and order in the region of Prussia' was duly announced on 20 July. The chancellor was appointed commissar for Prussia and empowered to use the authority vested in the Prussian prime minister, which in turn allowed him to remove Prussian ministers from their posts and entrust their duties to individuals appointed by him as 'Reich commissars'. At the same time a state of emergency was declared throughout Berlin and the province of Brandenburg, and executive powers were transferred to Lieutenant General Gerd von Rundstedt of the Reichswehr. On the morning of the 20th, Papen dismissed the Prussian prime minister, Otto Braun, and his minister of the interior, Carl Severing. During the afternoon Rundstedt instructed the newly appointed chief of police, Kurt Melcher, to arrest Melcher's predecessor, Albert Grzesinski, together with the assistant chief of police, Bernhard Weiß, who for years had been the target of Goebbels' anti-Semitic witch-hunt in Berlin, and the commander of the local police force, Magnus Heimannsberg. They were to be released only after they had given a written undertaking not to continue in office. During the days that followed countless high-ranking civil servants were pensioned off, and other changes of personnel were made before the state of emergency was lifted on 26 July.[93] 'To the astonishment of their perpetrators' these actions passed off 'without a hitch'. A Communist Party call for a general strike went unheeded. And the SPD, Reichsbanner and trades unions as well as the Prussian government failed to put up any appreciable resistance,[94] allowing Goebbels to note in his diary: 'Everything is going like clockwork. The Reds are out of the way. Their organizations are offering no resistance. [...] The Reds have missed their big chance. They'll never get another one.'[95]

Hitler himself was on the campaign trail – between 15 and 30 July 1932 he gave forty-nine speeches between Tilsit (now Sovetsk in western Russia) and Nuremberg. Or, rather, he repeated a single speech that underwent countless minor modifications. In it he referred only obliquely to Papen's 'Prussian coup' when he named the 'deposed' figures of Braun, Severing and Grzesinski. Nor did he give his reaction to the events of 20 July when he spoke at the SA Sports Festival in the Berlin Stadium a week later, saying only: 'How long is it since a Prussian prime minister declared that he would take steps to ensure that our movement never came to Prussia? Well, our movement is now here, and Herr Braun has gone.' According to *Der Angriff*, the event – advertised as 'Berlin's Hitler Day' – attracted 180,000 visitors, although Goebbels, in his diary, mentions the lower figure of 120,000. Whatever the true figure, it was the biggest open-air event that the NSDAP had held in the city. Every detail, from the music and gymnastics displays to the appearance of the National Socialists' air-force squadrons, revealed the extent to which the party had learnt to stage-manage and choreograph these mass rallies. As the applause died down at the end of Goebbels' speech, 'evening began to fall and the most extraordinary atmosphere settled upon the crowd,' according to the reporter for *Der Angriff*. 'Out of the shadows, will-o'-the-wisps rise up. Torchbearers cross the arena, glow-worms on long pieces of string. And in the greyish-blue sky, too, the first lights have been lit. A rally imbued with sentiment. The transfiguration of the summer solstice, dreams that last for minutes on end but which then pass', for, 'suddenly', the Führer is there, and the members of the SA and SS who have entered in serried ranks receive the order 'Halt!' 'Picked out by bright beams of light, the Führer's automobile does a lap of honour. It is a fantastic, stirring, indescribable sight. [...] Berlin is but one further sign that the day of resurrection is approaching with its golden dawn', for just as the Führer 'draws on the inexhaustible wellspring of German faith that gives him the strength to accomplish his mission, so the assembled crowd shares his faith and believes in him – in our greatest comrade of the people, Adolf Hitler!'[96]

The Reichstag elections on 31 July 1932 brought the expected increase in the NSDAP's share of the vote: at 37.4 per cent, it was almost twice as much as it had been in the Reichstag elections on 14 September 1930. Almost 13.8 million Germans voted for it. In Berlin, too, the party saw massive gains, attracting almost 757,000 votes as against 396,000 in 1930. With almost 28.7 per cent of the vote, it was now the most powerful party in Berlin, ahead of the SPD and KPD, both of which had polled around 722,000 votes. The greatest losses were suffered by the DNVP, which fell from 351,000 votes in 1930 to 219,000, while the Centre Party gained in popularity, up from 98,000 votes in 1930 to 130,000 in 1932. The parties of the bourgeois centre ground had lost all their former significance. But the success of the NSDAP is placed in perspective when we compare the results with those of the elections to the Landtag on 24 April 1932. The turnout on both occasions was more or less the same. In April the NSDAP had won 27.9 per cent of the vote – only marginally less than in July. Meanwhile, the KPD increased its share of the vote from 23.7 to 27.3 per cent.[97] With its post-election headlines 'Popular Verdict on Papen. No Right-Wing Majority', 'Nazis at a Standstill', 'Resurgence of Social Democrats' and 'Communist Gains', the SPD's official newspaper was not entirely wrong, therefore, and much the same could be said of the B. Z. am Montag with its lead story 'The Nation Has Decided: No Dictatorship!' Der Angriff, conversely, demanded: 'Hitler Must Come to Power!'[98] But even when the German Nationalists' thirty-seven seats were added to the 230 of the NSDAP, the 'nationalist bloc' still did not command an absolute majority in the 607-seat new Reichstag. Here, too, then there was an impasse.

On 1 August 1932 Hitler reacted to the election results with his usual open letters to the party as well as to the SA, SS, National Socialist Motorized Corps and Hitler Youth movement, on each occasion ending with an appeal to continue 'the struggle'.[99] He did not comment on possible political options such as sharing in government or taking on the chancellorship. In the immediate wake of the elections he himself was presumably unsure as to his course of action and is said to have briefly considered a coalition with the Centre Party, only to reject that possibility soon afterwards.[100] He left for his summer holidays in the Bavarian Alps but interrupted his stay there on 4 August, when he received news from Berlin that Schleicher wanted to discuss the situation with him. What followed was a repeat of the secret diplomacy that had taken place between Hitler and Schleicher three months earlier and that had ended with the fall of Brüning's government. Once again Hitler returned from the Obersalzberg to Munich and took the night train to Berlin, where he arrived on the morning of 5 August.[101] As before, his visit was kept secret, although news filtered out that immediately after his arrival he had held a meeting with Göring that was said to have been concerned only with 'party business'. He was then reported to have travelled on to Mecklenburg as a guest of the region's National Socialist prime minister, Walter Granzow.[102]

These were all in fact attempts to divert attention from the real aim of Hitler's visit and from Schleicher's wish to be kept informed about Hitler's next moves. The most obvious reason for the meeting was Schleicher's annoyance at certain actions by Hitler about which he had been informed by his subordinates and by his confidant Count Bodo von Alvensleben-Neugattersleben. On 26 July 1932 – before the elections on the 31st – Schleicher's successor as head of the ministerial office in the Defence Ministry, Ferdinand von Bredow, had summoned Göring and Röhm to answer charges that 'during or immediately after the elections the SA was planning something that pointed in the direction of the arming of the SA or to violent acts of terror'. Göring was unable simply to dismiss the evidence presented to him by Bredow but attempted to defend the measures that were being taken by the SA by claiming that they were not directed at the Reichswehr. According to the minutes of the meeting, Göring argued that, in the face of the NSDAP's expected victory in the elections, the left would not abandon power without a struggle and that the left-wing parties were 'planning something'. Indeed, he had proof that 'something' was afoot and that not only the National Socialists but also the government and, above all, the new government in Prussia were being targeted. The Iron Front was arming itself with the intention of carrying out a coup, which would undoubtedly take place on election night or, failing that, on the night of 1–2 August. Göring then summed up the position of the NSDAP and SA leadership as it had existed since the spring of 1932: 'The SA had to prepare for a countercoup, and it was necessary, therefore, to discuss its task in advance with the Reichswehr. The Reichswehr could not be activated straightaway, and the police would be too weak, with the result that the main burden would fall on the SA, which must be empowered to act.' It remains unclear whether Bredow realized that Göring was referring here to the 'three-day' model that he had already publicly threatened – three days when the SA and the SS were to be let loose on the streets to seek out all those with political affiliations to the Communists. He interrupted Göring's torrent of words and declared that this was a monstrous line of thought. Did Göring have unassailable proof that the left was making these preparations? According to the minutes of the meeting, Göring was unable to produce a single shred of evidence. 'He claimed that it was merely a matter of instinct.'

Bredow left Göring in no doubt about his attitude to the latter's casual manner: if the 'gentlemen' at the NSDAP were to carry out the illegal measures that they were planning, they would feel the full force of the country's instruments of power. The 'gentlemen' in question lost no time in assuring Bredow that neither the National Socialists nor the SA would take the law into their own hands in the aftermath of the election: 'But they believed that they had the right to avenge the harm caused by Marxism. The SA had for years been training to take revenge. Marxism must be destroyed root and branch.' Bredow's visitors ended by striking an emotionally bombastic note – he could not remember if it was Göring or Röhm who made this remark: 'You can place the greatest strain on us, you can leave us to starve, but we shall not allow anyone to rob us of the right to vengeance. Not even our Führer can do this!' Bredow reminded them that the armed forces needed no support from others and drew their attention to Hitler's declaration of loyalty to the army.[103] A few days later Bredow followed up this meeting by writing to all the chiefs of staff of the Reichswehr and insisting that, in the light of the NSDAP's current attempts to ensure 'an active role for the SA in the machinery of state', existing orders continued to remain in force: the SA must not be entrusted with weapons and the armed forces should not work with them in the event of any internal disturbances. On the other hand, 'the intrinsically gratifying attempts by the NSDAP to make contact with the Reichswehr and to achieve a more trusting relationship' meant that the armed forces should do everything in their power 'to avoid anything that might be construed as a rebuttal or insult'. The requisite reserve on the part of the Reichswehr should not give the NSDAP the impression that 'the armed forces had no sympathy or understanding for the patriotic and militaristic attitude of the National Socialist movement'.[104] In other words, 'requisite reserve' was not the same as neutrality, and Bredow's curtness signified no more than a clear pointer to the authority and inviolability of the Reichswehr's position of power.

In the Run-up to Power

Hitler's meeting with Schleicher took place on 5 or 6 August 1932, probably at Fürstenberg, 50 miles north of Berlin, a part of the country already under NSDAP control.[105] In the course of their discussion, he was evidently able to allay Schleicher's fears about an imminent SA putsch, even though the SA in Berlin had been placed on high alert shortly before polling day[106] and a new wave of SA terror had swept over Prussia's eastern provinces in the days after the election.[107] Worse, Schleicher seems to have succumbed to Hitler's powers of suggestion and to have abandoned his misgivings about the Führer's demands not only to be involved in any new government but also to take over as chancellor. 'I must now try to persuade the old man [Hindenburg] to accept Hitler as chancellor,' Schleicher is reported to have told a confidant following his meeting with Hitler.[108]

Back on the Obersalzberg, Hitler certainly struck a note of supreme confidence, announcing that all was going to plan and that the whole affair would be over within a week. On hearing of the outcome of the negotiations, Goebbels imagined what the future would look like:

> The Chief will be chancellor and prime minister of Prussia. Straßer minister of the interior in both Prussia and the country as a whole. Goebbels Prussian minister of culture and the country's minister of education. Darré agriculture in both. Frick secretary of state in the national Chancellery. Göring aviation. Justice will remain with us. [. . .] If the Reichstag refuses to pass the Enabling Act, it will be sent packing. [. . .] We shall never again give up power, they'll have to carry us out feet first. It will be a proper solution. It may mean bloodshed, but it will clear things up and purge the body politic. We'll make a good job of it.[109]

At a meeting with Papen on 10 August, however, Hindenburg would express his emphatic preference for a continuation of the 'presidential cabinet' under Papen rather than the transfer of the chancellorship to Hitler. In view of Hindenburg's lack of enthusiasm for Hitler as chancellor, Papen was beginning to have second thoughts. During the cabinet meeting that same day Papen suggested that the entry of National Socialists into government would 'necessarily lead to running battles between the National Socialists in government and units of the SS and SA', with the result that it was highly likely that the National Socialist leaders would rid themselves of their SS and SA divisions once they had entered government.[110]

By this date even a section of the middle-class press in Berlin thought it likely not only that Hitler would enter government but that he would be appointed chancellor. The newspaper *Tempo* – the latest of Ullstein's dailies – even headlined its 10 August issue: 'Before Hitler's Appointment. Planned: Hitler as Chancellor, Papen as Foreign Minister and Vice-Chancellor, Straßer as Minister of the Interior, Schleicher as Defence Minister.'[111] That same day the head of the SA in Berlin, Wolf-Heinrich Helldorf, issued an appeal to the various organizations under him, warning them against 'illegal actions'.[112] Such an injunction was in part a concession to the pressure placed

on the SA by three new draconian emergency measures that had been passed
by the government the previous day, extending the existing truce until
31 August, introducing special courts to deal promptly with acts of political
violence and threatening stricter penalties, including the death penalty.[113] At
the same time, Helldorf himself was brought back into line after emissaries
from Berlin had turned up at the holiday homes of Hitler and Goebbels and
reported that the SA in the capital was 'doing stupid things' and that Helldorf
had 'big plans'. 'He must be stopped', Goebbels wrote in his diary and the
following day discussed the 'Berlin question' with Röhm.[114] Helldorf's 'big
plans' were presumably his preparations for a putsch, something that the
National Socialist leadership was keen to avoid: far from having been demobi-
lized, the Berlin SA was 'drawing its noose tighter round Berlin' in the days
before and after 10 August. It was making the government 'very nervous.
That's the object of the exercise. They'll relent soon enough.' Or so Goebbels
hoped.[115]

Hitler left Berchtesgaden on 11 August and the next day travelled to Berlin,
a visit that he was determined to cloak in secrecy. As a result he arrived after
nightfall at Caputh to the south-west of the city, and it was here that he was
met by Goebbels and stayed the night. The next morning, the 13th, he travelled to Berlin with Röhm[116] for a meeting with Schleicher, who, much to his
surprise, conveyed to him Hindenburg's serious misgivings. He then drove to
the Chancellery with Röhm and Frick, the chairman of his party in the
Reichstag, for a meeting with Papen, where he was confronted by the news that
both Papen himself and Hindenburg were keen to abide by the principle of
presidential government but that Hitler could serve them as vice-chancellor,
the mere suggestion of which was enough to provoke an outburst of hysterical
rage on Hitler's part. The way in which the government was handling the
'system', Hitler declared, was fundamentally misguided; the parties that were
associated with it must be destroyed once and for all, no matter how much
blood was shed in achieving that aim. His use of the phrase 'mow down' left
Papen in no doubt as to the identity of the author of the demand that 'the SA
should be allowed to patrol the streets freely for three days'. The annihilation
of Marxism was his life's goal, Hitler went on, which was why he needed to
have complete control of the whole apparatus of government. He could rule
only according to his own methods. Papen attempted to propose a compromise, but in vain.[117] That afternoon Hitler, again accompanied by Röhm and
Frick, went to see Hindenburg for what he still believed was a crucial audience.
Hindenburg opened the proceedings by asking whether Hitler was prepared
'to place himself at the government's disposal in order to work with it'.[118]

Accounts of the rest of the meeting agree only that it was brief. Four different versions have come down to us in the form of two partial transcripts, a press release from the president's office[119] and Hitler's own divergent account.[120] Both the government and Hindenburg believed that Hitler had refused to work with them and was demanding that he and his party should take complete control of the government and the state. For his part, Hitler declared that the government had proposed a restructuring that he 'as the leader of the National Socialist movement was obliged to reject in its suggested form'. Conversely, his preconditions for the NSDAP's entry into government, of which Hindenburg had been apprised before the meeting, had already been rejected by the president. Moreover, he had not travelled to Berlin of his own volition but had been invited to attend the meeting and had certainly not 'sought to impose any demands on the gentlemen in Berlin'.[121]

Chancellor or Not?

Did these differences of opinion revolve around the question of whether Hitler was ultimately demanding the post of chancellor rather than simply agreeing to join a government that would embrace all 'nationally minded forces', as had previously been his aim? Were these simply more of the same misunderstandings 'that could have been resolved if the mood in both camps had been less frosty', as one observer, familiar with the details of the negotiations, noted at the time?[122] Was Hindenburg too 'bad-tempered', Papen too undiplomatic, Schleicher too devious and Hitler too irritable for the meeting to have gone well? And was Hitler simultaneously 'toying with the idea of a violent revolution'?[123] Years later he admitted that he had 'more than once had to deal with situations that suggested the idea of a coup d'état'.[124] And there are undoubtedly signs that point in that direction: on the eve of Hitler's meeting with Hindenburg, the Bavarian prime minister, Heinrich Held, apparently received a phone call from Berlin informing him that Hitler had assembled sixty thousand members of the SA in the immediate vicinity of the capital and that these troops were preparing to march on the city at night and force Hindenburg to make Hitler his chancellor. If Hindenburg were to refuse, he would be arrested and a 'National Revolution' would be declared, just as it had been at the Bürgerbräu in Munich in 1923.[125] Had the guards in the Wilhelmstraße and surrounding area not been issued with rifles since 8 August? Were not at least some of the SA's lower-ranking officers arming themselves for 'a march on a defiant Berlin'? Moreover, SA units had been seen prowling the streets of Hohenlychen just outside the city and waving machine guns, while in

Neuruppin they had tried to requisition lorries and had attempted to use force in seizing weapons from the surrounding estates.[126]

As for Berlin itself, the National Socialists' own account of the history of the SA in the city openly admits that

> the SA divisions were in their centres, awaiting their marching orders. For three days they waited. [. . .] And each man believed that the final struggle was at hand and that the Führer would be made the chancellor of the German people. And so there is a sense of cheerful disorder in all the storm centres, and everyone is waiting for the orders to attack. Uniforms are checked once again, the knapsack is packed, and haversack and flask are filled. In his mind's eye each of them can already see the Brandenburg Gate rising up as they march between its columns in serried ranks. [. . .] And then there comes the great disappointment: they will not be marching after all.[127]

On 18 August, the German correspondent of the Associated Press news agency, Louis P. Lochner, tackled Hitler on the subject of rumours about an imminent 'march on Berlin'. Hitler made fun of such reports. The question, he said, was not 'whether I shall march on Berlin but rather who will have to march out of Berlin. My Storm Troops are the best disciplined body and will not attempt an illegal march. Why should I march on Berlin when I am here already?' he asked. 'We hold strong positions in the Presidency of the Prussian Diet, and will capture others legally.'[128]

This renewed insistence on the desire for a 'legal' solution receives some support from the fact that, immediately after speaking to Hindenburg, Hitler and Röhm took steps to oppose the attempt on the part of a number of SA leaders to launch an attack. On 15 August they even sent the SA 'on leave' until the end of the month.[129] Why was it, then, that in an interview with the *Rheinisch-Westfälische Zeitung* Hitler repeated his earlier threat to national security by claiming an 'increased' right of self-defence?

> We have a right to defend ourselves that we shall never be talked into relinquishing by stupid phrases such as 'law and order'. As a result of this pathetic middle-class twaddle, not one of my dead comrades has been brought back to life, not one cripple has been healed, not one injured colleague has been helped. The National Socialist movement has gone to extreme lengths to fight legally, but the slaughter must end soon, or I shall see myself forced to order party comrades to defend themselves in a way that will sweep aside the methods of the Red Soviet political police with the speed of lightning.[130]

It is conceivable that, in making this declaration, Hitler was offering a sop to the SA, which was disappointed at having to interrupt its activities on 13 August and to which he was giving a licence to resume activities that had been growing increasingly violent since the beginning of the month.

The Potempa Affair

On 22 August, at a special hearing of the Beuthen District Court, five members of the SA were condemned to death for the brutal murder of an unemployed agricultural worker at Potempa on the night of 9–10 August. On hearing of the verdict, which was handed down in keeping with the more stringent laws in force since 10 August, Hitler sent a telegram to the condemned men: 'My comrades! In the light of this most appalling sentence, I feel bound to you in unlimited loyalty. From this moment onwards your freedom is a question of our honour, and it is our duty to struggle against a government under which this is possible.'[131] The *Berliner Tageblatt* opined that this was probably the first time in the history of any civilized nation that a major political party had adopted an official stance in support of murderers justly sentenced to death. It also contrasted the wording of Hitler's telegram with a passage from the statement in which the chairman of the court had justified its verdict:

> To the seriousness of the crime we must add the appalling violence and brutality with which it was carried out. According to the evidence of the court doctor, it is extremely rare to find an act of such violence in which the victim's larynx is smashed by being stamped on and the carotid artery severed, so that he must have died from these injuries.[132]

Goebbels then proceeded to add insult to injury by using the report in the *Berliner Tageblatt* as an excuse for a frontal attack on 'the Jews' in the city's newspaper district, describing them as 'pimps who think like those Red incendiaries and who sit in their editorial offices, safe and protected by police cordons, inciting German workers to take arms against German workers [. . .], these same Jews who openly and anonymously have ruled Germany for the past fourteen years'. He ended his article with an appeal: 'Never forget, comrades! Repeat it to yourselves a hundred times a day so that it pursues you even into your deepest dreams: the Jews are to blame!'[133]

These renewed anti-Semitic tirades were now combined not only with the usual polemical outbursts against the 'Marxist destroyers and corrupters' who deserved only to be 'annihilated', as Hitler demanded on 23 August,[134] but also with increasingly savage attacks on Papen's government. In a speech to the party's 230 representatives in the Reichstag that he gave at the Kaiserhof on 29 August 1932, Hitler referred to the present government as 'the system that rules us today'. The National Socialist movement, he told his audience, had the inestimable advantage of being 'the only factor capable of operating clearly'. As their leader, he would follow the path that 'brings our movement and, with it, our nation closer to its goal'.[135] At best this sounded like a qualification of his earlier insistence that he would follow only a legally orientated political course, but now that the NSDAP had adopted a frontline position 'in the fight against the racially alien rule of Papen's reactionary government'[136] and in the light of increased speculation about the imminent dissolution of the newly elected Reichstag,[137] the general public quickly forgot the events of 13 August and Hindenburg's rejection of Hitler's demands and failed to register that the SA in and around Berlin was still on high alert.

Not until several months later did the *Vossische Zeitung* publish the account of a politician who wisely chose to remain anonymous but who was said by the paper to be 'particularly well informed about the growth of the National Socialist party and the SA'. The piece appeared under the heading 'Adolf Hitler's Powerbase' and, according to the newspaper, it was intended to remind readers that in any negotiations 'extra-parliamentary factors' should not be overlooked. The anonymous writer began his account of the planned scenario by recalling Hitler's announcement that in the event of his assuming power in the country the streets were to be handed over to the SA and SS for a period of three whole days and the 'state's instruments of power were to be with-drawn'.[138] True, this demand had not been couched in such a way as to imply that the SA was to be given carte blanche to instigate a three-day reign of unbridled terror:

> Rather, brown battalions were to march through the streets of the capital with their eagles and swastikas as a sign that the party had seized power. For three whole days the regular march step of the Storm Troopers and the military music of their brass bands were to proclaim the movement's victory. And only 'to prevent clashes' were the state police to withdraw for this period. The police would have to restrict themselves to office duties and directing traffic. The SA and SS were to take over the duties of the police force.

There followed a detailed account of the scenario planned for August 1932, at least to the extent that the anonymous writer had been able to establish those events:

The burgher, roused from his sleep at first light, rubs his eyes in disbelief. The roar of lorries and motorbikes and the echoing steps of the vast army of marchers batter against the houses like waves breaking upon a beach. Armed as if for battle, with their combat packs in full view, the tight formations of Brownshirts march past, filling the approach roads from east and west, the National Socialist Motorized Corps at their head, whole fleets of lorries with motorcycles to the front and rear. Some 35,000 men, concentrated in and around Berlin, blockade the streets and squares. In the government quarter the brown masses build up – it is unclear if they are here to protect the various branches of government or to cut them off completely. A process begins that is designed to 'cleanse' the streets of elements that bear the signs of political associations [. . .] or whatever else they may have sniffed out with their suspicions. Shots are fired. The workers and the defence associations start to fight back. Barricades are erected, the forces of counteraction are formed. They are ruthlessly pursued, resistance repulsed. The SA's intelligence service is superbly organized. Street closures, the inner city cut off from the working-class districts, the transportation of Storm Troopers 'for special use' at places under particular threat. [. . .] The suppression of the 'Bolshevik uprising' has emphatically begun. In the circumstances it is vital to be certain of the heads of the resistance. The cleansing of the streets is followed by house-to-house searches. The cell representatives of the NSDAP who control blocks of five or six houses have already done a good job. More than three thousand names filled the proscription lists. [. . .] Among the first buildings to be occupied is Broadcasting House in the Masurenallee. [. . .] At the end of the three-day period the station will broadcast to the city and country, informing them of the 'outbreak of the Bolshevik uprising' and its violent suppression by the SA.

Thus the planned scenario. The anonymous writer went on:

A vision of overexcited nerves? Perhaps. But one that haunted the minds of the SA. This was more or less how the march on Berlin was to proceed in the summer of 1932: the forces of resistance were to be lured into the open, and their suppression was to mark the start of the 'total seizure of power'. No denial can alter the fact that this was the intention, and it would be fatal to overlook the fact that these intentions still exist.

But, the writer asked, had the state authorities watched all this without acting? Was it not their duty to prevent excesses that were bound to shake the state to its very foundations? And here the anonymous writer raised the crucial point:

It is said that these state authorities were hand in glove with the people who carried out these plans. They assumed that not only sovereignty in the country but also power over the Prussian state and, with it, control over the police were in the hands of members of the NSDAP. One should consider the possibility of the following line-up: Hitler as chancellor, Frick or Straßer as Prussian prime minister or commissar for Prussia. The deployment of the state's instruments of power would have been unthinkable with the front fighting against its own followers. Events would have followed hard on each other's heels, and the resistance, largely supported by the workers, would easily have given the impression to the outside world that they were part of a Bolshevik uprising. Once things had reached this point, there would have been no objection to the use of all available force with the aim of restoring law and order. [. . .] And whatever happened, it would have been 'legal'. After three days they would have reached their goal. [. . .] The plan would essentially have succeeded. And those people would have been proved right who claimed on the strength of their intimate knowledge of the situation that the SA was by no means as bad as it appeared. Although they would march, they would do so *with* the police, not *against* them.

The writer ended by insisting that the danger had not gone away: 'A situation could easily develop similar to the one presupposed by the SA leadership last August.' But no one wanted to attack the state's instruments of power as long as the right to wield those powers was not vested in them. They would wait. They saw in any coalition in which they themselves played a significant part 'a necessary evil – a springboard to real and total power'.[139] If this picture was accurate, then it followed that the SA would not undertake a putsch in the usual sense of the term, and certainly not against the Reichswehr. But following its seizure of power, it would become the principal instrument in the battle to destroy Marxism in the sense that Hitler understood that term, always assuming that the NSDAP gained access to the heart of the state's power in Prussia and, hence, in Berlin: the police. At the date when this article appeared in the *Vossische Zeitung*, where it occupied almost an entire page, the paper had a circulation of barely seventy thousand.[140] It is difficult to know if its readers would have given the piece more than the most cursory glance.

Hitler in Waiting

Hitler seized every opportunity that was offered to him to insist that he could wait and that time was on his side:

I shan't sell the party down the river in return for whatever title they propose to give me. I'd prefer to continue fighting! One year, two years, three years! And if the gentlemen tell me that I won't hold out? What lies ahead of me? My great adversary, the country's president, is eighty-five, I am forty-three, and I feel the very picture of good health, I can say that to the gentlemen. I am convinced that nothing will happen to me because I believe that Providence has destined me for my work.[141]

In the new Reichstag, where his 'political representative', Hermann Göring, was elected leader of the house on 30 August, Hitler engineered Papen's humiliation, guiding Göring's tactics from the latter's official residence during the parliamentary session on 12 September. Although Papen had already presented him with Hindenburg's signed order to dissolve the Reichstag, Göring, acting 'in agreement with the Führer', insisted on proceeding with the Communists' vote of no confidence in Papen's cabinet before the chancellor had had a chance to speak. The vote was carried by an overwhelming majority. Since it had taken place in violation of the constitution, the result was invalid. New elections for the Reichstag were fixed for 6 November 1932.[142]

Meanwhile the NSDAP was showing signs of the consequences of Hindenburg's rebuff of Hitler on 13 August. Goebbels noted in his diary that the whole of the party organization in Berlin was in a state of 'deep depression' and that everything must be done to raise the party's spirits.[143] Later, during the hustings, the first cracks became visible in the NSDAP: when Gregor Straßer addressed members of the National Socialist Operational Cells Organization (NSBO) in the Sportpalast on 20 October, the *Vossische Zeitung* noted that the speech reflected a particular trend in a party that was determined to come to power but without insisting on a total monopoly of power. According to the paper, the tactical aim of Straßer's speech was to calm the middles classes, who were turning away from the NSDAP in large numbers.[144] During the election campaign Hitler spoke only once in Berlin, appearing at the Sportpalast on 2 November. He evidently felt obliged to begin by explaining to his audience the reasons for his declining to enter government, but he also used the opportunity to elaborate the party narrative, claiming, for example: 'If in November 1918 I had had even a single corps under me, the revolution would never have succeeded!' His reason for refusing to enter government culminated in the claim: 'What I want is to lead!'[145] The speech was reproduced in *Der Angriff*, which spoke of the 'tremendous cheering' and 'storms of thunderous applause', whereas the *Vossische Zeitung* felt that Hitler had seemed 'drained' at the Sportpalast. 'His voice, hoarse from recent exertions, has lost much of its former charm, in spite of its familiar Austrian accent, and the applause no longer interrupted his speech as often and as noisily as in the past.' Perhaps his insistence 'I can wait', the paper concluded, was 'the first step on the road to renunciation'.[146]

But the main headlines in the *Vossische Zeitung* on 3 November concerned the start of a transport strike in Berlin. According to the paper, radical workers' groups in the form of the Communists and National Socialists had succeeded in carrying the workforce with them. Goebbels explained away the fact that both the NSBO and the Communist Revolutionary Trades Union Organization had called for the strike by claiming that the NSDAP had 'really had no choice in the matter'. If the party had withdrawn from the strike, 'our position of power among working people would have been undermined'.[147] Goebbels was no doubt right to make this claim for the party's participation in the strike in that it almost certainly helped to reduce the losses that the NSDAP suffered in the Reichstag elections on 6 November. The party lost a total of two million votes when compared with the results of 13 July, and the number of its representatives in the Reichstag fell from 230 to 196. In Berlin, on the other hand, its losses were relatively slight: throughout the country as a whole its share of the vote fell by 4.3 per cent, but in the capital this figure was only 2.4 per cent – 721,000 votes compared with 757,000 in July. As a result it was still the second-largest party and, as such, ahead of the SPD with 647,000 votes. The clear winners were the Communists, who raised their share of the vote to 31.3 per cent (861,000 votes as opposed to 722,000 in July) and were once again the most powerful party in Berlin.[148] A closer look at the NSDAP's results in the strongholds of the Communist Party reveals that, although the NSDAP had a considerable number of potential voters in Berlin's working-class areas by the end of 1932 as the 'nationalist alternative', it had still failed to make any 'inroads into the Marxist front'.[149]

A week after the elections, however, Papen invited Hitler to a meeting to discuss 'a new possibility of bringing together all the nationalist parties'. Hitler declined the invitation but declared himself willing under certain conditions to engage in a written 'exchange of ideas'. It was now Papen's turn to reject such a suggestion. Unable to achieve a broad-based 'nationalist consensus', Papen and his cabinet tendered their resignations on 17 November.[150] Hindenburg then summoned Hitler to a private audience and the latter flew to Berlin the very next day. After two face-to-face meetings, Hitler once again declared his preference for a written form of communication with the president and his secretary of state, Otto Meißner. His only meeting with Schleicher took place on 23 November.[151] He returned to Munich a week later.

So leben sie!
so leben sie alle Tage!

Hitlers Rechnung im Kaiserhof

1 Frühstück	Mk. 2.30	mal 12 für 10 Tage	276.– Mk.
1 Mittag	Mk. 5.00	mal 12 für 10 Tage	600.– Mk.
1 Zimmer	Mk. 24.00	mal 10 für 12 Tage	2880.– Mk.

Das sind die nationalen „sozialistischen Arbeiter", Young-
knechte, Streikbrecher und Arbeitermörder der NSDAP.

Hindenburg-Wahlausschuß prabt im Hotel Prinz-Albrecht

150 Mann verschlingen Fleisch, Gemüse, Kompott, Ananas,
Bowle, Likör, Zigarren, Zigaretten, Kognak usw. auf einer
Sitzung am 3. März für **1527.– Mk.**

Und ihr müßt hungern

Nazis und Stahlhelm, Deutschnationale und Volkspartei, Zentrum und Staatspartei,
ADGB.- und SPD.-Führer haben Euch zur Wahl von Hindenburg oder Hitler auf-
gefordert.

Arbeitslose, Frauen, Proletarier, Angestellte, Bauern
und Mittelstand gebt diesen Wahlschiebern, Patrioten,
Bolschewistenfressern die Quittung!

Macht Schluß mit diesem System!
Kämpft mit der KPD!
Wählt Kommunisten! Liste 4.

Verantwortlich für Inhalt und Herausgabe: Ernst Schneller, Berlin. — Druck: City-Druckerei AG, Berlin C 25

18 A Communist Party flyer (1932) complaining about Hitler's lavish lifestyle at the Kaiserhof

Berlin. Blick vom Kaiserhof zur Reichskanzlei

19 A view from the Kaiserhof showing the new extension to the Reich Chancellery on the Wilhelmplatz, postcard (c.1933)

20 Hitler at an election rally in the Lustgarten in Berlin. The man wearing a cap (to Hitler's right) is the chief of the SA in the city, Count Wolf-Heinrich Helldorf; behind to Hitler's left stands Joseph Goebbels (4 April 1932)

21 A special edition of *Vorwärts* (late June 1932) complaining about the SA's attacks on the paper

22 The cover of Joseph Goebbels' book *Der Angriff* (1923). The design by 'Mjölnir', the penname of Hans Herbert Schweitzer, dates from 1927

23 The Reich Chancellery extension in the Wilhelmstraße with Hitler's portrait as an insert, postcard (1933)

24 The Lustgarten, with the Cathedral to the right. Albert Speer planned to use it as a collection point for rallies, postcard (1936)

25 Plan of the government district (1936)

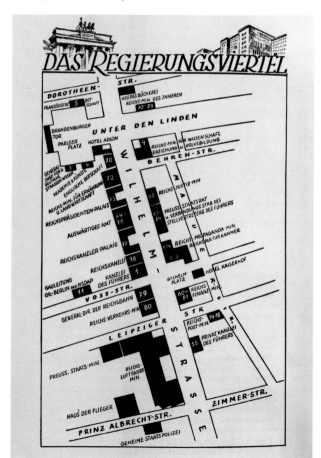

26 Hitler inspecting the Olympia Stadium, postcard (1936)

27 Unter den Linden decorated for Mussolini's visit, seen from the Brandenburg Gate, postcard (1937)

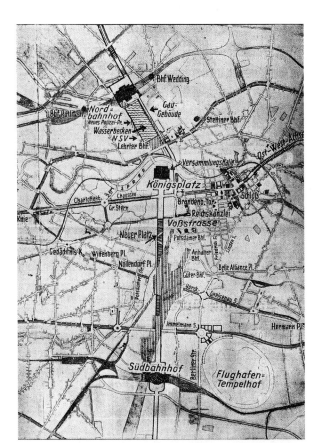

28 Line drawing based on a plan drawn up by the general inspector of buildings. The drawing was published in the Berlin press to indicate the extent of the plans to redevelop the inner city (January 1938)

29 A wall-sized photograph of Hitler at the exhibition 'Give Me Four Years' in the Berlin Exhibition Centre (1937)

30 Hitler's portrait outside the Altes Museum in the Lustgarten, postcard (1938)

6 Millionen Naziwähler: Futter für ein großes Maul

MIT GOTT FÜR HITLER UND KAPITAL

„Und den Fisch hab ich gewählt!"

31 *Six Million Nazi Voters: Food for a Big Mouth. 'And I voted for the fish!'* John Heartfield, photomontage (1930)

32 The New Chancellery in the Voßstraße, photographed from the south facing north (1939)

33 The Reich Chancellery extension on the Wilhelmplatz with the entrance to the New Chancellery in the middle of the picture (1945)

But when Hindenburg invited Schleicher to form a new government on 2 December, Hitler travelled back to Berlin and again stayed for a week at the Kaiserhof, consulting with leading officials from the NSDAP and discussing the new political situation. A row broke out when Gregor Straßer, the party's national organizer, declared his willingness to tolerate Schleicher and it turned out that Schleicher had already offered Straßer the post of vice-chancellor in his new cabinet. On 1 December Hitler had already told one of Schleicher's negotiators that, far from being willing to compromise, he even had conditions of his own, which Goebbels summarized as follows: 'Adjournment of the Reichstag until January, amnesty, streets free [for the SA and SS] and right of self-defence. If these conditions aren't met, then the battle will begin all over again. The choice is General Schleicher's.'[152]

On 5 December Hitler addressed the NSDAP's Reichstag representatives in Göring's official residence, informing his audience that no great movement had ever triumphed by making compromises. This was a jibe at both Schleicher and Straßer. The more that events forced a decision, the more victims that process would require, he went on, clearly referring to his 'three-day plan'. All that mattered in such a process, he concluded, was who was prepared to make the ultimate sacrifice and who was willing to bring his last remaining battalion to the field of battle.[153]

On 8 December Gregor Straßer wrote to Hitler and, much to the surprise of the party leadership, resigned from all his positions within the NSDAP. Significantly, he objected to the use of 'brute force in the party's confrontation with Marxism': such brutality should not be 'central to the internal political task'. It was 'false, dangerous and not in the Pan-German interest' to trust simply in 'chaos as the key to the party's hour of destiny'.[154] The result was a certain confusion among the upper echelons of the NSDAP but not an actual rift. On 9 December Hitler himself took over Straßer's functions and appointed Robert Ley his chief of staff responsible for the party's political organization.[155]

Hitler left Berlin on 10 December but was back in the city by the 16th to give a speech to the NSDAP members of the Prussian Landtag, again at Göring's official residence.[156] His toing and froing between Munich and Berlin eventually assumed a distinctly comic aspect as the focus of his political activities was now clearly Berlin, where he spent no fewer than thirty-six days between early November 1932 and the end of January 1933. In early December it was also decided to bring out a Berlin edition of the *Völkischer Beobachter*, which, starting on 1 January 1933, would appear each morning and thus complement the evening edition of *Der Angriff*.[157] At the height of Hitler's visits, which were generally shrouded in secrecy or at least hard for the general public to fathom, the Social Democratic *Vorwärts* expressed the widespread sense of unease in an article headed 'Everyone Is Pushing Everyone Else!':

> Hitler against Papen, Straßer against Schleicher, Hugenberg against Hitler, Papen against Hugenberg, Hugenberg against Hindenburg, Alvensleben pushing forwards, Thyssen pushing backwards, Straßer becoming vice-chancellor, Hitler wanting the Reich ministry, Schleicher inclined to accept this, Hindenburg inclined to accept that. Who can make any sense of this secret politicking, which is taking place behind the back of the German people?[158]

This secret politicking became more urgent on 4 January, when Hitler met Papen at the Cologne home of the banker Kurt von Schroeder in circumstances that can only be described as conspiratorial. The talks represented a resumption of the attempt to form a government of which Schleicher would no longer be a part.[159] Hitler returned to Berlin on 10 January, taking the night train from Bielefeld and arriving early in the morning at Friedrichstraße Station. It was his first visit to the capital in 1933. Again the trip was shrouded in secrecy. He held another meeting with Papen during the night of 10–11 January at Joachim von Ribbentrop's home at 9 Lentzeallee in Dahlem, seeking to distract attention from the meeting by giving an interview to his press chief, Otto Dietrich, on 11 January, in which he poured scorn on 'a certain section of the Berlin press': apart from his discussions with Göring at the latter's apartment at 34 Kaiserdamm in Charlottenburg and with 'other leading party comrades', he claimed that he had merely visited the new editorial offices of the *Völkischer Beobachter* at 88–90 Zimmerstraße in Kreuzberg and in the evening attended a 'splendid' performance of Verdi's *La traviata* at the Staatsoper Unter den Linden.[160] On 10 January Schleicher informed journalists that it was still completely impossible to negotiate with Hitler as he was sticking to his old demand and insisting that 'the Communists be handed over to him to be hunted down like wild animals'.[161]

Barely a week later Hitler returned to Berlin from a meeting of NSDAP Gauleiters in Weimar and on 17 January held a meeting at Göring's service flat in the presidential palace that was also attended by Alfred Hugenberg and Otto Schmidt-Hannover, who was the chairman of the German National People's Party in the Reichstag. The talks were designed to bring about a rapprochement with the German Nationalists. According to a report by one of the DNVP members of the Reichstag, Hitler had declared: 'I have to become chancellor, but I don't want to form a party government. I shall tolerate Schleicher if he hands over the streets to me. Marxism must be crushed, but not by the organs of the state.' In the event the discussions proved fruitless as the DNVP representatives refused to see 'the Prussian Ministry of the Interior and, with it, the Prussian police placed in the hands of the NSDAP'.[162]

A further meeting with Papen took place the next day, again at Ribbentrop's home, Ribbentrop himself recalling that Hitler continued to insist on the chancellorship, while Papen felt that it would be impossible to get this past Hindenburg.[163] 'The Führer is remaining in Berlin,' Goebbels noted on 19 January, 'and will intervene when the moment is right.' During the night of 20–21 January Hitler, Goebbels and Göring met in Göring's private apartment and discussed the line that they should take.[164]

The Plot Thickens

On the evening of 20 January 1933 leaders of the Berlin Gau met at the Sportpalast, where they were addressed by Hitler.[165] Two days later he unveiled a memorial plaque to Horst Wessel at the Nicolai Cemetery in Prenzlauer Berg. According to official estimates, some sixteen thousand members of the SA from Berlin and Brandenburg took part in the celebrations, starting by marching past the nearby Karl Liebknecht House – the Communist Party's central offices on the Bülowplatz – and then taking up their positions outside the cemetery. In his diary Goebbels described this deliberate act of provocation as a 'proud and heroic victory of the SA on behalf of the party' and as a 'terrible defeat' for the Communist Party, which had suffered 'a loss of prestige that could never again be made good'. In the side streets, he added, 'the Communists were consumed by impotent rage, incapable of causing any serious clashes. We have won a great battle.'[166] That same evening, a further ceremony was held in the Sportpalast, and in his speech Hitler praised 'those fanatics who are consumed by the great task of their age, who live for that task and who die for it'. These men would 'later be not only the martyrs of their struggle but also the seed from which the subsequent harvest' would spring.[167] The memorial service was followed by further talks at Ribbentrop's villa, where the National Socialists were represented by Ribbentrop himself, Hitler, Frick, Göring and the latter's secretary, Paul Körner, while the opposing party included Papen, Meißner and Oskar von Hindenburg, mockingly described as 'the son of the country's president and, as such, not provided for in the country's constitution'. Mindful of Oskar von Hindenburg's increasing influence on his father, Hitler spent two hours haranguing him. At the end of the meeting,

Papen told Hitler that he was now prepared to push through the latter's chancellorship.[168] On 23 January, finally, Hitler addressed a gathering of SA and SS leaders at the Kaiserhof and informed them that the political situation could now be described as 'highly favourable' for their movement. The results of the 'unprecedented tenacity and iron resolve' of the whole of the National Socialist leadership would become clear 'in the not too distant future'. As the 'political soldiers of the German people's uprising', the SA and SS would have a historic role to play.[169]

Hitler returned to Munich on the evening of 23 January 1933, while Schleicher met Hindenburg, only to be rebuffed when he suggested a further dissolution of the Reichstag and an indefinite delay to any new elections. In the meantime, he asked Hindenburg to entrust him with unlimited executive power throughout the whole of the country. Hindenburg refused to give him carte blanche and with that the trust that had existed between the two men was over.[170] When Schleicher returned to see Hindenburg on 28 January, the latter proved unwilling to accept any of his chancellor's suggestions. Hindenburg complained that Schleicher had failed to win a parliamentary majority and that he was now hoping for a cabinet that would be in a position to implement his own ideas. Schleicher responded by announcing the resignation of the entire government.[171] Hindenburg then invited Schleicher's predecessor, Franz von Papen, to 'clarify the political situation by entering into negotiations with all the various parties'.[172]

Hitler was back in Berlin by 27 January, at a time when the press was full of speculation about the imminent formation of a new national government under Papen that would include the DNVP.[173] In his discussions with Göring and Ribbentrop,[174] Hitler expressed his initial annoyance with the German Nationalists and, declaring that he had already told Hindenburg all he needed to, announced his intention of leaving again.[175] When Schleicher's cabinet resigned on the 28th and Papen sent word to him via Ribbentrop that his chancellorship now seemed a possibility, Hitler felt that fate was looking kindly on him and not only demanded the post of chancellor and the right to appoint National Socialists to the ministries of the interior in both Prussia and the country as a whole – these were the demands that he had already made in his talks with Hugenberg the previous day – but also insisted on the post of commissar for Prussia.[176]

In the hectic secret negotiations of the following forty-eight hours, the 'Prussian question' seemed to be the point on which Hitler's chancellorship still threatened to founder, even though Hindenburg gradually lost his earlier misgivings about Hitler's appointment.[177] For Hitler, however, having access to the Prussian police was indispensable: he would never have been content with just the chancellorship and the post of minister of the interior. A decision finally came on 29 January 1933.[178] During the morning Hitler and Göring met Papen in his apartment in the Ministry of the Interior in the Wilhelmstraße. Hitler named Frick as his preferred candidate for the post of minister of the interior and accepted a compromise on the 'Prussian question' whereby Göring would be commissar for the Prussian Ministry of the Interior. For his own part, he accepted Hindenburg's wish that Papen be appointed vice-chancellor and commissar for Prussia, but then repeated his demand that the Reichstag be dissolved and new elections held. As chancellor, he would ensure that in the new Reichstag there would be the necessary two-thirds majority for an Enabling Act that would transfer legislative authority to his new cabinet.[179] Papen continued to struggle to form a cabinet and in his discussions with others withheld various pieces of information: in his talks with Hugenberg and the head of the Stahlhelm, Franz Seldte, for example, he omitted to mention Hitler's demand for new elections. On the afternoon of 29 January he told Göring that the final obstacle had been removed, even though he had still not received Hindenburg's definitive approval of Hitler's appointment.[180]

By early evening rumours had spread like wildfire throughout the city: Schleicher was said to be threatening a 'countercoup', the Reichswehr was planning a putsch, the garrison at Potsdam had been placed on high alert and instructed to shoot on sight, the president was to be dispatched to his estates in Eastern Prussia or arrested, and so on. The rumours were no doubt triggered by a meeting that had taken place on the afternoon of 29 January between Hitler and General Kurt von Hammerstein, the chief of the army command.[181] Hitler later claimed that it was in order to prevent the attempted putsch that he had instructed Helldorf to place the whole of the Berlin SA on high alert. Moreover, Walther Wecke, 'the chief of police and known to be a person of trust', had been told to 'make the necessary arrangements for a rapid occupation of the Wilhelmstraße by six police battalions'.[182] Tipped off by Hitler, Papen lost no time in passing on the rumour to Hindenburg and his entourage, among others. The president's predictable reaction allowed Papen 'to pursue the course of events that he himself wanted. [. . .] He submitted his list of ministers to Hindenburg and on the evening of 29 January ensured that he had the president's agreement to swear in a cabinet under Hitler the very next morning.'[183] When, on the morning of 30 January, Hugenberg abandoned his opposition to the dissolution of the Reichstag, Hitler had achieved his aim. 'Proud, triumphant and victorious, Hitler strode along at the front of his delegation, with his goose-stepping henchmen behind him, and mounted the steps of the building on whose first floor the old man was already awaiting his new cabinet.'[184] At around 11:20 Hindenburg named Hitler chancellor 'in the name of the Reich' in the reception room of the old chancellery building at 77 Wilhelmstraße – the president's official residence was currently being renovated.[185]

At around midday Hitler returned to the Kaiserhof to celebrate his victory. During the early afternoon he held a meeting of the leaders of the SA, SS and Stahlhelm 'which drew up plans for the march that would bring the great day's events to a solemn conclusion: the whole of the SA and SS from Greater Berlin and sections of the SA and SS from Brandenburg totalling some twenty thousand men would march through the Brandenburg Gate with torches in their hands, and then file past the president and the Führer in the Wilhelmstraße.'[186]

It was no accident that the SA leadership chose a torch-lit procession to signal its sense of triumph and as a way of honouring Hitler, for such processions had a long and venerable tradition in Germany. On the evening of 17 June 1913, for example, seven thousand students from all the universities and colleges in Berlin marched from Moabit to the Royal Palace via Unter den Linden in order to mark the twenty-fifth anniversary of the reign of Kaiser Wilhelm II. A paper loyal to the Kaiser reported that 'the thousands of torches shone dark red against the cloudless evening sky, and a vast procession brought the memorable jubilee to an end'.[187] The SA, too, was an organization that, both brutal and bureaucratic in its military structure, had for years been marking special occasions with torch-lit processions for which detailed instructions were handed out in advance. In 1929, for instance, the supreme commander of the SA had issued a set of general instructions for group leaders at the 1929 NSDAP rally in Nuremberg. The instructions for torch-lit processions read as follows:

> Torches can be collected from the billets at 50 pfennigs each or in exchange for a voucher obtained in advance from the master of the ordnance. Assemble in the specified streets. Advance in closed preorganized columns. [...] Throughout the march keep your left hand on your belt buckle. No sticks! No smoking! Singing extremely desirable, but only songs that everyone can sing along with in a lusty tone of voice! [...] Obey any instructions from the traffic police. The following are banned: shouts of 'Up with' and 'Down with', 'Death to all Jews' and the like. The only chant that is permitted is 'Germany, Awake!', but only when the squad leader gives the order to do so in person. [...] The mass of torches will be lit only with the onset of darkness. They burn for approximately three hours.[188]

The SA leadership could fall back on these tried-and-tested rituals on 30 January 1933. As with all similar marches in recent years, nothing was left to chance by the present SA group leader, Wolf-Heinrich Helldorf. Hitler's appointment had been expected, and the whole of the Berlin SA had been on high alert since the previous evening. This was no spontaneous action improvised by Goebbels, no 'masterly achievement' that ostensibly prompted Hitler to ask how Goebbels had managed to 'round up so many torches in such a short space of time'.[189] The detailed advance planning is clear from the following report which appeared the next day in the new Berlin edition of the *Völkischer Beobachter*:

At the appointed time, 7:30, the units of the SA, SS and Stahlhelm assembled in order to take part in the torch-lit procession past the presidential palace. The West Berlin group assembled in the Lichtenstein-Allee, facing the Großer Stern, the East Berlin group in the Bellevue-Allee on the corner of the Charlottenburger Chaussee, facing the Kleiner Stern. The SA joined the march in the Kaiserin-Augusta-Straße, facing the Hofjäger-Allee, and the Stahlhelm in the northern section of the Sieges-Allee, facing the Charlottenburger Chaussee. At the same time the East Berlin Motorized Unit joined the East Berlin group. The Berlin-Brandenburg group and the Brandenburg staffs likewise took up their positions in front of the West Berlin group shortly before 7:30. Participants had been instructed to appear in their service uniforms, standards and flags were carried at the front of the procession. The route had been planned in consultation with the authorities and was as follows: Charlottenburger Chaussee, Pariser Platz, Wilhelmstraße, Kaiserhof, Mohrenstraße, Markgrafenstraße, Französische Straße, Werdersche Straße and Schleusenbrücke, with the Schloßfreiheit as the final destination. [...] At exactly 7:30 the vast columns of men set off, with the Fuhsel Band at their head. The front of the procession reached the Brandenburg Gate at around 8:15, having passed along the Charlottenburger Chaussee, which was densely lined with people. Traffic was paralysed. Large contingents of policemen kept the roads free. To shouts of wild acclamation, the head of the procession then turned into the Wilhelmstraße and at 8:22 marched past the presidential palace. In the right-hand wing at the front of the building the old field marshal [Hindenburg] was greeted with shouts of tremendous enthusiasm and kept bowing in gratitude. The cheering then swells to a hurricane. Behind the darkened windows of the Chancellery Germany's new leader appears, surrounded by his ministers. On the Wilhelmplatz the marchers wheel round outside the Kaiserhof. Here group leader Count Helldorf reviews the march-past. The processions move off in opposite directions to the Mohrenstraße and the Französische Straße. It was several hours before the end of the procession reached the Wilhelmstraße and the Kaiserhof and dispersed in the direction of the Lustgarten.

The Brandenburg Gate lies in the darkness of a January night. The quadriga above the sandstone columns is shrouded in mist. On the roofs of the low houses to the left and right of the victory gate are policemen with spotlights that pick out the black square as far as the Wilhelmstraße on one side and the Charlottenburger Chaussee on the other. The traffic, which has been allowed to circulate freely until eight, now has to be diverted for the head of the torch-lit procession has set off from the Großer Stern, and the reflection of their bright lights can be seen at the end of the long, broad road that glitters with the asphalt. Motorized squadrons roar up: 'The head of the procession is on the march!' At the sharp bend of Unter den Linden and the Wilhelmstraße the crush of people is almost a threat to life and limb. Not only is the broad promenade a dense mass of people as far as the other side of Unter den Linden, but thousands of men, women and children are standing on the corner, wedged tightly against each other, and the procession has no choice but to pass right in front of them in order to turn off to the presidential palace. The Wilhelmstraße, too, is black with people. Thick ropes keep the route of the march free. Countless photographers are positioned in front of the presidential palace. Newsreel trucks with floodlights and all their usual paraphernalia have arrived. On the steps to the government press office newspaper reporters have gathered. [. . .] Suddenly a cry goes up: the head of the torch-lit procession turns into the Wilhelmstraße, with its flickering lights. The drums roll, march music rings out and – here they are! The march-past begins!

You need to have been there. Only then will you understand that no words can capture the mood in which German Berlin saw this proud day in its history unfold on the evening of 30 January: history that was not written on parchment but hammered out in the weighty march steps of the many thousands of men who make up our brown battalions. German Berlin is on the march. [. . .] The SA is on the march! [. . .] Berlin and Germany are ours! [. . .] The head of the procession now reaches the furthest wing of the presidential palace. Suddenly a bright light flares up behind the previously darkened windows. Within the window frame can be seen the elderly field marshal, who is enthusiastically acclaimed. But then, three buildings away, is the Reich Chancellery. A floodlight suddenly appears out of nowhere, and crowds that cannot be held back, crowds afire with enthusiasm, burst through the police lines: at the window of the Reich Chancellery is our leader! Behind him stand his ministers. Hour after hour the brown battalions march past. A proud day for our proud Berlin![190]

The very next day the party leaders began to make preparations for the election campaign. In the course of a conversation with Hitler, Goebbels apparently established the guidelines 'for the fight against the Red terror'. 'For the present we shall avoid direct countermeasures. The attempt at a Bolshevik revolution first has to flare up. At the right moment we shall then strike,' Goebbels wrote in the version of his diary that he prepared for publication. In the unedited version we read: 'For the present no countermeasures. First let things flare up. And four weeks for the election campaign.'[191] If we take this literally, the date works out at 28 February 1933.

11

'A real and genuine capital'

1933 AND LATER: HITLER'S METROPOLIS

'We have hammered home our idea and forced our name on this city, imposing them both upon it. It has become a struggle for Berlin that has lasted eight years or so and cost rivers of blood and tears but which in spite of everything was started by a desperate minority, irresistibly drawing this vast metropolis into its sway and finally casting it down.'
Joseph Goebbels, 1934[1]

'But Berlin will be transformed by the greatest and most sweeping changes. Here it was not just a question of providing the city with a prestigious and imposing architectural centre but above all of building a capital worthy of the new Reich.'
Albert Speer, June 1939[2]

The Dictatorship Begins

Within hours of his appointment as chancellor, Hitler was holding his first cabinet meeting. He wasted no time on preliminaries but immediately raised the question of whether the new government should ban the Communist Party or aim, rather, at holding new elections. He was afraid that if the KPD were banned, there would be serious internal struggles and possibly even a general strike. At a time when the economy needed stability, a general strike, he argued, posed far greater risks than the uncertainty bound up with new elections. Alfred Hugenberg, the chairman of the DNVP and the new minister not only of trade and industry but also of food and agriculture, raised a dissenting voice. While he had no wish to see the country plunged into a general strike, he was convinced that there was no alternative to suppressing the KPD, especially as in the present case there was no threat of a strike. Otherwise they would never achieve a majority in the Reichstag, at least not a two-thirds majority. Once the KPD had been banned, it was entirely possible that the Reichstag would vote through an Enabling Act.

Hugenberg's opposition to the idea of new elections almost caused the collapse of the new government only hours after it had been formed. But on the afternoon of 30 January 1933 Hitler, taking advantage of the new political situation, played his trump card: a general strike was a very real cause for concern and as far as possible the army should not be used to suppress it. This was an astute move in that it won over the new minister of the armed forces, Werner von Blomberg, who promptly thanked Hitler for his intervention and, according to the minutes of the meeting, stressed that 'the soldier is used to seeing only an external enemy as his adversary'. Earlier, the leader of the Stahlhelm, Franz Seldte, who was now the labour minister, had pointed out how unfortunate it would be if the new government's first act was to ban the KPD and precipitate a general strike. Hugenberg was thus isolated within the cabinet. Hitler was keen not to snub him at this early stage in the proceedings but still wanted to press ahead with new elections, so he declared that the very next morning he would 'make contact with representatives of the Centre Party' and report back at a further cabinet meeting on the afternoon of 31 January 1933.[3] His negotiations with the Centre Party were, of course, a sham as the party's representatives would never have agreed to any long-term prorogation of the Reichstag.[4] He announced, therefore, that any further dealings with the Centre Party would be pointless, so that new elections were now unavoidable. Franz von Papen – now the chancellor's official representative in the cabinet and commissar for Prussia – proceeded to take the initiative and declared that it was best to make it clear that the coming elections to the Reichstag would be the last and that a return to the parliamentary system would henceforth be prevented. Hitler did not need to be told twice. He announced that he would give a binding promise that the outcome of new elections would not affect the make-up of the present government and that the forthcoming elections would be the last ones to the Reichstag. A return to the parliamentary system, he concluded, was to be avoided at all costs.[5]

By 1 February Hindenburg had dissolved the Reichstag 'now that the formation of a working majority had proved to be impossible'. In this way 'the German people' could 'have its say on the formation of a government of national unity'. The new elections were announced for 5 March 1933.[6]

Hitler had got his way. From now on he took every opportunity to limit his political opponents' freedom of movement. His first step was a 'Decree for the

Protection of the German People' that came into force on 4 February 1933 and that could be used to ban opposition newspapers and meetings.[7] Two days earlier a general ban on demonstrations by the KPD and a ban on an SPD demonstration in the Lustgarten had been announced, and on the 3rd the SPD's official newspaper, *Vorwärts*, was banned for a four-day period.[8] The appeal to the German people that was largely drafted by Hitler and broadcast by all the German radio stations on 1 February had already set the tone for the coming electoral campaign. Among other incendiary claims, it had declared:

> In an unprecedented onslaught of violence and determination, the Communist brand of madness is trying to poison and undermine a nation uprooted and shaken to its very depths. [...] Starting with the family and encompassing all our concepts of honour and fidelity, folk and fatherland, culture and finance, including even the eternal foundations of our morality and faith, nothing is safe from this entirely negative and destructive idea. Fourteen years of Marxism have ruined Germany.

On the one hand, Hitler's appeal was limited to a declaration of war on 'anarchic Communism' and of 'the need to counter the Communist corrosion of Germany', thereby tapping into the phobia of Communism that was widespread in middle-class circles, while, on the other hand, he announced that as a precondition for the country's 'political and economic revival' it was necessary 'once and for all to deal with the madness of the class system and put an end to class conflict'. Bound up with this – and here Hitler used one of his favourite phrases – was the 'restoration of a well-ordered body of the people'. His appeal culminated in a promise that quickly became a byword for Hitler and the NSDAP leadership: 'The parties of Marxism and its fellow travellers have had fourteen years to demonstrate their abilities. The result is a scene of devastation. Now, German people, give us four years, then judge and sentence us!'[9]

At the third cabinet meeting on the morning of 1 February Hitler had expressed his belief that a united front was being formed 'against the present government' and that it stretched from the trades unions to the KPD. Göring – now minister without portfolio, commissioner for air transport and Prussian minister of the interior – had backed his leader, claiming that the 'acts of terror on the part of the Communists' were increasing all the time.[10] True, a few serious clashes had taken place in Berlin on the evening of 30 January, and the Central Committee of the KPD was still calling – in vain – for a general strike. But otherwise there had been no systematic resistance from the KPD and, much to the annoyance of the NSDAP leadership, no attempt at insurrection.

Following Hitler's nomination as chancellor, the SPD leadership and the Social Democrat members of the Reichstag had in any case declared that they would continue their fight on a constitutional basis. If individual organizations or groups were to act on their own initiative, they argued, the whole of the working class would suffer immeasurably in consequence.[11] In the light of this, Hitler could do no more than issue an appeal for patience in his address to the NSDAP, SA and SS on 2 February:

> For thirteen years you have followed me with a rare display of discipline. For several days the Communist murderers have been agitating against the national uprising in the most irresponsible manner. No one should lose their nerve! Remain calm and maintain a sense of discipline! Do not allow spies and agents provocateurs to deter you from carrying out my orders! The hour when we shall destroy this reign of terror is at hand![12]

As always, Hitler was at pains not to antagonize the leaders of the armed forces, with the result that on that same evening we find him attending celebrations organized by the army chief of staff, General Kurt von Hammerstein-Equord, in the banqueting hall of the latter's official residence in the Bendlerstraße[13] and attended by the general's group commanders. Hitler took the opportunity to deliver himself of a speech in which he not only spelt out his administration's immediate goals and methods – 'the root-and-branch extermination of Marxism' and 'the most rigorous authoritarian leadership' – but also ensured himself of the good will of the military, not least by assuring his hosts that the SA would not encroach on the Reichswehr's military monopoly. Instead, the Reichswehr would become the most important institution in the new state. At the same time, the armed forces must be kept out of the country's internal politics.[14]

After a week spent fulfilling his duties as chancellor, Hitler returned to Munich, where the NSDAP press office issued a statement on 5 February to the effect that 'the Führer's visit to Munich is in the first instance a private affair but will then be directed at preparations for the elections to the Reichstag. As already explained, the leadership of the National Socialist movement will remain in Munich. Adolf Hitler, who is personally extremely fond of Munich, will retain his actual home here.'[15] His 'actual home' was his large nine-room apartment at 16 Prinzregentenplatz into which Hitler had moved in November 1929 thanks to the intervention of the local publisher Hugo Bruckmann. Covering an area of over 3,000 square feet, it was furnished by Bruckmann's architect, Paul Ludwig Troost, who in the process became Hitler's favourite architect, too.[16] (It should be added at this point that once Hitler had taken up his new office, his visits to Munich grew markedly less frequent and more cursory. Only during the early stages was he there almost every weekend.)[17] Hitler's refusal to find a place to live after he had taken up his new appointment in Berlin was also due, of course, to the situation in which he found himself in February 1933: since the summer of 1932 the presidential palace at 73 Wilhelmstraße had been undergoing repairs, with the result that the president was using the old chancellor's palace at 77 Wilhelmstraße as his temporary offices – this was the reason why Hitler's appointment had taken place there and why the members of the new cabinet had been sworn in there. Until May 1934 Hitler had to make do with the secretary of state's service flat on the fourth floor of Siedler's new extension to the Chancellery, which had been completed in 1930.[18] Only a few years later he was publicly describing this building as 'the offices on the Wilhelmplatz that give the impression from the outside of a warehouse or a municipal fire station', while the interior was said to resemble 'a sanatorium for consumptives'. In terms of its 'size and layout', the office space provided for the chancellor recalled 'the tasteless décor of the general representative of a modest cigar and tobacco company'.[19] But it was not merely questions of taste that prompted Hitler to ridicule the building's exterior and its interior design; there was also the consideration that it failed to reflect the standards that he applied to buildings designed for the exercise of state power: it was impossible to impress visitors with them, still less to inspire in them a sense of fear.

By 11 February Hitler was back in Berlin, where he replaced an indisposed Hindenburg at the official opening of the International Automobile and Motorcycle Exhibition at the Kaiserdamm in Charlottenburg. Hitler was a great fan of cars – in January 1942, while at his headquarters at the Wolfsschanze, he declared that 'My love is for the automobile, which has afforded me the most wonderful hours of my life'[20] – and he had long since taken an interest in the 'motorization of the world'. As early as 1927 he had insisted that the revolutionary change that had been brought about by this process was 'the result of the creative industry of the Aryans. [. . .] The inventor of the automobile is an Aryan.'[21] In this way he was even able to add an element of anti-Semitism to his enthusiasm for cars. But the opening of the motor show at Charlottenburg also gave him an opportunity as the newly appointed chancellor to gain the support of industrialists in a branch of industry that was particularly important to him. He used his speech, therefore, to announce tax breaks, a new and far-reaching road-building plan and the promotion of sporting events, for he was confident, he told his audience, that the motor car industry would be one of the leading factors in the country's coming economic upturn. Above all, however, he already knew by this date that this branch of industry would play a significant role in his plans for military rearmament. In the Charlottenburg exhibition halls he was able, therefore, to sing the praises of machines 'that can be described as true masterpieces of precision and also of aesthetic beauty'. He additionally praised the courage of the country's entrepreneurs, industrialists and businessmen, the inventiveness of German designers and technicians and, finally, the hard work and conscientiousness of German workers. In this way Hitler was able to cloak his desire for rearming the country as quickly as possible in an appeal to the 'community of the people' and by trumpeting his attempt to reduce unemployment. At the same time, Hitler's appearance at the IAA (Internationale Automobil-Ausstellung) exhibition in February 1933 marked the start of a new ritual: every year from now on he would open the motor show at the Charlottenburg exhibition centre and, alighting from his car, offer his 'German greeting' to the crowds lining the route from the Chancellery building via the Charlottenburger Chaussee and Bismarckstraße to the Kaiserdamm. And with each passing year the military aspect of the exhibition would increase, until in 1939 – the last of the IAA motor shows that Hitler officially opened – a periodical of the time could speak of the 'sense that has been woken in every section of the people of the need for Germany to defend itself' and of the way in which 'exhibition visitors were drawn in particularly large numbers to the German armed forces' stand'.[22]

Hitler's first official engagement at the exhibition centre was a part of his new election campaign, which had already begun – at least to the extent that the NSDAP allowed its opponents to campaign at all. As Goebbels noted in his diary on 3 February, it was

> easy for the party to fight as we can claim for ourselves all the resources of the state. Radio and press are at our disposal. [. . .] Nor, of course, are we short of money this time round. [. . .] We relay the radio broadcasts to the nation and in this way give listeners a graphic picture of what is taking place at our events. I myself shall introduce every speech by the Führer and will try to convey a sense of the magic and the atmosphere of our mass demonstrations.[23]

This new propaganda model had an initial airing during the first speech that Hitler gave at the Sportpalast on 10 February following his appointment as chancellor. It was broadcast not only by all the German radio stations but also by loudspeaker in ten squares in Berlin: the Kleiner Tiergarten, the

Wildenbruchplatz, the Wittenbergplatz, the Gendarmenmarkt, the Gartenplatz, the Lauterplatz, the Pistoriusplatz, the Küstriner Platz, the square in front of the Spandau Town Hall and the Schleidenplatz.[24] This added a new dimension to the National Socialists' ability to conquer and occupy the public arena. As for the contents of his speech, which lasted several hours, Hitler was for the most part happy to repeat remarks that he had already made in his address of 1 February, even repeating the phrase about the four years that the German people should give his government to prove itself. But he reserved his trump card for the end, concluding with words that were couched in the form of a veritable Lord's Prayer:

> For I cannot rid myself of my belief in my people, cannot gainsay the conviction that this nation will one day rise again, cannot distance myself from my love of this people of mine, and I firmly cherish the conviction that the hour will come once again when the millions who hate us today will stand behind us and together with us they will greet the new German Reich of greatness and honour, of strength and majesty and justice, a Reich that we shall have created together only after an embittered and effortful struggle. Amen.[25]

The Reichstag Fire

A second rally was held at the Sportpalast on 2 March, when Hitler again spoke. At the same time a further rally took place in one of the exhibition halls on the Kaiserdamm, where the main speaker was Hermann Göring. As before, Hitler's speech was broadcast by all the German radio stations and relayed to seven local squares: the square outside Gesundbrunnen Station, the Comeniusplatz, the Marktplatz at Pankow, the Viktoriaplatz in Lichtenberg, the Marktplatz in Friedrichshagen, the Marktplatz in Oberschöneweide and the Richardplatz in Neukölln[26] – generally, then, squares in working-class parts of the city. During this one-sided electoral campaign, both the KPD and the SPD held rallies in the Sportpalast, but it was almost impossible to advertise them. Neither was broadcast on the radio, and both were ended prematurely. According to the *Vossische Zeitung*:

> The Communist Party election meeting that took place in the Sportpalast [on 23 February] and that was attended by ten thousand party supporters was broken up by the police at around ten o'clock, when the speaker, the Communist deputy Wilhelm Pieck, criticized the introduction of religious

education in vocational schools and technical colleges. The detective who was supervising the event felt that Pieck was making disparaging remarks about religion and declared the meeting over.[27]

In much the same way a meeting called by the SPD on 27 February to mark the fiftieth anniversary of Karl Marx's death was broken up during a speech by Friedrich Stampfer, a member of the SPD committee. The next day the party's official newspaper quoted the offending passage: 'Even today I am still of the opinion that in order to be a true Marxist one has to know a great deal. But one thing I have learnt in the meantime: in order to be an anti-Marxist one need not know anything at all!' At this point the meeting was broken up by the police.[28]

By now the situation was deteriorating by the day, largely as a result of acts of terror perpetrated by a violently vindictive SA. In consequence, having their meetings broken up by the police during the month of February was among the least of the worries of the KPD and SPD. In his capacity as commissar for the Prussian Ministry of the Interior, Göring pursued a policy of removing republican sympathizers from the police[29] and administration and of filling important posts with National Socialists. On 15 February, for example, he appointed one of the NSDAP's representatives in the Reichstag, Rear Admiral Magnus von Levetzow, to the post of chief of police in Berlin. But Göring also aggravated the situation by issuing various decrees. On 17 February, for instance, he ordered the local police

> to use all the means in their power to support every activity undertaken in the national interest, whereas acts of Communist terror and similar attacks are to be rigorously resisted, if necessary with the use of weapons. Police officers who use their weapons when carrying out their duties will be protected by me without regard for the consequences of their use of those weapons. Conversely, anyone who out of a misguided sense of consideration fails to use his weapons will face disciplinary proceedings.[30]

This was effectively a shoot-to-kill policy. On 22 February Göring additionally ordered the 'auxiliary police' to be conscripted and deployed. Since the regular police were overworked and there was said to be a constant threat not only to public safety but to 'the lives and property of law-abiding citizens as a result of the increasing violence on the part of left-wing radicals, especially Communists', it was no longer possible to dispense with the 'voluntary services of suitable helpers, who can be used as auxiliary police officers'. For the present, the term 'auxiliary police' was defined as meaning only 'members of the SS, SA, Stahlhelm and German Nationalist Kampfring'.[31]

Subsequent events are best summed up by the official chronicle of the Berlin-Brandenburg SA published four years later:

> The extermination of Marxism in every shape and form is the first challenge that the SA must face and deal with in consultation with the state authorities. The fight against the last remaining attempts to create a reign of Red terror, the searches and the impounding of weapons and propaganda material last for a period of several months and are both difficult and bloody.

The first of the SA's auxiliary police forces in Berlin-Brandenburg was made up of 'two hundred old and proven SA men from all the different associations' and was under the 'direct command' of group leader Wolf-Heinrich Helldorf. Their 'accommodation' was an old warehouse at 178 Friedrichstraße in the Kreuzberg district of the city:

> Then the individual units and independent members of the Sturmbann set up SA auxiliary police detachments numbering between one hundred and 150 men each, who work closely with the relevant police stations. They are not in barracks. The SA auxiliary police officers carry pistols and on their upper left arm they wear a white armband with the words 'Auxiliary Police'.[32]

If these figures are accurate, then the Berlin SA ultimately fielded a total of between 1,500 and two thousand auxiliary police officers.

On 26 February the press reported on the results of a police search of the KPD central offices in the Karl-Liebknecht-Haus on the Bülowplatz (now the Rosa-Luxemburg-Platz). The building had already been searched on several previous occasions, but without any real results. On this occasion, however, there was talk of truly sensational discoveries – underground vaults containing large quantities of highly treasonable material, a subterranean passage and, indeed, even a whole labyrinth of corridors and secret rooms, together with leaflets calling for armed insurrection. It was said that it would take weeks to complete a detailed examination of all the rooms and of all the documents that had been uncovered.[33] But by the following evening the Reichstag fire was being reported. A twenty-four-year-old Dutch citizen and former member of the Dutch Communist Party, Marinus van der Lubbe, was arrested at the scene. He confessed to having started the blaze single-handedly using fire lighters and his own clothing and tablecloths. At his trial, he was found guilty, sentenced to death and executed on 10 January 1934.[34]

The controversy over the events surrounding the Reichstag fire shows no sign of abating and, indeed, has become even more intense in recent years.[35] It is impossible to find agreement even on such basic matters as the time of Hitler's arrival at the building. Ian Kershaw, who tends to subscribe to the theory that Van der Lubbe was acting on his own, believes that Hitler arrived on the scene at around 22:30, an hour after Göring, while other, more recent writers, arguing that the National Socialists were responsible for the fire or at least complicit in it, set out from a much earlier point in time.[36] Inconsistencies and contradictions were a feature of the original investigation from the very outset, with the result that Göring's claim, expressed at the scene of the crime and immediately and enthusiastically taken up by Hitler, that the arson attack was 'the most appalling act of Bolshevik terror ever to have been seen in Germany',[37] was met with considerable scepticism even on the part of those who were usually uncritical of the government's official pronouncements.

The British journalist Sefton Delmer, who was the Berlin correspondent of the *Daily Express* and who had already interviewed Hitler on several occasions, witnessed the Führer's initial reaction in the burning Reichstag building and reported on his experiences in a piece that appeared in the paper on 28 February. According to Delmer, Hitler had called out in some excitement: 'This is a God-given signal! If this fire, as I believe, turns out to be the handiwork of Communists then there is nothing that shall stop us now crushing out this murder pest with an iron fist.' Delmer continues his account:

> It was then that Hitler turned to me: 'God grant', he said, 'that this is the work of the Communists. You are witnessing the beginning of a great new epoch in German history. This fire is the beginning.' And then something touched the rhetorical spring in his brain. 'You see this flaming building,' he said, sweeping his hand dramatically around him. 'If this Communist spirit got hold of Europe for but two months it would be all aflame like this building.'[38]

At the cabinet meeting the following morning, Hitler picked up where he had left off and declared that 'an implacable confrontation with the KPD' was now 'unavoidable'. The minutes of the meeting record Hitler's remarks in reported speech:

> The psychologically right moment for this confrontation had now come. It was pointless to wait any longer. The KPD was resolved on extreme

measures. The war on them could not be dependent on legal considerations. Now that the arson attack on the Reichstag building had taken place, there could no longer be any doubt that the government would win a 51 per cent share of the vote in the elections. [...] There was an urgent need to issue a decree to protect society against the Communist danger.

It is worth recalling at this juncture that exactly four weeks earlier Hitler and Goebbels had agreed that for the time being they would avoid taking any steps against the 'Red terror': the 'Bolshevik attempt at revolution' must first be allowed to 'flare up'. They would then strike when the moment was right. Now Hitler was claiming that the 'psychologically right moment' had come for the NSDAP to confront the Communist Party. In much the same way, his earlier demand that for three days the streets of Berlin should be handed over to the SA in 1932 had presupposed a particular set of circumstances in which the SA would suppress a 'Bolshevik uprising' after it had already broken out.

At the cabinet meeting on 28 February Göring lost no time in taking up Hitler's cue. He did not think that the attack on the Reichstag had been prompted by the closure of the Karl-Liebknecht-Haus, as was being suggested, but that it was due, rather, to the fact that the Prussian police had impounded numerous secret files belonging to the KPD. According to Göring, it was clear from this material that the Communists were planning to form terrorist cells, to set fire to public buildings and to poison the food in soup kitchens, even if it meant sacrificing their own supporters. Finally, they were intending to abduct the wives and children of government ministers and other high-ranking figures and hold them hostage. Göring announced that as the minister responsible he had ordered the temporary closure of the local museums and taken steps to ensure that the government district was better protected. He had additionally banned not only the Communist press but also all Social Democrat newspapers throughout the country. All KPD offices and meeting rooms had been closed and all KPD deputies and officials had been arrested, at least to the extent that they could be traced. The police and CID had been placed on high alert. That very day some two thousand members of the SA and SS would march through Berlin.[39]

According to the next day's *Völkischer Beobachter*, Hitler 'and members of his closest staff' travelled straight from the cabinet meeting 'to the scene of devastation' in order to see for themselves the source of the blaze. The reporter was allowed to accompany Hitler on his tour of the building and struck a suitably overwrought note in his account of the visit:

The Führer stands silent and pensive, his arms folded, in front of the ruins, and his eyes scan the burnt-out hall. [. . .] The Führer does not speak, but his features reflect his feelings, and they bode ill for the culprits and for the paymasters who are behind these blind and criminal hooligans. [. . .] The Führer wanders through the rooms, climbs over the tangle of red firemen's hoses, over piles of rubble, through the scene of destruction, and in the rooms that are carefully guarded by the police he sees the sources of the fires that were lit and the traces of the Communist arsonists. The police are still examining the nooks and crannies of the rambling building. Perhaps they have still to find the odd culprit, who may have hidden himself away in his fear. Perhaps even now the one criminal who has been arrested will be confessing the names of his Communist accomplices. It will then be possible to refute the lie that is being put about, namely, that it was the National Socialists who incited the culprit to commit his crime, a lie eagerly peddled through the streets by the Jewish rabble. Then the long arm of the law will strike home! By this evening we shall know what the Führer has decided.[40]

Within twenty-four hours of the fire, it was already evident from the NSDAP's official newspaper that at least a part of the population thought that the National Socialists were responsible for the attack. The paper does not, however, reveal why Hitler found it necessary to return to the scene of the crime and to brood on the building's charred remains. A second article gives us an insight into the extent of the reprisals that were now under way. Here we read that '130 Bolshevik leaders' had been arrested and were in custody, as were many prominent individuals, 'foremost among whom, of course, are Jews'. Among those named in the article were the writer and general practitioner Max Hodann; two lawyers, Hans Litten (against whom Hitler bore a personal grudge) and Alfred Apfel ('who once defended the vile arsonist Max Hoelz'); the writer Ludwig Renn, famous for his novel *Krieg*; and the editor of *Die Weltbühne*, Carl von Ossietzky, described by the paper as 'the Red muckraker'. Ernst Torgler, too, was said to have been 'caught', although the leader of the Communists in the Reichstag, having been accused of starting the fire, had in fact handed himself in voluntarily. What the article failed to make clear was that 28 February 1933 was also 'the day on which the SA Auxiliary Police of Berlin-Brandenburg were deployed for the very first time'. According to the SA's official chronicle, their headquarters in the Friedrichstraße were used to accommodate 'a hundred political prisoners from the overflowing cells at the police headquarters'.[41] Also on 28 February the president issued a decree 'For the Protection of People and State' that was generally referred to as the

'Reichstag Fire Decree'. As a result, large sections of the country's constitution were rendered null and void 'until further notice', the rights of the regional governments and communities were curtailed, and the death penalty was introduced for a whole series of new offences. The Reichstag Fire Decree effectively summoned the Third Reich into existence. A second decree on 24 March consolidated Hitler's dictatorship in the form of the Enabling Act, described as an 'Act for the Removal of Distress from People and Reich'.[42]

SA Terror and Aryanization

Even before the Reichstag fire, it had been difficult to speak of an electoral campaign in Berlin. In the wake of the fire, there could no longer be any possibility of such a campaign. In spite of this, the turnout on 5 March 1933 was 87.3 per cent – substantially higher than in the last 'free' elections on 6 November 1932, when the figure had been 81.0 per cent. Given the conditions under which the election was held, the results in Berlin can only be described as astonishing: as was to be expected, the NSDAP added appreciably to its share of the vote and for the first time polled over a million votes (1,032,342, or 34.6 per cent of the total). The German Nationalists and Stahlhelm, campaigning on a single ticket as the 'Black-White-and-Red Battle Front', stagnated at 11 per cent, the SPD, with 21.7 per cent, recorded modest losses, whereas the KPD lost around a fifth of its votes, ending up on 24.5 per cent. The result was that the 'nationalist concentration' in Berlin managed only 45.6 per cent of the total. The NSDAP and Battle Front together won 1,359,309 votes, but when the votes of the two workers' parties were added together, the 'Red bloc' of the KPD and SPD actually polled 1,377,794 votes, marginally ahead of the National Socialist and German Nationalist coalition.

As usual, the most extreme result was recorded in the district of Wedding, where the KPD and SPD polled 147,094 votes against the 77,201 votes of the NSDAP and Battle Front.[43] If the NSDAP was to carry out Hitler's programme of 'exterminating Marxism root and branch', then it clearly needed to do more than merely gag the Communist and Social Democratic press. It was not even enough to have arrested hundreds of officials and organized a vendetta against left-wing intellectuals, journalists, writers and lawyers. Still less had it achieved its objective by sweeping away the personal liberties enshrined in the constitution, including freedom of speech, the right of assembly and other basic rights. To repeat Hitler's statement of intent from 1926: 'We shall not rest until the last remaining newspaper has been destroyed, the last remaining organization been rooted out, the last educational establishment been removed and the final

Marxist converted or annihilated. There is no halfway house.'[44] As it had done during the years of the 'struggle for Berlin', the SA assumed the task of implementing Hitler's programme. And just as the SA storm centres had been the hub from which these violent assaults on the 'Red bulwark' had been coordinated, so the city-wide network of centres and homes (the 'SA barracks'), together with the empty warehouses, factories, army barracks, hangars, cellars and attics that were impounded by the SA, now formed the infrastructure that was used in breaking down the city's proletarian organizations. The term 'unofficial concentration camps' quickly became established as a way of describing the places of torture where the opponents of the regime were incarcerated not just for a few days but throughout the summer and autumn of 1933 and in some cases even longer. Here a few thousand members of the SA exercised a reign of terror, torturing and murdering an untold number of victims. Such 'camps' planned and systematized the use of violence until such time as the SS under Heinrich Himmler took over this role. The significance of these unofficial concentration camps in establishing the National Socialist dictatorship, especially in the capital, was for a long time overlooked, and it was not until 1977 that the first attempt was made to list the SA centres and barracks that had served as concentration camps in Berlin in 1933. Only twenty-three such centres were identified. A revised list in 1983 concluded that there had been 105 unofficial concentration camps and places where torture had been routinely carried out.[45] Four years later new research came up with no fewer than 150 such camps.[46] It is likely that at least for a while there were two hundred such places in the capital.[47] In his memoirs, Rudolf Diels, who at the time in question was in charge of the Political Police at the police headquarters in Berlin and who went on to become the first head of the Gestapo, described the situation in March 1933 as follows:

> Hitler's success or failure depended on the decisions that were taken on the streets of the capital. [. . .] It was here that the dangers threatening him were to be found, here, too, that his chances lay. These streets were not only the headquarters of the Communist intelligentsia, here, too, the SA – triggered as a countermovement – was numerically at its most powerful, constantly prepared and organized along positively military lines. The hatred of the Berlin SA for the Communists was indescribable. It was an entirely personal, inextinguishable hatred of brother for brother and had been building up on the orders of their legal leader. [. . .] The great act of homage paid by the Berlin SA to its 'Führer and People's Chancellor' on the night of 30 January 1933 led initially to feelings of intoxication at the prospect of victory, and

even after the Reichstag fire the SA hesitated before striking out at its enemy. But the Reichstag elections marked the end of legality, and by early March the activities of the Berlin SA had assumed the most rabid forms. [. . .]

Each of these young lads had a long-standing hatred to express and was determined to settle old scores with individual Communists. Friend and foe lived in the same tenement buildings, at the back of the same blocks of flats, even in the same hallways in Britz and Pankow, Nowawes and Reinickendorf and Moabit, Fischerkietz and Wedding. None of the members of the Red Front who had beaten up an SA man or looked at him askance during the time of 'the struggle' escaped the private revenge of this victorious brown-shirted army. [. . .]

From every part of the city, rumours reached us at the Political Police, police reports, complaints and victorious accounts of the actions of the SA. Unlike the party, it was prepared for its seizure of power. It needed no unified leadership: the Gruppen-Stab [command staff] set an example but gave no orders. But at the storm centres there were carefully drawn-up plans for attacks on the Communist parts of the city. During those days in March, every SA man was hard on the heels of his enemy, everyone knew what to do. The storm centres purged their districts. They knew not only the houses where their enemies lived, they had also established where they met and where they would go to ground. [. . .] Not only the Communists but everyone who had ever spoken out against Hitler's movement was at risk. [. . .] SA men destroyed the fixtures and fittings at the home of the son of the country's president, Friedrich Ebert. They forced their way into the homes of the owners of the Ullstein and Mosse publishing houses and laid into anyone who got in their way. As for the staff of *Die Weltbühne* and *Das Tagebuch*, they dragged away anyone they could lay their hands on.[48]

Only in the rarest cases were the SA's actions concealed from public view. In general, the organization set little store by secrecy, and arrests were frequently carried out in broad daylight. In some instances the individuals who were arrested in this way were held up to public ridicule and mistreated in the places where they lived before being taken away to one of the city's unofficial concentration camps.[49] This is also true of one of the SA's most notorious acts, the 'Köpenick Week of Blood' at the end of June 1933, when more than five hundred men and women, mainly Social Democrats and Communists, were arrested and tortured. Nearly a hundred of them were murdered in a frenzy of bestial brutality.[50] It was not least in an effort to legitimize these acts of brutality on the part of the SA and, later, the Gestapo, and to justify them in the eyes of their middle-class supporters, that the NSDAP leaders sought to fuel existing phobias about Communists by means of further 'revelations', many of which bordered on the grotesque and were even involuntarily comical.

At a cabinet meeting on 2 March 1933, for example, Göring reported on 'the measures being taken against the Communists' and informed his cabinet colleagues that

> substantive documents concerning Communist plans had been found the previous night. [. . .] Two copies of a map of Berlin had been discovered indicating all the principal electricity stations, the underground network and converter stations. One copy had been in the possession of the party's central offices, the other had been cut up and distributed among individual groups. The plan had been photographed.[51]

As was the case with all the other 'evidence' said to have been uncovered at this time and that allegedly pointed to an 'attempted Communist uprising', no real proof was ever produced. The type of map mentioned by Göring was in any case very popular at this period and published in large quantities. Its main distinguishing feature was that it highlighted all the city's important buildings and transport links; its publication as 'evidence' of a plot would merely have made the cabinet look very foolish.

A propaganda tract published in huge numbers at this time claimed that a 'plan of action for the period after 5 March 1933' had been worked out 'by the general staff of the revolution' right down to the very last detail: 'Between 5 and 9 March 1933, railway bridges were to be blown up, power lines brought down and power stations shut down and destroyed. [. . .] The massed ranks of the unemployed were evidently intended to launch attacks and commit robberies in the exclusive residential district of Krumme Lanke.'[52]

The National Socialist propaganda machine had initially set its sights on the Communist Party or, more generally, 'Marxism', but by March 1933 it had added a further dimension in the form of anti-Semitism. Party officials, journalists and writers who were dragged away were particularly badly treated if it turned out that they were Jews ('You stinking Jewish carrion will get nothing to eat from me!' a guard at the SS's Columbia House Concentration Camp in Tempelhof screamed at the journalist Kurt Hiller).[53] Yet they had fallen into the hands of the SA and SS for political reasons – in other words, because they belonged to particular organizations or on account of their exposed position in public life. But by the second half of March at the latest, the wave of repressions had grown to include cases of individuals who were persecuted on racial grounds alone. Johann von Leers, whom Goebbels had 'discovered', specialized in concocting anti-Semitic insults in the NSDAP's propaganda bureau. In March, he published a mass-produced pamphlet titled *Our Present Demand: Jews Out!*, in which we read that

> The appointment of Adolf Hitler as chancellor of Germany constitutes the first great defeat of the Jews for centuries and as such it will go down in the history of the world. Despite the raging hatred of all Jews, Adolf Hitler has succeeded, as the world's only statesman to demonstrate his opposition to Jews, in assuming leadership of the nation in its open struggle against Jews – and he has done so in spite of all the resistance that he has been shown.

It was necessary, Leers went on, to 'evict all the East European Jews who are so detrimental to our country and to render the others harmless both politically and economically'.[54]

The distinction that Leers was at pains to draw here was by no means random, for on 9 March Hans Heinrich Lammers, the secretary of state at the Chancellery, had written to the minister of the interior 'at the chancellor's request' and passed on 'ideas' put forward by the Ministry of Trade and Industry, since the time had now come when they 'could begin to prepare for openly racial legislation'. It was particularly important, the writer continued, to 'take legal steps to curb the ever-increasing influx of East European Jews' and to 'remove at least some of the East European Jews who have come to this country and who have not been naturalized'.[55]

The way in which the state planned to deal with Jewish doctors emerges from the action undertaken at the Moabit General Hospital. On 13 March Göring appointed Julius Lippert – previously the NSDAP's party leader on the Berlin City Council and the editor of *Der Angriff* – to the post of state commissioner for Berlin, effectively making him the most powerful person in the city.[56] In turn, Lippert appointed Wilhelm Klein, a dentist from Wiesbaden, as the city's medical adviser. Working closely with Paul Schuder, who was 'state commissioner for overseeing the business of the district mayor' of Tiergarten, Klein began to 'purge' the Moabit General Hospital on 20 March, suspending several Jewish doctors and a whole series of trainees. By the following week he was preparing to dismiss every member of staff 'of Jewish extraction or otherwise belonging to the Marxist parties'. On 1 April the SA carried out its first raid on the hospital, and a number of Jewish doctors were taken away, still wearing their white coats. Loaded into waiting lorries, they were driven away, in some cases to the barracks in the General-Pape-Straße in Schöneberg, which the SA had commandeered for the occasion. Of the forty-seven doctors employed by the Moabit General Hospital, twenty-three were dismissed in late March and early April, another four in May and three more at the end of the year.[57]

Similar raids took place at Berlin's other hospitals[58] and, indeed, among medical-care providers in general. And so we find the *Völkischer Beobachter* reporting on 16 April that twenty-seven Jewish doctors working in public welfare in the district of Mitte were being relieved of their duties with effect from 30 June 1933.[59]

Of course, Hitler did not personally order these dismissals and cases of ill treatment, and yet they were all a direct result of the goal that he had proclaimed in the early 1920s, whereby 'the Jewish question' must be solved because the Jews were allegedly involved in an attempt to 'take control of all things German: in Berlin alone, 85 per cent of all doctors are Jewish', Hitler had announced at the end of 1922.[60] Two months later, on 26 February 1923, he had spoken of the 'plight of our students', arguing that if Jewish doctors and lawyers were driven 'from posts that they do not deserve, there will be enough room for the German intelligentsia'.[61] This was a clear pointer that, once the party was in power, organized anti-Semitism would take the form of the exclusion of Jews, initially from particular professions, and that there would be a vast programme designed to create jobs for the 'Aryan' rivals of Jewish civil servants, academics, businessmen and so forth. The first steps taken in this direction were the laws enacted on 7 April 1933 'to re-establish the professional class of civil servants' and to decide 'who should be admitted to the legal profession'.

The party's propaganda machine had prepared for this first wave of discriminatory laws and decrees by means of the 'boycott' of Jewish retailers, doctors, lawyers and so on of 1 April, an action organized in the main by the SA. At a cabinet meeting on 29 March, Hitler declared that he himself had instigated the previous day's appeal by inviting party members to engage in a 'defensive struggle against the appalling witch-hunt conducted by the Jews'.[62] The SA was to be permitted to 'fight' one more time:

Street by street we have dissected the list of Jewish shops, warehouses, doctors and lawyers, and not even the Jewish piano teacher has been forgotten – she too will find a guard positioned outside the door of her apartment. [. . .] A squad of SA cars appears, packed with banners. 'SA and civilians fall into line in two groups! Start counting!' The assignment begins:

Brunnenstraße. As many guards as there are Jewish shops. 'Five civilians, one SA man as the leader of the troop.' 'Three civilians, one SA man!' 'You'll stand guard at number so-and-so, you'll stand there, you'll stand over here!' 'Take your banners!' 'State your names!'

Next street. Everywhere is divided up, the whole area of tenement buildings, rear buildings, slums. For the rapacious Jew can be found everywhere among the hundred men and women who are hard at work: flaunting himself in his corner shop, luring passers-by into the cinema, hiding away in a cellar, furtively concealed at the very back of the building.

9:45. 'Move out.' Eyes flashing, banners waving, Adolf Hitler's fighters set to work, purging Germany of lies, witch-hunts and the Jewish plague. [. . .]

By the evening the impression left on everyone by the day's battle is that it has worked. Worked wonderfully well. We are dog-tired but happy! For we have won another battle![63]

The SA was allowed to continue to regard itself as the instrument of the 'national revolution' and as Hitler's warriors in his fight against Jewish piano teachers and the poorest slum-dwelling retailers. In point of fact, Hitler used the SA only as an auxiliary tool that could be deployed and reined in again depending on the situation. The boycott, which the Jewish population was bound to find traumatic, was planned to last only one day. As Hitler informed his cabinet on 31 March, this day of action was intended to be followed by 'a pause'.[64]

The Question of the Department Stores

In general Hitler avoided taking risks or striking a confrontational attitude during this early period, when his regime was still relatively unstable. Or at least he avoided risks when he could expect serious repercussions in terms of foreign policy and the domestic economy. On 16 March, for example, he had received Theodor Lewald, the head of the German Olympic Committee, in his offices in the Chancellery building and received a report on the state of preparations for the 1936 Olympic Games in Berlin. In early April, Lewald was then attacked in the National Socialist press – as far as the party was concerned, he was categorized as a 'half-Jew'. Hitler promptly instructed his chief press officer, Otto Dietrich, to desist from any further such attacks.[65] And when the International Olympic Committee, bridling at the regime's anti-Jewish measures, wrote to the German delegates on 3 May to point out that 'the Games are entrusted to a city, not to a country, and must bring together the amateurs of all nations on the basis of the greatest possible equality, i.e. they should not have a political, racial, national or denominational character', with the result that it would be better if Berlin withdrew its candidacy if these conditions 'do not meet with the chancellor's approval',[66] Hitler reacted furiously and was initially inclined to turn down the offer of the post of honorary chairman of the Olympic Games. But Berlin's mandate to present the Games was confirmed at the International Olympic Committee's meeting in Vienna on 7–9 June 1933 after the German delegation had given assurances that it was speaking on behalf of the German government and that the country would abide by every last one of the Olympic rules. In particular, German Jews would not be excluded from the German team.[67]

Another case affected the Jewish publishing house of Rudolf Mosse, which published not only the *Frankfurter Zeitung* but also the *Berliner Tageblatt* – internationally speaking, by far the most prestigious of all the German-language newspapers. As recently as the beginning of March, both the leading political editor, Wolfgang Bretholz, and the editor-in-chief, Theodor Wolff, had published a series of articles boldly speaking out in support of the Weimar Republic and against the National Socialists. Both were then forced to flee abroad.[68] On 10 March the *Berliner Tageblatt* was banned from appearing for four consecutive days 'in the interests of public safety and order'.[69] It would have been easy for the government to deliver the coup de grâce to the *Tageblatt* – there was no other paper in Berlin that Hitler hated as much – but the party contented itself with re-organizing the editorial offices over the coming months and aligning the paper with the regime, until it was finally indistin-guishable from any other National Socialist newspaper.[70] In the process, its circulation figures plummeted, and by the early summer of 1933 the publishing house, which had already gone into receivership in 1932 before being rescued by the Rudolf Mosse Foundation, again found itself on the brink of bank-ruptcy. The Dresdner Bank was willing to offer temporary credit facilities but only on condition that the government instructed it to do so.

There is something distinctly piquant about the fact that the affair was discussed at the same cabinet meeting as the one called to decide the fate of Hermann Tietz's department store, which was likewise in a state of crisis. It, too, moreover, was Jewish. The 'Tietz case' had in fact already been discussed at a cabinet meeting on 23 June, but no decision had been taken. The cabinet had already had to confront the same problem as early as 31 March, except that on that occasion it was the Karstadt chain that was under discussion. A non-Jewish organization, Karstadt needed 1.5 million marks of extra credit, other-wise it would have to close the very next day, with the loss of more than twenty thousand jobs. On that occasion Hitler had declared the loan irresponsible unless they first made an attempt to clarify the question of all the other department stores, which were said to be destroying tens of thousands of smaller businesses. The status quo, he argued, could not continue. Faced with the simple fact that the decision could no longer be deferred, he declared that 'in the circumstances' he would agree to the loan. But when the discussion turned to Hermann Tietz and his 17,450 employees, Hitler simply announced that it was clear from the company's debts, which had been accumulating for some time, that 'department stores' were 'no longer viable concerns. [. . .] Whatever steps he and his colleagues might take would serve only to delay the onset of the catastrophe.' The cabinet could take its decision only from the standpoint of the consequences that any collapse would entail.[71]

On 4 July, therefore, when the Tietz case again came up for discussion, Hitler summed up the situation as he saw it: the cabinet would raise no objections 'to any attempt to put the Mosse and Tietz businesses back on an even keel if that attempt were to be made on a commercial footing and without the involvement of the Reich; whether and to what extent such a rescue could be successfully carried out must be left to the banks to decide.'[72] Point 16 of the NSDAP programme, which allowed for 'the immediate communalization of large department stores and their leasing to small traders at a reduced cost', was thus rendered obsolete at a single stroke.

A sworn 'enemy of department stores', Hitler had merely facilitated their planned 'Aryanization'. In the Leipziger Straße and on the Alexanderplatz, Hermann Tietz became simply HERTIE, and shortly afterwards A. Wertheim AG, with its vast store on the Leipziger Platz and the Leipziger Straße – designed by the Jewish architect Alfred Messel, the building was one of the city's landmarks – and its branches in the Königstraße and the Rosenthaler Straße, became AWAG, a purely 'Aryan' concern. The Aryanized *Berliner Tageblatt* likewise survived only as long as the regime needed it to maintain a semblance of 'diversity'. Its final edition appeared on 31 January 1939, six years and a day after Hitler had been appointed chancellor. It contained a transcript of his notorious speech about the 'Pan-German Reichstag' in which he had announced 'the annihilation of the Jewish race in Europe'.[73] The headline was taken from the same speech, which Hitler had made the previous day: 'I believe in a long peace.'[74]

Press, Radio and Cinema

Following the Reichstag fire, the house met in the Kroll Opera,[75] which was modified to meet its new function. Wearing his uniform and brown shirt,

Hitler set forth his government's aims on 23 March 1933 and spoke of a 'far-reaching moral renewal of the body of the nation'. 'Every aspect of education, theatre, cinema, literature, press and radio', he declared, 'will be the means to achieve this end and will be valued accordingly.'[76] The *Gleichschaltung*, or alignment, of all these areas of culture was carried out during the weeks and months that followed. As such, it took place in parallel with the aforementioned creation of new posts for German academics. In the first instance, this involved replacing Jews and other politically unreliable individuals in higher and middle management, although such changes were sometimes also the result of voluntary 'self-realignment'. There was also a vast redistribution of wealth. Only those businesses were destroyed that were part of the organized workers' movement – publishing houses, printing works and so on – and their assets were impounded. In early May 1933, for example, the Free Trades Unions were disbanded and their funds poured into the German Workers' Front. In the same speech, however, Hitler also stressed that, to deal with the economic crisis, it was necessary to have 'unconditionally authoritarian leadership within the country in order to create a condition of trust in the stability of current conditions'.[77] Just as he was prepared to uphold this trust, not least on the part of foreign businesses in Germany, and not only allowed even the hated *Berliner Tageblatt* to continue to appear on the city's streets but also helped to save Jewish and non-Jewish department stores that he could easily have left to go under, he also proved accommodatingly opportunistic in terms of the nation's culture. His basic principle was to wind up unprofitable companies or branches of the same, while profitable concerns were placed, where possible, under the control of the party or state. Finally, prestigious organizations and institutions that could be exploited for their contacts with other countries were reorganized and kept afloat. To take a single example: Ullstein-Verlag, which was far more important than Mosse, was not renamed Deutscher Verlag until the end of 1937, while Ullstein's profit-making newspapers – above all, the *B. Z. am Mittag* and the *Berliner Morgenpost* – and the majority of the company's magazines, including the *Berliner Illustrirte Zeitung*, the *Grüne Post* and *Die Dame*, were allowed to continue to exist until Berlin lost its status as a city of newspapers. After all, not only could they be incorporated into the Third Reich's propaganda machinery, they even made a profit. On the other hand, the financially ailing *Tempo* appeared for the last time on the evening of 5 August 1933, while financial considerations forced the *Vossische Zeitung* to appear only once, rather than twice, a day from 1 November 1933; by 31 March 1934 it had ceased publication altogether.[78] A number of Jews were still able to maintain a toehold on the cultural scene at least for a little while longer. Backed by 'Aryan' colleagues, these included one of the editors at Mosse-Verlag, Gusti Hecht,[79] and the portrait and fashion photographer Yva (Else Neulaender-Simon), whose images continued to appear in fashion magazines until the beginning of 1938. Between 1936 and 1938 staff in her studio in the Schlüterstraße also included an apprentice by the name of Helmut Neustädter, who, driven into exile, later took the name of Helmut Newton.[80]

Conversely, many National Socialists who had previously concealed their true thoughts while working for democratic organizations were now able to say what they actually felt. Hermann Ullstein, who together with his brothers continued to run his own publishing business until they were forced to sell it, recalls a conversation that took place within days of Hitler's accession to power. The old editor with whom he was speaking suddenly launched into a National Socialist tirade and proudly declared that he had been a member of the party since 1923.[81] Hitler was always interested in what went on in the Ullstein stable, and in July 1933 he spoke to the company's newly appointed 'political director', Eduard Stadtler, who had joined the NSDAP from the German Nationalist Party on 9 June 1933.[82] In particular, he wanted to know about the progress that had been made in aligning the company with NSDAP policies. He also asked for a report to be drawn up on the possibility of a 'transfer of capital' through the president of the Reichsbank. Finally, at the end of October, he was interested to learn from Stadtler that

> the actual newspaper branch of the business has undergone profound changes in terms of its personal politics. The compromised gentlemen have left the editorial offices, and new members of staff have been taken on. The various titles have not become party newspapers – this, after all, was to be avoided – but have placed themselves in the service of the new state in the most loyal way imaginable. [. . .] The part of the business responsible for the company's magazines has likewise undergone a spiritual transformation. [. . .] Inasmuch as the magazines have a powerful impact abroad, this change is particularly welcome to the new government in the difficult situation that obtains at present with regard to its foreign policy. The extent of government interference in the two companies responsible for its newspapers and magazines emerges most clearly from the fact that since the beginning of the year more than seventy editors have lost their jobs.[83]

Within months, however, this willingness on the part of Ullstein's editorial departments to attune their thinking to the 'new idea of the state'[84] was no longer sufficient in the minds of Hitler, Goebbels and their kind, and it was made unmistakably clear to the Ullstein brothers that it was now time for them 'voluntarily' to sell their business. On 7 June 1934 the company was bought for a risible sum by the same trust company as the one that had acquired Mosse-Verlag only a short time previously. Not even the Ullsteins themselves discovered that the sale had been ordered by Hitler and the NSDAP.[85] Readers were to be tricked into not noticing that the enterprise had transmuted into one that was National Socialist to the core, allowing the NSDAP to dominate the newspaper scene in Berlin from now on. A leading National Socialist journalist summed up this situation in April 1934:

> The leadership of the [Berlin] Gau is of the view that the Ullstein papers should continue to exist. [. . .] The party can only gain from any collaboration between this concern and the Gau leadership, for in the process it has acquired, at no cost to itself, an extensive and, in monetary terms, extremely valuable press outlet. [. . .] For reasons of the party's foreign policy and to avoid further difficulties over the Jewish question, the Gau leadership believes that the name of Ullstein can be retained and that any changes under the first *Gleichschaltung* agreements should be made as silently and as unobtrusively as possible.[86]

Ullstein was taken over in the wake of the second wave of changes made in the name of *Gleichschaltung*, which assumed the form of the appropriation of assets. It was the most important such acquisition, but by no means the last. Between 1931 and 1939 the number of newspapers in Berlin shrank from forty-four to fifteen. Of these, ten were owned openly or covertly by the National Socialist Press Trust. Three others were published by Hugenberg's Scherl-Verlag, and these too were finally acquired by the NSDAP in the summer of 1944.[87]

If Berlin's newspapers needed time to fall into line, the same was emphatically not true of the local radio stations, which fell into the lap of the NSDAP like ripe fruit. Following an initial wave of dismissals combined with arrests and acts of open terror on the part of the SA, Goebbels – since 13 March 1933 minister for information and propaganda, an appointment made by Hindenburg at Hitler's bidding – assumed responsibility for 'surveillance of the radio', a task that until then had been carried out by the postmaster general.[88] This transfer inevitably led to arguments with other ministries and with the country's regions, with the result that on 6 July Hitler issued instructions placing the country's radio networks under the central control of Goebbels' new ministry, peremptorily announcing in a circular to regional governors on

15 July that 'in the field of broadcasting, the Reich must have unlimited control not only over the public radio network but also over the Reich Broadcasting Corporation and the other broadcasting corporations. [. . .] The radio is one of our chief ways of disseminating information and propaganda.'[89]

The cinema, too, was relatively easy to win over, and on 2 February – three days after his appointment as chancellor – Hitler, an enthusiastic cinema-goer, attended the premiere of Gustav Ucicky's *Dawn* at the Ufa-Palast: the showing was a kind of bridal gift to Hitler and his closest colleagues from Germany's biggest film company, Ufa, whose largest shareholder was Alfred Hugenberg. With its mystical approach to death, the film took up one of the core ideas of National Socialist ideology and in that way became a perfect expression of the country's future willing self-sacrifice to the aspirations of the Third Reich, which naturally included the mass medium of the cinema as well as the radio and press. The same trust company that in 1934 had swallowed up Mosse- and Ullstein-Verlag on the instructions of the NSDAP turned its attentions the following year to the film industry, starting with the nationalization of Tobis, before moving on to Ufa in March 1937. With this the two most important film companies in Germany came within the jurisdiction of the regime. By the early 1940s Germany's film companies had been almost entirely nationalized.[90]

In short, Hitler's access to the mass media and his complete control over them, including even their appropriation, was not a precondition of his 'far-reaching moral renewal of the body of the nation', which he had announced on 23 March 1933, but was a direct result of that aim. And this result had essentially been achieved by the outbreak of the Second World War, at the very moment when Hitler needed to have at his disposal a 'renewed body of the nation' to realize his ultimate dream. At the time most listeners had scarcely registered the remarks that had followed this announcement, or if they had done so, they would have dismissed them as a cultural irrelevance: 'Art will always be an expression and reflection of the longings and reality of an age. Cosmopolitan contemplation is rapidly disappearing. Heroism is rising up passionately as the characteristic that will shape and lead our political fates in the future. It is the task of art to express this defining spirit of the age.'[91]

Early Plaudits for Albert Speer

Some time was to pass before Hitler matched his actions to his words in Berlin and applied them to his favourite terrain in the field of the arts: architecture. In the short term, the heroism that he had proclaimed in his Reichstag address was confined to symbolic and ephemeral forms of expression within the local scene. The first opportunity to offer the city's inhabitants a suitably impressive spectacle was on 1 May 1933, National Labour Day, which had just been declared a public holiday. It was to be more than a repeat of the rallies that the party had held as recently as 1932, when Hitler had addressed his supporters at the Lustgarten, in the Grunewald Stadium and elsewhere.[92] The new public holiday was to be 'a visible symbol of the arrival of a new German national community',[93] and so the venue that was chosen for an evening rally was the Tempelhofer Feld to the south of the city centre, an area not yet fully developed by the city's airport and previously used as a parade ground for the troops of earlier generations of Germans. It was designed to surpass in every way the Youth Movement rally held that same morning in the Lustgarten. According to the advance programme, 'The entire population of the Reich's capital will take part in this rally. Among those who will be present will be the government and representatives of the armed forces and of the regional governments, the diplomatic corps and workers' delegations from the whole country.'[94] In his speech to the gathering, Hitler announced a 'vast programme that we do not intend to leave to posterity to bring about but which we must realize ourselves, a programme that will cost many millions. It is a programme for our new roads!' Hitler was referring to the start of work on the country's new network of motorways.[95]

The old parade ground at the Tempelhofer Feld was vast and was divided into an area for 'paying spectators' to the north of the road running through the airport and the actual parade ground to the south of the road. This area to the south was in turn divided into twelve sections. There was also an area 460 feet wide to the east that was open to 'invited guests'. The 'artistic design' of the area was based on sketches by Albert Speer, who had previously carried out a number of minor commissions for the NSDAP in Berlin, most recently the redevelopment of a Baroque palace on the Wilhelmplatz into the new headquarters for Goebbels' Ministry of Information. In his memoirs, Speer claims that it was more or less by chance that he was invited to design the buildings for the rally on 1 May and that during a visit to the ministry he had seen the city's plans for the evening event, which looked like the 'setting for a fair featuring shooting matches'. As a result he had produced his own designs that same night, and, according to Speer, these were immediately accepted, with the result that he found himself a further rung up the career ladder. Hitler, too, is said to have been delighted with his designs.[96] This is by no means the only occasion in his reminiscences when Speer suddenly and invol-untarily manages to clamber up the career ladder, frequently by means of sketches produced 'overnight'. But, like so much in his memoirs, this version of events deserves to be banished to the realm of fairy tale and legend. The execution of the designs, rather than their 'artistic supervision', lay in the hands of the Berlin municipal authorities, for the NSDAP or, to be more specific, Goebbels had reserved for themselves the right to organize this vast propaganda spectacle, which according to official estimates drew a crowd of 1.3 million. And Goebbels' new ministry was modelled in every way on the leadership of the party's propaganda machine. Moreover, it is clear from a volume that appeared in 1940 under the title *Berlin im Festschmuck* (Berlin in Festive Guise) that Speer was already 'a part of the Propaganda Ministry at this time'.[97]

The main building was a vast grandstand over 1,300 feet long with room for thirteen thousand spectators. Its focal point was a 'mountain of flags', a central stand rising to a height of over 30 feet and surmounted by three groups of flags towering 75 and 110 feet over the parade ground and lit by powerful spotlights. On each of the masts, a single black, white and red flag was framed by two swastika banners. According to the aforementioned guide, the 'practical realization of what until then was the largest mass rally' to be held in the city was possible 'only through the extensive use of one of the latest technical inventions, the loudspeaker'. Around 100 heavy-duty loudspeakers were distributed around the arena, which measured almost 5 million square feet in total. The vast dimensions of the event were also reflected in the firework display that followed the rally, with twenty different fronts extending over 1,300 feet.[98]

Further National Labour Day rallies designed by Speer took place at the Tempelhofer Feld on 1 May 1934 and 1935, although on these occasions the grandstand and the display of flags were changed: even larger flags were used and the central stand was enlarged, the 'Führer's pulpit' that Hitler used for his speech being moved significantly further forward and raised 10 feet above the stand that accommodated the members of his government in order to increase the theatrical impact of the speaker, who, picked out by spotlights, appeared to be floating high above the crowd.[99]

As with the 'traditional march of torchbearers' on 30 January – the day on which Hitler seized power – and as with his drive to the trade fair and his appearance at the motor show or the celebrations to mark his birthday on 20 April, the night-time ritual of these May rallies remained a fixed part of the National Socialists' year until 1939, emotionally charged events stage-managed as part of the 'public life of the nation'[100] and intended to invest the regime with a sense of mythic timelessness. In view of National Socialism's lack of any historical traditions, it had all the greater need of such solemn occasions.

Hence, it tried all the more frequently to present itself as an organization that would last for all eternity and Hitler was all the more determined to leave his mark on history while he was still alive. As was to become clear all too soon, it was Berlin that was to bear the brunt of this ambition. ·

Hitler the Architect

Within hours of the great Labour Day demonstration, the German trades unions were forcibly 'aligned'. On 23 June 1933 the Socialist Party was banned, and by the end of June and beginning of July the middle-class parties had disbanded of their own accord. The law prohibiting the formation of new parties that came into force on 14 July finally marked the end of Germany as a parliamentary state, the NSDAP being the only remaining party in the country. On 6 July, in a speech that he gave in Berlin, Hitler had informed his regional governors that the 'revolution' was over and that the party had 'now become the state'.[101] At the end of July he treated himself to a visit to the Bayreuth Festival, then left for the Obersalzburg. Here he not only enjoyed a break from his duties as chancellor, he also gave speeches and even held meetings. It was at this date that the Obersalzburg began to develop into a branch of the Chancellery in Berlin.[102] The 'Reich Party Day of Victory' was held in Nuremberg from 31 August to 3 September, and it was only after an absence of several weeks that Hitler returned to Berlin. It was presumably at this date, if not before, that he took his first major decision affecting the urban design of the historic heart of the city, when he approved the plans of the Reichsbank's director of buildings, Heinrich Wolff, for an extension to the bank's main building. The bank had announced a competition in February 1933 and invited thirty German architects to submit designs for a new building in the Friedrichswerder district of the city, not far from the Royal Palace and Lustgarten. Six designs were shortlisted, including one by Mies van der Rohe, but the jury felt unable to recommend any of them.[103] Heinrich Wolff had been asked at the end of 1932 to draw up plans for an extension to the building and had produced a preliminary draft of his own, but it had not been entered in the competition.

The situation was confused, and it is conceivable that either the directors of the Reichsbank or Hjalmar Schacht, who had been reappointed as the bank's president on 16 March 1933, asked Hitler to reach a decision for them. Whatever the case, contemporary publications state simply that 'in September 1933 the directors of the Reichsbank settled on a design drawn up by the bank's director of buildings, Heinrich Wolff, that had been approved by the

Führer and invited him to elaborate it and complete the commission'.[104] Wolff himself declared that the competition designs and models were 'presented to the Führer' at the same time as his own plans and that Hitler 'agreed that my design should be adopted not only on architectural grounds but also for reasons of urban planning'.[105]

This was the first time in modern German history that the judging of an architectural competition had been handed over to the head of government by the public body that had organized the competition in the first place. For the present, questions as to who approached Hitler and why and in what circumstances and whether it was Hitler himself who interfered in the decision-making process must remain unanswered, but it seems as if Hitler's decision in favour of Wolff's design was a decision in favour of the lesser of two evils, for the building, which was the first large building to be constructed in Berlin after 1933, 'has an undeniably functional rationale that underlies the design in general'. Although 'traditionalist in style and design', it was none the less 'modern in its construction and organization'.[106] As a pragmatic politician, Hitler was able to derive propagandist capital from the number of jobs created by the extensive demolition work involved in the project and from the ceremony accompanying the laying of the foundation stone on 5 May 1934. His intervention also prevented an ultra-modern building from springing up in the centre of the city under his chancellorship, a development that would undoubtedly have had a far-reaching symbolic impact. Instead, Hitler's decision signalled the fact that from now on all building projects of any importance in the city also needed to ensure that they commanded the Führer's support.

This point was fully understood by Berlin's municipal authorities. In the case of another project, they turned – as now became usual – to the secretary of state at the Chancellery and asked him to arrange a meeting with Hitler, a meeting that duly took place on 19 September 1933. The city's delegation was headed by the state commissioner, Julius Lippert, and the mayor, Heinrich Sahm, together with a delegation representing the country's railways, the Reichsbahn, and including its director general, Julius Dorpmüller, and his deputy, Wilhelm Kleinmann. Under discussion was the line linking the Stettin, Potsdam and Anhalt stations, which the Reichsbahn was planning as a way of linking the north and south of the city. Part of the stretch of line had given rise to an argument between the Reichsbahn and the city in the guise of its transport department. Hitler announced his decision, and with that the meeting might have ended, but instead he used the opportunity to deliver a kind of lecture on the principles that should govern future infrastructure and building projects in Berlin. Not only did the Potsdam and Anhalt stations 'have to be linked and relocated behind the Landwehrkanal', but perhaps it might also be possible to combine the two stations in a single 'South Station' with close links to the city's airport. Hitler then commented dismissively that the city was at present no more than a jumble of houses and business premises thrown together without any systematic plan and that the only monumental designs were Unter den Linden and the Royal Palace, together with their immediate vicinity. This part of the city had been constructed in around 1651, he informed his audience,

> and we must admire the liberality of the rulers at that time who designed this area in such a way that even now it remains the high point of the city of Berlin in terms of both its urban planning and its culture. But thereafter one building was thoughtlessly stuck on to the next one without any consideration for the city's future development away from this central nucleus.

He now regarded it as his special mission to make good what the city of Berlin had neglected to do in the past.

The city's representatives must have been taken aback when Hitler then went on to announce with something amounting to a flourish:

> As the capital of a country numbering 65 million souls, Berlin must be raised to such a height in respect of its urban planning and culture that it can compete with all the cities of the world. It must be helped and promoted so that there can never be any doubt that culturally, too, Berlin is the capital of the German Reich and that it can bear comparison with other cities such as London, Paris and Vienna.

To this end, he planned to ask the country's finance minister to make available the sum of 40 million marks a year for the next few years – within six months this figure had risen to 60 million each year over a period of twenty years.[107]

In the event, the city's representatives expressed enthusiasm at the idea, and later that same day they wrote to Lammers to thank Hitler for helping them to reach an agreement with the Reichsbahn. The chancellor, they went on, had used the opportunity to present the delegation with 'tremendous plans for redeveloping Berlin', plans designed to take the country's capital 'in a direction previously unsuspected' and that would turn it into 'the most illustrious metropolis in Europe'. They concluded by asking if Hitler would be 'kind enough' to include in his discussions 'those members of our administration who in all likelihood will have the task of implementing the chancellor's great plans in the not too distant future'.[108] It seems beyond doubt that the leaders of the Reichsbahn as well as the delegation from the municipal authorities were impressed by the competence that Hitler showed in addressing the question of the city's north–south rail link. Of course, only a few of his closest intimates knew that he had long been profoundly interested in architecture and town planning in general and in Berlin's urban landscape in particular. At the end of 1928, for example, his secretary, Rudolf Heß, had drawn attention to his plans and individual designs for 'turning Berlin into the great metropolis of the new German Reich', adding: 'We often laughed – but with a serious undertone – when he walked with us through Berlin, which he knew like the back of his hand, and with a wave of his hand demolished old and unattractive blocks of houses so that existing buildings or others yet to be constructed should have more space to create a better impression.'[109]

We have already seen that Hitler took an interest in contemporary architectural journals, although often enough it will have been sufficient for him simply to have read the newspapers. It can hardly have escaped his notice that in the summer of 1933 the *Berliner Beobachter* – a supplement to the Berlin edition of the *Völkischer Beobachter* – featured a number of articles that discussed the planned new rail link and also mentioned the problems associated with the route that the line was to follow.[110] One article even used the plans as an excuse to raise the question of a new central station. This would finally present Berlin with an opportunity to 'erect a monumental building that would be a symbol of the city's importance'.[111] The suggestion was intended to seize the moment inasmuch as the construction of the new rail link could be combined with the erection of a new and imposing central station, while at the same time putting an end to the existing system of terminus stations away from the city centre. And yet not even this proposal came close to Hitler's grandiose designs for the city's landscape, for all that those plans were still only crudely formulated. Even so, they were a step in the right direction and if necessary could provide a kind of a bridgehead in implementing Hitler's aims.

Olympic Buildings

Meanwhile, as the date of the official opening of the Olympic Games drew inexorably closer, the architectural and financial planning lagged behind. The building committee had agreed in the summer of 1933 that Otto March's German Stadium, which dated from 1913, and Werner March's neighbouring

Sports Forum of 1928–9 should be enlarged and converted to create the new Olympic Stadium. Hitler was kept informed of developments by his secretary of state, Heinrich Lammers, but evidently felt that insufficient progress was being made. On 5 October 1933, therefore, he inspected the entire site in the company of the minister of the interior, Wilhelm Frick. He began by examining the models of the Sports Forum and the redesigned Stadium. In his account of Hitler's visit, Theodor Lewald noted that

> with his well-known interest in architecture, the chancellor showed a clear-sighted understanding of the ideas and plans underlying the whole redevelopment programme. Throughout his visit to the Sports Forum and later in the Stadium, the architect Werner March and I were able to raise all the important questions. [. . .] I pointed out that the Stadium was now being used more for general political and other purposes than for sports and that as a result the city was making difficulties about the fact that the legal situation had yet to be clarified. The chancellor declared that the Stadium must be built by the Reich [. . .]; the whole world had been invited to attend, and so something grandiose and beautiful must be created. March had shown him various types of stone, and he declared that the [new Olympic] Stadium must be clad in evenly hewn stone blocks; if you had four million unemployed, you had to ensure that there was work, and a few million marks no longer mattered one way or the other. He invited March to visit him early the following week and bring with him all his plans, including those for the surrounding area, and to present him with an overall scheme.

Lewald was extremely pleased, for Hitler's declared aims went far beyond anything that he had expected from the visit. He ended by announcing: 'I believe that today we have taken the decisive step in realizing our boldest hopes and plans.'[112] Hitler himself summed up the arrangements that he had made:

> All the Olympia buildings in Grunewald will be taken over by the Reich. The actual Stadium is to be enlarged to seat 100,000 spectators. The Stadium site will also include a swimming pool and an arena for equestrian events. In connection with the extensions to the Stadium, it is also intended to include a parade ground large enough for mass demonstrations. A large open-air stage will be built in the delightful Murelle Gorge in the north-western part of the Stadium grounds. The German Sports Forum's gymnastics hall will be enlarged to include a new swimming pool, an accommodation block and,

above all, a large administrative block and teaching centre, the House of German Sport.[113]

Five days after Hitler's tour of the Olympic site, an 'internal discussion' took place at the Chancellery to which Goebbels was also invited. Hitler began by declaring that if the world was to be invited to the Olympics, then it needed to be shown exactly what the new Germany was capable of achieving culturally. Moreover, Berlin needed a 'vast site' for the sorts of gatherings and fairs that the present age necessarily brought with it. Hitler asked

> what sort of a crowd the [present] Stadium and the surrounding area could accommodate and was given a figure of 120,000–130,000, a figure that he declared was wholly inadequate. He asked the architect, Werner March, to provide him with a sketch of the site and in the western extension of the Stadium drew in an area that seemed to him large enough for assemblies, fairs and march-pasts. The architect reckoned that this would offer the potential for assemblies of almost half a million people and went on to note that it had already occurred to him that the Olympia Stadium should be cut into on its western curve, thereby opening up a view to the west. The Führer responded enthusiastically to this idea of an architectural link between the Olympia Stadium and the great festival arena and demanded that this too should have a fixed architectural frame to it.[114]

It is clear that by now Hitler was not just issuing general instructions but was interfering in plans in very specific ways, occasionally drawing on his own experiences – the final proposal mentioned here was no doubt influenced by his unfortunate experiences with the festival arena at the Tempelhofer Feld.

Known from now on as the Reichssportfeld, this new project was commissioned by the Reich in the person of Hans Pfundtner, the secretary of state at the Ministry of the Interior. The city of Berlin, which had previously been responsible for the scheme, was unceremoniously dismissed from its duties.[115] During a second visit to the Chancellery on 14 December 1933, March presented three different versions of his new design to Hitler. Of these, Hitler chose Proposal B, comprising a forecourt, a stadium, a parade ground and 'Führer Tower' (later renamed the Bell Tower) and the grandstand embankment, all of which were aligned along a dominant east–west axis. The swimming pool formed the northern extension of the counteraxis, which was created beside the Reichssportfeldstraße (renamed the Flatowallee in 1997) to the south of the stadium.[116] March later explained that he had complied with Hitler's 'basic demand' that it should be 'obvious from afar that the different-sized sites were linked to one another and attractively interrelated'. He had designed the biggest of the buildings, the Olympia Stadium, in such a way that it was central to the whole site and placed at the intersection of the two main approach roads. Although this meant that the new stadium had to be moved nearly 500 feet eastwards out of the hollow of the old stadium, it created an open space to the west for parades and for the grandstand embankment of the assembly ground, now known as the 'May Field': 'In this way the Olympia Stadium and the May Field with its Bell Tower and the approach road from the east could be developed along a straight east–west axis as the most monumental and spacious of designs.' In general, the overall picture that was created by the harmonious relationship between architecture and landscape reflected the Führer's stated aim 'that the Reichssportfeld, including all its buildings and open spaces, should also be the scene of great national celebrations'.[117] The Dietrich-Eckart Theatre (now the Waldbühne), the Langemarck Hall and the pieces of sculpture distributed over the site further burdened the Reichssportfeld with nationalist symbols. For Hitler, it was his first lesson in axial symmetry. In the wake of his second meeting with Werner March, he announced that he had given his definitive approval to the scheme and that building work on the site of the stadium could now begin: 'In this way Germany will acquire a sports facility that has no equal in the world.'[118]

The Autocratic Urban Planner

The fact that Hitler's interest in the fundamental shift that had taken place in plans for the Reichssportfeld was merely part of a wider concern for the city's future planning needs emerges from a letter addressed by the deputy mayor, Oskar Maretzky, to the secretary of state, Heinrich Lammers, on 5 December 1933. Maretzky wanted Benno Kühn, one of the city councillors responsible for urban planning, to be included in all discussions at which Hitler would 'speak on the subject of the urban planning of the capital' so that the position of the city authorities might be made clear. In order to lend more weight to his request, Maretzky included in his letter a list of all the planning projects in Berlin in which Hitler 'had repeatedly taken a lively interest' and in which he had shown 'an immediate concern':

The *conversion* of the Grunewald Stadium for the 1936 Olympiad;
the *extension* to the Reichsbank;
the *creation* of a new east–west transport link between the Kaiser Wilhelm Memorial Church and the Alexanderplatz (cutting through the Jägerstraße);

levelling the area covered by Anhalt and Potsdam stations and relocating the
mainline stations, goods stations and sidings;
the *creation* of a major north–south street axis using the area made available
by the removal of Anhalt Station and
the provision of a *link* between the airport and the Tempelhofer Feld and the
north–south rail axis.

As each plan was elaborated, so it became necessary, Maretzky argued, to
ensure that all of them were based on a grand unifying design, hence the desire
on the part of the municipal authorities 'that their plans for the future shape of
Berlin be kept in constant agreement with the chancellor's wishes'.[119] The
wording of Maretzky's letter reveals the seeds of the future discord between the
municipal authorities, on the one hand, and Hitler and his representatives, on
the other. The city had 'plans' for Berlin and, according to Maretzky, wanted to
square these with Hitler's 'wishes'. Clearly Maretzky had yet to understand the
*Führerprinzip** and was still tainted by the delusional, if vestigial, belief that the
council was a self-governing body operating within the rule of law. Above all,
he and the other members of the city council had failed to realize that where
urban planning was concerned, Hitler was by no means set upon merely
expressing his 'wishes', wishes that he and the local authorities might then
discuss as equals in order to reach some agreement. Hitler had more or less
clear ideas on the sort of plans that he intended to implement in Berlin, even
if, in 1933–4, his ideas had yet to acquire the rabid certainty that was later to
characterize all of his views on the subject. For the present he required an
architect who, acting as his spokesman, would couch these ideas in the
language of a professional, and an administration willing to execute these
plans. Hence he could happily dispense with a partner who claimed to want an
exchange of ideas in the form of an open dialogue. The city authorities did not
as yet know this for themselves, but they were to discover it soon enough.

At this stage, the 'big picture' that Hitler had in mind – in other words, the
programme of urban redevelopment that was beginning to take shape in his
thoughts – was barely recognizable as such, at least as far as the representatives
of the municipal council were concerned. Minutes of the next meeting at the
Chancellery on 29 March 1934 indicate that Hitler was acting as chancellor,
mayor, adviser on urban planning and chief city architect all rolled into one.[120]
He apparently opened the meeting

---

* The unbroken chain of command in the Third Reich.

by offering a detailed critique of the architectural model of the Horst-Wessel-Platz [as the Bülowplatz had been renamed on 26 May 1933]. He was not in agreement with the plans for the area in front of the Volksbühne, complaining that the central axis of the theatre and the open-air steps behind it were badly designed. The triangular forecourt must be kept open, and the guard houses could be moved slightly to the right and left. In answer to his question as to the location of the Karl-Liebknecht-Haus [the former headquarters of the Communist Party which had now been requisitioned by the SA], he decided that the Horst Wessel Memorial should be placed in the eastern Garden of Remembrance, whereas the memorial to the police officers [who had been shot on 9 August 1931] should be built in the western Garden of Remembrance. The memorial to the Hitler Youth movement could be positioned elsewhere.

Only after Hitler had gone into detail on these points was the subject of the 'north–south axis' and the 'east–west intersection' discussed. The city's planning officer answered questions relating to the plans that had already been officially set out and that reflected the current state of the authorities' thinking. Hitler again reacted by giving his immediate 'authorization', adding that the axis was correctly positioned and that he was in agreement with the plan's spaciousness and vast scale. He also agreed with the location of the new South Station and was pleased with the way in which it would be connected with the enlarged airport. He then raised the question of the function and design of the north–south axis, albeit still in extremely vague terms:

> Immediately to the north of the South Station, the Führer imagines a mighty triumphal arch lying on the major axis and celebrating the unconquered army of the World War. On what was the Königsplatz, opposite and to the side of the Reichstag, space should be found for the Defence Ministry and the Ministry of the Air Force and Navy. [. . .] At the northern end of the square, the Führer proposes two commemorative buildings for the heroes of the aerial and naval battles. On the new street leading south from the Skagerak-Platz he wants the central government buildings and the monumental buildings necessary for the party's intermediary staff.

Hitler expressed misgivings about the plans to cut through the Ministerial Gardens behind some of the Baroque buildings in the Wilhelmstraße since, although the ministries were to be relocated, the Chancellery was to remain here. As for the administrative buildings, Hitler had already given considerable thought to the layout and redevelopment of the city's museums, largely those situated around the Museumsinsel.* 'Passing to a third group of buildings, the Führer demands a new Winter Stadium and the erection of a very large assembly hall capable of accommodating 250,000 people.' Somewhat surprisingly, Hitler mentioned the latter building almost in passing and without regard to his plans for the 'north–south axis', implying that space for such a vast building could be found anywhere in the city. Conceivably he had not yet alighted on the building's subsequent site in a bend of the Spree, where it would form a fixed point on the north–south axis and correspond to the triumphal arch at the South Station.

Hitler then moved on to a fourth group of buildings, those of the university and scientific institutions. He had not yet made up his mind, he explained, whether such institutions could remain in the inner city or whether they would have to be moved to a location outside. But a decision could wait. In the course of the rest of the discussion, Hitler graciously 'approved' the plans to redevelop the Molkenmarkt, where Berlin's history may be said to have begun. Here the city's plans included the demolition of the Town Hall (the second Berlin Town Hall of 1902–11) and the construction of more administrative offices.[121] No doubt encouraged by this debate, Hitler 'spoke out in no uncertain terms against high-rise buildings', while conceding that the previous regime had completed a handful of successful projects, including the redevelopment of Schinkel's New Guard House as a memorial to the nation's dead. The debate then returned to the city's plans to encroach on the Ministerial Gardens, and here Hitler proposed that the Leipziger Straße be extended in a westerly direction.

Finally, Hitler turned his attention back to the Lustgarten, the layout of which he insisted should be changed. The statue of Friedrich Wilhelm III that had been erected on the central axis of the Old Museum was 'in completely the wrong place' and had to go. A suggestion by the head of the city's planning department that it should be repositioned close to the Old Apothecary wing of the Royal Palace and, as such, 'on the direct axis of Unter den Linden' was one that 'met with the Führer's sympathetic approval'. As if that were not enough, Hitler also offered to help in 'redeveloping' the old city and ended the meeting by declaring his support for the plans for the South Station and for a new line running north–south. The vast scope and sheer complexity of the subjects touched on during the meeting reinforces the idea that Hitler, who generally

---

* The northern part of the island of Cölln in Berlin's Spree River where five of the city's most prestigious museums are situated.

took the initiative in all discussions, must have been interested for some time past in questions of town planning and the general layout of the city. After all, in recent months he had been fully occupied in forcing through the acceptance of the power structures of the Third Reich. This assessment is confirmed by the course taken by a later discussion at the Chancellery on 5 June 1934, the agenda of which was every bit as full as it had been on 29 March, involving, as it did, the redevelopment of the Rolandblock, the Horst-Wessel-Platz, the Alexanderplatz, the Friedrichstraße Station forecourt, plans for the various museums, the north–south axis, variations on the east–west link and plans to cut through the Wilhelmplatz.[122] In this context – which appeared at first sight to be concerned only with questions of transport policy – Hitler argued that in his view it was necessary to tear down houses on the northern edge of the Voßstraße and replace them with a new building 'that might perhaps open up towards the Voßstraße in the manner of a forecourt and accommodate the central administrative authorities, middle management, parts of the Chancellery and other command centres immediately answerable to the chancellor'.[123] The plans that Hitler was already outlining here were to become the New Chancellery, which was built along the Voßstraße only a few years later, including the opening towards the street 'in the manner of a forecourt'. And in his divagations on the 'triumphal arch in honour of the unvanquished army' that he wanted built at the South Station he offered his first overtly political justification for the structure: once and for all, the arch was to 'free our brave nation of the pernicious idea that Germany lost the World War in every part and in every field'. And he went on to announce that in consultation with his minister of finance he was planning to transform Berlin into a capital worthy of the Reich and a metropolis of international standing. For the next twenty years he was setting aside an annual sum of 60 million marks from the annual budget, making a grand total of 1.2 billion marks.[124]

Berlin's representatives welcomed this news, for only a few weeks earlier they had heard Hitler strike a completely different note when discussing the city's amenities. On 8 March 1934 Julius Lippert had appealed to Hitler in his capacity as city commissioner, pointing out that the Städtische Oper in Charlottenburg was in receipt of an annual subsidy of 1.8 million marks but that the city was finding it increasingly difficult to ensure that the company was run along orderly lines. The city would therefore be most grateful if the Reich assumed responsibility for the company. Unfortunately the Ministry of Propaganda intended to requisition the company without offering the city a penny in return. 'I would therefore ask you most humbly, my Führer, either to decide to take out a long-term lease on the Städtische Oper or to pay the city an appropriate purchase price.' Lammers replied on 12 March, informing Lippert of Hitler's belief that 'even without the payment of a purchase price it is in the city's best interest to be relieved of the responsibility of running an organization that is not economically viable but which because of the need for a subsidy is in fact a burden on the city's finances'. The matter was discussed at a cabinet meeting on 22 March, when Goebbels' ministry received an increase in its allocation intended to cover the cost of rebuilding the Städtische Oper. As a result Goebbels was able to announce soon afterwards that the government had decided 'to take over the running of the company from the City of Berlin and transfer it to the Reich'. The 'financial means needed to this purpose' were 'already available'. The building was renamed the German Opera House[125] and was rebuilt between May and October 1935. A new reception room on the ground floor was designed for the sole use of members of the government, who could make their way from there to the private box in the grand tier. It was here that Hitler, Goebbels and Heß sat during the 'Kraft durch Freude' (Strength through Joy) conference in 1937.[126] The large foyer that served the grand tier was redesigned as a self-contained reception room 'in the stiffly formal style of the 1930s', with long mirrors, crystal chandeliers and a wide marble-clad door that led directly into the anteroom outside the government box.[127] In one of the picture albums that were popular with collectors at this period the caption to an illustration of the foyer indicates that 'the Führer' played an active role in redesigning it.[128]

Hand in Hand

On 5 July Hitler received representatives of the City of Berlin, the State Railways and the Ministry of Propaganda at the Chancellery. The meeting began with a report by Julius Lippert on various job-creation schemes that bore the distinctly martial name of 'Berlin's Battle for Work'. According to the minutes of the meeting, the atmosphere was entirely matter-of-fact, and at no point did Hitler mention that only two days earlier he had tabled a new law consisting of no more than a single sentence: 'The measures taken to suppress the treasonable attacks on 30 June and on 1 and 2 July 1934 are hereby declared legal as acts of national defence.'[129] These measures had consisted almost entirely of shootings. Even now, the misleading terms 'Röhm Putsch' or 'Röhm Revolt' continue to be used to describe these events. In Berlin alone there were two dozen deaths. The starting point had been the increasingly embittered attempts by the SA to remilitarize its organization and to establish itself as a kind of 'people's army' either alongside the Reichswehr or even in place of it.

In general, these moves represented a flaring up of the old problematic relationship between the SA and the NSDAP, on the one hand, and the Reichswehr, on the other. Hitler had for the most part been keen to get rid of the SA leadership, starting with its chief of staff, Ernst Röhm, and including individual regional leaders such as the group leader in Berlin, Karl Ernst. In Berlin, the move to oust the SA was led by Hermann Göring and was used as an opportunity to carry out a number of Hitler's private vendettas. Gregor Straßer, the NSDAP's former organizational leader, was murdered at the Gestapo's headquarters in the Prinz-Albrecht-Straße (now the Niederkirchnerstraße), while Hitler's predecessor as chancellor, Kurt von Schleicher, met his end, together with his wife, at home. General Ferdinand von Bredow, Schleicher's former secretary of state, was gunned down in the former cadet school in Lichterfelde. And Erich Klausener, who had at one time been head of the police department at the Prussian Ministry of the Interior, was butchered in his own office.[130] What was particularly striking about this killing spree in Berlin was the number of people killed who in the course of 1932 had tried in their various ways to resist or thwart the NSDAP's attempts to seize power. Be that as it may, the purge could be regarded as successful, at least from Hitler's standpoint, to the extent that the SA had been permanently weakened and was now little more than a sports organization, albeit one that could be mobilized, if need be, for anti-Semitic outrages. Above all, it was Himmler's SS that benefited from this move. Himmler had taken over the running of the Prussian Gestapo from Göring on 20 April 1934 and in the process had become the uncontested head of the Political Police in the country as a whole. On 20 July Hitler made the SS an independent organization within the NSDAP in recognition of the 'great service that it had rendered the party, especially in connection with the events of 30 June 1934'.[131] The following years witnessed the growth of the 'area around the ministries'[132] along the Prinz-Albrecht-Straße and the Wilhelmstraße. It was here that the headquarters of the National Socialists' surveillance, persecution and terror organizations were based. By the end of the 1930s the tasks faced by this state apparatus and, hence, the amount of space that it required had grown to such an extent that the SS's main offices and various departments were moved to other parts of the city. But Hitler left the SS to deal with its own requirements in this regard, and the same was true of the new ministry buildings for Göring and Goebbels. By the summer of 1934 the overall structure of the Third Reich and its internal divisions of labour were more clearly defined, as were its various positions of power and areas of influence. On 1 July the minister of the Reichswehr, Werner von Blomberg, thanked Hitler for his 'soldier-like determination and exemplary courage': 'As the arms' bearer of the entire nation, the armed forces, far from all internal political struggles, will thank you with their devotion and loyalty!'[133]

It is difficult to resist the conclusion that the new building plans for Berlin had an increasingly imperious and militaristic aspect to them – presuming that this, had not been Hitler's aim from the very beginning. In addition to stressing the public display of state power, Hitler was no doubt also motivated by a spirit of soldierly solidarity. Presumably the administrators, technicians and architects with whom he worked were not yet fully aware of this dimension to his thinking. Could such an attitude be inferred from the progress that was being made on the Reichssportfeld? Hitler inspected the site for a second time on 31 October 1934. On this occasion the architect Werner March used his various plans and models to explain his overall stratagem and also discussed his finished plans for individual buildings on the site. According to a press notice reporting on Hitler's visit:

> The Führer expressed his agreement with all the solutions that had been found for the questions concerning urban planning, transport and the landscaping of the site and also gave his basic approval to the plans that were submitted to him for individual buildings. [...] The Führer then made his way to the vast building site of the German Kampfbahn and the model of the arena building that had been erected there at an actual height of 50 feet, from the topmost platform of which he gained an impressive view of the overall site and its surroundings. The Führer gave a number of important pointers concerning the design of the buildings and the choice of ashlars that should be used for them.[134]

There seems little doubt that March revised his plans and models in the light of Hitler's 'pointers', for at the next meeting of the building committee he informed its other members that he had 'taken account of the Führer's wishes for a weightier design for the ring of columns by increasing their width from 2 feet to 2 feet 4 inches and their depth from 2 feet 9 inches to 3 feet 4 inches, considerably strengthening them in the process'.[135] Hitler had evidently expressed a wish to see other changes as well, with the result that Albert Speer became involved at this stage of the proceedings, as is made clear in a letter from Hans Pfundtner to Goebbels at the Ministry of Propaganda: 'As I have already indicated, Herr March has remained in close contact with Herr Speer while revising his designs and now hopes that he has taken full account of the Führer's suggestions'.[136] The contentious points evidently related to the design for the front of the 'arena building', which was later to become the Olympia

Stadium. In spite of repeated invitations from the building committee, it was not until the official opening of the Olympic Games that Hitler first set foot inside the stadium. But it is clear from a remark that he made in the middle of 1935 that the reason for this omission was a lack of time rather than any alleged disagreement with March.[137]

Hitler made a number of other basic remarks about his architectural ideas during a meeting held to discuss the state of preliminary work on the new airport at Tempelhof, another project that was particularly close to his heart. The planned airport was to be the biggest and most beautiful civilian airport in the world,[138] and money was not to be a consideration. Foreigners arriving both here at the airport and at the planned South Station were to be greeted by buildings whose sheer beauty and size would silence any possible criticisms of Germany. When he landed at Tempelhof now, Hitler remarked, the only building to catch his eye and impress him was Karstadt's department store. He found it shaming that, when he then drove into the city, the municipal buildings and ministries left such a pitiful impression in comparison. In this respect the Third Reich desperately needed to bring about a change.[139] These comments follow on seamlessly from the ideas on architecture and urban planning that Hitler had expressed in *Mein Kampf* some ten years earlier.

Julius Lippert as State Commissioner, Civic Leader and Mayor

Was there any point during the coming years when Hitler abandoned this path? His last known meeting with representatives of the City of Berlin and of the State Railways to discuss questions of urban planning was on 28 June 1935. Again there was complete agreement on both sides concerning the redevelopment of Unter den Linden and the relocation of the Central Market Hall. Particularly revealing are Hitler's comments on questions of overall planning. He assured his listeners, for example, that he was determined to make a genuinely grand contribution to the city. Every year for the next twenty years, he repeated, 60 million marks would be made available for this purpose. Never before had a state invested 1.2 billion marks in its capital city. Because of the country's rearmament programme, this sum would have been difficult to raise in the current fiscal year, 1935, but he had spoken to the minister of finance and resolved the issue to their mutual satisfaction. Asked by Julius Lippert if it was not time to establish the building commission planned by Hitler 'for the City of Berlin is dependent for its planning on the great ideas that the Führer has already proposed for the redevelopment of Berlin', Hitler replied that he had 'yet to find the right architect. [. . .] It was still not possible to say if Albert

Speer was the right man for the job. For the present he had to deal exclusively with questions of foreign policy, but he would continue to look round for a suitable architect.' Hitler then showed his visitors the models for the site of his planned party rallies in Nuremberg, while repeatedly returning to the topic of his plans to redevelop Berlin. 'But he was unable to find the time to give proper consideration to such plans while he was in Berlin. For that, he needed to go to the mountains. Perhaps he would ask his visitors to join him in the mountains for such a discussion.'[140] But his visitors never came, for they were never invited. At his New Year reception on 10 January 1936 Hitler asked Lippert to prepare plans for Berlin, including an account of the extent, type and distribution of publicly owned land. This took time, and it was not until several months later that Lippert asked for a meeting to discuss his ideas. Hitler replied that he was happy to hear Lippert's submission, and a date was agreed. But then Hitler decided during the summer that the meeting could be postponed until the autumn. The submission never took place, and in February 1937 the plans were filed away.[141]

Why was it so difficult to agree on a date for a meeting? Had Lippert done something wrong? To all appearances, he seems to have had a successful record. The National Socialist leaders of the city had cleaned up Berlin for the Olympic Games and, for the majority of visitors, the capital produced a superficial picture of apparent joie de vivre and bustling optimism. Notices proclaiming 'Jews forbidden' disappeared for the duration, as did displays of the anti-Semitic broadsheet Der Stürmer. Travel guides of the period proclaimed that Berlin, especially at night, had everything that the pleasure-seeking tourist could possibly desire. There were bars and nightclubs in abundance.[142] Quite apart from the Games themselves, there was a flawlessly organized and lavish accompanying programme. On the morning of 1 August, only hours before the Games were officially opened, a military march-past took place along the 'Via Triumphalis', which, lined with flags, extended from Unter den Linden westwards along the Charlottenburger Chaussee and the Knie – the western section of the east–west axis. There followed a church service for the International Olympic Committee and a reception hosted by Hermann Göring in his capacity as prime minister of Prussia, after which a wreath was laid at the national cenotaph at the New Guard House. Members of Berlin's Hitler Youth movement then welcomed the runner with the Olympic torch as he passed through the Lustgarten. The morning's events culminated in a reception at the Chancellery at which Hitler announced that archaeological excavations had resumed in Olympia.* Those who were unable to see the Führer in person were regaled with larger-than-life photographs bearing titles such as 'The Führer and his Followers' at the entrance to the German Exhibition. Or they could gaze in awe at the exhibition guide, which, designed by a former member of the Bauhaus, Herbert Bayer, was nothing if not ultra-modern in its design. The Reichssportfeld had been completed on time, and even as late as 1942 Hitler was still able to shake his head in disbelief at those members of his government who in 1933 had been unable to appreciate that 'putting on the Olympic Games' was 'a unique opportunity for us to gain hard currency and raise our standing abroad'.[143] 'I'm afraid the Nazis have succeeded with their propaganda,' William L. Shirer, the head of Universal News Service's Berlin office, wrote in his diary on 16 August 1936.[144]

On 1 January 1937 Lippert, previously state commissioner, became the mayor of Berlin, a post he filled in tandem with that of the city's president. In May–June the Exhibition Centre opposite Broadcasting House hosted an even more up-to-date exhibition under the title 'Give Me Four Years', at which images of Hitler, gazing confidently into the future, were reproduced on posters and in the exhibition catalogue. The editor of a photographic magazine of the period wrote enthusiastically that

> the walls on the southern and northern sides of the building are vast symbols: a thousand times its original size, the 60-foot-high head of the Führer, surrounded by larger-than-life workers and farmers, has its counterpart on the north wall, the two soldiers nearly 50 feet tall with rifles resting on their shoulders, while behind them, to their right and left, armies of men bearing all manner of arms can be seen on the march. Covered with photographs, these walls extend over an impressive area of 8,000 square feet, an area on which a house and garden could comfortably sit. Such large photographs have not been seen at any previous exhibitions.[145]

During the late summer of 1937 Lippert took charge of the celebrations marking the seven-hundredth anniversary of the city's foundation in 1237. Held between 14 and 22 August, the event turned out to be distinctly unimpressive when compared with the great propaganda exhibitions at the foot of the Radio Tower. Hitler spent this period commuting between Bayreuth and Nuremberg, where he was preparing for the party rally, and only had time to send Lippert the briefest of congratulatory telegrams.[146]

* Since the 1870s, the excavation of ancient Olympia had been the responsibility of the German Archaeological Institute in Athens.

Albert Speer as General Inspector of Buildings

All who had eyes to see must have been aware that in 1935–6 a new star was in the ascendant in National Socialist Berlin. Before 1933 Lippert had been a mediocre journalist, but thereafter he became an assiduous bureaucrat unconditionally devoted to Hitler and eager to carry out his new duties, an eagerness that brought him high office in the capital's municipal administration. But he was not capable of seizing his chance as an architect. Albert Speer, by contrast, had quickly worked his way up through the party hierarchy, initially accepting minor commissions from the leadership of the Berlin Gau and eventually becoming Hitler's architect of choice. It was Speer, for example, who was commissioned to produce the designs for the party's rally grounds in Nuremberg.[147] He also wrote an article on 'The Führer's Buildings' that appeared in the picture album produced by a famous cigarette-card manufacturer to which we have already referred. Here he appeared alongside 'old warriors' such as Goebbels, Robert Ley, Fritz Todt and Baldur von Schirach, penning prose that was positively purpureal: once the 'great building projects' that were 'so compelling that they can no longer be deferred' had been completed, then 'the monumental buildings of National Socialism will rise above the salubrious workers' dwellings and the clean factories of our cities just as the cathedrals of the Middle Ages once rose above the rooftops of the houses of private burghers'.[148] Lippert had taken up his new post on 1 January 1937, much as any white-collar worker or public servant would start his new job on the first of the month, whereas Speer was appointed general inspector of buildings for the country's capital on 30 January 1937, the fourth anniversary of Hitler's accession to power and, as such, a date that had long since been hallowed in the party's annals. According to the wording of his appointment, his task was 'systematically to plan the design of the country's capital, produce a new overall plan and ensure that all squares, thoroughfares and buildings that influence our view of the city are worthily implemented along uniform lines'.[149] In the Reichstag, Hitler additionally announced that he had appointed a general inspector of buildings for Berlin because he needed someone who would take responsibility for the architectural development of the capital and ensure that 'an overall vision be brought to the chaos of Berlin's architectural past, a vision that will do justice to the spirit of the National Socialist movement and to the character of the German capital'.[150] The establishment of this new municipal authority would help to turn Berlin into a 'real and genuine capital of the German Reich'.

In countless variations, these words were to be repeated in all the public pronouncements that were made during the years that followed, including the ceremonies accompanying the laying of the foundation stones of two major projects that formed part of this 'redevelopment programme' and which, even if they were not completed, at least reached the preliminary construction stage. On 27 November 1937 Hitler laid the foundation stone of the Faculty of Defence Technology at the Technical University in Berlin[151] and declared it the beginning of an architectural revolution that would determine the character of the city for a thousand years.[152] And on 14 June 1938 he performed a similar task at the House of German Foreign Transport at the planned Runder Platz, which was heralded as the first building on what was to be 'the greatest highway of the Reich's capital'.[153]

Writing in his memoirs, Speer naturally had an explanation to hand to account for the fact that Hitler had appointed him to his new post and abandoned years of collaboration with the municipal authorities in Berlin. According to Speer, it was because Lippert 'could not warm to Hitler's building plans'.[154] In fact, the documents cited above demonstrate the exact opposite. Hitler, Speer went on, had described Lippert as 'an incompetent, an idiot, a failure and a nonentity'. 'I don't know where to start with this city authority,' Hitler allegedly told Speer after the summer of 1936. 'From now on it will be you who will produce the designs.'[155] Speer's account must be treated with considerable scepticism, for the surviving transcripts of his various discussions give no indication that the atmosphere attending the negotiations between Hitler and the city authorities had grown noticeably cooler or that it reflected the tenor of the remarks imputed to the Führer. In his memoirs Speer also tried to imply that his years with Hitler had followed a two-stage process. First, there was the period when he had worked as an ultimately non-political architect and was a purely artistic and autonomous agent. Only afterwards did his work acquire a military dimension, when he became minister for armaments and production. Susanne Willems is only one of many writers to have examined the sources in detail and concluded that, even during his early years, when he initiated a scheme for the systematic demolition of 'Jewish apartments', working closely with the Gestapo and assisting with the deportations that began in Berlin in the autumn of 1941, Speer was anything but an architect and town planner operating solely within the sphere of art and holding exclusively aesthetic views.[156]

If Speer's autobiography inhabits the world of myth and legend in its accounts of Hitler's building projects in the capital, then Joachim Fest in his biography of Speer adds to the confusion when discussing

the axial arrangement that underlay the whole of the plans for redeveloping
the city:

> The starting point for their deliberations was entirely accurate when it argued
> that on the basis of its geological and historical conditions Berlin had a more
> or less continuous east–west link but not a corresponding connection
> running from north to south. More than a century earlier Karl Friedrich
> Schinkel had tried to remedy this regrettable situation, and a study dating
> from the 1920s had taken up these ideas and made them its own.[157]

It is certainly true that in 1840 Schinkel had put forward a plan for developing
an area that lay some distance outside the city gates – Berlin's industrial revolution was only just beginning at this date. But not until almost thirty years later
was the city wall torn down. Schinkel's aim was simply to develop an area of
the city that was still largely undeveloped.[158]

Moreover, it has often been supposed[159] that Hitler was inspired by Martin
Mächler's 'Development Plan for Greater Berlin' of 1917–19, a passage from
which was reproduced in the architectural section at the Great Berlin Art
Exhibition in 1927. The accompanying catalogue claimed that Mächler's ideas
'touch on the most controversial and decisive problem in the development of
Greater Berlin: namely, the question of creating a north–south link for the
major railway lines'.[160] But Hitler had told Speer that his idea 'of an abnormally
wide road' derived from his examination of 'inadequate plans of Berlin', which
in the 1920s had encouraged him to develop his own thoughts on the
subject.[161] This is the decisive point: even if Hitler had referred to Mächler, it
would still be misleading to speak of obvious 'similarities between Mächler's
ideas and Speer's Hitler-inspired plans for a north–south axis',[162] for any 'similarities' are purely superficial: Mächler's overall concept had evolved from
existing economic and architectural structures and was intended to fulfil the
city's potential as an international capital by exploiting its economic and
geographical situation. Hitler, conversely, wanted to impose on the city a form
that reflected his party's political principles. As Alfred Schinz observed when
discussing the plans for four circular roads around the city centre,

> the concept behind their design stemmed not so much from a realistic
> insight into the inner structure of the city's traffic and transport infrastruc-
> ture within an urban setting as from the desire to transfer to Berlin older
> models of absolutist urban layouts in a monumentalized form. It was believed
> that in this way visible order would finally be imposed on Berlin's 'chaotic'

urban landscape. All attempts to plan the manifold functions of a sprawling urban landscape were consciously neglected in favour of this primitive scheme.[163]

It is inappropriate to cite Schinkel and Mächler as Hitler's inspirational models, still less to seek to give his plans a semblance of legitimacy in this way. Above all, such an approach reveals a fundamental misunderstanding of Hitler's view of architecture and urban planning as weapons in his political armoury. Hitler had no desire to improve Berlin's urban landscape as such. In the first place, the claim made by Joachim Fest and others that Hitler and Speer 'started out' from the belief that Berlin lacked a north–south link and that all their plans for the city from the 1920s onwards came back to the idea of such a link, not least as a result of the capital's growing transport problems, is a grotesque misrepresentation of the discussions that actually took place at the time of the Weimar Republic and that were designed to deal with the problems of the city's urban planning.[164]

This debate was in fact dominated by the problem of the absence of a link between the capital's two great centres within the inner city: the first of these was the 'City', around the axis formed by the Leipziger Straße and the Friedrichstraße, while the second was the 'New West End', along the Tauentzienstraße and the Kurfürstendamm.[165] The discussion surrounding the 'eye of the needle', as the Potsdamer Platz became known, is typical of this whole attitude. All the suggestions that were made invariably took as their starting point the need to relieve the burden of traffic on certain thoroughfares, chiefly the Leipziger Straße, and generally found expression in plans to cut through other roads in an east–west direction.[166] Anyone wanting to travel northwards from the inner city in the direction of Wedding would use the existing north–south axis in the form of the Friedrichstraße and its extension, the Chausseestraße, or, alternatively, they could take the Brunnenstraße, while the streets running off from the Alexanderplatz gave access to the north-east of the city.

The New Chancellery

When the question of east–west links came up in internal discussions with the city administration, Hitler had expressed his opposition to the city's preferred option, which was to cut through the Ministerial Gardens that extended in a westerly direction behind the Chancellery, the Presidential Palace and various ministry buildings. Instead, he had proposed that the Leipziger Straße be extended towards the west. By the date of the topping-out ceremony of the New Chancellery in early August 1938 and certainly by 9 January 1939, when the building was officially handed over to him, the world at large had discovered the reasons for Hitler's opposition to these plans. And, once again, his ideas on urban planning were the result of essentially political choices. His decision to build the New Chancellery and the date at which the building was finished were directly related to the political events that had preceded them. In the course of his speech at the topping-out ceremony, Hitler had declared that he was keen that 'as far as possible Berlin should be seen as a representative of the German nation' and that the city must survive long into the future as 'the capital of the German Reich'. To this end, he wanted to 'build a beautiful, great and proud capital'. He then expressed his aims even more clearly: 'This year we have acquired a wonderfully beautiful, powerful and great German city [Vienna] as a part of our Reich, a very beautiful city, a city with a very great cultural heritage and wonderful buildings. For precisely this reason it is necessary for Berlin to change its aspect in order to reflect its great, new German mission.' It was simply unacceptable that 'as the representative of the German nation' and of the country's 75 million inhabitants he was obliged to welcome 'foreign representatives in unworthy slums'.[167] And in the speech that he gave in the Sportpalast on 9 January 1939 in the presence of eight thousand building workers and others involved in the construction of the New Chancellery,[168] he used the occasion to forge a link between the annexation of Austria and the creation of a 'Pan-German Reich', and to praise his architect Albert Speer. It was his intention, he explained, to give 'this new and, indeed, greatest Reich a worthy capital of which the German need no longer feel ashamed whenever he travels abroad':

> When I decided at the beginning of last year to provide an answer to a great German question that has long remained unresolved, namely, the annexation of German Austria, I invited our brilliant young architect to call on me at the end of January and told him that this great German Reich now needs another place to display itself and, above all, to work. I shall not have much time to perform this task. And so you, too, have little time. I know that it will be something quite unique. By 10 January next year at the latest the New Chancellery must be complete, for that is when I intend to receive foreign diplomats there. My general inspector of buildings asked to have a few hours to think things over, and that very evening he came to me with an appointments diary and announced: 'On such and such a date in March the houses will be demolished, the topping-out ceremony will take place on 1 August,

and on 9 February, my Führer, I shall report that the building has been completed!'[169]

In his memoirs Speer took over this version of events, adding that he wasted no time in demolishing the houses in the Voßstraße. Since the elongated strip of land invited such an approach, he had designed a succession of rooms along an extended axis, and Hitler had been impressed by Speer's 500-feet-long gallery 'as it was more than twice as long as the Hall of Mirrors at Versailles'.[170] But both Speer's account of his own contribution to the designs and his claim that the project was executed in such a short space of time are further legends put about by Speer himself and by contemporary National Socialist propagandists in an attempt to demonstrate just how efficient their system was.

In fact, Hitler had already spoken to representatives of the city authorities on 5 July 1934 and raised the question of widening the Voßstraße by tearing down all the buildings on the northern side of the street and, at the same time, he had discussed the possibility of building an extension to the Chancellery. As early as 1935 he had produced a sketch showing the front of the building, the forecourt-like extension overlooking the Voßstraße, the Wilhelmsplatz entrance through Siedler's new building of 1928–30 and the series of rooms leading to the reception room.[171] In answer to a question from the minister of finance concerning his interest in acquiring the Dresdner Bank's buildings at 2 Voßstraße, adjacent to the Chancellery, secretary of state Heinrich Lammers replied on 31 May 1935: 'The Führer wishes to buy the property.'[172] When the building was acquired by the state in December 1935, Hitler decided that the property next to it at no. 3, the Ministry of Justice, should likewise be taken over. Both buildings were torn down in March 1936, and on 18 May 1936 the Chancellery formally took charge of the site.[173]

In a letter dated 28 May 1936, Speer informed Lammers that, 'after a year or so's work, the preliminary design for the Voßstraße project has by and large been settled on and approved by the Führer and chancellor'.[174] Further plots of land were acquired in 1936, and the buildings at 4 and 5 Voßstraße were torn down in April 1937. It was at around this time that local newspapers reported for the first and last time on the building project, noting that the plans provided for an extension to the Chancellery.

The shell of the first stage of the project, covering 2–5 Voßstraße, was completed on 1 January 1938. There were no reports in the press on the laying of the foundation stone of the New Chancellery, for no such ceremony took place. Otherwise the laying of the foundation stone for every other major public building project was marked by elaborate ceremonies and was extensively covered by the press.[175] The way in which the public was manipulated – Hitler's speech at the topping-out ceremony remained unpublished – is explained by the shifts of power that were taking place in the background in the upper echelons of the regime and in the armed forces between November 1937 and early February 1938, culminating in the 'Decree concerning the Leadership of the Armed Forces', announced on 4 February, whereby Hitler arrogated to himself direct control over the whole of his country's armed forces.[176]

Great Plans, Half in Secret

In his speech at the topping-out ceremony in August 1938 Hitler had indicated that the New Chancellery would 'later fulfil a different aim' and that it would 'serve its present purpose for a period of only some ten or twelve years', after which it would be used for a different cause – 'a great national people's cause involving the whole country'. The building, Hitler went on, was 'not the only one' on which Speer had been working: during the same period he had also 'produced tremendous plans for the whole of Berlin'.[177] But in his present speech he refused to divulge anything more than these vague hints, and Speer himself later confirmed that 'Hitler was anxious that our plans should not be made public. Only parts of them were made known as we could not entirely exclude the general public from our work. [. . .] And so we granted outsiders only the occasional glimpse of harmless-seeming parts of our plans. The basic concept, as it related to the question of urban planning, was made public with Hitler's permission by means of an article that I myself wrote.'[178]

This, too, is less than the entire truth, for even before Speer's essay on 'New Plans for our Country's Capital' had appeared in the inaugural issue of a new architectural journal, *Der Deutsche Baumeister* (The German Architect), in January 1939, a number of glossy magazines and several dailies had already examined the subject in some detail. The popular weekly *Koralle*, for example, had run a report as long ago as May 1938 headed 'The Redevelopment of Berlin under Adolf Hitler' and announcing that the city was to acquire a new face worthy of the Pan-German Reich. It struck a monumental note: 'The grand lines of the building programme suggest that decisive action is to start within the next few days.' The article was accompanied by a simplified illustration of Schinkel's designs from 1840, but it also included an up-to-the-minute account of Speer's plans for a north–south axis between the North and South stations. The plans themselves were reproduced and accompanied by a passage reading as follows:

Here it has taken shape, this monumental north–south axis. The railway tracks of the Anhalt and Potsdam stations, which until now have driven a wedge into the city's road network and fatally inhibited its urban development, will disappear. From the new South Station the broad N–S Road will lead to the Königsplatz [until 1933 and after 1945 the Platz der Republik] and its great assembly building. Not far from the city's imposing centre, the intersection of two roads will form the focal point of Berlin's traffic. The north–south axis will then continue on its course and culminate in the great North Station.[179]

By far the most popular German illustrated publication of this period was the *Berliner Illustrirte Zeitung*, which in mid-December 1938 published an article headed 'The Führer's Idea as Shaped by the General Inspector of Buildings, Albert Speer: Berlin as the Reich's Great Capital'. [180] It discussed the 'first one thousand yards of the new north–south axis' and featured a bird's-eye view of the Runder Platz and its environs, including the House of German Foreign Transport, the foundation stone of which had been laid by Hitler on 14 June 1938, when he had declared that the roads that made up his axial plan were intended not for 1940 but for the coming centuries, for he believed that Germany would last forever 'just as he also believes in his capital!'[181] The diagram also showed that the north–south axis was to run along the lines of the former Siegesallee and cut across the Voßstraße in order to create a new link with the 'New West End' in the vicinity of the Memorial Church. The well-known architectural journal *Deutsche Bauzeitung*, finally, had published 'the programme for Berlin's redevelopment' in January 1938, describing the plan as 'magnificent in its composition and tremendous in its scope'. It required 'a closer examination of the details in order to grasp the full import of the plan'. The journal claimed to reproduce the exact wording of Speer's programme of planned changes:

1. All the important buildings in the Reich's capital will in future be brought together along a new street to produce a unique and powerful overall impression. This street will be sufficiently broad as to be appropriate to the future volume of traffic in an international city. It will run from north to south through the centre of today's Berlin.

2. A new South Station, to the west of the present Tempelhof Ring Station, will absorb the traffic from the Anhalt and Potsdam stations. In this way, an area at present covered by over 10 million square feet of railway tracks and necessary until now for the efficient running of these two mainline stations

will become available for building. The new north–south road will pass through this area previously occupied by the country's railways and in this way will open up the possibility of constructing numerous new buildings.

3. A new North Station between Putlitzstraße Station and Wedding Station will take over the mainline traffic from the Lehrter and the Stettin stations and also from the Municipal Railway. An area of six million square feet currently occupied by Lehrt Station will thereby become available.

4. The new road will link Berlin's two new central stations. [There follows a description of the proposed route of the road.]

5. The new road will be extended northwards and southwards to the city's outer ring road. [. . .] In total, this new north–south road will be 24 miles in length.

6. The east–west axis that currently runs from the Lustgarten to Staaken will be cut through from the Royal Palace, following the Kaiser-Wilhelm-Straße, in an easterly direction and will be extended in both directions as far as the outer ring road. [. . .] The east–west link will be a little over 30 miles long.

7. Four broad inner ring roads will complement the new Berlin axial system, largely using existing roads.

The Great Hall

The *Deutsche Bauzeitung* added that all the details concerning the centrepiece of the new plan for the city's redevelopment, namely the north–south axis, were already in place. It went on to quote Speer and his fellow workers, who claimed that their aim was 'to provide this greatest artery of Berlin's future traffic network not only with the most modern means of transport but to set it within an urban framework without precedent in urban planning'. The programme's main feature was then presented as follows:

Anyone who later leaves the great hall of the new South Station will see at the far end of Berlin's tremendous new road, some four miles away on the site of what is now the Alsenstraße, an assembly building at the very heart of the city, a building whose dimensions are a true reflection of the city's extended precincts and of the significance of Berlin as the capital of the Reich.

In front of this 'large-scale building', the Königsplatz, with its surface area of 2.25 million square feet, would enable the country to hold mass rallies involving up to one million participants. Further deadlines had already been 'agreed in principle by the Führer, and by 1950 the main challenges will have been met, with the single exception of the ring road'. The South Station would be completed in 1945, the North Station three years later. 'Since it will take longer to free the land that is currently built on,' the report concludes, 'most of the large-scale building work mentioned here will not begin until 1939.'[182]

None of the reports dealt in any detail with the 'large assembly hall' mentioned here. And in no case was there an illustration, whether in the form of an architectural sketch or a line drawing. Only the schematic ground plans gave any indication of its size. Although the rest of the scheme was described in considerable detail, illustrations offering an overview of the north–south axis ended well before the bend in the River Spree, which was the planned site of the new hall. Even a brief monograph about Speer written by one of his closest colleagues and published in early 1943 announces in only the baldest of terms that

> A number of large buildings involved in the redevelopment, including the focal point of the Great Road that is planned for the present Königsplatz, have been entrusted to the Führer's architect to be developed on his own. All these designs, on which Speer has been working for years in his small studio on the Obersalzberg, have been developed to the point where they can be realized immediately after the war. [. . .] Wartime makes it impossible to publish these brilliant plans at present. They are being held back until the day of our definitive victory.[183]

If the outer aspect of the project was known to only a handful of initiates, then its planned size was a better-kept secret, even though Hitler had already given at least an indirect hint in the course of a speech he delivered at the official opening of the Second German Architecture and Craft Exhibition in the House of German Art in Munich on 10 December 1938, when he had discussed the capacity of public buildings and cited Berlin Cathedral as an example. This building, he explained, served as a 'central church for the capital of the German Reich' for the 3.5 million Protestants who lived there. 'The cathedral has seating for 2,450. These seats are numbered and in that way can accommodate the country's leading Protestant families.' It was difficult, however, to see how the spiritual needs of around 3.5 million souls could be met in a church that could seat only 2,450 parishioners. The size of the building was by no means dictated by the constraints of construction technology but was 'the result of architectural considerations as petty as they are thoughtless. In reality this cathedral should hold 100,000 people.' Unlike the Church, the NSDAP, as a popular movement, must bear the people in mind when designing its buildings and construct halls 'for 150,000 or 200,000 people. In other words, we must build them as big as today's technical possibilities permit, and above all we must build for eternity!'[184]

It needed no great feat of the imagination to conclude that 'replanning' Berlin in general and building the 'Great Hall' in particular would consume vast sums of money. Of course, this subject was never broached in public – after 1937 press reports on official building projects were controlled with particular rigour by the Ministry of Propaganda.[185] Only in an out-of-the-way foreign publication was a figure apparently given:

> According to conservative estimates, the cost of the future metropolis has been set at 25 thousand million marks. When the architect, Minister Speer, who is also the general inspector of buildings in the Reich's capital, was asked where all this money was to come from, he replied: 'This is only a fraction of what we are unfortunately having to spend on a war that has been forced upon us against our will.'[186]

Triumphal Buildings for Military Triumphs

But it presumably struck the people responsible for these plans that between 1937 and 1939 it was advisable to say as little as possible about the Great Hall in public because it was no longer possible to deny the link between the erection of this cultic building in the tradition of medieval cathedrals, on the one hand, and Hitler's plans for another world war, on the other. The triumphal arch in front of the new South Station was to be dedicated to the memory of those German soldiers who had fallen in the First World War, so it made sense that the Great Hall marking the northern boundary of the north–south axis should ensure that Hitler's rewriting of history found its architectural counterpart in a quasi-religious edifice celebrating the victory of the troops of the 'Pan-German Reich' in the coming world war under Hitler's supreme command.[187] In his later monologues given in his hideaway headquarters, Hitler expressed this same idea by telling his listeners, as they sat round the table of an evening, that Berlin would one day be the capital of the world and that as a cosmopolitan capital it was comparable to ancient Egypt, Babylon and Rome.[188] Indeed, he even thought that it was appropriate to rename Berlin 'Germania'*, for such a name was well suited to the country's main city 'in its

---

* The home of the original Germanic tribes on the Lower Rhine who gave their name to Germany.

new and imposing form' and, in spite of the geographical distance that separated that erstwhile member of the Germanic racial nucleus from modern
Berlin, the name would none the less create a sense that they both belonged
together.[189]

By 1938 work had begun on tearing down buildings in the Alsen
district in the bend in the Spree in order to make way for the Great Hall.
Similar demolition work was started at the same date in the old Tiergarten
district to make way for the House for German Foreign Transport and the
proposed intersection with the Kaiser-Wilhelm-Straße that was part of the
east–west axis,[190] as well as at various other places in the city. There is something almost symbolic about the fact that it was at the same time – April and
May 1938 – that Goebbels launched his campaign against the Jews still
remaining in Berlin, his aim being to isolate them from the rest of the population and drive them from the city.[191] Moreover, the manner in which Hitler's
fiftieth birthday was marked in Berlin on 19 and 20 April 1939 reveals the
connection between the redevelopment of the city and the preparations for
war. At nine o'clock on the evening of the 19th the Führer drove the miles
along the completed section of the east–west axis, stopping at the Adolf-Hitler-
Platz (previously the Reichskanzlerplatz and now the Theodor-Heuss-Platz)
and then returning along the same route. The leaders of the city authorities
were waiting for him to the west of the Brandenburg Gate. Albert Speer
stepped forward and declared in a loud voice: 'My Führer, I should
like to report the completion of the east–west axis. May the work speak for
itself!'[192] At eleven o'clock the following morning the armed forces took part in
a march-past along the same stretch of road – now the Straße des 17. Juni. A
platform for Hitler had been erected opposite the main entrance of the
Technical University, which was itself a part of the plans for the city's facelift.
The birthday parade lasted four hours, a march-past of vast dimensions
designed to show off the new military might of all the armed forces'
weaponry.[193]

The End of 'Germania'

With the start of the Second World War building work was initially suspended,
then briefly resumed following the military victory in the Polish campaign.
Hitler's visit to defeated Paris in the early hours of 28 June 1940 revived his
desire to 'give Berlin a new face', and it was at his express command that the
building work started up again.[194] Speer used the opportunity to persuade
Hitler to issue a decree in which the latter declared:

In the shortest possible time Berlin must be redeveloped and acquire the form that is its due through the greatness of our victory as the capital of a powerful new empire. In the completion of what is now *the country's most important architectural task* [highlighted in the original] I see the most significant contribution to our final victory. I expect that it will be completed by the year 1950.[195]

In 1940 and 1941 Hitler repeatedly inspected Speer's model hall at 4 Pariser Platz (formerly the Academy of the Arts) and on each occasion he evinced his enthusiasm.[196] But after setbacks in his war on the Soviet Union, which he had intended should be a brief blitzkrieg, work on the various projects bound up with Berlin's urban redevelopment programme was finally abandoned in early March 1943.[197]

When Hitler took his own life in his Chancellery bunker on 30 April 1945, he took with him not only his plan for Germany's military domination of Europe but also his attempt to turn Berlin into the capital of the world, 'Germania' – the two plans were not only closely connected, each was a precondition and expression of the other. Berlin continues to the present day to bear the burden of both these foolhardy schemes.

Notes

Preface

1. Bernhard Sauer, 'Goebbels' "Rabauken": Zur Geschichte der SA in Berlin-Brandenburg', *Berlin in Geschichte und Gegenwart: Jahrbuch des Landesarchivs Berlin 2006*, ed. Uwe Schaper (Berlin 2006), 107–64. Together with Martin Schuster's unpublished dissertation, 'Die SA in der nationalsozialistischen "Machtergreifung" in Berlin und Brandenburg 1926–1934' (FU Berlin, 2005), Sauer's study at least provides a solid basis for a scholarly engagement with this important topic.
2. J. K. von Engelbrechten, *Eine braune Armee entsteht: Die Geschichte der Berlin-Brandenburger SA* (Munich 1937).
3. This is the chapter heading in Jochen Boberg, Tilman Fichter and Eckhardt Gillen (eds), *Die Metropole: Industriestruktur in Berlin im 20. Jahrhundert* (Munich 1986).
4. Hans Herzfeld, 'Berlin auf dem Wege zur Weltstadt', *Berlin: Neun Kapitel seiner Geschichte*, ed. Richard Dietrich (Berlin 1960), 239–71, esp. 263.
5. Joachim C. Fest, *Hitler: Eine Biographie* (Frankfurt am Main, Berlin and Vienna 1973), 204–5; trans. Richard and Clara Winston as *Hitler* (London 1974), 139–40.
6. Henry Picker, *Hitlers Tischgespräche im Führerhauptquartier*, 4th edn (Stuttgart 1983), 142 (entry of 25 March 1942).
7. Gerhard Kiersch and others, *Berliner Alltag im Dritten Reich* (Düsseldorf 1981), 47.
8. Peter Steinbach, 'Zwischen Bomben und Gestapo: Berlin als Reichshauptstadt und als Hauptstadt des deutschen Widerstandes', *Berlin als Faktor nationaler und internationaler Politik*, ed. Hannelore Horn (Berlin 1988), 23–43, esp. 27.
9. Sven Felix Kellerhoff, *Hitlers Berlin: Geschichte einer Hassliebe* (Berlin 2005), 20–3.
10. See the monograph published anonymously by the Bezirksamt Tempelhof-Schöneberg, *Der Schwerbelastungskörper: Mysteriöses Erbe der Reichshauptstadt* (Berlin 2005).

Chapter 1 · 1916–18: Hitler's early visits to Berlin

1. *Griebens Reiseführer Berlin*, abridged edn (Berlin 1917), 5.
2. Anton Joachimsthaler, *Hitlers Weg begann in München: 1913–1923* (Munich 2000), 346 n.504. Here the address of Richard Arendt's parents is incorrectly given as 'Berlin N 113, Schonnrische Str. 15/3', although it is unclear if this form already appears in Arendt's wartime muster roll or if it is the result of a transcriptional error on Joachimsthaler's part.
3. For further details, see Joachimsthaler, *Hitlers Weg* (note 2), 108–10.

4. See Joachimsthaler, *Hitlers Weg* (note 2), 346 n.504. According to Ian Kershaw, Hitler had invited his acquaintance Reinhold Hanisch to tell him 'tales of Berlin' as early as 1909, when he was living in a refuge for the homeless in Vienna. Even at this early date, Hitler was already enthusiastic about 'all things German'. See Ian Kershaw, *Hitler 1889–1936: Hubris* (London 1998), 53.

5. Joachimsthaler, *Hitlers Weg* (note 2), 169.

6. Page reproduced from BA NS 26/17 and quoted by Eberhard Jäckel and Axel Kuhn (eds), *Hitler: Sämtliche Aufzeichnungen 1905–1924* (Stuttgart 1980), 82; also reproduced by Werner Maser, *Hitlers Briefe und Notizen: Sein Weltbild in handschriftlichen Dokumenten*, 2nd edn (Düsseldorf 1973), 106–7. The identity of the image on the front of the postcard is not known.

7. Adolf Hitler, *Mein Kampf* (Munich 1933), 211; trans. Ralph Manheim as *Mein Kampf* (London 2002), 175.

8. Kershaw, *Hitler 1889–1936* (note 4), 29–32.

9. Hitler, *Mein Kampf* (note 7), 18–19; Engl. trans. 8–9.

10. Hitler, *Mein Kampf* (note 7), 138; Engl. trans. 116.

11. Kershaw, *Hitler 1889–1936* (note 4), 68–9.

12. Hitler, *Mein Kampf* (note 7), 138; Engl. trans. 116.

13. Statement made on 26 Feb. 1924, the first day of Hitler's trial before the People's Court in Munich, quoted from Lothar Gruchmann (ed.), *Der Hitler-Prozess 1924: Wortlaut der Hauptverhandlung vor dem Volksgericht München I* (Munich 1997–9), 19.

14. Joachimsthaler, *Hitlers Weg* (note 2), 34–5.

15. Joachimsthaler, *Hitlers Weg* (note 2), 110–14; and Kershaw, *Hitler 1889–1936* (note 4), 90.

16. Joachimsthaler, *Hitlers Weg* (note 2), 115–17; Kershaw, *Hitler 1889–1936* (note 4), 91.

17. Joachimsthaler, *Hitlers Weg* (note 2), 127; Kershaw, *Hitler 1889–1936* (note 4), 91. Kershaw argues that Hitler wanted to imply that he had spent the whole war in the trenches.

18. The best account is Fritz Wiedemann, *Der Mann, der Feldherr werden wollte: Erlebnisse und Erfahrungen des Vorgesetzten Hitlers im 1. Weltkrieg und seines späteren Persönlichen Adjutanten* (Velbert 1964), 25.

19. Joachimsthaler, *Hitlers Weg* (note 2), 129.

20. Joachimsthaler, *Hitlers Weg* (note 2), 133.

21. Thus Hitler in the Wolfsschanze in East Prussia on 13 October 1941, quoted by Heinrich Heim, *Monologe im Führerhauptquartier 1941–1944*, ed. Werner Jochmann (Hamburg 1980), 79.

22. Statements by Ignaz Westenkirchner and Ernst Schmidt reported by Joachimsthaler, *Hitlers Weg* (note 2), 156.

23. Wiedemann, *Der Mann, der Feldherr werden wollte* (note 18), 28; and Joachimsthaler, *Hitlers Weg* (note 2), 162–3.

24. Wiedemann, *Der Mann, der Feldherr werden wollte* (note 18), 28–9.

25. Wiedemann, *Der Mann, der Feldherr werden wollte* (note 18), 29.

26. Hitler, *Mein Kampf* (note 7), 209; Eng. trans. 173.

27. Joachimsthaler, *Hitlers Weg* (note 2), 164.

28. All quotations from Hitler, *Mein Kampf* (note 7), 210–11; Engl. trans. 174.

29. Allegedly the chief doctor, 'a Dr Stettiner, [...] a Jew', had criticized Hitler's reading matter, a book on military science, by saying 'I thought you were more sensible than that', a criticism that Hitler interpreted as a sign of declining standards of military discipline; see Gruchmann, *Der Hitler-Prozess 1924* (note 13), 21.

30. Joachimsthaler, *Hitlers Weg* (note 2), lower half of the seventh page of plates following p. 96.

31. Jäckel and Kuhn, *Hitler: Sämtliche Aufzeichnungen* (note 6), 77.

32. Hitler, *Mein Kampf* (note 7), 211; Engl. trans. 175.

33. All quotations are taken from the complete text of these reports in *Dokumente aus geheimen Archiven*, iv: *1914–1918. Berichte des Berliner Polizeipräsidenten zur Stimmung und Lage der Bevölkerung in Berlin 1914–1918* (Weimar 1987), 37, 45, 48–9, 53.

34. *Dokumente aus geheimen Archiven* (note 33), 61.

35. *Dokumente aus geheimen Archiven* (note 33), 94–5; see also Philipp Scheidemann's account in *Memoiren eines Sozialdemokraten* (Dresden 1928), quoted here from Dieter Glatzer and Ruth Glatzer, *Berliner Leben 1914–1918: Eine historische Reportage aus Erinnerungen und Berichten* (Berlin 1983), 224–5.

36. *Dokumente aus geheimen Archiven* (note 33), 102–3.

37. *Dokumente aus geheimen Archiven* (note 33), 111.

38. Hitler, *Mein Kampf* (note 7), 208; Engl. trans. 172. There is a remarkable similarity here and elsewhere between Hitler's accounts and the 'argumentation' put forward in the series of articles published in the *Süddeutsche Monatshefte* in 1924; see, for example, Hermann von Kuhl, 'Der Sommer 1918 an der Front', *Süddeutsche Monatshefte*, xxi/7 (April 1924), 38: 'Hundreds and thousands of men were lost in this way on the front.'

39. *Spartakusbriefe*, ed. Institut für Marxismus-Leninismus beim Zentralkomitee der Sozialistischen Einheitspartei Deutschlands (Berlin 1958), 165–7.

40. Richard Müller, *Vom Kaiserreich zur Republik: Ein Beitrag zur Geschichte der revolutionären Arbeiterbewegung während des Weltkrieges* [1924] (Berlin 1974), 63–5.

41. *Dokumente und Materialien zur Geschichte der deutschen Arbeiterbewegung*, Series II, vol. i, ed. Institut für Marxismus-Leninismus beim Zentralkomitee der Sozialistischen Einheitspartei Deutschlands (Berlin 1967), 490–2.

42. For further details, see Hellmut von Gerlach, *Von Rechts nach Links* (Zurich 1937).

43. *Dokumente aus geheimen Archiven* (note 33), 161 (report of 30 Sept. 1916).

44. Ulrich Cartarius (ed.), *Deutschland im Ersten Weltkrieg: Texte und Dokumente 1914–1918* (Munich 1982), 89 (letter from Hindenburg to the Reich Chancellor on the subject of the setting up of a Supreme War Office, 10 Oct. 1916).

45. *Dokumente aus geheimen Archiven* (note 33), 166 and passim.

46. *Dokumente aus geheimen Archiven* (note 33), 163.

47. *Adreßbuch für Berlin und seine Vororte 1917* (Berlin [1917]), 734.

48. *Adreßbuch für Berlin 1917* (note 47), 225.

49. Müller, *Vom Kaiserreich zur Republik* (note 40), 94.

50. See *Dokumente und Materialien* (note 41), 611 (letter from the Commander-in-Chief in the Marches to the Prussian War Ministry, 19 April 1917); see also Müller, *Vom Kaiserreich zur Republik* (note 40), 82, where the number of striking workers is reckoned to have been as high as 300,000.

51. Hitler, *Mein Kampf* (note 7), 213; Engl. trans. 176.

52. Hitler, *Mein Kampf* (note 7), 213; Engl. trans. 176–7.

53. For documentary details on the strike, see Herbert Michaelis and Ernst Schraepler (eds), *Ursachen und Folgen: Vom deutschen Zusammenbruch 1918 and 1945 bis zur staatlichen Neuordnung Deutschlands in der Gegenwart*, 25 vols (Berlin 1959), i.242–55.

54. See Müller, *Vom Kaiserreich zur Republik* (note 40), 100–111.

55. Hitler, *Mein Kampf* (note 7), 217; Engl. trans. 180.

56. Hitler, *Mein Kampf* (note 7), 219–20; Engl. trans. 182–3.

57. Hitler, *Mein Kampf* (note 7), 222–4; Engl. trans. 184–6.

58. Hitler, *Mein Kampf* (note 7), 225; Engl. trans. 187.

59. Kershaw, *Hitler 1889–1936* (note 4), 68–9; and John Lukacs, *The Hitler of History: Hitler's Biographers on Trial* (London 2002), 56.

60. Hitler, *Mein Kampf* (note 7), 138; Engl. trans. 116.

61. Joachimsthaler, *Hitlers Weg* (note 2), 127.

62. Hitler, *Mein Kampf* (note 7), 220; Engl. trans. 183.

63. Hitler, *Mein Kampf* (note 7), 7–8; Engl. trans. 10.

64. Hitler, *Mein Kampf* (note 7), 21; Engl. trans. 21.

65. Hitler, *Mein Kampf* (note 7), 206; Engl. trans. 171.
66. Joachimsthaler, *Hitlers Weg* (note 2), 96.
67. Heim, *Monologe im Führerhauptquartier* (note 21), 100.
68. Jäckel and Kuhn, *Hitler: Sämtliche Aufzeichnungen* (note 6), 82.
69. Whereas nowadays all of Berlin's museums are closed on Mondays, there was no consistent policy in Hitler's day. The National Gallery, for example, was closed on Thursdays, the Hohenzollern Museum at Schloß Monbijou and the Arsenal on Saturdays. See the table of museums and collections in *Griebens Reiseführer Berlin* (note 1), 38.
70. Jäckel and Kuhn, *Hitler: Sämtliche Aufzeichnungen* (note 6), 83.
71. Joachim C. Fest, *Hitler: Eine Biographie* (Frankfurt am Main, Berlin and Vienna 1973), 106–7; trans. Richard and Clara Winston as *Hitler* (London 1974), 71, where the adjective *lebenslanges* (lifelong) has been replaced by 'future' before the noun 'resentment'.
72. In defence of Fest, it must be acknowledged that he formulated his theory about Hitler's 'lifelong resentment' towards Berlin at a time when the above-mentioned sources were not yet available in published form.
73. Lukacs, *The Hitler of History* (note 59), 59.
74. Lukacs, *The Hitler of History* (note 59), 60.
75. Hitler, *Mein Kampf* (note 7), 179; Engl. trans. 150.
76. For a more detailed account, see Joachimsthaler, *Hitlers Weg* (note 2), 25–7; and Kershaw, *Hitler 1889–1936* (note 4), 68–9.
77. Hitler, *Mein Kampf* (note 7), 138; Engl. trans. 116.
78. Hitler, *Mein Kampf* (note 7), 135; Engl. trans. 113.
79. Hitler, *Mein Kampf* (note 7), 134, 39, 14; Engl. trans. 112, 35, 15.
80. On the following, see Lukacs, *The Hitler of History* (note 59), 63–5.
81. Jäckel and Kuhn, *Hitler: Sämtliche Aufzeichnungen* (note 6), 69; Engl. trans. from Kershaw, *Hitler 1889–1936* (note 4), 93–4.
82. Anton Joachimsthaler offers an overview of Hitler's relations with women in *Hitlers Liste: Ein Dokument persönlicher Beziehungen* (Munich 2003), 33–40; see also RSA iii/1.260 (letter to Else Vogl, 28 Nov. 1928).
83. Rudolf Olden, *Hitler* (Amsterdam 1935, reprinted Hildesheim 1981), 45.
84. On the following, see Otto Schilling, *Innere Stadt-Erweiterung* (Berlin 1921), 207–9; and Benedikt Goebel, *Der Umbau Alt-Berlins zum modernen Stadtzentrum: Planungs-, Bau- und Besitzgeschichte des historischen Berliner Stadtkerns im 19. und 20. Jahrhundert* (Berlin 2003), 128–30.
85. The Schloßfreiheit was the road immediately in front of the Castle. It was located on the second arm of the Spree.
86. Karl Scheffler, *Berlin: Wanderungen einer Stadt* (Berlin 1931), 95.
87. Peter Springer, *Schinkels Schloßbrücke in Berlin: Zweckbau und Monument* (Frankfurt, Berlin and Vienna 1981), 12 and 109–11.
88. On the following, see Dietmar Arnold and Ingmar Arnold, *Schloßfreiheit: Vor den Toren des Stadtschlosses* (Berlin 1998), 10–11 and 51–3.
89. Thomas Nipperdey, *Deutsche Geschichte 1866–1918*, 2nd edn, 2 vols (Munich 1991), i.739.
90. In Oct. 1941 Hitler announced that although Wilhelm II had had 'taste', it was of an extremely poor kind. And in Sept. 1942 he again referred to Wilhelm II's 'tasteless style'; see Heim, *Monologe im Führerhauptquartier* (note 21), 101 and 380. See also Klaus Backes, *Hitler und die bildenden Künste: Kulturverständnis und Kunstpolitik im Dritten Reich* (Cologne 1988), 14. Backes sets out from the premise that Hitler's stylistic predilections had changed 'by 1925/6 at the latest'. We shall return to this point in due course.
91. Jäckel and Kuhn, *Hitler: Sämtliche Aufzeichnungen* (note 6), 83.
92. Quoted by Jost Dülffer and others, *Hitlers Städte: Baupolitik im Dritten Reich. Eine Dokumentation* (Cologne and Vienna 1978), 90.
93. Hitler, *Mein Kampf* (note 7), 225; Engl. trans. 187.

Chapter 2 · 1919–25: A social climber from Munich on his way north

1. According to a report published in the *Berliner Tageblatt* on 6 March 1923 and headed 'What is banned and what is permitted in Munich', quoted in Eberhard Jäckel and Axel Kuhn (eds), *Hitler: Sämtliche Aufzeichnungen 1905–1924* (Stuttgart 1980), 843.

2. Quoted by Ernst Hanfstaengl, *Zwischen Weißem und Braunem Haus: Memoiren eines politischen Außenseiters* (Munich 1970), 109.

3. Greim became commanding general of an air force regiment in 1942 and, from Feb. 1943, commander-in-chief of the Sixth Fleet on the eastern front. On Hitler's orders he was appointed Göring's successor as commander-in-chief of the air force on 27 April 1945. He took his own life in allied custody in Salzburg on 24 May 1945. See Robert Wistrich, *Wer war wer im Dritten Reich: Ein biographisches Lexikon. Anhänger, Mitläufer, Gegner aus Politik, Wirtschaft, Militär, Kunst und Wissenschaft* (Munich 1983), 98.

4. See Erich Sturvetant, *Jüterbog: Ein Führer durch seine Sehenswürdigkeiten* (Jüterbog 1928), 468–70.

5. Together with Admiral Alfred von Tirpitz, Kapp founded the extreme right-wing Pan-German Fatherland Party in 1917. After the war was over, he became a member of the committee of the German National People's Party.

6. See the relevant documentation in Herbert Michaelis and Ernst Schraepler (eds), *Ursachen und Folgen: Vom deutschen Zusammenbruch 1918 und 1945 bis zur saatlichen Neuordnung Deutschlands in der Gegenwart*, 25 vols (Berlin 1959), iv.101. For an overview of the situation, see Hans J. Reichhardt, *Kapp-Putsch und Generalstreik März 1920 in Berlin: 'Tage der Torheit, Tage der Not'. Eine Ausstellung des Landesarchivs Berlin* (Berlin 1990); and for a detailed account, see Heinrich August Winkler, *Von der Revolution zur Stabilisierung: Arbeiter und Arbeiterbewegung in der Weimarer Republik 1918 bis 1924* (Berlin and Bonn 1984), 295–7.

7. Michaelis and Schraepler, *Ursachen und Folgen* (note 6), iv. 101.

8. Anton Joachimsthaler, *Hitlers Weg begann in München 1913–1923* (Munich 2000), 272–3; see also Otto Dietrich, *Zwölf Jahre mit Hitler* (Cologne 1955), 178–9.

9. Gottfried Grandel, report to the NSDAP Main Archives (22 Oct. 1941), BA NS/26514, fol. 1; see also Ian Kershaw, *Hitler 1889–1936: Hubris* (London 1999), 155. On Grandel's role, see Albrecht Tyrell, *Vom 'Trommler' zum 'Führer': Der Wandel von Hitlers Selbstverständnis zwischen 1919 und 1924 und die Entwicklung der NSDAP* (Munich 1975), 110. Edmund Rumpler, who was one of the best-known German airplane pioneers and who developed the Rumpler Taube (Dove), was in fact Jewish.

10. See Kurt Gosswiler, *Kapital, Reichswehr und NSDAP 1919–1924*, 2nd edn (Berlin 1984), 554–6 (letter from Karl Mayr to Wolfgang Kapp, 24 Sept. 1920). Kershaw's claim that Mayr was 'an important Bavarian link with the putschist Wolfgang Kapp in 1920' hits the nail on the head; Kershaw, *Hitler 1889–1936* (note 9), 122.

11. Konrad Heiden, *Adolf Hitler: Das Zeitalter der Verantwortungslosigkeit. Eine Biographie* (Zurich 1936), 138; John Toland, *Adolf Hitler* (Bergisch Gladbach 1977), 141; and Kurt Pätzold and Manfred Weißbecker, *Adolf Hitler: Eine politische Biographie* (Leipzig 1995), 63.

12. Walter Görlitz and Herbert A. Quint, *Adolf Hitler: Eine Biographie* (Stuttgart 1952), 142. John Lukacs describes this as 'the first serious German postwar biography of Hitler'; see Lukacs, *The Hitler of History: Hitler's Biographers on Trial* (London 2002), 11. Remarkably, later accounts fail to mention the party documents drawn up by Eckart and Hitler.

13. See Joachimsthaler, *Hitlers Weg* (note 8), 273. In view of the fact that even before the putsch there had already been close links between the two groups that were involved in the overthrow in Munich and Berlin, Pätzold and Weißbecker note with some surprise that 'little is known about this trip, a circumstance that is in itself remarkable in a life whose every recess has been explored in exhaustive detail': Pätzold and Weißbecker, *Adolf Hitler* (note 11), 63.

14. Kershaw, *Hitler 1889–1936* (note 9), 155.

15. See Margarete Plewnia, *Auf dem Weg zu Hitler: Der 'völkische' Publizist Dietrich Eckart* (Bremen 1970), 15–17.

16. Georg Franz-Willing, *Krisenjahr der Hitlerbewegung: 1923* (Preußisch Oldendorf 1975), 202. Franz-Willing's account is based on a personal communication from Pabst of 1 Nov. 1962. Walter Stennes recalled first seeing Hitler in Reventlow's house 'in the spring of 1920', when Countess Reventlow had greeted him – Stennes – with the words: 'My husband has been talking for some time to a man from Bavaria who will be the new Messiah – at least that is what people are saying in Munich.' See Charles Drage, *Als Hitler nach Canossa ging* (Berlin 1982), 101–2.

17. See Anton Joachimsthaler, *Hitlers Liste: Ein Dokument persönlicher Beziehungen* (Munich 2003), 63–102.

18. Görlitz and Quint, *Adolf Hitler* (note 12), 143–4. Tyrell offers no evidence to support his claim that there is no truth to the remark that 'Hitler got to know Ludendorff, Reventlow and possibly also the other leaders of the Pan-German League during his brief stay in Berlin towards the end of the Kapp Putsch': Tyrell, *Vom 'Trommler'* (note 9), 224 n.391.

19. See Joachimsthaler, *Hitlers Weg* (note 8), 182–4; and Kershaw, *Hitler 1889–1936* (note 9), 87–97.

20. Report from Lieutenant Bendt to Fourth Group Command (21 Aug. 1919), quoted by Joachimsthaler, *Hitlers Weg* (note 8), 243.

21. Joachimsthaler, *Hitlers Weg* (note 8), 244. Only at this point does Hitler become more forthcoming in *Mein Kampf,* claiming that his speeches guided thousands of his comrades back to their people and their fatherland; see Adolf Hitler, *Mein Kampf* (Munich 1933), 235; Engl. trans. Ralph Manheim as *Mein Kampf* (London 2002), 196.

22. Joachimsthaler, *Hitlers Weg* (note 8), 251; Hitler, *Mein Kampf* (note 21), 236; Engl. trans. 198. Wilhelm Hoegner states that Hitler had already been despatched to the DAP on 2 July 1919; see Wilhelm Hoegner, *Die verratene Republik: Geschichte der deutschen Gegenrevolution* (Munich 1958), 122. In a letter of 29 Nov. 1921, Hitler himself gives June 1919 as the date of his admission; see Jäckel and Kuhn, *Hitler: Sämtliche Aufzeichnungen* (note 1), 526.

23. Jäckel and Kuhn, *Hitler: Sämtliche Aufzeichnungen* (note 1), 91.

24. Jäckel and Kuhn, *Hitler: Sämtliche Aufzeichnungen* (note 1), 112.

25. Jäckel and Kuhn, *Hitler: Sämtliche Aufzeichnungen* (note 1), 119.

26. Speech at an NSDAP meeting in Rosenheim (17 June 1920), quoted by Jäckel and Kuhn, *Hitler: Sämtliche Aufzeichnungen* (note 1), 148.

27. Reichswehr report on a speech in Munich, quoted by Jäckel and Kuhn, *Hitler: Sämtliche Aufzeichnungen* (note 1), 267.

28. *Rosenheimer Tagblatt* (28 June 1920), quoted by Jäckel and Kuhn, *Hitler: Sämtliche Aufzeichnungen* (note 1), 150.

29. Speech at an NSDAP meeting in Munich on 13 Aug. 1920, quoted by Jäckel and Kuhn, *Hitler: Sämtliche Aufzeichnungen* (note 1), 189.

30. Speech at an NSDAP meeting in Munich on 19 Nov. 1920, quoted by Jäckel and Kuhn, *Hitler: Sämtliche Aufzeichnungen* (note 1), 260.

31. The message on the card is reproduced by Jäckel and Kuhn, *Hitler: Sämtliche Aufzeichnungen* (note 1), 256.

32. See Jäckel and Kuhn, *Hitler: Sämtliche Aufzeichnungen* (note 1), 255–6 and 257–8.

33. Joachimsthaler, *Hitlers Weg* (note 8), 371 n.869; Gottfried Grandel, report to the NSDAP Main Archives (22 Oct. 1941), BA NS/26514, fol. 3.

34. Thus Joachimsthaler, *Hitlers Weg* (note 8), 281. None the less, a further card from Hitler to Joseph Popp in Munich has survived in addition to the one mentioned in n.31 above. It too shows the Reichstag. It is not postmarked, but Jäckel and Kuhn assume on the basis of the numbering on it that it postdates the card of 3 Nov. 1920: see Jäckel and Kuhn, *Hitler: Sämtliche Aufzeichnungen* (note 1), 256, document 163. Walter Stennes

thought that he could recall Ludendorff introducing him to Hitler in 1920: see Drage, *Als Hitler nach Canossa ging* (note 16), 102.

35. Kershaw, *Hitler 1889–1936* (note 9), 160; and Tyrell, *Vom 'Trommler'* (note 9), 118. See also Dietrich, *Zwölf Jahre mit Hitler* (note 8), 178: 'Eckart knew a group of well-heeled citizens whom he called on with a view to enlisting their support for his newspaper and also introduced Hitler to them. They were the first sponsors to offer their help for reasons of general patriotism or, if one prefers it, the first to give money to Hitler. He himself later claimed more than once that Eckart often introduced him with the words: "This is the man who will one day liberate Germany."'

36. Joachimsthaler, *Hitlers Weg* (note 8), 285, dates Hitler's visit to '5 June to 9 July 1921'; Franz-Willing, *Krisenjahr der Hitlerbewegung* (note 16), 203, even speaks of a 'six-week' stay. But on a postcard sent to Fritz Lauböck, the son of the founder of the NSDAP branch in Rosenheim, and postmarked 25 June 1921, Hitler writes that 'this is my last day' in the city, and that he was visiting the Arsenal on Unter den Linden: see Jäckel and Kuhn, *Hitler: Sämtliche Aufzeichnungen* (note 1), 435.

37. Franz-Willing, *Krisenjahr der Hitlerbewegung* (note 16), 203.

38. Imanuel Geiss, *Geschichte des Rassismus* (Frankfurt 1988), 274.

39. See Thomas Friedrich, 'Die Politik des Hasses: Über den Aufstieg des Antisemitismus von der Ideologie zur Staatsdoktrin zu Lebzeiten Max Liebermanns', *Was vom Leben übrig bleibt, sind Bilder und Geschichten: Max Liebermann zum 150. Geburtstag. Rekonstruktion der Gedächtnisausstellung des Berliner Jüdischen Museums von 1936*, ed. Hermann Simon (Berlin 1997), 95–117, esp. 104–5.

40. Reminiscences of Fritz Geisler (9 Oct. 1936), quoted by Jäckel and Kuhn, *Hitler: Sämtliche Aufzeichnungen* (note 1), 530. On the other hand, Geisler dates the discussion to 'early 1922'.

41. Franz-Willing, *Krisenjahr der Hitlerbewegung* (note 16), 203 (letter from Hermann Esser to Georg Franz-Willing, 19 Feb. 1963).

42. *Baedeker: Berlin und Umgebung*, 19th edn (Berlin 1921), 3–5; *Griebens Reiseführer Berlin und Umgebung*, 61st edn (Berlin 1921/2), 18.

43. Tyrell, *Vom 'Trommler'* (note 9), 118.

44. On the postcard of 25 June 1921 that he sent from the Arsenal on Unter den Linden, Hitler reports that the 'trophies' – presumably items looted by the Germans during the First World War – had been 'stolen': see Jäckel and Kuhn, *Hitler: Sämtliche Aufzeichnungen* (note 1), 435.

45. Eckart and Gansser had got to know each other in Berlin during the First World War and soon became good friends; see Joachimsthaler, *Hitlers Weg* (note 8), 369 n.860. Gansser's membership number was 3061; see Albrecht Tyrell, *Führer befiehl . . . Selbstzeugnisse aus der 'Kampfzeit' der NSDAP: Dokumentation und Analyse* (Düsseldorf 1969), 23.

46. Quoted by Georg Franz-Willing, *Ursprung der Hitlerbewegung 1919–1922*, rev. edn (Preußisch Oldendorf 1974), 277–8.

47. Franz-Willing, *Ursprung der Hitlerbewegung* (note 46), 277.

48. Franz-Willing, *Ursprung der Hitlerbewegung* (note 46), 278.

49. Franz-Willing, *Ursprung der Hitlerbewegung* (note 46), 289. Konrad Heiden reports that shortly before Hitler's appointment as chancellor, 'Bechstein was open-handed whenever Hitler visited him in Berlin, as he often did, and complained about the difficulties encountered by the *Beobachter*': see Konrad Heiden, *Geburt des dritten Reiches: Die Geschichte des Nationalsozialismus bis Herbst 1933* (Zurich 1934), 144. According to information uncovered by the public prosecutor's office at the time of the Hitler-Ludendorff trial in 1924, the Daimler works at Marienfelde in Berlin also contributed to the NSDAP's funds: see Franz-Willing, *Ursprung der Hitlerbewegung* (note 46), 291.

50. On Gansser, see also Hanfstaengl, *Zwischen Weißem und Braunem Haus* (note 2), 66 and 69.

51. Heinrich Heim, *Monologe im Führerhauptquartier 1941–1944*, ed. Werner Jochmann (Hamburg 1980), 208.

52. *Völkischer Beobachter* (Berlin edn), liv/17 (17 Jan. 1941), 3. There is evidence that at the end of 1921 Berlin made a number of other attempts to contact the NSDAP in Munich. On 14 Nov. 1921, for example, Hitler wrote to a Fritz Körting in Dahlem; see Jäckel and Kuhn, *Hitler: Sämtliche Aufzeichnungen* (note 1), 519. The *Adreßbuch für Berlin und seine Vororte 1919* (i.1415) lists an engineer by the name of Fritz Körting at 80 Kronprinzenallee in Dahlem.

53. In their 1980 edition of Hitler's early correspondence, Jäckel and Kuhn stated that the identity of the recipient of this letter was 'unknown': *Hitler: Sämtliche Aufzeichnungen* (note 1), 525. It was left to Anton Joachimsthaler to demonstrate that the addressee was Gansser: *Hitlers Weg* (note 8), 335 n.255.

54. The club's rooms were at 6 Sommerstraße (now the Ebertstraße), not the Sonnenstraße, as Joachimsthaler states: *Hitlers Weg* (note 8), 66–7. It was officially launched on 2 Oct. 1919 at the Hotel Prinz Albrecht, 9 Prinz-Albrecht-Straße, the same building as the one occupied by the SS leadership under Heinrich Himmler in 1934: see Reinhard Rürup, *Topographie des Terrors: Gestapo, SS und Reichssicherheitshauptamt auf dem 'Prinz-Albrecht-Gelände'. Eine Dokumentation* (Berlin 1987), 13.

55. J. K. Engelbrechten and Hans Volz, *Wir wandern durch das nationalsozialistische Berlin: Ein Führer durch die Gedenkstätten des Kampfes um die Reichshauptstadt* (Munich 1937), 53. Fritz Geisler's recollections of 9 Oct. 1936, from which we have already quoted, differ slightly from the account given by Engelbrechten and Volz and claim that the discussion took place 'in early 1922': see Jäckel and Kuhn, *Hitler: Sämtliche Aufzeichnungen* (note 1), 530.

56. Engelbrechten and Volz, *Wir wandern* (note 55), 52–3; see also Hans Volz, *Daten der Geschichte der NSDAP*, 8th edn (Berlin and Leipzig 1938), 9; and Jäckel and Kuhn, *Hitler: Sämtliche Aufzeichnungen* (note 1), 530. Hitler and Esser also appeared as representatives of the NSDAP in a complaint against the ban on posters that was heard at the Reich's equivalent of the Home Office on 13 Dec. 1921; see Jäckel and Kuhn, *Hitler: Sämtliche Aufzeichnungen* (note 1), 531.

57. Engelbrechten and Volz, *Wir wandern* (note 55), 68. Hitler wrote to the NSDAP branch in Hagen on 6 March 1922, whereas the next written evidence of his presence in Munich is his speech to an NSDAP meeting in the city on 2 April 1922: see Jäckel and Kuhn, *Hitler: Sämtliche Aufzeichnungen* (note 1), 597–8. In a declaration of 10 April 1922, Hitler writes of a 'lengthy absence from Munich': see Jäckel and Kuhn, *Hitler: Sämtliche Aufzeichnungen* (note 1), 600. Kershaw's reference to a 'fund-raising trip that Hitler made to Berlin in April 1922' rests on a misunderstanding. Hanfstaengl, to whom Kershaw refers at this point, speaks repeatedly and explicitly of a visit to Berlin in April 1923; see Kershaw, *Hitler 1889–1936* (note 9), 189; and Hanfstaengl, *Zwischen Weißem und Braunem Haus* (note 2), 68.

58. The letter is reproduced in full in Gossweiler, *Kapital* (note 10), 558.

59. Gossweiler, *Kapital* (note 10), 559 (letter from Gansser to Burhenne, 2 Aug. 1922).

60. Engelbrechten and Volz, *Wir wandern* (note 55), 68. Joachimsthaler claims, without giving any evidence, that Hitler had been turned out of a pre-booked room at the Hotel Excelsior opposite the Anhalt Station and that the Bechsteins then offered to put him up in their town house at 6 Johannisstraße, a narrow side street off the Friedrichstraße north of the Weidendamm Bridge: see Joachimsthaler, *Hitlers Weg* (note 8), 67.

61. Tyrell, *Führer befiehl* (note 45), 46.

62. Jäckel and Kuhn, *Hitler: Sämtliche Aufzeichnungen* (note 1), 642. The text reproduced by Jäckel and Kuhn follows the original report drawn up by Fritz Geisler on 9 Oct. 1936 for Engelbrechten and Volz, *Wir wandern* (note 55). The version of the text reproduced in this last-named study was revised by Heinrich Lammers, the head of the Reich Chancellery, and supplemented by Volz on the basis of information that he received from others who had heard the speech.

63. Geisler's report quoted by Jäckel and Kuhn, *Hitler: Sämtliche Aufzeichnungen* (note 1), 643 n.6; Engelbrechten and Volz, *Wir wandern* (note 55), 54; Volz, *Daten der Geschichte*

der NSDAP (note 56), 9. See also Lammers' obituary of Emil Gansser in the *Völkischer Beobachter* (Berlin edn) (17 Jan. 1941), 3.

64. Gossweiler, *Kapital* (note 10), 345 (letter of Fritz Detert, 23 Oct. 1937); see also Heiden, *Geburt des dritten Reiches* (note 49), 146.

65. Franz-Willing, *Ursprung der Hitlerbewegung* (note 46), 133; Kershaw, *Hitler 1889–1936* (note 9), 172.

66. Circular from the DSP (10 May 1921) quoted from Franz-Willing, *Ursprung der Hitlerbewegung* (note 46), 133–4.

67. Jäckel and Kuhn, *Hitler: Sämtliche Aufzeichnungen* (note 1), 436; Kershaw, *Hitler 1889–1936* (note 9), 172.

68. For a comprehensive account of this episode, see Tyrell, *Vom 'Trommler'* (note 9), 119–21.

69. Jäckel and Kuhn, *Hitler: Sämtliche Aufzeichnungen* (note 1), 438; Tyrell, *Vom 'Trommler'* (note 9), 125–7; Kershaw, *Hitler 1889–1936* (note 9), 175.

70. See Tyrell, *Vom 'Trommler'* (note 9), 132–4.

71. The DSP was disbanded in the late autumn of 1922, when its members joined the NSDAP; see Franz-Willing, *Ursprung der Hitlerbewegung* (46), 136.

72. Jäckel and Kuhn, *Hitler: Sämtliche Aufzeichnungen* (note 1), 448.

73. Jäckel and Kuhn, *Hitler: Sämtliche Aufzeichnungen* (note 1), 692.

74. Jäckel and Kuhn, *Hitler: Sämtliche Aufzeichnungen* (note 1), 674 (speech in Passau on 7 Aug. 1922).

75. Engelbrechten and Volz, *Wir wandern* (note 55), 54.

76. Kershaw, *Hitler 1889–1936* (note 9), 194; Franz-Willing, *Krisenjahr der Hitlerbewegung* (note 16), 53; Werner Maser, *Die Frühgeschichte der NSDAP: Hitlers Weg bis 1924* (Frankfurt 1965), 383; Heiden, *Geburt des dritten Reiches* (note 49), 123. Kershaw and Franz-Willing date the discussion to 26 Feb. 1923, Heiden and Maser speak only of 'late February'. Since Hitler was present at an NSDAP meeting in Munich of 26 Feb., he cannot have been in Berlin before 27 Feb. 1923. He was back in Munich by 4 March. See Jäckel and Kuhn, *Hitler: Sämtliche Aufzeichnungen* (note 1), 835–7 and 842–4.

77. See the report on his speech of 12 Feb. 1923 in Jäckel and Kuhn, *Hitler: Sämtliche Aufzeichnungen* (note 1), 830.

78. Statement given by Hitler to the Munich People's Court on the third day of his trial (28 Feb. 1924) reproduced from Jäckel and Kuhn, *Hitler: Sämtliche Aufzeichnungen* (note 1), 1111.

79. 'National Socialist Party Rally', report in the *Münchner Neueste Nachrichten* (31 Jan. 1923); and police report on Hitler's speech at an SA meeting in Munich (4 March 1923) in Jäckel and Kuhn, *Hitler: Sämtliche Aufzeichnungen* (note 1), 826 and 842.

80. Fest, *Hitler* (note 5), 29–30; Engl. trans. 14.

81. Rudolf Herz, *Hoffmann & Hitler: Fotografie als Medium des Führer-Mythos* (Munich 1994), 94.

82. Otto Dietrich, *Mit Hitler in die Macht: Persönliche Erlebnisse mit meinem Führer* (Munich 1934), 52. Dietrich later claimed that for safety's sake Hitler systematically prevented photographers from taking photographs of him 'in order to prevent the police from recognizing him and also for political reasons'; see Dietrich, *Zwölf Jahre mit Hitler* (note 8), 198.

83. Hanfstaengl, *Zwischen Weißem und Braunem Haus* (note 2), 69–70.

84. Ulrich Graf, 'Wie ich den Führer kennen lernte', hectograph copy, IfZ Munich, Archives, sign. F14, p.55.

85. Graf, 'Wie ich den Führer kennen lernte' (note 84), 56–8.

86. *Simplicissimus*, xxviii/9 (28 May 1923), 107.

87. Heine was the only Jewish graphic artist on the editorial board. In 1933 he was forced off the board and driven into exile. He died in Stockholm in 1948.

88. As a Jewish artist, Heine used this question with particular skill to turn on its head the anti-Semitic cliché of the 'typically Jewish physiognomy', including, for example, the stereotypically hooked nose.

89. Konrad Heiden claimed that there was something that was 'truthful for all time' in these cartoons, which he incorrectly dates to 1922. Hitler, he concluded, was 'a German condition': Heiden, *Adolf Hitler* (note 11), 134–5. A completely different interpretation is offered by Claudia Schmölders, *Hitlers Gesicht: Eine physiognomische Biographie* (Munich 2000), 46–8.

90. Dietrich, *Zwölf Jahre mit Hitler* (note 8), 198. See also Baldur von Schirach's introduction to Heinrich Hoffmann's iconography, *Hitler wie ihn keiner kennt: 100 Bild-Dokumente aus dem Leben des Führers* (Berlin [1932]), 11–12.

91. Heiden, *Adolf Hitler* (note 11), 134. Heiden witnessed Hitler's political beginnings in Munich from 1919–20 onwards.

92. Hanfstaengl, *Zwischen Weißem und Braunem Haus* (note 2), 74–5. None the less, the photographer, Georg Pahl, is unlikely to have used a film at this date, as Hanfstaengl assumes, but will have used a glass plate to produce the negative.

93. Herz, *Hoffmann & Hitler* (note 81), 94.

94. Georg Pahl, 'Die Jagd nach dem ersten Hitlerbild', undated manuscript in the Picture Archives of the Bundesarchiv, quoted from Herz, *Hoffmann & Hitler* (note 81), 94.

95. Hanfstaengl, *Zwischen Weißem und Braunem Haus* (note 2), 75.

96. See the account in Tyrell, *Vom 'Trommler'* (note 9), 132–4.

97. Herz, *Hoffmann & Hitler* (note 81), 33.

98. Herz, *Hoffmann & Hitler* (note 81), 95–7.

99. *Berliner Illustrirte Zeitung*, xxxii/37 (16 Sept. 1923), 734 (upper left-hand corner).

100. *Berliner Illustrirte Zeitung*, xxxii/40 (7 Oct. 1923), 795.

101. *Berliner Illustrirte Zeitung*, xxxii/45 (11 Nov. 1923), 895. This photograph, however, was taken not by Heinrich Hoffmann but by the photojournalist Philipp Kester.

102. *Berliner Illustrirte Zeitung*, xxxii/46–7 (25 Nov. 1923), 914 (upper left-hand corner). When the image was reprinted, a half-length portrait was preferred and reproduced at a larger size.

103. The editors were the graphic designer John Heartfield, the publisher Wieland Herzfelde and the graphic artist George Grosz. The first two were members of the German Communist Party, which was founded during the winter of 1918/19, while Grosz was a sympathizer. Several issues were impounded before publication was finally banned altogether after the sixth issue in early 1920. Until 1922 the paper continued to appear as the satirical section of *Der Gegner*. Four issues were published illegally between July 1923 and June 1924, in part with the note 'Verlag: Unionsbuchhandlung Zürich', which was no doubt intended to confuse the authorities. For a fuller account, see Herzfelde's introduction to *Die Pleite: Illustrierte Halbmonatsschrift* (Leipzig 1986) (photo-mechanical reproduction of the original issues from 1919–24).

104. 'By tomorrow we shall either have a national government in Germany or we shall be dead.' Thus the wording of the report from Wolff's Telegraph Agency of 9 Nov. 1923.

105. Grosz's cartoons and caricatures appeared in book form and portfolios, most of which were published by Wieland Herzfelde's legendary Malik-Verlag. They include *God With Us* (1920), *The Face of the Ruling Class* (1921) and *The Reckoning is Coming* (1923).

106. The postcard is reproduced in Herz, *Hoffmann & Hitler* (note 81), 99.

107. Herz, *Hoffmann & Hitler* (note 81), 99.

108. When the drawing was reprinted – initially in *The New Face of the Ruling Class* published by Malik-Verlag in Berlin in 1930 – the title was changed to 'Hitler, the saviour'.

109. See also 'Celebration of Teutonic Ancestors' (1921), published in *Ecce homo* as pl. 43.

110. This and the previous quotations are taken from Hitler, *Mein Kampf* (note 21), 395–9; Engl. trans. 326–9. Even during the early weeks of 1922 – shortly before the Munich Party Rally of 29–30 Jan. 1922, Hitler had spoken dismissively of 'dreamers' and 'dangerous fools' in the *völkisch* movement. These people, he went on, 'believed that they could without further ado drive back an entire nation by a thousand years': see Jäckel and Kuhn, *Hitler: Sämtliche Aufzeichnungen* (note 1), 551.

111. See, in particular, Gerhard Schreiber, *Hitler: Interpretationne 1923–1983. Ergebnisse, Methoden und Probleme der Forschung* (Darmstadt 1984), 27–37.

112. *Dokumente und Materialien zur Geschichte der deutschen Arbeiterbewegung,* Series II, vol. vii/2, ed. Institut für Marxismus-Leninismus beim Zentralkomitee der Sozialistischen Einheitspartei Deutschlands (Berlin 1967), 471–2.

113. *Das Tage-Buch* was published in Berlin from 1920. In terms of its editorial profile, it was entirely comparable to *Die Weltbühne*, while its political allegiance may best be described as left-wing liberal to radically democratic with a smattering of socialism.

114. All the Bloch quotations are taken from *Das Tage-Buch,* v/15 (12 April 1924), 474–7. Bloch later revised the text when including it in his 1935 collection *Erbschaft dieser Zeit.*

115. Leo Lania, *Welt im Umbruch: Biographie einer Generation* (Frankfurt 1954), 233. Lania published a pamphlet on his involvement in the Hitler–Ludendorff trial and a book on his experiences and observations during the autumn of 1923 in Munich: Leo Lania, *Der Hitler-Ludendorff-Prozeß* (Berlin 1925).

116. *Berliner Tageblatt* (21 July 1923), quoted in Jäckel and Kuhn, *Hitler: Sämtliche Aufzeichnungen* (note 1), 950. It is significant that the report on the situation in Munich opines that 'No one will view it as a tragedy that at yesterday's meeting of the National Socialists the government was attacked in the strongest possible terms'.

117. Walther G. Oschilewski, *Zeitungen in Berlin im Spiegel der Jahrhunderte* (Berlin 1975), 197–8.

118. *Berliner Volks-Zeitung* (2 Sept. 1921), quoted from Carl von Ossietzky, *Sämtliche Schriften,* 8 vols (Reinbek 1994), i.537.

119. *Berliner Volks-Zeitung* (24 Sept. 1921), quoted from Ossietzky, *Sämtliche Schriften* (note 118), i.547.

120. *Berliner Volks-Zeitung* (27 Sept. 1921), quoted from Ossietzky, *Sämtliche Schriften* (note 118), i.550–1.

121. *Berliner Volks-Zeitung* (4 March 1923), quoted from Ossietzky, *Sämtliche Schriften* (note 118), ii.213.

122. *Berliner Volks-Zeitung* (19 July 1923), quoted from Ossietzky, *Sämtliche Schriften* (note 118), ii.278.

123. *Berliner Volks-Zeitung* (10 Nov. 1923), quoted from Ossietzky, *Sämtliche Schriften* (note 118), ii.309–10.

124. *Vorwärts,* xl/526 (9 Nov. 1923), title-page. As early as June 1920 the Social Democratic *Münchener Post* had reported on an NSDAP event in the Bürgerbräu: 'Among the speakers was Herr Adolf Hitler, who carried on like a stand-up comic.' See Jäckel and Kuhn, *Hitler: Sämtliche Aufzeichnungen* (note 1), 138.

125. Kershaw, *Hitler 1889–1936* (note 9), 223. See also Harold J. Gordon, Jr, *Hitler and the Beer Hall Putsch* (Princeton, NJ, 1972), 573: 'Outside the walls [of his prison] his stature increased daily'; and 580: 'The period after the Putsch was highlighted by Hitler's increasing significance.'

126. Richard F. Hamilton, *Who Voted for Hitler?* (Princeton, NJ, 1982), 78 and 476.

127. Bernd Kruppa, *Rechtsradikalismus in Berlin 1918–1928* (Berlin 1988), 298.

128. Kruppa, *Rechtsradikalismus* (note 127), 298.

129. The number of unemployed persons receiving support from the city's welfare office fell from 234,018 at the end of 1923 to 30,724 at the end of 1924. See *Statistisches Taschenbuch der Stadt Berlin,* 2nd edn (Berlin 1926), 96.

130. Election results from *Statistisches Taschenbuch* (note 129), 221; and Otto Büsch and Wolfgang Haus, *Berlin als Hauptstadt der Weimarer Republik 1919–1933* (Berlin and New York 1987), 70.

131. Kruppa, *Rechtsradikalismus* (note 127), 306.

132. 'Basic Guidelines for the Reconstitution of the National Socialist German Workers' Party' (26 Feb. 1925), reproduced in RSA i.7–9.

133. Volz, *Daten der Geschichte der NSDAP* (note 56), 20.

134. RSA i.37–8.

135. RSA i.38.
136. Winkler, *Der Schein der Normalität*, 235. The figures for Berlin are taken from the *Statistisches Taschenbuch der Stadt Berlin* (note 129), 223.
137. Kruppa, *Rechtsradikalismus* (note 127), 307; and RSA i.38, n.6. The headquarters of the reconstituted NSDAP were initially located at 45 Wiener Straße in the district of Kreuzberg.
138. Engelbrechten and Volz, *Wir wandern* (note 55), 32. Martin Broszat, by contrast, reckons that the number of members was between 100 and 200: see Martin Broszat, 'Die Anfänge der Berliner NSDAP 1926/27', *Vierteljahreshefte für Zeitgeschichte*, viii (1960), 85–118.
139. Kruppa, *Rechtsradikalismus* (note 127), 308.
140. See Kruppa, *Rechtsradikalismus* (note 127), 435 n.70.
141. Engelbrechten and Volz, *Wir wandern* (note 55), 32.
142. *Statistisches Taschenbuch der Stadt Berlin* (note 129), 225.
143. *Die Weltbühne*, xxi/11 (17 March 1925), 386–7.
144. Joachimsthaler, *Hitlers Weg* (note 8), 277.
145. Volz, *Daten der Geschichte der NSDAP* (note 56), 21.
146. Carl von Ossietzky, 'Parteienkrise', *Das Tage-Buch* (1 Nov. 1924), quoted from Ossietzky, *Sämtliche Schriften* (note 118), ii.391.
147. Hanfstaengl dates this visit to 1 April 1924 but it must have taken place at a later date as the court did not announce its verdict until 1 April; see Hanfstaengl, *Zwischen Weißem und Braunem Haus* (note 2), 157.
148. The cartoon uses the basic compositional elements of Ferdinand Keller's canvas *Kaiser Wilhelm the Victorious* (1888); see Jürgen Reiche, 'Symbolgehalt und Bedeutungswandel eines politischen Monuments', *Das Brandenburger Tor 1791–1991: Eine Monographie*, ed. Willmuth Arenhövel and Rolf Bothe (Berlin 1991), 270–316, esp. 278–9; and Schmölders, *Hitlers Gesicht* (note 89), 128–9.
149. Hanfstaengl, *Zwischen Weißem und Braunem Haus* (note 2), 158.
150. Jäckel and Kuhn, *Hitler: Sämtliche Aufzeichnungen* (note 1), 701. A similar point was made in a speech at an NSDAP meeting in Nuremberg on 3 Jan. 1923: 'And so this freedom movement must continue to evolve until the swastika flag wafts from the Berlin Palace as a symbol of the German will': Jäckel and Kuhn, *Hitler: Sämtliche Aufzeichnungen* (note 1), 780.
151. Speech at an NSDAP meeting in Munich on 30 Oct. 1923: Jäckel and Kuhn, *Hitler: Sämtliche Aufzeichnungen* (note 1), 1050.
152. Jäckel and Kuhn, *Hitler: Sämtliche Aufzeichnungen* (note 1), 1054.
153. Not until 1926 was the Königsplatz renamed the Platz der Republik.
154. Graf, 'Wie ich den Führer kennen lernte' (note 84), 57–8.

Chapter 3 · 1922–6: Setbacks in building up the NSDAP in Berlin

1. *Völkischer Beobachter* (Bavaria edn), xl/294 (21 Dec. 1927).
2. Arnolt Bronnen, *Roßbach* (Berlin 1920), 97.
3. *Berliner Tageblatt* (morning edn), cxxxv (24 March 1920), quoted in Bernd Kruppa, *Rechtsradikalismus in Berlin 1918–1928* (Berlin 1988), 123. See also Bronnen, *Roßbach* (note 2), 101: 'The weapons were quickly fetched from their hiding places, and the soldiers were mobilized at the Tiergarten Club while the party was still going on.'
4. Report written by the Prussian State Commissar for the Supervision of Public Order (26 May 1920), quoted in Kruppa, *Rechtsradikalismus* (note 3), 155–6. By far the best account of this whole complex of events is still Emil Julius Gumbel, *Verschwörer: Zur Geschichte und Soziologie der deutschen nationalistischen Geheimbünde 1918–1924* (Vienna 1924, reprinted Heidelberg 1979); see esp. 88–90 for details of Roßbach's organization.

5. Document dated 26 Sept. 1921 quoted in Kruppa, *Rechtsradikalismus* (note 3), 170. Roßbach's organization had an opportunity to do this during the fighting in the Upper Silesian industrial region in the spring of 1921.

6. Gumbel, *Verschwörer* (note 4), 33; see also Detlev Peukert, *Die Weimarer Republik: Krisenjahre der klassichen Moderne* (Frankfurt 1987), 83: 'Ideologically speaking, anti-Marxism, anti-liberalism and anti-Semitism produced an explosive amalgam.' See also Dominique Venner, *Söldner ohne Sold: Die deutschen Freikorps 1918–1923* (Vienna and Berlin 1974), 186–8, where the note of apology is all too apparent. A similar note is struck by Hannsjoachim W. Koch, *Der deutsche Bürgerkrieg: Eine Geschichte der deutschen und österreichischen Freikorps 1918–1923* (Berlin, Frankfurt and Vienna 1978), 322–4. A striking example of the extent to which anti-Semitism was already rampant in the Ehrhardt Brigade in 1919 is given by Helmut Plaas, 'Das Kapp-Unternehmen', *Der Kampf um das Reich*, ed. Ernst Jünger, 2nd edn (Essen [1931]), 164–89, esp. 170 and 174.

7. Werner Maser, *Die Frühgeschichte der NSDAP: Hitlers Weg bis 1924* (Frankfurt 1965), 236 and 266.

8. J. K. Engelbrechten and Hans Volz, *Wir wandern durch das nationalsozialistische Berlin: Ein Führer durch die Gedenkstätten des Kampfes um die Reichshauptstadt* (Munich 1937), 10.

9. Hans Volz, *Daten der Geschichte der NSDAP*, 8th edn (Berlin and Leipzig 1938), 10; Engelbrechten and Volz, *Wir wandern* (note 8), 10 and 181.

10. *Berliner Tageblatt* (morning edn), dccc (21 Nov. 1922).

11. *Göttinger Tagblatt* (9 Dec. 1922), quoted by Georg Franz-Willing, *Krisenjahr der Hitlerbewegung: 1923* (Preußisch Oldendorf 1975), 213–14.

12. Engelbrechten and Volz, *Wir wandern* (note 8), 10.

13. Gumbel, *Verschwörer* (note 4), 88. The original 'Roßbach Storm Troopers' were officially disbanded on 28 Jan. 1920: see Bernhard Sauer, 'Gerhard Roßbach – Hitlers Vertreter für Berlin: Zur Frühgeschichte des Rechtsradikalismus in der Weimarer Republik', *Zeitschrift für Geschichtswissenschaft*, l (2002), 5–21, esp. 7.

14. Kruppa, *Rechtsradikalismus* (note 5), 174.

15. Gumbel, *Verschwörer* (note 4), 88–9); and Sauer, 'Gerhard Roßbach' (note 13), 7.

16. Sauer, 'Gerhard Roßbach' (note 13), 15–16; see also Friedrich Glombowski, *Organisation Heinz: Das Schicksal der Kameraden Schlageters* (Berlin 1934), 127.

17. *Berliner Tageblatt* (14 Nov. 1922), quoted in Gumbel, *Verschwörer* (note 4), 90.

18. Quoted in Kruppa, *Rechtsradikalismus* (note 5), 199. According to Kruppa, the report was 'presumably' written at the end of 1922.

19. Franz-Willing, *Krisenjahr* (note 11), 219.

20. Kurt Caro and Walter Oehme, *Schleichers Aufstieg: Ein Beitrag zur Geschichte der Gegenrevolution* (Berlin 1933), 152: 'Roßbach is instructed to form local branches in north Germany.' See also Kruppa, *Rechtsradikalismus* (note 5), 198); Glombowski, *Organisation Heinz* (note 16), 127; and Hitler's 'Notes for a speech', Eberhard Jäckel and Axel Kuhn (eds), *Hitler: Sämtliche Aufzeichnungen 1905–1924* (Stuttgart 1980), 538.

21. Schlageter, a Freikorps leader in the fighting in the Baltic and Upper Silesia, was later active in resisting the French occupying forces in the Ruhr. He was condemned to death for spying by a French war tribunal and executed in Düsseldorf on 26 May 1923. Many in Germany – not just the chauvinist right – hailed him as a national hero, the NSDAP even treating him as a proto-martyr.

22. BA NS 26/33: Gau Berlin-Brandenburg, unpaginated; Engelbrechten and Volz, *Wir wandern* (note 8), 10; Franz-Willing, *Krisenjahr* (note 11), 219; and Kruppa, *Rechtsradikalismus* (note 5), 200.

23. Sauer, 'Gerhard Roßbach' (note 13), 18; see also *Berliner Tageblatt*, dxv (12 Nov. 1922).

24. Kruppa, *Rechtsradikalismus* (note 5), 201–3.

25. See Kurt Gossweiler, *Kapital, Reichswehr und NSDAP 1919–1924*, 2nd edn (Berlin 1984), 422.

26. Sauer, 'Gerhard Roßbach' (note 13), 18; Franz-Willing, *Krisenjahr* (note 11), 221–2.

27. Kruppa, *Rechtsradikalismus* (note 5), 227–9 and 231.

28. Kruppa, *Rechtsradikalismus* (note 5), 232–4; see also Sauer, 'Gerhard Roßbach' (note 13), 19–20.

29. Bronnen, *Roßbach*, 133.

30. Gumbel, *Verschwörer* (note 4), 96–7; see also John Dornberg, *Der Hitlerputsch, München, 8. und 9. November 1923* (Munich and Vienna 1983), 76.

31. Volz, *Daten der Geschichte der NSDAP* (note 9), 95; Gerhard Roßbach, *Mein Weg durch die Zeit: Erinnerungen und Bekenntnisse* (Weilburg-Lahn 1950), 87–8. Arnolt Bronnen ignores Roßbach's relations with Hitler after the November Putsch. See also Kruppa, *Rechtsradikalismus* (note 5), 314–15.

32. Franz-Willing, *Krisenjahr* (note 11), 220.

33. Anton Joachimsthaler, *Hitlers Weg begann in München: 1913–1923* (Munich 2000), 277.

34. Engelbrechten and Volz, *Wir wandern* (note 8), 18. They describe the Völkische Turnerschaften that were formed from members of the Freikorps and National Youth Movement between 1921 and 1923 as 'the first forerunners of the SA in Berlin' and claim that they had around 400 members. Conversely, Franz-Willing describes the Deutschvölkische Turnerschaften that Roßbach organized as 'kind of hall protection' and reckons that they belonged to the DVFP: see Franz-Willing, *Krisenjahr* (note 11), 222.

35. Joachimsthaler, *Hitlers Weg* (note 33), 312.

36. See Ulrich Graf, 'Wie ich den Führer kennen lernte', hectograph copy, IfZ Munich, Archives, sig. F 14.

37. *Völkischer Beobachter* (7 Sept. 1923), quoted by Jäckel and Kuhn, *Hitler: Sämtliche Aufzeichnungen* (note 20), 999.

38. Jäckel and Kuhn, *Hitler: Sämtliche Aufzeichnungen* (note 20), 1004. In an interview with a representative of the United Press news agency on 30 Sept. 1923 Hitler repeated this turn of phrase almost word for word: 'Our programme is that of the national dictatorship. If Munich does not march on Berlin when the time comes, then Berlin will march on Munich.' See Jäckel and Kuhn, *Hitler: Sämtliche Aufzeichnungen* (note 20), 1022.

39. Herbert Michaelis and Ernst Schraepler (eds), *Ursachen und Folgen: Vom deutschen Zusammenbruch 1918 and 1945 bis zur staatlichen Neuordnung Deutschlands in der Gegenwart*, 25 vols (Berlin 1959), v.203–6.

40. *Deutsche Allgemeine Zeitung*, cdlvii (3 Oct. 1923), reproduced in Michaelis and Schraepler, *Ursachen und Folgen* (note 39), v.207–8. See also Teschner's 'national-revolutionary' view of the putsch in 'Der Küstriner Putsch', *Der Kampf um das Reich*, ed. Ernst Jünger, 2nd edn (Essen [1931]), 277–80.

41. See Koch, *Der deutsche Bürgerkrieg* (note 6), 363; Francis A. Carsten, *The Reichswehr and Politics 1918–1933* (Berkeley, CA, and London 1973), 188; and Thilo Vogelsang, *Reichswehr, Staat und NSDAP: Beiträge zur deutschen Geschichte 1930–1932* (Stuttgart 1962), 36–41 on the complex relations between the Reichswehr and the 'Black Reichswehr'.

42. Koch, *Der deutsche Bürgerkrieg* (note 6), 364; and Vogelsang, *Reichswehr, Staat und NSDAP* (note 41), 41.

43. Koch, *Der deutsche Bürgerkrieg* (note 6), 360.

44. *Berliner Tageblatt* (morning edn), id (24 Oct. 1923), quoted by Kruppa, *Rechtsradikalismus* (note 5), 280.

45. Charles Drage, *Als Hitler nach Canossa ging* (Berlin 1982), 90–1; and Franz-Willing, *Krisenjahr* (note 11), 117.

46. *Berliner Tageblatt* (evening edn), dvi (27 Oct. 1923), quoted by Kruppa, *Rechtsradikalismus* (note 5), 280.

47. The Reich's commissar for the supervision of public order, Dr Kuenzer, in a report to the Reichstag's special committee, or Femeausschuss (26 Feb. 1929), quoted by Caro and Oehme, *Schleichers Aufstieg* (note 20), 134–5.

48. Franz-Willing, *Krisenjahr* (note 11), 308; and Kruppa, *Rechtsradikalismus* (note 5), 261.

49. Carl Mertens, *Verschwörer und Fememörder* (Charlottenburg 1926), 29.

50. Judgement of the jury trial in Landsberg an der Warthe (3 Nov. 1926) in the murder trial against Schiburr *et al.*, quoted by Carsten, *The Reichswehr and Politics* (note 41), 159.

51. Alfred Kruck, *Geschichte des Alldeutschen Verbandes 1890–1939* (Wiesbaden 1954), 197–8.

52. Report by Colonel von Seißer on discussions in Berlin (3 Nov. 1923), quoted by Carsten, *The Reichswehr and Politics* (note 41), 172.

53. Harold J. Gordon, Jr, *Hitler and the Beer Hall Putsch* (Princeton, NJ, 1972), 248.

54. Ian Kershaw, *Hitler 1889–1936: Hubris* (London 1998), 205.

55. *Völkischer Beobachter* (21–22 Oct. 1923), quoted in Jäckel and Kuhn, *Hitler: Sämtliche Aufzeichnungen* (note 20), 1039.

56. SA newsletter no. 2 (26 Oct. 1923), quoted in Jäckel and Kuhn, *Hitler: Sämtliche Aufzeichnungen* (note 20), 1043 (emphasis in original).

57. Maser, *Die Frühgeschichte der NSDAP* (note 7), 317–18.

58. Personal communication from Schlockermann quoted by Maser, *Die Frühgeschichte der NSDAP* (note 7), 458.

59. Thus Gordon, *Hitler and the Beer Hall Putsch* (note 53), 386.

60. *Vossische Zeitung* (morning edn), dxxxiii (10 Nov. 1923) ('Even Without Marching on Berlin').

61. *Völkischer Beobachter* (9 Nov. 1935), quoted by J. K. von Engelbrechten, *Eine braune Armee entsteht: Die Geschichte der Berlin-Brandenburger SA* (Munich 1937), 33; and Engelbrechten and Volz, *Wir wandern* (note 8), 32. Significantly, the fortresses at both Spandau and Fort Hahneberg were home to battalions of the 'Black Reichswehr', the latter under Walter Stennes; see Drage, *Als Hitler nach Canossa ging* (note 45), 85.

62. Gordon, *Hitler and the Beer Hall Putsch* (note 53), 383. Gordon also states that a former army captain by the name of Seydel – a close friend of Röhm – was sent to liaise with the Berlin organizations in the run-up to the planned putsch. Quoting press reports from Mannheim of 14 Nov. 1923, Maser claims that on 9 Nov. between six and seven hundred of Hitler's supporters rioted in the Alexanderplatz and Wilhelmplatz, shouting slogans such as 'Long live Hitler' and 'Kill the Jews', but there is no evidence for such claims in the Berlin press; Maser, *Die Frühgeschichte der NSDAP* (note 7), 462.

63. Kurt Finker, 'Bund Wiking (BW) 1923–1928', *Lexikon zur Parteiengeschichte 1789–1945*, ed. Dieter Fricke, 4 vols (Leipzig 1983–6), i.368–74, esp. 368–9; see also Georg Franz-Willing, *Putsch und Verbotszeit der Hitlerbewegung: November 1923 – Februar 1925* (Preußisch Oldendorf 1977), 34: 'Ehrhardt's task was to plan the march on Berlin.'

64. Kruppa, *Rechtsradikalismus* (note 5), 316.

65. RSA i.329.

66. Heinrich Heim, *Monologe im Führerhauptquartier 1941–1944*, ed. Werner Jochmann (Hamburg 1980), 169 (recorded in the Wolfsschanze on the night of 3/4 Jan. 1942).

67. Jäckel and Kuhn, *Hitler: Sämtliche Aufzeichnungen* (note 20), 1241.

68. See the documentation in Werner Jochmann, *Nationalsozialismus und Revolution: Ursprung und Geschichte der NSDAP in Hamburg 1922–1933. Dokumente* (Frankfurt 1963), 61–3.

69. Jäckel and Kuhn, *Hitler: Sämtliche Aufzeichnungen* (note 20), 1228.

70. Volz, *Daten der Geschichte der NSDAP* (note 9), 95; see also Kurt Finker, 'Frontbann 1924–1926', *Lexikon zur Parteiengeschichte 1789–1945*, ed. Dieter Fricke, 4 vols (Leipzig 1983–6), ii.716–18.

71. Heinrich Bennecke, *Hitler und die SA* (Munich 1962), 110–12 and 116–18; Franz-Willing, *Putsch und Verbotszeit* (note 63), 209–11; and Kershaw, *Hitler 1889–1936* (note 54), 229. See also Otto Gritschneder, *Bewährungsfrist für den Terroristen Adolf H. Der Hitler-Putsch und die bayerische Justiz* (Munich 1990), 107–9.

72. The complete wording of the guidelines is reproduced by Franz-Willing, *Putsch und Verbotszeit* (note 63), 209.

73. Thus the expression of Hagen Schulze, *Weimar: Deutschland 1917–1933*, 2nd edn (Berlin 1983), 268.

74. Heim, *Monologe im Führerhauptquartier* (note 66), 245 (recorded in the Wolfsschanze on the evening of 31 Jan. 1942).

75. Peter Longerich, *Geschichte der SA*, 2nd edn (Munich 2003), 51.

76. RSA ii/1.83–4. The letter was printed and forwarded by Pfeffer to the SA leaders as 'SABE 1 Sturmf[ührer]': see Bennecke, *Hitler und die SA* (note 71), 238.

77. See Kruppa, *Rechtsradikalismus* (note 5), 294. According to Kruppa, the Frontbann was the 'real' NSDAP in Berlin between 1924 and 1926.

78. Kruppa, *Rechtsradikalismus* (note 5), 312–14; Engelbrechten, *Eine braune Arme entsteht* (note 61), 34–5.

79. Kurt Daluege, 'Auf Vorposten für Adolf Hitler: Zehn Jahre Berliner S. A. Eine zeit-gemäße Erinnerung an die ersten Nationalsozialisten von Groß-Berlin', *Völkischer Beobachter* (Berlin edn/Edition A), il/82 (22 March 1936), 2.

80. [Waldemar] Geyer, 'Zum 10. Jahrestag der S. A.-Gruppe Berlin-Brandenburg', *Völkischer Beobachter* (Berlin edn/Edition A), il/82 (22 March 1936), 7.

81. RKO's report of April 1925, quoted by Kruppa, *Rechtsradikalismus* (note 5), 314.

82. Finker, 'Bund Wiking (BW)' (note 63), 369.

83. Walther G. Oschilewski, *Zeitungen in Berlin im Spiegel der Jahrhunderte* (Berlin 1975), 107.

84. Kruppa, *Rechtsradikalismus* (note 5), 315–16.

85. Otto-Ernst Schüddekopf, *Linke Leute von rechts: Die nationalrevolutionären Minderheiten und der Kommunismus in der Weimarer Republik* (Stuttgart 1960), 206–7; and Kruppa, *Rechtsradikalismus* (note 5), 319–21.

86. Quoted from Martin Broszat, 'Die Anfänge der Berliner NSDAP 1926/27', *Vierteljahrshefte für Zeitgeschichte*, viii (1960), 85–118, esp. 95.

87. Kruppa, *Rechtsradikalismus* (note 5), 328–9.

88. Schüddekopf, *Linke Leute von rechts* (note 85), 211; see also Vogelsang, *Reichswehr, Staat und NSDAP* (note 41), 47–9 and the documents reproduced on pp.408–13, detailing how Reichswehr strategists such as Schleicher and Hasse demanded a sober acceptance of the facts: 'We have a republic and cannot change it for practical and personal reasons, nor do we wish to change it,' Hasse explained in his statement to the chief of the army command (30 Nov. 1926): see Vogelsang, *Reichswehr, Staat und NSDAP* (note 41), 409.

89. Volker R. Berghahn, *Der Stahlhelm: Bund der Frontsoldaten* (Düsseldorf 1966). The number of Stahlhelm members rose from 100,000 in 1924 to 225,000 in 1928: see Bernhard Mahlke, 'Stahlhelm-Bund der Frontsoldaten (Stahlhelm) 1918–1935', *Lexikon zur Parteiengeschichte 1789–1945*, 4 vols, ed. Dieter Fricke (Leipzig 1983–6), iv.145–58, esp. 145.

90. See Louis Dupeux, *'Nationalbolschewismus' in Deutschland 1919–1933: Kommunistische Strategie und konservative Dynamik* (Munich 1985); and Armin Mohler, *Die Konservative Revolution in Deutschland 1918–1932: Ein Handbuch*, 3rd edn (Darmstadt 1989). Of some interest for the light that it sheds on the attitude of the NSDAP to the DNVP is a diary entry by the young Horst Wessel before he joined the NSDAP: 'What was initially the spirit of revolution – in other words, opposition to Weimar – soon turned into the gloomiest reaction that welcomed only the past and above all incomprehendingly ignored the workers' question'; quoted in Thomas Oertel, *Horst Wessel: Untersuchung einer Legende* (Cologne 1988), 29.

91. Daluege, 'Auf Vorposten für Adolf Hitler' (note 79); and Engelbrechten and Volz, *Wir wandern* (note 8), 18.

92. Engelbrechten, *Eine braune Armee entsteht* (note 61), 39. Conversely, a piece that appeared in 1934 claims that 'In March 1926, the newly founded SA, with barely three hundred men in the whole of Berlin, took up the fight for the Reich's capital city': see *Sturm 33 Hans Maikowski: Geschrieben von Kameraden des Toten* (Berlin-Schöneberg 1934), 17.

93. Engelbrechten, *Eine braune Armee entsteht* (note 61), 40.
94. Venner, *Söldner ohne Sold* (note 6), 301; Kruppa, *Rechtsradikalismus* (note 5), 441; and www.dhm.de/lemo/html/biografien/Daluege-Kurt.
95. Venner, *Söldner ohne Sold* (note 6), 300–2.
96. Kruppa, *Rechtsradikalismus* (note 5), 438; and Ortel, *Horst Wessel* (note 90), 31–3.
97. Engelbrechten, *Eine braune Armee entsteht* (note 61), 40.
98. Kurt Daluege, 'Sie hielten die Fahne! Zehn Jahre SA und SS in Berlin', *Völkischer Beobachter* (Berlin edn), il/302 (28 Oct. 1936).
99. Geyer, 'Zum 10. Jahrestag der SA-Gruppe Berlin-Brandenburg' (note 80).
100. Kruppa, *Rechtsradikalismus* (note 5), 310.
101. Kruppa, *Rechtsradikalismus* (note 5), 315 and 437.
102. Quoted from Broszat, 'Die Anfänge der Berliner NSDAP' (note 86), 93.
103. *Berliner Abendzeitung*, i/12 (26 May 1926), 2. Ignaz Wrobel was one of several pseudonyms used by Kurt Tucholsky.
104. *Berliner Arbeiterzeitung*, i/6 (11 April 1926), 3.
105. *Berliner Arbeiterzeitung*, i/6 (11 April 1926), 4.
106. *Berliner Arbeiterzeitung*, i/7 (18 April 1926), 2.
107. Broszat, 'Die Anfänge der Berliner NSDAP' (note 86), 89.
108. Julius Lippert, *Im Strom der Zeit: Erlebnisse und Eindrücke* (Berlin 1942), 112.
109. Broszat, 'Die Anfänge der Berliner NSDAP' (note 86), 90; and Gerhard Neuber, 'Faschismus in Berlin: Entwicklung und Wirken der NSDAP und ihrer Organisationen in der Reichshauptstadt 1920–1934' (diss. Univ. East Berlin, 1976), 60.
110. Quoted from Broszat, 'Die Anfänge der Berliner NSDAP' (note 86), 102–3.
111. See also Venner, *Söldner ohne Sold* (note 6), 260 and 303–4; Glombowski, *Organisation Heinz* (note 16), 127–8; and Sauer, 'Gerhard Roßbach' (note 13), 17–19.
112. Patrick Moreau, *Nationalsozialismus von links: Die 'Kampfgemeinschaft Revolutionärer Nationalsozialisten' und die 'Schwarze Front' Otto Strassers 1930–1935* (Stuttgart 1984), 18–20.
113. In May 1926 the Ruhr Gau had more members than any other outside Bavaria: it is said to have had 3,730; see Gerhard Schulz, *Aufstieg des Nationalsozialismus: Krise und Revolution in Deutschland* (Frankfurt, Berlin and Vienna 1976), 384–5.
114. Moreau, *Nationalsozialismus von links* (note 112), 26.
115. Elke Fröhlich (ed.), *Die Tagebücher von Joseph Goebbels*, Part I: *Aufzeichnungen 1923–1941*, 9 vols (Munich 1997–2006), i/2.55–6 (15 Feb. 1926).
116. Fröhlich, *Die Tagebücher von Joseph Goebbels* (note 115), i/2.72, 75, 96, 103 and 112–13.
117. Fröhlich, *Die Tagebücher von Joseph Goebbels* (note 115), i/2.126–7.
118. Appendix to the report of 26 Aug. 1926 reproduced by Helmut Heiber (ed.), *Das Tagebuch von Joseph Goebbels 1925/26* (Stuttgart [1961]), 111–12.
119. Fröhlich, *Die Tagebücher von Joseph Goebbels* (note 115), i/2.132 (entry of 17 Sept. 1926).
120. The full wording of the letter appears in Heiber, *Das Tagebuch von Joseph Goebbels* (note 118), 112–13.
121. Fröhlich, *Die Tagebücher von Joseph Goebbels* (note 115), i/2.141.
122. Fröhlich, *Die Tagebücher von Joseph Goebbels* (note 115), i/2.143.
123. Fröhlich, *Die Tagebücher von Joseph Goebbels* (note 115), i/2.143.
124. *Berliner Arbeiterzeitung*, i/36 (7 Nov. 1926), 8.

Chapter 4 · 1926: Goebbels takes over the running of the party in Berlin

1. Quoted from Ralf Georg Reuth, *Goebbels: Eine Biographie* (Munich and Zurich 1990), 114.
2. 'Der Gau Berlin steht!', *Berliner Arbeiterzeitung*, i/38 (21 Nov. 1926), 3.
3. Hermann Hillger (ed.), *Kürschners Deutscher Reichstag 1928* (Berlin n.d.), 526.

4. Goebbels wrote his doctorate at the University of Heidelberg on the minor dramatist and member of the Berlin Romantic generation Wilhelm von Schütz (1776–1847). His supervisor was the Jewish Germanist Max von Waldberg.

5. Joseph Goebbels, 'Vom Geiste unserer Zeit', *Westdeutsche Landeszeitung* (24 Jan. 1922), quoted from Reuth, *Goebbels* (note 1), 57.

6. Quoted from Reuth, *Goebbels* (note 1), 58.

7. Diary of Joseph Goebbels (1897–1923) in Elke Fröhlich (ed.), *Die Tagebücher von Joseph Goebbels: Sämtliche Fragmente*, 4 vols (Munich 1987), i/1.21–9.

8. Fröhlich, *Die Tagebücher von Joseph Goebbels* (note 7), i/1.25.

9. Under the heading 'From January to August 1923 in Cologne (Dresdner Bank'), in Fröhlich, *Die Tagebücher von Joseph Goebbels* (note 7), i/1.25–6.

10. Fröhlich, *Die Tagebücher von Joseph Goebbels* (note 7), i/1.28–9.

11. Reuth, *Goebbels* (note 1), 71; and Helmut Heiber, *Joseph Goebbels* (Berlin 1962), 40.

12. Elke Fröhlich (ed.), *Die Tagebücher von Joseph Goebbels*, Part I: *Aufzeichnungen 1923–1941*, 9 vols (Munich 1997–2006), i/1.155–6 (27 June 1924).

13. Fröhlich, *Die Tagebücher von Joseph Goebbels* (note 12), i/1.156 (30 June 1924).

14. Both quotations from Fröhlich, *Die Tagebücher von Joseph Goebbels* (note 12), i/1.157.

15. Fröhlich, *Die Tagebücher von Joseph Goebbels* (note 12), i/1.161 (4 July 1924).

16. Fröhlich, *Die Tagebücher von Joseph Goebbels* (note 12), i/1.201 (19 Aug. 1924).

17. Fröhlich, *Die Tagebücher von Joseph Goebbels* (note 12), i/1.199–201 (19 Aug. 1924).

18. Fröhlich, *Die Tagebücher von Joseph Goebbels* (note 12), i/1.206 (20 Aug. 1924).

19. Fröhlich, *Die Tagebücher von Joseph Goebbels* (note 12), i/1.218 (5 Sept. 1924).

20. Fröhlich, *Die Tagebücher von Joseph Goebbels* (note 12), i/1.227 (22 Sept. 1924).

21. Reuth, *Goebbels* (note 1), 87.

22. Fröhlich, *Die Tagebücher von Joseph Goebbels* (note 12), i/1.223 (15 Sept. 1924) and 284 (23 March 1925).

23. Joseph Goebbels, 'Politisches Tagebuch', *Völkische Freiheit* (1 Jan. 1925), quoted in Heiber, *Joseph Goebbels* (note 11), 44.

24. *Völkischer Beobachter* (17 July 1925), quoted in RSA i.118; see also Reuth, *Goebbels* (note 1), 90.

25. Fröhlich, *Die Tagebücher von Joseph Goebbels* (note 12), i/1.344 (21 Aug. 1925); similar remarks are found in the entries for 2 and 12 Oct. 1925 (i/1.360 and 364).

26. Fröhlich, *Die Tagebücher von Joseph Goebbels* (note 12), i/1.365 (14 Oct. 1925).

27. Fröhlich, *Die Tagebücher von Joseph Goebbels* (note 12), i/1.375 (6 Nov. 1925) and 379 (23 Nov. 1925).

28. On the subject of the NSDAP's peripatetic lecturers, see Udo Kissenkoetter, *Gregor Straßer und die NSDAP* (Stuttgart 1978), 31.

29. Reuth, *Goebbels* (note 1), 87.

30. Fröhlich, *Die Tagebücher von Joseph Goebbels* (note 12), i/1.241 (28 Oct. 1924), 243 (4 Nov. 1924) and 277 (8 March 1925).

31. Fröhlich, *Die Tagebücher von Joseph Goebbels* (note 12), i/1.380 (28 Nov. 1925). On 27 Nov. 1925 Goebbels spoke on the subject of the 'League of Nations and the Security Pact' at the Kriegervereinshaus on the Chausseestraße; see J. K. Engelbrechten and Hans Volz, *Wir wandern durch das nationalsozialistische Berlin: Ein Führer durch die Gedenkstätten des Kampfes um die Reichshauptstadt* (Munich 1937), 144.

32. Fröhlich, *Die Tagebücher von Joseph Goebbels* (note 12), i/2.52 (6 Feb. 1926).

33. Fröhlich, *Die Tagebücher von Joseph Goebbels* (note 12), i/2.94 (10 June 1926).

34. Joseph Goebbels, *Kampf um Berlin: Der Anfang*, 3rd edn (Munich 1934), 27.

35. RSA i.22.

36. On 22 May 1926, for example, Hitler inveighed against the 'international blood-sucking society' which at the end of the period of inflation in Germany emigrated to Paris from Berlin's Grenadierstraße 'with long flat soles'. He was referring to the East European Jews from the suburb of Spandau. In a speech at an NSDAP meeting in Schleiz on 18 Jan. 1927 he mentioned the Kurfürstendamm, whose shops contained 'no non-Jews', i.e. only Jews; see RSA ii/1.134.

37. Speech at an NSDAP meeting in Weimar on 28 Oct. 1925; RSA i.196.
38. Speech at an NSDAP meeting in Munich on 9 April 1929; RSA iii/2.190.
39. Fröhlich, *Die Tagebücher von Joseph Goebbels* (note 12), i/2.107 (15 July 1926).
40. Fröhlich, *Die Tagebücher von Joseph Goebbels* (note 12), i/1.196 (13 Aug. 1924) and 219 (8 Sept. 1924).
41. Fröhlich, *Die Tagebücher von Joseph Goebbels* (note 12), i/2.73 (13 April 1926).
42. Henry Picker, *Hitlers Tischgespräche im Führerhauptquartier*, 4th edn (Stuttgart 1983), 381–2 (entry of 24 June 1942).
43. Fröhlich, *Die Tagebücher von Joseph Goebbels* (note 12), i/2.144–5 (1 and 6 Nov. 1926).
44. Fröhlich, *Die Tagebücher von Joseph Goebbels* (note 12), i/2.146–7 (8 and 11 Nov. 1926).
45. Joseph Goebbels, *Das erwachende Berlin* (Munich 1934), 11 and 24–5.
46. Gert Sachs, 'Vom Roten Berlin zur Hauptstadt des Dritten Reiches: Eine Unterredung mit Dr. Goebbels', *Völkischer Beobachter* (Berlin edn) (29 Oct. 1936).
47. Goebbels, *Kampf um Berlin* (note 34), 33–4.
48. Fröhlich, *Die Tagebücher von Joseph Goebbels* (note 12), i/2.88 (24 May 1926).
49. Goebbels, *Kampf um Berlin* (note 34), 20.
50. Konrad Heiden, *Geburt des dritten Reiches: Die Geschichte des Nationalsozialismus bis Herbst 1933* (Zurich 1934), 229.
51. Goebbels, *Kampf um Berlin* (note 34), 21.
52. Martin Broszat, 'Die Anfänge der Berliner NSDAP 1926/27', *Vierteljahrshefte für Zeitgeschichte*, viii (1960), 85–118, esp. 104 (Reinhold Muchow's report for Nov. 1926 on the 'General political situation in Berlin and the struggle of the NSDAP'). The Kriegervereinshaus was a traditional meeting place for the extreme right wing in Berlin: see Bernd Kruppa, *Rechtsradikalismus in Berlin 1918–1928* (Berlin 1988), 44. The building in the Chausseestraße still exists.
53. Joseph Goebbels, *Vom Kaiserhof zur Reichskanzlei: Eine historische Darstellung in Tagebuchblättern* (Munich 1934), 204.
54. Fröhlich, *Die Tagebücher von Joseph Goebbels* (note 12), i/2.148 (12 Nov. 1926). Heinz Oskar Hauenstein had been one of the leaders of the NSDAP in Berlin in 1922/3 and had been in regular contact with Hitler. He was expelled from the party on 27 Oct. 1926, a move confirmed by Hitler on 5 Nov.
55. Goebbels, *Kampf um Berlin* (note 34), 23–4. On the particular conditions in Spandau, see Oliver C. Gliech, 'Die Spandauer SA 1926 bis 1933: Eine Studie zur nationalsozialistischen Gewalt in einem Berliner Bezirk', *Berlin-Forschungen III*, ed. Wolfgang Ribbe (Berlin 1988), 107–205, esp. 131–2; see also Kruppa, *Rechtsradikalismus in Berlin* (note 52), 297.
56. Fröhlich, *Die Tagebücher von Joseph Goebbels* (note 12), i/2.147 and 149 (11 and 15 Nov. 1926); and Reuth, *Goebbels* (note 1), 110–11.
57. This is indicated by an entry in the police surveillance records for this period: 'Stayed in Berlin from 9 to 12 Nov. 1926 incl. During this time held various discussions with Dr Göbbels [*sic*] and the National Socialist deputies about retaining the *völkisch* association': Institut für Zeitgeschichte – Archiv, F 19/17, Karte Nr. III.
58. Sachs, 'Vom Roten Berlin' (note 46); and Goebbels, *Kampf um Berlin* (note 34), 23.
59. Goebbels, *Kampf um Berlin* (note 34), 23.
60. Fröhlich, *Die Tagebücher von Joseph Goebbels* (note 12), i/1.282–4 (entries from 18 March 1925 onwards); see also Roger Manvell and Heinrich Fraenkel, *Doctor Goebbels: His Life and Death* (London and New York 2010), 52–4; and Reuth, *Goebbels* (note 1), 89–91.
61. Helmut Heiber (ed.), *Das Tagebuch von Joseph Goebbels 1925/26* (Stuttgart [1961]), 114 (letter from Erich Schmiedicke in Berlin to Joseph Goebbels in Elberfeld, 28 Oct. 1926).
62. The circular is reproduced in full in Heiber, *Das Tagebuch von Joseph Goebbels* (note 61), 115–16.

63. *Berliner Arbeiterzeitung*, i/38 (21 Nov. 1926), 3.
64. Fröhlich, *Die Tagebücher von Joseph Goebbels* (note 12), i/1.300–2 (entries for 2–12 May 1925).
65. Broszat, 'Die Anfänge der Berliner NSDAP' (note 52), 106 (Reinhold Muchow's report for Dec. 1926).
66. Goebbels, *Kampf um Berlin* (note 34), 32–3.
67. *Berliner Arbeiterzeitung*, i/8 (25 April 1926), 4 ('Groß-Berlin') and 6 ('Volksentscheid').
68. Otto Büsch and Wolfgang Haus, *Berlin als Hauptstadt der Weimarer Republik 1919–1933* (Berlin and New York 1987), 444.
69. J. K. von Engelbrechten, *Eine braune Armee entsteht: Die Geschichte der Berlin-Brandenburger SA* (Munich 1937), 49.
70. The book contains the copyright notice for 1932 but the first edition had already appeared in 1931. On 19 Nov. 1930 Goebbels noted in his diary that he was even thinking of writing a novel on the subject of the 'battle for Berlin'; see Fröhlich, *Die Tagebücher von Joseph Goebbels* (note 12), ii/1.285. His later colleague at the Propaganda Ministry, Wilfrid Bade, published a novelistic account of this period under the title *Die SA erobert Berlin* (Munich 1933). On p.24 he has Goebbels arriving at Friedrichstraße Station on 9 Nov. 1926.
71. Broszat, 'Die Anfänge der Berliner NSDAP' (note 52), 104 (Reinhold Muchow's report for Nov. 1926).
72. Quoted from Reuth, *Goebbels* (note 1), 113. Reuth's note 24 on p.635 makes it clear that the newspaper from which he is quoting is not the Social Democratic *Volksblatt*, as he erroneously claims.
73. Goebbels, *Kampf um Berlin* (note 34), 49 and 44.
74. Goebbels, *Kampf um Berlin* (note 34), 42.
75. Goebbels, *Kampf um Berlin* (note 34), 46 and 48.
76. *Berliner Arbeiterzeitung*, i/43 (26 Dec. 1926), 3.
77. *Berliner Arbeiterzeitung*, ii/1–2 (9 Jan. 1927), 2.
78. Goebbels, *Kampf um Berlin* (note 34), 60–1.
79. Broszat, 'Die Anfänge der Berliner NSDAP' (note 52), 108 (Reinhold Muchow's report for Jan. 1927).
80. Goebbels, *Kampf um Berlin* (note 34), 60–2.
81. *Spandauer Zeitung* quoted by Gliech, 'Die Spandauer SA' (note 55), 129.
82. 'Nationalsozialistische Deutsche Arbeiterpartei, Gau Berlin-Brandenburg, Dr. Goebbels, An die Freunde im Reich!', *Berliner Arbeiterzeitung*, ii/6 (6 Feb. 1927), 1.
83. Engelbrechten, *Eine braune Armee entsteht* (note 69), 53.
84. Broszat, 'Die Anfänge der Berliner NSDAP' (note 52), 109 (Reinhold Muchow's report for Jan. 1927).
85. Horst Wessel's diary jottings in the Bundesarchiv NS 26/1280 are quoted here from the facsimile and transcription in Thomas Oertel, *Horst Wessel: Untersuchung einer Legende* (Cologne 1988), after p.58.
86. Broszat, 'Die Anfänge der Berliner NSDAP' (note 52), 109 (Reinhold Muchow's report for Jan. 1927).
87. Goebbels, *Kampf um Berlin* (note 34), 28.
88. Reuth, *Goebbels* (note 1), 115.
89. In the Reichstag elections on 20 May 1928 the KPD increased its share of the vote from 29.3 per cent in 1924 to 40.4 per cent, while the SPD fell slightly from 34.4 to 34 per cent; see Büsch and Haus, *Berlin als Hauptstadt* (note 68), 378.
90. *Berliner Arbeiterzeitung*, ii/1–2 (9 Jan. 1927), 3.
91. Goebbels, *Kampf um Berlin* (note 34), 64.
92. Wolfgang Sauer, 'Die Mobilmachung der Gewalt', *Die nationalsozialistische Machtergreifung: Studien zur Errichtung des totalitären Herrschaftssystems in Deutschland 1933/34*, ed. Karl Dietrich Bracher and others, 2nd edn (Cologne and Opladen 1962), 685–966, esp. 831.

93. Eugen Hadamovsky, *Propaganda und nationale Macht: Die Organisation der öffentlichen Meinung für die nationale Politik* (Oldenburg 1933), 22, 39, 45 and 47–8. The book is dedicated to 'the master of political propaganda, Dr Joseph Goebbels'.
94. 'Nazionalsozialistische Deutsche Arbeiterpartei' (note 82) (emphasis in the original).
95. 'Goebbels, Parteigenossen und Parteigenossinnen! Nationalsozialisten aus Berlin! Kameraden der S. A.!', *Berliner Arbeiterzeitung*, ii/2 (6 Feb. 1927), 3 (emphasis in the original).
96. Broszat, 'Die Anfänge der Berliner NSDAP' (note 52), 111 (Reinhold Muchow's report for Feb. 1927).
97. Goebbels, *Kampf um Berlin* (note 34), 64–71.
98. Anon., *Der unbekannte SA-Mann* (Munich 1930), 42–3, quoted by Engelbrechten and Volz, *Wir wandern* (note 31), 139.
99. Goebbels, *Kampf um Berlin* (note 34), 75.
100. 'Zusammenstöße am Wedding: Zwischen Kommunisten und Nationalsozialisten', *Berliner Tageblatt* (morning edn) (12 Feb. 1927).
101. 'Blutige Kämpfe am Wedding: Faschisten und Schupo gegen Arbeiter', *Die Welt am Abend*, v/36 (12 Feb. 1927); and *Berliner Morgenpost* (12 Feb. 1927).
102. Heiber, *Das Tagebuch von Joseph Goebbels* (note 61), 118 (Bericht der Abteilung I A, Außendienst, VII. Geschäftsstelle, 28 March 1927).
103. Broszat, 'Die Anfänge der Berliner NSDAP' (note 52), 116–17 (Reinhold Muchow's special report on the events at Lichterfelde-Ost Station on 20 March 1927).
104. The Communist *Welt am Abend* published two photographs of the carriage on its front page on 22 March 1927, one of them depicting the outside, the other the inside. The photograph of the outside of the carriage shows not only the damage caused by the hail of stones thrown by the SA but also a number of bullet holes. According to the indictment of 9 Jan. 1928, there were twelve such holes. In other words, the SA not only threw stones at the carriage, but also shot at it.
105. Indictment of the Public Prosecutor at the District Court I (9 Jan. 1928): II P J 62/27, Landesarchiv Berlin, Rep. 58, Zug. 399, no. 302, vol. vi.
106. *Berliner Tageblatt* (evening edn) (21 March 1927). The report appeared not on the front page but on p.5 of the paper's main section. Its claim that 'some 250' National Socialists took part in the attack is a gross underestimation.
107. 'Schüsse auf Bahnhof Lichterfelde-Ost', *Vossische Zeitung* (22 March 1927), 4.
108. 'Zusammenstöße mit Nationalsozialisten', *Vorwärts* (evening edn), xliv/135 (21 March 1927).
109. *Die Welt am Abend*, v/67 (21 March 1927). Only the *Welt am Abend* and the Communist Party's central organ, *Rote Fahne*, reported the events on their front pages.
110. 'Kommunisten-Sturm auf einen Bahnhof', *Deutsche Zeitung* (21 March 1927).
111. 'Neue Verhaftungen von Rechtsradikalen', *Vossische Zeitung* (23 March 1927).
112. 'Die Ausschreitungen im Berliner Westen', *Berliner Tageblatt* (evening edn), lvi/139 (23 March 1927).
113. 'Die Exzesse im Berliner Westen: Waffensuche bei den Völkischen', *Berliner Tageblatt* (evening edn), lvi/137 (22 March 1927).
114. Broszat, 'Die Anfänge der Berliner NSDAP' (note 52), 118 (Reinhold Muchow's special report on the events at Lichterfelde-Ost Station on 20 March 1927). Goebbels was in his car at the head of the SA columns. In a witness statement dated 21 March 1927, he told the police that he wanted to study the mood of the passers-by: II P J 62/27, Landesarchiv Berlin, Rep. 58, Zug. 399, no. 201, vol. i.
115. Goebbels, *Kampf um Berlin* (note 34), 102.
116. Heiden, *Geburt des dritten Reiches* (note 50), 235.
117. Broszat, 'Die Anfänge der Berliner NSDAP' (note 52), 118 (Reinhold Muchow's special report on the events at Lichterfelde-Ost Station on 20 March 1927).
118. 'Ein Blutsonntag in Berlin', *Berliner Arbeiterzeitung*, ii/13 (27 March 1927), 5.

119. Bade, *Die SA erobert Berlin* (note 70), 86–9. Bade presumably used Goebbels' diary when drawing up his report.
120. Bade, *Die SA erobert Berlin* (note 70), 90.
121. Goebbels, *Kampf um Berlin* (note 34), 102.
122. 'Ein Blutsonntag in Berlin', *Berliner Arbeiterzeitung*, ii/13 (27 March 1927), 5.
123. Bade, *Die SA erobert Berlin* (note 70), 89.

Chapter 5 · 1927–8: The successes of a dangerously misjudged splinter group

1. Joseph Goebbels, 'Rund um die Gedächtniskirche', *Der Angriff*, ii/4 (23 Jan. 1928).
2. *Der Angriff*, ii/20 (14 May 1928).
3. In 1920 the party troops styled themselves the 'Gymnastics and Sports Division', but by 1922 at the latest the term *Sturmabteilung* (Storm Division) had already gained widespread currency. From then on the phrase 'Sports Division' was used only as a cover.
4. *Berliner Tageblatt*, lvi/204 (1 May 1927) (morning edn).
5. RSA ii/1.250, n.3.
6. RSA ii/1.283, nn.1–2.
7. See p. 48 above.
8. Anon., *Berlin für Kenner: Ein Bärenführer bei Tag und Nacht durch die deutsche Reichshauptstadt* (Berlin [1912]), 81.
9. Hans-Werner Klünner, 'Der Clou 1927 wieder der Clou', publicity brochure for Hoffmann & Retschlag for the 'Clou Concert Hall', *Berlin-Archiv*, supplement, BE 01162 (Braunschweig [*c.* 1994]).
10. 'Adolf Hitler bei uns', *Berliner Arbeiterzeitung*, ii/19 (8 May 1927) (emphasis in original); *Völkischer Beobachter* (3 May 1927); and Adolf Dresler (ed.), *Fritz Maier-Hartmann: Die Sammlung Rehse. Dokumente der Zeitgeschichte* (Munich 1928), 187.
11. *Völkischer Beobachter* (5 May 1927); 'Lord, let us not be cowards', quoted from RSA ii/1.287–90.
12. *Vossische Zeitung* (3 May 1927); *Berliner Tageblatt*, lvi/205 (2 May 1927) (evening edn). The official account of the party's history later claimed that 'Jewish gutter journalists' had had recourse 'to the basest lies and distortions' in reporting Hitler's speech at the Clou: see J. K. von Engelbrechten, *Eine braune Armee entsteht: Die Geschichte der Berlin-Brandenburger SA* (Munich 1937), 59.
13. *Vorwärts*, xliv/205 (2 May 1927) (evening edn).
14. *Die Welt am Abend*, v/101 (2 May 1927).
15. For an informative insight into the Reich's self-styled prophets, faith healers and sectarian leaders, see Rudolf Olden (ed.), *Das Wunderbare oder Die Verzauberten: Propheten in deutscher Krise* (Berlin 1932).
16. 'Adolf Hitlers Rede in Berlin', *Deutsche Zeitung* (2 May 1927) (evening edn).
17. Ian Kershaw, *The 'Hitler Myth': Image and Reality in the Third Reich* (Oxford 2001).
18. *Berliner Arbeiterzeitung*, ii/15 (10 April 1927); ii/16 (17 April 1927); and ii/17 (24 April 1927).
19. 'Adolf Hitler bei uns', *Berliner Arbeiterzeitung*, ii/19 (8 May 1927).
20. Carl von Ossietzky, 'Stahlhelm ante portas', *Die Weltbühne*, xxiii/18 (3 May 1927), 689; and xxiii/19 (10 May 1927), 730.
21. Artur Schweriner, 'Hitlers neueste Hochburg', *C. V.-Zeitung* (20 May 1927), 283.
22. *Berliner Lokal-Anzeiger* (2 May 1927) (evening edn). It is difficult to see how Reuth reached his conclusion that 'only a few regional papers' reported on Hitler's visit to Berlin, while the 'leading papers' ignored it because 'there were no violent demonstrations': see Ralf Georg Reuth, *Goebbels: Eine Biographie* (Munich and Zurich 1990), 119.
23. The Chief Public Prosecutor at District Court I, Berlin-Mitte (23 Nov. 1927); 1 J 372/27, LA Berlin, Rep. 58, Zug. 399, no. 27.

24. *Germania* (5 May 1927); and *Berliner Börsen-Courier* (5 May 1927). The quotations from the public prosecutor's indictment at Berlin's District Court I are from Dietz Bering, *Kampf um Namen: Bernhard Weiß gegen Joseph Goebbels* (Stuttgart 1991), 128–9.

25. *Deutsche Allgemeine Zeitung* (6 May 1927), quoted by Viktor Reimann, *Dr. Joseph Goebbels* (Vienna and Munich 1976), 94.

26. Indictment quoted by Bering, *Kampf um Namen* (note 24), 129.

27. Joseph Goebbels, *Kampf um Berlin: Der Anfang*, 3rd edn (Munich 1934), 146. In his own *Nationalsozialistische Briefe* (1 April 1927), Goebbels had already advised the chairmen of NSDAP meetings to respond to political opponents as follows whenever they asked to make a point of order: 'If you dare once more to disrupt the calm and objective course of the meeting, I cannot guarantee that an appropriate scalp massage won't make you a useful member of human society again'; quoted in *Vorwärts*, xliv/214 (7 May 1927) (morning edn).

28. Goebbels, *Kampf um Berlin* (note 27), 146 and 148.

29. *Berliner Tageblatt*, lvi/211 (5 May 1927) (evening edn). This article appeared under the headline 'The National Socialist Scandal' and was the first piece on Goebbels and the Berlin NSDAP that the *Berliner Tageblatt* published on its front page.

30. *Berliner Tageblatt*, lvi/212 (6 May 1927) (morning edn).

31. Goebbels, *Kampf um Berlin* (note 27), 152–3.

32. Hans Schwarz van Berk, 'Die Stimme der Verfolgten', in Joseph Goebbels, *Der Angriff: Aufsätze aus der Kampfzeit*, 2nd edn (Munich 1935), 17.

33. On 31 May 1927 former Lieutenant Edmund Heines was banned from the party following his criticism of the NSDAP and the SA leadership in Munich. Heines had joined the Roßbach Freikorps in 1918–19 and had been an SA leader in Munich since 1926–7; see RSA ii/1.320–2 and 333 (documents 130 and 137).

34. Konrad Heiden, *Geburt des dritten Reiches: Die Geschichte des Nationalsozialismus bis Herbst 1933* (Zurich 1934), 236.

35. RSA ii/1.419–20.

36. Goebbels, *Kampf um Berlin* (note 27), 153.

37. J. K. Engelbrechten and Hans Volz, *Wir wandern durch das nationalsozialistische Berlin: Ein Führer durch die Gedenkstätten des Kampfes um die Reichshauptstadt* (Munich 1937), 199.

38. 'Adolf Hitler vor dem Freiheitsbund', *Völkischer Beobachter* (8/9 May 1927), quoted in RSA ii/1.290; and 'Hitler im Freiheitsbund', *Berliner Arbeiterzeitung*, ii/19 (8 May 1927).

39. RSA ii/1.384.

40. Thus Reuth, *Goebbels* (note 22), 124 and 637 n.73, where he refers to minutes of the meeting kept by the Munich Political Police.

41. Reuth, *Goebbels* (note 22), 124 and 637 n.73.

42. Bayerisches Hauptstaatarchiv, Munich, Allg. StA, Sonderabgabe I, no. 1762, quoted by Ernst Deuerlein (ed.), *Der Aufstieg der NSDAP in Augenzeugenberichten* (Düsseldorf 1968), 286–7.

43. On 27 May 1927 the Munich police banned both the planned meeting of the Reichsbanner and the planned countermarches by the NSDAP and United Patriotic Associations after violent confrontations had taken place in Giesing two days earlier; see RSA ii/1.312 n.3 and 322 n.2. The Reichsbanner Schwarz-Rot-Gold was a largely socio-democratic organization that had been formed in 1924 to protect the Weimar Republic and the parliamentary system.

44. Undated report by the Munich police concerning the speech that Hitler gave at an NSDAP meeting in Munich on 23 May 1927, StA Munich, Polizeidirektion München 6737, quoted from RSA ii/1.313.

45. Adolf Hitler, *Mein Kampf* (Munich 1933), 613–16; Engl. trans. Ralph Manheim as *Mein Kampf* (London 2002), 498–9.

46. Goebbels, *Kampf um Berlin* (note 27), 180–2.

47. *Berliner Tageblatt*, lvi/224 (13 May 1927) (morning edn); and 'Die nationalsozialistischen Ausschreitungen', *Berliner Tageblatt*, lvi/225 (13 May 1927) (evening edn).
48. 'Nationalsozialistische Prügelhelden', *Berliner Tageblatt*, lvi/237 (20 May 1927) (evening edn); and 'Reichsbannerleute vogelfrei?', *Berliner Tageblatt*, lvi/242 (24 May 1927) (morning edn).
49. Elke Fröhlich (ed.), *Die Tagebücher von Joseph Goebbels*, Part I: *Aufzeichnungen 1923–1941*, 9 vols (Munich 1997–2006), i/2.139 (16 Oct. 1926); see also Erich Stockhorst, *5000 Köpfe: Wer war was im 3. Reich* (Wiesbaden n. d.), 418.
50. Report of Abteilung I A, Außendienst, quoted as Document 5 by Helmut Heiber (ed.), *Das Tagebuch von Joseph Goebbels 1925/26* (Stuttgart [1961]), 117–19, esp. 117. It is claimed here, however, that a section of the membership did not play an active role in the party's demonstrations and other meetings.
51. Thomas Oertel, *Horst Wessel: Untersuchung einer Legende* (Cologne 1988), 21, 31–2, 39–40 and 50–4.
52. Bundesarchiv MS 26/1280, quoted in Oertel, *Horst Wessel* (note 51), 51 and 59.
53. Bundesarchiv NS 26/1280, quoted in Oertel, *Horst Wessel* (note 51), 51 (letter of 23 Nov. 1926); see also Bernd Kruppa, *Rechtsradikalismus in Berlin 1918–1928* (Berlin 1988), 319.
54. Kruppa, *Rechtsradikalismus in Berlin* (note 53), 330; on Kube's change of allegiance, see also the *Völkischer Beobachter* (15 Dec. 1927).
55. *Berliner Arbeiterzeitung*, ii/7 (13 Feb. 1927); Albrecht Tyrell, *Führer befiehl . . . Selbstzeugnisse aus der 'Kampfzeit' der NSDAP: Dokumentation und Analyse* (Düsseldorf 1969), 145; translation from Ian Kershaw, *Hitler 1889–1936* (London 1998), 297.
56. Otto Büsch and Wolfgang Haus, *Berlin als Hauptstadt der Weimarer Republik 1919–1933* (Berlin and New York 1987), 323–4; and Kruppa, *Rechtsradikalismus in Berlin* (note 53), 330–1.
57. On the occasion of a speech to a general meeting of the NSDAP in Munich on 30 July 1927; see RSA ii/1.422.
58. Goebbels, *Kampf um Berlin* (note 27), 168 and 174.
59. Goebbels, *Kampf um Berlin* (note 27), 180. On p.169 a poster is reproduced inviting interested parties to a public 'election meeting of National Socialist deputies' in the Hohenzollern Rooms in Charlottenburg on 30 June 1927. The main speaker is 'Dr Goebbels'.
60. *B. Z. am Mittag* (13 May 1927).
61. Goebbels, *Kampf um Berlin* (note 27), 168–72. Goebbels did not consider it beneath himself to keep repeating this 'explanation': 'The necessary consequence of such bans [including those on the National Socialists' subsidiary organizations] was invariably recurrent political excesses in the streets. Many a Jew in Berlin's West End had his ears boxed during these demonstrations': Goebbels, *Kampf um Berlin* (note 27), 180.
62. Goebbels, *Kampf um Berlin* (note 27), 174.
63. Goebbels, *Kampf um Berlin* (note 27), 172.
64. Erich Koch, 'Folgen der Rassenvermischung', *Berliner Arbeiterzeitung*, ii/17 (24 April 1927); reproduced in the appendix to Heiber, *Das Tagebuch von Joseph Goebbels* (note 50), 120.
65. Heiber, *Das Tagebuch von Joseph Goebbels* (note 50), 121–3 (letter from Goebbels to Hitler, 5 June 1927).
66. Heiber, *Das Tagebuch von Joseph Goebbels* (note 50), 124.
67. Minutes of a meeting of party officials in Berlin on 10 June 1927, reproduced in Heiber, *Das Tagebuch von Joseph Goebbels* (note 50), 127 and 129.
68. Heiber, *Das Tagebuch von Joseph Goebbels* (note 50), 124–6 (letters from Gregor Straßer to Rudolf Heß, 15 and 18 June 1927).
69. Heiber, *Das Tagebuch von Joseph Goebbels* (note 50), 135–6 (letter from Emil Holtz to Hitler, 17 June 1927).
70. *Völkischer Beobachter* (25 June 1927), reproduced in RSA ii/1.385.

71. Heiber, *Das Tagebuch von Joseph Goebbels* (note 50), 136 (letter from Emil Holtz to Hitler, 17 June 1927). The *Berliner Arbeiterzeitung* ceased publication with its issue of 20 Dec. 1930.

72. Heiber, *Das Tagebuch von Joseph Goebbels* (note 50), 122 (letter from Goebbels to Hitler, 5 June 1927).

73. Heiber, *Das Tagebuch von Joseph Goebbels* (note 50), 124 (letter from Gregor Straßer to Rudolf Heß, 15 June 1927).

74. A week before Goebbels launched his own paper, the *Berliner Arbeiterzeitung* published the following appeal: 'As the only officially recognized organ of the NSDAP in Berlin-Brandenburg, we feel it is necessary that party comrades should inform us at once about incidents that take place at public events so that the appropriate press campaign may be initiated without delay'; *Berliner Arbeiterzeitung*, ii/26 (26 June 1927).

75. Goebbels, *Kampf um Berlin* (note 27), 183–4. Many accounts take over this version of events more or less uncritically: see, for example, Roger Manvell and Heinrich Fraenkel, *Doctor Goebbels: His Life and Death* (London and New York 2010), 80; Ernest Bramsted, *Goebbels and National Socialist Propaganda 1924–1945* (London 1965), 30 ('It became imperative for the Party to have at least a weekly newspaper of its own'); and Frank Hörnigk, 'Nationalsozialistischer "Kulturkampf" um Berlin 1926–1933', *Literarisches Leben in Berlin 1871–1933*, ed. Peter Wruck (Berlin 1987), 253–78, esp. 259 ('In this way he succeeded in consolidating an exchange of information with the party roots, an exchange that had been rendered difficult by the ban and sometimes even interrupted completely').

76. Helmut Heiber, *Joseph Goebbels* (Berlin 1962), 67.

77. Heiden, *Geburt des dritten Reiches* (note 34), 235.

78. *Berliner Arbeiterzeitung*, ii/37 (11 Sept. 1927): 'In it all aspects of public life will be examined in the form of lectures and discussions. Every German man and every German woman may take part.' It is not known if the local police attempted to prevent this National Socialist élite school from operating.

79. Goebbels, *Kampf um Berlin* (note 27), 194 and 196.

80. See, for example, Viktor Reimann, *Dr. Joseph Goebbels* (Vienna and Munich 1976), 101.

81. Julius Lippert, *Im Strom der Zeit: Erlebnisse und Eindrücke* (Berlin 1942), 120.

82. The posters are reproduced in facsimile in Goebbels, *Kampf um Berlin* (note 27), 195. Line reproductions are used, rather than photographs of the actual advertisement pillars. Conversely, far less important posters are reproduced by Goebbels from photographs taken of advertisement pillars in and around Berlin (pp.81 and 149). It has not been possible to locate any surviving copies of these posters in any German poster collection. See Sven Felix Kellerhoff, *Hitlers Berlin: Geschichte einer Hassliebe* (Berlin 2005), 204 n.20, who as proof of the existence of these posters refers in turn to Carin Kessemeier, *Der Leitartikler Goebbels in den NS-Organen 'Der Angriff' und 'Das Reich'* (Münster 1967), pl. 3. But Kessemeier's source for the image that she reproduces is Goebbels, *Kampf um Berlin* (note 27), 195. In spite of this, the evidence may still be allowed to stand.

83. Ignorance of the practices of the Berlin press at the time of the Weimar Republic continues to mislead historians and journalists into taking literally the subtitle 'The German Monday paper'; see, for example, Bering, *Kampf um Namen* (note 24), 133; and Kellerhoff, *Hitlers Berlin* (note 82), 58. But Goebbels' weekly newspaper no more appeared on a Monday than the *8-Uhr-Abendblatt* appeared every evening at eight or the *B. Z. am Mittag* appeared at midday. (It was published substantially earlier.) Berlin's 'Monday newspapers' were originally intended to fill the gap between the Sunday and Monday editions of the major newspapers, which as a rule appeared twelve times a week: see Peter de Mendelssohn, *Zeitungsstadt Berlin: Menschen und Mächte in der Geschichte der deutschen Presse*, 2nd edn (Frankfurt, Berlin and Vienna 1982), 331–2. Growing competition soon forced publishers to bring out their 'Monday editions' on Sunday evening. Goebbels claims that his readers already had copies in their hands on

the Saturday evening: Goebbels, *Kampf um Berlin* (note 27), 202 and 209. Straßer's *Berliner Arbeiterzeitung* was also published on a Saturday, underlining the importance of Goebbels' strategic move in establishing a rival publication.

84. Goebbels, *Kampf um Berlin* (note 27), 196–7.

85. Kellerhoff, *Hitlers Berlin* (note 82), 57–8.

86. Kessemeier, *Der Leitartikler Goebbels* (note 82), 46 and 290 n.15; and Goebbels, *Kampf um Berlin* (note 27), 198: 'When we began in July 1927 with a print run of two to three thousand [. . .].'

87. Jacques Albachary (ed.), *Albacharys Markt-Zahlen für Reklame-Verbraucher* (Berlin 1929), 18.

88. Goebbels' *Kampf um Berlin* alone reproduces a dozen such NSDAP posters from 1927 in the form of either facsimiles or photographs.

89. Artur Schweriner, 'Wie Herr Göbbels Berlin erobern will', *C. V.-Zeitung* (9 March 1928).

90. Goebbels, *Kampf um Berlin* (note 27), 45 and 201–2.

91. Thus Reimann, *Dr. Joseph Goebbels* (note 80), 102.

92. According to the official party history, his drawings 'reveal the intuition of pure genius in representing the typical National Socialist SA man from Berlin in his revolutionary implacability, his rigorous solidarity and his willingness to make the ultimate sacrifice. [. . .] It is the face of the fighter from the Freikorps and the Frontbann, the face of the eternal military German who has now become the political soldier of Adolf Hitler, the SA man'; see Engelbrechten, *Eine braune Armee entsteht* (note 12), 61.

93. Joseph Goebbels, 'Menschen, seid menschlich!', *Der Angriff* (28 Nov. 1927).

94. Quoted from the book version by Karl Martin Friedrich (ed.), *Der kesse Orje: Spaziergänge eines Berliner Jungen durch das System*, with an introduction by Goebbels and drawings by Mjölnir (Munich 1931), 14. Mjollnir was the hammer belonging to the Norse god Thor.

95. 'Ein Kampf um Berlin', *Der Angriff*, i/8 (22 Aug. 1927).

96. Goebbels, *Kampf um Berlin* (note 27), 198, 200 and 202.

97. Reimann, *Dr. Joseph Goebbels* (note 80), 103.

98. Kessemeier, *Der Leitartikler Goebbels* (note 82), 49.

99. Bering, *Kampf um Namen* (note 26), 133.

100. Goebbels, *Kampf um Berlin* (note 27), 209 and 204.

101. Engelbrechten, *Eine braune Armee entsteht* (note 12), 61–2. Even at a time when the party itself was banned, the South-West Sports Association – a cover for the Kreuzberg SA and the leaders of the SA in Berlin – continued to have use of a schoolroom and a gymnasium at 34 Hagelberger Straße, where it was able to hold exercises, discussions and weekly courses: see Engelbrechten and Volz, *Wir wandern* (note 37), 181.

102. Joseph Goebbels, 'Warum Angriff?', *Der Angriff*, i/1 (4 July 1927).

103. Hans Schwarz van Berk, 'Vorwort', in Goebbels, *Der Angriff* (note 32), 11.

104. *Berliner Arbeiterzeitung*, iii/1 (8 Jan. 1928).

105. *C. V.-Zeitung* (20 Jan. 1928).

106. Fröhlich, *Die Tagebücher von Joseph Goebbels* (note 49), i/2.358 (21 April 1928): 'Rousing march-pasts. A wonderful celebration. Long live Hitler! We've become one big family here in Berlin.'

107. *C. V.-Zeitung* (4 May 1928). The election leaflet was reproduced as a facsimile in the next issue of 11 May 1928. The points that were omitted by the Berlin poster company on the grounds of their anti-Semitic content are quoted from references to them in the issue of 4 May.

108. *Der Angriff*, ii/20 (14 May 1928).

109. Büsch and Haus, *Berlin als Hauptstadt* (note 56), 348–9, 354 and 378; and Engelbrechten und Volz, *Wir wandern* (note 37), 46.

110. Walter Görlitz and Herbert A. Quint, *Adolf Hitler: Eine Biographie* (Stuttgart 1952), 266.

111. Martin Broszat, 'Die Anfänge der Berliner NSDAP 1926/27', *Vierteljahrshefte für Zeitgeschichte*, viii (1960), 91.
112. Heiden, *Geburt des dritten Reiches* (note 34), 240.
113. In the original, the word *kleinbürgerlichen* (petty bourgeois) appears – presumably erroneously – as the meaningless *heimbürgerlichen*.
114. Quoted from Reinhard Kühnl, *Die nationalsozialistische Linke 1925–1930* (Meisenheim am Glan 1966), 344–5.
115. Joseph Goebbels, 'Die Schlacht ist geschlagen', *Der Angriff* (21 May 1928).
116. 'Joseph Goebbels, IdI.', *Der Angriff* (28 May 1928). His diary entry for 22 May 1928 reads: 'Immune, that's the main thing'; see Fröhlich, *Die Tagebücher von Joseph Goebbels* (note 49), i/2.373. He referred to the Reichstag as a 'Jewish school': Fröhlich, *Die Tagebücher von Joseph Goebbels* (note 49), i/3.37.
117. 'Die N.S.A.P.D. [*sic*] sucht Neuland', *C. V.-Zeitung* (29 June 1928).
118. Adolf Hitler, 'Der Siegesmarsch des Nationalsozialismus 1927', *Völkischer Beobachter* (1-2 Jan. 1928), quoted from RSA ii/2.588.
119. See Kruppa, *Rechtsradikalismus in Berlin* (note 53), 362.
120. Peter Longerich, *Geschichte der SA*, 2nd edn (Munich 2003), 72.
121. *C. V.-Zeitung* (29 June 1928); and Kruppa, *Rechtsradikalismus in Berlin* (note 53), 352.
122. Fröhlich, *Die Tagebücher von Joseph Goebbels* (note 49), i/3.40 and 46.
123. *Der Angriff*, ii/29 (16 July 1928).
124. *Völkischer Beobachter* (18 July 1928); and *Der Angriff*, ii/29 (16 July 1928).
125. RSA iii/1.11–13 and 21. Goebbels' diary entry on Hitler's speech is not exactly brimful of enthusiasm: 'The boss spoke in the evening. Packed hall. Wild enthusiasm. 37° C. In two parts from 8.30 till just before 12. Foreign policy. Familiar thesis. Masterly account. Imposing gathering': see Fröhlich, *Die Tagebücher von Joseph Goebbels* (note 49), i/3.53 (14 July 1928).
126. See the catalogue of the 1928 Great Berlin Art Exhibition organized by the Cartel of the United Association of Artists (Berlin 1928).
127. Gustav Böß, *Berlin von heute: Stadtverwaltung und Wirtschaft* (Berlin 1929), 35.

Chapter 6 · 1928–30: The breakthrough as the dominant party of the right

1. Elke Fröhlich (ed.), *Die Tagebücher von Joseph Goebbels*, Part I: *Aufzeichnungen 1923–1941*, 9 vols (Munich 1997–2006), i/3.339 (30 Sept. 1929).
2. Published under the pseudonym K. L. Gerstorff, 'Die Chancen des deutschen Faschismus', *Die Weltbühne*, xxvi/35 (26 Aug. 1930), 296.
3. Thus the lessee, Richard Mueck, following the renovations in the spring and summer of 1929, quoted by Christa Schreiber, 'Der Sportpalast in seiner baulichen Entwicklung', *Arena der Leidenschaften: Der Berliner Sportpalast und seine Veranstaltungen 1910–1973*, ed. Alfons Arenhövel (Berlin 1990), 16–38, esp. 28.
4. Arenhövel, *Arena der Leidenschaften* (note 3), 8–10, from which the quotation from the *Berliner Tageblatt* of 25 Nov. 1925 is taken.
5. Arenhövel, *Arena der Leidenschaften* (note 4), 10.
6. Kurt Tucholsky, *Gesammelte Werke*, 10 vols (Reinbek 1997), iii.229.
7. Egon Erwin Kisch, *Der rasende Reporter: Hetzjagd durch die Zeit. Wagnisse in aller Welt. Kriminalistisches Reisebuch* (Berlin and Weimar 1983), 227–31; see also Monika Peschken-Eilsberger, 'Der Berliner Sportpalast in der Literatur der zwanziger Jahre', *Arena der Leidenschaften* (note 4), 106–7, esp. 107.
8. Mehring's poem first appeared as part of the revue 'Europäische Nächte' of 1924 and was reprinted in Walter Mehring, *Chronik der Lustbarkeiten: Die Gedichte, Lieder und Chansons 1918–1933* (Düsseldorf 1981), 219–24; Weinert's poem was first printed in *Die Arena* in 1926: see Dietrich Pawlowski, 'He, he, he . . . Zum Radsport', *Arena der Leidenschaften* (note 4), 71–9, esp. 77 and 79 n.36.
9. Arenhövel, *Arena der Leidenschaften* (note 4), 11.

10. Klemens Klemmer, *Jüdische Baumeister in Deutschland: Architektur vor der Shoah* (Stuttgart 1998), 255.
11. Arenhövel, *Arena der Leidenschaften* (note 4), 11.
12. Fröhlich, *Die Tagebücher von Joseph Goebbels* (note 1), i/3.89 (24 Sept. 1928).
13. Fröhlich, *Die Tagebücher von Joseph Goebbels* (note 1), i/3.77 (6 Sept. 1928).
14. Arenhövel, *Arena der Leidenschaften* (note 4), 10.
15. Fröhlich, *Die Tagebücher von Joseph Goebbels* (note 1), i/3.52 (12 July 1928) and 54 (17 July 1928).
16. Fröhlich, *Die Tagebücher von Joseph Goebbels* (note 1), i/3.65 (8 Aug. 1928).
17. Fröhlich, *Die Tagebücher von Joseph Goebbels* (note 1), i/3.68 (13 Aug. 1928).
18. Fröhlich, *Die Tagebücher von Joseph Goebbels* (note 1), i/3.71 (24 Aug. 1928).
19. Reuth mixes up the dates when he states that Hitler spoke in the Friedrichshain Conference Rooms 'at the end of August': see Ralf Georg Reuth, *Goebbels: Eine Biographie* (Munich and Zurich 1990), 142. As we noted above (p. 136), Hitler had already spoken there on 13 July, making it impossible for the event to have had any connection with the crisis affecting the SA.
20. Fröhlich, *Die Tagebücher von Joseph Goebbels* (note 1), i/3.82 (14 Sept. 1928).
21. J. K. von Engelbrechten, *Eine braune Armee entsteht: Die Geschichte der Berlin-Brandenburger SA* (Munich 1937), 73.
22. Martin Schuster, 'Die SA in der nationalsozialistischen "Machtergreifung" in Berlin und Brandenburg 1926–1934' (FU Berlin, 2005), 49; and 'Geschichte der SA in Berlin', undated manuscript in BA Zwischenarchiv, ZB II, no. 3608.
23. *Der Angriff* (17 Sept. 1928).
24. Fröhlich, *Die Tagebücher von Joseph Goebbels* (note 1), i/3.89 (25 Sept. 1928).
25. Fröhlich, *Die Tagebücher von Joseph Goebbels* (note 1), i/3.271 (1 Oct. 1928).
26. *Der Angriff* (8 Oct. 1928).
27. Fröhlich, *Die Tagebücher von Joseph Goebbels* (note 1), i/3.95–6 (4–6 Oct. 1928).
28. Fröhlich, *Die Tagebücher von Joseph Goebbels* (note 1), i/3.100 (13 Oct. 1928).
29. Fröhlich, *Die Tagebücher von Joseph Goebbels* (note 1), i/3.101 (14 Oct. 1928).
30. Fröhlich, *Die Tagebücher von Joseph Goebbels* (note 1), i/3.107 (22 Oct. 1928).
31. Fröhlich, *Die Tagebücher von Joseph Goebbels* (note 1), i/3.122 (14 Nov. 1928).
32. Martin Broszat, *Die Machtergreifung: Der Aufstieg der NSDAP und die Zerstörung der Weimarer Republik* (Munich 1984), 94. Goebbels still recognized at this time that he tended 'to overrate meetings at the moment of success. It is good, then, if the next day brings with it calm and sober reflection'. At the same time, however, he needed 'success as a substitute for sheer numbers': see Fröhlich, *Die Tagebücher von Joseph Goebbels* (note 1), i/3.100 (13 Oct. 1928).
33. *C. V.-Zeitung* (16 Nov. 1928).
34. *Der Angriff* (12 Nov. 1928).
35. Fröhlich, *Die Tagebücher von Joseph Goebbels* (note 1), i/3.103 (16 Oct. 1928).
36. See the facsimile of the advertisement from *Der Angriff* and all the other relevant details in Arenhövel, *Arena der Leidenschaften* (note 4), 265.
37. 'Das erwachende Berlin', *Völkischer Beobachter* (18–19 Nov. 1928).
38. [Artur] Schweriner, 'Hitler spricht', *C. V.-Zeitung* (23 Nov. 1928).
39. The Berlin SS was founded in the summer of 1926. By 1929 it had about thirty-five members. Between then and the autumn of 1930 its numbers fluctuated wildly 'but between 1926 and 1930 it never had more than seventy-five members at most': see J. K. Engelbrechten and Hans Volz, *Wir wandern durch das nationalsozialistische Berlin: Ein Führer durch die Gedenkstätten des Kampfes um die Reichshauptstadt* (Munich 1937), 25.
40. Dax, 'Hitler spricht im Sportpalast', *Der Angriff*, ii/47 (19 Nov. 1928).
41. RSA iii/1.207–27, esp. 222 (speech to the NSDAP meeting in Munich, 9 Nov. 1928).
42. *Der Angriff*, ii/47 (19 Nov. 1928); reprinted in Joseph Goebbels, *Der Angriff: Aufsätze aus der Kampfzeit*, 2nd edn (Munich 1935), 217–18.

43. On the legend of Hitler as party member no. 7, see Albrecht Tyrell, *Vom 'Trommler' zum 'Führer': Der Wandel von Hitlers Selbstverständnis zwischen 1919 und 1924 und die Entwicklung der NSDAP* (Munich 1975), 27, 196 and 198-9 n.118; see also Anton Joachimsthaler, *Hitlers Weg begann in München: 1913-1923* (Munich 2000), 257-9.

44. See RSA iii/1.201-2, which gives only a summary of the contents of the speech as it appeared in the *Fränkischer Kurier* (4 Nov. 1928).

45. The *C. V.-Zeitung* had at its disposal a detailed account of Hitler's Nuremberg speech which, it claimed, 'showed Hitler's true face'. Its piece on Hitler's speech at the Sportpalast appeared on 23 Nov. 1928 with the subtitle: 'Retreat in Berlin – Fanfare in Nuremberg'.

46. All the quotations are taken from RSA iii/1.236-40.

47. Fröhlich, *Die Tagebücher von Joseph Goebbels* (note 1), i/3.124 (17 Nov. 1928).

48. RSA iii/1.284 and 286 ('Freedom and Bread': speech at the NSDAP rally in Hersbruck, 30 Nov. 1928).

49. Adolf Hitler, 'Politik der Woche', *Illustrierter Beobachter* (1 Dec. 1928), reprinted in RSA iii/1.291-2.

50. Adolf Hitler, 'Politik der Woche', *Illustrierter Beobachter* (26 Jan. 1929), reprinted in RSA iii/1.394-5.

51. See Wolfgang Ruge, 'Deutschnationale Volkspartei (DNVP) 1918-1933', *Lexikon zur Parteiengeschichte 1789-1945*, 4 vols, ed. Dieter Fricke (Leipzig 1983-6), ii.476-528, esp. 507-9.

52. Fröhlich, *Die Tagebücher von Joseph Goebbels* (note 1), i/3.177 (1 Feb. 1929) and 178 (2 Feb. 1929). A similar note was struck on 9 March 1929 in the context of a meeting at the Kriegervereinshaus: 'We've not had such a good attendance for a long time' (i/3.199).

53. Fröhlich, *Die Tagebücher von Joseph Goebbels* (note 1), i/3.181 (8 Feb. 1929) and 190 (22 Feb. 1929).

54. Fröhlich, *Die Tagebücher von Joseph Goebbels* (note 1), i/3.214 (29 March 1929).

55. Fröhlich, *Die Tagebücher von Joseph Goebbels* (note 1), i/3.245 (11 May 1929).

56. Marie-Luise Ehls, *Protest und Propaganda: Demonstrationen in Berlin zur Zeit der Weimarer Republik* (Berlin and New York 1927), 136.

57. [Artur] Schweriner, 'Hitler spricht', *C. V.-Zeitung* (23 Nov. 1928).

58. The membership figures for the Stahlhelm were 225,000 in 1928, 280,000 in 1931 and 340,000 in 1932; see Bernhard Mahlke, 'Stahlhelm-Bund der Frontsoldaten (Stahlhelm) 1918-1935', *Lexikon zur Parteiengeschichte 1789-1945*, 4 vols, ed. Dieter Fricke (Leipzig 1983-6), iv.145-58, esp. 145. In 1928 the DNVP had 696,000 members. At the Reichstag elections in May 1928 the party received 4.4 million votes: see Ruge, 'Deutschnationale Volkspartei' (note 51), 477.

59. Fröhlich, *Die Tagebücher von Joseph Goebbels* (note 1), i/3.205 (17 March 1929) and 211 (24 March 1929).

60. Fröhlich, *Die Tagebücher von Joseph Goebbels* (note 1), i/3.212 (26 March 1929) and 213 (28 March 1929).

61. Fröhlich, *Die Tagebücher von Joseph Goebbels* (note 1), i/3.221 (6 April 1929).

62. All quotations are taken from the slightly revised version of the text published by Goebbels in *Der Angriff: Aufsätze aus der Kampfzeit* (note 42), 291-4.

63. Joseph Goebbels, 'Einheitsfront', *Der Angriff* (27 May 1929), quoted from Goebbels, *Der Angriff: Aufsätze aus der Kampfzeit* (note 42), 289-91.

64. Fröhlich, *Die Tagebücher von Joseph Goebbels* (note 1), i/3.248 (16 May 1929).

65. For more on the abolition of the government's responsibility towards the Reichstag, the increasingly powerful position of the president and so on, see Volker R. Berghahn, *Der Stahlhelm: Bund der Frontsoldaten* (Düsseldorf 1966), 119-20 and 125-7.

66. RSA ii/2.219 and 232-3 (letter to the federal leadership of the Stahlhelm).

67. Fröhlich, *Die Tagebücher von Joseph Goebbels* (note 1), i/3.256-7 (29 May 1929).

68. Fröhlich, *Die Tagebücher von Joseph Goebbels* (note 1), i/3.258 (31 May 1929) and 259 (1 June 1929).
69. Fröhlich, *Die Tagebücher von Joseph Goebbels* (note 1), i/3.261 (5 June 1929). See also the entry for 7 June 1929: 'Gau Day. Read Hitler's memorandum against the Stahlhelm. Angry debate against the Stahlhelm. Everyone complaining about the politics of compromise adopted by the V[ölkischer] B[eobachter]. I have difficulty in calming the meeting. A good sign: the socialist revolutionaries are on guard. Against the "officers' camarilla" I'm on the side of the radicals. There's a lot that I too don't like. But one has to confront Hitler. That's the best way' (264).
70. Fröhlich, *Die Tagebücher von Joseph Goebbels* (note 1), i/3.281 (5 July 1929) and 271 (19 June 1929).
71. Fröhlich, *Die Tagebücher von Joseph Goebbels* (note 1), i/3.281 (5 July 1929).
72. Fröhlich, *Die Tagebücher von Joseph Goebbels* (note 1), i/3.283 (6 July 1929).
73. Hans Peter Bleuel and Ernst Klimmert, *Deutsche Studenten auf dem Weg ins Dritte Reich: Ideologien, Programme, Aktionen 1918–1935* (Gütersloh 1967), 196–9. The election results are quoted from 'Sieg der nationalen Studenten', *Berliner Lokal-Anzeiger* (7 July 1929) and 'Antwort der Berliner Studenten an Becker', *Der Tag* (7 July 1929).
74. *Illustrierter Beobachter*, iv/28 (13 July 1929).
75. 'Kampf um Berlin', *Der Angriff* (15 July 1929).
76. 'Entschließung', *Berliner Lokal-Anzeiger* (morning edn) (10 July 1929).
77. Adolf Hitler, 'Prinzip und Taktik: Zur Krise der Deutschnationalen Volkspartei', *Völkischer Beobachter* (9 April 1930), reprinted in RSA ii/3.152–6, esp. 156.
78. 3–4 Leipziger Straße. The sandstone building dates from 1898 to 1903 and was built in the style of the Italian High Renaissance. On its southern side it was connected to the Landtag (now the House of Representatives) in the Prinz-Albrecht-Straße (now the Niederkirchnerstraße). It now serves as the seat of the Bundesrat. Somewhat surprisingly, Engelbrechten and Volz fail to mention either Hitler's speech to the National Socialist Students' League at the Kriegervereinshaus on 5 July 1929 or his appearance at the Prussian Diet on 9 July, their chronology omitting everything between 26 May and 4 Aug.; see Engelbrechten and Volz, *Wir wandern* (note 39), 35. The topographical section of their study even omits all reference to the building itself. Instead, they refer merely to the adjoining Landtag and state only that 'Hitler never set foot in the Landtag during the whole time that the party was fighting for its survival' (69).
79. 'Nationale Einheitsfront für das Volksbegehren', *Berliner Lokal-Anzeiger* (morning edn) (10 July 1929).
80. 'Hitlers Kampf gegen die Feigheit', *Deutsche Zeitung* (23 July 1929), reprinted in RSA iii/2.290–92. The *Berliner Lokal-Anzeiger* reprinted the whole of Hugenberg's speech but devoted only twelve lines to Hitler's harangue.
81. 'Gloss' (11 July 1929), reprinted in Rumpelstilzchen [Adolf Stein], *Ja, hätt'ste . . .* (Berlin 1929), 360–1.
82. Fröhlich, *Die Tagebücher von Joseph Goebbels* (note 1), i/3.284–5 (12 July 1929).
83. Walther G. Oschilewski, *Zeitungen in Berlin im Spiegel der Jahrhunderte* (Berlin 1975), 163–4 and 216; and Peter de Mendelssohn, *Zeitungsstadt Berlin: Menschen und Mächte in der Geschichte der deutschen Presse*, 2nd edn (Frankfurt, Berlin and Vienna 1982), 240–2 and 331–3.
84. 'Die nationale Einheitsfront', *Berliner Lokal-Anzeiger* (Sunday edn) (22 Sept. 1929). Two other examples may be cited here: on the day of the elections to the municipal assembly (17 Nov. 1929), the *Berliner Lokal-Anzeiger* published the address, telephone numbers and office hours of the NSDAP headquarters, where callers would receive 'information and all the help necessary in deciding for whom to vote'; and on the following day (18 Nov. 1929), the *Berliner illustrierte Nachtausgabe* not only published a photograph of Goebbels on its front page, it also regaled readers with his own detailed account of the policies that the NSDAP would pursue if elected.

85. Fröhlich, *Die Tagebücher von Joseph Goebbels* (note 1), i/3.158 (5 Jan. 1929) and 159 (6 Jan. 1929). Only after 1 May 1930 was *Der Angriff* able to publish a ten-page issue: see Fröhlich, *Die Tagebücher von Joseph Goebbels* (note 1), i/3.127 (9 April 1930).
86. Engelbrechten and Volz, *Wir wandern* (note 39), 35. In the month of Oct. alone, Goebbels noted that there had been five hundred new members: Fröhlich, *Die Tagebücher von Joseph Goebbels* (note 1), i/3.361 (31 Oct. 1929).
87. Thomas Friedrich, 'Die Berliner Zeitungslandschaft am Ende der Weimarer Republic', *Berlin 1932: Das letzte Jahr der ersten deutschen Republik. Politik, Medien, Symbole*, ed. Diethart Kerbs and Henrick Stahr (Berlin 1992), 56–67. According to a report drawn up by the Gau's secretary, a Herr Wilke, the print run of *Der Angriff* rose by 30 per cent between Jan. and late Nov. 1929: see 'Kampf um Berlin', *Der Angriff* (28 Nov. 1929). Even so, the actual figures were not made known.
88. Appeal of 23 Dec. 1928 reproduced in RSA iii/1.374.
89. Fröhlich, *Die Tagebücher von Joseph Goebbels* (note 1), i/3.281 (5 July 1929); 333 (22 Sept. 1929); 343 (5 Oct. 1929); 353 (20 Oct. 1929); ii/1.62 (13 Jan. 1930); 71 (24 Jan. 1930); and 74 (29 Jan. 1930). Hitler's appeal of 3 Feb. 1930 ('Parteigenossen!') is reproduced in RSA iii/3.65; and his appeal of 14 Feb. 1930 ('Parteigenossen! Parteigenossinnen!') appears in RSA iii/3.87–8.
90. 'Kampf um Berlin', *Der Angriff* (28 Nov. 1929).
91. Arenhövel, *Arena der Leidenschaften* (note 4), 273–4 and 275; and Fröhlich, *Die Tagebücher von Joseph Goebbels* (note 1), i/3.337 (28 Sept. 1929) and 353–6 (20–23 Oct. 1929).
92. On the economic situation before 1929, see Heinrich August Winkler, *Der Schein der Normalität: Arbeiter und Arbeiterbewegung in der Weimarer Republik 1924 bis 1930* (Berlin and Bonn 1985), 26–45; on the susceptibility of white-collar workers to nationalist ideas, see Hans Speier, *Die Angestellten vor dem Nationalsozialismus: Ein Beitrag zum Verständnis der deutschen Sozialstruktur 1918–1933* (Göttingen 1977), 110–23.
93. Statistisches Amt der Stadt Berlin (ed.), *Statistisches Jahrbuch der Stadt Berlin*, vi (1930), 136; vii (1931), 105.
94. Cuno Horkenbach (ed.), *Das Deutsche Reich von 1918 bis heute* (Berlin 1930), 289. A detailed account of the whole affair, including its aftermath, is given by Christian Engeli, *Gustav Böß: Oberbürgermeister von Berlin 1921 bis 1930* (Stuttgart 1971), 230–74; see also Wolfgang Haus, 'Chance, Krise und Sturz der Demokratie im Berlin der Weimarer Republik', *Berlin als Hauptstadt der Weimarer Republik 1919–1933*, ed. Otto Büsch and Wolfgang Haus (Berlin and New York 1987), 161–264, esp. 223–5.
95. Engeli, *Gustav Böß* (note 94), 247.
96. Engeli, *Gustav Böß* (note 94), 87.
97. Adolf Hitler, 'Politik der Woche', *Illustrierter Beobachter* (19 Oct. 1929), quoted from RSA iii/2.407. Hitler also mentioned the Sklarek Scandal in the course of his speech in Munich on 25 Oct. 1929: see RSA iii/2.416.
98. Engeli, *Gustav Böß* (note 94), 243–4.
99. 'Pfui!', *Berliner Börsen-Courier*, lxii (morning edn) (2 Nov. 1929).
100. Fröhlich, *Die Tagebücher von Joseph Goebbels* (note 1), i/3.362 (1 Nov. 1929).
101. *Statistisches Jahrbuch der Stadt Berlin* (note 93), 347 and 349.
102. Haus, 'Chance, Krise und Sturz' (note 94), 224.
103. Fröhlich, *Die Tagebücher von Joseph Goebbels* (note 1), i/3.375 (18 and 19 Nov. 1929).
104. Together, the National Socialist Freedom Movement and the German Socialist Party won 4.8 per cent of the vote in Berlin in May 1924. In Zehlendorf, the figure of 9.8 per cent in May 1924 fell to 7.9 per cent in Nov. 1929.
105. Dü[rr], 'Hitler frißt Karl Marx!', *Der Angriff* (21 Nov. 1929).
106. Fröhlich, *Die Tagebücher von Joseph Goebbels* (note 1), ii/1.40 (13 Dec. 1929).
107. The comments that Hitler made at the end of a speech he gave in Munich on 24 Feb. 1929 shed light on his ideas about the political role of women in the National Socialist movement: 'Of course, this party is a fighting movement for men. But women need to

stand behind these men. They are part of this fighting front. Unlike the Communists we shall never send women to the top. But we want their spirit to be behind us. [. . .] Women must strengthen and support men': RSA iii/1.450.

108. Dü[rr], 'Hitler frißt Karl Marx!' (note 105).
109. The city's Town Hall was built between 1861 and 1869. A monumental brick structure, it was popularly known as the 'Red House' on account of the colour of its brickwork and terracotta decorations; see Karl Baedeker, *Berlin und Umgebung: Handbuch für Reisende*, 20th edn (Leipzig 1927), 143; and *Griebens Reiseführer: Berlin und Umgebung*, 66th edn (Berlin 1929), 119. The term 'Red Town Hall' – with obvious political connotations – did not become current until around 1948/9.
110. J. K. von Engelbrechten, *Eine braune Armee entsteht: Die Geschichte der Berlin-Brandenburger SA* (Munich 1937), 108.
111. Fröhlich, *Die Tagebücher von Joseph Goebbels* (note 1), ii/1.35 (7 Dec. 1929), 45 (19 Dec. 1929), 51 (29 Dec. 1929) and 57 (7 Jan. 1930). Engelbrechten and Volz mention neither the SA march on 18 Dec. nor the march-past of the KPD central offices on 28 Dec.: see Engelbrechten und Volz, *Wir wandern* (note 39). Engelbrechten mentions the SA march-past of the Karl-Liebknecht-Haus on 23 Aug. 1929 and a funeral service for Horst Wessel's brother, Werner, on 28 Dec., but does not say where this service took place: see Engelbrechten, *Eine braune Armee entsteht* (note 110), 98–9 and 112.
112. Fröhlich, *Die Tagebücher von Joseph Goebbels* (note 1), ii/1.64 (15 Jan. 1930). For a well-researched study of this whole incident, see Heinz Knobloch, *Der arme Epstein: Wie der Tod zu Horst Wessel kam* (Berlin 1993), 9–59; see also Thomas Oertel, *Horst Wessel: Untersuchung einer Legende* (Cologne 1988), 83–6.
113. Fröhlich, *Die Tagebücher von Joseph Goebbels* (note 1), ii/1.81 (6 Feb. 1930).
114. The complete list is reproduced by Hans Volz, *Daten der Geschichte der NSDAP*, 8th edn (Berlin and Leipzig 1938), 113–15. The 'murdered' men were Hans Kütemeyer, Gerhard Weber and Walter Fischer.
115. Erwin Reitmann, *Horst Wessel: Leben und Sterben* (Berlin 1936), 72–3.
116. 'Die Fahne hoch!', *Der Angriff* (27 Feb. 1930), quoted from Goebbels, *Der Angriff: Aufsätze aus der Kampfzeit* (note 42), 269–70.
117. 'Bis zur Neige', *Der Angriff* (6 March 1930), quoted from Goebbels, *Der Angriff: Aufsätze aus der Kampfzeit* (note 42), 272–4. According to the official party history, Wessel built up the SA in Friedrichshain because he had been sent there and entrusted with the local branch: Engelbrechten, *Eine braune Armee entsteht* (note 110), 91–2.
118. Fröhlich, *Die Tagebücher von Joseph Goebbels* (note 1), ii/1.97 (26 Feb. 1930), 99 (1 March 1930) and 150 (4 May 1930).
119. Ernst Hanfstaengl, *Zwischen Weißem und Braunem Haus: Memoiren eines politischen Außenseiters* (Munich 1970), 204.
120. Albrecht Tyrell, 'Der Wegbereiter: Hermann Göring als politischer Beauftragter Hitlers in Berlin 1930–1932/33', *Demokratie und Diktatur: Geist und Gestalt politischer Herrschaft in Deutschland und Europa. Festschrift für Karl-Dietrich Bracher*, ed. Manfred Funke and others (Bonn and Düsseldorf 1987), 178–97, esp. 183–5.
121. Adolf Hitler, 'Politik der Woche', *Illustrierter Beobachter*, v/10 (8 March 1930), 149.
122. RSA v/2.389–93; and *Der Angriff* (23 Jan. 1933).
123. Apart from the 1929 local elections in Berlin, the NSDAP also made considerable gains elsewhere: in the election for the Landtag in Baden on 27 Oct., for example, it won nearly 7 per cent of the vote; in the metropolitan council election in Lübeck on 10 Nov. the figure was 8.1 per cent; and in the Landtag elections in Thuringia on 8 Dec. the party gained 11.3 per cent of the vote: see Volz, *Daten der Geschichte der NSDAP* (note 114), 27.
124. Schuster, 'Die SA in der nationalsozialistischen "Machtergreifung"' (note 22), 49.
125. Fröhlich, *Die Tagebücher von Joseph Goebbels* (note 1), i/3.192 (26 Feb. 1929).
126. Detlef Schmiechen-Ackermann, *Nationalsozialismus und Arbeitermilieus: Der nationalsozialistische Angriff auf die proletarischen Wohnquartiere und die Reaktion in den*

sozialistischen Vereinen (Bonn 1998), 180. It must be said, however, the Schmiechen-Ackermann relies on a National Socialist source that seems to the present writer to be based on figures that have been massaged in the Nationalist Socialist interest.

127. Engelbrechten and Volz, *Wir wandern* (note 39), 13.

128. Engelbrechten, *Eine braune Armee entsteht* (note 110), 127.

129. Engelbrechten, *Eine braune Armee entsteht* (note 110), 103.

130. 'Berichtigung', *Völkischer Beobachter* (15 Jan. 1930), quoted from RSA ii/3.13–14.

131. See Heinz Pol, 'Gregor der Große', *Die Weltbühne*, xxvi/16 (15 April 1930), 563–6. Pol claims that Hitler was far more afraid of his popular Gauleiter in Berlin than of the defeated Gregor Straßer and that he therefore resolved the conflict in Straßer's favour (564).

132. Fröhlich, *Die Tagebücher von Joseph Goebbels* (note 1), ii/1.111 (16 March 1929) and 119 (28 March 1930).

133. Institut für Konjunkturforschung (ed.), *Konjunkturstatistisches Handbuch* (Berlin 1933), 15.

134. See Fritz Sternberg's contemporary account, *Der Niedergang des deutschen Kapitalismus* (Berlin 1932), esp. 243–5.

135. See Herbert Michaelis and Ernst Schraepler (eds), *Ursachen und Folgen: Vom deutschen Zusammenbruch 1918 and 1945 bis zur staatlichen Neuordnung Deutschlands in der Gegenwart*, 25 vols (Berlin 1959), vii.612–14.

136. Adolf Hitler, 'Politik der Woche', *Illustrierter Beobachter* (7 Dec. 1929), quoted from RSA ii/2.504.

137. Horkenbach, *Das Deutsche Reich* (note 94), 292–317; on the DNVP, see especially Ruge, 'Deutschnationale Volkspartei' (note 51), 509–12.

138. *Der Angriff* (9 Feb. 1930), quoted from Arenhövel, *Arena der Leidenschaften* (note 4), 280; Fröhlich, *Die Tagebücher von Joseph Goebbels* (note 1), ii/1.82 (8 Feb. 1930); Hitler's letter to the committee set up to discuss the demand for a public referendum (3 April 1930), reproduced in RSA iii/3.146–7; Arenhövel, *Arena der Leidenschaften* (note 4), 284 (entry for 2 April 1930); and Fröhlich, *Die Tagebücher von Joseph Goebbels* (note 1), ii/1.123 (3 April 1930) and 149 (3 May 1930). According to the police report, the Hitler rally on 2 May was attended by some fifteen thousand party members. The *Völkischer Beobachter* put the figure at sixteen thousand: see RSA iii/3.173 n.2. *Der Angriff* (4 May 1930) insisted that 'previous highs were far exceeeded' and that the true figure was around twenty thousand.

139. *Vossische Zeitung* (4 May 1930). A fortnight later Goebbels noted that 'two nights ago the Reds systematically attacked our own people and ended up with three dead. There's a bad atmosphere. But these little rascals have to be shown that they can't kill us and get away with it. Our people act in self-defence': Fröhlich, *Die Tagebücher von Joseph Goebbels* (note 1), ii/1.158 (18 May 1930).

140. Adolf Hitler, 'Wieder eine Verleumdung entlarvt', *Völkischer Beobachter* (7 May 1930). Hitler was responding to a piece that had appeared in the *Münchner Telegramm Zeitung* on 5 May 1930 under the title 'Der Riß im Hakenkreuz: Hitler contra Straßer'; see RSA iii/3.179 n.1.

141. 'Das Ergebnis der nationalsozialistischen Führertagung', *Rheinisch-Westfälische Zeitung* (28 April 1930), quoted from RSA iii/3.168.

142. Patrick Moreau, *Nationalsozialismus von links: Die 'Kampfgemeinschaft Revolutionärer Nationalsozialisten' und die 'Schwarze Front' Otto Strassers 1930–1935* (Stuttgart 1984), 30. Moreau rightly points out that the conflict was made worse by the metalworkers' strike in Saxony, which took place only a few weeks before the start of campaigning in the region, encouraging Hitler to think that Otto Straßer's support for the strike would result in the loss of financial support for his party among leading industrialists.

143. Joseph Goebbels, 'Halbe Bolschewisten', *Der Angriff* (27 April 1930).

144. RSA iii/3.168; Fröhlich, *Die Tagebücher von Joseph Goebbels* (note 1), ii/1.144 (28 April 1930).

145. Fröhlich, *Die Tagebücher von Joseph Goebbels* (note 1), ii/1.149 and 150 (3 and 4 May 1930).
146. Joseph Goebbels, 'Radikalismus der Literaten', *Der Angriff* (11 May 1930). When this article was republished in book form, the title was altered to 'Radikalismus am Schreibtisch': see Goebbels, *Der Angriff: Aufsätze aus der Kampfzeit* (note 42), 296–8.
147. Moreau, *Nationalsozialismus von links* (note 142), 31. Among those present in addition to Hitler and Otto Straßer were Rudolf Heß, Max Amann, the managing director of the party's publishing house in Munich, Gregor Straßer and Hans Hinkel, a co-owner of Kampf-Verlag: see Michaelis and Schraepler, *Ursachen und Folgen* (note 135), vii.390 n.1.
148. 'Aus einer Unterredung Otto Straßers mit Adolf Hitler am 22. Mai 1930', quoted by Michaelis and Schraepler, *Ursachen und Folgen* (note 135), vii.394–5 and 396. Otto Straßer published the contents of the discussion in the form of a pamphlet, *Ministersessel oder Revolution? Eine wahrheitsgemäße Darstellung meiner Trennung von der NSDAP.*
149. 'Ein Brief unseres Führers', *Berliner Arbeiter-Zeitung*, v/28 (13 July 1930), quoted from RSA iii/3.249–50.
150. Moreau, *Nationalsozialismus von links* (note 142), 38–40, 206 n.69 and 147–9. From the summer of 1931, Otto Straßer's group called itself the 'Black Front'.
151. 'Drei von 5000: General-Mitgliederversammlung des Gaues Groß-Berlin', *Berliner Arbeiterzeitung*, v/27 (6 July 1930).
152. Fröhlich, *Die Tagebücher von Joseph Goebbels* (note 1), ii/1.190 (3 July 1930).
153. Fröhlich, *Die Tagebücher von Joseph Goebbels* (note 1), ii/1.189 (2 July 1930); 'Nationalsozialisten im Sportpalast', *Berliner Lokal-Anzeiger* (evening edn) (2 July 1930).
154. Between 1 May 1930 and 1 Oct. 1932 the Berlin Gau's offices were at 10 Hedemannstraße in the Kreuzberg district of the city. As such, they were located not far from the government buildings in the Wilhelmstraße and not far from the southern end of the Friedrichstraße, where many film companies were based: see Engelbrechten and Volz, *Wir wandern* (note 39), 71.
155. Fröhlich, *Die Tagebücher von Joseph Goebbels* (note 1), ii/1.148 (3 May 1930).
156. Arenhövel, *Arena der Leidenschaften* (note 4), 286 and 289–90; *Völkischer Beobachter* (16 Sept. 1930).
157. Weigand von Miltenberg, *Adolf Hitler: Wilhelm III.* (Berlin 1930), 7.

Chapter 7 · 1930: The NSDAP between legitimate tactics and open violence

1. Goebbels' appeal to his supporters at the time of the first concerted attempt to disrupt the screening of *All Quiet on the Western Front* in the Mozartsaal cinema on the Nollendorfplatz in Schöneberg on 5 Dec. 1930, quoted by Martin Broszat, *Die Machtergreifung: Der Aufstieg der NSDAP und die Zerstörung der Weimarer Republik* (Munich 1984), 61.
2. Theodor Wolff, 'Parole: links!', *Berliner Tageblatt* (14 Sept. 1930).
3. Ernst Thälmann, *Reden und Aufsätze 1930–1933* (Cologne 1975), 17.
4. Elke Fröhlich (ed.), *Die Tagebücher von Joseph Goebbels*, Part I: *Aufzeichnungen 1923–1941*, 9 vols (Munich 1997–2006), ii/1.309 (23 Dec. 1930).
5. Fröhlich, *Die Tagebücher von Joseph Goebbels* (note 4), ii/1.240 (16 Sept. 1930).
6. Fröhlich, *Die Tagebücher von Joseph Goebbels* (note 4), ii/1.239 (15 Sept. 1930).
7. Fröhlich, *Die Tagebücher von Joseph Goebbels* (note 4), ii/1.245 (22 and 23 Sept. 1930).
8. *Der Angriff* (5 Oct. 1930), quoted by Broszat, *Die Machtergreifung* (note 1), 55.
9. See Goebbels' diary entry for 17 Oct. 1930: 'At the party meeting yesterday the obsessive desire to reach a compromise finally became intolerable. We shall soon have to stand up to it. The desire for power [*Wille zur Macht*] will soon lead us to the feeding trough': see Fröhlich, *Die Tagebücher von Joseph Goebbels* (note 4), ii/1.262 (17 Oct. 1930). Within days he was agreeing with Hitler on this point: 'Long discussion with the

Chief at the Sanssouci. He's not pleased with the parliamentary party. For that, I'm grateful to the pompous bigwigs in the Reichstag. Hitler was again entirely on my side'; Fröhlich, *Die Tagebücher von Joseph Goebbels* (note 4), ii/1.265 (21 Oct. 1930).

10. Broszat, *Die Machtergreifung* (note 1), 51.

11. Only a few weeks later we find Goebbels complaining that 'it seems they want to exclude me from the parliamentary party': see Fröhlich, *Die Tagebücher von Joseph Goebbels* (note 4), ii/1.298 (7 Dec. 1930).

12. Witness statement to the Fourth Criminal Division of the Court of Appeal in Leipzig (25 Sept. 1930), quoted in RSA iii/3.443–5.

13. Carl von Ossietzky, 'Gibt es noch eine Opposition?', *Die Weltbühne*, xxvi/2 (7 Jan. 1930), 40. Writing under the pseudonym of Ignaz Wrobel, Kurt Tucholsky was similarly dismissive of the NSDAP only a few weeks later. Asked about the role of 'Hitler's people', he placed the following words in the mouth of a 'clairvoyant': 'Not as bad as all that. A terrible amount of shouting, acts of brutality, pleasure in organized violence, delight in wearing a uniform and in lorries and marches [...] not as bad as all that. Extra team of horses at the front: when they've given the first tug on the reins, they'll be held back, the poor fellows.' Under any future half-dictatorial government, the radical sections of the Stahlhelm would be 'quickly suppressed. Herr Hitler, too, has paid his debt to society and can go. [...] A few prison sentences, [...] a few acts of violence against the Jews [...] and against a handful of republicans, [...] a ban on the KPD, but nothing more': Ignaz Wrobel, 'Der Hellseher', *Die Weltbühne*, xxvi/14 (1 April 1930), 499–501.

14. Friedrich Hussong, 'Vor und nach Tisch', *Berliner Lokal-Anzeiger*, xlviii/436 (16 Sept. 1930) (morning edn).

15. Carl von Ossietzky, 'Brüning darf nicht bleiben', *Die Weltbühne*, xxvi/39 (23 Sept. 1930), 463.

16. Quietus, 'Die Zukunft des Nationalsozialismus', *Die Weltbühne*, xxvi/39 (23 Sept. 1930), 478 and 480.

17. *Zeitungskatalog 1930*, Annoncen-Expedition Rudolf Mosse, 56th edn (Berlin n.d.), 264.

18. *A-I-Z*, ix/40 (1930), 783.

19. See Hanne Bergius, 'Der groteske Tod: Erscheinungsformen und Motivik bei Heartfield', *John Heartfield*, ed. Akademie der Künste zu Berlin (Cologne 1991), 56–64, esp. 62.

20. Bergius, 'Der groteske Tod' (note 19), 62.

21. The Political Office of the KPD was its highest executive body; see Hermann Weber, *Die Wandlung des deutschen Kommunismus: Die Stalinisierung der KPD in der Weimarer Republik*, 2 vols (Frankfurt 1969), ii.40–1.

22. 'Resolution des Polbüro der KPD über den Fascismus', *Die Rote Fahne* (15 June 1930), quoted by Hermann Weber (ed.), *Der deutsche Kommunismus: Dokumente* (Cologne and Berlin 1963), 151.

23. *Der Rote Aufbau: Halbmonatsschrift für Politik, Literatur, Wirtschaft, Sozialpolitik und Arbeiterbewegung*, v/4 (15 Feb. 1932), 147–9.

24. 'Der Weg zur Freiheit: Aus der Rede des Genossen Ernst Thälmann über die Aufgaben der KPD nach dem Wahlsieg vom 14. September', quoted in Thälmann, *Reden und Aufsätze 1930–1933* (note 3), 16–17.

25. The KPD won 739,235 votes (27.3 per cent), the SPD 738,094 (27.2 per cent): see Statistisches Amt der Stadt Berlin (ed.), *Statistisches Jahrbuch der Stadt Berlin*, vii (1931), 339.

26. *Statistisches Jahrbuch der Stadt Berlin* (note 25), 341; and Cuno Horkenbach (ed.), *Das Deutsche Reich von 1918 bis heute* (Berlin 1930), Table VII after p.472.

27. Otto Büsch and Wolfgang Haus, *Berlin als Hauptstadt der Weimarer Republik 1919–1933* (Berlin and New York 1987), 378.

28. Heinrich Brüning, *Memoiren 1918–1934* (Stuttgart 1970), 191–3.

29. Brüning, *Memoiren* (note 28), 196.

30. Fröhlich, *Die Tagebücher von Joseph Goebbels* (note 4), ii/1.255 (6 Oct. 1930).

31. *Berliner Lokal-Anzeiger*, xlviii/485 (14 Oct. 1930) (evening edn).

32. This was the experience of the present writer when curating the exhibition 'Vor aller Augen: Vorgeschichte, Verlauf und Folgen der "Reichskristallnacht" vom 9./10. November 1938', which was held at the Academy of the Arts in Berlin-Tiergarten in November 1988. The misattribution became apparent when the same photograph was discovered in Edmund Schultz's *Das Gesicht der Demokratie: Ein Bildwerk zur Geschichte der deutschen Nachkriegszeit*, a picture book full of nationalistic and anti-demoncratic texts that had been published in Leipzig as early as 1931, with an introduction by Friedrich Georg Jünger.

33. Horkenbach, *Das Deutsche Reich* (note 26), 325–6.

34. The Bismarck memorial was erected in 1901 directly opposite the Reichstag but was moved in 1938, when Albert Speer famously redeveloped the city along an east–west axis. Together with the statues of Moltke and Roon, it was relocated to the Großer Stern, which was intended in this way to become the 'Forum of the Second Reich'.

35. 'Der Hergang der Aufläufe', *Berliner Lokal-Anzeiger* (14 Oct. 1930) (morning edn); see also 'Der Schaufenstersturm in der Leipziger Straße', *Vossische Zeitung* (30 April 1931).

36. Dirk Walter, *Antisemitische Kriminalität und Gewalt: Judenfeindschaft in der Weimarer Republik* (Bonn 1999), 209.

37. 'Weltanschauung und Kommunalpolitik' (speech at an NSDAP rally in Munich), RSA iii/2.490; see also the remarks that Hitler made in the course of a speech in Munich on 18 Feb. 1929: 'Thanks to the economic policies of our Marxist and bourgeois parties, large department stores are shooting up out of the ground like mushrooms after a storm and are destroying the middle classes. A more general cultural decline can be seen to accompany these economic phenomena': 'Der Römische Friede und der Nationalsozialismus', RSA iii/1.427.

38. 'Keine Wiederholung der Krawalle: Heute vormittag alles ruhig. Eine neue Mitteilung des Polizeipräsidiums', *Berliner Lokal-Anzeiger* (14 Oct. 1930) (evening edn). In a later report the chief of police emended these figures slightly, claiming that there had been 103 arrests, including 39 members of the NSDAP, 58 sympathizers and 2 members of the Stahlhelm': see Walter, *Antisemitische Kriminalität*, 209 and 312 n.22.

39. Quoted from Walter, *Antisemitische Kriminalität* (note 36), 210.

40. Fröhlich, *Die Tagebücher von Joseph Goebbels* (note 4), ii/1.260–1 (14 Oct. 1930).

41. Fröhlich, *Die Tagebücher von Joseph Goebbels* (note 4), ii/1.258 (10 Oct. 1930); see also Ralf Georg Reuth, *Goebbels: Eine Biographie* (Munich and Zurich 1990), 179–80.

42. Fröhlich, *Die Tagebücher von Joseph Goebbels* (note 4), ii/1.260–1 (14 Oct. 1930).

43. We shall return to these events in late Aug. and early Sept. 1930 in the context of the second Stennes Putsch of early April 1931.

44. Fröhlich, *Die Tagebücher von Joseph Goebbels* (note 4), ii/1.214 (8 Aug. 1930): 'The gentlemen want to get into the Reichstag and refuse to submit to the parliamentary party, and since this has been turned down, they are starting a kind of miniature palace revolution.' See also Heinrich Bennecke, *Hitler und die SA* (Munich 1962), 148–9.

45. See the two decrees of 2 Sept. 1930 reproduced in RSA iii/3.380–1. See also Gerhard Schulz, *Aufstieg des Nationalsozialismus: Krise und Revolution in Deutschland* (Frankfurt, Berlin and Vienna 1976), 582–4; Peter Longerich, *Geschichte der SA in München*, 2nd edn (Munich 2003), 102–4; and Charles Drage, *Als Hitler nach Canossa ging* (Berlin 1982), 111–13. For more on the figure of Stennes, see Hsi-Huey Liang, *Die Berliner Polizei in der Weimarer Republik* (Berlin 1977), 98–101.

46. RSA iii/3.178–9 (letter from the Berlin chief of police to the police headquarters in Munich, 16 Sept. 1930).

47. Carl von Ossietzky, 'Die Blutlinie', *Die Weltbühne*, xxvi/43 (21 Oct. 1930), 603. Ossietzky is referring here to the first Stennes Mutiny of late Aug.–early Sept. 1930.

48. Walter, *Antisemitische Kriminalität* (note 36), 210.

49. *Berliner Lokal-Anzeiger* (14 Oct. 1930) (morning edn).
50. 'Treuekundgebung der 107 nationalsozialistischen Reichstagsabgeordneten für Adolf Hitler', *Völkischer Beobachter* (15 Oct. 1930). It was on this occasion that Hitler declared: 'We are no poor imitation of some other party but enter German history as a completely new movement': RSA iv/1.18. Goebbels was not represented among the leaders of the parliamentary party. The chairman of the party in the Reichstag was Wilhelm Frick, his second-in-command Hermann Göring, whom Hitler appointed personally to the post: see RSA iv/1.19 n.6.
51. Although all the windows of the Wertheim department store were smashed as part of a concerted attack, there were no reports of any looting here.
52. Interview with the International News Service (14 Oct. 1930), which also appeared in several German newspapers, including the *Berliner Lokal-Anzeiger* (15 Oct. 1930) (morning edn). See also RSA iv/1.19–20.
53. Adolf Hitler, 'Der Metallarbeiterstreik', *Illustrierter Beobachter*, v/44 (1 Nov. 1930), 765 and 767. On the strike itself, see Heinrich August Winkler, *Der Weg in die Katastrophe: Arbeiter und Arbeiterbewegung in der Weimarer Republik 1930 bis 1933* (Berlin and Bonn 1987), 232–4.
54. RSA iv/1.22 n.1.
55. 'Nazi Policy: Herr Hitler's Statement. Repudiation of Reparations', *The Times* (15 Oct. 1930), 12. See also RSA iv/1.22–3. A partial German translation appeared in the *C. V.-Zeitung*, ix/43 (24 Oct. 1930), 559–60.
56. 'Die Schuldfrage', *Berliner Lokal-Anzeiger*, xlviii/485 (14 Oct. 1930) (evening edn).
57. Friedrich Hussong, 'Greller Auftakt: Die gestrige Eröffnung des Reichstages', *Berliner Lokal-Anzeiger*, xlviii/484 (14 Oct. 1930) (morning edn).
58. At 32 Köthener Straße in the Kreuzberg district of Berlin, not far from the Museum of Arts and Crafts (now the Martin-Gropius-Bau).
59. Published by S. Fischer Verlag in Berlin in 1930.
60. Thomas Mann, 'Deutsche Ansprache', quoted from Bärbel Schrader and Jürgen Schebera, *Kunstmetropole Berlin: Dokumente und Selbstzeugnisse* (Berlin and Weimar 1987), 269.
61. Gertrud Bergmann, 'Thomas Mann bei den Juden', *Der Angriff* (23 Oct. 1930).
62. Bergmann, 'Thomas Mann bei den Juden' (note 61).
63. Z., 'Thomas Manns "deutsche Ansprache"', *Berliner Lokal-Anzeiger*, xlviii/492 (18 Oct. 1930) (morning edn), 3.
64. Curt Hotzel, 'Thomas Manns Kampf gegen das Leben: Ein Versagen vor den Forderungen der Nation', *Deutsche Tageszeitung* (6 Nov. 1930) (morning edn).
65. All the quotations from Bronnen's writings are taken from Arnolt Bronnen, *arnolt bronnen gibt zu protokoll: beiträge zur geschichte des modernen schriftstellers* (Hamburg 1954), 252–3.
66. Fröhlich, *Die Tagebücher von Joseph Goebbels* (note 4), ii/1.264 (18 Oct. 1930).
67. Bronnen, *arnolt bronnen gibt zu protokoll* (note 65), 256–7.
68. Fröhlich, *Die Tagebücher von Joseph Goebbels* (note 4), ii/1.282 (14 Nov. 1930); 287 (21 Nov. 1930); 294 (1 Dec. 1930); and 297 (5 Dec. 1930).
69. RSA iv/1.145 n.2. The text of Hitler's address has not survived. The editors of RSA again mistakenly describe the *Rheingold* wine bar as a hotel.
70. See RSA iv/1.145–7.
71. Albert Speer, *Erinnerungen* (Berlin 1969), 31–4; trans. Richard and Clara Winston as *Inside the Third Reich: Memoirs by Albert Speer* (London 1970), 14–16. For a critical assessment of Speer's reminiscences, see Matthias Schmidt, *Albert Speer: Das Ende eines Mythos. Speers wahre Rolle im Dritten Reich* (Bern and Munich 1982), 39–46. For a more recent documentary study, see Heinrich Breloer and Rainer Zimmer, *Die Akte Speer: Spuren eines Kriegsverbrechers* (Berlin 2006), 22–33; and Heinrich Breloer, *Speer und Er: Hitlers Architekt und Rüstungsminister* (Berlin 2005), 46–52.

72. Fröhlich, *Die Tagebücher von Joseph Goebbels* (note 4), ii/1.296–7 (4 and 5 Dec. 1930). Hitler's reproaches were directed at frictions within the party allegedly caused by one of Goebbels' former colleagues, a certain Herr Loepelmann.

73. Fröhlich, *Die Tagebücher von Joseph Goebbels* (note 4), ii/1.291–2 (27, 28 and 29 Nov. 1930).

74. Fröhlich, *Die Tagebücher von Joseph Goebbels* (note 4), ii/1.298 (7 Dec. 1930).

75. Fröhlich, *Die Tagebücher von Joseph Goebbels* (note 4), ii/1.295 (3 Dec. 1930).

76. Fröhlich, *Die Tagebücher von Joseph Goebbels* (note 4), i/3.287–8 (21 and 23 July 1929).

77. *Berliner Börsen-Courier* (6 Dec. 1930) (morning edn).

78. Fröhlich, *Die Tagebücher von Joseph Goebbels* (note 4), ii/1.298 (6 Dec. 1930).

79. Space precludes a more detailed assessment of the way in which the National Socialists' violence against the Remarque film was part of a wider and highly politicized cultural war: on 4 Dec. 1930, for example, the graphic artist George Grosz and his publisher Wieland Herzfelde were acquitted by the Berlin District Court of a charge of blasphemy brought following the publication of Grosz's drawing 'Christ with Gas Mask': see Lothar Fischer, *George Grosz* (Reinbek 1993), 104–6.

80. See the lavishly documented study by Peter Dörp, 'Goebbels' Kampf gegen Remarque: Eine Untersuchung über die Hintergründe des Hasses und der Agitation Goebbels' gegen den amerikanischen Spielfilm "Im Westen nichts Neues" nach dem gleichnamigen Bestsellerroman von Erich Maria Remarque', quoted here from the internet site www.erft.de/schulen/abtei-gym/remarque/soerp2.htm.

81. RSA iv/1.146 and 149.

82. Rumpelstilzchen, *Das sowieso!* (Berlin 1931), 116–18. (Rumpelstilzchen was the pen name of Adolf Stein.)

83. Fröhlich, *Die Tagebücher von Joseph Goebbels* (note 4), ii/1.300–1 (9 and 10 Dec. 1930).

84. *Deutsche Tageszeitung* (12 Dec. 1930) (morning edn).

85. RSA iv/1.164.

86. Fröhlich, *Die Tagebücher von Joseph Goebbels* (note 4), ii/1.302–5 (12, 13, 14 and 17 Dec. 1930).

87. Fröhlich, *Die Tagebücher von Joseph Goebbels* (note 4), ii/1.306 (18 Dec. 1930).

88. Horkenbach, *Das Deutsche Reich* (note 26), 340–1.

89. Carl von Ossietzky, 'Remarque-Film', *Die Weltbühne*, xxvi/51 (16 Dec. 1930).

Chapter 8 · 1931: The capital as the butt of ridicule and vituperation

1. RSA iv/1.195–6.

2. Elke Fröhlich (ed.), *Die Tagebücher von Joseph Goebbels*, Part I: *Aufzeichnungen 1923–1941*, 9 vols (Munich 1997–2006), ii/1.316 (3 Jan. 1931). According to the NSDAP's later official account of this incident on New Year's Eve 1930, 'Vastly superior numbers of the Reichsbanner attacked the National Socialist meeting room at 30 Hufelandstraße in the Prenzlauer Berg district. One SA man from Unit 2 drew his pistol in self-defence and shot two Reds'; see J. K. Engelbrechten, *Eine braune Armee entsteht: Die Geschichte der Berlin-Brandenburger SA* (Munich 1937), 146.

3. RSA iv/1.180 (statement made to Prince Friedrich zu Eulenburg-Hertefeld, 24 Jan. 1931). Eulenburg-Hertefeld joined the DNVP in 1918 but switched to the NSDAP in March 1931. In the course of the conversation Hitler was asked whether he would consider forming a coalition with the DNVP in order to achieve an absolute majority in the Reichstag. 'Yes, of course,' he replied, adding that he attached no conditions to the pact (RSA iv/1.179–80).

4. Engelbrechten, *Eine braune Armee entsteht* (note 2), 148.

5. Fröhlich, *Die Tagebücher von Joseph Goebbels* (note 2), ii/1.332 (24 Jan. 1931).

6. See above, p. 136.

7. Engelbrechten, *Eine braune Armee entsteht* (note 2), 149.

8. Engelbrechten, *Eine braune Armee entsteht* (note 2), 85. See also the excerpt from the reminiscences of another SA activist in Berlin in Detlef Schmiechen-Ackermann, *Nationalsozialismus und Arbeitermilieus: Der nationalsozialistische Angriff auf die proletarischen Wohnquartiere und die Reaktion in den sozialistischen Vereinen* (Bonn 1998), 377, where we read: 'The storm centres are a thorn in the flesh [of our enemies].'

9. Engelbrechten, *Eine braune Armee entsteht* (note 2), 150–2.

10. Wolf Rüdiger Heß (ed.), *Rudolf Heß: Briefe 1908–1933* (Munich and Vienna 1987), 369.

11. *Vossische Zeitung* (13 May 1927) (evening edn).

12. Fröhlich, *Die Tagebücher von Joseph Goebbels* (note 2), ii/1.109 (12 March 1930).

13. *Vossische Zeitung* (1 April 1931) (morning edn).

14. Ilse Maurer and Udo Wengst (eds), *Staat und NSDAP 1930–1932: Quellen zur Ära Brüning* (Düsseldorf 1977), XVLII, n.81. The claim by Hsi-Huey Liang that before 1933 the number of NSDAP supporters in the Berlin police was as little as two to three hundred rests on questionable evidence since he relies entirely on documents from 1933–4 in which the officers in question are named: see Hsi-Huey Liang, *Die Berliner Polizei in der Weimarer Republik* (Berlin 1977), 103.

15. Cuno Horkenbach (ed.), *Das Deutsche Reich von 1918 bis heute* (Berlin 1931), 54.

16. *Verhandlungen des Reichstages: Stenographische Berichte*, cdxliv.687–8 quoted by Ernst Deuerlein (ed.), *Der Aufstieg der NSDAP in Augenzeugenberichten* (Düsseldorf 1968), 347.

17. Adolf Hitler, *Mein Kampf* (Munich 1933), 773–4; Engl. trans. Ralph Manheim as *Mein Kampf* (London 2002), 621.

18. Hitler, *Mein Kampf* (note 17), 775; Engl. trans. 623 (emphasis in original).

19. See Chapter 3, n.76 above.

20. RSA ii/1.83.

21. RSA iii/3.170.

22. This idea was expressed with unintentional clarity by Ernst Röhm in a memorandum of 22 April 1931 shortly after Hitler had appointed him the SA's chief of staff. Röhm justified the deployment of SA units by arguing that only in this way was it possible to 'counter acts of terror from the lowest strata of society': see Thilo Vogelsang, *Reichswehr, Staat und NSDAP: Beiträge zur deutschen Geschichte 1930–1932* (Stuttgart 1962), 423.

23. Schmiechen-Ackermann, *Nationalsozialismus und Arbeitermilieus* (note 8), 169.

24. RSA iv/1.361.

25. *Berliner Tageblatt* (8 May 1931) (evening edn).

26. RSA iv/1.366–7. Barely a month earlier, on 2 April 1931, he had prefaced an order to Goebbels with the words: 'In November 1926, I invited you, my dear Herr Doctor, to take over the Berlin branch, which was then completely run down': RSA iv/1.246.

27. *Berliner Tageblatt* (9 May 1931) (morning edn); RSA iv/1.369–70.

28. Fröhlich, *Die Tagebücher von Joseph Goebbels* (note 2), ii/1.402 (9 May 1931). The second, expurgated edition was published by the NSDAP's own Eher-Verlag in Munich in 1929.

29. On Hans Litten, see Irmgard Litten, *A Mother Fights Hitler* (London 1940); Max Fürst, *Talisman Scheherezade: Die schwierigen zwanziger Jahre* (Munich and Vienna 1976); and Carlheinz von Brück, *Ein Mann, der Hitler in die Enge trieb: Hans Littens Kampf gegen den Faschismus*, 2nd edn (Berlin 1976).

30. Fröhlich, *Die Tagebücher von Joseph Goebbels* (note 2), ii/1.353–4 (26 and 27 Feb. 1931).

31. Fröhlich, *Die Tagebücher von Joseph Goebbels* (note 2), ii/1.357–8 (4 and 6 March 1931).

32. Fröhlich, *Die Tagebücher von Joseph Goebbels* (note 2), ii/1.373 (28 March 1931).

33. Herbert Michaelis and Ernst Schraepler (eds), *Ursachen und Folgen: Vom deutschen Zusammenbruch 1918 und 1945 bis zur staatlichen Neuordnung Deutschlands in der Gegenwart*, 25 vols (Berlin 1959), vii.398.

34. RSA iv/1.246–8.

35. RSA iv/1.253–5. Between now and 8 April 1931, there were five further appeals, orders and articles directed at Stennes and at other 'poisons' that had to be removed from the movement: RSA iv/1.276.

36. For a detailed overview, see Patrick Moreau, *Nationalsozialismus von links: Die 'Kampfgemeinschaft Revolutionärer Nationalsozialisten' und die 'Schwarze Front' Otto Strassers 1930–1935* (Stuttgart 1984), 82–93.

37. Peter H. Merkl, 'Formen der nationalsozialistischen Gewaltanwendung: Die SA der Jahre 1925–1933', *Sozialprotest, Gewalt, Terror: Gewaltanwendung durch politische und gesellschaftliche Randgruppen im 19. und 20. Jahrhundert*, ed. Wolfgang J. Mommsen and Gerhard Hirschfeld (Stuttgart 1982), 422–40, esp. 437.

38. Karl Martin Friedrich (ed.), *Der kesse Orje: Spaziergänge eines Berliner Jungen durch das System*, with an introduction by Joseph Goebbels and drawings by Mjölnir (Munich 1931), 9.

39. According to the 1927 Berlin *Baedeker* (20th edn, pp.4–5), the Kaiserhof was one of the 'best hotels' in Berlin but was also slightly cheaper and had fewer rooms than the Adlon on the Pariser Platz, the Esplanade on the Bellevuestraße/Potsdamer Platz and the Bristol on Unter den Linden.

40. See Michaelis and Schraepler, *Ursachen und Folgen* (note 33), vii.80 (letter from the Prussian prime minister relating to the argument over flags in the Berlin hotel industry, 25 Aug. 1927); see also Gottfried Korff (ed.), *Berlin, Berlin: Die Ausstellung zur Geschichte der Stadt* (Berlin 1987), 208 (exhibition catalogue).

41. Otto Dietrich, *Mit Hitler in die Macht: Persönliche Erlebnisse mit meinem Führer* (Munich 1934), 149–51.

42. Dietrich, *Mit Hitler in die Macht* (note 41), 152–4.

43. H. Hoffmann and E. Penkala, 'Hitlers Hauptquartier in Berlin', *Neue I. Z.*, viii/5 (28 Jan. 1932), 99–101. The first of the authors was presumably not Hitler's personal photographer Heinrich Hoffmann but the photojournalist Herbert Hoffmann, whose volume of photographs *Berlin vor fünfzig Jahren* was published in 1978.

44. *Die Welt am Montag*, xxxviii/14 (4 April 1932).

45. Fröhlich, *Die Tagebücher von Joseph Goebbels* (note 2), ii/1.394 (28 April 1931).

46. Fröhlich, *Die Tagebücher von Joseph Goebbels* (note 2), ii/1.409–10 (20 May 1931).

47. RSA iv/1.212 (article of 21 Feb. 1931, 'The Brown House').

48. Heß, *Briefe* (note 10), 369 (letter of 7 July 1925).

49. Henry Ashby Turner, Jr, *Hitler aus nächster Nähe: Aufzeichnungen eines Vertrauten 1929–1932* (Frankfurt, Berlin and Vienna 1978), 411; this passage is not included in the abridged American translation by Ruth Hein, *Hitler: Memoirs of a Confidant* (New Haven, CT, and London 1985).

50. RSA iv/2.245 n.5. Curiously enough, Goebbels had noted in his diary barely twelve months earlier: 'I can't work here in Munich. There's no order and organization here.' See Fröhlich, *Die Tagebücher von Joseph Goebbels* (note 2), ii/1.204 (23 July 1930).

51. RSA iv/1.VI–IX (documents 42–140).

52. It was located at 10 Hedemannstraße in Kreuzberg: see note 154 on p. 406 above.

53. See Horkenbach, *Das Deutsche Reich von 1918 bis heute* (note 15), 548–9 ('Political Parties'). A further exception to the rule was the tiny German Peasants' Party, whose headquarters were in Breslau.

54. RSA ii/1.408 ('Wesen und Ziele des Nationalsozialismus', speech to the Gau party convention of the Austrian NSDAP, Freilassing, 3 July 1927). See also the entirely positive references to Frederick the Great in Hitler's 'second book': RSA iiA.7, 32, 69–70, 99, 101, 127 and 132.

55. The paper headlined its report on Hitler's appearance 'Berlin's oath of loyalty to its leader Adolf Hitler': *Der Angriff* (20 May 1931).

56. RSA iv/1.389–90 (speech at an NSDAP meeting in Berlin, 19 May 1931).

57. See note 46 above.

58. Heinrich Heim, *Monologe im Führerhauptquartier 1941–1944*, ed. Werner Jochmann (Hamburg 1980), 100–2 (21–22 Oct. 1941).

59. Henry Picker, *Hitlers Tischgespräche im Führerhauptquartier*, 4th edn (Stuttgart 1983), 102 (entry of 4 Feb. 1942).

60. See Wolfgang Schivelbusch, *Die Kultur der Niederlage: Der amerikanische Süden 1865, Frankreich 1871, Deutschland 1918* (Berlin 2001), esp. 294–6. It is significant that Julius Langbehn, too, led the way in rejecting the 'lack of culture' of North America, noting many parallels with the United States in his critique of contemporary culture in Berlin: 'The restless spirit of industry characterizes the denizens of the Spree as surely as it does those who dwell on the banks of the Hudson. And in both cases this restlessness prevents the emergence of an independent spirit': see Julius Langbehn, *Rembrandt als Erzieher: Von einem Deutschen* (Leipzig 1922), 117.

61. RSA iv/1.85 (speech at an NSDAP meeting in Offenburg, 8 Nov. 1930).

62. RSA iv/1.334 (speech at an NSDAP meeting in Stuttgart, 24 April 1931).

63. RSA iv/1.191–2 (speech at an NSDAP meeting in Weimar, 8 Feb. 1931).

64. See Thomas Friedrich, ' "Alles kommt auf die Blickrichtung an" oder Geschichte im Prokrustesbett: Das "Revolutionstrauma" der Nationalsozialisten und der Umgang der NS-Bildpropaganda mit den Fotos der Novemberrevolution', *Revolution und Fotografie: Berlin 1918/19. Eine Ausstellung der Neuen Gesellschaft für Bildende Kunst* (Berlin 1989), 227–40 (exhibition catalogue).

65. Hitler, *Mein Kampf* (note 17), 246–8, 250 and 252; Engl. trans. 211–13.

66. See Thomas Friedrich, 'Regenerierter Volkskörper', *Tennis in Deutschland von den Anfängen bis 2002: Zum 100-jährigen Bestehen des Deutschen Tennis Bundes*, ed. Deutscher Tennis Bund (Berlin 2002), 126–33.

67. Hitler wrote 'His Majesty the Kaiser'.

68. Hitler, *Mein Kampf* (note 17), 255–7; Engl. trans. 213–14.

69. Hitler, *Mein Kampf* (note 17), 265–6; Engl. trans. 221–3. In this context Hitler specifically mentions the *Frankfurter Zeitung* and the *Berliner Tageblatt*.

70. Hitler, *Mein Kampf* (note 17), 279; Engl. trans. 237.

71. Hitler, *Mein Kampf* (note 17), 288–90; Engl. trans. 239–40.

72. BA R 43 II/1181 (copy of a report of the meeting held at the offices of Chancellor Adolf Hitler, 19 Sept. 1933).

73. Hitler, *Mein Kampf* (note 17), 646; Engl. trans. 525. See also his remarks on Munich: 'Not only has one not seen Germany if one does not know Munich – no, above all, one does not know German art if one has not seen Munich': *Mein Kampf* (note 17), 129; Engl. trans. 116.

74. Hitler, *Mein Kampf* (note 17), 18; Engl. trans. 18.

75. Hans Lehmbruch, 'Acropolis Germaniae: Der Königsplatz – Forum der NSDAP', *Bürokratie und Kult: Das Parteizentrum der NSDAP am Königsplatz in München. Geschichte und Rezeption*, ed. Iris Lauterbach (Munich 1995), 17–45; and Peter Köpf, *Der Königsplatz in München: Ein deutscher Ort* (Berlin 2005).

76. See note 1 and epigraph to this chapter.

77. Janos Frecot and Klaus-Jürgen Sembach, *Berlin im Licht: Photographien der nächtlichen Stadt* (Berlin 2002), 7–10; and Dietrich Neumann, *Archikektur der Nacht* (Munich 2002), 42.

78. Fröhlich, *Die Tagebücher von Joseph Goebbels* (note 2), i/3.102 (14 Oct. 1928).

79. Fröhlich, *Die Tagebücher von Joseph Goebbels* (note 2), i/3.101 (14 Oct. 1928).

80. Report from the Municipal Building Control Department to the Minister for National Welfare (25 Aug. 1924), quoted by Dietrich Neumann, 'Die ungebaute Stadt der Moderne', *Stadt der Architektur: Architektur der Stadt. Berlin 1900–2000*, ed. Thorsten Scheer, Josef Paul Kleihues and Paul Kahlfeldt (Berlin 2000), 161–73, esp. 161, where the case is treated at length.

81. Josef Paul Kleihues, Jan Gerd Becker-Schwering and Paul Kahlfeldt (eds), *Bauen in Berlin 1900–2000* (Berlin 2000), 108.

82. Werner Oechslin, 'Lichtarchitektur: Die Genese eines neuen Begriffs', *Architektur der Nacht*, ed. Neumann (note 77), 28–35, esp. 31–2, where several examples from Berlin are cited.

83. Ernst A. Busche, '1918–1933: Laboratorium. Wohnen und Weltstadt', *750 Jahre Architektur und Städtebau in Berlin: Die Internationale Bauausstellung im Kontext der Baugeschichte Berlins*, ed. Josef Paul Kleihues (Stuttgart 1987), 153–82, esp. 177–8.

84. Herbert Molderings described the volume as 'the modernist photography book par excellence, the first to give striking photographic expression to the philosophy of "Americanism" in Europe'; see *sehepunkte*, v/7–8 (15 July 2005). In the sixth impression of 1928 the photographic section was expanded to include one hundred photographs: see Martin Parr and Gerry Badger, *The Photobook: A History*, 2 vols (London 2004–6), i.76–7.

85. Erich Mendelsohn, *Amerika: Bilderbuch eines Architekten. Mit 77 photographischen Aufnahmen des Verfassers* (Berlin 1926), plate 5. Mendelsohn was by no means uncritical in his assessment of New York's night-time architecture. His caption to another night-time exposure reads: 'During the day the city is filled with energy, whereas at night all life evaporates in the network of automobile lights, in the illuminated appeal of the advertisements and in the verticals of the high-rise buildings. A circus of light is found only rarely, as here, in the rhythm of the architecture': pl. 25. But his comment on his photograph of Broadway by night (pl. 44) is far more enthusiastic: 'Still lacking in order because of its excesses, it is none the less filled with a fantastic beauty that will ultimately become perfect.'

86. Henry Russell-Hitchcock and Philip Johnson, *The International Style* (repr. New York and London, 1995).

87. Albert Speer, *Erinnerungen* (Berlin 1969), 54–5; Engl. trans. by Richard and Clara Winston as *Inside the Third Reich: Memoirs by Albert Speer* (London 1970), 41.

88. See, for example, the list of architects in Elisabeth M. Hajos and Leopold Zahn, *Berliner Architektur der Nachkriegszeit* (Berlin 1928), reprinted as *Berliner Architektur 1919 bis 1929: 10 Jahre Architektur der Moderne* (Berlin 1996), 111–30.

89. See the section 'Amerika – Deutschland!' in Dietrich Neumann, *'Die Wolkenkratzer kommen!' Deutsche Hochhäuser der zwanziger Jahre. Debatten, Projekte, Bauten* (Braunschweig 1995), 62–84.

90. *Deutsche Bauausstellung Berlin 1931: Amtlicher Katalog und Führer* (Berlin 1931), 97.

91. Hitler, *Mein Kampf* (note 17), 290–2; Engl. trans. 240–2.

92. RSA iii/2.144–6.

93. Kleihues and others, *Bauen in Berlin* (note 81), 88.

94. In other cases he simply ignored buildings such as Ludwig Hoffmann's Town Hall on the Molkenmarkt and the huge District and County Court buildings on the Neue Friedrichstraße (now the Littenstraße).

95. To the south of the Werderscher Markt, the Deutsche Reichsbank occupied an entire block, while in the Behrenstraße the most impressive complex of buildings was made up of the (surviving) offices of the Deutsche Bank, together with half a dozen other banks; see Karl Baedeker, *Berlin und Umgebung: Handbuch für Reisende*, 19th edn (Leipzig 1921), 29, 122 and 158.

96. Julius Posener, *Berlin auf dem Wege zu einer neuen Architektur. Das Zeitalter Wilhelms II.* (Munich 1979); Peter Stürzebecher, *Das Berliner Warenhaus: Bautypus, Element der Stadtorganisation, Raumsphäre der Warenwelt* (Berlin 1979); and Karl-Heinz Hüter, *Architektur in Berlin 1900–1933* (Berlin 1987), esp. 26, where he describes the building as an 'architectural masterpiece'.

97. Speer, *Erinnerungen* (note 87), 47; Engl. trans. 34.

98. Neumann, *'Die Wolkenkratzer kommen!'* (note 89), 62–3. In his search for a plot of land on which to build his Brown House, Hitler had initially considered a fourteen- to sixteen-storey high-rise building in Munich's inner city but then decided against it: 'In spite of the outward grandeur of such a high-rise building', the result would have been

an experiment 'whose models lie not within us but outside us. What is natural in New York is ultimately merely artificial in Munich': RSA iv/1.212.

99. Heinz Johannes, *Neues Bauen in Berlin: Ein Führer mit 168 Bildern* (Berlin 1931, repr. 1998).

100. See the illustration in Frecot and Sembach, *Berlin im Licht* (note 77), 91.

101. Johannes, *Neues Bauen in Berlin* (note 99), 16.

102. Dietrich Worbs, 'Das Columbushaus am Potsdamer Platz von Erich Mendelsohn, 1931/32', *Architektur-Experimente in Berlin und anderswo: Für Julius Posener*, ed. Sonja Günther and Dietrich Worbs (Berlin 1989), 82–101, esp. 101. In this context, Worbs cites Mendelsohn's *Amerika* photographic study of 1926.

103. 'Berliner Architektur unter jüdischem Einfluß', *Die Bauzeitung*, il/13 (1939), 188, quoted from Worbs, 'Das Columbushaus' (note 102), 93–4. Few would disagree with Regina Stephan when she writes that 'There is a universal consensus regarding the importance of the Columbus Building in the history of office architecture'; see Regina Stephan, *Studien zu Waren- und Geschäftshäusern Erich Mendelsohns in Deutschland* (Munich 1992), 170; see also the same writer's chapter 'Wir glauben an Berlin!' in her monograph *Erich Mendelsohn: Dynamik und Funktion. Realisierte Visionen eines kosmopolitischen Architekten* (Ostfildern-Ruit 1999), 144–65. According to the standard history of architecture in Berlin, 'In its outward appearance, the building is one of the most beautiful ever created by twentieth-century architecture': see Hans Joachim Stark, 'Bürohäuser der Privatwirtschaft', *Berlin und seine Bauten*, ed. Architekten- und Ingenieur-Verein zu Berlin, Part IX: *Industriebauten, Bürohäuser* (Berlin, Munich and Düsseldorf 1971), 115–82, esp. 159.

104. 'Bauelend und Kulturverödung im heutigen Staat', *Völkischer Beobachter* (19 Aug. 1930).

105. 'The view of the building is particularly beautiful from the bridge and the opposite side of the river': *Griebens Reiseführer*, vol. vi: *Berlin und Umgebung mit Angaben für Automobilisten* (Berlin 1932), 130. The abridged edition of this guide that was published shortly before the outbreak of the Second World War even describes the Shell Building as 'the most beautiful high-rise building in Berlin': see *Griebens Reiseführer Berlin und Umgebung: Kleine Ausgabe mit Angaben für Autofahrer* (Berlin 1939), 92.

106. Rainer Stommer, *Hochhaus: Der Beginn in Deutschland* (Marburg 1990), 161.

107. *Berlin und seine Bauten* (note 103), 157. The Shell Building features on the jacket of this volume.

108. Busche, 'Laboratorium' (note 83), 178.

109. On the gradual changes that have taken place in the character of the Tiergarten district, see Hartwig Schmidt, *Das Tiergartenviertel: Baugeschichte eines Berliner Villenviertels* (Berlin 1981), 300–2. The Shell Building replaced several houses from the 1850s and 1860s, some of which had had neo-Classical façades (329, 350).

110. The Königin-Augusta-Straße was renamed the Tirpitzufer in 1933 and the Reichpietschufer in 1947.

111. In fact the Von-der-Heydt-Brücke.

112. Renamed the Stauffenbergstraße on 20 July 1955.

113. Julius Posener, 'Immeuble Shell à Berlin', *L'architecture d'aujourd'hui* (Dec. 1932–Jan. 1933), 75–7.

114. It was in early Oct. 1931 that the first contact was made between Hitler and General Kurt von Schleicher, the head of the Ministerial Office in the Reichswehr Ministry. On 10 Oct. Hitler and his 'personal envoy in Berlin', Hermann Göring, 'spent one-and-a-half hours discussing questions of domestic and foreign policy' with President Hindenburg; see Hans Volz, *Daten der Geschichte der NSDAP*, 8th edn (Berlin and Leipzig 1938), 35–6; and Horkenbach, *Das Deutsche Reich* (note 15), 327 and 340.

115. Barbara Miller-Lane, *Architektur und Politik in Deutschland 1918–1945* (Braunschweig 1986), 142–3. Miller-Lane is right to point out that 'for many years' Hitler's

understanding of art 'had no real influence on party propaganda, which took account of contemporary art only when it could be used in its anti-Semitic campaigns. But in around 1928 the Nazis' propaganda underwent a fundamental shift, when the party press began to take an intellectual interest in literature, music and drama in its attempt to reach out to wider sections of the population.'

116. In 1929 the city's architectural adviser, Martin Wagner, even published a journal under the title *Das Neue Berlin: Grossstadtprobleme*. His editor-in-chief was the writer Adolf Behne. A complete reprint, with a foreword by Julius Posener, was published in 1988.

117. See Ludovica Scarpa, *Martin Wagner und Berlin: Architektur und Städtebau in der Weimarer Republik* (Braunschweig and Wiesbaden 1986), esp. 83–124.

118. A particularly good example of this is Goebbels' article 'Rund um die Gedächtniskirche', *Der Angriff* (23 Jan. 1928), reprinted in Joseph Goebbels, *Der Angriff: Aufsätze aus der Kampfzeit*, 2nd edn (Munich 1935), 338–40. On the percentage of Jews in the population of the individual districts in Berlin between 1910 and 1925, see Friedrich Leyden, *Groß-Berlin: Geographie der Weltstadt* (Breslau 1933, repr. 1995).

119. Christoph Heuter, *Emil Fahrenkamp 1885–1966: Architekt im rheinisch-westfälischen Industriegebiet* (Petersberg 2002), 164 and 208 n.735. Hitler's remark is confirmed not only by Fahrenkamp's daughter, Ursula Leussing, but also by his most famous pupil, Wilhelm Schmidt, who worked closely with Fahrenkamp over a period of many years (122, 149 and 199 n.504). In his de-Nazification trial in 1947, Fahrenkamp himself explained that 'Hitler rejected me as too modern for him, but I was later given exhibition buildings to design so that I wouldn't be passed over entirely' (199). In the light of the commissions that Fahrenkamp received after 1933 and especially after 1938 and in view of his dealings with Göring, Goebbels and Speer, this evasive reply was clearly meant as one of contrition.

120. Lauterbach, *Bürokratie und Kult* (note 75).

121. Ulrike Grammbitter, 'Vom "Parteiheim" in der Brienner Straße zu den Monumentalbauten am "Königlichen Platz". Das Parteizentrum der NSDAP am Königsplatz in München', *Bürokratie und Kult* (note 75), 61–87, esp. 63–4. Grammbitter discovered the letter in the Bavarian State Archives.

122. RSA iv/2.57–64, esp. 62–3 (letter to Karl Stützel, 7 Aug. 1931).

123. RSA iv.2.59–60 (letter to Karl Stützel, 7 Aug. 1931) (emphasis added).

124. The Schloßfreiheit was the road in front of the Royal Palace. The houses here were pulled down in the mid-1890s in order to make way for the national monument to Kaiser Wilhelm I that was unveiled in 1897: see p. 19 above; see also Dietmar Arnold and Ingmar Arnold, *Schloßfreiheit: Vor den Toren des Stadtschlosses* (Berlin 1998), esp. 43–5. It is clear from the passage quoted here that Hitler was unfamiliar with the history of this street and assumed that the picture of Berlin that it presented was much older than was in fact the case.

125. RSA iv/2.60–61.

126. RSA iv/2.61.

127. Fröhlich, *Die Tagebücher von Joseph Goebbels* (note 2), i/2.113 (25 July 1926).

128. Fröhlich, *Die Tagebücher von Joseph Goebbels* (note 2), ii/1.256 (9 Oct. 1930).

129. Heß, *Briefe* (note 10), 395.

130. Fröhlich, *Die Tagebücher von Joseph Goebbels* (note 2), ii/2.37 (12 June 1931).

131. Heß, *Briefe* (note 10), 413.

132. Fröhlich, *Die Tagebücher von Joseph Goebbels* (note 2), ii/2.40 and 75 (16 June and 12 Aug. 1931).

133. Volz, *Daten der Geschichte der NSDAP* (note 114), 35; and Horkenbach, *Das Deutsche Reich* (note 15), 273.

134. Kurt Pätzold and Manfred Weißbecker, *Geschichte der NSDAP 1920–1945* (Cologne 1998), 161.

135. Letter from Gregor Straßer to Ernst Schlange (12 Sept. 1931), quoted from Albrecht Tyrell, *Führer befiehl. . . Selbstzeugnisse aus der 'Kampfzeit' der NSDAP: Dokumentation und Analyse* (Düsseldorf 1969), 344.

136. Fröhlich, *Die Tagebücher von Joseph Goebbels* (note 2), ii/2.75 (12 Aug. 1931).

137. Dirk Walter, *Antisemitische Kriminalität und Gewalt: Judenfeindschaft in der Weimarer Republik* (Bonn 1999), 211. Walter's account is based for the most part on the extensive findings of the Charlottenburg County Court (23 Sept. 1931) and the appeal hearing of the Berlin District Court (9 Feb. 1932): see Walter, *Antisemitische Kriminalität*, 312–13 n.25.

138. *Berliner Tageblatt* (18 Sept. 1931) (evening edn), quoted from Heinrich Hannover and Elisabeth Hannover-Drück, *Politische Justiz 1918–1933* (Frankfurt 1966), 284.

139. *C. V.-Zeitung*, x/38 (18 Sept. 1931), 457.

140. *Völkischer Beobachter* (29 Sept. 1931).

141. *C. V.-Zeitung*, x/39 (25 Sept. 1931), 467–8.

142. For a detailed examination of the journalistic and legalistic controversies, see Walter, *Antisemitische Kriminalität* (note 137), 212–14.

143. Heinrich Brüning, *Memoiren 1918–1934* (Stuttgart 1970), 411; see also Ted Harrison, '"Alter Kämpfer" im Widerstand: Graf Helldorf, die NS-Bewegung und die Opposition gegen Hitler', *Vierteljahrshefte für Zeitgeschichte*, xlv (1997), 385–423, esp. 392–3.

144. Walter, *Antisemitische Kriminalität* (note 137), 216–17; and Hannover and Hannover-Drück, *Politische Justiz* (note 138), 285–7.

145. Walter, *Antisemitische Kriminalität* (note 137), 217.

146. 'Graf Helldorf freigesprochen: Das Urteil im Kurfürstendamm-Prozeß', *Vossische Zeitung* (10 Feb. 1932) (morning edn).

147. RSA iv/2.106 n.16 (letter VI/N 2325/31 from the Munich Police Headquarters to the Berlin Police Headquarters, 14 Jan. 1932).

148. Martin Schuster, 'Die SA in der nationalsozialistischen "Machtergreifung" in Berlin und Brandenburg 1926–1934' (FU Berlin, 2005), 51.

149. Schuster, 'Die SA' (note 148), 51.

150. Thus the title of a volume of essays published by the Leo Baeck Institute under the editorship of Werner E. Mosse in 1965. (A second edition followed in 1966.)

151. H[ubert] R[enfro] Knickerbocker, *The German Crisis* (1932). A German translation by Franz Fein appeared under the title *Deutschland so oder so?*. Knickerbocker was the foreign correspondent of the *New York Evening Post*.

Chapter 9 · 1932: The start of a decisive year

1. *Die Welt am Montag*, xxxviii/1 (4 Jan. 1932).

2. Rumpelstilzchen, *Nu wenn schon!* (Berlin 1932), 229.

3. Details from the ninth edition of the *Statistisches Jahrbuch der Stadt Berlin* (Berlin 1933), 10 and 105; see also Ingo Materna and Wolfgang Ribbe, *Berlin: Geschichte in Daten*, 2nd edn (Wiesbaden 2003), 169.

4. See Herbert Michaelis and Ernst Schraepler (eds), *Ursachen und Folgen: Vom deutschen Zusammenbruch 1918 und 1945 bis zur staatlichen Neuordnung Deutschlands in der Gegenwart*, 25 vols (Berlin 1959), viii.323.

5. J. K. von Engelbrechten, *Eine braune Armee entsteht: Die Geschichte der Berlin-Brandenburger SA* (Munich 1937), 197.

6. Quoted from the 'Memorandum of the Prussian Ministry of the Interior concerning the National Socialist German Workers' Party', excerpts from which are reproduced in Ilse Maurer and Udo Wengst (eds), *Staat und NSDAP 1930–1932: Quellen zur Ära Brüning* (Düsseldorf 1977), 296.

7. *Vorwärts* (9 Jan. 1932), quoted from Alfons Arenhövel, *Arena der Leidenschaften: Der Berliner Sportpalast und seine Veranstaltungen 1910–1973* (Berlin 1990), 314.

8. Arenhövel, *Arena der Leidenschaften* (note 7), 314.

9. 'Hindenburgs Funk-Appell: Die Silvester-Ansprache des Reichspräsidenten', *Vossische Zeitung* (1 Jan. 1932) (morning edn).

10. RSA iv/3.9.

11. Quoted from Axel Steinhage and Thomas Flemming, *Chronik 1932: Tag für Tag in Wort und Bild* (Dortmund 1989), 13.

12. T[heodor] W[olff], 'So oder so', *Berliner Tageblatt*, lxi/4 (3 Jan. 1932) (morning edn).

13. Heinrich Brüning, *Memoiren 1918–1934* (Stuttgart 1970), 460–2.

14. *Vossische Zeitung* (7 Jan. 1932) (evening edn). In his biography of Hitler, Konrad Heiden describes the alleged scene in Munich on 6 Jan., when Groener's telegram arrived: Hitler apparently stuffed it into his pocket as if it were some trophy, exclaiming: 'Now I have it in my pocket! You've acknowledged that I'm someone you can do business with!': see Konrad Heiden, *Adolf Hitler: Das Zeitalter der Verantwortungslosigkeit. Eine Biographie* (Zurich 1936), 293.

15. Konrad Heiden, *Geburt des dritten Reiches: Die Geschichte des Nationalsozialismus bis Herbst 1933* (Zurich 1934), 52.

16. Brüning, *Memoiren* (note 13), 501.

17. Joseph Goebbels, *Vom Kaiserhof zur Reichskanzlei: Eine historische Darstellung in Tagebuchblättern* (Munich 1934), 20 (7 Jan. 1932). The entries in this volume, which was intended not least as a vehicle for party propaganda, take the form of a diary, but, as Elke Fröhlich has pointed out in her two editions of Goebbels' private diaries, they are often at odds with those in his private jottings, which were not intended for public consumption.

18. J. K. Engelbrechten and Hans Volz, *Wir wandern durch das nationalsozialistische Berlin: Ein Führer durch die Gedenkstätten des Kampfes um die Reichshauptstadt* (Munich 1937), 63. There were also shorter visits that Hitler paid to Berlin, for public appearances and the like, when he did not stay at the Kaiserhof. This was particularly true of the secret meetings that he held in Berlin or when he travelled through the capital for similar meetings in the surrounding area.

19. Heiden, *Geburt des dritten Reiches* (note 15), 53: 'Hitler understood that to agree to Brüning's plan was to support the chancellor himself since his agreement would have consolidated the chancellor's standing with the country's president to a quite exceptional degree.'

20. RSA iv/3.43 (letter to Heinrich Brüning, 15 Jan. 1932). For the description of Hindenburg, see RSA iv/3.44. The German Nationalist leader, Alfred Hugenberg, had already given a similar reason for turning down Brüning's proposal; see the wording of his reply in 'Hugenbergs "Nein"', *Berliner Lokal-Anzeiger* (12 Jan. 1932) (evening edn).

21. Otto Meißner, *Staatssekretär unter Ebert – Hindenburg – Hitler: Der Schicksalsweg des deutschen Volkes von 1918–1945, wie ich ihn erlebte* (Hamburg 1950), 216–17; Ian Kershaw, *Hitler 1889–1936: Hubris* (London 1998), 394; and Goebbels, *Vom Kaiserhof* (note 17), 24 (12 Jan. 1932).

22. 'Hitler antwortet. Zwei Briefe: an Hindenburg und Brüning', *Berliner Tageblatt* (13 Jan. 1932) (morning edn).

23. In an article headed 'Adolf Hitler's Day of Reckoning with the Rebels' that appeared in the *Völkischer Beobachter* (4 April 1931), Hitler had declared that 'I consider any man who tries to incite a completely unarmed organization to commit an act of violence against today's state to be either a fool or a criminal or an agent provocateur!' RSA iv/1.256. Walter Stennes was a former chief of police, a point that Hitler never ceased to stress in his attempts to belittle his enemy following his expulsion from the party. From 1919 to 1922 he commanded a special operations police squad and from 1925 to 1930 advised the Foreign Ministry and Defence Ministry, also acting as their spokesman: see RSA iv/1.248 n.1.

24. See the statement to the County Court in Berlin-Mitte (16 Jan. 1932) in RSA iv/3.45.

25. *Berliner Lokal-Anzeiger*, l/27 (16 Jan. 1932) (evening edn).

26. *Berliner Tageblatt*, lxi/27 (16 Jan. 1932) (evening edn).

27. Gottfried Feder's brochure *Das Programme der N.S.D.A.P. und seine weltanschaulichen Grundlagen* was first published by the party in 1927. By 1932 it had sold more than 395,000 copies.
28. The wording of the speech, at least to the extent that it was reproduced in *Der Angriff* (18 Jan. 1932), appears in RSA iv/3.49–52.
29. RSA iv/3.51 n.13.
30. RSA iv/3.52.
31. The author may have been the arts editor of the *Vossische Zeitung*, Otto Ernst Hesse.
32. H., 'Das Weltanschauungsplakat', *Vossische Zeitung* (18 Jan. 1932) (evening edn).
33. Olden also worked as a defence lawyer. Among his clients was Carl von Ossietzky in his two *Weltbühne* trials. For more on Olden and his tragic death in exile, see *Der Deutsche PEN-Club im Exil 1933–1948: Eine Ausstellung der Deutschen Bibliothek Frankfurt am Main* (Frankfurt am Main 1980), esp. 192–4.
34. Rudolf Olden (ed.), *Das Wunderbare oder Die Verzauberten: Propheten in deutscher Krise* (Berlin 1932). The book was published by Rowohlt, which was still based in Berlin at this time.
35. Olden, 'Über das Wunderbare', *Das Wunderbare* (note 34), 11.
36. Olden, 'Über das Wunderbare', *Das Wunderbare* (note 34), 16–17 and 20.
37. *Vossische Zeitung* (24 Jan. 1932) (morning edn). The paper later published a correction, placing the total number of students at fourteen thousand.
38. See the report of the law student Walter Loeb in the *C. V.-Zeitung*, xi/5 (29 Jan. 1932): 'Our enemies lashed out at us with riding whips, keys and belt buckles. Many of us were injured and thrown to the ground, one of our number collapsed, covered in blood, and had to be taken to the rescue station. [. . .] They did not even shy away from roaming the halls of science: "When Jewish blood sprays from the knife, then that's as good as it gets." From every quarter cries could be heard: "Death to the Jews!" and "Jews out!" Most repugnant of all was the behaviour of the female National Socialist students, who egged on their comrades by shouting the most vulgar obscenities, encouraging them to commit further acts of brutality and singing inflammatory songs.'
39. Cuno Horkenbach (ed.), *Das Deutsche Reich von 1918 bis heute* (Berlin 1932), 49; and *Vossische Zeitung* (9 Feb. 1932) (morning edn).
40. Engelbrechten, *Eine braune Arme entsteht* (note 5), 201. Three pages later Engelbrechten quotes an SA veteran, Erich Kruschwitz, who reports that the SA closed ranks and protected its members from prosecution: 'Many of our comrades in the SA who had used their weapons in self-defence and who now had to escape the attention of the Republic's police or the public prosecutor were spirited away into the country by job-creation schemes and given refuge with friendly landowners, especially in Mecklenburg.'
41. *Vossische Zeitung* (8 Feb. 1932) (evening edn).
42. *Völkischer Beobachter* (11 Feb. 1932); and Arenhövel, *Arena der Leidenschaften* (note 7), 318–19.
43. Hitler was alluding to an article in the morning edition of the *Berliner Tageblatt* (29 July 1931) that had claimed he was planning to dismiss Ernst Röhm – the SA's chief of staff since 1 Jan. 1931 – on the grounds of his homosexuality. See also Hitler's declaration of 30 July 1931 in which he dismissed the article of the '*Berliner Tageblatt* liar' as 'a fabrication and a lie from start to finish': RSA iv/2.41–2.
44. All quotations from the speech of 9 Feb. 1932 are taken from RSA iv/3.118–22.
45. Goebbels, *Vom Kaiserhof* (note 17), 26 (19 Jan. 1932) and 43 (9 Feb. 1932).
46. 'Weshalb SA-Appell? Der Diktator und seine Partetruppe', *Vossische Zeitung* (11 Feb. 1932) (morning edn).
47. *Der Angriff* (10 Feb. 1932).
48. *Völkischer Beobachter* (12 Feb. 1932).
49. Gerhard Mondt, *Herbert Norkus: Das Tagebuch der Kameradschaft Beusselkietz. Mit einem Geleitwort von Baldur von Schirach* (Berlin 1941), 87–8.

50. RSA iv/3.122 (emphasis in the original). According to J. K. Engelbrechten, 'This is the arm of the movement in the capital: 22,000 enthusiastic men and youths willing to spill their last drop of blood'; Engelbrechten, *Eine braune Armee entsteht* (note 5), 206.

51. Goebbels, *Vom Kaiserhof* (note 17), 43 (9 Feb. 1932).

52. Goebbels, *Vom Kaiserhof* (note 17), 43–4 (10 Feb. 1932).

53. Goebbels, *Vom Kaiserhof* (note 17), 51 (23 Feb. 1932).

54. Goebbels, *Vom Kaiserhof* (note 17), 44 (11 Feb. 1932); and RSA iv/3.125 n.14.

55. Horkenbach, *Das Deutsche Reich* (note 39), 32. According to the declaration issued by the Central Committee, its own candidacy would be used 'to unmask and combat the parties of the fascist and bourgeois dictatorship and its reliable prop, the Social Democrats – these parties will be exposed as the mortal enemies of the working class'.

56. Horkenbach, *Das Deutsche Reich* (note 39), 51.

57. Horkenbach, *Das Deutsche Reich* (note 39), 56. The appeal invited all those Germans to vote for Duersterberg 'who are resolved to fight for autochthonous Christian culture, for family and for the German way of life; against open and veiled godlessness; for the organic state of German blood; against Weimar democracy and international Marxism; for German military sovereignty against pacifist emasculation; for the protection of property and private business; for an end to unemployment and protection of the workplace'; quoted by Horkenbach, *Das Deutsche Reich* (note 39), 56.

58. RSA iv/3.129.

59. Goebbels, *Vom Kaiserhof* (note 17), 48 (19 Feb. 1932).

60. RSA iv/3.133–5.

61. Goebbels, *Vom Kaiserhof* (note 17), 48 (19 Feb. 1932).

62. Goebbels, *Vom Kaiserhof* (note 17), 49 (21 Feb. 1932): 'Hugenberg was with the Führer. As candidates he proposes Vögler [the leading Dortmund industrialist Albert Vögler] and Prince Oskar of Prussia. Remarkable how unfamiliar he is with the soul of the people! The German National Party remains the organization of reactionary forces.'

63. See Hitler's witness statement to the committee of enquiry of the Thuringian Landtag (15 March 1932) in RSA iv/3.227–9.

64. See the minutes reporting Hitler's appointment (26 Feb. 1932) in RSA iv/3.136–7.

65. See Hitler's letters to the Braunschweig Embassy in Berlin (28 Feb. and 10 March 1932) in RSA iv/3.151 and 200.

66. André François-Poncet, *Botschafter in Berlin 1931–1938* (Berlin and Mainz 1962), 40.

67. Goebbels, *Vom Kaiserhof* (note 17), 49–50 (22 Feb. 1932). The passage from the Sportpalast speech is quoted from Horkenbach, *Das Deutsche Reich* (note 39), 57. A slightly different version appears in Michaelis and Schraepler, *Ursachen und Folgen* (note 4), viii.395.

68. Goebbels, *Vom Kaiserhof* (note 17), 50 (22 Feb. 1932). In his entry of 23 Feb. 1932 (p.51), Goebbels expressly mentions the presence of the Braunschweig minister of the interior and member of the NSDAP, Dietrich Klagge: 'Let's hope he'll be able to account for his actions.'

69. 'Das Signal zum Angriff. Eröffnung des Entscheidungskampfes durch Adolf Hitler. Die Wahlproklamation der NSDAP im Berliner Sportpalast', *Völkischer Beobachter* (Feb. 1932) (special issue no. 22); also reproduced as 'Speech at the NSDAP Rally in Berlin, 27 Feb. 1932' in RSA iv/3.138–44.

70. *Völkischer Beobachter* (Feb. 1932) (special issue no. 22); also RSA iv.3.139. In the special issue of the paper, the NSDAP's electoral gambit is praised as an 'overwhelming expression of the living will' that flows through the National Socialist movement 'like a river' and, as such, is altogether different from the 'paper power of our enemies' press, enemies who seek in vain to gull the people with the most reprehensible measures and to conceal from them their desperate situation'.

71. On 4 Feb. 1932 the German supreme court met to consider lifting the ban on *Der Angriff*, which had been in place since 8 Jan. 1932, and decided that the term 'rotary

synagogue' did not constitute an insult to the Jewish religion: see Horkenbach, *Das Deutsche Reich* (note 39), 46.

72. Thomas Friedrich, 'Die Berliner Zeitungslandschaft am Ende der Weimarer Republic', *Berlin 1932: Das letzte Jahr der ersten deutschen Republik. Politik, Medien, Symbole*, ed. Diethart Kerbs and Henrick Stahr (Berlin 1992), 56–67. The circulation figures mentioned there for the *Berliner Tageblatt* have been corrected in the light of the information provided by the paper itself in 1932, while the figures for *Der Angriff* have been corrected in order to conform with those given by Goebbels in a diary entry of 12 Aug. 1931: see Elke Fröhlich (ed.), *Die Tagebücher von Joseph Goebbels*, Part I: *Aufzeichnungen 1923-1941*, 9 vols (Munich 1997–2006), ii/1.75 (12 Aug. 1931).
73. Goebbels, *Vom Kaiserhof* (note 17), 54 (29 Feb. 1932).
74. RSA iv/3.96 and 106–7.
75. Goebbels, *Vom Kaiserhof* (note 17), 40.
76. See Berthold Grzywatz, 'Der Beusselkiez', *Tiergarten*, ii: *Moabit*, ed. Helmut Engel, Stefi Jersch-Wenzel and Wilhelm Treue (Berlin 1987), 33–49.
77. See Christian Striefler, *Kampf um die Macht: Kommunisten und Nationalsozialisten am Ende der Weimarer Republik* (Berlin 1993), 363. Ralf Georg Reuth describes the incident as an act of vengeance designed to avenge the assault that had taken place a few days earlier, when members of the SA had attacked a group of Communists at the 'Felseneck Colony': see Ralf Georg Reuth, *Goebbels: Eine Biographie* (Munich and Zurich 1990), 211–12.
78. Engelbrechten and Volz, *Wir wandern* (note 18), 124.
79. Manfred von Killinger, *Die SA in Wort und Bild* (Leipzig 1933), quoted from Peter Longerich, *Geschichte der SA*, 2nd edn (Munich 2003), 117; see also Gerhard Paul, *Aufstand der Bilder: Die NS-Propaganda vor 1933* (Bonn 1992), 133–4.
80. Paul, *Aufstand der Bilder* (note 79), 138.
81. Karl Aloys Schenzinger, *Der Hitlerjunge Quex: Roman* (Berlin 1932), 5–8 and 45–8.
82. Schenzinger, *Der Hitlerjunge Quex* (note 81), 261–4; see also Hans Volz, *Daten der Geschichte der NSDAP*, 8th edn (Berlin and Leipzig 1938), 108. The novel was filmed in 1933, when the director was Hans Steinhoff. In spite of frequent claims to the contrary, neither the novel nor the film depicts the life of Herbert Norkus. Only the settings are identical: Beusselkietz in Moabit and neighbouring parts of Berlin. The film was shown for the first time at the Ufa-Palast in Munich on 12 Sept. 1933 in the presence of Hitler himself. See Rolf Giesen and Manfred Hobsch, *Hitlerjunge Quex, Jud Süß und Kolberg: Die Propagandafilme des Dritten Reiches. Dokumente und Materialien zum NS-Film* (Berlin 2005), 31–4.
83. Schenzinger, *Der Hitlerjunge Quex* (note 81), 98–100. In his study of the careers of members of the NSDAP, Peter H. Merkl has noted the large percentage of those who were motivated to join either the SA or the party by their anti-Marxist feelings: 'The anti-Marxists tended to live either in Berlin or in rural areas': see Peter H. Merkl, *Political Violence under the Swastika: 581 Early Nazis*, 8th edn (Princeton, NJ, 1975), 522–3.
84. Longerich, *Geschichte der SA* (note 79), 117.
85. Reproduced in the *Berliner Tageblatt* (12 March 1932) (morning edn).
86. *Vossische Zeitung* (12 March 1932) (morning edn).
87. *Das 12 Uhr Blatt* (14 March 1932).
88. Heinrich August Winkler, *Der Weg in die Katastrophe: Arbeiter und Arbeiterbewegung in der Weimarer Republik 1930 bis 1933* (Berlin and Bonn 1987), 189 and 519–20.
89. Paul, *Aufstand der Bilder* (note 79), 97; see also Otto Dietrich, *Mit Hitler in die Macht: Persönliche Erlebnisse mit meinem Führer* (Munich 1934), 60–2.
90. *Statistisches Jahrbuch der Stadt Berlin*, 8th edn (Berlin 1932), 258; see also Otto Büsch and Wolfgang Haus, *Berlin als Hauptstadt der Weimarer Republik 1919-1933* (Berlin and New York 1987), 70–1. As before, the NSDAP recorded its best results in Steglitz, where it won 35.2 per cent of the vote. Even as late as 1935 an official history of the

party's 'years of struggle' was forced to admit that workers and peasants were still underrepresented in the 'workers' party'. According to these figures, workers represented 32.1 per cent of the party against 46.3 per cent in the population as a whole. Peasants made up 10.7 per cent of the party's membership in comparison with 20.7 per cent in the country as a whole. Conversely, white-collar workers were overrepresented, with 20.6 per cent (12.4 per cent), as were the self-employed with 20.2 per cent (9.6 per cent) and civil servants with 13.0 per cent (4.8 per cent). See *Aufbruch und Kampf der Partei: Der Schulungsbrief*, v (1938), 287.

91. Resolution of the Central Committee of the KPD in *Die Rote Fahne* (27 March 1932); see also Thomas Weingartner, *Stalin und der Aufstieg Hitlers: Die Deutschlandpolitik der Sowjetunion und der Kommunistischen Internationale 1929–1934* (Berlin 1970), 104–6.

92. These appeals are reproduced in RSA iv/3.223–5 and 226.

93. Veit Valentin, 'Gegen-Angriff!', *Vossische Zeitung* (15 March 1932) (morning edn).

94. T[heodor] W[olff], 'Der erste Schlag', *Berliner Tageblatt* (15 March 1932) (morning edn).

95. RSA iv/3.257 n.2.

96. Albert Krebs, *Tendenzen und Gestalten der NSDAP: Erinnerungen an die Frühzeit der Partei* (Stuttgart 1959), 152–4.

97. From 20 March to 3 April 1932: see Horkenbach, *Das Deutsche Reich* (note 39), 83.

98. Interview with the *Daily Express* in RSA iv/3.258–60.

99. Kershaw, *Hitler 1889–1936* (note 21), 363; Paul, *Aufstand der Bilder* (note 79), 97 and 204–6. The text of these speeches is reproduced in RSA v/1.16–48.

100. Heinrich Hoffmann (ed.), *Hitler über Deutschland* (Munich 1932), 3. (The text was written by Josef Berchtold.)

101. See Paul, *Aufstand der Bilder* (note 79), 70–2.

102. Fröhlich, *Die Tagebücher von Joseph Goebbels* (note 72), ii/2.238 (10 March 1932). Whereas the *Berliner Lokal-Anzeiger*, in its morning edition of 10 March 1932, spoke of a 'very large audience', the headline in the morning edition of the *Berliner Tageblatt* on the same day read: 'Failed Hitler Rally in the Lustgarten'.

103. Adolf Hitler, *Mein Kampf* (Munich 1933), 552; Engl. trans. Ralph Manheim as *Mein Kampf* (London 2002), 448. Sven Felix Kellerhoff thinks that the demonstration that was described by Hitler was 'clearly the official burial of the workers who died in the riots on 9 November', which took place on 20 Nov. 1918 and which Hitler could have attended on his way back to Munich from hospital in Pomerania. If so, he must have walked from Stettin Station to Anhalt Station: see Kellerhoff, *Hitlers Berlin: Geschichte einer Hassliebe* (Berlin 2005), 19–20. I consider this to be unlikely not least because the procession came from Unter den Linden and turned off right into the Schloßfreiheit in front of the Lustgarten, before passing the National Memorial and finally crossing over the Schloßplatz: see the illustrations in the exhibition catalogue *Revolution und Fotografie: Berlin 1918/19. Eine Ausstellung der Neuen Gesellschaft für Bildende Kunst* (Berlin 1989), 253. Moreover, it was a genuine funeral procession and had none of the belligerent character ascribed to it by Hitler in *Mein Kampf*. It is far more likely that Hitler was describing an incident that took place in 1922/3, during a period when he was frequently in Berlin (see above pp. 21–34).

104. *Berlin Handbuch: Das Lexikon der Bundeshauptstadt*, ed. Presse- und Informationsamt des Landes Berlin (Berlin 1992), 788–9; see also Annemarie Lange, *Berlin in der Weimarer Republik* (Berlin 1987), 295, 415, 442, 801, 822–3, 1026 and 1028.

105. Count Harry Kessler, *Tagebücher 1918–1937*, ed. Wolfgang Pfeiffer-Belli (Frankfurt 1961), 324.

106. Goebbels, *Vom Kaiserhof* (note 17), 59 (9 March 1932).

107. See Paul, *Aufstand der Bilder* (note 79), 98.

108. The brief summary of the speech that appeared in the *Völkischer Beobachter* (6 April 1932) is reproduced in RSA v/1.20–1.

109. The text of the speech appeared in the *Potsdamer Tageszeitung* (5 April 1932) and is reproduced in RSA v/1.23.
110. The last two quotations are taken from Hoffmann, *Hitler über Deutschland* (note 100), 10.

Chapter 10 · 1932–3: The road to power

1. Joseph Goebbels, *Vom Kaiserhof zur Reichskanzlei: Eine historische Darstellung in Tagebuchblättern* (Munich 1934), 93.
2. Count Harry Kessler, *Tagebücher 1918–1937*, ed. Wolfgang Pfeiffer-Belli (Frankfurt 1961), 676.
3. Quoted from RSA v/2.375 n.2.
4. Heinrich August Winkler, *Der Weg in die Katastrophe: Arbeiter und Arbeiterbewegung in der Weimarer Republik 1930 bis 1933* (Berlin and Bonn 1987), 519 and 528.
5. *B. Z. am Mittag* (11 April 1932).
6. Statistisches Amt der Stadt Berlin (ed.), *Statistisches Jahrbuch der Stadt Berlin*, 8th edn (Berlin 1932), 259.
7. *Berliner Tageblatt* (17 March 1932) (evening edn).
8. *Vossische Zeitung* (17 March 1932) (evening edn).
9. *Berliner Tageblatt* (17 March 1932) (evening edn).
10. Goebbels, *Vom Kaiserhof* (note 1), 60 (entry of 11 March 1932).
11. *Berliner Tageblatt* (17 March 1932) (evening edn).
12. *Berliner Tageblatt* (6 April 1932) (evening edn).
13. See the minutes of the meeting at the Ministry of the Interior, reproduced in Ilse Maurer and Udo Wengst (eds), *Staat und NSDAP 1930–1932: Quellen zur Ära Brüning* (Düsseldorf 1977), 304–9 (document 63) and Gerhard Schulz's introduction to the same volume, VII–LXX, esp. LVIII–LX.
14. Maurer and Wengst, *Staat und NSDAP* (note 13), 305 and 308–9; see also Thilo Vogelsang, *Reichswehr, Staat und NSDAP: Beiträge zur deutschen Geschichte 1930–1932* (Stuttgart 1962), 160–2.
15. Cuno Horkenbach (ed.), *Das Deutsche Reich von 1918 bis heute* (Berlin 1932), 110–11. See also Gotthard Jasper, *Die gescheiterte Zähmung: Wege zur Machtergreifung Hitlers 1930–1934* (Frankfurt 1986), 84–5; Vogelsang, *Reichswehr, Staat und NSDAP* (note 14), 171–4; and the minutes taken by secretary of state Hermann Pünder on 30 May 1932 relating to the discussions concerning a ban on the SA held at the Chancellery on 30 May 1932 in Maurer and Wengst, *Staat und NSDAP* (note 13), 322–6.
16. Kurt Caro and Walter Oehme, *Schleichers Aufstieg: Ein Beitrag zur Geschichte der Gegenrevolution* (Berlin 1933), 229.
17. Maurer and Wengst, *Staat und NSDAP* (note 13), 319 (document 69).
18. Goebbels, *Vom Kaiserhof* (note 1), 79 (entry of 11 April 1932).
19. 'Storm Troops Threatened', *Daily Express* (13 April 1932), quoted in RSA v/1.54.
20. RSA v/1.54–6, esp. 56.
21. J. K. von Engelbrechten, *Eine braune Armee entsteht: Die Geschichte der Berlin-Brandenburger SA* (Munich 1937), 217.
22. Heinrich Hoffmann (ed.), *Hitler über Deutschland* (Munich 1932), 39.
23. RSA v/1.88–90, esp. 90 (speech at the NSDAP rally in Frankfurt an der Oder, 22 April 1932).
24. *MM Der Montagmorgen*, x/17 (25 April 1932).
25. *Statistisches Jahrbuch der Stadt Berlin* (note 6), 259–60.
26. See Winkler, *Der Weg in die Katastrophe* (note 4), 547.
27. T[heodor] W[olff], 'Vor der Tür', *Berliner Tageblatt* (26 April 1932) (morning edn).
28. See Francis L. Carsten, *The Reichswehr and Politics 1918–1933* (Berkeley, CA, and London 1973), 338–50.
29. Goebbels, *Vom Kaiserhof* (note 1), 80 (entry of 14 April 1932).

30. Ted Harrison, '"Alter Kämpfer" im Widerstand: Graf Helldorf, die NS-Bewegung und die Opposition gegen Hitler', *Vierteljahrshefte für Zeitgeschichte*, xlv/3 (July 1997), 385–423, esp. 393.

31. Helldorf told Goebbels about his discussions with Schleicher, prompting Goebbels to note: 'Discussion with Count Helldorf. He was with Schleicher, who has his own ideas about National Socialism. But of course he can't understand us': Goebbels, *Vom Kaiserhof* (note 1), 84 (entry of 23 April 1932); and 'Count Helldorf was with Schleicher. He wants a change of direction': Goebbels, *Vom Kaiserhof* (note 1), 88 (entry of 26 April 1932). See also Caro and Oehme, *Schleichers Aufstieg* (note 16), 229–30.

32. Goebbels, *Vom Kaiserhof* (note 1), 88 (entry of 26 April 1932).

33. Goebbels, *Vom Kaiserhof* (note 1), 89 (entries of 28 and 29 April 1932).

34. Winkler, *Der Weg in die Katastrophe* (note 4), 576. Winkler draws attention to Schleicher's role since the middle of April 1932 and concludes that Schleicher 'conspired with Hitler from the end of April'.

35. Caro and Oehme, *Schleichers Aufstieg* (note 16), 232. Their preface is dated Dec. 1932. Two years earlier the same two authors had published a well-researched book on the NSDAP under the title *Kommt 'Das Dritte Reich'?*. A second edition appeared in 1931.

36. The headlines in the evening edition of the *Berliner Tageblatt* of 3 May 1932 read: 'Rumours of a crisis. Brüning sees Hindenburg. – Resignation of finance minister Warmbold.' The paper declared that it could not be denied that since the disbandment of the SA and his emphatic refusal to disband the Reichsbanner there had been constant attempts to turn Hindenburg against Groener.

37. RSA v/1.108 n.29; Goebbels, *Vom Kaiserhof* (note 1), 92–3 (entries of 6 and 8 May 1932).

38. Among others, Hindenburg's secretary of state, Otto Meißner; see Meißner, *Staatssekretär unter Ebert – Hindenburg – Hitler: Der Schicksalsweg des deutschen Volkes von 1918–1945, wie ich ihn erlebte* (Hamburg 1950), 230.

39. Goebbels, *Vom Kaiserhof* (note 1), 93–5 (entries of 8, 9 and 10 May 1932).

40. Vogelsang, *Reichswehr, Staat und NSDAP* (note 14), 189.

41. Albert Krebs, *Tendenzen und Gestalten der NSDAP: Erinnerungen an die Frühzeit der Partei* (Stuttgart 1959), 155.

42. The journalist in question was Helmut Klotz, who had published letters from Ernst Röhm revealing the latter's homosexuality; see Winkler, *Der Weg in die Katastrophe* (note 4), 563–4.

43. Horkenbach, *Das Deutsche Reich* (note 15), 143–8.

44. *Berliner Tageblatt* (13 May 1932) (evening edn).

45. Wolfgang Bretholz, 'Die Nutzniesser', *Berliner Tageblatt* (13 May 1932) (evening edn); see also Goebbels, *Vom Kaiserhof* (note 1), 97 (entry of 13 May 1932).

46. In 1934 the hotel was turned into the 'SS House' and became, among other things, the headquarters of the SS; see Reinhard Rürup, *Topographie des Terrors: Gestapo, SS und Reichssicherheitshauptamt auf dem 'Prinz-Albrecht-Gelände'. Eine Dokumentation* (Berlin 1987), 11, 13, 30 and Illus. 44–6.

47. RSA v/1.110–11. An explanation that was published subsequently and that adopted almost exactly the same wording elicited the following comment from the *Berliner Tageblatt*: 'The nature of these "cold and calculating" considerations and the way in which the National Socialists view their activities in Prussia are not made clear from this explanation, which is given over, rather, to calls of "Heil Hitler", declarations of loyalty and organizational subtleties'; 'Die Fraktion von Hitlers Gnaden', *Berliner Tageblatt* (20 May 1932) (morning edn).

48. RSA v/1.111–86.

49. Horkenbach, *Das Deutsche Reich* (note 15), 160–6. For an account of the events that led to Brüning's fall from power, see Karl Dietrich Bracher, *Die Auflösung der Weimarer Republik: Eine Studie zum Problem des Machtverfalls in der Demokratie*, 3rd edn (Villingen 1960), 511–17.

50. Vogelsang, *Reichswehr, Staat und NSDAP* (note 14), 196.
51. Carsten, *The Reichswehr and Politics* (note 28), 335 (letter from Groener to Gerold von Gleich, 22 May 1932).
52. Carsten, *The Reichswehr and Politics* (note 28), 394 (official record of Hindenburg's discussions concerning the formation of a new government, 30 and 31 May 1932).
53. Carsten, *The Reichswehr and Politics* (note 28), 366; Hans Volz, *Daten der Geschichte der NSDAP*, 8th edn (Berlin and Leipzig 1938), 41; and Otto Dietrich, *Mit Hitler in die Macht: Persönliche Erlebnisse mit meinem Führer* (Munich 1934), 97 and 112–13.
54. Horkenbach, *Das Deutsche Reich* (note 15), 168–9 and 173; Bracher, *Die Auflösung der Weimarer Republik* (note 49), 545–7; and Goebbels, *Vom Kaiserhof* (note 1), 106–8 (entries of 4, 5 and 6 June 1932). In a leading article in the *Berliner Tageblatt*, one of the paper's editors expressed the view that in adopting this new measure Papen's government 'is showing that it is in fact acting only according to the instructions of Adolf Hitler, the secret chancellor, and that the struggle with this cabinet is synonymous with the fight against National Socialism, which praises it and which sees in this regime a preliminary stage on the road to its own seizure of power'; Wolfgang Bretholz, 'Der heimliche Kanzler', *Berliner Tageblatt* (7 June 1932) (evening edn).
55. Horkenbach, *Das Deutsche Reich* (note 15), 172.
56. Goebbels, *Vom Kaiserhof* (note 1), 110 (entry of 13 June 1932); and Vogelsang, *Reichswehr, Staat und NSDAP* (note 14), 214–16.
57. Goebbels, *Vom Kaiserhof* (note 1), 111 (entry of 14 June 1932).
58. Horkenbach, *Das Deutsche Reich* (note 15), 195–7.
59. RSA v/1.186 and 188.
60. RSA v/1.209 (speech in Munich, 3 July 1932).
61. Engelbrechten, *Eine braune Armee entsteht* (note 21), 225.
62. 'Die Ursachen der Straßenkrawalle', *Berliner Tageblatt* (23 June 1932).
63. The article by Hans Jäger, 'Die Nationalsozialistische Deutsche Arbeiterpartei', that appeared in the *Internationale Pressekorrespondenz* on 3 June 1932 (pp.1427–31) is notable for its greater grasp of reality and its refusal to toe the party line. The article is reproduced in part in Theo Pirker (ed.), *Komintern und Faschismus: Dokumente zur Geschichte und Theorie des Faschismus*, 2nd edn (Stuttgart 1966), 158–67.
64. Ernst Thälmann, 'Die Antifaschistische Aktion im Anmarsch', *Internationale Pressekorrespondenz* (14 June 1932), 1553, quoted from Hermann Weber (ed.), *Der deutsche Kommunismus: Dokumente* (Cologne and Berlin 1963), 195.
65. After the NSDAP won 48.9 per cent of the votes and an absolute majority in the regional elections in Mecklenburg-Schwerin, it won 43.9 per cent in the regional elections in Hesse on 19 June, narrowly failing to secure an outright majority taking thirty-two out of seventy seats; see Volz, *Daten der Geschichte der NSDAP* (note 53), 42.
66. Horkenbach, *Das Deutsche Reich* (note 15), 204.
67. See the details in n.70 below.
68. In *Vorwärts* Schleicher wrote that 'a lasting and productive government is possible only if it does not resist the trends that imbue the mass of the people. Rather, it must know how to create a broad basis of trust from the living and forward-looking powers of the people'; quoted from 'Schleicher über den neuen Kurs', *Vossische Zeitung* (20 June 1932) (evening edn).
69. *Vossische Zeitung* (20 June 1932) (evening edn).
70. *Vossische Zeitung* (18 June 1932) (morning edn); 22 June 1932 (morning edn); 24 June 1932 (evening edn); 26 June 1932 (morning edn); 29 June 1932 (evening edn); 1 July 1932 (evening edn); 5 July 1932 (morning edn); 9 July 1932 (evening edn).
71. Horkenbach, *Das Deutsche Reich* (note 15), 212. Typical of the way in which these events were reported by the German Nationalist newspapers that were part of the Hugenberg empire is the article headed 'Bloody incident outside the *Vorwärts* building' that appeared in the *Berliner Lokal-Anzeiger* on 26 June 1932 (Sunday edn). Here as much space was devoted to the NSDAP's version of events as to the chief of police's

report. But whereas the police report was presented as something altogether unbelievable, the SA men were held up as victims. At the same time, the SA's earlier attack on a Social Democrat newspaper vendor was not mentioned at all by the paper.

72. Quoted from the *C. V.-Zeitung*, xi/27 (1 July 1932), 274.
73. 'Attacke gegen Preußens Polizei: Rechtsradikale Täuschungsmanöver um den Lustgarten-Krawall', *Vossische Zeitung* (29 June 1932) (evening edn).
74. c. m. [Carl Misch], 'Nicht auf die Spitze!', *Vossische Zeitung* (24 June 1932) (evening edn).
75. Goebbels, *Vom Kaiserhof* (note 1), 119–20 (entries of 26 and 27 June 1932).
76. *Vossische Zeitung* (30 June 1932) (evening edn) and 15 July 1932 (morning edn).
77. Special edition of *Der Angriff* (mid-July 1932), in which appeared Goebbels' appeal of 8 July 1932.
78. Goebbels, *Vom Kaiserhof* (note 1), 124–5 (entry of 8 July 1932).
79. Vogelsang, *Reichswehr, Staat und NSDAP* (note 14), 219.
80. 'Der Gruppenführer spricht zu seinen Kameraden: "Wir wollen alles oder nichts!"', *Der Angriff*, vi/141 (11 July 1932).
81. Horkenbach, *Das Deutsche Reich* (note 15), 237; see also 'Goebbels gegen Gayl', *Vossische Zeitung* (9 July 1932) (morning edn) and 'Propaganda-Trick: Goebbels' Kampfansage an Gayl', *Vossische Zeitung* (10 July 1932) (morning edn).
82. All quotations are taken from the version of the text that was published in *Der Angriff* (11 July 1932). The poet to whom Goebbels refers here is Theodor Körner (1791–1813), whose poem 'Männer und Buben' opens with the words 'Das Volk steht auf'. He died fighting in the Napoleonic Wars.
83. *Völkischer Beobachter* (17–18 July 1932) (Bavarian edn), quoted from 'Drohung mit Bewaffnung: Die Nationalsozialisten verlangen "freie Hand"', *Vossiche Zeitung* (16 July 1932) (evening edn).
84. *Vossische Zeitung* (16 July 1932).
85. On the following, see Vogelsang, *Reichswehr, Staat und NSDAP* (note 14), 235–7; and Bracher, *Die Auflösung der Weimarer Republik* (note 49), 576–8. For a good example of the demands of the whole of the right-wing press, see the article 'Hugenberg fordert Reichskommissar für Preußen', *Berliner Lokal-Anzeiger* (19 July 1932) (morning edn).
86. For an account of the wider picture, see Christoph Graf, *Politische Polizei zwischen Demokratie und Diktatur: Die Entwicklung der preußischen Politischen Polizei vom Staatsschutzorgan der Weimarer Republik zum Geheimen Staatspolizeiamt des Dritten Reiches* (Berlin 1983), 54–64.
87. See the line of argument adopted by the minister of the interior in the ministerial discussion on 11 July 1932, reproduced in part in Herbert Michaelis and Ernst Schraepler (eds), *Ursachen und Folgen: Vom deutschen Zusammenbruch 1918 und 1945 bis zur staatlichen Neuordnung Deutschlands in der Gegenwart*, 25 vols (Berlin 1959), viii.560.
88. Vogelsang, *Reichswehr, Staat und NSDAP* (note 14), 244.
89. Dirk Blasius, *Weimars Ende: Bürgerkrieg und Politik 1930–1933* (Göttingen 2005), 66. On the events in Altona, see also Carl Severing, *Mein Lebensweg*, 2 vols (Cologne 1950), ii.345–6; and Albert Grzesinski, *Im Kampf um die deutsche Republik: Erinnerungen eines Sozialdemokraten* [1933] (Munich 2001), 264–5.
90. For a good overview of the course of events as well as a perceptive account of the situation that led up to it, see Winkler, *Der Weg in die Katastrophe* (note 4), 650–2. Winkler's study is based on an earlier monograph by Wolfgang Kopitzsch.
91. RSA v/1.237.
92. The letter from Kerrl and Papen's reply to it are reproduced in Michaelis and Schraepler, *Ursachen und Folgen* (note 87), viii.566–9.
93. Michaelis and Schraepler, *Ursachen und Folgen* (note 87), viii.558 and 570–72; see also Horkenbach, *Das Deutsche Reich* (note 15), 248–50; and Hagen Schulze, *Weimar: Deutschland 1917–1933*, 2nd edn (Berlin 1983), 378–80.

94. Michaelis and Schraepler, *Ursachen und Folgen* (note 87), viii.558; see also Vogelsang, *Reichswehr, Staat und NSDAP* (note 14), 247; and Winkler, *Der Weg in die Katastrophe* (note 4), 656–8. On the discussion concerning the question of the possibility of resisting the 'Prussian coup', see Grzesinski, *Im Kampf um die deutsche Republik* (note 89), 274–7; Severing, *Mein Lebensweg* (note 89), ii.352–9; Karl Dietrich Bracher, 'Dualismus oder Gleichschaltung: Der Faktor Preußen in der Weimarer Republik', *Die Weimarer Republik 1918–1933: Politik–Wirtschaft–Gesellschaft*, ed. Karl Dietrich Bracher, Manfred Funke and Hans-Adolf Jacobsen (Düsseldorf 1987), 535–51, esp. 541–7; Winkler, *Der Weg in die Katastrophe* (note 4), 671–80; and Heinrich August Winkler, *Der lange Weg nach Westen: Deutsche Geschichte 1806–1933*, 2 vols (Munich 2000), i.513–15.

95. Goebbels, *Vom Kaiserhof* (note 1), 132–3 (entry of 21 July 1932).

96. All quotations are taken from *Der Angriff* (28 July 1932) (emphasis in original); see also Goebbels, *Vom Kaiserhof* (note 1), 134 (entry of 27 July 1932).

97. Winkler, *Der Weg in die Katastrophe* (note 4), 684; *Statistisches Jahrbuch der Stadt Berlin* (note 6), 259–60; and Statistisches Amt der Stadt Berlin, *Statistisches Jahrbuch der Stadt Berlin*, 9th edn (Berlin 1933), 262–3. Goebbels summed up the results of the election as follows: 'In Berlin suffered somewhat from the mendacious campaign [of the Reds]. Result: we now have to gain power and exterminate Marxism'; Elke Fröhlich (ed.), *Die Tagebücher von Joseph Goebbels*, Part I: *Aufzeichnungen 1923–1941*, 9 vols (Munich 1997–2006), ii/2.330 (1 Aug. 1932).

98. *Vorwärts* (1 Aug. 1932) (morning edn); *B. Z. am Mittag* (1 Aug. 1932); and *Der Angriff* (1 Aug. 1932).

99. RSA v/1.294–5.

100. Ian Kershaw, *Hitler 1889–1936: Hubris* (London 1998), 370.

101. *Berliner Lokal-Anzeiger* (6 Aug. 1932) (morning edn): 'Yesterday evening there were widespread rumours in Berlin to the effect that Adolf Hitler had arrived here by train at 7:15. The Brown House has officially declared that Hitler is recovering in the Bavarian mountains.'

102. Thus the account in the *Vossische Zeitung* (6 Aug. 1932) (evening edn).

103. Note taken by Ferdinand von Bredow (26 July 1932) and quoted from Vogelsang, *Reichswehr, Staat und NSDAP* (note 14), 475–6.

104. Letter from Bredow to all the chiefs of staff (5 Aug. 1932) quoted from Vogelsang, *Reichswehr, Staat und NSDAP* (note 14), 476–8.

105. Opinions differ as to the time and place of this meeting. Thilo Vogelsang thinks that it 'must have taken place on 5 August': Vogelsang, *Reichswehr, Staat und NSDAP* (note 14), 257; Konrad Heiden writes that 'he met General Schleicher at Fürstenberg during manoeuvres': Konrad Heiden, *Geburt des dritten Reiches: Die Geschichte des Nationalsozialismus bis Herbst 1933* (Zurich 1934), 77; Görlitz and Quint claim that 'Hitler and Schleicher met on 6 August at the home of the Mecklenburg prime minister, Walter Granzow': Walter Görlitz and Herbert A. Quint, *Adolf Hitler: Eine Biographie* (Stuttgart 1952), 347; Heinrich August Winkler states that Hitler 'met the defence minister near Berlin for a long secret conversation on 6 August': Winkler, *Der lange Weg nach Westen* (note 94), 517; and Ian Kershaw argues that 'The secret negotiations with Reichswehr Minister Schleicher, at Fürstenberg, fifty miles north of Berlin, lasted for several hours on 6 August': Kershaw, *Hitler 1889–1936* (note 100), 370.

106. 'It looks as if things are going to get serious in the next few days' and 'Tense atmosphere. The SA is on high alert': Goebbels, *Vom Kaiserhof* (note 1), 134 (entries of 27 and 28 July 1932).

107. See Winkler, *Der Weg in die Katastrophe* (note 4), 698–9.

108. Vogelsang, *Reichswehr, Staat und NSDAP* (note 14), 258.

109. Fröhlich, *Die Tagebücher von Joseph Goebbels* (note 97), ii/2.334 (7 Aug. 1932).

110. Walter Görlitz, *Hindenburg: Ein Lebensbild* (Bonn 1953), 381; minutes of ministerial discussion in the Chancellery on 10 Aug. 1932 in Michaelis and Schraepler, *Ursachen und Folgen* (note 87), viii.613–18, esp. 617.

111. *Tempo: Berliner Abend-Zeitung* (10 Aug. 1932).

112. *Völkischer Beobachter* (12 Aug. 1932) (Bavarian edn), quoted from Edgar von Schmidt-Pauli, *Hitlers Kampf um die Macht: Der Nationalsozialismus und die Ereignisse des Jahres 1932*, 2nd edn (Berlin 1933), 95. In his appeal, Helldorf admitted that 'some units [of the SA] have been practising how to defend themselves and doing exercise drills designed to protect them from attack'.

113. Horkenbach, *Das Deutsche Reich* (note 15), 282–3. The wave of terror that had continued after polling day was caused almost exclusively by the SA and increasingly included bombings. See the leading article by O. S., 'Acht Tage zu spät', *Berliner Tageblatt* (9 Aug. 1932) (evening edn): 'It is as if a button were being pressed every day in some secret central location, so that explosions take place now here, now there with uncanny precision, spreading fear and terror all round.'

114. Fröhlich, *Die Tagebücher von Joseph Goebbels* (note 97), ii/2.335–6 (9 and 10 Aug. 1932).

115. Fröhlich, *Die Tagebücher von Joseph Goebbels* (note 97), ii/2.337 (11 Aug. 1932). See also Harrison, '"Alter Kämpfer"' (note 30), 393. Harrison suspects that Helldorf 'was planning a violent coup'.

116. Fröhlich, *Die Tagebücher von Joseph Goebbels* (note 97), ii/2.338 (12 Aug. 1932).

117. Schmidt-Pauli, *Hitlers Kampf um die Macht* (note 112), 106–8; Heiden, *Geburt des dritten Reiches* (note 105), 78–9; and Vogelsang, *Reichswehr, Staat und NSDAP* (note 14), 263–4.

118. RSA v/1.300 (discussions in the Chancellery in Aug. 1932).

119. In addition to the internal minutes (RSA v/1.300–2), an official communiqué was also published (RSA v/1.303 n.2). Moreover, Otto Meißner kept a note of the meeting in his capacity as secretary of state: see Michaelis and Schraepler, *Ursachen und Folgen* (note 87), viii.618–19.

120. RSA v/1.303 (Hitler's letter to Kurt von Schleicher, Otto Meißner and Erwin Planck, 13 Aug. 1932); see also Hitler's interview with the *Rheinisch-Westfälische Zeitung* (16 Aug. 1932) in RSA, v/1.304–9.

121. RSA v/1.304–5.

122. Schmidt-Pauli, *Hitlers Kampf um die Macht* (note 112), 115; see also 'Hitler gegen Hitler: Der Hofberichterstatter plaudert aus der Schule', *Berliner Tageblatt* (17 Aug. 1932) (evening edn).

123. Rainer Zitelmann, *Hitler: Selbstverständnis eines Revolutionärs*, 3rd edn (Darmstadt 1990), 86.

124. Henry Picker, *Hitlers Tischgespräche im Führerhauptquartier*, 4th edn (Stuttgart 1983), 323 (evening of 21 May 1942).

125. Zitelmann, *Hitler* (note 123), 87–8, who refers here to the 1955 reminiscences of Baron Erwein von Aretin.

126. Vogelsang, *Reichswehr, Staat und NSDAP* (note 14), 262; and Schmidt-Pauli, *Hitlers Kampf um die Macht* (note 112), 88 and 93.

127. Engelbrechten, *Eine braune Armee entsteht* (note 21), 238.

128. RSA v/1.316 (interview with Associated Press, 18 Aug. 1932).

129. Vogelsang, *Reichswehr, Staat und NSDAP* (note 14), 266; and Schmidt-Pauli, *Hitlers Kampf um die Macht* (note 112), 115.

130. RSA v/1.309 (interview with the *Rheinisch-Westfälische Zeitung*, 16 Aug. 1932).

131. RSA v/1.317.

132. 'Das Todesurteil: Hitler deckt die verurteilten Mörder', *Berliner Tageblatt* (23 Aug. 1932) (evening edn).

133. Joseph Goebbels, 'Die Juden sind schuld!', *Der Angriff* (24 Aug. 1932) quoted from Joseph Goebbels, *Wetterleuchten* (Munich 1939), 323–5. In a speech that he gave on

7 Sept. 1932, Hitler himself claimed that 'Berlin's Jews and Gentlemen's Club imagine that they can still rescue the situation at the very last moment': RSA v/1.341–2.

134. Published in *Der Angriff* (23 Aug. 1932) and quoted here from RSA v/1.319.

135. RSA v/1.321.

136. This was the summary of Hitler's Sportpalast speech of 1 Sept. 1932 that appeared in the *Völkischer Beobachter* on 3 Sept. The speech was entirely given over to a polemical attack on Papen's government: see RSA v/1.325–9.

137. See, for example, 'Wird der neue Reichstag wieder aufgelöst?', *Berliner Lokal-Anzeiger* (25 Aug. 1932) (evening edn).

138. 'Drei Tage Straße frei: Wie es sich Hitler dachte', *Vossische Zeitung* (3 Oct. 1932) (evening edn). The article quotes word for word from a piece that had appeared in the Stahlhelm's official newspaper, *Stahlhelm*.

139. 'Adolf Hitlers Hausmacht', *Vossische Zeitung* (22 Nov. 1932) (morning edn) (emphasis in original). It has unfortunately proved impossible to identify the writer.

140. Thomas Friedrich, 'Die Berliner Zeitungslandschaft am Ende der Weimarer Republik', *Berlin 1932: Das letzte Jahr der ersten deutschen Republik. Politik, Medien, Symbole*, ed. Diethart Kerbs and Henrick Stahr (Berlin 1992), 58.

141. RSA v/1.339–50, esp. 349 ('Die politische Lage': speech delivered at the NSDAP rally in Munich, 7 Sept. 1932).

142. Volz, *Daten der Geschichte der NSDAP* (note 53), 44; Horkenbach, *Das Deutsche Reich* (note 15), 320–5 and 329; Konrad Heiden, *Adolf Hitler: Das Zeitalter der Verantwortungslosigkeit. Eine Biographie* (Zurich 1936), 313; and Winkler, *Der lange Weg nach Westen* (note 94), i.521–2.

143. Goebbels, *Vom Kaiserhof* (note 1), 161 (entry of 10 Sept. 1932).

144. 'Strassers Beruhigungspillen: Freundlichkeiten für Hugenberg und Leipart', *Vossische Zeitung* (22 Oct. 1932) (morning edn).

145. 'Deutschland ist auf dem Marsch', special edition of *Der Angriff* (Nov. 1932) reproduced from RSA v/2.149–66, esp. 158 and 163 (speech at NSDAP rally in Berlin, 2 Nov. 1932).

146. 'Prominentenabend im Sportpalast', *Vossische Zeitung* (3 Nov. 1932) (evening edn).

147. Goebbels, *Vom Kaiserhof* (note 1), 191 (entry of 2 Nov. 1932). None the less, Goebbels was forced to admit that many of the 'old party comrades' were 'confused' about involvement in the strike. Even so, the party had to 'hold out and remain firm'. If it changed course, it would 'lose everything': Goebbels, *Vom Kaiserhof* (note 1), 192.

148. *Statistisches Jahrbuch der Stadt Berlin*, 1933 edition (note 97), 264–5; Volz, *Daten der Geschichte der NSDAP* (note 53), 44; and RSA v/2.185 n.2.

149. This is confirmed by the analysis of Jürgen W. Falter, 'Wahlen und Wählerverhalten unter besonderer Berücksichtigung des Aufstiegs der NSDAP nach 1928', *Die Weimarer Republik 1918–1933: Politik–Wirtschaft–Gesellschaft*, ed. Karl Dietrich Bracher, Manfred Funke and Hans-Adolf Jacobsen (Düsseldorf 1987), 484–504, esp. 503–4. Apart from the supporters of the country's two Catholic parties, it was above all KPD voters who remained 'largely immune' to the NSDAP. On the other hand, the KPD's electoral success on 6 Nov. 1932 was only relative: with 16.8 per cent of the votes, it failed to achieve even the result of the USPD (18.2 per cent) in the Reichstag elections of 6 June 1920: see the diagram on the front endpapers of Schulze, *Weimar* (note 93).

150. Michaelis and Schraepler, *Ursachen und Folgen* (note 87), viii.675–80; and RSA v/2.188–93; see also Franz von Papen, *Der Wahrheit eine Gasse* (Munich 1952), 241–52.

151. RSA v/2.194–207; Schmidt-Pauli, *Hitlers Kampf um die Macht* (note 112), 171–80; and Meißner, *Staatssekretär* (note 38), 247–9.

152. Goebbels, *Vom Kaiserhof* (note 1), 212–13 and 216–17 (entries of 1 and 5 Dec. 1932); and Meißner, *Staatssekretär* (note 38), 250–2. See also the comprehensive account by Udo Kissenkoetter, *Gregor Straßer und die NSDAP* (Stuttgart 1978), 159–71.

153. RSA v/2.248 (Hitler's speech of 7 Dec. 1932).

154. Based on the written draft of Straßer's letter of resignation, quoted by Kissenkoetter, *Gregor Straßer* (note 152), 172 and 202–3.
155. RSA v/2.251.
156. RSA v/2.279–82.
157. Goebbels, *Vom Kaiserhof* (note 1), 203 and 215 (entries of 15 Nov. and 3 Dec. 1932).
158. *Vorwärts* (20 Jan. 1933) (evening edn).
159. Dietrich, *Mit Hitler in die Macht* (note 53), 169–70; Papen, *Der Wahrheit eine Gasse* (note 150), 255–6; and Michaelis and Schraepler, *Ursachen und Folgen* (note 87), viii.743–4.
160. RSA v/2.345–8, together with nn.1–3, 7–11 and 13–14.
161. RSA v/2.347 n.14.
162. Thus Vogelsang, *Reichswehr, Staat und NSDAP* (note 14), 368.
163. Reinhold Quaatz, *Die Deutschnationalen und die Zerstörung der Weimarer Republik: Aus dem Tagebuch von Reinhold Quaatz 1928–1933* (Munich 1989), 223 (entry of 17 Jan. 1933) quoted from RSA v/2.371 n.5; see also Joachim von Ribbentrop, *Zwischen London und Moskau: Erinnerungen und letzte Aufzeichnungen*, ed. Annelies von Ribbentrop (Leoni 1953), 39.
164. Goebbels, *Vom Kaiserhof* (note 1), 244 (entry of 19 Jan. 1933).
165. In his speech he returned to one of his favourite topics, the ostensible continuation of Prussian traditions by the NSDAP: 'What our movement has achieved in these fourteen years since the collapse of 1918 is exactly the same as Prussia achieved following the decline of the old German Empire': RSA v/2.375–87, esp. 377.
166. Goebbels, *Vom Kaiserhof* (note 1), 246–7 (entry of 22 Jan. 1933). The KPD responded with a counterdemonstration on 25 Jan. 1933, when it is said that 130,000 people took part in this 'tremendous show of strength against fascism': see Ralf Georg Reuth, *Goebbels: Eine Biographie* (Munich and Zurich 1990), 251.
167. RSA v/2.391–2.
168. Ribbentrop, *Zwischen London und Moskau* (note 163), 39, quoted from RSA v/2.393 n.9; see also Vogelsang, *Reichswehr, Staat und NSDAP* (note 14), 372; and Papen, *Der Wahrheit eine Gasse* (note 150), 265–6, who gives a completely different account of the conversation, claiming that neither he nor Meißner nor Hindenburg raised the possibility of Hitler's chancellorship on this particular occasion.
169. RSA v/2.393–4.
170. Meißner, *Staatssekretär* (note 38), 253–5; and Vogelsang, *Reichswehr, Staat und NSDAP* (note 14), 372–4.
171. Anton Golecki (ed.), *Das Kabinettt von Schleicher: 3. Dezember 1932 bis 30. Januar 1933* (Boppard 1986), 306–9, esp. 308–9 (minutes of ministerial discussion at 11:30 on 28 Jan. 1933).
172. Golecki, *Das Kabinett von Schleicher* (note 171), LXVIII. For a fuller account of the following events, see Henry Ashby Turner, Jr, *Hitler's Thirty Days to Power: January 1933* (London 1996), 135–62.
173. RSA v/2.395 n.1.
174. Ribbentrop did not join the NSDAP until May 1932. Thanks to his excellent contacts with 'leading circles' in Berlin society, he was able to act as intermediary with Papen, Hugenberg and others.
175. Ribbentrop, *Zwischen London und Moskau* (note 163), 40; see also Goebbels, *Vom Kaiserhof* (note 1), 249 (entry of 27 Jan. 1933).
176. Turner, *Hitler's Thirty Days* (note 172), 139–40.
177. Turner, *Hitler's Thirty Days* (note 172), 143–4.
178. Turner, *Hitler's Thirty Days* (note 172), 148.
179. Ribbentrop, *Zwischen London und Moskau* (note 163), 42; Turner, *Hitler's Thirty Days* (note 172), 148–9; and Vogelsang, *Reichswehr, Staat und NSDAP* (note 14), 390.
180. Turner, *Hitler's Thirty Days* (note 172), 150; and Vogelsang, *Reichswehr, Staat und NSDAP* (note 14), 391.

181. See the notes taken by Kurt von Hammerstein (28 Jan. 1935), in Bracher, *Die Auflösung der Weimarer Republik* (note 49), 733–4; and Vogelsang, *Reichswehr, Staat und NSDAP* (note 14), 392–6.

182. Thus Hitler on the evening of 21 May 1942 in his special train to Berlin, quoted by Picker, *Hitlers Tischgespräche* (note 124), 327. Wecke was far from being a 'Berlin police officer with National Socialist sympathies', as he is described in the German edition of Turner's study: Henry Ashby Turner, Jr, *Hitlers Weg zur Macht: Der Januar 1933* (Munich 1996), 198. (This passage is not in the English edition.) Wecke was a former army officer and a member of the Freikorps. He had joined the NSDAP in 1922 and had close contacts with Göring; for a brief biography of Wecke, see Graf, *Politische Polizei zwischen Demokratie und Diktatur* (note 86), 389.

183. Turner, *Hitler's Thirty Days* (note 172), 154–6. Turner rightly points out that Papen deliberately tricked Hindenburg, even to the extent of presenting him with a list of ministers. See also Papen, *Der Wahrheit eine Gasse* (note 150), 273; and Meißner, *Staatssekretär* (note 38), 268–9.

184. Theodor Duersterberg, *Der Stahlhelm und Hitler* (Wolfenbüttel and Hanover 1949), 41. Duersterberg was deputy chairman of the Stahlhelm and, as such, an eyewitness of the events that unfolded on the morning of 30 Jan. 1933.

185. The text of Hitler's nomination of 30 Jan. 1933 is reproduced in RSA v/2.395.

186. Engelbrechten, *Eine braune Armee entsteht* (note 21), 257.

187. *Festliche Tage im Kaiserhause Berlin 1913* (special issue of *Die Woche* [Berlin 1913]), 6.

188. The order is reproduced in facsimile in Walter Oehme and Kurt Caro, *Kommt 'Das Dritte Reich'?*, 2nd edn (Berlin 1931), 33–4, esp. 34.

189. Thus Heinrich Hoffmann, *Hitler wie ich ihn sah: Aufzeichnungen seines Leibfotografen* (Munich and Berlin 1974), 49.

190. Herbert Seehofer, 'Das erwachte Berlin marschiert: Der Aufmarsch der braunen Front', *Völkischer Beobachter* (31 Jan. 1933) (Berlin edn).

191. Goebbels, *Vom Kaiserhof* (note 1), 254 (entry of 31 Jan. 1933); and Fröhlich, *Die Tagebücher von Joseph Goebbels* (note 97), ii/3.121 (1 Feb. 1933).

Chapter 11 · 1933 and later: Hitler's metropolis

1. Joseph Goebbels, *Das erwachende Berlin* (Munich 1934), 16.

2. Albert Speer, 'Städtebauliche Entwicklung im Dritten Reich: Deutsches Wollen', *Zeitschrift der Auslands-Organisation der NSDAP*, i/6 (1 June 1939), 8–9, esp. 9.

3. *Akten der Reichskanzlei: Regierung Hitler 1933–1938* (hereafter ARH), ed. Konrad Repgen and Hans Booms (Boppard 1983), i/1. For an unsurpassed account of the general situation in Berlin at the start of the Third Reich, see Karl Dietrich Bracher, Wolfgang Sauer and Gerhard Schulz, *Die nationalsozialistische Machtergreifung: Studien zur Errichtung des totalitären Herrschaftssystems in Deutschland 1933/34*, 2nd edn (Cologne and Opladen 1962), 47–50.

4. Bracher, Sauer and Schulz, *Die nationalsozialistische Machtergreifung* (note 3), 49; see also Herbert Michaelis and Ernst Schraepler (eds), *Ursachen und Folgen: Vom deutschen Zusammenbruch 1918 und 1945 bis zur staatlichen Neuordnung Deutschlands in der Gegenwart*, 25 vols (Berlin 1959), ix.9–15.

5. See the ministerial discussion on 31 Jan. 1933 in ARH i/1.5–6.

6. Cuno Horkenbach (ed.), *Das Deutsche Reich von 1918 bis heute* (Berlin 1935), 35.

7. Horkenbach, *Das Deutsche Reich* (note 6), 43.

8. Horkenbach, *Das Deutsche Reich* (note 6), 41.

9. Horkenbach, *Das Deutsche Reich* (note 6), 35–7.

10. ARH i/1.9.

11. Michaelis and Schraepler, *Ursachen und Folgen* (note 4), ix.7–9.

12. *Völkischer Beobachter* (3 Feb. 1933), quoted from Max Domarus, *Hitler: Reden und Proklamationen 1932–1945* (Munich 1965), i/1.195.

13. Now the Stauffenbergstraße. Other sources speak of a meal in the general's service apartment in Dahlem: see, for example, Anton Joachimsthaler, *Hitlers Liste: Ein Dokument persönlicher Beziehungen* (Munich 2003), 90.
14. Heinz Höhne, *Die Zeit der Illusionen: Hitler und die Anfänge des Dritten Reiches 1933–1936* (Düsseldorf, Vienna and New York 1991), 55–6. In its edition of 6 Feb. 1933, the *Völkischer Beobachter* published only a brief communiqué that fell far short of a summary of Hitler's speech. Hitler expressed himself in similar terms in cabinet: on 8 Feb. 1933, for example, he announced that the next five years must be devoted to 'rearming' the German people and that every measure designed to create jobs must be judged from this point of view: ARH i/1.50–1.
15. Wolff Telegraphisches Bureau report of 5 Feb. 1933, quoted from Domarus, *Hitler: Reden und Proklamationen* (note 12), i/1.200.
16. Winfried Nerdinger, *Ort und Erinnerung: Nationalsozialismus in München* (Salzburg and Munich 2006), 65. With his nomination as chancellor, and especially after 1939, Hitler stayed increasingly infrequently at the Prinzregentenplatz. As Nerdinger points out, Hitler had by the early 1930s 'transferred his private refuge to the Obersalzberg near Berchtesgaden, later turning it into his second residence after the Chancellery in Berlin' (65).
17. Wolfgang Schuster, 'Hitler in München – privat?', *München – 'Hauptstadt der Bewegung'* (Munich 1993), 125–30, esp. 130.
18. Hans Wilderotter, *Alltag der Macht: Berlin Wilhelmstraße* (Berlin 1998), 74.
19. Adolf Hitler, 'Die Reichskanzlei', *Die Kunst im Deutschen Reich*, iii/9 (Sept. 1939), 277–80, esp. 277.
20. Heinrich Heim, *Monologe im Führerhauptquartier 1941–1944*, ed. Werner Jochmann (Hamburg 1980), 192.
21. RSA ii/1.386–403, esp. 395 (speech given at the NSDAP rally in Dörflas, 26 June 1927, under the title 'Freiheit und Brot').
22. *Motorschau: Monatsschrift für Kraft- und Luftfahrt*, iv/2 (Feb. 1940), 120; on Hitler's appearance on 11 Feb. 1932, see also Ian Kershaw, *Hitler 1889–1936: Hubris* (London 1998), 450–2.
23. Joseph Goebbels, *Vom Kaiserhof zur Reichskanzlei: Eine historische Darstellung in Tagebuchblättern* (Munich 1934), 256–7.
24. *Der Angriff* (9 Feb. 1933), quoted from Alfons Arenhövel (ed.), *Arena der Leidenschaften: Der Berliner Sportpalast und seine Veranstaltungen 1910–1973* (Berlin 1990), 335.
25. *Völkischer Beobachter* (11/12 Feb. 1933), quoted from Domarus, *Hitler: Reden und Proklamationen* (note 12), i/1.207–8.
26. *Der Angriff* (1 and 3 March 1933), quoted from Arenhövel, *Arena der Leidenschaften* (note 24), 337.
27. *Vossische Zeitung* (24 Feb. 1933), quoted from Arenhövel, *Arena der Leidenschaften* (note 24), 336.
28. *Vorwärts* (28 Feb. 1933), quoted from Arenhövel, *Arena der Leidenschaften* (note 24), 337.
29. 'Sensational dismissal of high-ranking officials at the Police Headquarters in Berlin' was the headline in the Berlin edition of the NSDAP's official newspaper, *Völkischer Beobachter* (19/20 Feb. 1933).
30. Michaelis and Schraepler, *Ursachen und Folgen* (note 4), ix.38–9.
31. Michaelis and Schraepler, *Ursachen und Folgen* (note 4), ix.39–41.
32. J. K. von Engelbrechten, *Eine braune Armee entsteht: Die Geschichte der Berlin-Brandenburger SA* (Munich 1937), 265–7.
33. *Deutsche Allgemeine Zeitung* (26 Feb. 1933), quoted from Michaelis and Schraepler, *Ursachen und Folgen* (note 4), ix.47–8. At the cabinet meeting on 27 Feb. Göring made no mention of the results of these searches but mentioned only the activities of the Communist Party in Hamburg: see ARH i/1.124–5.

34. See van der Lubbe's account of his actions during his police interrogation on 1/2 March 1933 and the announcement of his sentence on 23 Dec. 1933 in Michaelis and Schraepler, *Ursachen und Folgen* (note 4), ix.54–7 and 70.

35. In their own detailed account of the events surrounding the fire, Bahar and Kugel seek to counter the view that van der Lubbe was solely responsible: Alexander Bahar and Wilfried Kugel, *Der Reichstagsbrand: Wie Geschichte gemacht wird* (Berlin 2001). In the fourth volume of his *Deutsche Gesellschaftsgeschichte*, conversely, Hans-Ulrich Wehler argues that van der Lubbe was solely to blame, a view shared by Richard J. Evans in the first volume of his three-volume study of the Third Reich. Current thinking on the subject is summarized by Dieter Deiseroth in his collection of essays *Der Reichstagsbrand und der Prozess vor dem Reichsgericht* (Berlin 2006), 9.

36. Bahar and Kugel, *Der Reichstagsbrand* (note 35), 137–43.

37. Thus the wording of the first official account of the fire that was issued by the Prussian Press Agency on the night of 27/28 Feb. 1933: see Horkenbach, *Das Deutsche Reich* (note 6), 72; see also the contemporary critique by Konrad Heiden, *Geburt des dritten Reiches: Die Geschichte des Nationalsozialismus bis Herbst 1933* (Zurich 1934), 120–31.

38. Sefton Delmer, 'Nothing Shall Stop Us Now', *The Daily Express* (28 Feb. 1933).

39. Hitler's and Göring's reactions are reproduced in ARH i/1.128–30.

40. Herbert Seehofer, 'Mit dem Führer an der Brandstätte: Das furchtbare Bild der Zerstörung', *Völkischer Beobachter* (Berlin edn) (1 March 1933).

41. Engelbrechten, *Eine braune Armee entsteht* (note 32), 267.

42. The wording of the 'Reichstag Fire Decree' and of the Enabling Act may be found in Michaelis and Schraepler, *Ursachen und Folgen* (note 4), ix.53–4 and 156–7.

43. All figures are taken from the ninth edition of the *Statistisches Jahrbuch der Stadt Berlin* (Berlin 1933), 264–6.

44. RSA i.325 (from the speech to the 1919 National Club in Hamburg, 28 Feb. 1926).

45. Laurenz Demps, 'Konzentrationslager in Berlin 1933 bis 1945', *Jahrbuch des Märkischen Museums III/1977*, ed. Herbert Hampe and Hans-Joachim Beeskow (Berlin 1977), 7–19, esp. 16–17; and Demps, 'Berlin als Eperimentierfeld des Terrorismus im Jahr 1933', *1933 – Wege zur Diktatur: Rahmenprogramm – Vortragsreihe* (Berlin 1984), 105–15, esp. 114–15.

46. Helmut Bräutigam and Oliver C. Gliech, 'Nationalsozialistische Zwangslager in Berlin I. Die "wilden" Konzentrationslager und Folterkeller 1933/34', *Berlin-Forschungen II*, ed. Wolfgang Ribbe (Berlin 1987), 141–78; see also Kurt Schilde, Rolf Scholz and Sylvia Walleczek, *SA-Gefängnis Papestraße: Spuren und Zeugnisse* (Berlin 1996).

47. Adalbert Rückerl, *NS-Verbrechen vor Gericht: Versuch einer Vergangenheitsbewältigung*, 2nd edn (Heidelberg 1984), 25 n.10. For an exemplary account of conditions in an unofficial camp (the Maikowski House in Berlin-Charlottenberg), as well as in the SS-run Columbia House in Berlin-Tempelhof and the concentration camp at Oranienburg, see Stefan Szende, *Zwischen Gewalt und Toleranz: Zeugnisse und Reflexionen eines Sozialisten* (Frankfurt and Cologne 1975), 15–53.

48. Rudolf Diels, *Lucifer ante portas: Zwischen Severing und Heydrich* (Zurich [1950]), 157–8 and 164–5. Diels' apologetic tone when discussing SA atrocities stems from his desire to relativize his own role as an accomplice in the NSDAP's crimes and as a manager during the early stages of Hitler's dictatorship in 1933/4. Instead, he sought to present himself as a defender of a vestigial legality. But this does not make his account factually inaccurate. For more on Diels, see Christoph Graf, *Politische Polizei zwischen Demokratie und Diktatur: Die Entwicklung der preußischen Politischen Polizei vom Staatsschutzorgan der Weimarer Republik zum Geheimen Staatspolizeiamt des Dritten Reiches* (Berlin 1983), 54–66 and 317–29.

49. Bräutigam and Gliech, 'Nationalsozialistische Zwangslager' (note 46), 150–1.

50. Bräutigam and Gliech, 'Nationalsozialistische Zwangslager' (note 46), 151 and 153; see also Kurt Werner and Karl Heinz Biernat, *Die Köpenicker Blutwoche 1933* (Berlin 1960). On 19 July 1950 the Criminal Division of the (East) Berlin District Court passed

sentence on those accused of complicity in the 'week of bloodshed in Köpenick', sentencing fifteen of them to death and the remaining forty-one to terms between five years and life. By this date, ten of those who had been sentenced to death and fifteen of the others had fled or were living in West Germany: see Senate of Berlin (ed.), *Berlin: Ringen um Einheit und Wiederaufbau 1948–1951* (Berlin 1962), 723. With the exception of a single trial, which had already taken place in 1948/9, there were no further prosecutions in the matter of Berlin's unofficial concentration camps.

51. ARH, i/1.146 (ministerial discussion of 2 March 1933). At the later session, Hitler declared that it would have been better 'if the culprit [van der Lubbe] had been hanged at once': see ARH i/1.147.

52. Adolf Ehrt, *Bewaffneter Aufstand! Enthüllungen über den kommunistischen Umsturzversuch am Vorabend der nationalen Revolution*, 2nd rev. edn (Berlin and Leipzig 1933).

53. Kurt Hiller, *Leben gegen die Zeit* (Reinbek 1969), 257.

54. Dr [Johann von] Leers, *Forderung der Stunde: Juden raus!* (Berlin [1933]), 22.

55. Michaelis and Schraepler, *Ursachen und Folgen* (note 4), ix.383; see also Saul Friedländer, *Nazi Germany and the Jews*, vol. i: *The Years of Persecution 1933–1939* (New York 1997). Since the measures designed to 'eradicate Marxism' were clearly instigated by Hitler, and inasmuch as it was Hitler who proposed that steps be taken against the Jews in the present case as well, questions must surround Ian Kershaw's claim that 'Scarcely any of the transformations of Germany during the spring and summer of 1933 had followed direct orders from the Reich Chancellery. Hitler had rarely been personally involved': see Kershaw, *Hitler 1889–1936* (note 22), 483.

56. Horkenbach, *Das Deutsche Reich* (note 6), 111. In the elections to the municipal assembly on 12 March 1933, the NSDAP won 38.3 per cent of the vote; see *Statistisches Jahrbuch der Stadt Berlin* (note 43), 268.

57. Christian Pross and Rolf Winau, *Nicht misshandeln: Das Krankenhaus Moabit* (Berlin 1984), 182–94.

58. In the Friedrichshain Hospital, for example. Following the dismissal of almost all its Jewish doctors on 18 May 1933, it was renamed the Horst Wessel Hospital.

59. *Das Schwarzbuch: Tatsachen und Dokumente. Die Lage der Juden in Deutschland 1933* (Paris 1934, reprinted Frankfurt, Berlin and Vienna 1983), 212.

60. Eberhard Jäckel and Axel Kuhn (eds), *Hitler: Sämtliche Aufzeichnungen 1905–1924* (Stuttgart 1980), 775.

61. Jäckel and Kuhn, *Hitler: Sämtliche Aufzeichnungen* (note 60), 837.

62. ARH i/1.270–1; see also the documentation on the 'April boycott' in Michaelis and Schraepler, *Ursachen und Folgen* (note 4), ix.387–92.

63. 'Nachklang zum Boykott: Wie die Propaganda-Maschinerie arbeitete', *Völkischer Beobachter* (Berlin edn) (5 April 1933).

64. ARH i/1.277.

65. ARH i/1.234–6 and 284–6.

66. ARH i/1.432–5.

67. ARH i/1.453–4.

68. Wolfgang Bretholz, 'Im Namen der Freiheit', *Berliner Tageblatt* (4 March 1933), reproduced in Margret Boveri, *Wir lügen alle: Eine Hauptstadtzeitung unter Hitler* (Olten and Freiburg im Breisgau [1965]), 71–3; and Theodor Wolff, 'Wahlkampf?', *Berliner Tageblatt* (5 March 1933), reproduced in Bernd Sösemann (ed.), *Theodor Wolff: Der Journalist, Berichte und Leitartikel* (Düsseldorf 1993), 361–3.

69. Walther G. Oschilewski, *Zeitungen in Berlin im Spiegel der Jahrhunderte* (Berlin 1975), 189–91. After the publisher and editorial staff had declared their allegiance to the new regime, the paper was able to resume publication on 12 March; see Boveri, *Wir lügen alle* (note 68), 76–7.

70. See Boveri, *Wir lügen alle* (note 68), 76–104.

71. ARH i/1.278–9 (ministerial discussion of 31 March 1933 concerning Karstadt); and ARH i/1.585–7 (cabinet meeting on 23 June 1933 concerning Hermann Tietz).

72. ARH i/1.615–17.

73. Domarus, *Hitler* (note 12), ii/1.1047–67, esp. 1058.

74. *Berliner Tageblatt* (31 Jan. 1939) (morning edn).

75. See Stephan Speicher, *Ort der deutschen Geschichte: Der Reichstag in Berlin* (Berlin [1995]), 159.

76. Domarus, *Hitler* (note 12), i/1.232.

77. Domarus, *Hitler* (note 12), i/1.232.

78. See Peter de Mendelssohn, *Zeitungsstadt Berlin: Menschen und Mächte in der Geschichte der deutschen Presse*, 2nd edn (Frankfurt, Berlin and Vienna 1982), 391–435.

79. Until she emigrated to South Africa at the end of 1934 or beginning of 1935; see Boveri, *Wir lügen alle* (note 68), 89–91.

80. Marion Beckers and Elisabeth Moortgat, *Yva: Photographien 1925–1938* (Berlin 2001), 148–9, 152–3 and 196; and Helmut Newton, *Autobiography* (London 2003).

81. Peter de Mendelssohn, 'Als die Presse gefesselt war', *Hundert Jahre Ullstein*, ed. W. Joachim Freyburg and Hans Wallenberg, 4 vols (Frankfurt, Berlin and Vienna 1977), iii.193–243, esp. 205.

82. Horkenbach, *Das Deutsche Reich* (note 6), 248–9.

83. Quoted from Robert M. W. Kempner, 'Hitler und die Zerstörung des Hauses Ullstein', *Hundert Jahre Ullstein*, ed. W. Joachim Freyburg and Hans Wallenberg, 4 vols (Frankfurt, Berlin and Vienna 1977), iii.267–92, esp. 272–6.

84. Thus the new chairman of Ullstein's board of directors, Ferdinand Bausback, in a letter to the Reich Chancellery (12 Oct. 1933), quoted by Kempner, 'Hitler und die Zerstörung des Hauses Ullstein' (note 83), 275.

85. See Mendelssohn, *Zeitungsstadt Berlin* (note 78), 401–2 and 436–48; see also Kempner, 'Hitler und die Zerstörung des Hauses Ullstein' (note 83), 278–83; and Margot Lindemann and Kurt Koszyk, *Geschichte der deutschen Presse*, Part 3: *Deutsche Presse 1914–1945* (Berlin 1972), 403–5.

86. Kempner, 'Hitler und die Zerstörung des Hauses Ullstein' (note 83), 286–9 (letter from Fritz Geisler to the secretary of state at the Reich Chancellery, Hans Heinrich Lammers, 14 April 1934).

87. Mendelssohn, *Zeitungsstadt Berlin* (note 78), 465 and 476–7.

88. Horkenbach, *Das Deutsche Reich* (note 6), 130.

89. Ansgar Diller, *Rundfunkpolitik im Dritten Reich* (Munich 1980), 84–93, esp. 92.

90. Klaus Kreimeier, *Die Ufa-Story: Geschichte eines Filmkonzerns* (Munich and Vienna 1992), 303–6.

91. Hitler's government declaration on the occasion of the passing of the Enabling Act on 23 March 1933, quoted by Domarus, *Hitler* (note 12), i/1.229–37, esp. 232.

92. According to Albert Speer, 'Whereas at an earlier date the state's instruments of power would parade up and down in the course of great national celebrations, [. . .] nowadays it is millions of members of the awakened people who march. The capacity of the venues that have been used hitherto for assemblies in Berlin – the Stadium and the Lustgarten – is no longer adequate for demonstrations of this kind': see Albert Speer, 'Die Aufbauten auf dem Tempelhofer Feld in Berlin zum 1. Mai 1933', *Baugilde: Zeitschrift des Bundes Deutscher Architekten*, xv/13 (10 July 1933), 613.

93. Thus the reason belatedly given by the Ministry of the Interior on 21 April, justifying the law establishing National Labour Day on 10 April 1933: see ARH i/1.312 n.2.

94. Supplement to the *Völkischer Beobachter* (Berlin edn) (30 April 1933).

95. 'Hitler's speech at the Tempelhofer Feld, 1 May 1933' in Axel Friedrichs (ed.), *Die nationalsozialistische Revolution 1933* (Berlin 1935), 143–51, esp. 150. This was also the first time that Hitler had appealed to 'the blessing of Providence' in one of his speeches.

96. Albert Speer, *Erinnerungen* (Berlin 1969), 40. Speer's own description of the site is inaccurate. See André François-Poncet's account of the impression left on him by the rally in *Botschafter in Berlin 1931–1938* (Berlin and Mainz 1962), 127–30.

97. Heinz Weidner, *Berlin im Festschmuck: Vom 15. Jahrhundert bis zur Gegenwart* (Berlin 1940), 139.

98. Weidner, *Berlin im Festschmuck* (note 97), 139.

99. Weidner, *Berlin im Festschmuck* (note 97), 140.

100. See Karlheinz Schmeer, *Die Regie des öffentlichen Lebens im Dritten Reich* (Munich 1956), 68–101.

101. Friedrichs, *Die nationalsozialistische Revolution* (note 95), 44–8 and 58–9.

102. Thus the phrase used by Domarus, *Hitler* (note 12), i/1.293.

103. [Friedrich] P[aulsen], 'Der Reichsbank-Wettbewerb', *Bauwelt*, xxxi (1933), 1.

104. *Festschrift zur Feier der Grundsteinlegung für den Erweiterungsbau der Reichsbank* (Berlin 1934), 13. An almost identical formulation occurs in 'Die Erweiterungsbau der Reichshauptbank', *Kunst dem Volk*, xi/5 (May 1940), 10.

105. Heinrich Wolff, 'Der Erweiterungsbau der Reichshauptbank', *Monatshefte für Baukunst und Städtebau*, ix (Sept. 1937), 291.

106. Wolfgang Schäche, '1933–1945: Bauen im Nationalsozialismus: Dekoration der Gewalt', *750 Jahre Archhitektur und Städtebau in Berlin: Die Internationale Bauausstellung im Kontext der Baugeschichte Berlins*, ed. Josef Paul Kleihues (Stuttgart 1987), 183–212, esp. 187–8. Schäche ascribes a 'monumental attitude' to the building, whereas Andrea Mesecke argues that there can be no question of monumentalism here as the building fails to leave a sublime impression and its scale is entirely clear to the observer: see Andrea Mesecke, 'Zur Spezifik der Repräsentationsarchitektur im Nationalsozialismus', *Stadt der Architektur, Architektur der Stadt: Berlin 1900–2000*, ed. Thorsten Scheer, Josef Paul Kleihues and Paul Kahlfeldt (Berlin 2000), 186–99, esp. 189. Until 1989 the building was the headquarters of the Central Committee of the Sozialistische Einheitspartei Deutschlands (SED). It was reopened in 2000 after substantial rebuilding work and is now part of the Foreign Office.

107. 'Bericht [vom 25 September 1933] über die am Dienstag, 19. September 1933 bei dem Herrn Reichskanzler Adolf Hitler stattgefundene Konferenz', reproduced in facsimile in Wolfgang Schäche, *Architektur und Städtebau in Berlin zwischen 1933 und 1945: Planen und Bauen unter der Ägide der Stadtverwaltung* (Berlin 1991), 526–9; see also Jost Dülffer, Jochen Thies and Josef Henke, *Hitlers Städte: Baupolitik im Dritten Reich. Eine Dokumentation* (Cologne and Vienna 1978), 90–3.

108. The letter signed by Lippert and Maretzky is reproduced in facsimile by Schäche, *Architektur und Städtebau* (note 107), 524–5 and by Dülffer, Thies and Henke, *Hitlers Städte* (note 107), 88–9.

109. Wolf Rüdiger Heß (ed.), *Rudolf Heß: Briefe 1908–1933* (Munich and Vienna 1987), 305–6 (letter from Rudolf to Fritz Heß, 18 Dec. 1928).

110. 'Lebenswichtige Nord-Süd-Verbindung! Der Grundgedanke der Planung für die neue S-Bahn-Strecke Anhalter – Stettiner Bahnhof', *Berliner Beobachter*, daily supplement to the *Völkischer Beobachter* (12 Aug. 1933).

111. Hachtmann, 'Pläne der Reichsbahn: Die neue Nord-Süd-Stadtbahn', *Berliner Beobachter*, daily supplement to the *Völkischer Beobachter* (5 July 1933).

112. ARH i/2.894–5 (Theodor Lewald's drawing enclosed with letter to secretary of state Hans Pfundtner, 5 Oct. 1933); see also Werner March, *Bauwerk Reichssportfeld* (Berlin 1936).

113. Quoted from Hans Pfundtner, 'Die Gesamtleitung der Errichtung des Reichssportfeldes', *Das Reichssportfeld: Eine Schöpfung des Dritten Reiches für die Olympischen Spiele und die Deutschen Leibesübungen*, ed. Reichsministerium des Innern (Berlin 1936), 11–26, esp. 13–14.

114. Quoted from Organisationskomitee für die Olympischen Spiele Berlin 1936 (ed.), *XI. Olympiade Berlin 1936: Amtlicher Bericht* (Berlin 1936), i.55.

115. Wolfgang Schäche and Norbert Szymanski, *Das Reichssportfeld: Architektur im Spannungsfeld von Sport und Macht* (Berlin 2001), 56.

116. Schäche and Szymanski, *Das Reichssportfeld* (note 115), 58.

117. Werner March, 'Die baukünstlerische Gestaltung des Reichssportfeldes', *Das Reichssportfeld: Eine Schöpfung des Dritten Reiches für die Olympischen Spiele und die Deutschen Leibesübungen*, ed. Reichsministerium des Innern (Berlin 1936), 27–55, esp. 31 and 41.

118. *Völkischer Beobachter* (15 Dec. 1933), quoted from ARH i/2.895 n.6.

119. Letter from Maretzky to Lammers (5 Dec. 1933), quoted from Schäche, *Architektur und Städtebau* (note 107), 530–2.

120. The following quotations are taken from the transcript of the discussion in the Chancellery on 29 March 1934 reproduced in facsimile by Schäche, *Architektur und Städtebau* (note 107), 533–6 and by Dülffer, Thies and Henke, *Hitlers Städte* (note 107), 97–100.

121. On this point, see Benedikt Goebel, *Der Umbau Alt-Berlins zum neuen Stadtzentrum: Planungs-, Bau- und Besitzgeschichte des historischen Berliner Stadtkerns im 19. und 20. Jahrhundert* (Berlin 2003), 242–56.

122. See the transcript of the discussion in the Reich Chancellery on 5 July 1934 reproduced in facsimile by Schäche, *Architektur und Städtebau* (note 107), 537–43 and by Dülffer, Thies and Henke, *Hitlers Städte* (note 107), 101–7.

123. Schäche, *Architektur und Städtebau* (note 107), 541 and Dülffer, Thies and Henke, *Hitlers Städte* (note 107), 105.

124. Schäche, *Architektur und Städtebau* (note 107), 540 and 542 and Dülffer, Thies and Henke, *Hitlers Städte* (note 107), 104 and 106.

125. ARH i/2.1205 nn.22 and 23.

126. Helmut Engel, Stefi Jersch-Wenzel and Wilhelm Treue (eds), *Charlottenburg*, Part 1: *Die historische Stadt* (Berlin 1986), 444.

127. Irmgard Wirth, *Die Bauwerke und Kunstdenkmäler von Berlin: Stadt und Bezirk Charlottenburg. Textband* (Berlin 1961), 316–17.

128. Cigaretten-Bilderdienst (ed.), *Adolf Hitler: Bilder aus dem Leben des Führers* (Altona and Bahrenfeld 1936), 76.

129. ARH i/2.1358.

130. See the documentation in Michaelis and Schraepler, *Ursachen und Folgen* (note 4), x.138–224; see also Peter Longerich, *Geschichte der SA*, 2nd edn (Munich 2003), 206–9; and Charles Bloch, *Die SA und die Krise des NS-Regimes 1934* (Frankfurt 1970).

131. Michaelis and Schraepler, *Ursachen und Folgen* (note 4), x.221.

132. Reinhard Rürup, *Topographie des Terrors: Gestapo, SS und Reichssicherheitshauptamt auf dem 'Prinz-Albrecht-Gelände'. Eine Dokumentation* (Berlin 1987), 11–15.

133. Michaelis and Schraepler, *Ursachen und Folgen* (note 4), x.195.

134. Press notice quoted from Schäche and Szymanski, *Das Reichssportfeld* (note 115), 66.

135. Schäche and Szymanski, *Das Reichssportfeld* (note 115), 67.

136. Letter from Pfundtner to Goebbels (21 Feb. 1935) quoted in Schäche and Szymanski, *Das Reichssportfeld* (note 115), 69.

137. Transcript of a meeting on 28 June 1935 by the City of Berlin quoted by Schäche, *Architektur und Städtebau* (note 107), 555 and Dülffer, Thies and Henke, *Hitlers Städte* (note 105), 115. In his memoirs (94), Speer reports an argument between Hitler and March and claims that he himself later salvaged the situation and, with it, the 1936 Berlin Games, but his account is rightly dismissed as implausible by Schäche and Szymanski, *Das Reichssportfeld* (note 115), 78–81.

138. Under the headline 'Berlin gets the most up-to-date airport', the *Völkischer Beobachter* of 5 May 1937 was the first to break the news about the plans for a new airport. The article included a photograph of the latest model. Hitler decided on 26 March 1936 that plans to develop the airport at Tempelhof would no longer form part of his more grandiose plans to redevelop the city, announcing that he agreed instead to the

expansion of the airport at the expense of arms production: see ARH iii.832; for a fuller account, see Elke Dittrich, *Der Flughafen Tempelhof in Entwurfszeichnungen und Modellen 1935–1944*, 2nd edn (Berlin 2006).

139. ARH iii.129–30 (submission by the chairman of the Berlin Airport Society to Hitler, 29 Oct. 1934).

140. The City of Berlin's transcript of a discussion with Hitler on 28 June 1938 concerning transport problems arising from the redevelopment of the city, quoted in Schäche, *Architektur und Städtebau* (note 107), 552–6; see also Dülffer, Thies and Henke, *Hitlers Städte* (note 107), 112–16.

141. Schäche, *Architektur und Städtebau* (note 107), 570–1 (Lippert's letter to Hitler, 23 April 1936); and ARH iii.849 and 871.

142. *Griebens Reiseführer: Berlin und Umgebung*, 70th edition (Berlin 1936), advertising section 19–21.

143. Henry Picker, *Hitlers Tischgespräche im Führerhauptquartier*, 4th edn (Stuttgart 1983), 216 (morning of 12 April 1942).

144. William L. Shirer, *Berlin Diary 1934–1941: The Rise of the Third Reich* (New York 1997), 39.

145. E. Trieb. '"Gebt mir vier Jahre Zeit!" und die Fotografie', *Fotografische Rundschau und Mitteilungen*, lxxiv/10 (15 May 1937), 169.

146. See Gerhard Riecke, 'Das Lichten des Dschungels', *Die Metropole: Industriekultur in Berlin im 20. Jahrhundert*, ed. Jochen Boberg, Tilman Fischer and Eckhart Gillen (Munich 1986), 232–7; see also Felix Escher, 'Berlins 700-Jahr-Feier 1937: Bemerkungen zur Entwicklung des Gedankens eines Stadtjubiläums', *Berlin in Geschichte und Gegenwart: Jahrbuch des Landesarchivs Berlin 1986*, ed. Hans J. Reichhardt (Berlin 1986), 177–90.

147. See Heinrich Breloer and Rainer Zimmer, *Die Akte Speer: Spuren eines Kriegsverbrechers* (Berlin 2006), 34–9.

148. Albert Speer, 'Die Bauten des Führers', *Adolf Hitler: Bilder aus dem Leben des Führers*, ed. Cigaretten-Bilderdienst (Altona and Bahrenfeld 1936), 72–7, esp. 77.

149. The decree is reproduced in facsimile in Breloer and Zimmer, *Die Akte Speer* (note 147), 49.

150. Domarus, *Hitler* (note 15), i/2.674.

151. The shell of the building is now beneath the pile of rubble out of which the Teufelsberg grew after the Second World War.

152. The text of the speech is reproduced in Domarus, *Hitler* (note 15), i/2.765–6.

153. For the text of the speech, see Domarus, *Hitler* (note 15), i/2.873–4.

154. Speer, *Erinnerungen* (note 96), 87.

155. Speer, *Erinnerungen* (note 96), 87.

156. Susanne Willems, *Der entsiedelte Jude: Albert Speers Wohnungsmarktpolitik für den Berliner Hauptstadtbau* (Berlin 2000).

157. Joachim C. Fest, *Speer: Eine Biographie*, 2nd edn (Berlin 1999), 104.

158. Paul Ortwin Rave, *Karl Friedrich Schinkel: Lebenswerk. Berlin, Stadtbaupläne, Brücken, Straßen, Tore, Plätze* (Berlin 1981), 29–31.

159. Most recently by Sven Felix Kellerhoff, *Hitlers Berlin: Geschichte einer Hassliebe* (Berlin 2005), 122. In his memoirs (533) Speer admits that he got to know Mächler's plans only while reading Alfred Schinz's 1964 monograph, *Berlin: Stadtschicksal und Städtebau*, in prison in Spandau.

160. *Große Berliner Kunstausstellung 1927* (Berlin 1927), 105.

161. Speer, *Erinnerungen* (note 96), 87.

162. Thus the formulation in Kellerhoff, *Hitlers Berlin* (note 159), 122.

163. Schinz, *Berlin* (note 159), 191–3.

164. Fest, *Speer* (note 157), 103–4.

165. Apart from the shopping centre between the major stores owned by Wertheim on the Leipziger Platz and by Hermann Tietz on the Dönhoffplatz, this 'city' included the

centre of the clothing industry on the Hausvogteiplatz, the newspaper district in the southern part of the Friedrichstadt, the banking quarter to the south of Unter den Linden and, of course, the government district in the Wilhelmstraße and its immediate vicinity; see Rudolf Krause, *Die Berliner City: Frühere Entwicklung / Gegenwärtige Situation / Mögliche Perspektiven* (Berlin 1958); and, more recently, Dorothea Zöbl, *Das periphere Zentrum: Ort und Entwicklung der Bundes- und Reichsbehörden im Groß-Berliner Stadtraum 1866/67–1914* (Potsdam 2001), who rightly notes a 'geographical dichotomy between east and west' in the inner city.

166. See Goebel, *Der Umbau Alt-Berlins* (note 121), 200–5; Laurenz Demps, *Berlin-Wilhelmstraße: Eine Topographie preußisch-deutscher Macht* (Berlin 1994), 185–98; and Dieter Hoffmann-Axthelm and Ludovica Scarpa, *Berliner Mauern und Durchbrüche* (Berlin 1987), 75–84. A particularly original suggestion came from Georg Opitz and Werner Kallmorgen, *Der Tiergartenring: Eine Städtebaustudie* (Berlin 1928).

167. Hitler's speech at the topping-out ceremony of the New Chancellery in the Deutschlandhalle on 2 Aug. 1938 is quoted by Angela Schönberger, *Die Neue Reichskanzlei von Albert Speer: Zum Zusammenhang von nationalsozialistischer Ideologie und Architektur* (Berlin 1981), 177–82, esp. 179 and 181. The topping-out ceremony took place in the Deutschlandhalle, which Hitler had officially opened on 29 Oct. 1935. On 2 Aug. 1938 he spoke to some 4,500 building workers and others who had been involved in the construction work. In the case of the Deutschlandhalle, too, Hitler had taken a personal interest in the project. At the end of 1934, when plans for the building had been submitted to him, he 'raised no objections' to its dual use as a sports venue and also as a party meeting place. Nor, according to a note by the secretary of state at the Chancellery, did he have any objections to the design of the front of the building: see ARH ii/2.1051. Building work on the Deutschlandhalle was initiated and supervised by the NSDAP. For further details, see the monograph published by its architect, Fritz Wiemer, as an offprint of his article, 'Deutschlandhalle Berlin', in the *Deutsche Bauzeitung* for 1935.

168. See Alfons Arenhövel (ed.), *Arena der Leidenschaften: Der Berliner Sportpalast und seine Veranstaltungen 1910–1973* (Berlin 1990), 395.

169. Hitler's speech on the occasion of the official handing over of the Chancellery at the Sportpalast on 9 Jan. 1939, quoted from Schönberger, *Die Neue Reichskanzlei* (note 167), 183–6, esp. 185.

170. Speer, *Erinnerungen* (note 96), 116–17.

171. Schönberger, *Die Neue Reichskanzlei* (note 167), 38–40.

172. ARH ii/2.1092.

173. Schönberger, *Die Neue Reichskanzlei* (note 167), 40; and ARH ii/2.1163.

174. Quoted by Schönberger, *Die Neue Reichskanzlei* (note 167), 40–1.

175. Schönberger, *Die Neue Reichskanzlei* (note 167), 41–5.

176. Johannes Hohlfeld (ed.), *Dokumente der Deutschen Politik und Geschichte von 1848 bis zur Gegenwart*, vol. iv: *Die Zeit der nationalsozialistischen Diktatur 1933–1945. Aufbau und Entwicklung 1933–1938* (Berlin n.d.), 385–6; and Schönberger, *Die Neue Reichskanzlei* (note 167), 46–50.

177. Schönberger, *Die Neue Reichskanzlei* (note 167), 179 and 181.

178. Speer, *Erinnerungen* (note 96), 154.

179. *Koralle: Wochenschrift für Unterhaltung, Wissen, Lebensfreude*, New Series, vi/20 (22 May 1938), 701.

180. *Berliner Illustrirte Zeitung*, xlvii/50 (15 Dec. 1938), 2047–9.

181. Domarus, *Hitler* (note 15), i/2.873.

182. 'Der Zwölfjahresplan für die Neugestaltung Berlins', *Deutsche Bauzeitung*, lxxii/5 (2 Feb. 1938), B 105–8.

183. Rudolf Wolters, *Albert Speer* (Oldenburg 1943), 55.

184. *Die Kunst im Dritten Reich*, iii/1 (Jan. 1939) (Edition A), 4–15, esp. 7.

185. Otto Thomae, *Die Propaganda-Maschinerie: Bildende Kunst und Öffentlichkeitsarbeit im Dritten Reich* (Berlin 1978), 143–8.

186. 'Plan zum Neuaufbau Berlins – 150 Architekten entwerfen Europas neueste Stadt', *Donau-Zeitung* (9 Jan. 1944), quoted by Joseph Wulf, *Die Bildenden Künste im Dritten Reich: Eine Dokumentation* (Gütersloh 1963), 239. None the less, the source seems to me somewhat problematic. On the question of ways of financing the scheme, see the overview in Hans J. Reichhardt and Wolfgang Schäche, *Von Berlin nach Germania: Über die Zerstörungen der 'Reichshauptstadt' durch Albert Speers Neugestaltungsplanungen* (Berlin 1998), 192–5.

187. For an overview of the plans for the 'Great Hall', see Reichhardt and Schäche, *Von Berlin nach Germania* (note 186), 109–17.

188. Heinrich Heim, *Monologe im Führerhauptquartier 1941–1944*, ed. Werner Jochmann (Hamburg 1980), 102 (21–22 Oct. 1941) and 318 (11/12 March 1942).

189. Picker, *Hitlers Tischgespräche* (note 143), 366 (8 June 1942).

190. Goebel, *Der Umbau Alt-Berlins* (note 121), 232–42.

191. See Peter Longerich, *'Davon haben wir nichts gewusst!' Die Deutschen und die Judenverfolgung 1933–1945* (Munich 2006), 112–13 and 117.

192. Speer, *Erinnerungen* (note 96), 163.

193. Domarus, *Hitler* (note 15), ii/1.1145–6; see also Heinrich Hoffmann (ed.), *Ein Volk ehrt seinen Führer: Der 20. April 1939 im Bild* (Berlin 1939).

194. Reichhardt and Schäche, *Von Berlin nach Germania* (note 186), 65.

195. Quoted from the facsimile of the document, which is dated by hand 25 June 1940 and which is reproduced by Speer, *Erinnerungen* (note 96), before p.193.

196. Minutes of two 'visits made by the Führer', quoted in Breloer and Zimmer, *Die Akte Speer* (note 147), 118–24.

197. Reichhardt and Schäche, *Von Berlin nach Germania* (note 186), 65.

Bibliography

Newspapers and Magazines

Das 12 Uhr Blatt
Der Angriff
Arbeiter-Illustrierte-Zeitung (A-I-Z)
L'architecture d'aujourd'hui
Baugilde: Zeitschrift des Bundes Deutscher Architekten
Bauwelt: Zeitschrift für das gesamte Bauwesen
Berliner Arbeiterzeitung
Berliner Börsen-Courier
Berliner illustrierte Nachtausgabe
Berliner Illustrirte Zeitung
Berliner Lokal-Anzeiger
Berliner Morgenpost
Berliner Tageblatt
Berliner Volks-Zeitung
B. Z. am Mittag
Corriere della Sera
C. V.-Zeitung: Blätter für Deutschtum und Judentum
Daily Express
Die Dame
Deutsche Allgemeine Zeitung
Der Deutsche Baumeister
Deutsche Bauzeitung
Deutsche Tageszeitung
Deutsche Treue
Deutsche Zeitung
Deutsches Tageblatt
Deutsches Wochenblatt
Deutsches Wollen: Zeitschrift der Auslands-Organisation der NSDAP
Frankfurter Zeitung
Germania
Giornale d'Italia
Die Grüne Post
Illustrierter Beobachter
Internationale Pressekorrespondenz

Koralle: Wochenschrift für Unterhaltung, Wissen, Lebensfreude
Die Kunst im Dritten Reich
Kunst dem Volk
Monatshefte für Baukunst und Städtebau
Der Montag
MM Montag Morgen
Münchner Telegramm Zeitung
Der Nationale Sozialist
Nationalsozialistische Briefe
Das Neue Berlin: Großstadtprobleme
Neue I. Z.
Neue Preußische [Kreuz-]Zeitung
Die Pleite
Potsdamer Tageszeitung
Reichswart
Rheinisch-Westfälische Zeitung
Rosenheimer Tagblatt
Der Rote Aufbau
Die Rote Fahne
Scherl's Magazin
Simplicissimus
Der Stahlhelm
Der Stürmer
Der Tag
Das Tage-Buch
Tempo: Berliner Abend-Zeitung
Völkische Freiheit
Völkischer Beobachter
Vorwärts
Vossische Zeitung
Wahrer Jacob
Die Welt am Abend
Die Welt am Montag
Die Weltbühne
Westdeutsche Landeszeitung
Die Woche

Secondary Literature and Published Sources

Adreßbuch für Berlin und seine Vororte (Berlin 1917 and 1918)
Akten der Reichskanzlei: Regierung Hitler 1933–1938. Die Regierung Hitler (ARH), vol. i: 1933–4, part 1: 30 Jan. to 31 Aug. 1933, part 2: 12 Sept. to 27 Aug. 1934, ed. Konrad Repgen and Hans Booms (Boppard 1983)
Akten der Reichskanzlei: Regierung Hitler 1933–1938. Die Regierung Hitler (ARH), vol. ii: 1934–5, part 1: Aug. 1934 to May 1935, part 2: June to Dec. 1935, ed. Hans Günter Hockerts and Friedrich P. Kahlenberg (Munich 1999)
Akten der Reichskanzlei: Regierung Hitler 1933–1938. Die Regierung Hitler (ARH), vol. iii: 1936, ed. Hans Günter Hockerts and Hartmut Weber (Munich 2002)
Akten der Reichskanzlei: Regierung Hitler 1933–1938. Die Regierung Hitler (ARH), vol. iv: 1937, ed. Hans Günter Hockerts and Hartmut Weber (Munich 2005)
Arenhövel, Alfons (ed.). *Arena der Leidenschaften: Der Berliner Sportpalast und seine Veranstaltungen 1910–1973* (Berlin 1990)
Arnold, Dietmar and Ingmar. *Schloßfreiheit: Vor den Toren des Stadtschlosses* (Berlin 1998)

Backes, Klaus. *Hitler und die bildenden Künste: Kulturverständnis und Kunstpolitik im Dritten Reich* (Cologne 1988)

Bade, Wilfrid. *Die S. A. erobert Berlin* (Munich 1933)

Baedeker, Karl. *Berlin und Umgebung: Handbuch für Reisende*, 19th edn (Leipzig 1921) and 20th edn (Leipzig 1927)

Bahar, Alexander, and Wilfried Kugel. *Der Reichstagsbrand: Wie Geschichte gemacht wird* (Berlin 2001)

Beckers, Marion, and Elisabeth Moortgat. *Yva: Photographien 1925–1938* (Berlin 2001)

Bennecke, Heinrich. *Hitler und die SA* (Munich 1962)

Berendt, Erich F. *Soldaten der Freiheit: Ein Parolenbuch des Nationalsozialismus 1918–1925* (Berlin 1935)

Berghahn, Volker R. *Der Stahlhelm: Bund der Frontsoldaten* (Düsseldorf 1966)

Bergius, Hanne. 'Der groteske Tod: Erscheinungsformen und Motivik bei Heartfield', *John Heartfield*, ed. Akademie der Künste zu Berlin (Cologne 1991), 56–64 (exhibition catalogue)

Bergmann, Klaus. *Agrarromantik und Großstadtfeindschaft* (Meisenheim 1970)

Bering, Dietz. *Kampf um Namen: Bernhard Weiß gegen Joseph Goebbels* (Stuttgart 1991)

Berlin, Berlin: Die Ausstellung zur Geschichte der Stadt, ed. Gottfried Korff (Berlin 1987) (exhibition catalogue)

Berlin für Kenner: Ein Bärenführer bei Tag und Nacht durch die deutsche Reichshauptstadt (Berlin [1912])

Berlin und seine Bauten, ed. Architekten- und Ingenieur-Verein zu Berlin, part 9: *Industriebauten, Bürohäuser* (Berlin, Munich and Düsseldorf 1971)

Berlin Senate (ed.). *Berlin: Ringen um Einheit und Wiederaufbau 1948–1951* (Berlin 1962)

Bezirksamt Tempelhof-Schöneberg von Berlin (ed.). *Der Schwerbelastungskörper: Mysteriöses Erbe der Reichshauptstadt* (Berlin 2005)

Blasius, Dirk. *Weimars Ende: Bürgerkrieg und Politik 1930–1933* (Göttingen 2005)

Bleuel, Hans Peter, and Ernst Klinnert. *Deutsche Studenten auf dem Weg ins Dritte Reich: Ideologien, Programme, Aktionen 1918–1935* (Gütersloh 1967)

Bloch, Charles. *Die SA und die Krise des NS-Regimes 1934* (Frankfurt 1970)

Bloch, Ernst. *Erbschaft dieser Zeit*, rev. edn (Frankfurt 1977) (= *Gesamtausgabe in 16 Bänden*, vol. iv)

Boberg, Jochen, Tilman Fichter and Eckhart Gillen (eds). *Die Metropole: Industriekultur in Berlin im 20. Jahrhundert* (Munich 1986)

Böß, Gustav. *Berlin von heute: Stadtverwaltung und Wirtschaft* (Berlin 1929)

Boveri, Margret. *Wir lügen alle: Eine Hauptstadtzeitung unter Hitler* (Olten and Freiburg im Breisgau [1965])

Bracher, Karl Dietrich. *Die Auflösung der Weimarer Republik: Eine Studie zum Problem des Machtverfalls in der Demokratie*, 3rd edn (Villingen 1960)

—. 'Dualismus oder Gleichschaltung: Der Faktor Preußen in der Weimarer Republik', *Die Weimarer Republik 1918–1933: Politik – Wirtschaft – Gesellschaft*, ed. Karl Dietrich Bracher, Manfred Funke and Hans-Adolf Jacobsen (Düsseldorf 1987), 535–51

—, Manfred Funke and Hans-Adolf Jacobsen (eds). *Die Weimarer Republik 1918–1933: Politik – Wirtschaft – Gesellschaft* (Düsseldorf 1987)

—, Wolfgang Sauer and Gerhard Schulz. *Die nationalsozialistische Machtergreifung: Studien zur Errichtung des totalitären Herrschaftssystems in Deutschland 1933/34*, 2nd edn (Cologne and Opladen 1962)

Bramsted, Ernest. *Goebbels and National Socialist Propaganda 1924–1945* (London 1965)

Bräutigam, Helmut, and Oliver C. Gliech. 'Nationalsozialistische Zwangslager in Berlin. I. Die "wilden" Konzentrationslager und Folterkeller 1933/34', *Berlin-Forschungen II*, ed. Wolfgang Ribbe (Berlin 1987), 141–78

Breloer, Heinrich, and Rainer Zimmer. *Die Akte Speer: Spuren eines Kriegsverbrechers* (Berlin 2006)

—. *Speer und Er: Hitlers Architekt und Rüstungsminister* (Berlin 2005)

Bronnen, Arnolt. *Arnolt bronnen gibt zu protokoll: beiträge zur geschichte des modernen schriftstellers* (Hamburg 1954)

—. *Roßbach* (Berlin 1930)

Broszat, Martin. 'Die Anfänge der Berliner NSDAP 1926/27', *Vierteljahrshefte für Zeitgeschichte*, viii (1960), 85–118

—. *Die Machtergreifung: Der Aufstieg der NSDAP und die Zerstörung der Weimarer Republik* (Munich 1984)

Brück, Carlheinz von. *Ein Mann, der Hitler in die Enge trieb: Hans Littens Kampf gegen den Faschismus*, 2nd edn (Berlin 1976)

Brüning, Heinrich. *Memoiren 1918–1934* (Stuttgart 1970)

Büsch, Otto, and Wolfgang Haus. *Berlin als Hauptstadt der Weimarer Republik 1919–1933* (Berlin and New York 1987)

Busche, Ernst A. '1918–1933. Laboratorium: Wohnen und Weltstadt', *750 Jahre Architektur und Städtebau in Berlin: Die Internationale Bauausstellung im Kontext der Baugeschichte Berlins*, ed. Josef Paul Kleihues (Stuttgart 1987), 153–82

Caro, Kurt, and Walter Oehme. *Schleichers Aufstieg: Ein Beitrag zur Geschichte der Gegenrevolution* (Berlin 1933)

Carsten, Francis A. *The Reichswehr and Politics 1918–1933* (Berkeley and London 1973)

Cartarius, Ulrich (ed.). *Deutschland im Ersten Weltkrieg: Texte und Dokumente 1914–1918* (Munich 1982)

Cigaretten-Bilderdienst (ed.). *Adolf Hitler: Bilder aus dem Leben des Führers* (Altona and Bahrenfeld 1936)

Deiseroth, Dieter (ed.). *Der Reichstagsbrand und der Prozess vor dem Reichsgericht* (Berlin 2006)

Demps, Laurenz. 'Berlin als Experimentierfeld des Terrorismus im Jahr 1933', *1933 – Wege zur Diktatur: Rahmenprogramm – Vortragsreihe* (Berlin 1984), 105–15

—. *Berlin-Wilhelmstraße: Eine Topographie preußisch-deutscher Macht* (Berlin 1994)

—. 'Konzentrationslager in Berlin 1933 bis 1945', *Jahrbuch des Märkischen Museums III/1977*, ed. Herbert Hampe and Hans-Joachim Beeskow (Berlin 1977), 7–19

Deuerlein, Ernst (ed.). *Der Aufstieg der NSDAP in Augenzeugenberichten* (Düsseldorf 1968)

Deutsche Bauausstellung Berlin 1931: Amtlicher Katalog und Führer (Berlin 1931)

Der deutsche PEN-Club im Exil 1933–1948: Eine Ausstellung der Deutschen Bibliothek Frankfurt am Main (Frankfurt 1980)

Diels, Rudolf. *Lucifer ante portas: Zwischen Severing und Heydrich* (Zurich [1950])

Dietrich, Otto. *Mit Hitler in die Macht: Persönliche Erlebnisse mit meinem Führer* (Munich 1934)

—. *Zwölf Jahre mit Hitler* (Cologne 1955)

Diller, Ansgar. *Rundfunkpolitik im Dritten Reich* (Munich 1980)

Dittrich, Elke. *Der Flughafen Tempelhof in Entwurfszeichnungen und Modellen 1935–1944*, 2nd edn (Berlin 2006)

Dokumente aus geheimen Archiven, vol. iv: 1914–1918: *Berichte des Berliner Polizeipräsidenten zur Stimmung und Lage der Bevölkerung in Berlin 1914–1918* (Weimar 1987)

Dokumente und Materialien zur Geschichte der deutschen Arbeiterbewegung, series 2, vol. i, ed. Institut für Marxismus-Leninismus beim Zentralkomitee der Sozialistischen Einheitspartei Deutschlands (Berlin 1967)

Dollinger, Hans (ed.). *Der Erste Weltkrieg in Bildern und Dokumenten* (Munich 1965)

Domarus, Max. *Hitler: Reden und Proklamationen 1932–1945. Kommentiert von einem deutschen Zeitgenossen* (Munich 1965)

Dornberg, John. *Der Hitlerputsch: München, 8. und 9. November 1923* (Munich and Vienna 1983)

Dörp, Peter. 'Goebbels' Kampf gegen Remarque: Eine Untersuchung über die Hintergründe des Hasses und der Agitation Goebbels' gegen den amerikanischen Spielfilm "Im Westen nichts Neues" nach dem gleichnamigen Bestsellerroman von Erich Maria Remarque', www.erft.de/schulen/abtei-gym/remarque/doerp2.htm

Drage, Charles. *Als Hitler nach Canossa ging* (Berlin 1982)

Dresler, Adolf (ed.). *Fritz Maier-Hartmann: Die Sammlung Rehse. Dokumente der Zeitgeschichte* (Munich 1938)

Duesterberg, Theodor. *Der Stahlhelm und Hitler* (Wolfenbüttel and Hanover 1949)

Dülffer, Jost, Jochen Thies and Josef Henke. *Hitlers Städte: Baupolitik im Dritten Reich. Eine Dokumentation* (Cologne and Vienna 1978)

Dupeux, Louis. *'Nationalbolschewismus' in Deutschland 1919–1933: Kommunistische Strategie und konservative Dynamik* (Munich 1985)

Ehls, Marie-Luise. *Protest und Propaganda: Demonstrationen in Berlin zur Zeit der Weimarer Republik* (Berlin and New York 1997)

Ehrt, Adolf. *Bewaffneter Aufstand! Enthüllungen über den kommunistischen Umsturzversuch am Vorabend der nationalen Revolution*, 2nd edn (Berlin and Leipzig 1933)

Engel, Helmut, Stefi Jersch-Wenzel and Wilhelm Treue (eds). *Charlottenburg*, part 1: *Die historische Stadt* (Berlin 1986)

—. *Tiergarten*, part 2: *Moabit* (Berlin 1987) (= *Geschichtslandschaft Berlin: Orte und Ereignisse*, vol. ii)

Engelbrechten, J. K. von. *Eine braune Armee entsteht: Die Geschichte der Berlin-Brandenburger SA* (Munich 1937)

Engelbrechten, J. K., and Hans Volz. *Wir wandern durch das nationalsozialistische Berlin: Ein Führer durch die Gedenkstätten des Kampfes um die Reichshauptstadt* (Munich 1937)

Engeli, Christian. *Gustav Böß: Oberbürgermeister von Berlin 1921 bis 1930* (Stuttgart 1971)

Escher, Felix. 'Berlins 700-Jahr-Feier 1937: Bemerkungen zur Entwicklung des Gedankens eines Stadtjubiläums', *Berlin in Geschichte und Gegenwart: Jahrbuch des Landesarchivs Berlin 1986*, ed. Hans J. Reichhardt (Berlin 1986), 177–90

Evans, Richard J. *The Coming of the Third Reich* (London 2003)

—. *The Third Reich in Power* (London 2005)

—. *The Third Reich at War* (London 2008)

Falter, Jürgen W. 'Wahlen und Wählerverhalten unter besonderer Berücksichtigung des Aufstiegs der NSDAP nach 1928', *Die Weimarer Republik 1918–1933: Politik – Wirtschaft – Gesellschaft*, ed. Karl Dietrich Bracher, Manfred Funke and Hans-Adolf Jacobsen (Düsseldorf 1987), 484–504

Fest, Joachim C. *Hitler: Eine Biographie* (Frankfurt, Berlin and Vienna 1973 and 1978); trans. Richard and Clara Winston as *Hitler* (London 1974)

—. *Speer: Eine Biographie*, 2nd edn (Berlin 1999)

Festschrift zur Feier der Grundsteinlegung für den Erweiterungsbau der Reichshauptbank (Berlin 1934)

Finker, Kurt. 'Bund Wiking (BW) 1923–1928', *Lexikon zur Parteiengeschichte 1789–1945*, ed. Dieter Fricke, 4 vols (Leipzig 1983–6), i.368–73

—. 'Frontbann 1924–1926', *Lexikon zur Parteiengeschichte 1789–1945*, ed. Dieter Fricke, 4 vols (Leipzig 1983–6), ii.716–18

—. 'Olympia 1920–1926', *Lexikon zur Parteiengeschichte 1789–1945*, ed. Dieter Fricke, 4 vols (Leipzig 1983–6), iii.548

Fischer, Lothar. *George Grosz* (Reinbek 1993)

François-Poncet, André. *Botschafter in Berlin 1931–1938* (Berlin and Mainz 1962)

Franz-Willing, Georg. *Krisenjahr der Hitlerbewegung: 1923* (Preußisch Oldendorf 1975)

—. *Putsch und Verbotszeit der Hitlerbewegung: November 1923–Februar 1925* (Preußisch Oldendorf 1977)

—. *Ursprung der Hitlerbewegung: 1919–1922*, 2nd edn (Preußisch Oldendorf 1974)

Frecot, Janos, and Klaus-Jürgen Sembach. *Berlin im Licht: Photographien der nächtlichen Stadt* (Berlin 2002)

Freyburg, W. Joachim, and Hans Wallenberg (eds). *Hundert Jahre Ullstein*, 4 vols (Frankfurt, Berlin and Vienna 1977)

Friedländer, Saul. *Nazi Germany and the Jews*, vol. i: *The Years of Persecution 1933–1939* (New York 1997)

Friedrich, Karl Martin (ed.). *Der kesse Orje: Spaziergänge eines Berliner Jungen durch das System*, with an introduction by Joseph Goebbels and line drawings by Mjölnir (Munich 1931)

Friedrich, Thomas. ' "Alles kommt auf die Blickrichtung an" oder Geschichte im Prokrustesbett. Das "Revolutionstrauma" der Nationalsozialisten und der Umgang der NS-Bildpropaganda mit den Fotos der Novemberrevolution', *Revolution und Fotografie: Berlin 1918/19. Eine Ausstellung der Neuen Gesellschaft für Bildende Künste* (Berlin 1989), 227–40 (exhibition catalogue)

—. 'Die Berliner Zeitungslandschaft am Ende der Weimarer Republik', *Berlin 1932: Das letzte Jahr der ersten deutschen Republik. Politik, Medien, Symbole*, ed. Diethart Kerbs and Henrick Stahr (Berlin 1992), 56–67

—. 'Die Politik des Hasses: Über den Aufstieg des Antisemitismus von der Ideologie zur Staatsdoktrin zu Lebzeiten Max Liebermanns', *Was vom Leben übrig bleibt, sind Bilder und Geschichten: Max Liebermann zum 150. Geburtstag. Rekonstruktion der Gedächtnisausstellung des Berliner Jüdischen Museums von 1936*, ed. Hermann Simon (Berlin 1997), 95–117 (exhibition catalogue)

—. 'Regenerierter Volkskörper', *Tennis in Deutschland von den Anfängen bis 2002: Zum 100-jährigen Bestehen des Deutschen Tennis Bundes*, ed. Deutscher Tennis Bund (Berlin 2002), 126–33

Friedrichs, Axel (ed.). *Die nationalsozialistische Revolution 1933* (Berlin 1935) (= *Dokumente der deutschen Politik*, vol. i)

Fröhlich, Elke. Joseph Goebbels: Der Propagandist', *Die braune Elite I. 22 biographische Skizzen*, ed. Ronald Smelser and Rainer Zitelmann, 3rd edn (Darmstadt 1994), 52–68

— (ed.). *Die Tagebücher von Joseph Goebbels: Sämtliche Fragmente*, 4 vols (Munich 1987)

— '(ed.). *Die Tagebücher von Joseph Goebbels*, part 1: *Aufzeichnungen 1923–1941*, 9 vols in 14 parts (Munich 1997–2006), i/1 (Oct. 1923–Nov. 1925) and i/2 (Dec. 1925–May 1928), ed. Elke Fröhlich (2004 and 2005); i/3 (June 1928–Nov. 1929) and ii/1 (Dec. 1929–May 1931), ed. Anne Munding (2004 and 2005); ii/2 (June 1931–Sept. 1932) and ii/3 (Oct. 1932–March 1934), ed. Angela Hermann (2004 and 2006)

Fürst, Max. *Talisman Scheherezade: Die schwierigen zwanziger Jahre* (Munich and Vienna 1976)

Geiss, Imanuel. *Das Deutsche Reich und der Erste Weltkrieg* (Munich and Zurich 1985)

—. *Geschichte des Rassismus* (Frankfurt 1988)

Gerlach, Hellmut von. *Von Rechts nach Links* (Zurich 1937)

Giesen, Rolf, and Manfred Hobsch. *Hitlerjunge Quex, Jud Süß und Kolberg: Die Propagandafilme des Dritten Reiches. Dokumente und Materialien zum NS-Film* (Berlin 2005)

Glatzer, Dieter and Ruth. *Berliner Leben 1914–1918: Eine historische Reportage aus Erinnerungen und Berichten* (Berlin 1983)

Gliech, Oliver C. 'Die Spandauer SA 1926 bis 1933: Eine Studie zur nationalsozialistischen Gewalt in einem Berliner Bezirk', *Berlin-Forschungen III*, ed. Wolfgang Ribbe (Berlin 1988), 107–205

Glombowski, Friedrich. *Organisation Heinz: Das Schicksal der Kameraden Schlageters* (Berlin 1934)

Goebbels, Joseph. *Der Angriff: Aufsätze aus der Kampfzeit*, 2nd edn (Munich 1935)

—. *Das erwachende Berlin* (Munich 1934)

—. *Kampf um Berlin: Der Anfang*, 3rd edn (Munich 1934)

—. *Vom Kaiserhof zur Reichskanzlei: Eine historische Darstellung in Tagebuchblättern* (Munich 1934)

—. *Wetterleuchten* (Munich 1939)

Goebel, Benedikt. *Der Umbau Alt-Berlins zum modernen Stadtzentrum: Planungs-, Bau- und Besitzgeschichte des historischen Berliner Stadtkerns im 19. und 20. Jahrhundert* (Berlin 2003)

Golecki, Anton (ed.). *Das Kabinett von Schleicher: 3. Dezember 1932 bis 30. Januar 1933* (Boppard 1986)

Görlitz, Walter (i.e. Otto Julius Frauendorf). *Hindenburg: Ein Lebensbild* (Bonn 1953)

—, and Herbert A. Quint (i.e. Richard von Frankenberg). *Adolf Hitler: Eine Biographie* (Stuttgart 1952)

Gordon, Harold J., Jr. *Hitler and the Beer Hall Putsch* (Princeton, NJ 1972)

Gossweiler, Kurt. *Kapital, Reichswehr und NSDAP 1919–1924*, 2nd edn (Berlin 1984)

Graf, Christoph. *Politische Polizei zwischen Demokratie und Diktatur: Die Entwicklung der preußischen Politischen Polizei vom Staatsschutzorgan der Weimarer Republik zum Geheimen Staatspolizeiamt des Dritten Reiches* (Berlin 1983)

Grammbitter, Ulrike. 'Vom "Parteiheim" in der Brienner Straße zu den Monumentalbauten am "Königlichen Platz": Das Parteizentrum der NSDAP am Königsplatz in München', *Bürokratie und Kult: Das Parteizentrum der NSDAP am Königsplatz in München. Geschichte und Rezeption*, ed. Iris Lauterbach (Munich 1995), 61–87

Griebens Reiseführer Berlin. Kleine Ausgabe, 59th edn (Berlin 1917)

Griebens Reiseführer Berlin und Umgebung, 61st edn (Berlin 1921–2), 66th edn (Berlin 1929) and 70th edn (Berlin 1936)

Gritschneder, Otto. *Bewährungsfrist für den Terroristen Adolf H. Der Hitler-Putsch und die bayerische Justiz* (Munich 1990)

Große Berliner Kunstausstellung 1927 (Berlin 1927) (exhibition catalogue)

Grosz, George. *Ecce homo* (New York 1966) (facsimile of first edn of 1923 with a foreword by Günther Anders)

Gruchmann, Lothar (ed.). *Der Hitler-Prozess 1924: Wortlaut der Hauptverhandlung vor dem Volksgericht München I* (Munich 1997–9)

Grzesinski, Albert. *Im Kampf um die deutsche Republik: Erinnerungen eines Sozialdemokraten* [1933] (Munich 2001)

Gumbel, Emil Julius. *Verschwörer: Zur Geschichte und Soziologie der deutschen nationalistischen Geheimbünde 1918–1924* (Vienna 1924, reprinted Heidelberg 1979)

Hadamovsky, Eugen. *Propaganda und nationale Macht: Die Organisation der öffentlichen Meinung für die nationale Politik* (Oldenburg 1933)

Hajos, Elisabeth M., and Leopold Zahn. *Berliner Architektur der Nachkriegszeit* (Berlin 1928), reprinted under the title *Berliner Architektur 1919 bis 1929: 10 Jahre Architektur der Moderne* (Berlin 1996)

Hamilton, Richard Frederick. *Who Voted For Hitler?* (Princeton, NJ 1982)

Hanfstaengl, Ernst. *Zwischen Weißem und Braunem Haus: Memoiren eines politischen Außenseiters* (Munich 1970)

Hannover, Heinrich, and Elisabeth Hannover-Drück. *Politische Justiz 1918–1933* (Frankfurt 1966)

Harrison, Ted. '"Alter Kämpfer" im Widerstand: Graf Helldorf, die NS-Bewegung und die Opposition gegen Hitler', *Vierteljahrshefte für Zeitgeschichte*, vl (1995), 385–423

Haus, Wolfgang. 'Chance, Krise und Sturz der Demokratie im Berlin der Weimarer Republik', *Berlin als Hauptstadt der Weimarer Republik 1919–1933*, ed. Otto Büsch and Wolfgang Haus (Berlin and New York 1987), 161–264

Heiber, Helmut. *Joseph Goebbels* (Berlin 1962)

— (ed.). *Das Tagebuch von Joseph Goebbels 1925/26* (Stuttgart [1961])

Heiden, Konrad. *Adolf Hitler: Das Zeitalter der Verantwortungslosigkeit. Eine Biographie* (Zurich 1936)

—. *Geburt des dritten Reiches: Die Geschichte des Nationalsozialismus bis Herbst 1933* (Zurich 1934)

—. *Geschichte des Nationalsozialismus: Die Karriere einer Idee* (Berlin 1933)

Heim, Heinrich. *Monologe im Führerhauptquartier 1941–1944*, ed. Werner Jochmann (Hamburg 1980)

Herz, Rudolf. *Hoffmann & Hitler: Fotografie als Medium des Führer-Mythos* (Munich 1994)

Herzfeld, Hans. 'Berlin auf dem Wege zur Weltstadt', *Berlin: Neun Kapitel seiner Geschichte*, ed. Richard Dietrich (Berlin 1960), 239–71

Heß, Wolf Rüdiger (ed.). *Rudolf Heß: Briefe 1908–1933* (Munich and Vienna 1987)

Heuter, Christoph. *Emil Fahrenkamp 1885–1966: Architekt im rheinisch-westfälischen Industriegebiet* (Petersberg 2002)

Hiller, Kurt. *Leben gegen die Zeit* (Reinbek 1969)

Hillger, Hermann (ed.). *Kürschners Deutscher Reichstag 1928* (Berlin n.d.)

Hitler, Adolf. *Mein Kampf. Zwei Bände in einem Band*, 26th edn (Munich 1933); trans. Ralph Manheim as *Mein Kampf* (London 2002)

Hitler: Reden, Schriften, Anordnungen Februar 1925 bis Januar 1933 (RSA), ed. Institut für Zeitgeschichte, 6 vols in 12 parts, plus Index and one supplementary vol. in 4 parts (Munich 1991–2003)

Hoegner, Wilhelm. *Die verratene Republik: Geschichte der deutschen Gegenrevolution* (Munich 1958)

Hoffmann, Heinrich (ed.). *Hitler wie ich ihn sah: Aufzeichnungen seines Leibfotografen* (Munich and Berlin 1974)

—. *Hitler wie ihn keiner kennt. 100 Bild-Dokumente aus dem Leben des Führers* (Berlin [1932])

— (ed.). *Hitler über Deutschland*. Text by Josef Berchtold (Munich 1932)

— (ed.). *Ein Volk ehrt seinen Führer: Der 20. April 1939 im Bild* (Berlin 1939)

Hoffmann, Herbert. *Berlin vor fünzig Jahren: Ein Fotoreporter sieht seine Stadt und ihre Menschen* (Berlin 1978)

Hoffmann-Axthelm, Dieter, and Ludovica Scarpa. *Berliner Mauern und Durchbrüche* (Berlin 1987)

Hohlfeld, Johannes (ed.). *Dokumente der Deutschen Politik und Geschichte von 1848 bis zur Gegenwart*, vol. iv: *Die Zeit der nationalsozialistischen Diktatur 1933–1945. Aufbau und Entwicklung 1933–1938* (Berlin n.d.)

Höhne, Heinz. *Die Zeit der Illusionen: Hitler und die Anfänge des Dritten Reiches 1933–1936* (Düsseldorf, Vienna and New York 1991)

Horkenbach, Cuno (ed.). *Das Deutsche Reich von 1918 bis heute* (Berlin 1930), with supplementary vols for 1931, 1932 and 1933 (Berlin 1932–5)

Hörnigk, Frank. 'Nationalsozialistischer "Kulturkampf" um Berlin 1926–1933', *Literarisches Leben in Berlin 1871–1933*, ed. Peter Wruck (Berlin 1987), 253–78

Hüter, Karl-Heinz. *Architektur in Berlin 1900–1933* (Berlin 1987)

Institut für Konjunkturforschung (ed.). *Konjunkturstatistisches Handbuch* (Berlin 1933)

Jäckel, Eberhard, and Axel Kuhn (eds). *Hitler: Sämtliche Aufzeichnungen 1905–1924* (Stuttgart 1980)

Jasper, Gotthard. *Die gescheiterte Zähmung: Wege zur Machtergreifung Hitlers 1930–1934* (Frankfurt 1986)

Joachimsthaler, Anton. *Hitlers Liste: Ein Dokument persönlicher Beziehungen* (Munich 2003)

—. *Hitlers Weg begann in München: 1913–1923* (Munich 2000)

Jochmann, Werner. *Nationalsozialismus und Revolution: Ursprung und Geschichte der NSDAP in Hamburg 1922–1933. Dokumente* (Frankfurt 1963)

Johannes, Heinz. *Neues Bauen in Berlin: Ein Führer mit 168 Bildern* (Berlin 1931, reprinted Berlin 1998)

Kellerhoff, Sven Felix. *Hitlers Berlin: Geschichte einer Hassliebe* (Berlin 2005)

Kempner, Robert M. W. 'Hitler und die Zerstörung des Hauses Ullstein', *Hundert Jahre Ullstein*, ed. W. Joachim Freyburg and Hans Wallenberg, 4 vols (Frankfurt, Berlin and Vienna 1977), iii.267–92

Kershaw, Ian. *Hitler 1889–1936: Hubris* (London 1998)

—. *The 'Hitler Myth': Image and Reality in the Third Reich* (Oxford 2001)

Kessemeier, Carin. *Der Leitartikler Goebbels in den NS-Organen 'Der Angriff' und 'Das Reich'* (Münster 1967)

Kessler, Count Harry. *Tagebücher 1918–1937*, ed. Wolfgang Pfeiffer-Belli (Frankfurt 1961)

Kiersch, Gerhard, Rainer Klaus, Wolfgang Kramer and Elisabeth Reichardt-Kiersch. *Berliner Alltag im Dritten Reich* (Düsseldorf 1981)

Kisch, Egon Erwin. *Der rasende Reporter: Hetzjagd durch die Zeit. Wagnisse in aller Welt. Kriminalistisches Reisebuch* (Berlin and Weimar 1983)

Kissenkoetter, Udo. *Gregor Straßer und die NSDAP* (Stuttgart 1978)

Kleihues, Josef Paul, Jan Gerd Becker-Schwering and Paul Kahlfeldt (eds). *Bauen in Berlin 1900–2000* (Berlin 2000)

Klemmer, Klemens. *Jüdische Baumeister in Deutschland: Architektur vor der Shoah* (Stuttgart 1998)

Knickerbocker, H[ubert] R[enfro]. *The German Crisis* (New York 1932); trans. into German by Franz Fein as *Deutschland so oder so?* (Berlin 1932)

Knobloch, Heinz. *Der arme Epstein: Wie der Tod zu Horst Wessel kam* (Berlin 1993)

Koch, Hannsjoachim W. *Der deutsche Bürgerkrieg: Eine Geschichte der deutschen und österreichischen Freikorps 1918–1923* (Berlin, Frankfurt and Vienna 1978)

Köpf, Peter. *Der Königsplatz in München: Ein deutscher Ort* (Berlin 2005)

Krause, Rudolf. *Die Berliner City: Frühere Entwicklung / Gegenwärtige Situation / Mögliche Perspektiven* (Berlin 1958)

Krebs, Albert. *Tendenzen und Gestalten der NSDAP: Erinnerungen an die Frühzeit der Partei* (Stuttgart 1959)

Kreimeier, Klaus. *Die Ufa-Story: Geschichte eines Filmkonzerns* (Munich and Vienna 1992)

Kruck, Alfred. *Geschichte des alldeutschen Verbandes 1890–1939* (Wiesbaden 1954)

Kruppa, Bernd. *Rechtsradikalismus in Berlin 1918–1928* (Berlin 1988)

Kühnl, Reinhard. *Die nationalsozialistische Linke 1925–1930* (Meisenheim am Glan 1966)

Lange, Annemarie. *Berlin in der Weimarer Republik* (Berlin 1987)

Lania, Leo. *Welt im Umbruch: Biographie einer Generation* (Frankfurt 1954)

Lauterbach, Iris (ed.). *Bürokratie und Kult: Das Parteizentrum der NSDAP am Königsplatz in München. Geschichte und Rezeption* (Munich 1995)

Leers, Dr [Johann von]. *Forderung der Stunde: Juden raus!* (Berlin [1933])

Lehmbruch, Hans. 'Acropolis Germaniae: Der Königsplatz – Forum der NSDAP', *Bürokratie und Kult: Das Parteizentrum der NSDAP am Königsplatz in München. Geschichte und Rezeption*, ed. Iris Lauterbach (Munich 1995), 17–45

Lexikon zur Parteigeschichte 1789–1945, ed. Dieter Fricke, 4 vols (Leipzig 1983–6)

Leyden, Friedrich. *Groß-Berlin: Geographie der Weltstadt* (Breslau 1933, reprinted Berlin 1995)

Liang, Hsi-Huey. *Die Berliner Polizei in der Weimarer Republik* (Berlin 1977)

Lienhard, Fritz. *Die Vorherrschaft Berlins: Litterarische Anregungen*, 2nd edn (Berlin 1902)

Lindemann, Margot, and Kurt Koszyk. *Geschichte der deutschen Presse*, part 3: *Deutsche Presse 1914–1945* (Berlin 1972)

Lippert, Julius. *Im Strom der Zeit: Erlebnisse und Eindrücke* (Berlin 1942)

Litten, Irmgard. *A Mother Fights Hitler* (London 1940)

Longerich, Peter. *'Davon haben wir nichts gewusst!' Die Deutschen und die Judenverfolgung 1933–1945* (Munich 2006)

—. *Geschichte der SA*, 2nd edn (Munich 2003)

Lukacs, John. *The Hitler of History: Hitler's Biographers on Trial* (London 2002)

Machtan, Lothar. *Hitlers Geheimnis: Das Doppelleben eines Diktators* (Berlin 2001)

Mahlke, Bernhard. 'Stahlhelm-Bund der Frontsoldaten (Stahlhelm) 1918–1935', *Lexikon zur Parteiengeschichte 1789–1945*, ed. Dieter Fricke, 4 vols (Leipzig 1983–6), iv.145–58

Manvell, Roger, and Heinrich Fraenkel, *Doctor Goebbels: His Life and Death* (London and New York 2010)

March, Werner. 'Die baukünstlerische Gestaltung des Reichssportfeldes', *Das Reichssportfeld: Eine Schöpfung des Dritten Reiches für die Olympischen Spiele und die Deutschen Leibesübungen*, ed. Reichsministerium des Innern (Berlin 1936), 27–55

—. *Bauwerk Reichssportfeld* (Berlin 1936)

Maser, Werner. *Die Frühgeschichte der NSDAP: Hitlers Weg bis 1924* (Frankfurt 1965)

—. *Hitlers Briefe und Notizen: Sein Weltbild in handschriftlichen Dokumenten*, 2nd edn (Düsseldorf 1973)

Materna, Ingo, and Wolfgang Ribbe. *Berlin: Geschichte in Daten*, 2nd edn (Wiesbaden 2003)

Maurer, Ilse, and Udo Wengst (eds). *Staat und NSDAP 1930-1932: Quellen zur Ära Brüning* (Düsseldorf 1977)

Mehring, Walter. *Chronik der Lustbarkeiten: Die Gedichte, Lieder und Chansons 1918-1933* (Düsseldorf 1981)

Meißner, Otto. *Staatssekretär unter Ebert - Hindenburg - Hitler: Der Schicksalsweg des deutschen Volkes von 1918-1945, wie ich ihn erlebte* (Hamburg 1950)

Mendelsohn, Erich. *Amerika: Bilderbuch eines Architekten. Mit 77 photographischen Aufnahmen des Verfassers* (Berlin 1926)

Mendelssohn, Peter de. 'Als die Presse gefesselt war', *Hundert Jahre Ullstein*, ed. W. Joachim Freyburg and Hans Wallenberg, 4 vols (Frankfurt, Berlin and Vienna 1977), iii.193-243

—. *Zeitungsstadt Berlin: Menschen und Mächte in der Geschichte der deutschen Presse*, 2nd edn (Frankfurt, Berlin and Vienna 1982)

Merkl, Peter H. 'Formen der nationalsozialistischen Gewaltanwendung: Die SA der Jahre 1925-1933', *Sozialprotest, Gewalt, Terror: Gewaltanwendung durch politische und gesellschaftliche Randgruppen im 19. und 20. Jahrhundert*, ed. Wolfgang J. Mommsen and Gerhard Hirschfeld (Stuttgart 1982), 422-40

—. *Political Violence under the Swastika: 581 Early Nazis*, 8th edn (Princeton, NJ 1975)

Mertens, Carl. *Verschwörer und Fememörder* (Charlottenburg 1926)

Mesecke, Andrea. 'Zur Spezifik der Repräsentationsarchitektur im Nationalsozialismus', *Stadt der Architektur, Architektur der Stadt: Berlin 1900-2000*, ed. Thorsten Scheer, Josef Paul Kleihues and Paul Kahlfeldt (Berlin 2000), 186-99

Michaelis, Herbert, and Ernst Schraepler (eds). *Ursachen und Folgen: Vom deutschen Zusammenbruch 1918 und 1945 bis zur staatlichen Neuordnung Deutschlands in der Gegenwart*, 25 vols (Berlin 1959)

Michalka, Wolfgang, and Gottfried Niedhart (eds). *Die ungeliebte Republik: Dokumentation zur Innen- und Außenpolitik Weimars 1918-1933* (Munich 1980)

Miller-Lane, Barbara. *Architektur und Politik in Deutschland 1918-1945* (Braunschweig 1986)

Miltenberg, Weigand von. *Adolf Hitler, Wilhelm III* (Berlin 1930)

Mohler, Arnim. *Die Konservative Revolution in Deutschland 1918-1932: Ein Handbuch*, 3rd edn (Darmstadt 1989)

Mondt, Gerhard. *Herbert Norkus: Das Tagebuch der Kameradschaft Beusselkietz. Mit einem Geleitwort von Baldur von Schirach* (Berlin 1941)

Moreau, Patrick. *Nationalsozialismus von links: Die 'Kampgemeinschaft Revolutionärer Nationalsozialisten' und die 'Schwarze Front' Otto Strassers 1930-1935* (Stuttgart 1984)

Müller, Richard. *Vom Kaiserreich zur Republik: Ein Beitrag zur Geschichte der revolutionären Arbeiterbewegung während des Weltkrieges* [1924] (Berlin 1974)

Nerdinger, Winfried (ed.). *Ort und Erinnerung: Nationalsozialismus in München* (Salzburg and Munich 2006)

Neuber, Gerhard. 'Faschismus in Berlin: Entwicklung und Wirken der NSDAP und ihrer Organisationen in der Reichshauptstadt 1920-1934' (diss. Univ. East Berlin, 1976)

Neumann, Dietrich. (ed.). *Architektur der Nacht* (Munich 2002)

—. 'Die ungebaute Stadt der Moderne', *Stadt der Architektur, Architektur der Stadt: Berlin 1900-2000*, ed. Thorsten Scheer, Josef Paul Kleihues and Paul Kahlfeldt (Berlin 2000), 161-73

— 'Die Wolkenkratzer kommen!' *Deutsche Hochhäuser der zwanziger Jahre: Debatten, Projekte, Bauten* (Braunschweig 1995)

Newton, Helmut. *Autobiography* (London 2003)

Nipperdey, Thomas. *Deutsche Geschichte 1866-1918*, vol. i: *Arbeitswelt und Bürgergeist*, 2nd edn (Munich 1991)

Oechslin, Werner. 'Lichtarchitektur: Die Genese eines neuen Begriffs', *Architektur der Nacht*, ed. Dietrich Neumann (Munich 2002), 28–35

Oehme, Walter, and Kurt Caro. *Kommt 'Das Dritte Reich'?*, 2nd edn (Berlin 1931)

Oertel, Thomas. *Horst Wessel: Untersuchung einer Legende* (Cologne 1988)

Olden, Rudolf. *Hitler* (Amsterdam 1935, reprinted Hildesheim 1981)

—. *Das Wunderbare oder die Verzauberten: Propheten in deutscher Krise* (Berlin 1932)

Opitz, Georg, and Werner Kallmorgen. *Der Tiergartenring: Eine Städtebaustudie* (Berlin 1928)

Organisationskomitee für die Olympischen Spiele Berlin 1936 (ed.). *XI. Olympiade Berlin 1936: Amtlicher Bericht* (Berlin 1936)

Oschilewski, Walther G. *Zeitungen in Berlin im Spiegel der Jahrhunderte* (Berlin 1975)

Ossietzky, Carl von. *Sämtliche Schriften: Oldenburger Ausgabe* (Reinbek 1994)

Papen, Franz von. *Der Wahrheit eine Gasse* (Munich 1952)

Parr, Martin, and Gerry Badger. *The Photobook: A History*, 2 vols (London 2004–6)

Pätzold, Kurt, and Manfred Weißbecker. *Adolf Hitler: Eine politische Biographie* (Leipzig 1995)

—. *Geschichte der NSDAP 1920–1945* (Cologne 1998)

Paul, Gerhard. *Aufstand der Bilder. Die NS-Propaganda vor 1933* (Bonn 1992)

Pawlowski, Dietrich. 'He, he, he . . . Zum Radsport', *Arena der Leidenschaften: Der Berliner Sportpalast und seine Veranstaltungen 1910–1973*, ed. Alfons Arenhövel (Berlin 1990), 71–9

Peschken-Eilsberger, Monika. 'Der Berliner Sportpalast in der Literatur der zwanziger Jahre', *Arena der Leidenschaften: Der Berliner Sportpalast und seine Veranstaltungen 1910–1973*, ed. Alfons Arenhövel (Berlin 1990), 106–7

Peukert, Detlev. *Die Weimarer Republik: Krisenjahre der klassichen Moderne* (Frankfurt 1987)

Pfundtner, Hans. 'Die Gesamtleitung der Errichtung des Reichssportfeldes', *Das Reichssportfeld: Eine Schöpfung des Dritten Reiches für die Olympischen Spiele und die Deutschen Leibesübungen*, ed. Reichsministerium des Innern (Berlin 1936), 11–26

Picker, Henry. *Hitlers Tischgespräche im Führerhauptquartier*, 4th rev. edn (Stuttgart 1983)

Pirker, Theo (ed.). *Komintern und Faschismus: Dokumente zur Geschichte und Theorie des Faschismus*, 2nd edn (Stuttgart 1966)

Plaas, Hartmut. 'Das Kapp-Unternehmen', *Der Kampf um das Reich*, ed. Ernst Jünger, 2nd rev. edn (Essen [1931]), 164–89

Platz der Republik: Vom Exerzierplatz zum Regierungsviertel (Berlin 1992) (exhibition catalogue)

Die Pleite: Illustrierte Halbmonatsschrift: Fotomechanischer Neudruck der Originalausgaben 1919–24 (Leipzig 1986)

Plewnia, Margarete. *Auf dem Weg zu Hitler: Der 'völkische' Publizist Dietrich Eckart* (Bremen 1970)

Posener, Julius. *Berlin auf dem Wege zu einer neuen Architektur: Das Zeitalter Wilhelms II.* (Munich 1979)

—. 'Immeuble Shell à Berlin', *L'architecture d'aujourd'hui* (Dec. 1932–Jan. 1933), 75–7

Presse- und Informationsamt des Landes Berlin (ed.). *Berlin Handbuch: Das Lexikon der Bundeshauptstadt* (Berlin 1992)

Pross, Christian, and Rolf Winau. *Nicht misshandeln: Das Krankenhaus Moabit* (Berlin 1984)

Quaatz, Reinhold. *Die Deutschnationalen und die Zerstörung der Weimarer Republik: Aus dem Tagebuch von Reinhold Quaatz 1928–1933* (Munich 1989)

Rave, Paul Ortwin. *Karl Friedrich Schinkel: Lebenswerk. Berlin, Stadtbaupläne, Brücken, Straßen, Tore, Plätze* (Berlin 1981)

Reiche, Jürgen. 'Symbolgehalt und Bedeutungswandel eines politischen Monuments', *Das Brandenburger Tor 1791–1991: Eine Monographie*, ed. Willmuth Arenhövel and Rolf Bothe (Berlin 1991), 270–316

Reichhardt, Hans J. *Kapp-Putsch und Generalstreik März 1920 in Berlin: 'Tage der Torheit, Tage der Not'. Eine Ausstellung des Landesarchivs Berlin* (Berlin 1990) (exhibition catalogue)

—, and Wolfgang Schäche. *Von Berlin nach Germania: Über die Zerstörungen der 'Reichshauptstadt' durch Albert Speers Neugestaltungsplanungen* (Berlin 1998)

Reichsministerium des Innern (ed.). *Das Reichssportfeld: Eine Schöpfung des Dritten Reiches für die Olympischen Spiele und die Deutschen Leibesübungen* (Berlin 1936)

Reimann, Viktor. *Dr. Joseph Goebbels* (Vienna and Munich 1976)

Reitmann, Erwin. *Horst Wessel: Leben und Sterben* (Berlin 1936)

Rembrandt als Erzieher: Von einem Deutschen [Julius Langbehn], 47th edn (Leipzig 1906)

Reuth, Ralf Geog. *Goebbels: Eine Biographie* (Munich and Zurich 1990)

Revolution und Fotografie: Berlin 1918/19. Eine Ausstellung der Neuen Gesellschaft für Bildende Kunst (Berlin 1989) (exhibition catalogue)

Ribbentrop, Joachim von. *Zwischen London und Moskau: Erinnerungen und letzte Aufzeichnungen*, ed. Annelies von Ribbentrop (Leoni 1953)

Riecke, Gerhard. 'Das Lichten des Dschungels', *Die Metropole: Industriekultur in Berlin im 20. Jahrhundert*, ed. Jochen Boberg, Tilman Fischer and Eckhart Gillen (Munich 1986), 232–7

Rossbach, Gerhard. *Mein Weg durch die Zeit: Erinnerungen und Bekenntnisse* (Weilburg-Lahn 1950)

RSA *see Hitler: Reden, Schriften, Anordnungen*

Rückerl, Adalbert. *NS-Verbrechen vor Gericht: Versuch einer Vergangenheitsbewältigung*, 2nd rev. edn (Heidelberg 1984)

Ruge, Wolfgang. 'Deutschnationale Volkspartei (DNVP) 1918–1933', *Lexikon zur Parteiengeschichte 1789–1945*, ed. Dieter Fricke, 4 vols (Leipzig 1983–6), ii.476–528

Rühle, Gerd. *Das Dritte Reich: Dokumentarische Darstellung des Aufbaues der Nation. Die Kampfjahre 1918–1933* (Berlin 1936)

Rumpelstilzchen (i.e. Adolf Stern), *Ja, hätt'ste . . .* (Berlin 1929)

—. *Nu wenn schon!* (Berlin 1932)

—. *Das sowieso!* (Berlin 1931)

Rürup, Reinhard. *Topographie des Terrors: Gestapo, SS und Reichssicherheitshauptamt auf dem 'Prinz-Albrecht-Gelände': Eine Dokumentation* (Berlin 1987)

Russell-Hitchcock, Henry, and Philip Johnson. *The International Style. With a New Foreword by Philip Johnson* (New York and London 1995)

Salomon, Ernst von. *Die Geächteten: Roman* (Berlin 1930)

Sauer, Bernhard. 'Gerhard Roßbach: Hitlers Vertreter für Berlin. Zur Frühgeschichte des Rechtsradikalismus in der Weimarer Republik', *Zeitschrift für Geschichtswissenschaft*, 1 (2002), 5–21

—. 'Goebbels' Rabauken': Zur Geschichte der SA in Berlin-Brandenburg', *Berlin in Geschichte und Gegenwart: Jahrbuch des Landesarchivs Berlin 2006*, ed. Uwe Schaper (Berlin 2006), 107–64

Sauer, Wolfgang. 'Die Mobilmachung der Gewalt', *Die nationalsozialistische Machtergreifung: Studien zur Errichtung des totalitären Herrschaftssystems in Deutschland 1933/34*, ed. Karl Dietrich Bracher, Wolfgang Sauer and Gerhard Schulz, 2nd edn (Cologne and Opladen 1962), 685–966

Scarpa, Ludovica. *Martin Wagner und Berlin: Architektur und Städtebau in der Weimarer Republik* (Braunschweig and Wiesbaden 1986)

Schäche, Wolfgang. '1933–1945: Bauen im Nationalsozialismus. Dekoration der Gewalt', *750 Jahre Architektur und Städtebau in Berlin: Die Internationale Bauausstellung im Kontext der Baugeschichte Berlins*, ed. Josef Paul Kleihues (Stuttgart 1987), 183–212

—. *Architektur und Städtebau in Berlin zwischen 1933 und 1945: Planen und Bauen unter der Ägide der Stadtverwaltung* (Berlin 1991)

—, and Norbert Szymanski. *Das Reichssportfeld: Architektur im Spannungsfeld von Sport und Macht* (Berlin 2001)

Scheffler, Karl. *Berlin: Wandlungen einer Stadt* (Berlin 1931)

Schenzinger, Karl Aloys. *Der Hitlerjunge Quex: Roman* (Berlin 1932)

Schilde, Kurt, Rolf Scholz and Sylvia Walleczek. *SA-Gefängnis Papestraße: Spuren und Zeugnisse* (Berlin 1996)

Schilling, Otto. *Innere Stadt-Erweiterung* (Berlin 1921)

Schinz, Alfred. *Berlin: Stadtschicksal und Städtebau* (Braunschweig 1964)

Schivelbusch, Wolfgang. *Die Kultur der Niederlage: Der amerikanische Süden 1865, Frankreich 1871, Deutschland 1918* (Berlin 2001)

Schmeer, Karlheinz. *Die Regie des öffentlichen Lebens im Dritten Reich* (Munich 1956)

Schmidt, Hartwig. *Das Tiergartenviertel: Baugeschichte eines Berliner Villenviertels* (Berlin 1981)

Schmidt, Matthias. *Albert Speer: Das Ende eines Mythos. Speers wahre Rolle im Dritten Reich* (Berne and Munich 1982)

Schmidt-Pauli, Edgar von. *Hitlers Kampf um die Macht: Der Nationalsozialismus und die Ereignisse des Jahres 1932*, 2nd edn (Berlin 1933)

Schmiechen-Ackermann, Detlef. *Nationalsozialismus und Arbeitermilieus: Der national-sozialistische Angriff auf die proletarischen Wohnquartiere und die Reaktion in den sozialistischen Vereinen* (Bonn 1998)

Schmölders, Claudia. *Hitlers Gesicht: Eine physiognomische Biographie* (Munich 2000)

Schönberger, Angela. *Die Neue Reichskanzlei von Albert Speer: Zum Zusammenhang von nationalsozialistischer Ideologie und Architektur* (Berlin 1981)

Schrader, Bärbel, and Jürgen Schebera. *Kunstmetropole Berlin: Dokumente und Selbstzeugnisse* (Berlin and Weimar 1987)

Schreiber, Christa. 'Der Sportpalast in seiner baulichen Entwicklung', *Arena der Leidenschaften: Der Berliner Sportpalast und seine Veranstaltungen 1910–1973*, ed. Alfons Arenhövel (Berlin 1990), 16–38

Schreiber, Gerhard. *Hitler: Interpretationen 1923–1983. Ergebnisse, Methoden und Probleme der Forschung* (Darmstadt 1984)

Schüddekopf, Otto-Ernst. *Linke Leute von rechts: Die nationalrevolutionären Minderheiten und der Kommunismus in der Weimarer Republik* (Stuttgart 1980)

Schulz, Gerhard. *Aufstieg des Nationalsozialismus: Krise und Revolution in Deutschland* (Frankfurt, Berlin and Vienna 1976)

Schulze, Hagen. *Weimar: Deutschland 1917–1933*, 2nd edn (Berlin 1983)

Schumacher, Martin (ed.). *M. d. R. Die Reichtagsabgeordneten der Weimarer Republik in der Zeit des Nationalsozialismus. Politische Verfolgung, Emigration und Ausbürgerung 1933–1945. Eine biographische Dokumentation*, 2nd edn (Düsseldorf 1992)

Schuster, Martin. 'Die SA in der nationalsozialistischen "Machtergreifung" in Berlin und Brandenburg 1926–1934' (diss., Berlin 2004)

Schuster, Wolfgang. 'Hitler in München – privat?', *München – 'Hauptstadt der Bewegung'* (Munich 1993), 125–30 (exhibition catalogue)

Schwarz van Berk, Hans. 'Vorwort' and 'Die Stimme der Verfolgten', in Joseph Goebbels, *Der Angriff: Aufsätze aus der Kampfzeit*, 2nd edn (Munich 1935), 9–17

Das Schwarzbuch: Tatsachen und Dokumente. Die Lage der Juden in Deutschland 1933 (Paris 1934, reprinted Frankfurt, Berlin and Vienna 1983)

Severing, Carl. *Mein Lebensweg*, 2 vols (Cologne 1950)

Shirer, William L. *Berlin Diary 1934–1941: The Rise of the Third Reich* (New York 1997)

Sösemann, Bernd (ed.). *Theodor Wolff: Der Journalist, Berichte und Leitartikel* (Düsseldorf 1993)

Spartakusbriefe, ed. Institut für Marxismus-Leninismus beim Zentralkomitee der Sozialistischen Einheitspartei Deutschlands (Berlin 1958)

Speer, Albert. 'Die Bauten des Führers', *Adolf Hitler: Bilder aus dem Leben des Führers*, ed. Cigaretten-Bilderdienst (Altona and Bahrenfeld 1936), 72–7

—. *Erinnerungen* (Berlin 1969)

Speicher, Stephan. *Ort der deutschen Geschichte: Der Reichstag in Berlin* (Berlin [1995])

Speier, Hans. *Die Angestellten vor dem Nationalsozialismus: Ein Beitrag zum Verständnis der deutschen Sozialstruktur 1918–1933* (Göttingen 1977)

Springer, Peter. *Schinkels Schloßbrücke in Berlin: Zweckbau und Monument* (Frankfurt, Berlin and Vienna 1981)

Stark, Hans Joachim. 'Bürohäuser der Privatwirtschaft', *Berlin und seine Bauten*, ed. Architekten- und Ingenieur-Verein zu Berlin, part 9 (Berlin, Munich and Düsseldorf 1971), 115–82

Statistisches Jahrbuch der Stadt Berlin, ed. Statistisches Amt der Stadt Berlin, vols vi–ix (Berlin 1930–3)

Statistisches Taschenbuch der Stadt Berlin, 2nd edn (Berlin 1926)

Steinbach, Peter. 'Zwischen Bomben und Gestapo: Berlin als Reichshauptstadt und als Hauptstadt des deutschen Widerstandes', *Berlin als Faktor nationaler und internationaler Politik*, ed. Hannelore Horn (Berlin 1988), 23–43

Steinhage, Axel, and Thomas Flemming. *Chronik 1932: Tag für Tag in Wort und Bild* (Dortmund 1989)

Stephan, Regina. *Studien zu Waren- und Geschäftshäusern Erich Mendelsohns in Deutschland* (Munich 1992)

—. 'Wir glauben an Berlin!', *Erich Mendelsohn, Dynamik und Funktion: Realisierte Visionen eines kosmopolitischen Architekten*, ed. Regina Stephan (Ostfildern-Ruit 1999), 144–65

Stern, Fritz. *Kulturpessimismus als politische Gefahr: Eine Analyse nationaler Ideologie in Deutschland* (Berne, Stuttgart and Vienna 1963)

Sternberg, Fritz. *Der Niedergang des deutschen Kapitalismus* (Berlin 1932)

Stockhorst, Erich. *5000 Köpfe: Wer war was im 3. Reich* (Wiesbaden n.d.)

Stommer, Rainer. *Hochhaus: Der Beginn in Deutschland* (Marburg 1990)

Striefler, Christian. *Kampf um die Macht: Kommunisten und Nationalsozialisten am Ende der Weimarer Republik* (Berlin 1993)

Sturm 33 Hans Maikowski: Geschrieben von Kameraden des Toten (Berlin-Schöneberg 1934)

Sturtevant, Erich. *Jüterbog: Ein Führer durch seine Sehenswürdigkeiten* (Jüterbog 1928)

Stürzebecher, Peter. *Das Berliner Warenhaus: Bautypus, Element der Stadtorganisation, Raumsphäre der Warenwelt* (Berlin 1979)

Szende, Stefan. *Zwischen Gewalt und Toleranz: Zeugnisse und Reflexionen eines Sozialisten.* With a preface by Willy Brandt (Frankfurt and Cologne 1975)

Teschner, General a. D. 'Der Küstriner Putsch', *Der Kampf um das Reich*, ed. Ernst Jünger, 2nd edn (Essen [1931]), 277–80

Thaer, Albrecht von. *Generalstabdienst an der Front und in der OHL: Aus Briefen und Tagebuchaufzeichnungen 1915–1919* (Göttingen 1958)

Thälmann, Ernst. *Reden und Aufsätze 1930–1933* (Cologne 1975)

Thomae, Otto. *Die Propaganda-Maschinerie: Bildende Kunst und Öffentlichkeitsarbeit im Dritten Reich* (Berlin 1978)

Toland, John. *Adolf Hitler* (Bergisch Gladbach 1977)

Tucholsky, Kurt. *Gesammelte Werke*, vol. iii: *1921–1924* (Reinbek 1990)

Turner, Henry Ashby, Jr. *Hitler aus nächster Nähe: Aufzeichnungen eines Vertrauten 1929–1932* (Frankfurt, Berlin and Vienna 1978), 411; abridged trans. by Ruth Hein as *Hitler: Memoirs of a Confidant* (New Haven, CT and London 1985)

—. *Hitler's Thirty Days to Power: January 1933* (London 1996)

Tyrell, Albrecht. *Führer befiehl ... Selbstzeugnisse aus der 'Kampfzeit' der NSDAP: Dokumentation und Analyse* (Düsseldorf 1969)

—. *Vom 'Trommler' zum 'Führer': Der Wandel von Hitlers Selbstverständnis zwischen 1919 und 1924 und die Entwicklung der NSDAP* (Munich 1975)

—. 'Der Wegbereiter: Hermann Göring als politischer Beauftragter Hitlers in Berlin 1930–1932/33', *Demokratie und Diktatur: Geist und Gestalt politischer Herrschaft in Deutschland und Europa. Festschrift für Karl-Dietrich Bracher*, ed. Manfred Funke and others (Bonn and Düsseldorf 1987), 178–97

Venner, Dominique. *Söldner ohne Sold: Die deutschen Freikorps 1918–1923* (Vienna and Berlin 1974)

Vogelsang, Thilo. *Reichswehr, Staat und NSDAP: Beiträge zur deutschen Geschichte 1930–1932* (Stuttgart 1962)

Volz, Hans. *Daten der Geschichte der NSDAP*, 8th edn (Berlin and Leipzig 1938)

Walter, Dirk. *Antisemitische Kriminalität und Gewalt: Judenfeindschaft in der Weimarer Republik* (Bonn 1999)

Weber, Hermann (ed.). *Der deutsche Kommunismus: Dokumente* (Cologne and Berlin 1963)

—. *Die Wandlung des deutschen Kommunismus: Die Stalinisierung der KPD in der Weimarer Republik* (Frankfurt 1969)

Wehler, Hans-Ulrich. *Deutsche Gesellschaftsgeschichte*, vol. iv: *Vom Beginn des Ersten Weltkrieges bis zur Gründung der beiden deutschen Staaten 1914–1949* (Munich 2003)

Weidner, Heinz. *Berlin im Festschmuck: Vom 15. Jahrhundert bis zur Gegenwart* (Berlin 1940)

Weingartner, Thomas. *Stalin und der Aufstieg Hitlers: Die Deutschlandpolitik der Sowjetunion und der Kommunistischen Internationale 1929–1934* (Berlin 1970)

Weißbecker, Manfred. 'Kampfgemeinschaft Revolutionärer Nationalsozialisten (KG) 1930–1937/38', *Lexikon zur Parteiengeschichte 1789–1945*, ed. Dieter Fricke, 4 vols (Leipzig 1983–6), iii.172–8

Werner, Kurt, and Karl Heinz Biernat. *Die Köpenicker Blutwoche 1933* (Berlin 1960)

Wiedemann, Fritz. *Der Mann, der Feldherr werden wollte: Erlebnisse und Erfahrungen des Vorgesetzten Hitlers im 1. Weltkrieg und seines späteren persönlichen Adjutanten* (Velbert 1964)

Wilderotter, Hans. *Alltag der Macht: Berlin Wilhelmstraße* (Berlin 1998)

Willems, Susanne. *Der entsiedelte Jude: Albert Speers Wohnungsmarktpolitik für den Berliner Hauptstadtbau* (Berlin 2000)

Winkler, Heinrich August. *Von der Revolution zur Stabilisierung: Arbeiter und Arbeiterbewegung in der Weimarer Republik 1918 bis 1924* (Berlin and Bonn 1984)

—. *Der Schein der Normalität: Arbeiter und Arbeiterbewegung in der Weimarer Republik 1924 bis 1930* (Berlin and Bonn 1985)

—. *Der Weg in die Katastrophe: Arbeiter und Arbeiterbewegung in der Weimarer Republik 1930 bis 1933* (Berlin and Bonn 1987)

—. *Der lange Weg nach Westen: Deutsche Geschichte 1806–1933*, 2 vols (Munich 2000)

Wirth, Irmgard. *Die Bauwerke und Kunstdenkmäler von Berlin: Stadt und Bezirk Charlottenburg. Textband* (Berlin 1961)

Wistrich, Robert. *Wer war wer im Dritten Reich: Ein biographisches Lexikon. Anhänger, Mitläufer, Gegner aus Politik, Wirtschaft, Militär, Kunst und Wissenschaft* (Munich 1983)

Wolters, Rudolf. *Albert Speer* (Oldenburg 1943)

Worbs, Dietrich. 'Das Columbushaus am Potsdamer Platz von Erich Mendelsohn, 1931/32', *Architektur-Experimente in Berlin und anderswo: Für Julius Posener*, ed. Sonja Günther and Dietrich Worbs (Berlin 1989), 82–101

Wulf, Joseph. *Die Bildenden Künste im Dritten Reich: Eine Dokumentation* (Gütersloh 1963)

Zitelmann, Rainer. *Hitler: Selbstverständnis eines Revolutionärs*, 3rd edn (Darmstadt 1990)

Zöbl, Dorothea. *Das periphere Zentrum: Ort und Entwicklung der Bundes- und Reichsbehörden im Groß-Berliner Stadtraum 1866/67–1914* (Potsdam 2001)

Index

NOTE: English terms are used for political parties and organizations; there are cross-references from some abbreviations; for a full list of abbreviations and German terms see the list on page vii. Page numbers followed by *n* refer to a numbered note.